LATE AUGUSTAN PROSE

Prentice-Hall Periods of English Literature Series

MAYNARD MACK, *editor*

LATE

AUGUSTAN

PROSE

Edited by PATRICIA MEYER SPACKS

Wellesley College

Prentice-Hall, Inc., Englewood Cliffs, New Jersey

Prentice-Hall Periods of English Literature Series
Maynard Mack, editor

C 13-524132-4
P 13-524124-3

Library of Congress Catalog Card Number: 74-126826
Printed in the United States of America

Current Printing (last digit):
10 9 8 7 6 5 4 3 2 1

PRENTICE-HALL INTERNATIONAL, INC., London
PRENTICE-HALL OF AUSTRALIA, PTY. LTD., Sydney
PRENTICE-HALL OF CANADA, LTD., Toronto
PRENTICE-HALL OF INDIA PRIVATE LIMITED, New Delhi
PRENTICE-HALL OF JAPAN, INC., Tokyo

ACKNOWLEDGEMENTS

I am indebted and thankful to many for help in annotation: to Grazia Avitabile, Walter Jackson Bate, Pamela Benbow, Bertrand Bronson, Katherine Geffcken, Sally Graham, Ralph Hodgkinson, Katherine Lever, Florence McCulloch, John Middendorf, Charles Ryskamp, Albrecht Strauss and Margaret Taylor. I am also grateful to Carolyn Magid, for intelligent and assiduous clerical help; to Virginia Fanger, for her critical readings of part of the manuscript; to Maynard Mack, for stern but illuminating supervision; and to my husband, for perceptive criticism and unflagging support.

CONTENTS

vii

LATE AUGUSTAN PROSE

INTRODUCTION

When I had thus inquired into the original of words, I resolved to show likewise my attention to things; to pierce deep into every science, to inquire the nature of every substance of which I inserted the name, to limit every idea by a definition strictly logical, and exhibit every production of art or nature in an accurate description, that my book might be in place of all other dictionaries, whether appellative or technical.

Samuel Johnson, describing his original plans for his dictionary—actually published, in rather less ambitious form than Johnson had projected, in 1755—reveals an essential optimism of his age, its belief in the possibility of extraordinary individual accomplishment. The *Dictionary* expresses a single powerful intelligence, a single sensibility; if that intelligence takes all knowledge to be its province, it does not display the Renaissance avidity for incorporating information, but rather interests itself in expounding, elucidating, analyzing. Johnson thought it possible to uncover the assumptions embedded in language, to discover the relation between word and thing, to bring logic definitively to bear on "every idea," to describe whatever might exist. The scope of his imagination suggests the imaginative range of his period, an era of great prose which investigates some of its own assumptions while resting secure on others; which vividly expresses individual personalities, yet assumes the paramount importance of social solidarity and of universality as an aesthetic criterion.

In 1738, on the other hand, Alexander Pope wrote in a final footnote to his *Epilogue to the Satires*:

> This was the last poem of the kind printed by our author, with a resolution to publish no more; but to enter thus, in the most plain and solemn manner he could, a sort of PROTEST against that insuperable corruption and depravity of manners, which he had been so unhappy as to live to see. Could he have hoped to have amended any, he had continued those attacks; but bad men were grown so shameless and so powerful, that Ridicule was become as unsafe as it was ineffectual.

Almost half a century later, in a letter to a friend, Johnson himself wrote, "I have no national news that is not in the papers, and almost all news is bad. Perhaps no nation not absolutely conquered has declined so much in so short a time. We seem to be sinking."

The point is not that in the eighteenth century some men felt optimistic, others pessimistic; nor that the same men felt at different times optimistic and pessimistic: such points could be made of all centuries. But the quotations, in conjunction with the earlier one from Johnson, illuminate significant grounds for hope and for gloom. The "insuperable corruption and depravity of manners," the "national news" that is almost all bad—these refer to public affairs and imply generalizing judgments; Johnson's vision of imaginative and intellectual possibility is a private one. This is not, yet, that conflict between "society and the individual" with which we have become familiar. It is a clash between potentiality and actuality: the divergence that had earlier impelled Jonathan Swift's bitter satire of men who, capable of reason, refused its responsibilities. Johnson, Gibbon, Boswell could feel the possibility of meaningful achievement; yet around them they saw a nation in moral disorder. Johnson wrote his dismal letter in 1782, when England had been defeated (if "not absolutely conquered") by a colonial uprising which developed into a world war. He wrote with a consciousness of widespread public unrest, manifested in the Gordon Riots of 1780, when unruly mobs stormed the Houses of Parliament in protest over the prospect of liberalized anti-Catholic laws for Scotland, and by the continuing disorders in Ireland, where the people fought for the independence of their parliament. Lord North's government at home had collapsed at the news of Cornwallis's Yorktown surrender. Still in the future was the French Revolution, which was to make yet more apparent the cumulative weakening of hierarchy and subordination; but already there was abundant evidence to suggest that private standards did not operate in the public sphere. Wordsworth was to feel it bliss to be alive in the "dawn" of the 1790's; some saw not dawn but gathering conflagration.

The society that Dr. Johnson inhabited seems, from the perspective of the twentieth century, secure and orderly. Until the American Revolution, England held a world position of unquestioned naval and political supremacy. She was a great power with growing wealth and commercial resources, but a land, Oliver Goldsmith believed, "Where wealth accumulates and men decay." To a conservative temperament, signs of decay seemed abundant. Not even the Protestant Succession established by the Glorious Revolution of 1688 was secure; there were hints that inglorious revolutions might be in store. The abortive Jacobite uprising of 1715—intended to place James Stuart, son of King James II, on the throne of England—had been followed by a more serious revolt in 1745, when James Stuart's son, "Bonnie Prince Charlie," and his troops of Highlanders penetrated as far south as Derby on their way to London to re-establish the Catholic Stuart monarchy. The aspirations of autocratic George III and the increasing popular dissatisfaction with the procedures of Parliament (suggested, for example, by the repeated re-election of John Wilkes as Middlesex representative when he was under indictment for libel of the King and refused his seat in Parliament) challenged from opposite sides the principle of parliamentary supremacy which had been established at the accession of William of Orange. It survived both challenges, but not without strain.

In Ireland violent agitation for civil rights began around the mid-century. In England such reformers as William Oglethorpe and John Howard called attention to the horrors of prisons and the plight of the poor. In India Warren Hastings, as governor-general, used high-handed methods to raise money; he was indicted in 1787 for alleged misconduct and cruelty, and acquitted, after much oratory, in 1795. As industrialization increased, the English peasantry migrated to the cities, where they existed often in brutal poverty, prey to gin and disease and the cruel penal laws which decreed the death penalty for petty theft. England's Arcadia existed no longer—if, indeed, it ever had.

These representative phenomena of the eighteenth century may seem from the perspective of the twentieth to be indices of progress. The Wilkes affair marked the beginning of a movement for parliamentary reform which culminated—after interruptions—in the Reform Bill of 1832; the Irish agitation produced liberalizing change. Prisons were improved, criminal laws softened; the responsibilities of England's imperial role were newly assessed. Industrialization means economic progress; and the changes in the countryside that drove away peasants improved agriculture.

To the eyes of a thoughtful man of the time, however, change was often obscured by the chaos that produced it and by the question of whether it was movement in a desirable direction. The civil rights riots of our own era may someday seem an index and a portent of hopeful change; as they occur, we are only aware of their horror. All men in all periods must try to reconcile the values of the past with those of the future. They may hope to abandon the past or to refuse the future, but they cannot avoid its challenge. For us of the twentieth century, more tempted by the claims of progress than of tradition, it is difficult to imagine how alive the values of the past seemed to many in the eighteenth century. Pope could bitterly satirize the popular identification of George II with the Roman emperor Augustus, but to some people that identification seemed not at all ludicrous: England in her era of prosperity and power resembled Rome in her great days, and the enthusiasm with which such analogies were formed and pursued suggests how vital were classical standards. Eighteenth-century education, like all English education since the Renaissance, was classical education; eighteenth-century standards of personal conduct were Christianized versions of the standards of Seneca and Cicero; the century's easy literary references were to Horace, Virgil, Ovid, Juvenal; its oratory followed Quintilian's rules; its rhetoric and its language reflected Latin models. The corruption Juvenal found in Rome (which his translator Robert Lowell was to find in the United States), Johnson discovered in London. Juvenal could advocate only stoicism as a response to life's inevitable misery; Johnson could insist on Christian as well as classical standards, on the moral obligation to create (with the aid of divine grace) order, serenity, even happiness. As public affairs seemed increasingly shaped by the expediency or narrow self-interest of politicians or by popular pressure, the split between the private and the public could be seen as being not only between morality and amorality but between respect for tradition and abandonment of it. Robert Walpole appears in history as a great statesman; however, to many of his contemporaries his venality seemed more significant than his political accomplishment.

The century's moral philosophers, considering problems of conduct, codified an optimism that rested on faith in the saving power of emotion and suggested the possibility that individuals might reconcile public and private claims. Thomas Hobbes, in *Leviathan* (1651), had maintained that human life was nasty, mean, brutish, and short, and that the natural condition of mankind was for all men to be at war with one another. Before a century had passed, this view yielded to its opposite: that self-love, properly understood, was identical with love for mankind. David Hume (*Enquiry Concerning Human Understanding*, 1748; *Enquiry Concerning the Principles of Morals*, 1751) agreed with Hobbes that morality is an artificial creation of man, not a natural law. He maintained, however, that the natural propensities of man included "limited generosity" and such "natural virtues" as affection, kindliness, gratitude, compassion. Man naturally feels *sympathy*, an instinctive interest in others which does not depend on particular knowledge of individuals. He can use such emotions as the foundation of a moral system, in which reason should be sub-ordinated to feeling. Adam Smith shared Hume's belief in the value of emotion; his *Theory of Moral Sentiments* (1759) argues that "immediate sense and feeling" produce moral distinctions, that "good" feelings lead to good activity. David Hartley (*Observations on Man*, 1749) deviated even more from faith in reason: his elaborate hierarchy of pleasures, moving through the aesthetic, intellectual, ethical, and religious, rests on a base of the fundamental physical pleasures, from which all others derive. Al-though philosophers less eminent than Hume and Smith—such men as Richard Price, Thomas Reid, Dugald Stewart—reasserted the primacy of reason, the necessity of rational guidance for moral action, their voices were less resounding than Hume's. The central achievement of philosophic reason in the last two-thirds of the eighteenth century was its denial of reason's centrality. There had never been a period when reason in fact controlled human actions, but late in the seventeenth century and early in the eighteenth, some men had thought that the strait and narrow path to secular salvation was the path of reason. Even then, Lord Shaftesbury insisted on the instinctiveness of altruistic impulses; Pope, in the *Essay on Man*, identified reason as the "card" by which man may direct his perilous life voyage, but passions as the "gale" without which he lies becalmed. The importance of that gale became more apparent as the century continued.

The investigations of epistemology corroborated the view that reason was not dependable. Hume, carrying to a logical conclusion the theories of John Locke and George Berkeley, demonstrated that we cannot even prove our own existence, much less the reality of the external universe, of God, or of such abstractions as causality and immortality. As he doggedly follows out the implications of his every idea, he exemplifies the century's impulse to classify, organize, and analyze, displayed not only in Johnson's *Dictionary* but in many scientific investigations. This was the era of Carl Linnaeus, whose system of botanical classification still survives; of Captain James Cook, whose voyages enlarged the naturalist's sphere; of Gilbert White, whose investigations of his own countryside dramatized the scientific and imaginative possibilities of close observation. The line between science and imagination hardly existed. The word *science* still meant *knowledge*; for Erasmus Darwin the material of botany was the material of poetry, and if his achievement failed to justify his theory, the failure was perhaps due mainly to lack of poetic talent. Hume's empiricism emphasized what could not be known, but the empirical method was also a way toward knowledge, and a way enthusiastically used by writers and artists as well as by scientists and philosophers. Reason might not be trustworthy; experience must be, although the interpretation of experience allowed room for rational fallacy.

The artistic records of eighteenth-century experience stress, positively or negatively, the divergence between empirically grasped reality and theoretically held ideal. William Hogarth's satiric paintings and engravings of contemporary life depict humanity as grotesque to the point of terror. The portraits of Sir Joshua Reynolds, Thomas Gainsborough, George Romney, although alive with a sense of the individual's uniqueness, imply the accession of individual to idealized type: noble warrior, aristocratic lady, innocent child. Even Hogarth's vicious renditions suggest his awareness of this potential. Their exact observation of physical and social degradation seems realistic, but their element of caricature implies a vision of human possibility that existing social life and customs deny.

Other forms of the same dichotomy manifest themselves in the century's novels: Samuel Richardson, author of *Pamela* and *Clarissa*, presents a sentimentalized, idealized version of reality; his immediate contemporary Henry Fielding, in *Joseph Andrews* and *Tom Jones*, provides a more robust account of the world through fictional caricature. Life is a comedy to Fielding, who thinks: He measures his characters and his own writing by classical standards, laughs at their deviations from the norm, yet invites his readers to ponder the significance of the divergence between ancient and modern. Richardson, exemplar of the feeling man, finds life more grim; in *Clarissa*, even tragic. He provides heroines of supernal virtue, then allows his readers to perceive the minute agonies and vacillations of idealized figures confronted with real moral problems.

But the dichotomy is more apparent than real: The balance is different in each novelist; the values are similar. Fielding does not merely think; he manipulates his plots and characters to evoke rich emotional response, and he is capable of sentimentality over Parson Adams or Sophia Western. Richardson's acute psychological observation, his awareness of moral and social subtlety, suggest intellectual power and an approach that is more than emotional. In the novel, an evolving form, its standards not yet defined, its potential subject matter as broad as life, various complex balances had to work themselves out: realism, satire, and low comedy in the work of Tobias Smollett; fluctuating proportions of sense and sensibility in Fanny Burney and later Jane Austen; the sublime and the pathetic in the Gothic novels. In *Tristram Shandy*, Laurence Sterne achieved the most remarkable fusion of all, producing a work which purposefully illustrated Locke's theory of random association, which descended to depths of vulgar comedy and achieved heights of pathos and sentimentality, which dealt with contemporary subject matter but employed techniques that still seem fresh in twentieth-century experimental fiction. The possibilities for fiction seemed boundless.

The ideal of regularity in landscape gardening yielded to that of naturalness: "nature methodized" was urged toward artful wildness. In architecture, fanciful experiments in the "Gothic," pseudomedieval modes suggested that buildings might entertain, titillate, or otherwise heighten the emotions of their occupants. Yet the classical Palladian style also flourished, affirming in its simplicity and clarity, its ordered proportions, the dignity of man. In aesthetic theory, high regard for the "sublime"—artistic or natural phenomena that embodied grandeur, elevation, even terror—competed with stress on the "picturesque," whose admirers valued the natural insofar as it resembled the pictorial, approving landscapes that looked as though they belonged in a painting, and consequently enjoying effects more measured than those of the sublime.

Poetry also displayed great variety: Samuel Johnson and Oliver Goldsmith wrote in sonorous couplets of classic dignity; Thomas Gray experimented with English versions of the Pindaric ode; William Collins wrote lyrics whose subject was the aesthetic power of emotion. Christopher Smart and William Blake created new forms for outbursts of lyric intensity; Robert Burns and William Cowper, at the century's end, evolved a new poetry of rural life. The century's movement was from poetry of action to poetry of image, and from public stance, affirming and defending social values, to private introspections, displaying with increasing directness the poet's sensibility.

Even so cavalier a summary of the aesthetic situation in the final two-thirds of the eighteenth century suggests the variety, vitality, and excitement of the world Johnson, Boswell, and Burke inhabited. The conflicting possibilities and opposed values which created interesting tensions and fusions in art reflected conflicts whose nonaesthetic manifestations seemed rather more sinister. The discursive prose of the late eighteenth century was highly responsive to the immediate political, social, and aesthetic situation; it concerned itself with all the areas of activity and all the problems sketched above. Many men hoped in their writing to close the gap between the operative values of the cultivated private man and those of governments and societies. Depending on their interpretation of tradition and the grounds of their faith, they found conservative or revolutionary solutions. The revolutionaries, exemplified by William Godwin and Thomas Paine at the century's end, would bridge the gulf between public and private by eliminating all government and trusting the rationality of individual men; they returned, with rather touching naiveté, to faith in the saving possibilities of reason. The conservatives, believing with Johnson that "the mind can only repose on the stability of truth," trusted traditional solutions; instead of overturning governments, they sought to influence individuals toward a more meaningful sense of public responsibility. They wrote with their ancestors looking over their shoulders, with the weight of a respected rhetorical tradition, with a sense of continuity and of the need for asserting its value. The luminaries of the previous era, Swift and Pope, had been masters of satire; Johnson and Gibbon and Burke, deft ironists all, rarely wrote satire, though often polemic. Perhaps they felt, with Pope, that the times were too corrupt for satire to be effective (but Pope, five years after disclaiming further satiric intent, published his enlarged version of *The Dunciad*). Perhaps they wished to support positive values rather than to attack corrupt ones; but Gibbon's mode of support was a meticulous account of human folly and frailty, Johnson condemned as much as he praised (and wrote *Rasselas*, an extended philosophic satire); Burke poured ridicule on his enemies. More often than their predecessors, for whatever reasons, such men as Burke and Johnson rejected the ambiguity of satiric indirection, speaking out for the value of moral self-analysis and analysis of the past for the lessons it contained. The truths men needed, they believed, had been recorded; it was necessary only to rediscover and understand them.

During this time, many men wrote prose so serious, so assertive, so commanding that it retains its energy undiminished today. Prose is the traditional medium for an era's self-investigation. It is the language of analysis and of proclamation. The best prose of the eighteenth century records human responses to the anomalies of the age; it is the product of deep assurance pressed to react to immediate and demanding questions. The passion and power of Johnson, Burke, and Gibbon derive from minds engaged in the search for truth, still believing in the existence of truth and the possibility of finding it. Although this was the era of Hume, its dominant tone, as we have seen, is not skeptical; if some of the writers here represented suffered private agonies of doubt, most yet assumed that their dilemmas were personal, reflecting no uncertainties in the universe, only difficulties of the individual psyche. And the individual psyche was still far less important, in the minds of these thinkers, than external reality: social, political, historical, theological, literary.

II

Political Writing: Burke

In Horace Walpole's record of day-to-day political activity in the reign of George III, members of Parliament appear to be a meretricious lot. They are awarded peerages for dubious reasons; they maneuver to get an exceptionally stupid lord off the scene so that he will not ruin a parliamentary debate; they quarrel like schoolboys over the conduct of the American Revolution. We admire Walpole's history because of its unmistakable air of life, but the life it reveals is often petty and ridiculous. The major political writing of the late eighteenth century, on the other hand, occupies a high plane. There were reasons enough for cynicism in the political corruption of the time, but Burke and Paine and Godwin are not cynical. They see individual phenomena as reflections of large principles; they refer small concerns to vast contexts, in the characteristic intellectual fashion of their time, and compel their readers to understand the ramifying implications of every trivial stand taken.

The strong provocation of two great revolutions, the American and the French, produced the century's most vibrant political writing, after Swift. Edmund Burke, who had defended the rights of the American colonists, found in the French upheavals the stimulus to formulate and propound his own deepest convictions. His opposition to the use of force against the colonies, best articulated in his "Conciliation Speech," is practical, not theoretical: He recognizes the limited possibilities for success in a policy of strong repression, the superior advantages achievable by gentler methods. He uses traditional political rhetoric ("Those who wield the thunder of the state"; "winged ministers of vengeance") with ironic overtones; the energy of his speech comes not so much from the power of his language as from the power of his clear perception of political realities.

Like most pieces of persuasion, Burke's argument in the "Conciliation Speech" depends upon his apparent assumption of solidarity with his auditors. His psychological and political acuteness emerge in the diverse grounds of solidarity he asserts, moving from the idealistic to the practical, from the theoretical to the specific and concrete. The opening stages of his argument demonstrate his deftness. Early he appeals to his listeners' desire for simplicity, cutting through complex issues in a way likely to move a twentieth-century American reader conscious of his nation's Asian entanglements. "The proposition is Peace. Not Peace through the medium of War; not Peace to arise out of universal discord . . . ; not Peace to depend on . . . the precise marking the shadowy boundaries of a complex Government. It is simple Peace . . . . "

This is strong emotional argument, which will hardly bear the pressure of rational investigation. Burke continues it by associating his plan with pure, personal virtues ("plain good intention," "genuine simplicity of heart") and by rejecting as corrupt unnamed alternatives (which appeal "to the pruriency of curious ears," are merely "new and captivating" and full of meretricious "Splendor"). He has offered neither rational nor practical grounds for his position, but it has become, by the laws of association, the position of virtue.

At this point he inserts hints of tough-mindedness. Although he is willing to conciliate the colonies, he sees that England has a position of force; he argues, on the basis of national experience, that only a nation with strength can afford conciliation. Appealing to national pride in England's military supremacy, he argues that this supremacy makes a mild policy safe: "Such an offer from such a power will be attributed to magnanimity." Then, without further developing his thesis, he shifts ground, urging the necessity "to consider distinctly the true nature and the peculiar circumstances" of the case. And his argument becomes severely practical, an argument of enlightened self-interest, as he details, with abundant statistical evidence, the commercial advantages that the colonies offer the parent-nation. He offers equally cogent arguments against the use of force as a mode of repression, and then examines the causes for the colonists' love of freedom.

The first of these is their English origins. Although the others are more limited (the institution of slavery in the South, the nature of American education, the remoteness of the colonies' physical situation, etc.), the reverberations of Burke's first cause have their effect. "The question is," he claims, "not whether their spirit deserves praise or blame;—what, in the name of God, shall we do with it?" The sentence exemplifies the complexity and the moral effectiveness of his tone. Superficially, it is the tone of the irritated, practical man, unconcerned with moral judgment, wishing only an efficient means of dealing with the problem at hand. But the problem at hand has been demonstrated, by implication, to be a moral one. No British reader, reminded of the proud national tradition of freedom and reminded that the colonists' devotion to liberty is part of their tie to England ("The Colonists . . . are therefore not only devoted to Liberty, but to Liberty according to English ideas, and on English principles."), could fail to realize that the American spirit is praiseworthy; if he accepts this realization, Burke's case is won.

The merging of moral and practical considerations through subtleties of tone, the alternation between the moral and the practical as the substance of argument—these are crucial techniques of the speech. Burke engineers assent on many fronts at once. His sympathy for the colonists is not for revolutionaries but for men who have a rightful claim, supported by reason and emotion, and as he goes on to demonstrate through his review-histories of Ireland, Wales, Chester, and Durham, by English tradition as well. What reason and feeling and morality and tradition demand, he believes, must be done; to worry about the consequences of a right action is pusillanimous. "The question with me is, . . . not, what a lawyer tells me I *may* do; but what humanity, reason, and justice, tells me I ought to do."

At the same time that Burke draws his listeners or readers toward necessary assent, he mocks them for dissent. This speech, masterful in its persuasion, is equally authoritative in its irony. "Then, Sir, you keep up revenue laws which are mischievous, in order to preserve trade laws that are useless." Although the formal balance of the sentence emphasizes its ironic bite, the irony is more than verbal. It derives from Burke's passionate recognition of what seems to him national hypocrisy. A nation that prates of virtue governs its collective activities by the most short-sighted perceptions of self-interest. It claims to uphold an ordered structure of law without examining the quality of the laws upheld; it contemplates encouraging American slaves to rebel and claim their freedom without realizing its own dependence on the trade that created slavery; its parliament, like the dog in *Alice in Wonderland* (" 'I'll be judge, I'll be jury,' Said cunning old Fury: 'I'll try the whole cause and condemn you to death' ") sits in judgment on an issue that intimately involves its own self-interest. At such phenomena Burke directs his irony. Even trivial and obvious verbal tricks reflect his sense of a split in values. He inserts such qualifiers as *really* or *rather* in contexts that demand unqualified response; his diction pays tribute to an ideal of decorum while his relentless detailing of facts insists that traditional standards of politeness are irrelevant, even immoral, in the face of immediate political exigencies.

By simultaneously supporting and questioning his readers' assumptions (we are all willing to declare ourselves in favor of peace, simplicity, and good intentions, and opposed to pruriency, mere novelty, and meaningless complexity; but being human, we also find ourselves involved in unexamined pieties which conceal splits of value), Burke creates a kind of relevance that extends far beyond the immediate political situation. Although Burke did not know it, the battles of Lexington and Concord had already been fought when he spoke; the course of events that was to lead to American independence was inexorably in motion. Moreover, the House of Commons soon rejected all the crucial propositions of his speech. Its political effect was minimal; yet it survives as a masterpiece of rhetoric, supported by moral and practical clarity, and a masterpiece that speaks to issues still of concern.

In his bitter attacks on the principles and practice of the French Revolution, Burke mainfests the same grasp of the immediate existential situation as that which dominates his "Conciliation Speech." The facts of the case move him and form his attitude, based first on knowledge, only then on conservative theory. Both the form and the substance of his utterances manifest his intelligence, vigor, integrity, imaginative scope. Burke shows himself master of a rhetoric that accurately reflects the intricacies of his thought. The close link between rhetoric and meaning in the best political writing of the eighteenth century—a link that has virtually disappeared in modern political prose—is a reason for its abiding power.

One of Burke's important devices is the extended metaphor. Here is a characteristic excerpt from *Reflections on the French Revolution:*

> The speculative line of demarcation, where obedience ought to end, and resistance must begin, is faint, obscure, and not easily definable. It is not a single act, or a single event, which determines it. Governments must be abused and deranged indeed, before it can be thought of; and the prospect of the future must be as bad as the experience of the past. When things are in that lamentable condition, the nature of the disease is to indicate the remedy to those whom nature has qualified to administer in extremities this critical, ambiguous, bitter potion to a distempered state.

The commonplace metaphor of the "line of demarcation"—here made into a visual image by the adjectives Burke applies to it—yields to the dominant image of sickness. This sickness may be insanity ("abused and deranged"), but the "distemper" is not incurable, although the cure may be almost as dangerous as the disease. The adjectives describing the curative "potion" exemplify Burke's technique. All three combine a specific medical meaning with a more general and abstract application. *Critical* means "relating to the crisis of a disease; determining the issue of a disease"; it also means "of the nature of, or constituting, a crisis; involving suspense as to the issue." *Ambiguous* means "doubtful, not clearly defined," but also "not to be trusted"; *bitter* describes both a taste and an emotional reaction. Similarly, *extremities* in its general sense means "conditions of extreme urgency," but it also conveys the metaphorical meaning (*in extremis*) of being near death.

At every point Burke thus emphasizes the detailed relevance of that metaphor of disease and medicine which recurs frequently in his work, stressing the analogy between governments and individuals so vital to his thought, and suggesting the seriousness of what may go wrong with governments. Governments, like men, can die or be murdered; they can also be cured. But only doctors are likely to cure disease; Burke's metaphor suggests not just the danger of the potion but the fact that it can be known only "to those whom nature has qualified." In *Letter to a Noble Lord*, his reply to an accusation of venality, Burke sees himself as the doctor and England as the diseased victim. The danger of internal corruption to the state, the responsibility of those concerned with her welfare (such as Burke himself), make the English situation analogous to that of Frame.

Governments are composed of human beings, they deal with human problems, but they transcend human limitations. The relative value of the government and the individual was a crucial problem for the late eighteenth century, a special case of that central philosophical issue of the relation between the general and the particular. For Burke, with his strong classic bias, the general was more significant than the particular; governments, which could avoid the weakness of individuals, might provide models for men. The language in which he describes the operations of government is that of conventional moral adjuration. It is the proper goal of every man, in the eighteenth-century scheme of things, to oppose his sovereign reason to will and to caprice, to make opinion, fancy, and inclination yield to the control of reason. Such a goal, as every serious thinker had realized, was not fully attainable by the individual. Gulliver may dream of becoming a Houyhnhmn, but he makes himself ridiculous by the dream. Burke believes, however, that governments can achieve a comparable ideal: "I have ever abhorred, since the first dawn of my understanding to this its obscure twilight, all the operations of opinion, fancy, inclination, and will, in the affairs of government, where only a sovereign reason, paramount to all forms of legislation and administration, should dictate. Government is made for the very purpose of opposing that reason to will and to caprice, in the reformers or in the reformed, in the governors or in the governed, in kings, in senates, or in people."

This quotation from *Letter to a Noble Lord* demonstrates Burke's commitment to the kind of paradox that supplies tension to some of the best writing of his time. It manifests his faith that government is more than governors, that transcendent reason resides mysteriously in the institution, not in the men who compose it. But it depends on a *should*, describes a goal to be aimed for, not one achieved. If a government is more than the sum of its parts, the nature of the parts is still crucial.

Burke poises himself between his sense of the grandeur, the near-sacredness, of the state as an institution and his awareness that bad men produce bad governments. The French National Assembly, where unqualified men have more power than their betters, fills him with horror. "Whenever the supreme authority is vested in a body so composed, it must evidently produce the consequence of supreme authority placed in the hands of men not taught habitually to respect themselves; who had no previous fortune in character at stake; who could not be expected to bear with moderation, or to conduct with discretion, a power, which they themselves, more than any others, must be surprised to find in their hands." Self-respect is a noble virtue, "character" the most meaningful wealth; lacking these qualities men should not presume to govern. Power belongs to those accustomed to its use; hierarchy should

control the political world as it does the natural universe. Power, to be
borne and wielded, is a burden as well as a force. Moderation and discretion should govern state and individual alike. In Burke's descriptive as well
as his admonitory prose, he vividly displays his central moral convictions,
insisting on their relevance to the public sphere.

The passion of *Reflections on the French Revolution* is not fully ex-
plicable by the individual situation that provoked it; it is the passion of
a man defending his deepest beliefs. He stands for tradition ("People will
not look forward to posterity, who never look backward to their ancestors"), order (implying hierarchy), reason, moderation, good sense,
dignity—the best values of his time. He perceives that the cry for equality,
the new belief in "the rights of man" (a belief tragically separated, he
feels, from awareness of man's responsibilities), the desire for sudden
change, oppose these central values, foretell chaos, imply reduction to
the lowest human denominator. He believes that an attack on himself for
accepting a government pension is an attack on traditional values; the
energy of *Letter to a Noble Lord*, too, is that of fundamental conviction.
Defending himself, he defends also a great faith.

Burke's most powerful metaphor for the state is a cosmic analogy
which both includes and transcends the analogies he has drawn between
governments and men. Government is, he concludes, like the natural
world itself, "a permanent body composed of transitory parts." Giving
due weight to both its aspects, in *Letter to a Noble Lord* he dramatizes the
Augustan belief in the value of the universal: Commitment to large realities helps men to avoid the penalties of their own smallness.

> Our political system is placed in a just correspondence and symmetry with
> the order of the world, and with the mode of existence decreed to a perma-
> nent body composed of transitory parts; wherein, by the disposition of a
> stupendous wisdom, moulding together the great mysterious incorporation
> of the human race, the whole, at one time, is never old, or middle-aged, or
> young, but, in a condition of unchangeable constancy, moves on through
> the varied tenour of perpetual decay, fall, renovation, and progression.

The assurance of Burke's comparison between the organization
and meaning of government and that of the universe is striking; so is the
sonority and authority of his sentence, in rhythm and diction. He records
his vision of universal hierarchy: The "stupendous wisdom" that governs
the universe corresponds to the wisdom inherent in proper government;
"the great mysterious incorporation of the human race" duplicates on a

larger scale the mysterious incorporation of diverse people in one nation. For Burke the idea of ordered government has natural sanctions so profound that they become in effect supernatural.

III

History: Gibbon

The critical eye which men of the eighteenth century turned on their own political affairs could direct itself with equal searchingness (and disagreement) toward the past. In 1752 Viscount Bolingbroke published his *Letters on History*, the central principle of which was the ancient maxim, "history is philosophy teaching by example." The *Letters* were extremely popular, partly because they enunciated a fashionable but devoutly held doctrine. Given the prevailing belief in the power of reason, men could feel it possible to profit by the example of the past, to avoid its mistakes. Given belief in the universality of character—men were thought to have been essentially the same in all times and places, although socially-caused differences, of course, existed—history provided the best insight into psychology. The sense of intellectual mastery which many eighteenth-century thinkers shared readily focused on history; important writers of the period (notably Hume and Smollett) wrote history with a vivid belief in its immediate moral relevance.

Edward Gibbon investigated the decline and fall of the Roman Empire with full awareness of the subject's significance to his own time. He interested himself less in facts than in causality. In his search for reasons for the collapse of the Empire, his belief in the existence of determinable chains of cause and effect produced an interpretation of unequaled authority, rhetorical force, and erudition.

The relation between particular facts and general principles is an issue in history as in political writing. Gibbon's interpretations reveal his values: "The freedom of the mind, the source of every generous and rational sentiment, was destroyed by the habits of credulity and submission; and the monk, contracting the vices of a slave, devoutly followed the faith and passions of his ecclesiastical tyrant." This is part of his discussion of monastic life. Accusations of atheism thundered upon Gibbon after the publication of the first volume of *The Decline and Fall*, which concluded with the famous Chapters XV and XVI, overt attacks on early Christianity as being responsible—along with "barbarism"—for the Empire's fall.

Gibbon's bias against Christianity is implicit in his classical humanistic values. He admires "rational sentiment"; he values generosity and consequently "freedom of the mind," a state of being which Burke and Dr. Johnson would also have ardently upheld without meaning by it anything like what Paine or Godwin might have implied. Because "submission" has become for Gibbon the opposite of "freedom"—for Dante, it was actually one expression of our freedom: *In la sua voluntad' è nostra pace* ("In His will is our peace")—he condemns monasticism, not merely as the encourager of blind faith and indulged passion, but as an institution that subordinates the faith and passions of many to those of one: the Pope or the Abbot of a monastery. The monastic system, quasi-military in its stress on obedience, seemed to him to oppose the sort of government envisioned also by Burke, in which reason controls by superior right, not by arbitrary authority.

Gibbon begins his discussion of monasticism in Chapter XXXVII by announcing,

> The indissoluble connexion of civil and ecclesiastical affairs has compelled and encouraged me to relate the progress, the persecutions, the establishment, the divisions, the final triumph, and the gradual corruption of Christianity. I have purposely delayed the consideration of two religious events, interesting in the study of human nature, and important in the decline and fall of the Roman empire: (I) The institution of the monastic life; and, (II) The conversion of the northern Barbarians.

The summary list with which he opens, first reiterating as fact what is the essence of his interpretation ("the indissoluble connexion of civil and ecclesiastical affairs") is characteristic. He organizes his prodigious mass of fact by repeated summaries which make the whole matter seem simple, orderly, under control. The formulation, "compelled and encouraged," is also typical, in its unexpectedness and in its curious logic. For most writers, *compelled*—as a motive and as an explanation—would be sufficient. But Gibbon's ideas dominate not only his mind—through which, as a rational man, he is "compelled"—but his emotions: he feels desire as well as compulsion to complete his task in the ambitious form in which he imagines it. He places the interest of the religious events for "the study of human nature" before their significance in the decline and fall of the Empire, thus indicating an important theme of his book. While he displays the interest these events have for him as an individual human being, he also conveys, through his tone and sentence structure, his acceptance of the social role of the historian; dispassionate, comprehensive, detached.

These qualities—Gibbon's handling of masses of material; his concern with "human nature"; his complex, personal yet public attitude toward his subject; his masterful style—are absorbing throughout *The Decline and Fall*. Gibbon is a master of impressive statistics as a technique for dealing with detail: five thousand anchorites and fifty monasteries south of Alexandria, fourteen hundred monks on the Island of Tabenne, fifty thousand "religious persons" gathering at Easter, ten thousand females and twenty thousand males "of the monastic profession" in the city of Oxyrinchus alone. He concludes a paragraph of such figures by suggesting that posterity might apply to the monks a saying which had formerly referred to sacred animals: "that, in Egypt, it was less difficult to find a god than a man." The specificity of the numbers both emphasizes the scope of monastic influence and prepares for a judgment on that influence. These figures enumerate a mass eager to deny all that made them meaningfully human ("rational sentiment," "freedom of mind"), and even willing to reduce themselves to animals (some, Gibbon explains, actually ate grass) by presuming to be more than men. This is one of Gibbon's most vital arguments against the effects of Christianity. He announces a little later that he abuses the name of man by applying it to the extreme ascetics.

Gibbon makes facts convincing by making them vivid:

> They sank under the painful weight of crosses and chains; and their emaciated limbs were confined by collars, bracelets, gauntlets, and greaves, of massy and rigid iron. All superfluous incumbrance of dress they contemptuously cast away; and some savage saints of both sexes have been admired, whose naked bodies were only covered by their long hair. They aspired to reduce themselves to the rude and miserable state in which the human brute is scarcely distinguished above his kindred animals; and a numerous sect of Anachorets [that is, Anchorites] derived their name from their humble practice of grazing in the fields of Mesopotamia with the common herd.

Here he works through suggestive detail, and he calculates his conjunctions: the implicit equation of crosses with chains as important only for their "painful weight," the use of ornaments ("collars, bracelets") and armor ("gauntlets, and greaves") as equivalent in substance and in meaning, the increasing stress on animality which reaches its climax in the final clause, the revealing oxymorons ("savage saints," "aspired to reduce themselves," "human brute").

Every sentence of Gibbon's here quoted has begun with a noun or pronoun—usually the subject—closely followed by a verb. This is Gibbon's typical sentence structure. It conveys absolute sureness; there is no need to qualify. Also characteristic is the compound or compound-complex structure, in which the first main clause makes a more general statement than the second, which offers more specific or interpretative detail. Gibbon thus creates measured, logical progressions; he seems to meditate every piece of evidence. The compelling rhythms of his sentences help to engineer conviction; the dignified diction, even while it dwells on specific details, directs attention to general significance. The assurance, the control implicit in all Gibbon's devices create an aura of godlike authority and wisdom.

From this perspective he investigates the operations of human nature, hardly seeming to belong to the species he examines.

> The indignant father bewailed the loss, perhaps, of an only son; the credulous maid was betrayed by vanity to violate the laws of nature; and the matron aspired to imaginary perfection, by renouncing the virtues of domestic life. Paula yielded to the persuasive eloquence of Jerom; and the profane title of mother-in-law of God tempted that illustrious widow to consecrate the virginity of her daughter Eustochium.

Nominally these sentences concern the vagaries of human psychology, but in terms suggested by Gibbon's pervasive interest in chains of cause and effect: For every effect he supplies a comprehensible human cause—credulity, vanity, desire for superhuman status or for perfection (and, implicitly, boredom with routine domesticity). The judgments are perceptive but they lack sympathy; the awareness they demonstrate is convincing but neither full nor sufficiently complex.

Gibbon's detachment is both a weakness and a strength. It is part of his air of authority; conveying his lack of involvement, he suggests his lack of bias. This can be entertaining, as in his ironic footnotes. He tells us that the daily ration of bread in a certain monastery was twelve ounces, and appends in a footnote, without comment, a recommendation by the reformer John Howard that the minimum humane allowance of bread in prisons should be twenty-four ounces a day; or his footnote reports that a monk claims to have gained enormous power by his vow of obedience and vast wealth through his vow of poverty, then adds, "I forget the con-

sequences of his vow of chastity." The spirit of a judging mind, which
dominates *The Decline and Fall*, is one of the book's conspicuous virtues.
This is history ordered, made rational, judged by a penetrating intelligence of which one never loses consciousness.

On the other hand, the distant irony, the dispassionate tone, the
authoritative rhetoric may finally make a modern reader uneasy. Can
history be as orderly as Gibbon makes it; do such clear sequences of cause
and effect exist? What were the hopes, despairs, exaltations, disappoint-
ments of these credulous maids, illustrious widows, and savage saints?
What would their destinies have been had they not become brides
and mothers-in-law and devotees of God? How many men and women
lived lives far more brutal under secular tyrannies far more tyrannical?
Rarely does Gibbon examine such possible alternatives. For him interpretation and facts are virtually inseparable; in spite of his frequent summaries, the structure of his arguments is sometimes difficult to uncover or
to remember. Convinced without knowing exactly why, we may become suspicious of our conviction—suspicious perhaps finally of the
eighteenth-century faith in "truth." Gibbon, believing that truth exists,
single, unchangeable, must believe that it is discoverable; the assumption
of *The Decline and Fall* is that he has discovered the truth of a span of
history. It is not an assumption that we necessarily share. The operations
of Gibbon's powerful mind compel interest; that mind demonstrates the
value of the eighteenth-century belief both in discernible truth and in the
pre-eminent importance of general ideas as modes of understanding
particular events. It also suggests the limitation of such beliefs in action.

IV

Personal Records:
Cowper, Gray, Walpole,
Chesterfield, Boswell, Gibbon

Political and historical prose concerns large events and issues; but
what of the records of individual sensibilities in an age that deprecated the
importance of the individual sensibility and believed in the overriding
significance of general truth? The eighteenth century has left us letters,
journals, and autobiographies in which men directly describe their own
thoughts and feelings, and one great biography which combines self-
revelation with insight into its subject. Such records enlarge our under-

standing of eighteenth-century life and values, suggest why social life was so important at that time, and expose some remarkable personalities.

The letter writers in this volume record a varied range of experience. William Cowper lived in the complete seclusion of a country village; Thomas Gray led the less secluded life of the academic; Lord Chesterfield and Horace Walpole inhabited the world of diplomacy and aristocracy. All concern themselves with the gossip of their several worlds and believe their relations with others to be of central importance.

COWPER

William Cowper was a religious fanatic, intermittently insane, a man isolated from the significant life of his time, a proponent of nature tamed. He loved his greenhouse, his hares, his kittens, his cup of tea. His horizon was small, his vision limited. His letters display no sophistication, and only the mildest irony. Yet his correspondence remains moving and revealing.

"Every thing I see in the fields is to me an object, and I can look at the same rivulet, or at a handsome tree, every day of my life, with new pleasure." "To say truth, it would be but a shocking vagary, should the mariners on board a ship buffeted by a terrible storm, employ themselves in fiddling and dancing; yet sometimes much such a part act I." Here are the poles of Cowper's personality which his letters expose. In one mood, he seems simple, pure, almost mystical; his prose is limpid. Aware of the narrowness of his experience, he converts it into breadth by the intensity of his perception: he can contemplate the same rivulet day after day, finding—and conveying—constantly new pleasure in it. At the other extreme, his writing becomes more self-conscious, his prose employs the metaphors of his poetry (not always, but it is always more studied and rhetorical than his "happier" prose), and he presents himself as miserable, damned, his capacity to take and give pleasure merely "fiddling and dancing." The letters' alternations between these extremes dramatize the conflict that governed Cowper's life and his poetry. We participate both in his joyous sanity and in his melancholic insanity.

Cowper's correspondence reveals a man of delicate sensibility and neurotic intensity. Neither trait would he reveal directly: the letters of the eighteenth century, however fully they expose their authors, are governed, like other forms of prose, by a special decorum. One feels this decorum's control in the variety of styles Cowper has at his disposal. He

is master of a Biblical simplicity and weight: "This is just as it should
be. We are all grown young again, and the days that I thought I should
see no more, are actually returned." Such a style is both dignified and
poignant. It seems to conceal nothing; it has patriarchal authority.
Cowper is also capable of arch mock-seriousness:

> In point of size she is likely to be a kitten always, being extremely small of
> her age, but time I suppose, that spoils everything, will make her also a cat.
> You will see her I hope before that melancholy period shall arrive, for no
> wisdom that she may gain by experience and reflection hereafter, will
> compensate the loss of her present hilarity. She is dressed in a tortoise-shell
> suit, and I know that you will delight in her.

This passage, like the preceding one, responds to a perception of
mutability, but its tone and technique temper the meaning with gentle
mockery, as Cowper adapts large concerns to small uses, employs the
language of morality and of human reference to characterize a kitten. It is
not surprising that he can make a small mock-epic out of giving Lady
Hesketh directions about the best roads to Olney.

These examples suggest how important to the effect of eighteenth-
century correspondence in general, and to Cowper's letters in particular,
is the controlling decorum of style. A letter, however private its purpose,
was a literary performance. This recognition meant that self-pity, self-
obsession, and malice must be modified and restrained by a style that in
its lucidity and strength affirmed the Augustan faith in the dignity of man.

GRAY

The appeal of Gray's letters, too, derives partly from the personality
revealed by them, partly from the value system they expose. Much of his
correspondence concerning literary questions demonstrates his acute
awareness of linguistic nuance. He felt his nation's language to be in flux,
and he felt his responsibility to the language. He believed that expression
was more important than content:

> Now I insist, that Sense is nothing in poetry, but according to the dress she
> wears, & the scene she appears in. if you should lead me into a superb
> Gothic building with a thousand cluster'd pillars, each of them half a mile
> high, the walls all cover'd with fretwork, & the windows full of red & blue
> Saints, that had neither head, nor tail; and I should find the Venus of Medici
> in person perk'd up in a long nich over the high altar, as naked as ever she

was born, do you think it would raise, or damp my devotions?

The freedom of this critical pronouncement makes it revealing. Gray's obvious delight in the metaphor of the "superb Gothic building" becomes a key element in his argument for free imaginative expression, "superior wildness, more barbaric fancy," as he says a few lines later. He indulges in gay exaggeration ("a thousand cluster'd pillars, each of them half a mile high," the naked Venus "in person"), in self-mockery (over his own enthusiasm for the Gothic, the saints with "neither head, nor tail"), in an offhand vigor of expression ("perk'd up in a long nich . . . as naked as ever she was born"), and in a studied anticlimax of structure. His argument is serious, though his tone is not; the possibility of such an argument in such a tone existed, in his time, only within the special conventions of the letter.

The tone of ironic persiflage concealing serious meaning is characteristic of Gray's correspondence. He uses it to cover his hurt feelings at the unfavorable or uncomprehending critical reception of his odes, to accommodate his interest in gossip of duels or attempts at clandestine marriage, to complain about a vulgar property owner: " . . . a fat young Man with a head & face much bigger than they are usually worn." Through it one discerns his large capacity for feeling, and the extent to which feeling associates itself for him with experiences of art of or nature. His disapproval of the "fat young Man" focuses on that man's desecration of nature for the sake of an artificial conception of "landscape":

> Behold the Trees are cut down to make room for flowering shrubs, the rock is cut up, till it is as smooth & as sleek as sattin . . . . Even the poorest bits of nature, that remain, are daily threatened, for he says (& I am sure, when the Greatheads are once set upon a thing, they will do it) he is determined, it shall be *all new*. These were his words, & they are Fate.

With the poet's perception of the broad implications of isolated experience, he elevates poor Mr. Greathead into a symbol of the *nouveaux riches*; his very name becomes a Bunyanesque emblem of his nature, and his words, "all new," reverberate with implications he never intended or dreamed of.

As his distaste for Greathead suggests, Gray's interest in nature is not, like Cowper's, in nature methodized but in the wilder—and therefore more imaginatively compelling—aspects of the external universe: the Highlands of Scotland, for example. The imaginative power of his letters, in their language and their conception, is the index of their quality.

WALPOLE

Horace Walpole's letters, like Gibbon's history, reveal his sense of himself as both public and private man. Reporting the trial of lords who had participated in a Jacobite uprising, he initially observes that "this sight at once feasted one's eyes and engaged all one's passions." He speaks of arming himself with resolution to endure the trial's emotional rigors; he reports himself "shocked" by his first sight of the prisoners. His meticulous rendering of detail—down to the appearance of a prisoner's hair—seems partly dictated by a desire to communicate the causes and the substance of his private emotion. On the other hand, his reference to such public standards as "the humane dignity of the law of England," his interest in relationships and in individual histories, his clear consciousness that he is reporting a great event—these suggest Walpole's awareness of his function as historian of his own time, a function he also fulfilled in his *Memoirs*. The public and the private role merge effectively in letters which preserve with full vitality the details, significant and petty, of eighteenth-century life.

CHESTERFIELD

Another version of fused roles emerges in the letters of Lord Chesterfield, whose central subject is the private endeavor necessary to maintain an effective public "image," as we would call it today. His letters both advocate and exemplify decorum. "Remember," he warns his godson, "that a man who does not generally please is nobody, and that constant endeavours to please, will infallibly please, to a certain degree, at least." He here reveals his constant awareness of social reality and necessity—a man defines himself as "somebody" only by pleasing others ("good-breeding is the art of pleasing," wrote Fielding); his faith in the good results of determined effort; yet his modifying realism—although he is sure one can please by constant endeavor, he is equally sure that one will please only "to a certain degree," less than one had hoped. Lord Chesterfield's letters are unlike those from men to their friends in that they are written rather to his protegés, to his son and his godson, and for the avowed purpose of instruction. They reveal a great deal, not about the man in psychic undress, but about the values that governed sophisticated social intercourse.

The belief in the possibility of achieving truth takes a new form in these letters. As ardently as his contemporaries, Lord Chesterfield believed in that possibility, but his version of truth is limited and pragmatic. He thinks that by hard work and "minute attention" one can understand human nature, "which is pretty much the same in all human creatures," and can use that understanding to establish and maintain a position in the world. In addition to understanding, one needs virtue; but more important than virtue is reputation, "that solid foundation" upon which one builds character. Man can be a flashy "meteor" or have the solid value of "currency"; Chesterfield's advice assumes the desirability of the latter state. His letters, in addition to their constant adjurations to study the ways of the world, are lavish in particular advice, frequently cynical, about conduct and about human nature. He exemplifies the ideal he advocates: to penetrate the disguises of others while preserving an impenetrably pleasing façade.

BOSWELL

It is difficult to imagine someone more unlike Lord Chesterfield than the young James Boswell, unconfident, socially awkward, satisfying himself with prostitutes and reaping consequences that Chesterfield warns of, neither rich, distinguished, nor secure. Instead of wishing to understand others while himself remaining impenetrable, Boswell yearned to have others understand him. Rarely did he write only for his own eye: His intimate *London Journal*, for example, was mailed in weekly installments to his friend John Johnston. Boswell displayed his character to the world, figuring conspicuously (often foolishly) in his great *Life* of Samuel Jonhson and in his account of the tour of the Hebrides, luxuriating in his melancholy in *The Hypochondriack*, wondering, for Johnston's benefit and his own, about his possibilities of success and about the impression he was making. But there was, after all, some similarity between him and Lord Chesterfield: Both interested themselves in the truth of character. Such interest was growing in the last half of the eighteenth century; Chesterfield's attentive inspection and Boswell's equally attentive introspection are two aspects of a single phenomenon.

Boswell's self-absorption produces fictionalizing and heightening in his accounts of himself. "I have discovered that we may be in some degree whatever character we choose," he writes with elation on November 21, 1762. "Besides, practice forms a man to anything. I was now happy to find myself cool, easy, and serene." Four days later: "I lay abed very gloomy. I thought London did me no good. I rather disliked it; and I thought of going back to Edinburgh immediately. In short, I was most miserable." Apparently he could no longer choose his character; but his pleasure in his own misery, the satisfaction with which he offers first the details of his mental process, then the categorical summary, "I was most miserable," for the moment replaces his desire for rational control. And if he is happy to find himself "cool, easy, and serene," he is equally pleased with himself when he stops his chaise to bow to the crown of Scotland and other national emblems. "Having thus gratified my agreeable whim and superstitious humour, I felt a warm glow of satisfaction. Indeed, I have a strong turn to what the cool part of mankind have named superstition. But this proceeds from my genius for poetry, which ascribes many fanciful properties to everything." He alternates between opposed visions of himself, sometimes praising himself as "cool"; again, scorning that "cool part of mankind" which would see his romantic enthusiasm as superstition.

The *London Journal* is not merely a record of egotism, nor is the appropriate reaction to it simple amusement at Boswell's posturing. The journal opens with its author's explanation that it is a way of following the classic injunction, "know thyself." It seems in part a genuine effort at self-awareness; it demonstrates a tireless if rarely successful attempt to reconcile personality with principle, individual perception with general standards. The effort at such reconciliation dominates Boswell's life and writings. "I was hurt to find even such a temporary feebleness," he writes in the *Journal of a Tour to the Hebrides*, "and that I was so far from being that robust wise man who is sufficient for his own happiness. I felt a kind of lethargy of indolence. I did not exert myself to get Dr. Johnson to talk, that I might not have the labour of writing down his conversation." To be "hurt" by his own feebleness is most Boswellian. So is the detail about his mental state; and so is his implicit guilt over his failure to make Dr. Johnson talk, a responsibility which in many moods he seems to feel is central. One justification for his obsession with Johnson was that the great critic seemed, more fully than anyone else Boswell knew, to reconcile in his life as in his work the claims of general standards and individual response. Boswell is always delighted to supply evidence of Johnson's achievement; but he also enjoyed recording deviations from the ideal, presenting his hero as a man individual and peculiar to the point of eccentricity. His mode of self-presentation is not dissimilar; although he provides a clear vision of what he wishes to become, he is unsparing in setting down his violations of his own standards.

We do not read Boswell for his value system, but because we relish the immediate sense of life he communicates. He does not awaken our historical awareness; he makes his own time and place seem like ours by concentrating on people who appear to have been much the same two hundred years ago. The *London Journal* is full of vivid humanity: Boswell's tutor ridiculing a thirteen-year-old's passion "by setting his teeth together and giving hard thumps on the knees of his breeches"; the old day laborer Michael Cholmondeley who sold himself as a slave for seven years; Boswell himself, interrupted as he is about to consummate his passion for Louisa, reflecting "that I had been at no place of worship today" and excusing himself to go to church.

His record of the affair with Louisa displays his narrative brilliance at its height. Like the novels of Richardson—but with how different a perspective!—it recounts minute events and minute shifts of feeling, building the reader's interest and suspense. At times Boswell uses the language of the novelist: "a sweet elevation of the charming petticoat"; "I fanned the flame by pressing her alabaster breasts and kissing her delicious lips." But such sentimental heightening exists in comic juxtaposition with matter-of-fact records of his self-obsession. His primary concern with Louisa seems to be to display his sexual powers: "I was unhappy at being prevented from the completion of my wishes, and yet I thought that I had saved my credit for prowess, that I might through anxiety have not acted a vigorous part . . . . " He plots to arrange appropriate time and place; fate thwarts him. Finally, on January 12, 1763 (in a passage later than the ones here included), he enjoys the "supreme rapture" of possession, having set off for an inn with Louisa in a hackney coach, supplied with macaroons and night clothes. "Good heavens," he observes, "what a loose did we give to amorous dalliance!" Louisa is duly impressed with his virility and his sense of himself is accordingly invigorated. The drama has dealt as much with the problem of masculine self-esteem as with the joys of sexual love; its honesty of self-revelation generates an air of absolute authenticity.

Boswell tells us that he finds "a great difficulty in describing visible objects." His supreme literary achievement was not to make things visible, but to make people come alive, himself and others—an enterprise in key with the developing values of his time. Dr. Johnson, in his *Rambler* essay on biography (No. 60), maintained that the small details of a man's life and habits make him real to us. Boswell demonstrates the truth of that assertion in his *Life of Johnson*, with its meticulous rendering of Johnson's idiosyncrasies. Johnson as a public figure had first interested Boswell, but as he came to know the great man his interest shifted to the private—the "real"—person and that person's relation to the public figure. His almost novelistic sense of the interesting makes him shift constantly between presentations of Johnson filling his public role as literary dictator and formidable conversationalist and Johnson in the intimacy of friendship. We come to realize that there is little conflict, almost no dichotomy, between Johnson the public and Johnson the private man, and this fact itself accounts for much of his fascination—for Boswell and for us. Johnson seems a man of genuine integrity, whose public persona exaggerates some of his private characteristics (his wide range of interest, his combativeness, his sense of authority, his Christian orientation) but disguises little.

Boswell makes his subject memorable by presenting every encounter as a little drama. First he sets the scene ("my lodging in Old Bond-street") and distributes the characters on stage ("Garrick played around him with a fond vivacity, taking hold of the breasts of his coat, and, looking up in his face with a lively archness . . . "; "Goldsmith, to divert the tedious minutes, strutted about, bragging of his dress"); then he brings them into verbal conflict, resolved by Johnson's final, definitive pronouncement. Over and over he duplicates the pattern; every conversation is a contest. If no clash of values or attitudes develops naturally, Boswell functions as *provocateur* to make one: "If, Sir, you were shut up in a castle, and a new-born child with you, what would you do?" Johnson's practicality, humanity, hatred of sentimental sham emerge as a result; so do his high literary standards and his unwillingness to be defeated. His sense of the drama of his own public role seems as strong as Boswell's; he is eager to perform.

Boswell, too, is a character in his drama. He will seem a fool if necessary, be Johnson's straight man and foil for the sake of dramatic revelation. In response to his complexity of role, the great man assumes a variety of postures. When Boswell reports, in elaborate detail, Johnson's responses to a series of searching questions about Catholicism, he concludes, "I thus ventured to mention all the common objections against the Roman Catholic Church, that I might hear so great a man upon them . . . . But it is not improbable that if one had taken the other side, he might have reasoned differently." Earlier, he reports Johnson's confession that in his boyhood he used always to choose the wrong side in a debate, because it allowed him to say more ingenious things. One often feels, in his reported conversations, this spirit of intellectual opposition.

The fundamental form of Johnson's relationship with Boswell was mentor-pupil, with Johnson, thirty-one years Boswell's senior, assuming the father role. (At one point Boswell speculates aloud about why he gets along so well with Johnson, so badly with his own father. Johnson explains complacently that since he is a man of the world, he can deal with Boswell as the insular Lord Auchinleck cannot.) But occasional reversals of role startle us. The second time Boswell encountered Johnson, the older man told him that he seldom came home at night before 2:00 A.M. "I took the liberty," says the biographer, "to ask if he did not think it wrong to live thus, and not make more use of his great talents. He owned it was a bad habit." After longer acquaintance, Johnson confessed to the young man his own struggles with melancholy. Boswell's openness, his tendency to self-castigation, and his respect for authority seem to have provoked Johnson to self-revelation.

Johnson's confessions of melancholy and his unwillingness to go to bed at night remind us that he was not Boswell's opposite (a role in which the young man frequently cast him). Although Boswell often defined a polarity against which he could set himself, he also provided analogies for Johnson's experience and problems. His own explanation for Johnson's interest in him was that the critic, an examiner of the human mind, was pleased by Boswell's "undisguised display of what had passed in it"; in return Johnson provided his own display. Many appealing moments of the biography describe him playing a part, providing a public demonstration of his wit or cantankerousness: announcing that he would have HUGGED Adam Smith had he known of his advocacy of rhyme; pointing out that it was worthwhile being a dunce in Pope's day, given the prospect of poetic immortality in *The Dunciad*, then adding to a hapless bystander, "You should have lived then"; urging Boswell, who had demurred about the uselessness of a proposed project, "Never mind the use, do it." But the most moving sections are those in which Boswell's own awareness of the anguish of psychic conflict forms his interpretation of Johnson. "His mind resembled the vast amphitheatre, the Colisæum at Rome. In the centre stood his judgment, which, like a mighty gladiator, combated those apprehensions that, like the wild beasts of the *Arena*, were all around in cells, ready to be let out upon him. After a conflict, he drove them back into their dens; but not killing them, they were still assailing him."

Boswell's judgment was perhaps not so mighty a gladiator, and its foes were inclinations more often than apprehensions. But the struggle between reason and feeling was central in his own life, and consciousness of this centrality informs his compassionate yet admiring portrayal of Johnson.

Boswell was anxious to learn from his great mentor, even more anxious to display the accomplishments of one to whom he refers quite naturally as "the sage." He frequently manifests his pride in the closeness of the association between himself and the greatest literary figure of his time. His tone vacillates: We find the elevation of the dispassionate biographer, moments of personal malice (as in the accounts of Goldsmith's vanity), unself-conscious zest in the immediate occasion, humility before the great man, and mock-humility designed to stimulate response from Johnson. It is part of Johnson's triumph that public and private roles seem to have merged more nearly for him than for most men; it is Boswell's triumph that he achieved no such fusion, that the lofty biographer yields often to the engagingly vulnerable man who makes his world vivid by his involvement in it.

GIBBON

Edward Gibbon, who, unlike Boswell, wrote his autobiography consciously for publication—who, indeed, wrote six versions of it—operated on assumptions far different from Boswell's. The thirst for self-revelation implicit in the idea of autobiography is concealed by his judicious, dignified approach. Boswell defines himself and others by their inner conflicts; Gibbon defines himself by his profession and accomplishments. His expressed interest in his private life is minimal. Thus he dismisses in eight words the struggle between him and his father over his desire to marry Suzanne Curchod: "A lover's wishes reluctantly yielded to filial duty." The sentence continues, "time and absence produced their effect; but my choice has been justified by the virtue of Mademoiselle C[urchod] (now Madame N[ecker]) in the most humble and the most splendid fortune." (The final clause refers to the fact that Mlle. Curchod, a simple country girl when he knew her, later married Jacques Necker, who became French director-general of finances; she was the mother of Mme. de Staël and held an important social position.) Self-justification seems to be the real issue, not recollection of Gibbon's personal emotion, and he feels transparent satisfaction at the flattering light cast upon his taste by Mme. Necker's prominence. Or is the sentence ironic? And if so, how ironic? At whose expense? Perhaps we are to read it as a commentary on youthful passion, which yields inevitably to time and absence, or as a wry observation on the universal need for public justification. The cool, distant tone of *The Decline and Fall* dominates the autobiography as well, and a sense of irony is rarely far distant. It may be difficult to locate in isolated instances, but its over-all effect is vivid: It insists on the unimportance of individual lives, including that of the author, in the vastness of time and space. Gibbon sums up his life by comparing it with the common lot: "The far greater part of the globe is overspread with barbarism or slavery; in the civilized world the most numerous class is condemned to ignorance and poverty, and the double fortune of my birth in a free and enlightened country, in an honourable and wealthy family, is the lucky chance of an unit against millions." No suspicion of irony here: In one way or another—in an aristocrat's way, or a historian's—Gibbon is always aware of the millions.

His self-awareness involves self-presentation in distancing guises. In the sentence about the frustration of his love, he refers to a clash, not between himself and his father, but between "a lover's wishes" and "filial duty." Only for that sentence does he exist as lover. He also provides glimpses of himself as student at Magdalen College, Oxford ("where I lost fourteen valuable months of my youth. The reader will ascribe this loss to my own incapacity, or to the vices of that ancient institution"), as militia officer ("my present acquaintance will smile when I assure them that I was once a very tolerable officer . . . ; and the Captain of Grenadiers [they may again smile] has not been useless to the historian of the Roman Empire"), as bereaved son ("I revere the memory of my father, his errors I forgive, nor can I repent of the important sacrifices which were chearfully offered by filial piety"). The feelings one expects about each successive role are masked by irony or dignified by linguistic heightening. When Gibbon tries to express intimate feeling, he is likely to strike a false note—"I feel a tear of gratitude trickling down my cheek"—so much do his typical effects depend upon emotional restraint or concealment.

Emotional restraint need not mean lack of expressiveness. Gibbon writes of himself as historian, for example, with astonishing force. In this role he found personal justification and emotional release. Despite diction as dignified and structure as measured as the rest of the narrative, his accounts of the controversy that attended his great book are vibrant with energy. The famous passages that explain the origin and describe the completion of *The Decline and Fall* are also cases in point. "It was in Rome, on the fifteenth of October, 1764, as I sat musing amidst the ruins of the Capitol, while the barefooted fryars were singing Vespers in the temple of Jupiter, that the idea of writing the decline and fall of the City first started to my mind. After Rome has kindled and satisfied the enthusiasm of the Classic pilgrim, his curiosity for all meaner objects insensibly subsides."

The narrative of the manuscript's completion is more personal, but this skeletal description of its conception is equally moving. It suggests Gibbon's awareness of the vibrancy of the outer world, capable of both kindling and satisfying enthusiasm, and his sense of the mystery of artistic inspiration: The crucial idea starts into the historian's mind as though it were not of his origin. The ironies of the conjunction of barefoot friars, ruined Capitol, and temple of Jupiter are central to *The Decline and Fall*. The presentation of this conjunction in visual rather than theoretical form is peculiarly effective: We realize that Gibbon was obsessed by an image ("his curiosity for all meaner objects" thereafter insensibly subsiding) as well as an idea. One contemplates the disproportion between the accidental scene and the vast work it inspired, yet is led to realize how much of the work is implicit in the scene. Like much in Gibbon, the passage is a tour de force of understatement.

Of all these writers about people, Boswell seems most representative of the ambiguities of his time. In his interest in individual personality he foreshadows Romanticism, as does Cowper in his intense perception of nature, Gray in his concentration on the value of imagination. But in his sometimes wistful belief in absolute standards, Boswell—like Cowper in his stylistic, and Gibbon in his emotional, self-discipline; Chesterfield in his awareness of society's power; Walpole in his sense of history; Gray in his ironic impenetrability—looks back to the values that had dominated his century. His Janus stance is exemplary of the age.

v

The Literature of Observation:
Goldsmith, Johnson

Letters, journals, and biographies make the eighteenth century real to us, but quite another sort of writing made it real to itself. "Our complaints against the society we live in, our criticisms of it, always make more or less discernible our idea of the perfect society," writes a modern social historian.[1] The social criticism of the late eighteenth century was more intense than that of the *Tatler* and *Spectator*; moral issues and social ones merge in this time of developing social conscience. Some criticism was implicit in descriptive accounts; some was more directly offered. Both kinds suggest visions of ideal social order.

GOLDSMITH

In *The Citizen of the World* Oliver Goldsmith used the classic satiric device of the persona to provide moral perspective. The persona here is a Chinese visitor to London; his wondering observations on English social and literary life gain force from the prevalent assumption that human nature is the same in all times and places: hence the seriousness of his indictment of English deviations from proper norms. Sometimes the Chinese gentleman displays his incapacity for understanding the English, as in *Citizen* VIII, where he relates his encounters with prostitutes under the illusion that these are women of extraordinary graciousness and compassion. In the next essay, he professes that his eyes have been opened; he understands now what is going on and records it with naïve directness: " . . . the laws are cemented with blood, praised, and disregarded"; "As for the magistrates, the country-justices and squires, they are employed first in debauching young virgins, and then punishing the transgression"; "Upon proper occasions, he looks excessively tender. This is performed by laying his hand upon the heart, shutting his eyes, and showing his teeth." The technique is that of *Gulliver's Travels*, where Gulliver withholds judgment of what he sees when judgment is conspicuously required. Goldsmith, like Swift, forces his readers' awareness of the judgments that should be made. The calculated anticlimax of "cemented . . . praised, and disregarded" depends on the reader's frustrated expectation that the verbs will increase in emphasis; the moral incompatibility between debauching virgins and punishing them for debauchery demands the reader's awareness and judgment; the disparity between real tenderness and its purported physical manifestations, mechanical and grotesque, insists that the reader be aware of incongruity and attempt to resolve it, an act only to be achieved by moral judgment. Goldsmith's

---

[1] Martin Green, *The Problem of Boston: Some Readings in Cultural History* (New York: W. W. Norton & Company, Inc., 1966), p. 19.

prose, in the satiric essays, is economical and forceful. His sentences are usually short; he manipulates a subtle balance of concrete detail and weighty abstraction.

Not all the *Citizen of the World* essays are satiric; Goldsmith also uses his foreign visitor as a direct mode of social, literary, and political commentary. England's "Johnsons and Smolletts," he writes, "are truly poets; though, for all I know, they never made a single verse in their whole lives." This judgment derives unconventionally from the conventional assumption that poetry involves "glowing sentiment, striking imagery, concise expression, natural description, and modulated periods." Goldsmith's persona—functioning now as protection rather than disguise—frees his imagination to produce this strikingly original judgment of contemporary prose.

Goldsmith's most commanding tone mingles the satiric and the serious, as in this view of the didactic literature of his time: "The dullest writer tells of virtue and liberty, and benevolence with esteem; tells his true story, filled with good and wholesome advice; warns against slavery, bribery, or the bite of a mad dog, and dresses up his little useful magazine of knowledge and entertainment, at least with a good intention." This is descriptively accurate and satirically just. Its effectiveness depends on its suggestion that the speaker is compassionate as well as mocking. He gives the dullards their due, freely grants their high regard for virtue while hinting at their indiscriminate exploitation of any likely cause ("slavery, bribery, or the bite of a mad dog")and the unavoidable triviality ("little useful magazine") of their accomplishment. The combination of human gentleness with critical sharpness is one of Goldsmith's great gifts. It implies his adherence to diverse standards of value, his reconciliation of the claims of broad humanity and of critical integrity.

In *The Bee* Goldsmith assumes an English persona whose character is not dissimilar to that of the Chinese observer. Like Lien Chi Altangi, *The Bee*'s narrator is benevolent, naive, alienated from some of the ways and the values of the fashionable world. He, too, is a sharp observer and a judicious phrasemaker. His accounts of English feminine dress or of the social exigencies of poverty are leisurely and penetrating, their satiric implications modified by their warmth and gentleness of tone.

The gifts Goldsmith displays in these essays are a novelist's: sharp eye for detail, vivid sense of character, awareness of revealing action. To comment on the extravagances of fashion he contrives a little narrative about his friend, "a good-natured old man," and the friend's cousin

Hannah, "some years older than himself," whom he mistakes from the back, by her dress, for a girl of fifteen. The situation between the two becomes increasingly ludicrous. The exposure of the lady's bosom, which "had felt no hand, but the hand of time, these twenty years," offends her cousin; his unfashionable wig and muff displease her. But his attachment to the muff is as strong and as irrational as hers to her finery, so they cannot come to terms. Together they observe London life, the old man seeing all as a spectacle, the old woman seeing everywhere a rival. Hannah provides running commentary, disapproving of fashionable trains because if one was stepped on its wearer might suffer a bad fall, "and then you know, cousin,—her cloaths may be spoiled." The two part, having sustained their mutual incomprehension, and Goldsmith offers no further commentary.

The implicit commentary which the tale itself supplies is psychological as well as social; even more penetrating in this respect is the essay "On the Use of Language," which deals with language as disguise and as social convenience. It has been said that the novel as a form concerns itself with the intersection of the psychological and the social; Goldsmith's interest in the two in conjunction is another suggestion of his novelistic impulse. Periodical essays can hardly develop character or situation in full fictional terms, and the "characters" in *The Bee* are types rather than individuals. Yet Goldsmith's awareness of the misery of the man too poor to buy his own dinner, unable because of his poverty to achieve the social leverage that would procure a dinner invitation, is more than a knowledge of how society operates; it is an understanding of how *people* operate. Goldsmith's types seem real people; his understanding of the interplay of general and particular, the laws that govern society and those that control individuals, helps to make him a brilliant social critic.

JOHNSON

Dr. Johnson is more heavy-handed in his periodical essays in the *The Rambler* and *The Idler*. Goldsmith can use a metaphor with complete lightheartedness: "A French woman is a perfect architect in dress; she never, with Gothic ignorance, mixes the orders . . . . " Johnson's imagery may be less conspicuous; it is never so gay. He writes always as a moralist, his social observation and criticism imbued by his clear sense of values. He considers the problems of a new periodical (*The Idler*) from the perspective of the ages, observing that "every truth brought newly to light, impoverishes the mine, from which succeeding intellects are to dig their treasures." But he is capable of a less portentous tone, and when he takes upon himself the task of characterizing a "buyer of bargains," the dignity of his prose provides amusing counterpoint to the triviality of the subject matter. He exploits the contrast to heighten the ridiculousness of the woman he describes; he displays also his own vivid sense of detail.

The desperation of the rational man confronted by total irrationality provides much of the account's comedy (*Idler* 35): "I had often observed that advertisements set her on fire, and therefore, pretending to emulate her laudable frugality, I forbad the news-paper to be taken any longer; but my precaution is vain; I know not by what fatality, or by what confederacy, every catalogue of 'genuine furniture' comes to her hand . . . . " Irrationality triumphs; the woman survives, surrounded by her possessions, and her hapless husband (the persona Johnson adopts for this essay) can only speculate wildly about the possibility of having an auction of the entire accumulation. His lucid style has "placed" the bargain hunter and her habits, but it cannot control her. The essay embodies this truth, has no further pretensions, and survives as a fine piece of observant comedy.

The essays on Dick Minim, the critical equivalent of a poetaster, also manifest Johnson's observation of the social scene, although here he turns his attention to phenomena of clearer immediate significance than the bargain hunter. Perhaps because Dick Minim and his kind represent a genuine threat to literary values, Johnson's tone in dealing with them approaches real sharpness. As the bargain hunter becomes memorable by the clarity with which she is defined, Minim survives because of the precise observation Johnson turns on him. Johnson shows him in the very act of corrupting language, and once more the energy, balance, and lucidity of Johnsonian prose provide the standard by which the subject is judged.

Judgment always informs observation in the social commentary of Goldsmith and Johnson, as in Gibbon's history. The control of the sharp eye by the responsible judgment, the referral of every phenomenon to the appropriate assumed context—these provide the authority and dignity of the eighteenth century's literature of observation; awareness of context, of the enormous shifts of custom and assumption, supplies that literature's charm.

VI

Literary Criticism and Aesthetic Theory: Johnson to Wordsworth

The conflict between rationality and empiricism discernible in large outline in the philosophy of the late eighteenth century was an immediate issue for literary critics, commentators on art, writers on aesthetics. Dr. Johnson, the century's greatest critic, reconciles the opposing approaches in his own critical practice. A firm believer in the existence of truth, rational and permanent, Johnson also understood the necessity for close examination of individual texts in the formation of literary judgments. Both the style and the content of his pronouncements suggest the close relation between the issue of rationality versus empiricism and that of generality versus particularity in literary practice. In *Rasselas*, Johnson suggested that the poet is not to number the streaks of the tulip but to recapitulate the nature of tulips in general. His own poetry, concerned with general issues, employs rich particularity of imagery; his criticism poises itself between the generalizations to which reason leads and particularity of observation on individual texts. This balance reminds us that for men like Johnson no sharp dichotomy existed between rationality and empiricism. They achieve generalization through reason's meditation on experience; they reach particularity by close attention to experience in the light of reason's truth. Not all critics achieved such a fusion, but the fusion was a triumph of the age.

Johnson's unexamined assumptions—from his point of view, rational truths—establish his criticism's atmosphere. He complains that Shakespeare "sacrifices virtue to convenience" in his plays:

> From his writings, indeed, a system of social duty may be selected, for he that thinks reasonably must think morally; but his precepts and axioms drop casually from him; he makes no just distribution of good or evil, nor is always careful to show in the virtuous a disapprobation of the wicked; he carries his persons indifferently through right and wrong, and, at the close, dismisses them without further care, and leaves their examples to operate by chance. This fault the barbarity of his age cannot extenuate; for it is always a writer's duty to make the world better, and justice is a virtue independent of time or place.

Rhetorical authority here generates conviction. The series of parallel clauses, with their cumulative weight, prepares for the fine scorn of "dismisses them without further care" and "operate by chance," which imply a carelessness in Shakespeare diametrically opposed to Johnson's meticulous care. But the power of this prose derives more from its moral vocabulary than from its structure. *Virtue* and *virtuous, reasonably, morally, just* and *justice, duty* are the key terms. It is no accident that the language of morality is also the language of Johnson's criticism. His argument against Shakespeare as a writer is founded on stated moral assumptions: "he that thinks reasonably must think morally"; "it is always a writer's duty to make the world better"; "justice is a virtue independent of time or place." Such assumptions, which seemed to Johnson self-evident and unarguable, contrast with those of the relativistic twentieth century; when the nature of justice seems a vexed question, many writers believe their responsibilities to be more personal than social, and the clear connection between reason and morality has vanished.

Johnson's critical prose is full of such authoritative general pronouncements offered as obvious truths. The two first ones from the paragraph about Shakespeare reappear, in various forms, throughout his criticism; but his critical generalizations are not invariably moral, and they are equally assured when they are clearly wrong: attacks on rhyme or on pastoral, resounding *non sequiturs* ("since the end of poetry is pleasure, that cannot be unpoetical with which all are pleased"). The sources of assurance lie deeper than rhetorical *expertise*, which is an effect, not a cause, of Johnson's conviction. The conviction itself seems a product of his intellectual and moral commitments, part of the absolute integrity—in the root sense—of his thought. His thought is not without inconsistencies, but it conveys a wholeness that absorbs inconsistency. "Poetry is the art of uniting pleasure with truth, by calling imagination to the help of reason." Each abstraction reverberates in such a statement, for the *Lives of the Poets*, the essays on Shakespeare, the *Ramblers* have explored exactly these abstractions. To investigate one of them, *pleasure*, is to discover something of Johnson's range. "He who pleases many must have some species of merit"—this his only kind word for Pomfret, whom Johnson dismisses, with his work (biography, characterization, criticism) in a single page. At the other extreme, he remarks of Shakespeare that his works "are read without any other reason than the desire of pleasure, and are, therefore, praised only as pleasure is obtained." The works of David Mallet, because they convey "little information, and giv[e] no great pleasure, must soon give way." Young's "conceits please only when they surprise."

Almost all Johnson's critical essays consider the pleasure a work induces. Yet the great moralist was far from a hedonist. The pleasure principle, he believed, tested a work's power to move its readers. Pleasure seemed a reliable index of value because—convinced of the ultimate sanity of the universe—Johnson believed that what pleases must be inherently pleasing, that pleasure must have some external cause. Such a criterion forces him into a sort of critical relativism: The more people a work pleases, the more merit it presumably has. As a criterion, pleasure defines a vast emotional range: The surprising conceits of Young and the simplicities of "Namby-Pamby" Philips "please"; so do the characters in Shakespeare's plays; both the slight and the great are legitimate sources of pleasure. Ultimately Johnson's moral absolutism absorbs the relativistic implication of pleasure as a standard: "Nothing can please many, and please long, but just representations of general nature." Poetry unites pleasure with truth, and truth—objective and unchanging—is the source of the fullest pleasure.

Truth for Johnson involves totality; it is partly for this reason that he can assert, "Great thoughts are always general, and consist in positions not limited by exceptions, and in descriptions not descending to minuteness." The genuinely "great" thought must be comprehensive. But such thoughts will be familiar: "Great things cannot have escaped former observation." Thus, the artist must learn how to communicate freshly. "Known truths however may take a different appearance, and be conveyed to the mind by a new train of intermediate images." The images in their specificity are literally "intermediate"; they mediate between the ungraspable or commonplace generality and the individual sensibility. they are means to a vital end; "great thoughts" could not be communicated without them. And they are particular: One of Johnson's most characteristic rhetorical devices is to restate a general truth immediately in particular terms. *Rambler* 60, on biography, offers a typical example: "No species of writing seems more worthy of cultivation than biography, since none can be more delightful or more useful, none can more certainly enchain the heart by irresistible interest, or more widely diffuse instruction to every diversity of condition." The general truth that literature should please and instruct is a commonplace. That biography is particularly pleasing and instructive is less obvious, but hardly stimulating; so Johnson provides a gloss for his critical terms: *delightful*, in this instance means "enchain[ing] the heart by irresistible interest"; *useful* mean, "diffus[ing] instruction to every diversity of condition." One adjective stresses power; the other emphasizes scope. Both have been freshened by Johnson's fusion of the general truth with the particularization of metaphor.

This kind of fusion is the foundation of Johnson's critical method. It provides a structural principle for the *Lives of the Poets*, which alternately record the details Johnson believed essential to biography and assert the large truths the details illuminate. It accounts for the technique of his critical writings on Shakespeare, which suggest that the playwright's greatness lies in his superb exemplification of literary truths. The generalizations that emerge from meticulous examination of Shakespeare transcend such limiting principles as the classic dramatic unities; by Johnson's standards, the largeness of the generalizations suggests their truth. If investigating Shakespeare's plays failed to elucidate such generalizations, the investigation would be of dubious value. The particular without the general is relatively meaningless; the general without the particular is uninteresting. Reason requires experience; experience demands reason.

Johnson's conviction of the unalterable value of truth is an aspect of the faith that supports his thought. This is not in the usual sense religious faith, although he was a devout Christian whose ultimate sanctions were those of his church. Nor is it optimism. "Man is not born for happiness," Johnson asserts, with the economy and conviction of the ancient Greeks, as he prepares to describe Collins's descent into insanity. His faith is not in happiness or in the comprehensibility of the universe or in the goodness of men. He believes in the intrinsic value of hard work. "Diligence is never wholly lost," he writes; and "what we hope ever to do with ease we may first learn to do with diligence"; and "what is easy is seldom excellent." He believes that life is hard, accomplishment uncertain, appropriate reward for accomplishment more uncertain still. Man is weak, fallible, corrupt, his intellectual capacities restricted by his emotional and physical weaknesses. The vanity of human wishes is apparent; only death is sure. Yet the man who submits to his fate, who becomes numb to the horror of his own inevitable death, is by Johnson's standard a weakling: "This is to submit tamely to the tyranny of accident, and to suffer our reason to lie useless' (*Rambler* 78). Later in the same essay he sounds a characteristic battle cry: "To neglect at any time preparation for death, is to sleep on our post at a siege, but to omit it in old age, is to sleep at an attack." The metaphor of battle—explicit here, implicit in the quotation just above—is typical and revealing. Life is struggle; in this lies its hardship and its glory. Man cannot win the battle, but he can demonstrate his fitness for it. Every achievement of the human mind, every work of art, every sensitive and responsible act of criticism is a triumph.

The virtues Johnson demands in other writing he demonstrates in his own. "Nature gives no man knowledge," he writes, but adds, "There is a vigilance of observation and accuracy of distinction which books and precepts cannot confer; from this almost all native and original excellence proceeds." He finds in Shakespeare both the knowledge achieved only by experience and native "vigilance" and "accuracy," gifts of reason; he displays in his criticism (and in his moralizing) the same gifts. By his practice more than his assertion he maintains the grandeur of criticism; the scope of his concern gives his voice authority. His awareness of that scope, and of the impossibility of achieving understanding over so vast a range, creates energy and helps to convey the sense of an active mind, which dominates Johnson's prose. His pronouncements about specific pieces of writing are worked out before the reader's eyes. Even the large moral and critical assertions which seem to him self-evident convey a sense of mental activity in the economy and precision of their phrasing.

Johnson's criticism is compelling not because of its literary principles, which are standard classical ones (art is imitation of nature, the functions of literature are to please and to instruct, general truths are more universally relevant than particulars), but because of the vitality of the mind that applies those principles, mingles them with moral truths, demonstrates the revelatory power of intelligence committed to the search for truth and the significance of experience when illuminated by that intelligence.

Johnson's critical contemporaries demonstrate neither the stylistic nor the intellectual complexity which gives Johnson's writing unique life and relevance. Yet other critics too, in their theoretical pronouncements or their specific analysis (few combine the two as Johnson does), document the period's shifts of sensibility and reveal the seriousness of its search for "truth."

Sir Joshua Reynolds, a friend of Johnson's and the most distinguished English painter of his time, made a concerted attempt to define the truths of art. He states a belief in the "rules" far more extreme than Johnson's. "What we now call genius begins, not where rules, abstractedly taken, end; but where known vulgar and trite rules have no longer any place. It must of necessity be, that even works of genius, like every other effect, as they must have their cause, must likewise have their rules." "Rules," as Sir Joshua imagines them, need not be mere mechanical prescriptions; they may even, he goes on to say, be virtually inexpressible in words. If a successful artist seems to break them, the fact means only that he has gone beyond their previously known limitations. Johnson's account of Shakespeare suggests that genius may rise above rules, finding infinitely varied specific embodiments. Reynolds is more strictly classical, expounding his principles with passionate conviction, with wide scope of artistic reference, with the authority of his own successful practice. He has Johnsonian faith in the value of work and study and in the achievement they produce; his scorn for "inspiration" and for those who believe in it is equally intense. Art is the "full result of long labour and application of an infinite number and infinite variety of acts." Genius is "the child of imitation," not of a spark from heaven. Painting, Reynolds's primary subject, is "a literate and liberal profession"; to preserve its standards is a sacred duty.

In vocabulary and in structure, Reynolds's prose is less individual and less compelling than Johnson's. Lucid and forceful, it carefully defines theoretical positions, subordinating all specific instances—all references to particular painters—to general truths. Its relatively commonplace imagery is nonetheless revealing. In his sixth discourse, Reynolds uses some familiar "romantic" metaphors. He refers to the "fire" of genius and to the "fire and splendour" of the great masters. Nature is an inexhaustible fountain, "from which all excellences must originally flow." The monuments of antiquity are a "fountainhead" for the modern artist. The mind is a soil which must be fertilized from without; great works of art "impregnate" it. "Barrenness" is the artist's great enemy.

This imagery of fire, fountain, and fertility stresses the active, the fructifying, the energetic. But the fountain, in Reynolds's metaphor, is not art, and the fountainhead is not the artistic impulse. Great works impregnate the mind not with inspiration but with "kindred ideas": Only thus does the mind become "fruitful in resources." The sources of energy are outside the individual, but they are neither supernatural nor mysterious. Reynolds's artistic world teems with vitality; the individual must learn to make use of it, by study and by imitation. The romantic metaphors have unromantic applications.

Qualifying and enriching this metaphorical pattern is a quite different series of metaphors. "The fire of the artist's own genius operating upon these materials which have been thus diligently collected, will enable him to make new combinations, perhaps, superior to what had ever before been in the possession of the art: as in the mixture of the variety of metals, which are said to have been melted and run together at the burning of Corinth, a new and till then unknown metal was produced, equal in value to any of those that had contributed to its composition." The student can learn even from inferior art: "He will pick up from dung-hills what by a nice chemistry, passing through his own mind, shall be converted into pure gold." The "genuine materials" obtained from the artists of the past may be "wrought up and polished to elegance."

These metaphors of workmanship evoke the mystery of the artistic process which seems previously to have been denied. The "fire of genius" may produce something "new and till then unknown"—no one knows how. The "nice chemistry" by which refuse becomes gold is as unaccountable as the process that produces Corinthian brass. In both cases, the process is less important than the tangible substance it produces, which is also the gauge of value in the work of the craftsman who has "wrought up and polished" his materials. But the process is *more* important than its starting point in "genius" (although Reynolds believes in the reality of genius; he defines it in his seventh discourse) or in the mind of the less remarkable artist. It is judged by what it creates, something objective, an artifact—not a flower or an oak but an elegant and polished shape of metal.

"By a spirit of *Imitation* we counteract nature, and thwart her design." Fifteen years before Reynolds published his *Discourses* (chronology is of limited help in understanding the critical movements of the late eighteenth century), Edward Young made this statement in *Conjectures on Original Composition*, which gives to originality the status Reynolds accords to imitation. "All eminence, and distinction, lies out of the beaten road," Young believes, and his tone becomes polemical as he urges modern writers to strive for freshness. He deprecates learning and rules as means of creation and praises genius, "that god within," which we are to "revere," which "inspires; and is itself inspired," which has its origin in heaven. Young depends heavily on imagery of fountains, suns, stars. The contrast between him and Reynolds is exemplified by a metaphoric comment by Young on originality versus imitation: "An *Original* may be said to be of a *vegetable* nature; it rises spontaneously from the vital root of genius; it *grows*, it is not *made*: *Imitations* are often a sort of *manufacture* wrought up by those *mechanics*, *art*, and *labour*, out of pre-existent materials not their own." Reynolds, believing that all works of art are in fact creations out of pre-existent materials, would think the analogy between art and nature a serious falsification. From his point of view a poem, resembling polished metal, is totally unlike a flower.

Meyer Abrams has demonstrated how revealing a period's analogues for art and for the artistic process may be.[2] The coexistence of such different views of art as those of Reynolds and Young suggests the critical ferment of the late eighteenth century. Classical unanimity of assumption, if it had ever really exsited, was vanishing. Theorists and practical critics alike had to face basic aesthetic questions; because the resulting criticism also involves the reader in fundamental issues, it retains vitality.

One central problem was how the successful work of art achieved its effects. The matter of "rules" is obviously relevant, and the critics who consider this issue can be divided into those who believe that abstract theoretical principles can explain aesthetic impact and those who derive their principles from investigation of art's psychological effects. (Most critics in fact combine the two attitudes.)

Consideration of the psychological effects of literature raised the question of the validity of taste. If the reader's responses were to be the index of quality, were all responses of all men equally significant? The philosopher David Hume was one of many to investigate the problem. Opinion, he believes, is either right or wrong; there is one proper opinion about everything. But taste consists of individual aesthetic response, the registration of a phenomenon on a specific sensibility; if we condemn a man's taste, we damn his sensibility. Is there, then, no standard of taste? Logically, perhaps not; in practice we readily say that the man who prefers Ogilby to Milton has poor taste. What is the basis of such a judgment? The bulk of Hume's essay "On the Standard of Taste" attempts to answer this question. Its argument depends on such vague terms as *delicacy* and on familiar classical assumptions: moral principles are fixed and unchanging, reason should control all operations of the sensibility, human beings are essentially the same in all times and places. It follows that "the general principles of taste are uniform in human nature," although Hume grants uneasily that peculiarities of an epoch or a person may modify the application of these principles. For him, "whoever would assert an equality of genius . . . between . . . Bunyan and Addison, would be thought to defend no less an extravagance than if he had maintained a molehill to be as high as Teneriffe." Two hundred years have passed,

---

2 Meyer Abrams, *The Mirror and the Lamp* (New York: W.W. Norton & Company, Inc., 1958).

and the assertion no longer seems extravagant; this fact itself lends pathos to Hume's necessarily futile effort to reconcile unalterable principles with the diversity of individual sensibilities. His argument seems plausible, but experience belies it; the overturn of many of the eighteenth century's specific critical judgments in succeeding centuries suggests that the power of the individual sensibility or of the peculiarities of an era is greater than Hume wished to grant. On the other hand, the persistence through centuries and even millenia of impassioned admiration for Homer or the Parthenon or Egyptian sculpture or the Book of Job suggests that his views were not altogether illusory—that he saw, in fact, one side of the matter very clearly. His recognition of the problem of taste is itself indicative of the new self-consciousness of the late eighteenth century. This consciousness was to develop, as the nineteenth century progressed, into an increasingly powerful belief that the individual sensibility was the only meaningful index of value.

Goldsmith's critical writing, unlike that of any of the other critics we have considered, seems rooted in a sense of the immediate literary situation and its exigencies. A flavor of literary controversy survives in some chapters of his early work, *On Polite Learning in Europe*. He inveighs against critics, identifying himself rather with poets and playwrights, and he makes his own values clear. The proper end of literature is to give pleasure; no rule should interfere with the author's obligation to entertain his readers. The "disgusting solemnity of manner" of contemporary poetry, Goldsmith maintains, is its greatest weakness. "Agreeable trifling" should be the artist's goal; only thus can he "deceive us into instruction." In a sentence that exemplifies his literary convictions and his forceful, matter-of-fact tone, Goldsmith urges, "Let us, instead of writing finely, try to write naturally." He recognizes that—as Pope had put it—"True Ease in Writing comes from Art, not Chance": We can write finely with little effort, we are told only to *try* to write naturally. Goldsmith's belief in the value of ease, the lack of pretension, forms both his style and his principles.

His knowledge of practical psychology emerges as he attempts to draw theoretical distinctions between wit and humor, finding the response to wit based on admiration for an author; that to humor, on self-admiration and a feeling of superiority to the butt of the joke. The winning quality of his criticism is its air of honesty. If his pronouncements on humor do not survive as definitive statements, one is at least convinced that they are authentic records of self-analysis and of observation.

Often one feels an element of self-interest in Goldsmith's commentary. His concern with content in drama must derive from his personal predilection for writing unfashionably comic comedies. He uses his knowledge of psychology as a basis for ridiculing the contemporary taste for "weeping comedy" in his essay on the theater. Invoking classical sanctions, he yet stresses his awareness of the workings of the human heart, and appeals to equivalent awareness in his readers. He rests his case on his understanding of general psychological predispositions, but it originates in his immediate personal response to his own experience. Boswell and others mocked Goldsmith for his vanity and transparent self-interest, but transmuted in his criticism, it becomes a source of vitality. It lends immediacy to his writing: The impropriety of stage censorship, the value of laughter, the nature of wit are for him personal issues. Less judicious than Johnson, less committed to rationality, dominated by feelings and upholding the value of feeling, Goldsmith demonstrates, for readers of his own time and of ours, that literary criticism concerns not the abstract and theoretical but the real and immediate, that it can touch the borderlands of politics as well as of philosophy.

Like Boswell, Goldsmith foretells the nineteenth century while supporting some of the eighteenth century's values. The intellectual shift from the eighteenth to the nineteenth century was most crucially one in emphasis and interpretation. After *Lyrical Ballads* (1798), men continued to concern themselves with truth, but "truth" meant something new. Like Boswell and Gray and Goldsmith, they were interested in their own sensibilities; gradually individual sensibilities began to seem more significant than universal laws. The personal, the subjective, the visionary were increasingly important. "Truth" could be private rather than public; the visions of a madman or an opium addict might be recognized as more penetrating, more valid, than any official doctrine or "universal law." The communal vision seemed less meaningful. The ideal of freedom remained vital, but it no longer coexisted with the vibrant sense of tradition which Burke, for example, had considered its necessary control. The mind could repose less readily than Johnson had assumed on the stability of truth. The beginning of all these developments is apparent in the writing of the eighteenth century. The principles of continuity and of change together form the standards and techniques that developed from the early years of the eighteenth century to the Romantic Age—as, indeed, they form the standards and techniques of every period.

EDWARD YOUNG

(1683–1765)

Edward Young was in his own time best known as a poet and a writer of tragedies. Born near Winchester, he attended Winchester and Oxford, where he took degrees in law. He subsequently was ordained and became chaplain to George II in 1728 and rector of Welwyn in 1730. In 1761 he was named "clerk of the closet" to the Princess Dowager. *The Universal Passion*, a series of satires on the love of fame (1725), established his poetic reputation, which for a time almost equalled Pope's. *The Complaint; or Night Thoughts on Life, Death, and Immortality* (1742), in a romantic, melancholy vein, helped to establish the "graveyard school" of poetry. *Conjectures on Original Composition* (1759) is his only significant work of criticism. Johnson thought its maxims commonplace, but it has been generally considered to mark a new critical trend.

Young, seventy-five years old when he wrote this book, here displays a young man's uncritical enthusiasm for the idea of "originality." His notion of this term's implications is rather superficial, however; he seems unable to grasp the enriching power of tradition or to conceive of alternatives between total freshness and servile imitation. The only kind of "copying" of which he approves is duplication of general method. Even this is not fully acceptable: The "genius"—Young argues that genius is more common than one might suppose—is a magician rather than an architect, and Young fully accepts the implications of this metaphor, thus

47

denying the need for ordinary materials or comprehensible methods in the achievement of art.

Logical and coherent thought is not Young's talent. The *Conjectures* seems
more a rhapsody than an argument; or to put it another way, its argument depends
heavily on its enthusiastic tone. The capacity for excitement over literature here
displayed is inspiriting. Insisting on the importance of "genius" and of self-
knowledge, Young suggests that the artist must turn to nature—to the actual
world and to universally acknowledged truths—rather than to previous literary
models for inspiration. He enunciates a doctrine that was to become increasingly
important.

Conjectures on Original Composition in a Letter to the Author of Sir Charles
Grandison (London, 1759) is the source of the present text.

Biography and Criticism

McKillop, Alan D., "Richardson, Young, and the *Conjectures*," *Modern Philology*,
XXII (1925), 391–404.
Shelley, Henry C., *The Life and Letters of Edward Young*, 1914.

Conjectures
on Original Composition
in a letter to the Author of
Sir Charles Grandison[1]

(1759)

Dear Sir,

We confess the follies of youth without a blush; not so, those of age.
However, keep me a little in countenance, by considering, that age wants
amusements more, tho' it can justify them less, than the preceding periods
of life. How you may relish the pastime here sent you, I know not. It is
miscellaneous in its nature, somewhat licentious[2] in its conduct; and,

---

1 For critical treatment of this work, see introduction, pp. 43–44. The author of *Sir
Charles Grandison* is the novelist Samuel Richardson (1689–1761), a friend of Young's.
2 Disregarding accepted rules, especially of grammar or style.

perhaps, not over important in its end. However, I have endeavoured to make some amends, by digressing into subjects more important, and more suitable to my season of life. A serious thought standing single among many of a lighter nature, will sometimes strike the careless wanderer after amusement only, with useful awe: as monumental marbles scattered in a wide pleasure-garden (and such there are) will call to re-collection those who would never have sought it in a churchyard-walk of mournful yews.

To one such monument I may conduct you, in which is a hidden lustre, like the sepulchral lamps of old; but not like those will This be extinguished, but shine the brighter for being produced, after so long concealment, into open day.

You remember that your worthy patron, and our common friend,[3] put some questions on the *Serious Drama*, at the same time when he desired our sentiments on *Original*, and on *Moral* Composition. Tho' I despair of breaking thro' the frozen obstructions of age, and care's incumbent cloud, into that flow of thought, and brightness of expression, which subjects so polite require; yet will I hazard some conjectures on them.

I begin with *Original* Composition; and the more willingly, as it seems an original subject to me, who have seen nothing hitherto written on it: But, first, a few thoughts on Composition in general. Some are of opinion, that its growth, at present, is too luxuriant; and that the Press is overcharged. Overcharged, I think, it could never be, if none were admitted, but such as brought their Imprimatur[4] from *sound Under-standing*, and the *Public Good*. Wit, indeed, however brilliant, should not be permitted to gaze self-enamoured on its useless Charms, in that Fountain of Fame (if so I may call the Press), if beauty is all that it has to boast; but, like the first *Brutus*,[5] it should sacrifice its most darling off-spring to the sacred interests of virtue, and real service of mankind.

This restriction allowed, the more composition the better. To men of letters, and leisure, it is not only a noble amusement, but a sweet refuge; it improves their parts, and promotes their peace: It opens a back-door out of the bustle of this busy, and idle world, into a delicious garden of moral and intellectual fruits and flowers; the key of which is denied to the rest of mankind. When stung with idle anxieties, or teazed

---

3 This reference is only a fiction. Richardson himself invited Young to enter on the discussion.

4 Literally, license to print; figuratively, sanction.

5 Lucius Junius Brutus (fl. 510 B.C.), a leader in expelling the Tarquins from Rome, sentenced to death his two sons, who had conspired to restore the Tarquins.

with fruitless impertinence, or yawning over insipid diversions, then we perceive the blessing of a letter'd recess. With what a gust[6] do we retire to our disinterested, and immortal friends in our closet, and find our minds, when applied to some favourite theme, as naturally, and as easily quieted, and refreshed, as a peevish child (and peevish children are we all till we fall asleep) when laid to the breast? Our happiness no longer lives on charity; nor bids fair for a fall, by leaning on that most precarious, and thorny pillow, another's pleasure, for our repose. How independent of the world is he, who can daily find new acquaintance, that at once entertain, and improve him, in the little world, the minute but fruitful creation, of his own mind?

These advantages *Composition* affords us, whether we write ourselves, or in more humble amusement peruse the works of others. While we bustle thro' the thronged walks of public life, it gives us a respite, at least, from care; a pleasing pause of refreshing recollection. If the country is our choice, or fate, there it rescues us from *sloth* and *sensuality*, which, like obscene vermin, are apt gradually to creep unperceived into the delightful bowers of our retirement, and to poison all its sweets. Conscious guilt robs the rose of its scent, the lilly of its lustre; and makes an *Eden* a deflowered, and dismal scene.

Moreover, if we consider life's endless evils, what can be more prudent, than to provide for consolation under them? A consolation under them the wisest of men have found in the pleasures of the pen. Witness, among many more, *Thucydides, Xenophon, Tully, Ovid, Seneca, Pliny* the younger,[7] who says, *In uxoris infirmitate, & amicorum periculo, aut morte turbatus, ad studia, unicum doloris levamentum, confugio.*[8] And why not add to these their modern equals, *Chaucer, Rawleigh, Bacon, Milton, Clarendon,*[9] under the same shield, unwounded by misfortune, and nobly smiling in distress?

---

6 Keen relish or enjoyment.

7 Thucydides (471–c. 401 B.C.) and Xenophon (c. 430–c. 355 B.C.), Greek historians; Tully, Marcus Tullius Cicero (106–43 B.C.), Roman orator, politician, philosopher; Ovid, Publius Ovidius Naso (43 B.C.–A.D. 18), Latin poet; Lucius Annaeus Seneca (c. 3 B.C. –A.D. 65), Roman philosopher, dramatist, statesman; Pliny the younger, Caius Plinius Caecilius Secundus (c. 62–c. 113), Roman orator and statesman.

8 "Distracted by the ill-health of my wife and by the dangerous illness or the death of my friends, I flee for succor to my studies, the most potent assuagers of my grief" (*Epistles,* VIII. xix. 1, considerably altered).

9 Geoffrey Chaucer (c. 1340–1400), English poet; Sir Walter Raleigh (c. 1552–1618), statesman and man of letters; Francis Bacon (1561–1621), philosopher, scientist, statesman;

Composition was a cordial to these under the frowns of fortune; but evils there are, which her smiles cannot prevent, or cure. Among these are the languors of old age. If those are held honourable, who in a hand benumbed by time have grasped the just sword in defence of their country; shall they be less esteemed, whose unsteady pen vibrates to the last in the cause of religion, of virtue, of learning? Both These are happy in *this*, that by fixing their attention on objects most important, they escape numberless little anxieties, and that *tedium vitae*[10] which often hangs so heavy on its evening hours. May not this insinuate some apology for my spilling ink, and spoiling paper, so late in life?

But there are, who write with vigor, and success, to the world's delight, and their own renown. These are the glorious fruits where genius prevails. The mind of a man of genius is a fertile and pleasant field, pleasant as *Elysium*, and fertile as *Tempe*;[11] it enjoys a perpetual spring. Of that spring, *Originals* are the fairest flowers: *Imitations* are of quicker growth, but fainter bloom. *Imitations* are of two kinds; one of nature, one of authors: The first we call *Originals*, and confine the term *Imitation* to the second. I shall not enter into the curious enquiry of what is, or is not, strictly speaking, *Original*, content with what all must allow, that some compositions are more so than others; and the more they are so, I say, the better. *Originals* are, and ought to be, great favourites, for they are great benefactors; they extend the republic of letters, and add a new province to its dominion: *Imitators* only give us a sort of duplicate of what we had, possibly much better, before; increasing the mere drug of books, while all that makes them valuable, *knowlege* and *genius*, are at a stand. The pen of an *original* writer, like *Armida's* wand, out of a barren waste calls a blooming spring:[12] Out of that blooming spring an *Imitator* is a transplanter of laurels, which sometimes die on removal, always languish in a foreign soil.

John Milton (1608–1674), poet; Edward Hyde, Earl of Clarendon (1609–1674), statesman and historian who died in exile. All suffered personal or political misfortune: Chaucer and Raleigh were imprisoned; Bacon was barred from office for taking bribes; Milton was blind; Clarendon was exiled.

10 "Weariness of life."

11 The Vale of Tempe, between Mount Olympus and Mount Ossa in Greece, was famed for its beauty and sacred to Apollo; Elysium, or the Elysian Fields, refers to the happy other world in Greek religion reserved for heroes favored by the gods.

12 Armida was the enchantress who opposed the Crusaders in Tasso's *Jerusalem Delivered* (1575). In Canto XV she creates a lovely garden to beguile her foes; she later restores it to wasteland.

But suppose an *Imitator* to be most excellent (and such there are), yet still he but nobly builds on another's foundation; his debt is, at least, equal to his glory; which therefore, on the balance, cannot be very great. On the contrary, an *Original*, tho' but indifferent (its *Originality* being set aside), yet has something to boast; it is something to say with him in *Horace*,

> Meo *sum Pauper in aere;*[13]

and to share ambition with no less than *Caesar*, who declared he had rather be the first in a village, than the second at *Rome*.[14]

Still farther: An *Imitator* shares his crown, if he has one, with the chosen object of his imitation; an *Original* enjoys an undivided applause. An *Original* may be said to be of a *vegetable* nature; it rises spontaneously from the vital root of genius; it *grows*, it is not *made: Imitations* are often a sort of *manufacture* wrought up by those *mechanics*, *art*, and *labour*, out of pre-existent materials not their own.

Again: We read *Imitation* with somewhat of his languor, who listens to a twice-told tale: Our spirits rouze at an *Original; that* is a perfect stranger, and all throng to learn what news from a foreign land: And tho' it comes, like an *Indian* prince, adorned with feathers only, having little of weight; yet of our attention it will rob the more solid, if not equally new: Thus every telescope is lifted at a new-discovered star; it makes a hundred astronomers in a moment, and denies equal notice to the sun. But if an *Original*, by being as excellent, as new, adds admiration to surprize, then are we at the writer's mercy; on the strong wing of his imagination, we are snatched from *Britain* to *Italy*, from climate to climate, from pleasure to pleasure; we have no home, no thought, of our own; till the magician drops his pen: And then falling down into ourselves, we awake to flat realities, lamenting the change, like the beggar who dreamt himself a prince.

It is with thoughts, as it is with words; and with both, as with men; they may grow old, and die: Words tarnished, by passing thro' the mouths of the vulgar, are laid aside as inelegant, and obsolete. So thoughts, when become too common, should lose their currency; and we should send new metal to the mint, that is, new meaning to the press.

---

13 "I am poor but live on my own means" (*Epistles*, II. ii. 2).
14 See Plutarch, *Lives*, "Caesar," XI. 2.

The division of tongues at *Babel* did not more effectually debar men from *making themselves a name* (as the Scripture speaks,[15]) than the too great concurrence, or union of tongues will do for ever. We may as well grow good by another's virtue, or fat by another's food, as famous by another's thought. The world will pay its debt of praise but once; and instead of applauding, explode a second demand, as a cheat.

If it is said, that most of the *Latin* classics, and all the *Greek*, except, perhaps, *Homer*, *Pindar*, and *Anacreon*,[16] are in the number of *Imitators*, yet receive our highest applause; our answer is, That they, tho' not *real*, are *accidental Originals*; the works they imitated, few excepted, are lost: They, on their father's decease, enter as lawful heirs, on their estates in fame: The fathers of our copyists are still in possession; and secured in it, in spite of *Goths*, and Flames, by the perpetuating power of the Press. Very late must a modern *Imitator's* fame arrive, if it waits for their decease.

An *Original* enters early on reputation: *Fame*, fond of new glories, sounds her trumpet in triumph at its birth; and yet how few are awaken'd by it into the noble ambition of like attempts? Ambition is sometimes no vice in life; it is always a virtue in Composition. High in the towering *Alps* is the fountain of the *Po*; high in fame, and in antiquity, is the fountain of an *Imitator's* undertaking; but the river, and the imitation, humbly creep along the vale. So few are our *Originals*, that, if all other books were to be burnt, the letter'd world would resemble some metropolis in flames, where a few incombustible buildings, a fortress, temple, or tower, lift their heads, in melancholy grandeur, amid the mighty ruin. Compared with this conflagration, old *Omar*[17] lighted up but a small bonfire, when he heated the baths of the Barbarians, for eight months together, with the famed *Alexandrian* library's inestimable spoils, that no prophane book might obstruct the triumphant progress of his holy *Alcoran* round the globe.

But why are *Originals* so few? not because the writer's harvest is over, the great reapers of antiquity having left nothing to be gleaned after

---

15 A reference to Genesis 11: 4: "Let us build us a city and a tower . . .; and let us make us a name, lest we be scattered abroad upon the face of the whole earth."

16 Pindar, greatest lyric poet of Greece (c. 520–c. 442 B.C.); Anacreon, Greek amatory lyric poet (c. 560–c. 445 B.C.).

17 Omar I, the second caliph or successor of Mohammed the Prophet, in 640 or 641 had the great library at Alexandria burned on the ground that if its books agreed with the Koran (the holy book of Islam—identical with "Alcoran," below) they were unnecessary, and if they disagreed they were pernicious.

them; nor because the human mind's teeming time is past, or because it is incapable of putting forth unprecedented births; but because illustrious examples *engross, prejudice,* and *intimidate.* They *engross* our attention, and so prevent a due inspection of ourselves; they *prejudice* our judgment in favour of their abilities, and so lessen the sense of our own; and they *intimidate* us with the splendor of their renown, and thus under diffidence bury our strength. Nature's impossibilities, and those of diffidence, lie wide asunder.

Let it not be suspected, that I would weakly insinuate any thing in favour of the moderns, as compared with antient authors; no, I am lamenting their great inferiority. But I think it is no *necessary* inferiority; that it is not from divine destination, but from some cause far beneath the moon: I think that human souls, thro' all periods, are equal; that due care, and exertion, would set us nearer our immortal predecessors than we are at present; and he who questions and confutes this will show abilities not a little tending toward a proof of that equality, which he denies.

After all, the first ancients had no merit in being *Originals*: They could *not* be *Imitators.* Modern writers have a *choice* to make; and therefore have a merit in their power. They may soar in the regions of *liberty,* or move in the soft fetters of easy *imitation*; and *imitation* has as many plausible reasons to urge, as *Pleasure* had to offer to *Hercules. Hercules* made the choice of an hero, and *so* became immortal.[18]

Yet let not assertors of classic excellence imagine, that I deny the tribute it so well deserves. He that admires not antient authors, betrays a secret he would conceal, and tells the world, that he does not understand them. Let us be as far from neglecting, as from copying, their admirable compositions: Sacred be their rights, and inviolable their fame. Let our understanding feed on theirs; they afford the noblest nourishment: But let them nourish, not annihilate, our own. When we read, let our imagination kindle at their charms; when we write, let our judgment shut them out of our thoughts; treat even *Homer* himself, as his royal admirer was treated by the cynic;[19] bid him stand aside, nor shade our Composition from the beams of our own genius; for nothing *Original* can rise, nothing immortal, can ripen, in any other sun.

---

18 Hercules' immortality was a reward for his acceptance of the Twelve Labors imposed on him by Eurystheus.

19 Alexander the Great found the philosopher Diogenes lying in the sun. When the king asked him whether he wanted in anything, he replied, "Yes, I would have you stand from between me and the sun." See Plutarch, *Lives,* "Alexander," XIV. 1–3.

Must we then, you say, not imitate antient authors? Imitate them, by all means; but imitate aright. He that imitates the divine *Iliad*, does not imitate *Homer*; but he who takes the same method, which *Homer* took, for arriving at a capacity of accomplishing a work so great. Tread in his steps to the sole fountain of immortality; drink where he drank, at the true *Helicon*, that is, at the breast of nature: Imitate; but imitate not the *Composition*, but the *Man*. For may not this paradox pass into a maxim? *viz.* "The less we copy the renowned antients, we shall resemble them the more."

But possibly you may reply, that you must either imitate *Homer*, or depart from nature. Not so: For suppose you was to change place, in time, with *Homer*; then, if you write naturally, you might as well charge *Homer* with an imitation of you. Can you be said to imitate *Homer* for writing *so*, as you would have written, if *Homer* had never been? As far as a regard to nature, and sound sense, will permit a departure from your great predecessors; so far, ambitiously, depart from them; the farther from them in *similitude*, the nearer are you to them in *excellence*; you rise by it into an *Original*; become a noble collateral, not an humble descendant from them. Let us build our Compositions with the spirit, and in the taste, of the antients; but not with their materials: Thus will they resemble the structures of *Pericles* at *Athens*, which *Plutarch* commends for having had an air of antiquity as soon as they were built.[20] All eminence, and distinction, lies out of the beaten road; excursion, and deviation, are necessary to find it; and the more remote your path from the highway, the more reputable; if, like poor *Gulliver* (of whom anon) you fall not into a ditch, in your way to glory.[21]

What glory to come near, what glory to reach, what glory (presumptuous thought!) to surpass, our predecessors? And is that then in nature absolutely impossible? Or is it not, rather, contrary to nature to fail in it? Nature herself sets the ladder, all wanting is our ambition to climb. For by the bounty of nature we are as strong as our predecessors; and by the favour of time (which is but another round in nature's scale) we stand on higher ground. As to the *first*, were *they* more than men? Or are *we* less? Are not our minds cast in the same mould with those before the flood?

---

20 See Plutarch, *Lives*, "Pericles," XIII. 3.

21 Gulliver, in fact, never falls into a ditch. He has various misadventures among the giant Brobdinagians which contradict his sense of his own importance, including an episode in which he becomes emmired in cow dung as a result of an indiscreet leap. Young may have had this event in mind.

The flood affected matter; mind escaped. As to the *second*; though we are moderns, the world is an antient; more antient far, than when they, whom we most admire, filled it with their fame. Have we not their beauties, as stars, to guide; their defects, as rocks, to be shunn'd; the judgment of ages on both, as a chart to conduct, and a sure helm to steer us in our passage to greater perfection than theirs? And shall we be stopt in our rival pretensions to fame by this just reproof?

> *Stat contra, dicitque tibi tua pagina,*
> Fur *es.*
>
>   Mart.[22]

It is by a sort of noble contagion from a general familiarity with their writings, and not by any particular sordid theft, that we can be the better for those who went before us. Hope we, from plagiarism, any dominion in literature; as that of *Rome* arose from a nest of thieves?[23]

Rome was a powerful ally to many states; antient authors are our powerful allies; but we must take heed, that they do not succour, till they enslave, after the manner of *Rome.* Too formidable an idea of their superiority, like a spectre, would fright us out of a proper use of our wits; and dwarf our understanding, by making a giant of theirs. Too great awe for them lays genius under restraint, and denies it that free scope, that full elbow-room, which is requisite for striking its most masterly strokes. Genius is a master-workman, learning is but an instrument; and an instrument, tho' most valuable, yet not always indispensable. Heaven will not admit of a partner in the accomplishment of some favourite spirits; but rejecting all human means, assumes the whole glory to itself. Have not some, tho' not famed for erudition, so written, as almost to persuade us, that they shone brighter, and soared higher, for escaping the boasted aid of that proud ally?

Nor is it strange; for what, for the most part, mean we by genius, but the power of accomplishing great things without the means generally reputed necessary to that end? A *genius* differs from a *good understanding,* as a magician from a good architect; *that* raises his structure by means

---

22 "Your page stares you in the face, and calls you thief" (Martial, *Epigrams,* I. liii. 12).
23 Romulus, founder of the city that was to bear his name, made it a refuge for runaway slaves and homicides.

invisible; *this* by the skilful use of common tools. Hence genius has ever been supposed to partake of something divine.

Nemo unquam vir magnus fuit, sine aliquo afflatu divino.[24]

Learning, destitute of this superior aid, is fond, and proud, of what has cost it much pains; is a great lover of rules, and boaster of famed examples: As beauties less perfect, who owe half their charms to cautious art, learning inveighs against natural unstudied graces, and small harmless inaccuracies, and sets rigid bounds to that liberty, to which genius often owes its supreme glory; but the no-genius its frequent ruin. For unprescribed beauties, and unexampled excellence, which are characteristics of *genius*, lie without the pale of *learning's* authorities, and laws; which pale, genius must leap to come at them: But by that leap, if genius is wanting, we break our necks; we lose that little credit, which possibly we might have enjoyed before. For rules, like crutches, are a needful aid to the lame, tho' an impediment to the strong. A *Homer* casts them away; and, like his *Achilles*,

Fur a negat sibi nata, nihil non arrogat,[25]

by native force of mind. There is something in poetry beyond prose-reason; there are mysteries in it not to be explained, but admired; which render mere prose-men infidels to their divinity. And here pardon a second paradox; *viz.* "*Genius* often then deserves most to be praised, when it is most sure to be condemned; that is, when its excellence, from mounting high, to weak eyes is quite out of sight."

If I might speak farther of learning, and genius, I would compare genius to virtue, and learning to riches. As riches are most wanted where there is least virtue; so learning where there is least genius. As virtue without much riches can give happiness, so genius without much learning can give renown. As it is said in *Terence, Pecuniam negligere interdum maximum est lucrum;*[26] so to neglect of learning, genius sometimes owes its greater glory. Genius, therefore, leaves but the second place, among men

---

24 "No one was ever a great man without some divine inspiration" (Cicero, *Of the Nature of the Gods*, II. lxvi).

25 "He denies that laws were made for him; there is nothing he does not claim" (Horace, *Art of Poetry*, 122).

26 "To neglect money is sometimes the greatest profit" (*Adelphi*, II. ii. 8).

of letters, to the learned. It is their merit, and ambition, to fling light on the works of genius, and point out its charms. We most justly reverence their informing radius for that favour; but we must much more admire the radiant stars pointed out by them.

A star of the first magnitude among the moderns was *Shakespeare*; among the antients, *Pindar*; who (as *Vossius* tells us[27]) boasted of his no-learning, calling himself the eagle, for his flight above it. And such genii as these may, indeed, have much reliance on their own native powers. For genius may be compared to the natural strength of the body; learning to the superinduced accoutrements of arms: if the first is equal to the proposed exploit, the latter rather encumbers, than assists; rather retards, than promotes, the victory. *Sacer nobis inest Deus*, says *Seneca*.[28] With regard to the moral world, *conscience*, with regard to the intellectual, *genius*, is that god within. Genius can set us right in Composition, without the rules of the learned; as conscience sets us right in life, without the laws of the land: *This*, singly, can make us good, as men: *that*, singly, as writers, can, sometimes, make us great.

I say, sometimes, because there is a genius, which stands in need of learning to make it shine. Of genius there are two species, an earlier, and a later; or call them *infantine*, and *adult*. An adult genius comes out of nature's hand, as *Pallas* out of *Jove's* head, at full growth and mature: *Shakespeare's* genius was of this kind: On the contrary, *Swift* stumbled at the threshold, and set out for distinction on feeble knees: His was an infantine genius; a genius, which, like other infants, must be nursed, and educated, or it will come to nought: Learning is its nurse, and tutor; but this nurse may overlay with an indigested load, which smothers common sense; and this tutor may mislead, with pedantic prejudice, which vitiates the best understanding: As too great admirers of the fathers of the church have sometimes set up their authority against the true sense of Scripture; so too great admirers of the classical fathers have sometimes set up their authority, or example, against reason.

> *Neve minor, neu sit quinto productior actu*
> *Fabula.*[29]

---

27 Gerard Jan Vossius, *De Artis Poeticae Natura, ac Constitutione Liber* (Amsterdam, 1647), p. 24, referring to Pindar's *Olympian*, II. 86–88.

28 "Sacred to us is the god within." Young is almost certainly misremembering "*Sacer intra nos spiritus sedet*" (*Epistles*, XLI. 2).

29 "Let no play be either shorter or longer than five acts" (Horace, *Art of Poetry*, 189–90).

So says *Horace*, so says antient example. But reason has not subscribed. I know but one book that can justify our implicit acquiescence in it: And (by the way) on that book a noble disdain of undue deference to prior opinion has lately cast, and is still casting, a new and inestimable light.

But, superstition for our predecessors set aside, the classics are for ever our rightful and revered masters in *Composition*; and our understandings bow before them: But when? When a master is wanted; which, sometimes, as I have shown, is not the case. Some are pupils of nature only, nor go farther to school: From such we reap often a double advantage; they not only rival the reputation of the great antient authors, but also reduce the number of mean ones among the moderns. For when they enter on subjects which have been in former hands, such is their superiority, that, like a tenth wave, they overwhelm, and bury in oblivion all that went before: And thus not only enrich and adorn, but remove a load, and lessen the labour, of the letter'd world.

"But," you say, "since *Originals* can arise from genius only, and since genius is so very rare, it is scarce worth while to labour a point so much, from which we can reasonably expect so little." To show that genius is not so very rare as you imagine, I shall point out strong instances of it, in a far distant quarter from that mentioned above. The minds of the schoolmen were almost as much cloistered as their bodies; they had but little learning, and few books; yet may the most learned be struck with some astonishment at their so singular natural sagacity, and most exquisite edge of thought. Who would expect to find *Pindar* and *Scotus*, *Shakespeare* and *Aquinas*,[30] of the same party? Both equally shew an *original*, unindebted, energy; the *vigor igneus*, and *coelestis origo*,[31] burns in both; and leaves us in doubt whether genius is more evident in the sublime flights and beauteous flowers of poetry, or in the profound penetrations, and marvelously keen and minute distinctions, called the thorns of the schools. There might have been more able consuls called from the plough, than ever arrived at that honour: Many a genius, probably, there has been, which could neither write, nor read. So that genius, that supreme lustre of literature, is less rare than you conceive.

By the praise of genius we detract not from learning; we detract

---

30 Duns Scotus (c. 1265–1308) and Thomas Aquinas (c. 1225–1274) were scholastic theologians, leaders of rival sects. Young implies that one would not expect of "schoolmen" the imaginative energy of poets.

31 "Fiery vigor" and "divine source" (*Aeneid*, VI. 730).

not from the value of gold, by saying that diamond has greater still. He who disregards learning, shows that he wants its aid; and he that over-values it, shows that its aid has done him harm. Overvalued indeed it cannot be, if genius, as to *Composition*, is valued more. Learning we thank, genius we revere; That gives us pleasure, This gives us rapture; That informs, This inspires; and is itself inspired; for genius is from heaven, learning from man: *This* sets us above the low, and illiterate; *That*, above the learned, and polite. Learning is borrowed knowlege; genius is knowlege innate, and quite our own. Therefore, as *Bacon* observes, it may take a nobler name, and be called Wisdom; in which sense of wisdom, some are born wise.[32]

But here a caution is necessary against the most fatal of errors in those automaths, those self-taught philosophers of our age, who set up genius, and often, mere *fancied* genius, not only above human learning, but divine truth. I have called genius wisdom; but let it be remembered, that in the most renowned ages of the most refined heathen wisdom (and theirs is not Christian)

> the world by wisdom knew not God, and it pleased God by the foolish-ness of preaching to save those that believed.[33]

In the fairyland of fancy, genius may wander wild; there it has a creative power, and may reign arbitrarily over its own empire of chimeras. The wide field of nature also lies open before it, where it may range unconfined, make what discoveries it can, and sport with its infinite objects uncontrouled, as far as visible nature extends, painting them as wantonly as it will: But what painter of the most unbounded and exalted genius can give us the true portrait of a seraph? He can give us only what by his own, or others eyes, has been seen; tho' that indeed infinitely compounded, raised, burlesqued, dishonoured, or adorned: In like manner, who can give us divine truth unrevealed? Much less should any presume to set aside divine truth when revealed, as incongruous to their own sagacities.—Is this too serious for my subject? I shall be more so before I close.

Having put in a caveat against the most fatal of errors, from the too great indulgence of genius, return we now to that too great suppression

---

32 Young may be referring to Bacon's remark, in his essay *Of Studies*, that studies "teach not their own use; but that is a wisdom without them, and above them."

33 I Corinthians 1: 21.

of it, which is detrimental to Composition; and endeavour to rescue the writer, as well as the man. I have said, that some are born wise; but they, like those that are born rich, by neglecting the cultivation and produce of their own possessions, and by running in debt, may be beggared at last; and lose their reputations, as younger brothers estates, not by being born with less abilities than the rich heir, but at too late an hour.

Many a great man has been lost to himself, and the publick, purely because great ones were born before him. *Hermias*,[34] in his collections on *Homer*'s blindness, says, that *Homer* requesting the gods to grant him a sight of *Achilles*, that hero rose, but in armour so bright, that it struck *Homer* blind with the blaze.[35] Let not the blaze of even *Homer*'s muse darken us to the discernment of our own powers; which may possibly set us above the rank of *Imitators;* who, though most excellent, and even immortal (as some of them are) yet are still but *Dii minorum gentium*,[36] nor can expect the largest share of incense, the greatest profusion of praise, on their secondary altars.

But farther still: a spirit of *Imitation* hath many ill effects; I shall confine myself to three. *First*, It deprives the liberal and politer arts of an advantage which the mechanic enjoy: In these, men are ever endeavouring to go beyond their predecessors; in the former, to follow them. And since copies surpass not their *Originals*, as streams rise not higher than their spring, rarely so high; hence, while arts mechanic are in perpetual progress, and increase, the liberal are in retrogradation, and decay. *These* resemble pyramids, are broad at bottom, but lessen exceedingly as they rise; *Those* resemble rivers which, from a small fountainhead, are spreading ever wider and wider, as they run. Hence it is evident, that different portions of understanding are not (as some imagine) allotted to different periods of time; for we see, in the same period, understanding rising in one set of artists, and declining in another. Therefore *nature* stands absolved, and our inferiority in Composition must be charged on ourselves.

Nay, so far are we from complying with a necessity, which nature lays us under, that, *Secondly*, by a spirit of *Imitation* we counteract nature, and thwart her design. She brings us into the world all *Originals:* No two faces, no two minds, are just alike; but all bear nature's evident mark of

---

34 A friend and patron of Aristotle (died c. 345 B.C.).
35 See Leo Allatius, *De Patria Homeri* (1640), pp. 145–47.
36 "Minor gods "

separation on them. Born *Originals*, how comes it to pass that we die *Copies*? That meddling ape *Imitation*, as soon as we come to years of *Indiscretion* (so let me speak), snatches the pen, and blots out nature's mark of separation, cancels her kind intention, destroys all mental individuality; the letter'd world no longer consists of singulars, it is a medly, a mass; and a hundred books, at bottom, are but One. Why are Monkies such masters of mimickry? Why receive they such a talent at imitation? Is it not as the *Spartan* slaves received a licence for ebriety; that their betters might be ashamed of it?[37]

The *Third* fault to be found with a spirit of *Imitation* is, that with great incongruity it makes us poor, and proud; makes us think little, and write much; gives us huge folios, which are little better than more reputable cushions to promote our repose. Have not some sevenfold volumes put us in mind of *Ovid's* sevenfold channels of the *Nile* at the conflagration?

> *Ostia septem*
> *Pulverulenta vacant septem sine flumine valles.*[38]

Such leaden labours are like *Lycurgus's*[39] iron money, which was so much less in value than in bulk, that it required barns for strong-boxes, and a yoke of oxen to draw five hundred pounds.

But notwithstanding these disadvantages of *Imitation*, imitation must be the lot (and often an honourable lot it is) of most writers. If there is a famine of *invention* in the land, like *Joseph's* brethren, we must travel far for food;[40] we must visit the remote, and rich, Antients; but an inventive genius may safely stay at home; that, like the widow's cruse, is divinely replenished from within;[41] and affords us a miraculous delight. Whether our own genius be such, or not, we diligently should inquire; that we may not go a begging with gold in our purse. For there is a

---

37 The Spartans forced their slaves to drink to excess, then led them into the public halls so that the children might see what a sight a drunken man is. See Plutarch, *Lives*, "Lycurgus," XXVIII. 4.

38 "The seven mouths lie empty, filled with dust; seven broad channels, all without a stream" (Ovid, *Metamorphoses*, II. 255–56).

39 Lycurgus, famous Spartan lawgiver, lived in the ninth century B.C.

40 See Genesis 42: 1–6.

41 Elijah in the wilderness was fed by ravens; he drank of the brook. When the brook dried up, God ordered him to go to Zarephath, where a widow would sustain him. The widow, nearly destitute, had only a handful of meal and a little oil in a cruse; by a miracle the meal and the oil, divinely replenished, lasted many months. See I Kings 17: 7–16.

mine in man, which must be deeply dug ere we can conjecture its contents. Another often sees that in us, which we see not ourselves; and may there not be that in us which is unseen by both? That there may, chance often discovers, either by a luckily chosen theme, or a mighty premium, or an absolute necessity of exertion, or a noble stroke of emulation from another's glory; as that on *Thucydides* from hearing *Herodotus* repeat part of his history at the *Olympic* games: Had there been no *Herodotus*, there might have been no *Thucydides*, and the world's admiration might have begun at *Livy*[42] for excellence in that province of the pen. *Demosthenes* had the same stimulation on hearing *Callistratus*; or *Tully*[43] might have been the first of consummate renown at the bar.

Quite clear of the dispute concerning *antient and modern learning*, we speak not of performance, but powers. The modern powers are equal to those before them; modern performance in general is deplorably short. How great are the names just mentioned? Yet who will dare affirm, that as great may not rise up in some future, or even in the present age? Reasons there are why talents may not *appear*, none why they may not *exist*, as much in one period as another. An evocation of vegetable fruits depends on rain, air, and sun; an evocation of the fruits of genius no less depends on externals. What a marvellous crop bore it in *Greece*, and *Rome?* And what a marvellous sunshine did it there enjoy? What encouragement from the nature of their governments, and the spirit of their people? *Virgil* and *Horace* owed their divine talents to Heaven; their immortal works, to men; thank *Maecenas* and *Augustus*[44] for them. Had it not been for these, the genius of those poets had lain buried in their ashes. *Athens* expended on her theatre, painting, sculpture, and architecture, a tax levied for the support of a war. *Caesar* dropt his papers when *Tully* spoke; and *Philip*[45] trembled at the voice of *Demosthenes*: And has there arisen but one *Tully*, one *Demosthenes*, in so long a course of years? The powerful eloquence of them both in one stream, should never bear me down into the melancholy persuasion, that several have not been born,

---

42 Herodotus (c. 484–c. 443 B.C.), Greek historian of the wars of Greeks and Persians; Thucydides (471–c. 401 B.C.), Greek historian of the Peloponnesian War; Livy (59 B.C.–A.D. 17), Roman historian.

43 Callistratus was an eloquent Athenian orator (died 356 B.C.) who inspired the emulation of Demosthenes (385–322 B.C.). Tully is Marcus Tullius Cicero, famous orator of Rome.

44 Patrons of Virgil and Horace.

45 Philip, King of Macedonia (382–336 B.C.). In 339 B.C. he was compelled to raise a siege against Perinthus and Byzantium because the appeals of Demosthenes had stimulated his opponents to powerful resistance.

tho' they have not emerged. The sun as much exists in a cloudy day, as in a clear; it is outward, accidental circumstances that with regard to genius either in nation, or age,

> *Collectas fugat nubes, solemque reducit.*

Virg.[46]

As great, perhaps, greater than those mentioned (presumptuous as it may sound) may, possibly, arise; for who hath fathomed the mind of man? Its bounds are as unknown, as those of the creation; since the birth of which, perhaps, not One has so far exerted, as not to leave his possibilities beyond his attainments, his powers beyond his exploits. Forming our judgments, altogether by what *has* been done, without knowing, or at all inquiring, what possibly *might* have been done, we naturally enough fall into too mean an opinion of the human mind. If a sketch of the divine Iliad before *Homer* wrote, had been given to mankind, by some superior being, or otherwise, its execution would, probably, have appeared beyond the power of man. Now, to surpass it, we think impossible. As the first of these opinions would evidently have been a mistake, why may not the second be so too? Both are founded on the same bottom[47]; on our ignorance of the possible dimensions of the mind of man.

Nor are we only ignorant of the dimensions of the human mind in general, but even of our own. That a man may be scarce less ignorant of his own powers, than an oyster of its pearl, or a rock of its diamond; that he may possess dormant, unsuspected abilities, till awakened by loud calls, or stung up by striking emergencies, is evident from the sudden eruption of some men, out of perfect obscurity, into publick admiration, on the strong impulse of some animating occasion; not more to the world's great surprize, than their own. Few authors of distinction but have experienced something of this nature, at the first beamings of their yet unsuspected genius on their hitherto dark Composition: The writer starts at it, as at a lucid meteor in the night; is much surprized; can scarce believe it true. During his happy confusion, it may be said to him, as to *Eve* at the lake,

> *What there thou seest, fair creature, is thyself.*

Milt.[48]

---

46 "Puts to flight the gathered clouds and brings back the sun" (*Aeneid*, I. 143).
47 Foundation.
48 *Paradise Lost*, IV. 468.

Genius, in this view, is like a dear friend in our company under disguise; who, while we are lamenting his absence, drops his mask, striking us, at once, with equal surprize and joy. This sensation, which I speak of in a writer, might favour, and so promote, the fable of poetic inspiration: A poet of a strong imagination, and stronger vanity, on feeling it, might naturally enough realize the world's mere compliment, and think himself truly inspired. Which is not improbable; for enthusiasts of all kinds do no less.

Since it is plain that men may be strangers to their own abilities; and by thinking meanly of them without just cause, may possibly lose a name, perhaps a name immortal; I would find some means to prevent these evils. Whatever promotes virtue, promotes something more, and carries its good influence beyond the *moral* man: To prevent these evils, I borrow two golden rules from *ethics*, which are no less golden in *Composition*, than in life. 1. *Know thyself*; 2dly, *Reverence thyself*. I design to repay ethics in a future letter, by two rules from rhetoric for its service.

1st. *Know thyself.* Of ourselves it may be said, as *Martial* says of a bad neighbour,

Nil tam prope, proculque nobis.[49]

Therefore dive deep into thy bosom; learn the depth, extent, biass, and full fort of thy mind; contract full intimacy with the stranger within thee; excite and cherish every spark of intellectual light and heat, however smothered under former negligence, or scattered through the dull, dark mass of common thoughts; and collecting them into a body, let thy genius rise (if a genius thou hast)as the sun from chaos; and if I should then say, like an *Indian, Worship it*, (though too bold) yet should I say little more than my second rule enjoins, (*viz.*) *Reverence thyself.*

That is, let not great examples, or authorities, browbeat thy reason into too great a diffidence of thyself: Thyself so reverence, as to prefer the native growth of thy own mind to the richest import from abroad; such borrowed riches make us poor. The man who thus reverences himself, will soon find the world's reverence to follow his own. His works will stand distinguished; his the sole property of them; which property alone can confer the noble title of an *author*; that is, of one who (to speak accurately) *thinks*, and *composes*; while other invaders of the

---

49 "No one so near and yet so far from us" (Martial, *Epigrams*, I. lxxxvi. 10).

press, how voluminous, and learned soever, (with due respect be it spoken) only *read*, and *write*.

This is the difference between those two luminaries in literature, the well-accomplished scholar, and the divinely-inspired enthusiast; the *first* is, as the bright morning star; the *second*, as the rising sun. The writer who neglects those two rules above will never stand alone; he makes one of a group, and thinks in wretched unanimity with the throng: Incumbered with the notions of others, and impoverished by their abundance, he conceives not the least embryo of new thought; opens not the least vista thro' the gloom of ordinary writers, into the bright walks of rare imagination, and singular design; while the true genius is crossing all publick roads into fresh untrodden ground; he, up to the knees in antiquity, is treading the sacred footsteps of great examples, with the blind veneration of a bigot saluting the papal toe; comfortably hoping full absolution for the sins of his own understanding, from the powerful charm of touching his idol's infallibility.

Such meanness of mind, such prostration of our own powers, proceeds from too great admiration of others. Admiration has, generally, a degree of two very bad ingredients in it; of ignorance, and of fear; and does mischief in Composition, and in life. Proud as the world is, there is more superiority in it *given*, than *assumed*: And its grandees of all kinds owe more of their elevation to the littleness of others' minds, than to the greatness of their own. Were not prostrate spirits their voluntary pedestals, the figure they make among mankind would not stand so high. *Imitators* and *Translators* are somewhat of the pedestal-kind, and sometimes rather raise their *Original's* reputation, by showing him to be by them inimitable, than their own. *Homer* has been translated into most languages; *Ælian* tells us,[50] that the *Indians*, (hopeful tutors!) have taught him to speak their tongue. What expect we from them? Not *Homer's Achilles*, but something, which, like *Patroclus*,[51] assumes his name, and, at its peril, appears in his stead; nor expect we *Homer's Ulysses*, gloriously bursting out of his cloud into royal grandeur,[52] but an *Ulysses* under disguise, and

---

[50] *Varia Historia*, XII. 48.

[51] In *Iliad*, XVI, Achilles' friend Patroclus dresses in the hero's armor and terrifies the Trojans by appearing in the guise of Achilles. He loses his life in the battle.

[52] In *Odyssey*, VII, Athene disguises Odysseus in a cloud, from which he emerges in royal grandeur at the Court of Alcinous. Young may, however, be referring to *Odyssey*, XVI. 172–76, where Athene touches Odysseus with her wand to transform him from a beggar into a godlike figure. A similar episode occurs in *Odyssey*, XXIII. 156–58.

a beggar to the last. Such is that inimitable father of poetry, and oracle of all the wise, whom *Lycurgus* transcribed; and for an annual public recital of whose works *Solon*[53] enacted a law; that it is much to be feared, that his so numerous translations are but as the publish'd testimonials of so many nations, and ages, that this author so divine is untranslated still.

But here,

> *Cynthius aurem*
> *Vellit,*—

                                                                    Virg.[54]

and demands justice for his favourite, and ours.[55] Great things he has done; but he might have done greater. What a fall is it from *Homer's* numbers, free as air, lofty and harmonious as the spheres, into childish shackles, and tinkling sounds! But, in his fall, he is still great—

> *Nor appears*
> *Less than archangel ruin'd, and the excess*
> *Of glory obscur'd.*—

                                                                    Milt.[56]

Had *Milton* never wrote, *Pope* had been less to blame: But when in *Milton's* genius, *Homer*, as it were, personally rose to forbid *Britons* doing him that ignoble wrong; it is less pardonable, by that *effeminate* decoration, to put *Achilles* in petticoats a second time:[57] How much nobler had it been, if his numbers had rolled on in full flow, through the various modulations of *masculine* melody, into those grandeurs of solemn sound, which are indispensably demanded by the native dignity of heroick song? How much nobler, if he had resisted the temptation of that *Gothic* daemon,[58] which modern poesy tasting, became mortal? O how unlike the deathless, divine harmony of three great names (how justly join'd!), of *Milton*, *Greece*, and *Rome?* His verse, but for this little speck of mor-

---

53 Athenian lawgiver (c. 639–c. 559 B.C.). For Lycurgus, see note 39, above.

54 "Apollo twitches at my ear" (i.e., gives warning) (*Eclogues*, VI. 4–5).

55 I.e., Alexander Pope (1688–1744), translator of the *Iliad* (1715–1720) and the *Odyssey* (1725–1726).

56 *Paradise Lost*, I. 592–94.

57 To protect her son Achilles from death at Troy, Thetis disguised him as a girl and established him at the court of Lycomedes of Scyros.

58 Young means that Pope resorted to rhyme, which he associates with the medieval ("Gothic") as opposed to the classical.

tality, in its extreme parts, as his hero had in his heel;[59] like him, had been invulnerable, and immortal. But, unfortunately, *that* was undipt in *Helicon*; as *this*, in *Styx*. Harmony as well as eloquence is essential to poesy; and a murder of his musick is putting half *Homer* to death. *Blank* is a term of diminution; what we mean by blank verse, is, verse unfallen, uncurst; verse reclaim'd, reinthron'd in the true *language of the gods*; who never thunder'd, nor suffer'd their *Homer* to thunder, in rhime; and therefore, I beg you, my Friend, to crown it with some nobler term; nor let the greatness of the thing lie under the defamation of such a name.

But supposing *Pope's Iliad* to have been perfect in its kind; yet it is a *Translation* still; which differs as much from an *Original*, as the moon from the sun.

> —*Phoeben alieno jusserat igne*
> *Impleri, solemque suo.*
>
> Claud.[60]

But as nothing is more easy than to write originally wrong; Originals are not here recommended, but under the strong guard of my first rule—*Know thyself. Lucian*, who was an Original, neglected not this rule, if we may judge by his reply to one who took some freedom with him. He was, at first, an apprentice to a statuary; and when he was reflected on as such, by being called *Prometheus*, he replied, "I am indeed the inventor of new work, the model of which I owe to none; and, if I do not execute it well, I deserve to be torn by twelve vulturs, instead of one."[61]

If so, O *Gulliver!* dost thou not shudder at thy brother *Lucian's* vulturs hovering o'er thee? Shudder on! they cannot shock thee more, than decency has been shock'd by thee. How have thy *Houyhnhunms* thrown thy judgment from its seat, and laid thy imagination in the mire? In what ordure hast thou dipt thy pencil? What a monster hast thou made of the

> —*Human face divine?*
>
> Milt.[62]

---

[59] Thetis tried to make Achilles immortal by dipping him in the River Styx. He became invulnerable except for the heel by which she held him.

[60] "He had decreed that the moon should be filled with a fire not her own, but that the sun should be filled with his own fire" (Claudian, *Against Rufinus*, I. 9–10).

[61] *To One Who Said "You're A Prometheus in Words,"* Section 3. Lucian in fact says he should be torn by *sixteen* vultures if he did ugly work.

[62] *Paradise Lost*, III. 44.

This writer has so satirised human nature, as to give a demonstration in himself, that it deserves to be satirised. But, say his wholesale admirers, Few could *so* have written; true, and Fewer *would*. If it required great abilities to commit the fault, greater still would have saved him from it. But whence arise such warm advocates for such a performance? From hence, *viz.* before a character is established, merit makes fame; afterwards fame makes merit. *Swift* is not commended for this piece, but this piece for *Swift*. He has given us some beauties which deserve all our praise; and our comfort is, that his faults will not become common; for none can be guilty of them, but who have wit as well as reputation to spare. His wit had been less wild, if his temper had not jostled his judgment. If his favourite *Houyhnhnms* could write, and *Swift* had been one of them, every horse with him would have been an ass, and he would have written a panegyrick on mankind, saddling with much reproach the present heroes of his pen: On the contrary, being born amongst men, and, of consequence, piqued by many, and peevish at more, he has blasphemed a nature little lower than that of angels, and assumed by far higher than they: But surely the contempt of the world is not a greater virtue, than the contempt of mankind is a vice. Therefore I wonder that, though forborn by others, the laughter-loving *Swift* was not reproved by the venerable Dean,[63] who could sometimes be very grave.

For I remember, as I and others were taking with him an evening's walk, about a mile out of *Dublin*, he stopt short; we passed on; but perceiving that he did not follow us, I went back; and found him fixed as a statue, and earnestly gazing upward at a noble elm, which in its uppermost branches was much withered, and decayed. Pointing at it, he said, "I shall be like that tree, I shall die at top." As in this he seemed to prophesy like the Sybils; if, like one of them, he had burnt part of his works, especially *this* blasted branch of a noble genius, like her too, he might have risen in his demand for the rest.[64]

Would not his friend *Pope* have succeeded better in an *original* attempt? Talents untried are talents unknown. All that I know, is, that,

---

63 That is, by the religious side of himself. Swift was Dean of St. Patrick's Cathedral, Dublin.

64 An old woman came to King Tarquin the Proud and said that she wished to sell him the oracles of the gods in nine books for a large price. Tarquin laughed at her; she then burned three of the books and offered the remaining six at the same price. When he laughed again, she burned three more and finally sold him the remaining three for the price she had originally asked for all nine. The story is told by Aulus Gellius, *Attic Nights*, I. xix. 1–11, and by other classic authors.

contrary to these sentiments, he was not only an avowed professor of imitation, but a zealous recommender of it also. Nor could he recommend any thing better, except emulation, to those who write. One of these all writers must call to their aid; but aids they are of unequal repute. Imitation is inferiority confessed; emulation is superiority contested, or denied; imitation is servile, emulation generous; that fetters, this fires; that may give a name; this, a name immortal: This made *Athens* to succeeding ages the rule of taste, and the standard of perfection. Her men of genius struck fire against each other; and kindled, by conflict, into glories, which no time shall extinguish. We thank *Eschylus* for *Sophocles*; and *Parrhasius* for *Zeuxis*;[65] *emulation*, for both. That bids us fly the general fault of *imitators*; bids us not be struck with the loud report of former fame, as with a knell, which damps the spirits; but, as with a trumpet, which inspires ardour to rival the renown'd. Emulation exhorts us, instead of learning our discipline for ever, like raw troops, under antient leaders in composition, to put those laurel'd veterans in some hazard of losing their superior posts in glory.

Such is emulation's high-spirited advice, such her immortalizing call. *Pope* would not hear, pre-engaged with imitation, which blessed him with all her charms. He chose rather, with his namesake of *Greece*,[66] to triumph in the old world, than to look out for a new. His taste partook the error of his religion; it denied not worship to saints and angels; that is, to writers, who, canonized for ages, have received their apotheosis from established and universal fame. True poesy, like true religion, abhors idolatry; and though it honours the memory of the exemplary, and takes them willingly (yet cautiously) as guides in the way to glory; real, though unexampled, excellence is its only aim; nor looks it for any inspiration less than divine.

Though *Pope*'s noble muse may boast her illustrious descent from *Homer, Virgil, Horace*, yet is an *Original* author more nobly born. As *Tacitus* says of *Curtius Rufus*,[67] an *Original* author is born of himself, is his own progenitor, and will probably propagate a numerous offspring of

---

65 Sophocles, who followed Aeschylus as a writer of tragedy, is here said to be indebted to his predecessor in the same way that Zeuxis (fl. 5th cen. B.C.) was indebted to Parrhasius of Ephesus (fl. c. 400 B.C.), an earlier Greek painter.

66 Alexander the Great (356–323 B.C.), king of Macedonia, who conquered all of Greece, Persia, and India.

67 Tacitus quotes Tiberius as saying, "*Curtius Rufus videtur mihi ex se natura*": "Curtius Rufus I regard as the creation of himself" (*Annals*, XI. xxi).

imitators, to eternize his glory; while mule-like imitators die without issue. Therefore, though we stand much obliged for his giving us an *Homer*, yet had he doubled our obligation, by giving us—a *Pope*. Had he a strong imagination, and the true sublime? That granted, we might have had two *Homers* instead of one, if longer had been his life; for I heard the dying swan talk over an epic plan a few weeks before his decease.

Bacon, under the shadow of whose great name I would shelter my present attempt in favour of *Originals*, says, "Men seek not to know their own stock, and abilities; but fancy their possessions to be greater, and their abilities less, than they really are."[68] Which is, in effect, saying, "That we ought to exert more than we do; and that, on exertion, our probability of success is greater than we conceive."

Nor have I *Bacon*'s opinion only, but his assistance too, on my side. His mighty mind travelled round the intellectual world; and, with a more than eagle's eye, saw, and has pointed out, blank spaces, or dark spots in it, on which the human mind never shone: Some of these have been enlightened since; some are benighted still.

Moreover, so boundless are the bold excursions of the human mind, that in the vast void beyond real existence, it can call forth shadowy beings, and unknown worlds, as numerous, as bright, and, perhaps, as lasting, as the stars; such quite-original beauties we may call paradisaical,

Natos sine semine flores.

Ovid.[69]

When such an ample area for renowned adventure in *original* attempts lies before us, shall we be as mere leaden pipes, conveying to the present age small streams of excellence from its grand reservoir in antiquity; and those too, perhaps, mudded in the pass? *Originals* shine, like comets; have no peer in their path; are rival'd by none, and the gaze of all: All other compositions (if they shine at all) shine in clusters; like the stars in the galaxy; where, like bad neighbours, all suffer from all; each particular being diminished, and almost lost in the throng.

If thoughts of this nature prevailed; if antients and moderns were no longer considered as masters and pupils, but as hard-matched rivals for renown; then moderns, by the longevity of their labours, might, one day,

---

68 I have been unable to locate this quotation.
69 "Flowers produced without seed" (*Metamorphoses*, I. 108).

become antients themselves: And old time, that best weigher of merits, to keep his balance even, might have the golden weight of an *Augustan* age[70] in both his scales: Or rather our scale might descend; and that of antiquity (as a modern match for it strongly speaks) might *kick the beam*.[71]

And why not? For, consider, *since* an impartial Providence scatters talents indifferently, as thro' all orders of persons, so thro' all periods of time; *since*, a marvellous light, unenjoy'd of old, is pour'd on us by revelation, with larger prospects extending our understanding, with brighter objects enriching our imagination, with an inestimable prize setting our passions on fire, thus strengthening every power that enables composition to shine; *since*, there has been no fall in man on this side *Adam*, who left no works, and the works of all other antients are our auxiliars against themselves, as being perpetual spurs to our ambition, and shining lamps in our path to fame; *since*, this world is a school, as well for intellectual, as moral, advance; and the longer human nature is at school, the better scholar it should be; *since*, as the moral world expects its glorious milennium, the world intellectual may hope, by the rules of analogy, for some superior degrees of excellence to crown her later scenes; nor may it only hope, but must enjoy them too; for *Tully, Quintilian,*[72] and all true critics allow, that virtue assists genius, and that the writer will be more able, when better is the man—All these particulars, I say, considered, why should it seem altogether impossible, that heaven's latest editions of the human mind may be the most correct, and fair; that the day may come, when the moderns may proudly look back on the comparative darkness of former ages, on the children of antiquity; reputing *Homer* and *Demosthenes*, as the dawn of divine genius; and *Athens* as the cradle of infant fame; what a glorious revolution would this make in the rolls of renown?

What a rant, say you, is here?—I partly grant it: Yet, consider, my friend! knowlege physical, mathematical, moral, and divine, increases; all arts and sciences are making considerable advance; with them, all the accommodations, ornaments, delights, and glories of human life; and these are new food to the genius of a polite writer; these are as the root, and composition, as the flower; and as the root spreads, and thrives, shall the flower fail? As well may a flower flourish, when the root is dead. It

---

70 The Augustan Age of Rome, under the rule of Augustus (63 B.C.–A.D. 14), first Roman emperor, was a period in which architecture and literature flourished. Eighteenth-century men sometimes referred to their own era in history as a new Augustan Age.

71 The "modern match" is *Paradise Lost*, from which (IV. 1004) the phrase is taken.

72 Roman rhetorician (c. 35–c. 95), known for his beautiful Latin style.

is prudence to read, genius to relish, glory to surpass, antient authors; and wisdom to try our strength, in an attempt in which it would be no great dishonour to fail.

Why condemn'd *Maro* his admirable epic to the flames?[73] Was it not because his discerning eye saw some length of perfection beyond it? And what he saw, may not others reach? And who bid fairer than our countrymen for that glory? Something new may be expected from *Britons* particularly; who seem not to be more sever'd from the rest of mankind by the surrounding sea, than by the current in their veins; and of whom little more appears to be required, in order to give us *Originals*, than a consistency of character, and making their compositions of a piece with their lives. May our genius shine; and proclaim us in that nobler view!

—*minimâ contentos nocte Britannos.*

Virg.[74]

And so it does; for in polite composition, in natural, and mathematical, knowlege, we have great *Originals* already: *Bacon, Boyle,*[75] *Newton, Shakespeare, Milton,* have showed us, that all the winds cannot blow the *British* flag farther, than an original spirit can convey the *British* fame; their names go round the world; and what foreign genius strikes[76] not as they pass? Why should not their posterity embark in the same bold bottom of new enterprize, and hope the same success? Hope it they may; or you must assert, either that those *Originals,* which we already enjoy, were written by angels, or deny that we are men. As *Simonides* said to *Pausanias,* reason should say to the writer, "Remember thou art a man."[77] And for man not to grasp at all which is laudable within his reach, is a dishonour to human nature, and a disobedience to the divine; for as heaven does nothing in vain, its gift of talents implies an injunction of their use.

---

73 Virgil is said to have wished the *Aeneid* burned after his death because it had not been completely revised.

74 "Britons satisfied with the shortest night" (not Virgil but Juvenal: *Satires,* II. 161).

75 Robert Boyle (1627–1691), British chemist who formulated Boyle's Law concerning the relation between volume and pressure in gases.

76 This verb continues the metaphor of the flag: to *strike* a flag is to lower it.

77 Plutarch tells how Pausanias, boastful king of the Lacedaimonians, challenged the poet Simonides of Ceon to tell him a wise saying, whereupon the poet advised him to remember that he was only a man (*Letter to Apollonius,* 105A).

A friend of mine has obeyed that injunction;[78] he has relied on himself, and with a genius, as well *moral*, as *original* (to speak in bold terms), has cast out evil spirits; has made a convert to virtue of a species of composition, once most its foe. As the first Christian emperors expell'd daemons, and dedicated their temples to the living God.

But you, I know, are sparing in your praise of this author; therefore I will speak of one, which is sure of your applause. *Shakespeare* mingled no water with his wine, lower'd his genius by no vapid imitation. *Shakespeare* gave us a *Shakespeare*, nor could the first in antient fame have given us more. *Shakespeare* is not their son, but brother; their equal; and that, in spite of all his faults. Think you this too bold? Consider, in those antients what is it the world admires? Not the fewness of their faults, but the number and brightness of their beauties; and if *Shakespeare* is their equal (as he doubtless is) in that, which in them is admired, then is *Shakespeare* as great as they; and not impotence, but some other cause, must be charged with his defects. When we are setting these great men in competition, what but the comparative size of their genius is the subject of our inquiry? And a giant loses nothing of his size, tho' he should chance to trip in his race. But it is a compliment to those heroes of antiquity to suppose *Shakespeare* their equal only in dramatic powers; therefore, though his faults had been greater, the scale would still turn in his favour. There is at least as much genius on the *British* as on the *Grecian* stage, tho' the former is not swept so clean; so clean from violations not only of the *dramatic*, but *moral* rule; for an honest heathen, on reading some of our celebrated scenes, might be seriously concerned to see, that our obligations to the religion of nature were cancel'd by Christianity.

Johnson,[79] in the serious drama, is as much an imitator, as *Shakespeare* is an original. He was very learned, as *Sampson* was very strong, to his own hurt: Blind to the nature of tragedy, he pulled down all antiquity on his head, and buried himself under it; we see nothing of *Johnson*, nor indeed, of his admired (but also murdered) antients; for what shone in the historian is a cloud on the poet; and *Cataline* might have been a good play, if *Salust*[80] had never writ.

Who knows whether *Shakespeare* might not have thought less, if

---

78 Probably Richard Steele (1672–1729), who, concerned about the immorality of the stage, wrote consciously "moral," sentimental dramas.

79 I.e., Ben Jonson.

80 Sallust (86–34 B.C.), Roman historian, wrote a *History of the Conspiracy of Catiline;* Jonson wrote a tragic drama, *Catiline* (first acted 1611).

he had read more? Who knows if he might not have laboured under the load of *Johnson*'s learning, as *Enceladus* under *Ætna?*[81] His mighty genius, indeed, through the most mountainous oppression would have breathed out some of his inextinguishable fire; yet, possibly, he might not have risen up into that giant, that much more than common man, at which we now gaze with amazement, and delight. Perhaps he was as learned as his dramatic province required; for whatever other learning he wanted, he was master of two books, unknown to many of the profoundly read, though books, which the last conflagration alone can destroy; the book of nature, and that of man. These he had by heart, and has transcribed many admirable pages of them, into his immortal works. These are the fountain-head, whence the *Castalian* streams[82] of *original* composition flow; and these are often mudded by other waters, tho' waters in their distinct chanel, most wholesome and pure: As two chymical liquors, separately clear as crystal, grow foul by mixture, and offend the sight. So that he had not only as much learning as his dramatic province required, but, perhaps, as it could safely bear. If *Milton* had spared some of his learning, his muse would have gained more glory, than he would have lost, by it.

Dryden, destitute of *Shakespeare*'s genius, had almost as much learning as *Johnson*, and, for the buskin,[83] quite as little taste. He was a stranger to the pathos, and, by numbers, expression, sentiment, and every other dramatic cheat, strove to make amends for it; as if a saint could make amends for the want of conscience; a soldier, for the want of valour; or a vestal, of modesty. The noble nature of tragedy disclaims an equivalent; like virtue, it demands the heart; and *Dryden* had none to give. Let epic poets *think*, the tragedian's point is rather to *feel*; such distant things are a tragedian and a poet, that the latter indulged, destroys the former. Look on *Barnwell*, and *Essex*,[84] and see how as to these distant characters *Dryden* excells, and is excelled. But the strongest demonstration of his no-taste for the buskin, are his tragedies fringed with rhyme; which, in epic poetry, is a sore disease, in the tragic, absolute death. To

---

81 Enceladus, one of the giants of Greek mythology who rebelled against the gods, was punished by imprisonment under Mt. Etna.

82 Castalia was a spring on Mt. Parnassus, sacred to Apollo and the Muses, regarded as a source of inspiration.

83 The thick-soled boot worn by classic actors in tragedy; hence an emblem of tragedy.

84 George Barnwell was the central character of George Lillo's prose tragedy, *The London Merchant* (1731); the Earl of Essex figures in Shakespeare's *King John* (1596–1597).

Dryden's enormity, *Pope*'s was a light offence. As lacemen[85] are foes to mourning, these two authors, rich in rhyme, were no great friends to those solemn ornaments, which the noble nature of their works required.

Must rhyme then, say you, be banished? I wish the nature of our language could bear its intire expulsion; but our lesser poetry stands in need of a toleration for it; it raises that, but sinks the great; as spangles adorn children, but expose men. Prince *Henry* bespangled all over in his oylet-hole suit,[86] with glittering pins; and an *Achilles*, or an *Almanzor*,[87] in his *Gothic* array; are very much on a level, as to the majesty of the poet, and the prince. *Dryden* had a great, but a general capacity; and as for a general genius, there is no such thing in nature: A genius implies the rays of the mind concenter'd, and determined to some particular point; when they are scatter'd widely, they act feebly, and strike not with sufficient force, to fire, or dissolve, the heart. As what comes from the writer's heart, reaches ours; so what comes from his head, sets our brains at work, and our hearts at ease. It makes a circle of thoughtful critics, not of distressed patients; and a passive audience, is what tragedy requires. Applause is not to be given, but extorted; and the silent lapse of a single tear, does the writer more honour, than the rattling thunder of a thousand hands. Applauding hands, and dry eyes (which during *Dryden*'s theatrical reign often met) are a satire on the writer's talent, and the spectator's taste. When by such judges the laurel is blindly given, and by such a poet proudly received, they resemble an intoxicated hoste, and his tasteless guests, over some sparkling adulteration, commending their Champaign.

But *Dryden* has his glory, tho' not on the stage: What an inimitable *original* is his ode?[88] A small one, indeed, but of the first lustre, and without a flaw; and, amid the brightest boasts of antiquity, it may find a foil.

Among the brightest of the moderns, Mr. *Addison* must take his place. Who does not approach his character with great respect? They who refuse to close with the public in his praise, refuse at their peril. But, if men will be fond of their own opinions, some hazard must be run.

---

85 I.e., lace sellers oppose the wearing of unadorned garments of mourning.

86 Eyelet-embroidered.

87 The point here is obscure. Almanzor is the hero of *The Conquest of Granada*, a rhymed tragedy by Dryden (1670); Achilles appears in *Troilus and Cressida*, which Dryden adapted, in blank verse, from Shakespeare's version in 1679. Prince Henry may be the Hal of Shakespeare's *Henry IV*.

88 *Alexander's Feast* (1697), Dryden's second ode for St. Cecilia's Day, which he himself thought his best poem.

He had, what *Dryden* and *Johnson* wanted,[89] a warm, and feeling heart; but, being of a grave and bashful nature, thro' a philosophic reserve, and a sort of moral prudery, he conceal'd it, where he should have let loose all his fire, and have show'd the most tender sensibilities of heart. At his celebrated *Cato*,[90] few tears are shed, but *Cato*'s own; which, indeed, are truly great, but unaffecting, except to the noble few, who love their country better than themselves. The bulk of mankind want virtue enough to be touched by them. His strength of genius has reared up one glorious image, more lofty, and truly golden, than that in the plains of *Dura*,[91] for cool admiration to gaze at, and warm patriotism (how rare!) to worship; while those two throbbing pulses of the drama, by which alone it is shown to live, *terror* and *pity*, neglected thro' the whole, leave our unmolested hearts at perfect peace. Thus the poet, like his hero, thro' mistaken excellence, and virtue overstrain'd, becomes a sort of suicide; and that which is most dramatic in the drama, dies. All his charms of poetry are but as funeral flowers, which adorn; all his noble sentiments but as rich spices, which embalm, the tragedy deceased.

Of tragedy, pathos is not only the life and soul, but the soul inextinguishable; it charms us thro' a thousand faults. Decorations, which in this author abound, tho' they might immortalize other poesy, are the *splendida peccata*[92] which damn the drama; while, on the contrary, the murder of all other beauties is a venial sin, nor plucks the laurel from the tragedian's brow. Was it otherwise, *Shakespeare* himself would run some hazard of losing his crown.

Socrates frequented the plays of *Euripides*; and, what living *Socrates* would decline the theatre, at the representation of *Cato*? *Tully*'s assassins found him in his litter,[93] reading the *Medea* of the *Grecian* poet, to prepare himself for death. Part of *Cato* might be read to the same end. In the weight and dignity of moral reflection, *Addison* resembles that poet,[94] who was called the dramatic philosopher; and is himself, as he says of

---

89 I.e., lacked.

90 A famous tragedy by Addison (1713).

91 "Nebuchadnezzar the king made an image of gold, whose height was threescore cubits, and the breadth thereof six cubits: he set it up on the plain of Dura, in the province of Babylon" (Daniel 2: 1).

92 "Splendid sins."

93 Marcus Tullius Cicero (b. 106 B.C.) was assassinated in 43 B.C., after Mark Antony, his political enemy, had offered a reward for his death and that of others.

94 I.e., Euripides.

Cato, ambitiously sententious.[95] But as to the singular talent so remarkable in *Euripides*, at melting down hearts into the tender streams of grief and pity, there the resemblance fails. His beauties sparkle, but do not warm; they sparkle as stars in a frosty night. There is, indeed, a constellation in his play; there is the philosopher, patriot, orator, and poet; but where is the tragedian? And, if that is wanting,

> *Cur in theatrum Cato severe venisti?*
>
> Mart.[96]

And, when I recollect what passed between him and *Dryden*, in relation to this drama, I must add the next line,

> *An ideo tantum veneras, ut exires?*[97]

For, when *Addison* was a student at *Oxford*, he sent up this play to his friend *Dryden*, as a proper person to recommend it to the theatre, if it deserved it; who returned it, with very great commendation; but with his opinion, that, on the stage, it could not meet with its deserved success. But tho' the performance was denied the theatre, it brought its author on the public stage of life. For persons in power inquiring soon after of the head of his college for a youth of parts, *Addison* was recommended, and readily received, by means of the great reputation which *Dryden* had just then spread of him above.

There is this similitude between the poet and the play; as this is more fit for the closet than the stage; so, that shone brighter in private conversation than on the public scene. They both had a sort of *local* excellency, as the heathen gods a local divinity; beyond such a bound *they*, unadmired; and *these*, unadored. This puts me in mind of *Plato*, who denied *Homer* to the public;[98] that *Homer*, which, when in his closet, was rarely out of his hand. Thus, tho' *Cato* is not calculated to signalize himself in the warm emotions of the theatre, yet we find him a most amiable companion, in our calmer delights of recess.

Notwithstanding what has been offered, this, in many views, is an exquisite piece. But there is so much more of art, than nature in it, that I can scarce forbear calling it, an exquisite piece of statuary,

---

95 *Cato*, I. ii. 47.
96 "Why, severe Cato, do you come to the theater?" (*Epigrams*, I, prologue).
97 "Did you then enter only to leave?"
98 In *The Republic*, II. 377.

Where the smooth chisel all its skill has shown,
To soften into flesh the rugged stone.

Addison.[99]

That is, where art has taken great pains to labour undramatic matter into dramatic life; which is impossible. However, as it is, like *Pygmalion*,[100] we cannot but fall in love with it, and wish it was alive. How would a *Shakespeare*, or an *Otway*,[101] have answered our wishes? They would have outdone *Prometheus*, and, with their heavenly fire, have given him not only life, but immortality. At their dramas (such is the force of nature) the poet is out of sight, quite hid behind his *Venus*,[102] never thought of, till the curtain falls. Art brings our author forward, he stands before his piece; splendidly indeed, but unfortunately; for the writer must be forgotten by his audience, during the representation, if for ages he would be remembered by posterity. In the theatre, as in life, delusion is the charm; and we are undelighted, the first moment we are undeceived. Such demonstration have we, that the theatre is not yet opened, in which solid happiness can be found by man; because none are more than comparatively good; and folly has a corner in the heart of the wise.

A genius fond of *ornament* should not be wedded to the tragic muse, which is in *mourning*: We want not to be diverted at an entertainment, where our greatest pleasure arises from the depth of our concern. But whence (by the way) this odd generation of pleasure from pain? The movement of our melancholy passions is pleasant, when we ourselves are safe: We love to be at once, miserable, and unhurt: So are we made; and so made, perhaps, to show us the divine goodness; to show that none of our passions were designed to give us pain, except when being pain'd is for our advantage on the whole; which is evident from this instance, in which we see, that passions the most painful administer greatly, sometimes, to our delight. Since great names have accounted otherwise for this particular, I wish this solution, though to me probable, may not prove a mistake.

---

99 *A Letter from Italy*, 85–86.

100 In Greek mythology, a king of Cyprus who fell in love with an ivory image of a woman which he had made. In some accounts, the figure is that of Aphrodite or Venus.

101 Thomas Otway (1652–1685) wrote many famous tragedies; *The Orphan* (1680) and *Venice Preserved* (1682) are among his best-known works.

102 A further reference to the Pygmalion myth.

To close our thoughts on *Cato:* He who sees not much beauty in it, has no taste for poetry; he who sees nothing else, has no taste for the stage. Whilst it justifies censure, it extorts applause. It is much to be admired, but little to be felt. Had it not been a tragedy, it had been immortal; as it is a tragedy, its uncommon fate somewhat resembles his, who, for conquering gloriously, was condemn'd to die.[103] Both shone, but shone fatally; because in breach of their respective laws, the laws of the drama, and the laws of arms. But how rich in reputation must that author be, who can spare a *Cato*, without feeling the loss?

That loss by our author would scarce be felt; it would be but dropping a single feather from a wing, that mounts him above his cotemporaries. He has a more refined, decent, judicious, and extensive genius, than *Pope*, or *Swift*. To distinguish this triumvirate from each other, and, like *Newton*, to discover the different colours in these genuine and meridian rays of literary light, *Swift* is a singular wit, *Pope* a correct poet, *Addison* a great author. *Swift* looked on wit as the *jus divinum*[104] to dominion and sway in the world; and considered as usurpation, all power that was lodged in persons of less sparkling understandings. This inclined him to tyranny in wit; *Pope* was somewhat of his opinion, but was for softening tyranny into lawful monarchy; yet were there some acts of severity in his reign. *Addison*'s crown was elective, he reigned by the public voice:

—*Volentes*
Per populos dat jura, viamque affectat Olympo.

Virg.[105]

But as good books are the medicine of the mind, if we should dethrone these authors, and consider them, not in their royal, but their medicinal capacity, might it not then be said, that *Addison* prescribed a wholesome and pleasant regimen, which was universally relished, and did much good; that *Pope* preferred a purgative of satire, which, tho' wholesome, was too painful in its operation; and that *Swift* insisted on a large dose of ipecacuanha,[106] which, tho' readily swallowed from the fame of the physician, yet, if the patient had any delicacy of taste, he threw up the remedy, instead of the disease?

---

103 I have been unable to identify this figure.
104 "Divine right."
105 "Assigning laws to the willing nations, and assaying on earth the path to heaven" (*Georgics*, IV. 561–62).
106 An emetic drug.

Addison wrote little in verse, much in sweet, elegant, *Virgilian*, prose; so let me call it, since *Longinus* calls *Herodotus* most *Homeric*, and *Thucydides* is said to have formed his style on *Pindar*.[107] *Addison*'s compositions are built with the finest materials, in the taste of the antients, and (to speak his own language) on truly *Classic ground*: And tho' they are the delight of the present age, yet am I persuaded that they will receive more justice from posterity. I never read him, but I am struck with such a disheartening idea of perfection, that I drop my pen. And, indeed, far superior writers should forget his compositions, if they would be greatly pleased with their own.

And yet (perhaps you have not observed it) what is the common language of the world, and even of his admirers, concerning him? They call him an *elegant* writer: That elegance which shines on the surface of his compositions, seems to dazzle their understanding, and render it a little blind to the depth of sentiment, which lies beneath: Thus (hard fate!) he loses reputation with them, by doubling his title to it. On subjects the most interesting, and important, no author of his age has written with greater, I had almost said, with equal weight: And they who commend him for his elegance, pay him such a sort of compliment, by their abstemious praise, as they would pay to *Lucretia*, if they should commend her only for her beauty.[108]

But you say, that you know his value already—You know, indeed, the value of his writings, and close with the world in thinking them immortal; but, I believe, you know not, that his name would have deserved immortality, tho' he had never written; and that, by a better title than the pen can give: You know too, that his life was amiable; but, perhaps, you are still to learn, that his death was triumphant: That is a glory granted to very few: And the paternal hand of Providence, which, sometimes, snatches home its beloved children in a moment, must convince us, that it is a glory of no great consequence to the dying individual; that, when it is granted, it is granted chiefly for the sake of the surviving

---

107 The historian Herodotus (c. 484–c. 443 B.C.) is said to have a prose style resembling the verse of the poet Homer; the historian Thucydides (471–c. 401 B.C.), to have modeled himself on the poet Pindar (c. 518–438 B.C.), writer of triumphal odes. The Herodotus-Homer equation is made by Longinus, *On the Sublime*, XIII. 3; I have not located the source of the other.

108 In Roman legend, Lucretia (or Lucrece) was a virtuous matron who, raped by Sextus, begged her husband to avenge her and then killed herself. The ensuing revolt drove the Tarquins, the Etruscan family to which Sextus belonged, from Rome.

world, which may profit by his pious example, to whom is indulged the strength, and opportunity to make his virtue shine out brightest at the point of death: And, here, permit me to take notice, that the world will, probably, profit more by a pious example of lay-extraction, than by one born of the church; the latter being, usually, taxed with an abatement of influence by the bulk of mankind: Therefore, to smother a bright example of this superior good influence, may be reputed a sort of murder injurious to the living, and unjust to the dead.

Such an example have we in *Addison*; which, tho' hitherto suppressed, yet, when once known, is insuppressible, of a nature too rare, too striking to be forgotten. For, after a long, and manly, but vain struggle with his distemper, he dismissed his physicians, and with them all hopes of life: But with his hopes of life he dismissed not his concern for the living, but sent for a youth nearly related, and finely accomplished,[109] yet not above being the better for good impressions from a dying friend: He came; but life now glimmering in the socket, the dying friend was silent: After a decent, and proper pause, the youth said, "Dear Sir! you sent for me: I believe, and I hope, that you have some commands; I shall hold them most sacred:" May distant ages not only hear, but feel, the reply! Forcibly grasping the youth's hand, he softly said, "See in what peace a Christian can die." He spoke with difficulty, and soon expired. Thro' grace divine, how great is man! Thro' divine mercy, how stingless death! Who would not thus expire?

What an inestimable legacy were those *few dying words* to the youth beloved? What a glorious supplement to his own valuable fragment on the truth of Christianity?[110] What a full demonstration, that his fancy could not feign beyond what his virtue could reach? For when he would strike us most strongly with the grandeur of *Roman* magnanimity, his dying hero is ennobled with this sublime sentiment,

While yet I live, let me not live in vain.

Cato.[111]

But how much more sublime is that sentiment when realized in life; when dispelling the languors, and appeasing the pains of a last hour; and brightening with illustrious action the dark avenue, and all-awful

---

109 The youth was Addison's stepson, Edward Henry, Earl of Warwick (1698–1721).
110 *The Evidences of the Christian Religion* (1721; reissued in enlarged form 1730).
111 *Cato*, V. iv. 82.

confines of an eternity? When his soul scarce animated his body, strong faith, and ardent charity, animated his soul into divine ambition of saving more than his own. It is for our honour, and our advantage, to hold him high in our esteem: For the better men are, the more they will admire him; and the more they admire him, the better will they be.

By undrawing the long-closed curtain of his death-bed, have I not showed you a stranger in him whom you knew so well? Is not this of your favourite author,

> —*Notâ major imago?*
>
> Virg.[112]

His compositions are but a noble preface; the grand work is his death: That is a work which is read in heaven: How has it join'd the final approbation of angels to the previous applause of men? How gloriously has he opened a splendid path, thro' fame immortal, into eternal peace? How has he given religion to triumph amidst the ruins of his nature? And, stronger than death, risen higher in virtue when breathing his last?

If all our men of genius had so breathed their last; if all our men of genius, like him, had been men of genius for *eternals*; *then*, had we never been pained by the report of a latter end—oh! how unlike to this? But a little to balance our pain, let us consider, that such reports as make us, at once, adore, and tremble, are of use, when too many there are, who must tremble before they will adore; and who convince us, to our shame, that the surest refuge of our endanger'd virtue is in the fears and terrors of the disingenuous human heart.

"But reports," you say, "may be false"; and you farther ask me, "If all reports were true, how came an anecdote of so much honour to human nature, as mine, to lie so long unknown? What inauspicious planet interposed to lay its lustre under so lasting and so surprising an eclipse?"

The fact is indisputably true; nor are you to rely on me for the truth of it: My report is but a second edition: It was published before, tho' obscurely, and with a cloud before it. As clouds before the sun are often beautiful; so, this of which I speak. How finely pathetic are those two lines, which this so solemn and affecting scene inspired?

> *He taught us how to live; and, oh! too high*

---

112 "A form larger than his characteristic one" (*Aeneid*, II. 773).

A price for knowlege, taught us how to die.

Tickell.[113]

With truth wrapped in darkness, so sung our oracle to the public, but explained himself to me: He was present at his patron's death, and that account of it here given, he gave to me before his eyes were dry: By what means *Addison taught us how to die*, the poet left to be made known by a late, and less able hand; but one more zealous for his patron's glory: Zealous, and impotent, as the poor *Ægyptian*, who gather'd a few splinters of a broken boat, as a funeral pile for the great *Pompey*, studious of doing honour to so renown'd a name:[114] Yet had not this poor plank (permit me, here, so to call this imperfect page) been thrown out, the chief article of his patron's glory would probably have been sunk for ever, and late ages have received but a fragment of his fame: A fragment glorious indeed, for his genius how bright! But to commend him for composition, tho' immortal, is detraction *now*; if there our encomium ends: Let us look farther to that concluding scene, which spoke human nature not unrelated to the divine. To that let us pay the long, and large arrear of our greatly posthumous applause.

This you will think a long digression; and justly; if that may be called a digression, which was my chief inducement for writing at all: I had long wished to deliver up to the public this sacred deposit, which by Providence was lodged in my hands; and I entered on the present undertaking partly as an introduction to that, which is more worthy to see the light; of which I gave an intimation in the beginning of my letter: For this is the *monumental marble* there mentioned, to which I promised to conduct you; this is the *sepulchral lamp*, the long-hidden lustre of our accomplished countryman, who now rises, as from his tomb, to receive the regard so greatly due to the dignity of his death; a death to be distinguished by tears of joy; a death which angels beheld with delight.

And shall that, which would have shone conspicuous amid the resplendent lights of Christianity's glorious morn, by these dark days be dropped into oblivion? Dropped it is; and dropped by our sacred, august, and ample register of renown, which has entered in its marble-memoirs the dim splendor of far inferior worth: Tho' so lavish of praise, and so talkative of the dead, yet is it silent on a subject, which (if any) might have

---

113 Thomas Tickell, *Epitaph. On the Death of Mr. Addison*, 81–82, slightly altered.
114 See Plutarch, *Lives*, "Pompey," LXXX. 2.

taught its unletter'd stones to speak: If powers were not wanting, a monument more durable than those of marble, should proudly rise in this ambitious page, to the new, and far nobler *Addison*, than that which you, and the public, have so long, and so much admired: Nor this nation only, for it is *Europe*'s *Addison*, as well as ours; tho' *Europe* knows not half his title to her esteem; being as yet unconscious that the *dying Addison* far outshines her *Addison immortal*: Would we resemble him? Let us not limit our ambition to the least illustrious part of his character; heads, indeed, are crowned on earth; but hearts only are crowned in heaven: A truth, which, in such an *age of authors*, should not be forgotten.

It is piously to be hoped, that this narrative may have some effect, since all listen, when a death-bed speaks; and regard the person departing as an actor of a part, which the great master of the drama has appointed us to perform to-morrow: This was a *Roscius*[115] on the stage of life; his exit how great? Ye lovers of virtue! *plaudite*:[116] And let us, my friend! ever "remember his end, as well as our own, that we may never do amiss." I am,

Dear Sir,
Your most obliged,
humble Servant.

P.S.   How far *Addison* is an *Original*, you will see in my next;[117] where I descend from this consecrated ground into his sublunary praise: And great is the descent, tho' into noble heights of *intellectual* power.

---

115 Quintus Roscius (c. 126–62 B.C.), greatest Roman actor of his day.
116 "Applaud."
117 Never written.

PHILIP DORMER STANHOPE,
Fourth Earl of Chesterfield

(1694–1773)

Lord Chesterfield (who succeeded to his title at the age of 32) lived from his early youth in the company of the great. He was gentleman of the bedchamber to the Prince of Wales (afterwards George II) and became a Member of Parliament before he was 21 years old. As ambassador to The Hague, he arranged the marriage of the Prince of Orange with Anne, princess royal of England, and negotiated important treaties. He was a friend of Alexander Pope and John Gay, visited and corresponded with Voltaire, and eulogized Johnson's *Dictionary* in spite of the fact that he had earlier neglected the great lexicographer.

From 1737 Lord Chesterfield maintained an almost daily correspondence with his illegitimate son, Philip, in letters intended to form the youth for a diplomatic career. In spite of his efforts, his son remained undistinguished and awkward; he died at the age of 36. Chesterfield's letters were early renowned for their cynicism and worldliness (they displayed "the morals of a whore, and the manners of a dancing master," said Dr. Johnson), but they uphold genuine values of self-knowledge and self-discipline. Their realistic awareness of the dichotomy between idealism and practicality in society, politics, and diplomacy reminds one of the perceptiveness of Burke and Gibbon. Beginning in 1761, Lord Chesterfield wrote similar letters to his godson and heir-presumptive, yet another Philip Stanhope, who was destined to fill minor diplomatic offices. Like the letters to his natural son, this correspondence also reveals with clarity the standards and assumptions of sophisticated life in the mid-eighteenth century.

The letters here printed offer characteristically precise accounts of the nature and demands of civilized social intercourse. Advising his son about European travel, Lord Chesterfield makes it clear that the value of the Grand Tour, in his view, is the knowledge it provides of people and politics in action. Interested always in the way men deal with one another, he reveals to his protegés how the intricacies of human relationships may be turned to their advantage.

The source of the present text is *Letters of Chesterfield*, ed. Bonamy Dobree, 6 vols. (London: Eyre and Spottiswoode, 1932). Used by permission of the publishers.

Biography and Criticism

Connelly, Willard, *The True Chesterfield*, 1939.

Coxon, Roger, *Chesterfield and His Critics*, 1925.

Craig, W. H., *Life of Lord Chesterfield*, 1907.

Lucas, F. L., *The Search for Good Sense: Four Eighteenth-Century Characters*, 1958.

Price, Cecil, "'The Art of Pleasing': The Letters of Chesterfield, *The Familiar Letter in the Eighteenth Century*, eds. Howard Anderson, Philip Daghlian, Irvin Ehrenpreis, 1966, pp. 92–107.

Shellabarger, Samuel, *Lord Chesterfield and His World*, 1951.

The Letters of
Lord Chesterfield[1]

LETTER CXXIX.   *London, September the 5th, O. S. 1748*

Dear Boy,[2]

I have received yours, with the inclosed German letter to Mr. Grevenkop,[3] which he assures me is extremely well written, considering

---

1 See Introduction, pp. 24–25.

2 Chesterfield's illegitimate son, Philip, whose mother was Mlle. du Bouchet. Lord Chesterfield had met her during his embassy to The Hague. Philip was at this time 16 years old.

3 Gaspar Grevenkop, a Danish gentleman in the service of Lord Chesterfield.

the little time that you have applied yourself to that language. As you have now got over the most difficult part, pray go on diligently, and make yourself absolutely master of the rest. Whoever does not entirely possess a language will never appear to advantage, or even equal to himself, either in speaking or writing it: his ideas are fettered, and seem imperfect or confused, if he is not master of all the words and phrases necessary to express them. I therefore desire that you will not fail writing a German letter once every fortnight to Mr. Grevenkop; which will make the writing of that language familiar to you: and, moreover, when you shall have left Germany and be arrived at Turin, I shall require you to write even to me in German, that you may not forget with ease what you have with difficulty learned. I likewise desire that, while you are in Germany, you will take all opportunities of conversing in German, which is the only way of knowing that or any language accurately. You will also desire your German master to teach you the proper titles and superscriptions to be used to people of all ranks, which is a point so material in Germany, that I have known many a letter returned unopened because one title in twenty has been omitted in the direction.

St. Thomas's day[4] now draws near, when you are to leave Saxony and go to Berlin; and I take it for granted, that if anything is yet wanting to complete your knowledge of the state of that Electorate, you will not fail to procure it before you go away. I do not mean, as you will easily believe, the number of churches, parishes, or towns; but I mean the constitution, the revenues, the troops, and the trade of that Electorate. A few questions sensibly asked of sensible people will procure you the necessary informations; which I desire you will enter in your little book. Berlin will be entirely a new scene to you, and I look upon it in a manner as your first step into the great world: take care that step be not a false one, and that you do not stumble at the threshold. You will there be in more company than you have yet been; manners and attentions will therefore be more necessary. Pleasing in company is the only way of being pleased in it yourself. Sense and knowledge are the first and necessary foundations for pleasing in company; but they will by no means do alone, and they will never be perfectly welcome if they are not accompanied with manners and attentions. You will best acquire these by frequenting the companies of people of fashion; but then you must resolve to acquire them in those companies by proper care and observation; for I have

---

4 Probably October 3, the day of St. Thomas of Hereford.

known people who, though they have frequented good company all their lifetime, have done it in so inattentive and unobserving a manner as to be never the better for it, and to remain as disagreeable, as awkward, and as vulgar, as if they had never seen any person of fashion. When you go into good company (by good company is meant the people of the first fashion of the place) observe carefully their turn, their manners, their address, and conform your own to them. But this is not all, neither; go deeper still; observe their characters, and pry, as far as you can, into both their hearts and their heads. Seek for their particular merit, their predominant passion, or their prevailing weakness; and you will then know what to bait your hook with to catch them. Man is a composition of so many and such various ingredients, that it requires both time and care to analyse him, for, though we have all the same ingredients in our general composition, as reason, will, passion, and appetites; yet the different proportions and combinations of them in each individual, produce that infinite variety of characters which in some particular or other distinguishes every individual from another. Reason ought to direct the whole, but seldom does. And he who addresses himself singly to another man's reason, without endeavouring to engage his heart in his interest also, is no more likely to succeed, than a man who should apply only to a King's nominal minister and neglect his favourite. I will recommend to your attentive perusal, now you are going into the world, two books, which will let you as much into the characters of men as books can do. I mean *Les Réflexions Morales de Monsieur de La Rochefoucald*, and *Les Caractères de La Bruyère:*[5] but remember at the same time that I only recommend them to you as the best general maps to assist you in your journey, and not as marking out every particular turning and winding that you will meet with. There, your own sagacity and observation must come to their aid. La Rochefoucauld is I know blamed, but I think without reason, for deriving all our actions from the source of self-love. For my own part, I see a great deal of truth and no harm at all in that opinion. It is certain that we seek our own happiness in everything we do; and it is as certain that we can only find it in doing well, and in conforming all our actions to the rule of right reason, which is the great law of nature. It is only a mistaken self-love that is a blameable motive, when we take the immediate and

5 *Réflexions ou sentences et maximes morales* (1665), by François, duc de La Rochefoucauld (1613–1680), which considers selfishness the mainspring of human behavior; *Les Caractères* (1688), by Jean de La Bruyère (1645–1696), a group of character sketches, maxims, and essays.

indiscriminate gratification of a passion or appetite for real happiness. But am I blameable if I do a good action, upon account of the happiness which that honest consciousness will give me? Surely not. On the contrary, that pleasing consciousness is a proof of my virtue. The reflection which is the most censured in Monsieur de La Rochefoucauld's books, as a very ill-natured one, is this: *On trouve dans le malheur de son meilleur ami, quelque chose qui ne déplaît pas.*[6] And why not? Why may I not feel a very tender and real concern for the misfortune of my friend, and yet at the same time feel a pleasing consciousness of having discharged my duty to him, by comforting and assisting him to the utmost of my power in that misfortune? Give me but virtuous actions, and I will not quibble and chicane about the motives. And I will give anybody their choice of these two truths, which amount to the same thing: He who loves himself best is the honestest man; or, The honestest man loves himself best.

The characters of La Bruyère are pictures from the life; most of them finely drawn, and highly coloured. Furnish your mind with them first; and when you meet with their likeness, as you will every day, they will strike you the more. You will compare every feature with the original; and both will reciprocally help you to discover the beauties and the blemishes.

As women are a considerable, or at least a pretty numerous part, of company; and as their suffrages go a great way towards establishing a man's character in the fashionable part of the world (which is of great importance to the fortune and figure he proposes to make in it), it is necessary to please them. I will therefore, upon this subject, let you into certain *arcana*,[7] that will be very useful for you to know, but which you must, with the utmost care, conceal, and never seem to know. Women, then, are only children of a larger growth;[8] they have an entertaining tattle and sometimes wit; but for solid, reasoning good-sense, I never in my life knew one that had it, or who reasoned or acted consequentially for four-and-twenty hours together. Some little passion or humour always breaks in upon their best resolutions. Their beauty neglected or controverted, their age increased, or their supposed understandings depreciated, instantly kindles their little passions, and overturns any system of consequential conduct, that in their most reasonable moments they

---

6 "One finds something not displeasing in the misfortune of one's best friend."
7 Mysteries.
8 Cf. Dryden's "Men are but children of a larger growth" (*All for Love*, IV. i. 44).

might have been capable of forming. A man of sense only trifles with them, plays with them, humours and flatters them, as he does with a sprightly, forward child; but he neither consults them about, nor trusts them with, serious matters; though he often makes them believe that he does both; which is the thing in the world that they are proud of; for they love mightily to be dabbling in business (which, by the way, they always spoil); and being justly distrustful that men in general look upon them in a trifling light, they almost adore that man who talks more seriously to them, and who seems to consult and trust them; I say, who seems; for weak men really do, but wise ones only seem to do it. No flattery is either too high or too low for them. They will greedily swallow the highest, and gratefully accept of the lowest; and you may safely flatter any woman, from her understanding down to the exquisite taste of her fan. Women, who are either indisputably beautiful, or indisputably ugly, are best flattered upon the score of their understandings; but those who are in a state of mediocrity, are best flattered upon their beauty, or at least their graces; for every woman who is not absolutely ugly, thinks herself handsome; but, not hearing often that she is so, is the more grateful, and the more obliged to the few who tell her so; whereas a decided and conscious beauty looks upon every tribute paid to her beauty, only as her due; but wants to shine, and to be considered on the side of her understanding; and a woman who is ugly enough to know that she is so, knows that she has nothing left for it but her understanding, which is consequently (and probably in more senses than one) her weak side. But these are secrets which you must keep inviolably, if you would not, like Orpheus,[9] be torn to pieces by the whole sex; on the contrary, a man who thinks of living in the great world must be gallant, polite, and attentive to please the women. They have, from the weakness of men, more or less influence in all Courts; they absolutely stamp every man's character in the *beau monde*,[10] and make it either current, or cry it down, and stop it in payments. It is, therefore, absolutely necessary to manage, please, and flatter them; and never to discover the least marks of contempt, which is what they never forgive; but in this they are not singular, for it is the same with men; who will much sooner forgive an injustice than an insult. Every man is not ambitious, or covetous, or passionate; but every

---

9 Mythical poet and musician, torn to pieces by the women of Thrace, who believed he scorned them.

10 Lit. "Fine world," i. e., the world of high society.

man has pride enough in his composition to feel and resent the least slight and contempt. Remember, therefore, most carefully to conceal your contempt, however just, wherever you would not make an implacable enemy. Men are much more unwilling to have their weaknesses and their imperfections known, than their crimes; and, if you hint to a man that you think him silly, ignorant, or even ill-bred or awkward, he will hate you more, and longer, than if you tell him plainly that you think him a rogue. Never yield to that temptation, which to most young men is very strong, of exposing other people's weaknesses and infirmities, for the sake either of diverting the company, or of showing your own superiority. You may get the laugh on your side by it, for the present; but you will make enemies by it forever; and even those who laugh with you then will, upon reflection, fear, and consequently hate you; besides that, it is ill-natured, and a good heart desires rather to conceal than expose other people's weaknesses or misfortunes. If you have wit, use it to please, and not to hurt: you may shine like the sun in the temperate zones, without scorching. Here it is wished for: under the line[11] it is dreaded.

These are some of the hints which my long experience in the great world enables me to give you; and which, if you attend to them, may prove useful to you in your journey through it. I wish it may be a prosperous one; at least, I am sure that it must be your own fault if it is not.

Make my compliments to Mr. Harte,[12] who, I am very sorry to hear, is not well. I hope by this time he is recovered. Adieu.

LETTER CXCIII   *London, May the 17th, O. S. 1750*

My Dear Friend,

Your apprenticeship is near out, and you are soon to set up for yourself; that approaching moment is a critical one for you, and an anxious one for me. A tradesman who would succeed in his way must begin by establishing a character of integrity and good manners; without the former, nobody will go to his shop at all; without the latter, nobody will go there twice. This rule does not exclude the fair arts of trade. He may sell his goods at the best price he can within certain bounds. He may avail himself of the humour, the whims, and the fantastical tastes of his

---

11 I.e., the equator.
12 The Rev. Walter Harte (1709–1774), poet and essayist who at this time was acting as guide and tutor to Philip Stanhope.

customers; but what he warrants to be good must be really so, what he seriously asserts must be true, or his first fraudulent profits will soon end in a bankruptcy. It is the same in higher life, and in the great business of the world. A man who does not solidly establish and really deserve a character of truth, probity, good manners, and good morals, at his first setting out in the world, may impose and shine like a meteor for a very short time, but will very soon vanish, and be extinguished with contempt. People easily pardon, in young men, the common irregularities of the senses; but they do not forgive the least vice of the heart. The heart never grows better by age; I fear rather worse, always harder. A young liar will be an old one, and a young knave will only be a greater knave as he grows older. But should a bad young heart, accompanied with a good head (which, by the way, very seldom is the case), really reform in a more advanced age from a consciousness of its folly, as well as of its guilt, such a conversion would only be thought prudential and political, but never sincere. I hope in God, and I verily believe, that you want no moral virtue. But the possession of all the moral virtues, *in actu primo*, as the logicians call it, is not sufficient; you must have them in *actu secundo*[1] too; nay, that is not sufficient neither; you must have the reputation of them also. Your character in the world must be built upon that solid foundation, or it will soon fall, and upon your own head. You cannot therefore be too careful, too nice, too scrupulous, in establishing this character at first, upon which your whole depends. Let no conversation, no example, no fashion, no *bon mot*, no silly desire of seeming to be above, what most knaves and many fools call prejudices, ever tempt you to avow, excuse, extenuate, or laugh at the least breach of morality; but show upon all occasions, and take all occasions to show, a detestation and abhorrence of it. There, though young, you ought to be strict; and there only, while young, it becomes you to be strict and severe. But there, too, spare the persons, while you lash the crimes. All this relates, as you easily judge, to the vices of the heart, such as lying, fraud, envy, malice, detraction, etc.; and I do not extend it to the little frailties of youth, flowing from high spirits and warm blood. It would ill become you, at your age, to declaim against them, and sententiously censure a gallantry, an accidental excess of the table, a frolic, an inadvertency; no, keep as free from them yourself as you can, but say nothing against them in others. They certainly

---

1 In scholastic terminology, "in the first act" (*in actu primo*) means "in the will"; "in the second act" means "in the operation of the will."

mend by time, often by reason; and a man's worldly character is not affected by them, provided it be pure in all other respects.

To come now to a point of much less, but yet of very great consequence, at your first setting out. Be extremely upon your guard against vanity, the common failing of inexperienced youth; but particularly against that kind of vanity that dubs a man a coxcomb; a character which, once acquired, is more indelible than that of the priesthood. It is not to be imagined by how many different ways vanity defeats its own purposes. One man decides peremptorily upon every subject, betrays his ignorance upon many, and shows a disgusting presumption upon the rest. Another desires to appear successful among the women; he hints at the encouragement he has received from those of the most distinguished rank and beauty, and intimates a particular connection with some one; if it is true, it is ungenerous; if false, it is infamous; but in either case he destroys the reputation he wants to get. Some flatter their vanity by little extraneous objects which have not the least relation to themselves; such as being descended from, related to, or acquainted with, people of distinguished merit, and eminent characters. They talk perpetually of their grandfather such-a-one, their uncle such-a-one, and their intimate friend Mr. such-a-one, with whom, possibly, they are hardly acquainted. But admitting it all to be as they would have it, what then? Have they the more merit for these accidents? Certainly not. On the contrary, their taking up adventitious, proves their want of intrinsic merit; a rich man never borrows. Take this rule for granted, as a never-failing one; that you must never seem to affect the character in which you have a mind to shine. Modesty is the only sure bait when you angle for praise. The affectation of courage will make even a brave man pass only for a bully; as the affectation of wit will make a man of parts pass for a coxcomb. By this modesty I do not mean timidity and awkward bashfulness. On the contrary, be inwardly firm and steady, know your own value, whatever it may be, and act upon that principle; but take great care to let nobody discover that you do know your own value. Whatever real merit you have other people will discover; and people always magnify their own discoveries, as they lessen those of others.

For God's sake revolve all these things seriously in your thoughts before you launch out alone into the ocean of Paris. Recollect the observations that you have yourself made upon mankind, compare and connect them with my instructions, and then act systematically and consequentially from them; not *au jour la journée*.[2] Lay your little plan now, which you

---

2 "From day to day"; i.e., without forethought.

will hereafter extend and improve by your own observations, and by the advice of those who can never mean to mislead you; I mean Mr. Harte and myself.

LETTER CCI *London, November the 8th, O. S. 1750*

My Dear Friend,

Before you get to Paris, where you will soon be left to your own discretion, if you have any, it is necessary that we should understand one another thoroughly; which is the most probable way of preventing disputes. Money, the cause of much mischief in the world, is the cause of most quarrels between fathers and sons; the former commonly thinking that they cannot give too little, and the latter that they cannot have enough; both equally in the wrong. You must do me the justice to acknowledge, that I have hitherto neither stinted nor grudged any expense that could be of use or real pleasure to you; and I can assure you, by the way, that you have travelled at a much more considerable expense than I did myself; but I never so much as thought of that while Mr. Harte was at the head of your finances, being very sure that the sums granted were scrupulously applied to the uses for which they were intended. But the case will soon be altered, and you will be your own receiver and treasurer. However, I promise you that we will not quarrel singly upon the *quantum*,[1] which shall be cheerfully and freely granted; the application and appropriation of it will be the material point, which I am now going to clear up, and finally settle with you. I will fix, or even name, no settled allowance, though I well know in my own mind what would be the proper one; but I will first try your drafts, by which I can in a good degree judge of your conduct. This only I tell you in general, that, if the channels through which my money is to go are the proper ones, the source shall not be scanty; but should it deviate into dirty, muddy, and obscure ones (which, by the bye, it cannot do for a week without my knowing it), I give you fair and timely notice, that the source will instantly be dry. Mr. Harte, in establishing you at Paris, will point out to you those proper channels; he will leave you there upon the foot[2] of a man of fashion, and I will continue you upon the same. You will have your coach, your valet

---

1 Amount.
2 Footing.

de chambre, your own footman, and a valet de place[3] which, by the way, is one servant more than I had. I would have you very well dressed, by which I mean, dressed as the generality of people of fashion are—that is, not to be taken notice of, for being either more or less fine than other people; it is by being well dressed, not finely dressed, that a gentleman should be distinguished. You must frequent *les spectacles*,[4] which expense I shall willingly supply. You must play, *à des petits jeux de commerce*,[5] in mixed companies; that article is trifling; I shall pay it cheerfully. All the other articles of pocket-money are very inconsiderable at Paris, in comparison of what they are here; the silly custom of giving money wherever one dines or sups, and the expensive importunity of subscriptions, not being yet introduced there. Having thus reckoned up all the decent expenses of a gentleman, which I will most readily defray, I come now to those which I will neither bear nor supply. The first of these is gaming, which though I have not the least reason to suspect you of, I think it necessary eventually to assure you, that no consideration in the world shall ever make me pay your play-debts; should you ever urge to me that your honour is pawned, I shall most immovably answer you, that it was your honour, not mine, that was pawned, and that your creditor might e'en take the pawn for the debt.

Low company and low pleasures are always much more costly than liberal and elegant ones. The disgraceful riots of a tavern are much more expensive, as well as dishonourable, than the (sometimes pardonable) excesses in good company. I must absolutely hear of no tavern scrapes and squabbles.

I come now to another and very material point; I mean women; and I will not address myself to you upon this subject, either in a religious, a moral, or a parental style. I will even lay aside my age, remember yours, and speak to you, as one man of pleasure, if he had parts too, would speak to another. I will, by no means, pay for whores, and their never-failing consequences, surgeons; nor will I, upon any account, keep singers, dancers, actresses, and *id genus omne*;[6] and, independently of the expense,

---

3 A courier, a traveling servant with responsibility for making all arrangements for the journey; "*valet de chambre*," above, is a personal attendant.

4 Plays and public entertainments.

5 "At little games of trade"—i.e., social gambling.

6 "All that tribe"; refers to a phrase in Horace's *Satires* (I. ii. 2) which sums up, as Pope was to translate it,
The Tribe of Templars, Play'rs, Apothecaries,
Pimps, Poets, Wits, Lord *Fanny*'s, Lady *Mary*'s.

I must tell you, that such connections would give me, and all sensible people, the utmost contempt for your parts[7] and address;[8] a young fellow must have as little sense as address, to venture, or more properly to sacrifice his health, and ruin his fortune, with such sort of creatures; in such a place as Paris especially, where gallantry is both the profession and the practice of every woman of fashion. To speak plainly, I will not forgive your understanding claps and poxes; nor will your constitution forgive them you. These distempers, as well as their cures, fall nine times in ten upon the lungs. This argument, I am sure, ought to have weight with you;[9] for I protest to you, that if you meet with any such accident, I would not give one year's purchase for your life. Lastly, there is another sort of expense that I will not allow, only because it is a silly one; I mean the fooling away your money in baubles at toy-shops. Have one handsome snuff-box (if you take snuff) and one handsome sword; but then no more very pretty and very useless things.

By what goes before, you will easily perceive, that I mean to allow you whatever is necessary, not only for the figure, but for the pleasures of a gentleman, and not to supply the profusion of a rake. This, you must confess, does not savour of either the severity or parsimony of old age. I consider this agreement between us as a subsidiary treaty on my part for services to be performed on yours. I promise you, that I will be as punctual in the payment of the subsidies as England has been during the last war;[10] but then I give you notice at the same time, that I require a much more scrupulous execution of the treaty on your part than we met with on that of our Allies; or else that payment will be stopped. I hope that all that I have now said, was absolutely unnecessary, and that sentiments more worthy and more noble than pecuniary ones, would of themselves have pointed out to you the conduct I recommend; but, in all events, I resolved to be once for all explicit with you, that in the worst that can happen, you may not plead ignorance, and complain that I had not sufficiently explained to you my intentions.

Having mentioned the word rake, I must say a word or two more

7 Abilities, capacities, talents.

8 Skill, adroitness.

9 Around 1750 (the date of this letter), the young man had suffered a severe attack of inflammation of the lungs.

10 The War of the Austrian Succession, a contest over the claim of Maria Theresa to the Hapsburg lands. England paid subsidies to the young queen to help her in the war; the original subsidy of £300,000 voted in 1741 was raised a year later to £500,000.

upon that subject, because young people too frequently, and always fatally, are apt to mistake that character for that of a man of pleasure; whereas, there are not in the world two characters more different. A rake is a composition of all the lowest, most ignoble, degrading, and shameful vices; they all conspire to disgrace his character and to ruin his fortune; while wine and the pox contend which shall soonest and most effectually destroy his constitution. A dissolute, flagitious footman, or porter, makes full as good a rake as a man of the first quality. By the bye, let me tell you that in the wildest part of my youth, I never was a rake, but, on the contrary, always detected and despised the character.

A man of pleasure, though not always so scruplous as he should be, and as one day he will wish he had been, refines at least his pleasures by taste, accompanies them with decency, and enjoys them with dignity. Few men can be men of pleasure, every man may be a rake. Remember that I shall know every thing you say or do at Paris, as exactly as if, by the force of magic, I could follow you everywhere, like a sylph or a gnôme, invisible myself. Seneca says, very prettily, that one should ask nothing of God, but what one should be willing that men should know; nor of men, but what one should be willing that God should know[11]; I advise you to say or do nothing at Paris, but what you would be willing that I should know. I hope, nay I believe, that will be the case. Sense, I dare say, you do not want; instruction, I am sure, you have never wanted; experience, you are daily gaining; all which together must inevitably (I should think) make you both *respectable et aimable*,[12] the perfection of a human character. In that case, nothing shall be wanting on my part, and you shall solidly experience all the extent and tenderness of my affection for you; but dread the reverse of both! Adieu.

P.S.   When you get to Paris, after you have been to wait on Lord Albemarle,[13] go to see Mr. Yorke,[14] whom I have particular reasons for desiring that you should be well with, as I shall hereafter explain to you.

---

[11] *Epistle* X. 5. Seneca's formulation, however, is less epigrammatic than Chesterfield's.

[12] "Respectable and loveable."

[13] William Anne Keppel, second Earl of Albermarle (1702–1754), the English ambassador at Paris.

[14] Joseph Yorke, third son of Lord Chancellor Hardwicke, at this time secretary of the embassy at Paris.

Let him know that my orders, and your own inclinations, conspired to make you desire his friendship and protection.

LETTER CXLI   *21 January 1766*

My Dear Little Boy,[1]

I have more than once recommended to you, in the course of our correspondence, *Attention*, but I shall frequently recurr to that subject, which is as inexhaustible as it is important. Attend carefully in the first place to human nature in general, which is pretty much the same in all human creatures, and varies chiefly by modes, habits, education and example. Analyse, and if I may use the expression, anatomise it. Study your own, and that will lead you to know other people's. Carefully observe the words, the looks, and gestures of the whole company you are in, and retain all their little singularities, humours, tastes, antipathies and affections; which will enable you to please or avoid them occasionally as your judgment may direct you. I will give you the most trifling instance of this that can be imagined, and yet will be sure to please. If you invite anybody to dinner, you should take care to provide those things which you have observed them to like more particularly, and not to have those things which you know they have an antipathy to. These trifling things go a great way in the art of pleasing, and the more so from being so trifling, that they are flattering proofs of your regard for the persons, even to *minutes*.[2] These things are what the French call *des attentions*, which (to do them justice) they study and practise more than any people in Europe. Attend to and look at whoever speaks to you, and never seem *distrait* or *rêveur*,[3] as if you did not hear them at all, for nothing is more contemptuous, and consequently more shocking. It is true, you will by these means often be obliged to attend to things not worth anybody's attention, but it is a necessary sacrifice to be made to good manners in society. A minute attention is also necessary to time, place, and characters. A *bon mot* in one company, is not so in another, but on the contrary may prove offensive. Never joke with those whom you observe to be at that time pensive and grave; and on the other hand do not preach and moralize in a company full of mirth and gaiety. Many people come into company, full

---

1 Chesterfield's godson, also Philip Stanhope (1755–1815), the son of his distant cousin, Arthur Charles Stanhope. This Philip was to succeed as the fifth Earl of Chesterfield.
2 "Trifles."
3 "Distracted" or "dreamy."

of what they intend to say in it themselves, without the least regard to others, and thus charged up to the muzzle, are resolved to let it off at any rate. I knew a man, who had a story about a gun, which he thought a good one and that he told it very well; he tried all means in the world to turn the conversation upon guns, but if he failed in his attempt, he started in his chair, and said he heard a gun fired, but when the company assured him that they heard no such thing, he answered, perhaps then I was mistaken, but however, since we are talking of guns,—and then told his story, to the great indignation of the company. Become, as far as with innocence and honour you can, all things to all men, and you will gain a great many. Have *des prévenances*[4] too, and say or do, what you judge beforehand will be most agreeable to them without their hinting at or expecting it. It would be endless to specify the numberless opportunities that every man has of pleasing if he will but make use of them. Your own good sense will suggest them to you, and your good nature, and even your interest will induce you to practise them. Great attention is to be had to times and seasons, for example at meals, talk often but never long at a time; for the frivolous bustle of the servants, and often the more frivolous conversation of the guests, which chiefly turns upon kitchen-stuff and cellar-stuff, will not bear any long reasonings or relations. Meals are and were always reckoned the moments of relaxation of the mind, and sacred to easy mirth, and social cheerfulness. Conform to this custom, and furnish your quota of good humour, but be not induced by example, to the frequent excess of gluttony or intemperance. The former inevitably produces dullness, the latter, madness. Observe the *apropos* in every thing you say or do. In conversing with those who are much your superiors, however easy and familiar you may and ought to be with them, preserve the respect that is due to them. Converse with your equals, with an easy familiarity and at the same time with great civility and decency. But too much familiarity, according to the old saying, often breeds contempt, and sometimes quarrels; and I know nothing more difficult in common behaviour than to fix due bounds to familiarity; too little implies an unsociable formality, too much destroys all friendly and social intercourse. The best rule I can give you to manage familiarity, is never to be more familiar with anybody, than you would be willing, and even glad that he should be with you; on the other hand avoid that uncomfortable reserve and coldness, which is generally the shield of cun-

---

4 I.e., be obliging, engaging.

ning, or the protection of dullness. The Italian maxim is a wise one, *Volto sciolto e pensieri stretti*; that is, let your countenance be open, and your thoughts be close. To your inferiors, you should use a hearty benevolence in your words and actions, instead of a refined politeness, which would be apt to make them suspect that you rather laughed at them. For example, you must show civility to a mere country gentleman in a very different manner from what you do to a man of the world. Your reception of him should seem hearty, and rather coarse, to relieve him from the embarrassment of his own *mauvaise honte*.[5] Have attention even in company of fools, for though they are fools, they may perhaps drop, or repeat something worth your knowing, and which you may profit by. Never talk your best in the company of fools, for they would not understand you, and would perhaps suspect that you jeered them, as they commonly call it, but talk only the plainest common-sense to them, and very gravely, for there is no jesting, nor *badinage* with them. Upon the whole, with Attention, and *les attentions*, you will be sure to please, without them you will be as sure to offend.

---

5 "Bashfulness."

SAMUEL JOHNSON

(1709–1784)

Samuel Johnson, the most famous literary figure of his age, was born in Lichfield, the son of a bookseller. He went to London in 1737, becoming a contributor to the *Gentleman's Magazine*, for which he compiled records of Parliamentary debates, imaginative reconstructions of the activities of Parliament, where reporters were not at this time allowed. His marriage to a widow much older than himself bewildered his friends, who thought her both physically and spiritually unattractive; Johnson, however, was grief-stricken at her death. In 1755 he published his great *Dictionary*, which became the standard authority for more than a century. The impress of his personality is apparent even in such a work, which combines a lexicon, a guide to correct usage, and a group of illustrations from Elizabethan times to the eighteenth century. The illustrations are a record of Johnson's taste; the definitions sometimes record his prejudices.

Johnson wrote in many genres: poetry (most importantly two long imitations of Juvenal in heroic couplets), political discussion, a travel book, fiction (*Rasselas*, an account of an Eastern prince whose experience demonstrates the vanity of human wishes, was his most popular work), and the periodical essays, biography, and literary criticism for which he is best known today. In every form, his accomplishment was extraordinary, and he was renowned in his own time as a conversationalist, forceful personality, and writer. He was buried in Westminster Abbey.

Johnson's prose is marked by its stylistic brilliance, its range of concern, its authority and energy. It exemplifies the values Johnson upheld—integrity, dis-

cipline, balance—and demonstrates the fusion of reason and imagination which
was the century's greatest literary achievement. With surpassing skill it mingles
the abstract and concrete, the moral and the critical.

The Yale University Press is currently issuing a complete edition of Johnson's works, which is, however, far from complete. No good modern edition
now exists. The best edition available is *The Works of Samuel Johnson*, 9 vols.
(Oxford: Oxford University Press, 1825).

Biography and Criticism

Alkon, Paul K., *Samuel Johnson and Moral Discipline*, 1967.

Bate, W. J., *The Achievement of Samuel Johnson*, 1955.

Clifford, J. L., *Young Sam Johnson*, 1955.

Fussell, Paul, *The Rhetorical World of Augustan Humanism*, 1965 (good also on Burke
and Gibbon).

Hagstrum, Jean, *Samuel Johnson's Literary Criticism*, 1952.

Hilles, F. W., *New Light on Dr. Johnson*, 1959.

Krutch, Joseph Wood, *Samuel Johnson*, 1944.

Watkins, W. B. C., *The Perilous Balance*, 1939.

Wimsatt, W. K., *Philosophical Words, A Study of Style and Meaning in the Rambler
and Dictionary of Samuel Johnson*, 1948.

—— *The Prose Style of Samuel Johnson*, 1941.

THE RAMBLER[1]

(1750–1752)

*T*he *Rambler*, conceived as a biweekly series of essays in the tradition of Addison's *Spectator*, was almost entirely a one-man enterprise. Johnson's emphasis in these essays is strongly moralistic. His tone is elevated and often remote; he makes no attempt to achieve the lightness, sophistication, or gaiety that often mark Addison's essays. Instead, he manages a kind of weightiness and dignity peculiar to himself. In none of his other work are the possibilities of his rhetoric so elaborately displayed. The balanced, swelling sentences, the polysyllabic vocabulary, the measured tone contribute to the immense authority of these essays, which seem a record of profound conviction.

The text for the excerpts that follow is reprinted, by permission, from the Yale Edition of *The Rambler*, ed. W.J. Bate and A.B. Strauss, *copyright* © 1969, Yale University.

The Rambler

NUMBER 4   *Saturday, 31 March 1750*

Simul et jucunda et idonea dicere vitae.

HORACE, Ars Poetica, 1. 334.
And join both profit and delight in one.

CREECH.[2]

*T*he works of fiction, with which the present generation seems more particularly delighted, are such as exhibit life in its true state, diversified only by accidents that daily happen in the world, and influenced by passions and qualities which are really to be found in conversing with mankind.[3]

This kind of writing may be termed not improperly the comedy of

---

1 See Introduction, pp. 37–41.
2 Thomas Creech (1659–1700), who translated the works of Horace in 1684.
3 Johnson is referring to such novels as Richardson's *Pamela* (1740) and *Clarissa* (1747–1748), Fielding's *Joseph Andrews* (1742) and *Tom Jones* (1749), and Smollett's *Roderick Random* (1748).

romance, and is to be conducted nearly by the rules of comic poetry. Its province is to bring about natural events by easy means, and to keep up curiosity without the help of wonder: it is therefore precluded from the machines and expedients of the heroic romance,[4] and can neither employ giants to snatch away a lady from the nuptial rites, nor knights to bring her back from captivity; it can neither bewilder its personages in desarts, nor lodge them in imaginary castles.

I remember a remark made by Scaliger upon Pontanus,[5] that all his writings are filled with the same images; and that if you take from him his lillies and his roses, his satyrs and his dryads, he will have nothing left that can be called poetry. In like manner, almost all the fictions of the last age will vanish, if you deprive them of a hermit and a wood, a battle and a shipwreck.

Why this wild strain of imagination found reception so long, in polite and learned ages, it is not easy to conceive; but we cannot wonder that, while readers could be procured, the authors were willing to continue it: for when a man had by practice gained some fluency of language, he had no further care than to retire to his closet, let loose his invention, and heat his mind with incredibilities; a book was thus produced without fear of criticism, without the toil of study, without knowledge of nature, or acquaintance with life.

The task of our present writers is very different; it requires, together with that learning which is to be gained from books, that experience which can never be attained by solitary diligence, but must arise from general converse, and accurate observation of the living world. Their performances have, as Horace expresses it, *plus oneris quantum veniae minus*, little indulgence, and therefore more difficulty.[6] They are engaged in portraits of which every one knows the original, and can detect any deviation from exactness of resemblance. Other writings are safe, except from the malice of learning, but these are in danger from every common reader; as the slipper ill executed was censured by a shoemaker who happened to stop in his way at the Venus of Apelles.[7]

---

4 French heroic romances were particularly popular; notable among them were Mlle. de Scudéry's *Artamenes, or the Grand Cyrus* (tr. English 1653–1655) and *Almahide* (tr. 1677). English imitations included Roger Boyle's *Parthenissa* (1654–1669).

5 Julius Caesar Scaliger (1484–1558) commented on Giovanni Gioviano Pontano or Pontanus (1426–1503), Italian poet, author, and statesman, in his *Poetics*, VI. iv.

6 *Epistles*, II. i. 170.

7 Pliny the Younger (*Natural History*, XXXV. 36. 85) reports that the celebrated Greek painter Apelles (fl. 330 B.C.) once corrected his drawing of a sandal in response to a shoemaker's criticism.

But the fear of not being approved as just copyers of human manners, is not the most important concern that an author of this sort ought to have before him. These books are written chiefly to the young, the ignorant, and the idle, to whom they serve as lectures of conduct, and introductions into life. They are the entertainment of minds unfurnished with ideas, and therefore easily susceptible of impressions; not fixed by principles, and therefore easily following the current of fancy; not informed by experience, and consequently open to every false suggestion and partial account.

That the highest degree of reverence should be paid to youth, and that nothing indecent should be suffered to approach their eyes or ears; are precepts extorted by sense and virtue from an ancient writer, by no means eminent for chastity of thought.[8] The same kind, tho' not the same degree of caution, is required in every thing which is laid before them, to secure them from unjust prejudices, perverse opinions, and incongruous combinations of images.

In the romances formerly written, every transaction and sentiment was so remote from all that passes among men, that the reader was in very little danger of making any applications to himself; the virtues and crimes were equally beyond his sphere of activity; and he amused himself with heroes and with traitors, deliverers and persecutors, as with beings of another species, whose actions were regulated upon motives of their own, and who had neither faults nor excellencies in common with himself.

But when an adventurer is levelled with the rest of the world, and acts in such scenes of the universal drama, as may be the lot of any other man; young spectators fix their eyes upon him with closer attention, and hope by observing his behaviour and success to regulate their own practices, when they shall be engaged in the like part.

For this reason these familiar histories may perhaps be made of greater use than the solemnities of professed morality, and convey the knowledge of vice and virtue with more efficacy than axioms and definitions. But if the power of example is so great, as to take possession of the memory by a kind of violence, and produce effects almost without the intervention of the will, care ought to be taken that, when the choice is unrestrained, the best examples only should be exhibited; and that which

---

8 Juvenal, *Satire* XIV, particularly ll. 38–40.

is likely to operate so strongly, should not be mischievous or uncertain in its effects.

The chief advantage which these fictions have over real life is, that their authors are at liberty, tho' not to invent, yet to select objects, and to cull from the mass of mankind, those individuals upon which the attention ought most to be employ'd; as a diamond, though it cannot be made, may be polished by art, and placed in such a situation, as to display that lustre which before was buried among common stones.

It is justly considered as the greatest excellency of art, to imitate nature; but it is necessary to distinguish those parts of nature, which are most proper for imitation: greater care is still required in representing life, which is so often discoloured by passion, or deformed by wickedness. If the world be promiscuously described, I cannot see of what use it can be to read the account; or why it may not be as safe to turn the eye immediately upon mankind, as upon a mirror which shows all that presents itself without discrimination.

It is therefore not a sufficient vindication of a character, that it is drawn as it appears, for many characters ought never to be drawn; nor of a narrative, that the train of events is agreeable to observation and experience, for that observation which is called knowledge of the world, will be found much more frequently to make men cunning than good. The purpose of these writings is surely not only to show mankind, but to provide that they may be seen hereafter with less hazard; to teach the means of avoiding the snares which are laid by Treachery for Innocence, without infusing any wish for that superiority with which the betrayer flatters his vanity; to give the power of counteracting fraud, without the temptation to practise it; to initiate youth by mock encounters in the art of necessary defence, and to increase prudence without impairing virtue.

Many writers, for the sake of following nature, so mingle good and bad qualities in their principal personages, that they are both equally conspicuous; and as we accompany them through their adventures with delight, and are led by degrees to interest ourselves in their favour, we lose the abhorrence of their faults, because they do not hinder our pleasure, or, perhaps, regard them with some kindness for being united with so much merit.

There have been men indeed splendidly wicked, whose endowments threw a brightness on their crimes, and whom scarce any villainy made perfectly detestable, because they never could be wholly divested of their excellencies; but such have been in all ages the great corrupters of the world, and their resemblance ought no more to be preserved, than the art of murdering without pain.

Some have advanced, without due attention to the consequences of this notion, that certain virtues have their correspondent faults, and therefore that to exhibit either apart is to deviate from probability. Thus men are observed by Swift to be "grateful in the same degree as they are resentful."[9] This principle, with others of the same kind, supposes man to act from a brute impulse, and persue a certain degree of inclination, without any choice of the object; for, otherwise, though it should be allowed that gratitude and resentment arise from the same constitution of the passions, it follows not that they will be equally indulged when reason is consulted; yet unless that consequence be admitted, this sagacious maxim becomes an empty sound, without any relation to practice or to life.

Nor is it evident, that even the first motions to these effects are always in the same proportion. For pride, which produces quickness of resentment, will obstruct gratitude, by unwillingness to admit that inferiority which obligation implies; and it is very unlikely, that he who cannot think he receives a favour will acknowledge or repay it.

It is of the utmost importance to mankind, that positions of this tendency should be laid open and confuted; for while men consider good and evil as springing from the same root, they will spare the one for the sake of the other, and in judging, if not of others at least of themselves, will be apt to estimate their virtues by their vices. To this fatal error all those will contribute, who confound the colours of right and wrong, and instead of helping to settle their boundaries, mix them with so much art, that no common mind is able to disunite them.

In narratives, where historical veracity has no place, I cannot discover why there should not be exhibited the most perfect idea of virtue; of virtue not angelical, nor above probability, for what we cannot credit we shall never imitate, but the highest and purest that humanity can reach, which, exercised in such trials as the various revolutions of things shall bring upon it, may, by conquering some calamities, and enduring others, teach us what we may hope, and what we can perform. Vice, for vice is necessary to be shewn, should always disgust; nor should the

9 Swift-Pope *Miscellanies*, II (1727), 354. I owe this note to the Yale Edition of *The Rambler*, which in turn credits Professor Irvin Ehrenpreis.

graces of gaiety, or the dignity of courage, be so united with it, as to reconcile it to the mind. Wherever it appears, it should raise hatred by the malignity of its practices, and contempt by the meanness of its stratagems; for while it is supported by either parts or spirit, it will be seldom heartily abhorred. The Roman tyrant was content to be hated, if he was but feared;[10] and there are thousands of the readers of romances willing to be thought wicked, if they may be allowed to be wits. It is therefore to be steadily inculcated, that virtue is the highest proof of understanding, and the only solid basis of greatness; and that vice is the natural consequence of narrow thoughts, that it begins in mistake, and ends in ignominy.

NUMBER 60   *Saturday, 13 October 1750*

—*Quid sit pulchrum, quid turpe, quid utile, quid non,*
Plenius et melius Chrysippo et Crantore dicit.

HORACE, Epistles, I. 2. 3–4.

Whose works the beautiful and base contain;
Of vice and virtue more instructive rules,
Than all the sober sages of the schools.

FRANCIS.[1]

All joy or sorrow for the happiness or calamities of others is produced by an act of the imagination, that realises the event however fictitious, or approximates it however remote, by placing us, for a time, in the condition of him whose fortune we contemplate; so that we feel, while the deception lasts, whatever motions would be excited by the same good or evil happening to ourselves.

Our passions are therefore more strongly moved, in proportion as we can more readily adopt the pains or pleasures proposed to our minds, by recognising them as once our own, or considering them as naturally incident to our state of life. It is not easy for the most artful writer to give us an interest in happiness or misery, which we think ourselves never likely to feel, and with which we have never yet been made acquainted. Histories of the downfall of kingdoms, and revolutions of empires, are

---

10 The Emperor Caligula (Suetonius, *Lives of the Caesars*, "Caligula," 30. i).
1 Philip Francis (1708?–1773), miscellaneous writer and translator.

read with great tranquillity; the imperial tragedy pleases common auditors only by its pomp of ornament, and grandeur of ideas; and the man
whose faculties have been engrossed by business, and whose heart never
fluttered but at the rise or fall of stocks, wonders how the attention can be
seized, or the affection agitated by a tale of love.

Those parallel circumstances, and kindred images, to which we
readily conform our minds, are, above all other writings, to be found in
narratives of the lives of particular persons; and therefore no species of
writing seems more worthy of cultivation than biography, since none
can be more delightful or more useful, none can more certainly enchain
the heart by irresistible interest, or more widely diffuse instruction to
every diversity of condition.

The general and rapid narratives of history, which involve a thousand fortunes in the business of a day, and complicate innumerable incidents in one great transaction, afford few lessons applicable to private
life, which derives its comforts and its wretchedness from the right or
wrong management of things which nothing but their frequency makes
considerable, *Parva, si non fiant quotidie*, says Pliny,[2] and which can have
no place in those relations which never descend below the consultation of
senates, the motions of armies, and the schemes of conspirators.

I have often thought that there has rarely passed a life of which a
judicious and faithful narrative would not be useful. For, not only every
man has, in the mighty mass of the world, great numbers in the same
condition with himself, to whom his mistakes and miscarriages, escapes
and expedients, would be of immediate and apparent use; but there is
such an uniformity in the state of man, considered apart from adventitious
and separable decorations and disguises, that there is scarce any possibility
of good or ill, but is common to human kind. A great part of the time of
those who are placed at the greatest distance by fortune, or by temper,
must unavoidably pass in the same manner; and though, when the claims
of nature are satisfied, caprice, and vanity, and accident, begin to produce
discriminations and peculiarities, yet the eye is not very heedful, or quick,
which cannot discover the same causes still terminating their influence in
the same effects, though sometimes accelerated, sometimes retarded, or
perplexed by multiplied combinations. We are all prompted by the same
motives, all deceived by the same fallacies, all animated by hope, ob-
structed by danger, entangled by desire, and seduced by pleasure.

---

2 "Of little value if they be not done daily" (Pliny, *Epistles*, III. i).

It is frequently objected to relations of particular lives, that they are not distinguished by any striking or wonderful vicissitudes. The scholar who passed his life among his books, the merchant who conducted only his own affairs, the priest, whose sphere of action was not extended beyond that of his duty, are considered as no proper objects of publick regard, however they might have excelled in their several stations, whatever might have been their learning, integrity, and piety. But this notion arises from false measures of excellence and dignity, and must be eradicated by considering, that, in the esteem of uncorrupted reason, what is of most use is of most value.

It is, indeed, not improper to take honest advantages of prejudice, and to gain attention by a celebrated name; but the business of the biographer is often to pass slightly over those performances and incidents, which produce vulgar greatness, to lead the thoughts into domestick privacies, and display the minute details of daily life, where exterior appendages are cast aside, and men excel each other only by prudence and by virtue. The account of Thuanus is, with great propriety, said by its author to have been written, that it might lay open to posterity the private and familiar character of that man, *cujus ingenium et candorem ex ipsius scriptis sunt olim semper miraturi*, whose candour and genius will to the end of time be by his writings preserved in admiration.[3]

There are many invisible circumstances which, whether we read as enquirers after natural or moral knowledge, whether we intend to enlarge our science, or increase our virtue, are more important than publick occurrences. Thus Salust, the great master of nature, has not forgot, in his account of Catiline, to remark that "his walk was now quick, and again slow," as an indication of a mind revolving something with violent commotion.[4] Thus the story of Melancthon affords a striking lecture on the value of time, by informing us, that when he made an appointment, he expected not only the hour, but the minute to be fixed, that the day might not run out in the idleness of suspense;[5] and all the plans and enterprizes of De Wit are now of less importance to the world, than that part of his personal character which represents him as "careful of his health, and negligent of his life."[6]

---

3 Jacques Auguste de Thou (1553–1617), French historian and statesman. Johnson quotes from Nicholas Rigault's preface to de Thou's *Observations* (1620).

4 Sallust was a Roman historian (86–34 B.C.). The reference is to his *History of the Conspiracy of Catiline*, XV. 5.

5 Joachim Camerarius, *Vita Melancthonis*, ed. G. T. Strobol (Halle, 1777), p. 62.

6 Sir William Temple, *Works* (ed. 1770), III. 244.

But biography has often been allotted to writers who seem very little acquainted with the nature of their task, or very negligent about the performance. They rarely afford any other account than might be collected from publick papers, but imagine themselves writing a life when they exhibit a chronological series of actions or preferments; and so little regard the manners or behaviour of their heroes, that more knowledge may be gained of a man's real character, by a short conversation with one of his servants, than from a formal and studied narrative, begun with his pedigree, and ended with his funeral.

If now and then they condescend to inform the world of particular facts, they are not always so happy as to select the most important. I know not well what advantage posterity can receive from the only circumstance by which Tickell has distinguished Addison from the rest of mankind, "the irregularity of his pulse":[7] nor can I think myself overpaid for the time spent in reading the life of Malherb, by being enabled to relate, after the learned biographer, that Malherb had two predominant opinions; one, that the looseness of a single woman might destroy all her boast of ancient descent; the other, that the French beggars made use very improperly and barbarously of the phrase "noble Gentleman," because either word included the sense of both.[8]

There are, indeed, some natural reasons why these narratives are often written by such as were not likely to give much instruction or delight, and why most accounts of particular persons are barren and useless. If a life be delayed till interest and envy are at an end, we may hope for impartiality, but must expect little intelligence; for the incidents which give excellence to biography are of a volatile and evanescent kind, such as soon escape the memory, and are rarely transmitted by tradition. We know how few can portray a living acquaintance, except by his most prominent and observable particularities, and the grosser features of his mind; and it may be easily imagined how much of this little knowledge may be lost in imparting it, and how soon a succession of copies will lose all resemblance of the original.

If the biographer writes from personal knowledge, and makes haste to gratify the publick curiosity, there is danger lest his interest, his fear, his gratitude, or his tenderness, over-power his fidelity, and tempt

---

7 Thomas Tickell (1686–1740), in preface to Addison's *Works* (1721), I. xvi.

8 François de Malherbe (1555–1628), French poet. His life was written by Honorat de Bueil, Marquis de Racan (1651). See Racan, *Oeuvres Complètes* (1857), I. 258–59, 265.

him to conceal, if not to invent. There are many who think it an act of piety to hide the faults or failings of their friends, even when they can no longer suffer by their detection; we therefore see whole ranks of characters adorned with uniform panegyrick, and not to be known from one another, but by extrinsick and casual circumstances. "Let me remember," says Hale, "when I find myself inclined to pity a criminal, that there is likewise a pity due to the country."[9] If we owe regard to the memory of the dead, there is yet more respect to be paid to knowledge, to virtue, and to truth.

NUMBER 78   *Saturday, 15 December 1750*

———— *Mors sola fatetur*
Quantula sint hominum corpuscula.

JUVENAL, X. 172–73.

Death only this mysterious truth unfolds,
The mighty soul how small a body holds.

DRYDEN.

Corporal sensation is known to depend so much upon novelty, that custom takes away from many things their power of giving pleasure or pain. Thus a new dress becomes easy by wearing it, and the palate is reconciled by degrees to dishes which at first disgusted it. That by long habit of carrying a burden we lose, in great part, our sensibility of its weight, any man may be convinced by putting on for an hour the armour of our ancestors; for he will scarcely believe that men would have had much inclination to marches and battles, encumbered and oppressed, as he will find himself with the ancient panoply. Yet the heroes that overran regions, and stormed towns in iron accoutrements, he knows not to have been bigger, and has no reason to imagine them stronger than the present race of men; he therefore must conclude, that their peculiar powers were conferred only by peculiar habits, and that their familiarity with the dress of war enabled them to move in it with ease, vigour, and agility.

Yet it seems to be the condition of our present state, that pain

---

[9] Gilbert Burnet, *Life and Death of Sir Matthew Hale* (1682), pp. 58–59.

should be more fixed and permanent than pleasure. Uneasiness gives way by slow degrees, and is long before it quits its possession of the sensory; but all our gratifications are volatile, vagrant, and easily dissipated. The fragrance of the jessamine bower is lost after the enjoyment of a few moments, and the Indian wanders among his native spices without any sense of their exhalations. It is, indeed, not necessary to shew by many instances what all mankind confess, by an incessant call for variety, and restless pursuit of enjoyments, which they value only because unpossessed.

Something similar, or analogous, may be observed in effects produced immediately upon the mind; nothing can strongly strike or affect us, but what is rare or sudden. The most important events, when they become familiar, are no longer considered with wonder or solicitude, and that which at first filled up our whole attention, and left no place for any other thought, is soon thrust aside into some remote repository of the mind, and lies among other lumber of the memory, over-looked and neglected. Thus far the mind resembles the body, but here the similitude is at an end.

The manner in which external force acts upon the body is very little subject to the regulation of the will; no man can at pleasure obtund[1] or invigorate his senses, prolong the agency of any impulse, or continue the presence of any image traced upon the eye, or any sound infused into the ear. But our ideas are more subjected to choice; we can call them before us, and command their stay, we can facilitate and promote their recurrence, we can either repress their intrusion, or hasten their retreat. It is therefore the business of wisdom and virtue, to select among numberless objects striving for our notice, such as may enable us to exalt our reason, extend our views, and secure our happiness. But this choice is to be made with very little regard to rareness or frequency; for nothing is valuable merely because it is either rare or common, but because it is adapted to some useful purpose, and enables us to supply some deficiency of our nature.

Milton has judiciously represented the father of mankind, as seized with horror and astonishment at the sight of death, exhibited to him on the mount of vision.[2] For surely, nothing can so much disturb the passions, or perplex the intellects of man, as the disruption of his union with visible nature; a separation from all that has hitherto delighted or en-

---

1 Dull, blunt, deaden.
2 *Paradise Lost*, XI. 461–65.

gaged him; a change not only of the place, but the manner of his being; an entrance into a state not simply which he knows not, but which perhaps he has not faculties to know; an immediate and perceptible communication with the supreme Being, and, what is above all distressful and alarming, the final sentence, and unalterable allotment.

Yet we to whom the shortness of life has given frequent occasions of contemplating mortality, can without emotion, see generations of men pass away, and are at leisure to establish modes of sorrow, and adjust the ceremonial of death. We can look upon funeral pomp as a common spectacle in which we have no concern, and turn away from it to trifles and amusements, without dejection of look, or inquietude of heart.

It is, indeed, apparent from the constitution of the world, that there must be a time for other thoughts; and a perpetual meditation upon the last hour, however it may become the solitude of a monastery, is inconsistent with many duties of common life. But surely the remembrance of death ought to predominate in our minds, as an habitual and settled principle, always operating, though not always perceived; and our attention should seldom wander so far from our own condition, as not to be recalled and fixed by sight of an event, which must soon, we know not how soon, happen likewise to ourselves, and of which, though we cannot appoint the time, we may secure the consequence.

Every instance of death may justly awaken our fears and quicken our vigilance, but its frequency so much weakens its effect, that we are seldom alarmed, unless some close connexion is broken, some scheme frustrated, or some hope defeated. Many therefore seem to pass on from youth to decrepitude without any reflection on the end of life, because they are wholly involved within themselves, and look on others only as inhabitants of the common earth, without any expectation of receiving good, or intention of bestowing it.

Events, of which we confess the importance, excite little sensibility, unless they affect us more nearly than as sharers in the common interest of mankind; that desire which every man feels of being remembered and lamented, is often mortified when we remark how little concern is caused by the eternal departure even of those who have passed their lives with publick honours, and been distinguished by extraordinary performances. It is not possible to be regarded with tenderness except by a few. That merit which gives greatness and renown, diffuses its influence to a wide compass, but acts weakly on every single breast; it is placed at a distance from common spectators, and shines like one of the remote stars, of

which the light reaches us, but not the heat. The wit, the hero, the philosopher, whom their tempers or their fortunes have hindered from intimate relations, die without any other effect than that of adding a new
topic to the conversation of the day. They impress none with any fresh
conviction of the fragility of our nature, because none had any particular
interest in their lives, or was united to them by a reciprocation of benefits
and endearments.

Thus it often happens, that those who in their lives were applauded
and admired, are laid at last in the ground without the common honour
of a stone; because by those excellencies with which many were delighted,
none had been obliged, and, though they had many to celebrate, they had
none to love them.

Custom so far regulates the sentiments at least of common minds,
that I believe men may be generally observed to grow less tender as they
advance in age. He, who, when life was new, melted at the loss of every
companion, can look in time without concern, upon the grave into which
his last friend was thrown, and into which himself is ready to fall; not that
he is more willing to die than formerly, but that he is more familiar to the
death of others, and therefore is not alarmed so far as to consider how
much nearer he approaches to his end. But this is to submit tamely to the
tyranny of accident, and to suffer our reason to lie useless. Every funeral
may justly be considered as a summons to prepare for that state, into
which it shews us that we must sometime enter; and the summons is more
loud and piercing, as the event of which it warns us is at less distance. To
neglect at any time preparation for death, is to sleep on our post at a
siege, but to omit it in old age, is to sleep at an attack.

It has always appeared to me one of the most striking passages in the
visions of Quevedo, which stigmatises those as fools who complain that
they failed of happiness by sudden death. "How," says he, "can death be
sudden to a being who always knew that he must die, and that the time of
his death was uncertain?"[3]

Since business and gaiety are always drawing our attention away
from a future state, some admonition is frequently necessary to recall it to
our minds, and what can more properly renew the impression than the
examples of mortality which every day supplies? The great incentive to

---

[3] Francisco de Quevedo y Villegas (1580–1645), Spanish satirist and novelist. The
quotation is from his *Visions*, tr. Sir Roger L'Estrange (1702), pp. 173–74 (Vision VI). I am
indebted for this reference to Walter Jackson Bate and his annotation of *The Rambler* for the
Yale Edition.

virtue is the reflection that we must die; it will therefore be useful to
accustom ourselves, whenever we see a funeral, to consider how soon we
may be added to the number of those whose probation is past, and whose
happiness or misery shall endure for ever.

NUMBER 89   *Tuesday, 22 January 1751*

Dulce est desipere in loco.
HORACE, Odes, IV. 12. 28.
Wisdom at proper times is well forgot.

Locke, whom there is no reason to suspect of being a favourer of
idleness or libertinism, has advanced, that whoever hopes to employ any
part of his time with efficacy and vigour, must allow some of it to pass in
trifles.[1] It is beyond the powers of humanity to spend a whole life in profound study and intense meditation, and the most rigorous exacters of
industry and seriousness have appointed hours for relaxation and amusement.

It is certain, that, with or without our consent, many of the few
moments allotted us will slide imperceptibly away, and that the mind
will break, from confinement to its stated task, into sudden excursions.
Severe and connected attention is preserved but for a short time, and
when a man shuts himself up in his closet, and bends his thoughts to the
discussion of any abstruse question, he will find his faculties continually
stealing away to more pleasing entertainments. He often perceives himself
transported, he knows not how, to distant tracts of thought, and returns
to his first object as from a dream, without knowing when he forsook it,
or how long he has been abstracted from it.

It has been observed that the most studious are not always the most
learned. There is, indeed, no great difficulty in discovering that this
difference of proficiency may arise from the difference of intellectual
powers, of the choice of books, or the convenience of information. But I
believe it likewise frequently happens that the most recluse are not the
most vigorous prosecutors of study. Many impose upon the world, and
many upon themselves, by an appearance of severe and exemplary dili-

---

1 Probably a reference to *Some Thoughts Concerning Education*, pars. 206–9. I am once
more indebted to the Yale Edition.

gence, when they, in reality, give themselves up to the luxury of fancy, please their minds with regulating the past, or planning out the future; place themselves at will in varied situations of happiness, and slumber away their days in voluntary visions. In the journey of life some are left behind, because they are naturally feeble and slow; some because they miss the way, and many because they leave it by choice, and instead of pressing onward with a steady pace, delight themselves with momentary deviations, turn aside to pluck every flower, and repose in every shade.

There is nothing more fatal to a man whose business is to think, than to have learned the art of regaling his mind with those airy gratifications. Other vices or follies are restrained by fear, reformed by admonition, or rejected by the conviction which the comparison of our conduct with that of others, may in time produce. But this invisible riot of the mind, this secret prodigality of being, is secure from detection, and fearless of reproach. The dreamer retires to his apartments, shuts out the cares and interruptions of mankind, and abandons himself to his own fancy; new worlds rise up before him, one image is followed by another, and a long succession of delights dances round him. He is at last called back to life by nature, or by custom, and enters peevish into society, because he cannot model it to his own will. He returns from his idle excursions with the asperity, tho' not with the knowledge, of a student, and hastens again to the same felicity with the eagerness of a man bent upon the advancement of some favourite science. The infatuation strengthens by degrees, and, like the poison of opiates, weakens his powers, without any external symptom of malignity.

It happens, indeed, that these hypocrites of learning are in time detected, and convinced by disgrace and disappointment of the difference between the labour of thought, and the sport of musing. But this discovery is often not made till it is too late to recover the time that has been fooled away. A thousand accidents may, indeed, awaken drones to a more early sense of their danger and their shame. But they who are convinced of the necessity of breaking from this habitual drowsiness, too often relapse in spite of their resolution; for these ideal seducers are always near, and neither any particularity of time nor place is necessary to their influence; they invade the soul without warning, and have often charmed down resistance before their approach is perceived or suspected.

This captivity, however, it is necessary for every man to break, who has any desire to be wise or useful, to pass his life with the esteem of others, or to look back with satisfaction from his old age upon his earlier years. In order to regain liberty, he must find the means of flying from himself; he must, in opposition to the Stoick precept, teach his desires to fix upon external things; he must adopt the joys and the pains of others, and excite in his mind the want of social pleasures and amicable communication.

It is, perhaps, not impossible to promote the cure of this mental malady, by close application to some new study, which may pour in fresh ideas, and keep curiosity in perpetual motion. But study requires solitude, and solitude is a state dangerous to those who are too much accustomed to sink into themselves. Active employment, or publick pleasure, is generally a necessary part of this intellectual regimen, without which, though some remission may be obtained, a compleat cure will scarcely be effected.

This is a formidable and obstinate disease of the intellect, of which, when it has once become radicated by time, the remedy is one of the hardest tasks of reason and of virtue. Its slightest attacks, therefore, should be watchfully opposed; and he that finds the frigid and narcotick infection beginning to seize him, should turn his whole attention against it, and check it at the first discovery by proper counteraction.

The great resolution to be formed, when happiness and virtue are thus formidably invaded, is, that no part of life be spent in a state of neutrality or indifference; but that some pleasure be found for every moment that is not devoted to labour; and that, whenever the necessary business of life grows irksome or disgusting,[2] an immediate transition be made to diversion and gaiety.

After the exercises which the health of the body requires, and which have themselves a natural tendency to actuate and invigorate the mind, the most eligible amusement of a rational being seems to be that interchange of thoughts which is practised in free and easy conversation; where suspicion is banished by experience, and emulation by benevolence; where every man speaks with no other restraint than unwillingness to offend, and hears with no other disposition than desire to be pleased.

There must be a time in which every man trifles; and the only choice that nature offers us, is, to trifle in company or alone. To join profit with pleasure, has been an old precept among men who have had very different conceptions of profit. All have agreed that our amusements should not terminate wholly in the present moment, but contribute more or less to future advantage. He that amuses himself among well chosen

---

2 Offensive to the sensibilities.

companions, can scarcely fail to receive, from the most careless and obstreperous merriment which virtue can allow, some useful hints; nor can converse on the most familiar topicks, without some casual information. The loose sparkles of thoughtless wit may give new light to the mind, and the gay contention for paradoxical positions rectify the opinions.

This is the time in which those friendships that give happiness or consolation, relief or security, are generally formed. A wise and good man is never so amiable as in his unbended and familiar intervals. Heroic generosity, or philosophical discoveries, may compel veneration and respect, but love always implies some kind of natural or voluntary equality, and is only to be excited by that levity and chearfulness which disencumbers all minds from awe and solicitude, invites the modest to freedom, and exalts the timorous to confidence. This easy gaiety is certain to please, whatever be the character of him that exerts it; if our superiors descend from their elevation, we love them for lessening the distance at which we are placed below them; and inferiors, from whom we can receive no lasting advantage, will always keep our affections while their sprightliness and mirth contributes to our pleasure.

Every man finds himself differently affected by the sight of fortresses of war, and palaces of pleasure; we look on the height and strength of the bulwarks with a kind of gloomy satisfaction, for we cannot think of defence without admitting images of danger; but we range delighted and jocund through the gay apartments of the palace, because nothing is impressed by them on the mind but joy and festivity. Such is the difference between great and amiable characters; with protectors we are safe, with companions we are happy.

NUMBER 131   *Tuesday, 18 June 1751*

—————*Fatis accede deisque,*
Et cole felices; miseros fuge. Sidera coelo
Ut distant, et flamma mari, sic utile recto.

Lucan, Pharsalia, VIII. 486–88.

Still follow where auspicious fates invite;
Caress the happy, and the wretched slight.
Sooner shall jarring elements unite,

Than truth with gain, than interest with right.

F. LEWIS.[1]

There is scarcely any sentiment in which, amidst the innumerable varieties of inclination that nature or accident have scattered in the world, we find greater numbers concurring than in the wish for riches; a wish indeed so prevalent that it may be considered as universal and transcendental, as the desire in which all other desires are included, and of which the various purposes which actuate mankind are only subordinate species and different modifications.

Wealth is the general center of inclination, the point to which all minds preserve an invariable tendency, and from which they afterwards diverge in numberless directions. Whatever is the remote or ultimate design, the immediate care is to be rich; and in whatever enjoyment we intend finally to acquiesce, we seldom consider it as attainable but by the means of money. Of wealth therefore all unanimously confess the value, nor is there any disagreement but about the use.

No desire can be formed which riches do not assist to gratify. He that places his happiness in splendid equipage or numerous dependents, in refined praise or popular acclamations, in the accumulation of curiosities or the revels of luxury, in splendid edifices or wide plantations, must still either by birth or acquisition possess riches. They may be considered as the elemental principles of pleasure, which may be combined with endless diversity; as the essential and necessary substance, of which only the form is left to be adjusted by choice.

The necessity of riches being thus apparent, it is not wonderful that almost every mind has been employed in endeavours to acquire them; that multitudes have vied in arts by which life is furnished with accommodations, and which therefore mankind may reasonably be expected to reward.

It had indeed been happy, if this predominant appetite had operated only in concurrence with virtue, by influencing none but those who were zealous to deserve what they were eager to possess, and had abilities to improve their own fortunes by contributing to the ease or happiness of others. To have riches and to have merit would then have been the same,

---

1 I have been unable to identify this translation or the translator. The British Museum Catalogue lists only three English translations of Lucan before 1751, none of them by Lewis. Johnson included Nicholas Rowe's translation in his collection of English poetry, but Rowe is not the source for this quotation.

and success might reasonably have been considered as a proof of excellence.

But we do not find that any of the wishes of men keep a stated proportion to their powers of attainment. Many envy and desire wealth, who can never procure it by honest industry or useful knowledge. They therefore turn their eyes about to examine what other methods can be found of gaining that which none, however impotent or worthless, will be content to want.

A little enquiry will discover that there are nearer ways to profit than through the intricacies of art, or up the steeps of labour; what wisdom and virtue scarcely receive at the close of life, as the recompence of long toil and repeated efforts, is brought within the reach of subtilty and dishonesty by more expeditious and compendious measures: the wealth of credulity is an open prey to falshood; and the possessions of ignorance and imbecility are easily stolen away by the conveyances of secret artifice, or seized by the gripe of unresisted violence.

It is likewise not hard to discover, that riches always procure protection for themselves, that they dazzle the eyes of enquiry, divert the celerity of pursuit, or appease the ferocity of vengeance. When any man is incontestably known to have large possessions, very few think it requisite to enquire by what practices they were obtained; the resentment of mankind rages only against the struggles of feeble and timorous corruption, but when it has surmounted the first opposition, it is afterwards supported by favour, and animated by applause.

The prospect of gaining speedily what is ardently desired, and the certainty of obtaining by every accession of advantage an addition of security, have so far prevailed upon the passions of mankind, that the peace of life is destroyed by a general and incessant struggle for riches. It is observed of gold, by an old epigrammatist, that "to have it is to be in fear, and to want it is to be in sorrow."[2] There is no condition which is not disquieted either with the care of gaining or of keeping money; and the race of man may be divided in a political estimate between those who are practising fraud, and those who are repelling it.

If we consider the present state of the world, it will be found, that all confidence is lost among mankind, that no man ventures to act where money can be endangered, upon the faith of another. It is impossible to see the long scrolls in which every contract is included, with all their

---

2 *Greek Anthology*, IX. 394 (Palladas). The Yale Edition is the source of this reference.

appendages of seals and attestation, without wondering at the depravity of those beings, who must be restrained from violation of promise by such formal and publick evidences, and precluded from equivocation and subterfuge by such punctilious minuteness. Among all the satires to which folly and wickedness have given occasion, none is equally severe with a bond or a settlement.

Of the various arts by which riches may be obtained, the greater part are at the first view irreconcileable with the laws of virtue; some are openly flagitious, and practised not only in neglect, but in defiance of faith and justice; and the rest are on every side so entangled with dubious tendencies, and so beset with perpetual temptations, that very few, even of those who are not yet abandoned, are able to preserve their innocence, or can produce any other claim to pardon than that they have deviated from the right less than others, and have sooner and more diligently endeavoured to return.

One of the chief characteristicks of the golden age, of the age in which neither care nor danger had intruded on mankind, is the community of possessions: strife and fraud were totally excluded, and every turbulent passion was stilled, by plenty and equality. Such were indeed happy times, but such times can return no more. Community of possession must include spontaneity of production; for what is obtained by labour, will be of right the property of him by whose labour it is gained. And while a rightful claim to pleasure or to affluence must be procured either by slow industry or uncertain hazard, there will always be multitudes whom cowardice or impatience incite to more safe and more speedy methods, who strive to pluck the fruit without cultivating the tree, and to share the advantages of victory without partaking the danger of the battle.

In later ages, the conviction of the danger to which virtue is exposed while the mind continues open to the influence of riches, has determined many to vows of perpetual poverty; they have suppressed desire by cutting off the possibility of gratification, and secured their peace by destroying the enemy whom they had no hope of reducing to quiet subjection. But by debarring themselves from evil, they have rescinded many opportunities of good; they have too often sunk into inactivity and uselessness; and though they have forborn to injure society, have not fully paid their contributions to its happiness.

While riches are so necessary to present convenience, and so much more easily obtained by crimes than virtues, the mind can only be secured

from yielding to the continual impulse of covetousness by the pre-
ponderation of unchangeable and eternal motives. Gold will turn the
intellectual balance, when weighed only against reputation; but will be
light and ineffectual when the opposite scale is charged with justice,
veracity, and piety.

THE IDLER[1]

(1758–1760)

Six years after he had stopped writing *The Rambler*, which had contributed importantly to his reputation, Dr. Johnson was requested to compose essays for a newspaper, *The Universal Chronicle*. Under the title *The Idler*, he wrote nearly a hundred essays; the work presumably distracted him from the hard labor of his great edition of Shakespeare.

The *Idler* essays are shorter and lighter in tone than those of *The Rambler;* they are more closely modeled on the periodical essays of Addison and Steele. Although some of them seem trivial in comparison with Johnson's weightier work, many are charming, entertaining, even whimsical. They often provide sharp glimpses of the life of the time.

The present text is from Samuel Johnson, *The Idler and The Adventurer*, eds. W. J. Bate, John M. Bullitt, L. F. Powell (New Haven, Conn.: Yale University Press, 1963). Used by permission of the publishers.

The Idler

NUMBER 3   *Saturday, 29 April 1758*

Otia vitae
Solamur cantu.[2]

STATIUS, Silvae, IV. 4. 49–50.

It has long been the complaint of those who frequent the theatres, that all the dramatick art has been long exhausted, and that the vicissitudes of fortune, and accidents of life, have been shewn in every possible combination, till the first scene informs us of the last, and the play no sooner opens, than every auditor knows how it will conclude. When a con-

---

1 See Introduction, pp. 35–36.
2 "We beguile a leisured life with song "

spiracy is formed in a tragedy, we guess by whom it will be detected; when a letter is dropt in a comedy, we can tell by whom it will be found. Nothing is now left for the poet but character and sentiment, which are to make their way as they can, without the soft anxiety of suspense, or the enlivening agitation of surprize.

A new paper lies under the same disadvantages as a new play. There is danger lest it be new without novelty. My earlier predecessors had their choice of vices and follies, and selected such as were most likely to raise merriment or attract attention; they had the whole field of life before them, untrodden and unsurveyed; characters of every kind shot up in their way, and those of the most luxuriant growth, or most conspicuous colours, were naturally cropt by the first sickle. They that follow are forced to peep into neglected corners, to note the casual varieties of the same species, and to recommend themselves by minute industry, and distinctions too subtle for common eyes.

Sometimes it may happen, that the haste or negligence of the first inquirers, has left enough behind to reward another search; sometimes new objects start up under the eye, and he that is looking for one kind of matter, is amply gratified by the discovery of another. But still it must be allowed, that, as more is taken, less can remain, and every truth brought newly to light, impoverishes the mine, from which succeeding intellects are to dig their treasures.

Many philosophers imagine that the elements themselves may be in time exhausted. That the sun, by shining long, will effuse all its light; and that, by the continual waste of aqueous particles, the whole earth will at last become a sandy desart.[3]

I would not advise my readers to disturb themselves by contriving how they shall live without light and water. For the days of universal thirst and perpetual darkness are at a great distance. The ocean and the sun will last our time, and we may leave posterity to shift for themselves.

But if the stores of nature are limited, much more narrow bounds must be set to the modes of life; and mankind may want a moral or amusing paper, many years before they shall be deprived of drink or daylight. This want, which to the busy and the inventive may seem easily remediable by some substitute or other, the whole race of Idlers will feel with all the sensibility that such torpid animals can suffer.

When I consider the innumerable multitudes that, having no motive

---

3 A common speculation throughout the seventeenth century.

of desire, or determination of will, lie freezing in perpetual inactivity, till some external impulse puts them in motion; who awake in the morning, vacant of thought, with minds gaping for the intellectual food, which some kind essayist has been accustomed to supply; I am moved by the commiseration with which all human beings ought to behold the distresses of each other, to try some expedients for their relief, and to inquire by what methods the listless may be actuated, and the empty be replenished.

There are said to be pleasures in madness known only to madmen. There are certainly miseries in idleness, which the Idler only can conceive. These miseries I have often felt and often bewailed. I know, by experience, how welcome is every avocation that summons the thoughts to a new image; and how much languor and lassitude are relieved by that officiousness[4] which offers a momentary amusement to him who is unable to find it for himself.

It is naturally indifferent to this race of men what entertainment they receive, so they are but entertained. They catch, with equal eagerness, at a moral lecture, or the memoirs of a robber; a prediction of the appearance of a comet, or the calculation of the chances of a lottery.

They might therefore, easily be pleased, if they consulted only their own minds; but those who will not take the trouble to think for themselves, have always somebody that thinks for them; and the difficulty in writing is to please those from whom others learn to be pleased.

Much mischief is done in the world with very little interest or design. He that assumes the character of a critick, and justifies his claim by perpetual censure, imagines that he is hurting none but the author, and him he considers as a pestilent animal, whom every other being has a right to persecute; little does he think how many harmless men he involves in his own guilt, by teaching them to be noxious without malignity, and to repeat objections which they do not understand; or how many honest minds he debars from pleasure, by exciting an artificial fastidiousness, and making them too wise to concur with their own sensations. He who is taught by a critick to dislike that which pleased him in his natural state, has the same reason to complain of his instructor, as the madman to rail at his doctor, who, when he thought himself master of Peru, physick'd him to poverty.

If men will struggle against their own advantage, they are not to expect that the Idler will take much pains upon them; he has himself to

4 Readiness to do kind offices.

please as well as them, and has long learned, or endeavoured to learn, not to make the pleasure of others too necessary to his own.

NUMBER 35   *Saturday, 16 December 1758*

To The Idler

Mr. Idler,

If it be difficult to persuade the idle to be busy, it is likewise, as experience has taught me, not easy to convince the busy that it is better to be idle. When you shall despair of stimulating sluggishness to motion, I hope you will turn your thoughts towards the means of stilling the bustle of pernicious activity.

I am the unfortunate husband of a "buyer of bargains." My wife has somewhere heard, that a good housewife "never" has any thing to "purchase when it is wanted." This maxim is often in her mouth, and always in her head. She is not one of those philosophical talkers that speculate without practice, and learn sentences of wisdom only to repeat them; she is always making additions to her stores; she never looks into a broker's shop, but she spies something that may be wanted some time; and it is impossible to make her pass the door of a house where she hears "Goods selling by auction."

Whatever she thinks cheap, she holds it the duty of an oeconomist to buy; in consequence of this maxim, we are incumbered on every side with useless lumber. The servants can scarcely creep to their beds thro' the chests and boxes that surround them. The carpenter is employed once a week in building closets, fixing cupboards, and fastening shelves, and my house has the appearance of a ship stored for a voyage to the colonies.

I had often observed that advertisements set her on fire, and therefore, pretending to emulate her laudable frugality, I forbad the newspaper to be taken any longer; but my precaution is vain; I know not by what fatality, or by what confederacy, every catalogue of "genuine furniture" comes to her hand, every advertisement of a warehouse newly opened is in her pocket-book, and she knows before any of her neighbours, when the stock of any man "leaving off trade" is to be "sold cheap for ready money."

Such intelligence, is to my dear one the Siren's song. No engagement, no duty, no interest can withold her from a sale, from which she always returns congratulating herself upon her dexterity at a bargain; the porter lays down his burden in the hall, she displays her new acquisitions, and spends the rest of the day in contriving where they shall be put.

As she cannot bear to have any thing uncomplete, one purchase necessitates another; she has twenty feather-beds more than she can use, and a late sale has supplied her with a proportionable number of Witney blankets,[1] a large roll of linnen for sheets, and five quilts for every bed, which she bought because the seller told her, that if she would clear his hands he would let her have a bargain.

Thus by hourly encroachments my habitation is made narrower and narrower; the dining-room is so crouded with tables that dinner scarcely can be served; the parlour is decorated with so many piles of china, that I dare not step within the door; at every turn of the stairs I have a clock, and half the windows of the upper floors are darkened that shelves may be set before them.

This, however, might be borne, if she would gratify her own inclinations without opposing mine. But I who am idle am luxurious,[2] and she condemns me to live upon salt provision. She knows the loss of buying in small quantities, we have therefore whole hogs and quarters of oxen. Part of our meat is tainted before it is eaten, and part is thrown away because it is spoiled; but she persists in her system, and will never buy any thing by single pennyworths.

The common vice of those who are still grasping at more, is to neglect that which they already possess; but from this failing my charmer is free. It is the great care of her life that the pieces of beef should be boiled in the order in which they are bought; that the second bag of pease shall not be opened till the first are eaten; that every feather-bed shall be lain on in its turn; that the carpets should be taken out of the chests once a month and brushed, and the rolls of linnen opened now and then before the fire. She is daily enquiring after the best traps for mice; and keeps the rooms always scented by fumigations to destroy the moths. She employs workmen, from time to time, to adjust six clocks that never go, and clean five jacks[3] that rust in the garret; and a woman in the next alley lives by scouring the brass and pewter, which, are only laid up to tarnish again.

---

1 Blankets of heavy wool made in Witney, Oxfordshire.
2 Given to luxury or self-indulgence.
3 Probably smoke-jacks, machines for turning the spit in roasting meat.

She is always imagining some distant time in which she shall use whatever she accumulates; she has four looking-glasses which she cannot hang up in her house, but which will be handsome in more lofty rooms; and pays rent for the place of a vast copper in some warehouse, because when we live in the country we shall brew our own beer.

Of this life I have long been weary, but know not how to change it; all the married men whom I consult advise me to have patience; but some old bachelors are of opinion, that since she loves sales so well, she should have a sale of her own, and I have, I think, resolved to open her hoards, and advertise an auction.

> I am, Sir,
> Your very humble servant,
> *Peter Plenty.*

NUMBER 36   *Saturday, 23 December 1758*

The great differences that disturb the peace of mankind, are not about ends but means. We have all the same general desires, but how those desires shall be accomplished will for ever be disputed. The ultimate purpose of government is temporal, and that of religion is eternal happiness. Hitherto we agree; but here we must part, to try, according to the endless varieties of passion and understanding combined with one another, every possible form of government, and every imaginable tenet of religion.

We are told by Cumberland, that "rectitude," applied to action or contemplation, is merely metaphorical; and that as a "right" line describes the shortest passage from point to point, so a "right" action effects a good design by the fewest means; and so likewise a "right" opinion is that which connects distant truths by the shortest train of intermediate propositions.[1]

To find the nearest way from truth to truth, or from purpose to effect, not to use more instruments where fewer will be sufficient, not to move by wheels and levers what will give way to the naked hand, is the great proof of a healthful and vigorous mind, neither feeble with helpless ignorance, nor over-burdened with unwieldy knowledge.

---

[1] Richard Cumberland, *Philosophical Enquiry into the Laws of Nature* (ed. 1750 [first published, 1672; English trans. 1679]), Prolegomena, pp. xlii n. and xlv–xlvi.

But there are men who seem to think nothing so much the characteristick of a genius, as to do common things in an uncommon manner; like Hudibras to "tell the clock by algebra,"[2] or like the lady in Dr. Young's satires, "to drink tea by stratagem."[3] To quit the beaten track only because it is known, and take a new path, however crooked or rough, because the strait was found out before.

Every man speaks and writes with intent to be understood, and it can seldom happen but he that understands himself might convey his notions to another, if, content to be understood, he did not seek to be admired; but when once he begins to contrive how his sentiments may be received, not with most ease to his reader, but with most advantage to himself, he then transfers his consideration from words to sounds, from sentences to periods,[4] and as he grows more elegant becomes less intelligible.

It is difficult to enumerate every species of authors whose labours counteract themselves. The man of exuberance and copiousness, who diffuses every thought thro' so many diversities of expression, that it is lost like water in a mist. The ponderous dictator of sentences, whose notions are delivered in the lump, and are, like uncoined bullion, of more weight than use. The liberal illustrator, who shews by examples and comparisons what was clearly seen when it was first proposed; and the stately son of demonstration, who proves with mathematical formality what no man has yet pretended to doubt.

There is a mode of style for which I know not that the masters of oratory have yet found a name, a style by which the most evident truths are so obscured that they can no longer be perceived, and the most familiar propositions so disguised that they cannot be known. Every other kind of eloquence is the dress of sense, but this is the mask, by which a true master of his art will so effectually conceal it, that a man will as easily mistake his own positions if he meets them thus transformed, as he may pass in a masquerade his nearest acquaintance.

This style may be called the "terrifick," for its chief intention is to terrify and amaze; it may be termed the "repulsive," for its natural effect is to drive away the reader; or it may be distinguished, in plain English, by the denomination of the "bugbear style," for it has more terror than

2 Samuel Butler, *Hudibras*, I. i. 125–26.
3 Edward Young, *Satires*, VI. 188.
4 *Period:* "A complete sentence; esp. one of several clauses, grammatically connected, and rhetorically constructed" (*OED*).

danger, and will appear less formidable, as it is more nearly approached.

A mother tells her infant, that "two and two make four," the child remembers the proposition, and is able to count four to all the purposes of life, till the course of his education brings him among philosophers, who fright him from his former knowledge, by telling him that four is a certain aggregate of unites; that all numbers being only the repetition of an unite, which, though not a number itself, is the parent, root, or original of all number, "four" is the denomination assigned to a certain number of such repetitions. The only danger is, lest, when he first hears these dreadful sounds, the pupil should run away; if he has but the courage to stay till the conclusion, he will find that, when speculation has done its worst, two and two still make four.

An illustrious example of this species of eloquence, may be found in *Letters Concerning Mind*.[5] The author begins by declaring, that "the sorts of things are things that now are, have been, and shall be, and the things that strictly Are." In this position, except the last clause, in which he uses something of the scholastick language, there is nothing but what every man has heard and imagines himself to know. But who would not believe that some wonderful novelty is presented to his intellect, when he is afterwards told, in the true "bugbear" style, that "the Ares, in the former sense, are things that lie between the Have-beens and Shall-bes. The Have-beens are things that are past; the Shall-bes are things that are to come; and the things that Are, in the latter sense, are things that have not been, nor shall be, nor stand in the midst of such as are before them or shall be after them. The things that have been, and shall be, have respect to present, past, and future. Those likewise that now Are have moreover place; that, for instance, which is here, that which is to the east, that which is to the west."

All this, my dear reader, is very strange; but though it be strange, it is not new; survey these wonderful sentences again, and they will be found to contain nothing more than very plain truths, which till this author arose had always been delivered in plain language.

NUMBER 37   *Saturday, 30 December 1758*

Those who are skilled in the extraction and preparation of metals,

---

5 By John Petvin (1691–1745), vicar of Islington, Devon; pub. 1750; p. 40.

declare, that iron is every where to be found; and that not only its proper ore is copiously treasured in the caverns of the earth, but that its particles are dispersed throughout all other bodies.

If the extent of the human view could comprehend the whole frame of the universe, I believe it would be found invariably true, that Providence has given that in greatest plenty, which the condition of life makes of greatest use; and that nothing is penuriously imparted or placed far from the reach of man, of which a more liberal distribution, or more easy acquisition would increase real and rational felicity.

Iron is common, and gold is rare. Iron contributes so much to supply the wants of nature, that its use constitutes much of the difference between savage and polished life, between the state of him that slumbers in European palaces, and him that shelters himself in the cavities of a rock from the chilness of the night, or the violence of the storm. Gold can never be hardened into saws or axes; it can neither furnish instruments of manufacture, utensils of agriculture, nor weapons of defence; its only quality is to shine, and the value of its lustre arises from its scarcity.

Throughout the whole circle, both of natural and moral life, necessaries are as iron, and superfluities as gold. What we really need we may readily obtain; so readily, that far the greater part of mankind has, in the wantonness of abundance, confounded natural with artificial desires, and invented necessities for the sake of employment, because the mind is impatient of inaction, and life is sustained with so little labour, that the tediousness of idle time cannot otherwise be supported.

Thus plenty is the original cause of many of our needs, and even the poverty which is so frequent and distressful in civilized nations, proceeds often from that change of manners which opulence has produced. Nature makes us poor only when we want necessaries, but custom gives the name of poverty to the want of superfluities.

When Socrates passed through shops of toys and ornaments, he cried out, "How many things are here which I do not need."[1] And the same exclamation may every man make who surveys the common accommodations of life.

Superfluity and difficulty begin together. To dress food for the stomach is easy, the art is to irritate the palate when the stomach is sufficed. A rude hand may build walls, form roofs, and lay floors, and provide all that warmth and security require; we only call the nicer artificers to carve the cornice, or to paint the ceilings. Such dress as may

---

1 Diogenes Laertius, *Lives*, "Socrates," II. 25.

enable the body to endure the different seasons the most unenlightened nations have been able to procure, but the work of science begins in the ambition of distinction, in variations of fashion, and emulation of elegance. Corn grows with easy culture, the gardiner's experiments are only employed to exalt the flavours of fruits and brighten the colours of flowers.

Even of knowledge, those parts are most easy, which are generally necessary. The intercourse of society is maintained without the elegancies of language. Figures, criticisms, and refinements are the work of those whom idleness makes weary of themselves. The commerce of the world is carried cn by easy methods of computation. Subtilty and study are required only when questions are invented merely to puzzle, and calculations are extended to shew the skill of the calculator. The light of the sun is equally beneficial to him, whose eyes tell him that it moves, and to him whose reason persuades him that it stands still. And plants grow with the same luxuriance, whether we suppose earth or water the parent of vegetation.

If we raise our thoughts to nobler enquiries, we shall still find facility concurring with usefulness. No man needs stay to be virtuous till the moralists have determined the essence of virtue; our duty is made apparent by its proximate consequences, tho' the general and ultimate reason should never be discovered. Religion may regulate the life of him to whom the Scotists and Thomists[2] are alike unknown, and the asserters of fate and free-will, however different in their talk, agree to act in the same manner.

It is not my intention to depreciate the politer arts or abstruser studies. That curiosity which always succeeds ease and plenty, was undoubtedly given us as a proof of capacity which our present state is not able to fill, as a preparative for some better mode of existence, which shall furnish employment for the whole soul, and where pleasure shall be adequate to our powers of fruition. In the mean time let us gratefully acknowledge that Goodness which grants us ease at a cheap rate, which changes the seasons where the nature of heat and cold has not been yet examined, and gives the vicissitudes of day and night to those who never marked the tropicks, or numbered the constellations.

---

2 Scotists are followers of John Duns Scotus, a thirteenth-century theologian whose views opposed those of Thomas Aquinas, leader of the Thomists.

Criticism is a study by which men grow important and formidable at very small expence. The power of invention has been conferred by nature upon few, and the labour of learning those sciences which may, by mere labour, be obtained, is too great to be willingly endured; but every man can exert such judgment as he has upon the works of others; and he whom nature has made weak, and idleness keeps ignorant, may yet support his vanity by the name of a critick.

I hope it will give comfort to great numbers who are passing thro' the world in obscurity, when I inform them how easily distinction may be obtained. All the other powers of literature are coy and haughty, they must be long courted, and at last are not always gained; but criticism is a goddess easy of access and forward of advance, who will meet the slow and encourage the timorous; the want of meaning she supplies with words, and the want of spirit she recompenses with malignity.

This profession has one recommendation peculiar to itself, that it gives vent to malignity without real mischief. No genius was ever blasted by the breath of criticks. The poison which, if confined, would have burst the heart, fumes away in empty hisses, and malice is set at ease with very little danger to merit. The critick is the only man whose triumph is without another's pain, and whose greatness does not rise upon another's ruin.

To a study at once so easy and so reputable, so malicious and so harmless, it cannot be necessary to invite my readers by a long or laboured exhortation; it is sufficient, since all would be criticks if they could, to shew by one eminent example that all can be criticks if they will.

Dick Minim, after the common course of puerile studies, in which he was no great proficient, was put apprentice to a brewer, with whom he had lived two years, when his uncle died in the city, and left him a large fortune in the stocks. Dick had for six months before used the company of the lower players,[1] of whom he had learned to scorn a trade, and being now at liberty to follow his genius, he resolved to be a man of wit and humour. That he might be properly initiated in his new character, he frequented the coffee-houses near the theatres, where he listened very diligently, day after day, to those who talked of language and sentiments,

---

1 I.e., common actors.

and unities and catastrophes, till by slow degrees he began to think that he understood something of the stage, and hoped in time to talk himself.

But he did not trust so much to natural sagacity, as wholly to neglect the help of books. When the theatres were shut, he retired to Richmond[2] with a few select writers, whose opinions he impressed upon his memory by unwearied diligence; and when he returned with other wits to the town, was able to tell, in very proper phrases, that the chief business of art is to copy nature; that a perfect writer is not to be expected, because genius decays as judgment increases; that the great art is the art of blotting,[3] and that according to the rule of Horace every piece should be kept nine years.[4]

Of the great authors he now began to display the characters, laying down as an universal position that all had beauties and defects. His opinion was, that Shakespear, committing himself wholly to the impulse of nature, wanted that correctness which learning would have given him; and that Johnson,[5] trusting to learning, did not sufficiently cast his eye on nature. He blamed the stanza of Spenser, and could not bear the hexameters of Sidney.[6] Denham and Waller he held the first reformers of English numbers, and thought that if Waller could have obtained the strength of Denham, or Denham the sweetness of Waller,[7] there had been nothing wanting to complete a poet. He often expressed his commiseration of Dryden's poverty, and his indignation at the age which suffered him to write for bread; he repeated with rapture the first lines of *All for Love;*[8] but wondered at the corruption of taste which could bear any thing so unnatural as rhyming tragedies. In Otway he found uncommon powers of moving the passions, but was disgusted by his general negligence, and blamed him for making a conspirator his hero; and never concluded his disquisition, without remarking how happily the sound of the

---

2 Now a London suburb; in Johnson's time a nearby village.

3 Cf. Pope's *Essay on Criticism*, 68, 253–54, 256–57; and *Imitations of Horace*, II. i. 281.

4 *Art of Poetry*, 388.

5 I.e., Ben Jonson (1572–1637). Dick Minim is parroting the critical clichés of the period.

6 Sir Philip Sidney (1554–1586) interspersed in his *Arcadia* (1590) some poems in hexameters, six-stress lines, which exemplify his attempt to introduce Greek and Latin meters into English.

7 Sir John Denham (1615–1669), author of *Cooper's Hill* (1642); Edmund Waller (1606–1687), whose most famous poem is *Go, Lovely Rose*. Minim's judgments about these poets are also clichés of the period, as are those that follow.

8 By John Dryden (1678), a tragedy in blank verse.

clock is made to alarm the audience.[9] Southern[10] would have been his favourite, but that he mixes comick with tragick scenes, intercepts the natural course of the passions, and fills the mind with a wild confusion of mirth and melancholy. The versification of Rowe[11] he thought too melodious for the stage, and too little varied in different passions. He made it the great fault of Congreve,[12] that all his persons were wits, and that he always wrote with more art than nature. He considered *Cato*[13] rather as a poem than a play, and allowed Addison to be the complete master of allegory and grave humour, but paid no great deference to him as a critick. He thought the chief merit of Prior was in his easy tales and lighter poems, tho' he allowed that his *Solomon* had many noble sentiments elegantly expressed.[14] In Swift he discovered an inimitable vein of irony, and an easiness which all would hope and few would attain. Pope he was inclined to degrade from a poet to a versifier, and thought his numbers[15] rather luscious than sweet. He often lamented the neglect of *Phaedra and Hippolitus*,[16] and wished to see the stage under better regulations.

These assertions passed commonly uncontradicted; and if now and then an opponent started up, he was quickly repressed by the suffrages of the company, and Minim went away from every dispute with elation of heart and increase of confidence.

He now grew conscious of his abilities, and began to talk of the present state of dramatick poetry; wondered what was become of the comick genius which supplied our ancestors with wit and pleasantry, and why no writer could be found that durst now venture beyond a farce. He saw no reason for thinking that the vein of humour was exhausted, since we live in a country where liberty suffers every character to spread itself to its utmost bulk, and which therefore produces more originals

---

9 Thomas Otway (1652–1685) wrote *Venice Preserv'd* (1682), in which the hero, Jaffier, joins a conspiracy against the state. In Act V, not the sound of a clock but the tolling of a bell alarms the audience; contemporary critics found this an awe-inspiring effect.

10 Thomas Southerne (1660–1746), author of *The Fatal Marriage* (1694) and *Oroonoko* (1696).

11 Nicholas Rowe (1674–1718), author of *The Fair Penitent* (1703).

12 William Congreve (1670–1729), author of *The Way of the World* (1700).

13 By Joseph Addison (1713).

14 Matthew Prior (1664–1721), author of much light verse and of *Solomon on the Vanity of the World* (1718), a dignified, long poem in heroic couplets.

15 Metrics.

16 A play by Edmund Smith (1707).

than all the rest of the world together. Of tragedy he concluded business
to be the soul, and yet often hinted that love predominates too much upon
the modern stage.

He was now an acknowledged critick, and had his own seat in the
coffee-house, and headed a party in the pit.[17] Minim has more vanity than
ill-nature, and seldom desires to do much mischief; he will perhaps murmur a little in the ear of him that sits next him, but endeavours to influence the audience to favour, by clapping when an actor exclaims "ye
Gods," or laments the misery of his country.

By degrees he was admitted to rehearsals, and many of his friends
are of opinion, that our present poets are indebted to him for their
happiest thoughts; by his contrivance the bell was rung twice in *Barba-
rossa*,[18] and by his persuasion the author of *Cleone*[19] concluded his play
without a couplet; for what can be more absurd, said Minim, than that
part of a play should be rhymed, and part written in blank verse? and by
what acquisition of faculties is the speaker who never could find rhymes
before, enabled to rhyme at the conclusion of an act!

He is the great investigator of hidden beauties, and is particularly
delighted when he finds "the sound an echo to the sense."[20] He has read
all our poets with particular attention to this delicacy of versification, and
wonders at the supineness with which their works have been hitherto
perused, so that no man has found the sound of a drum in this distich,

> When pulpit, drum ecclesiastic,
> Was beat with fist instead of a stick;[21]

and that the wonderful lines upon honour and a bubble have hitherto
passed without notice.

> Honour is like the glassy bubble,
> Which costs philosophers such trouble,
> Where one part crack'd, the whole does fly,
> And wits are crack'd to find out why.[22]

---

17 The part of the theater that is on the floor of the house.
18 By Dr. John Brown (1754).
19 By Robert Dodsley (1758).
20 Pope, *Essay on Criticism*, 365.
21 *Hudibras*, I. i. 11–12.
22 *Hudibras*, II. ii. 385–88 (with minor changes).

In these verses, says Minim, we have two striking accommodations of the sound to the sense. It is impossible to utter the two lines emphatically without an act like that which they describe; "bubble" and "trouble" causing a momentary inflation of the cheeks by the retention of the breath, which is afterwards forcibly emitted, as in the practice of "blowing bubbles." But the greatest excellence is in the third line, which is "crack'd" in the middle to express a crack, and then shivers into monosyllables. Yet has this diamond lain neglected with common stones, and among the innumerable admirers of *Hudibras* the observation of this superlative passage has been reserved for the sagacity of Minim.

NUMBER 61   *Saturday, 16 June 1759*

Mr. Minim had now advanced himself to the zenith of critical reputation; when he was in the pit, every eye in the boxes was fixed upon him, when he entered his coffee-house, he was surrounded by circles of candidates, who passed their noviciate of literature under his tuition; his opinion was asked by all who had no opinion of their own, and yet loved to debate and decide; and no composition was supposed to pass in safety to posterity, till it had been secured by Minim's approbation.

Minim professes great admiration of the wisdom and munificence by which the academies of the continent were raised, and often wishes for some standard of taste, for some tribunal, to which merit may appeal from caprice, prejudice, and malignity. He has formed a plan for an academy of criticism, where every work of imagination may be read before it is printed, and which shall authoritatively direct the theatres what pieces to receive or reject, to exclude or to revive.

Such an institution would, in Dick's opinion, spread the fame of English literature over Europe, and make London the metropolis of elegance and politeness, the place to which the learned and ingenious of all countries would repair for instruction and improvement, and where nothing would any longer be applauded or endured that was not conformed to the nicest rules, and finished with the highest elegance.

Till some happy conjunction of the planets shall dispose our princes or ministers to make themselves immortal by such an academy, Minim contents himself to preside four nights in a week in a critical society selected by himself, where he is heard without contradiction, and whence his judgment is disseminated through the great vulgar and the small.

When he is placed in the chair of criticism, he declares loudly for the noble simplicity of our ancestors, in opposition to the petty refinements, and ornamental luxuriance. Sometimes he is sunk in despair, and perceives false delicacy daily gaining ground, and sometimes brightens his countenance with a gleam of hope, and predicts the revival of the true sublime. He then fulminates his loudest censures against the monkish barbarity of rhyme;[1] wonders how beings that pretend to reason can be pleased with one line always ending like another; tells how unjustly and unnaturally sense is sacrificed to sound; how often the best thoughts are mangled by the necessity of confining or extending them to the dimensions of a couplet; and rejoices that genius has, in our days, shaken off the shackles which had encumbered it so long. Yet allows that rhyme may sometimes be borne, if the lines be often broken, and the pauses judiciously diversified.

From blank verse he makes an easy transition to Milton, whom he produces as an example of the slow advance of lasting reputation. Milton is the only writer whose books Minim can read for ever without weariness. What cause it is that exempts this pleasure from satiety he has long and diligently enquired, and believes it to consist in the perpetual variation of the numbers, by which the ear is gratified and the attention awakened. The lines that are commonly thought rugged and unmusical, he conceives to have been written to temper the melodious luxury of the rest, or to express things by a proper cadence: for he scarcely finds a verse that has not this favourite beauty; he declares that he could shiver in a hot-house when he reads that

> the ground
> Burns frore, and cold performs th' effect of fire.[2]

And that when Milton bewails his blindness, the verse

> So thick a drop serene has quench'd these orbs,[3]

has, he knows not how, something that strikes him with an obscure sensation like that which he fancies would be felt from the sound of darkness.

Minim is not so confident of his rules of judgment as not very

---

1 See Young's *Conjectures*, above, pp. 67–68.
2 *Paradise Lost*, II. 594–95 ("the ground" is substituted for "the parching air").
3 *Paradise Lost*, III. 25 ("has quench'd these" is substituted for "hath quench'd their").

eagerly to catch new light from the name of the author. He is commonly so prudent as to spare those whom he cannot resist, unless, as will sometimes happen, he finds the publick combined against them. But a fresh pretender to fame he is strongly inclined to censure, 'till his own honour requires that he commend him. 'Till he knows the success of a composition, he intrenches himself in general terms; there are some new thoughts and beautiful passages, but there is likewise much which he would have advised the author to expunge. He has several favourite epithets, of which he has never settled the meaning, but which are very commodiously applied to books which he has not read, or cannot understand. One is "manly," another is "dry," another "stiff," and another "flimzy"; sometimes he discovers delicacy of style, and sometimes meets with "strange expressions."

He is never so great, or so happy, as when a youth of promising parts is brought to receive his directions for the prosecution of his studies. He then puts on a very serious air; he advises the pupil to read none but the best authors, and, when he finds one congenial to his own mind, to study his beauties, but avoid his faults, and, when he sits down to write, to consider how his favourite author would think at the present time on the present occasion. He exhorts him to catch those moments when he finds his thoughts expanded and his genius exalted, but to take care lest imagination hurry him beyond the bounds of nature. He holds diligence the mother of success, yet enjoins him, with great earnestness, not to read more than he can digest, and not to confuse his mind by pursuing studies of contrary tendencies. He tells him, that every man has his genius, and that Cicero[4] could never be a poet. The boy retires illuminated, resolves to follow his genius, and to think how Milton would have thought; and Minim feasts upon his own beneficence till another day brings another pupil.

---

4 Marcus Tullius Cicero (106–43 B.C.), Roman orator, politician, philosopher.

PREFACE TO SHAKESPEARE[1]

(1765)

Johnson's *Proposals* for an edition of Shakespeare appeared in 1756, but he took nine years to produce the work he had promised. Six critical editions of Shakespeare had already appeared in the eighteenth century; Johnson included prefaces from them in the first volume of his richly inclusive work. He attempted textual collation, although the texts available to him were not sufficient to make his comparisons thorough; he explicated difficult passages with wisdom and common sense; unlike some of his predecessors, he demonstrated a healthy respect for Shakespeare's text and avoided wanton emendation. In his preface he provided a weighty and careful critical estimate of the playwright, an estimate that displays his moral as well as his critical principles.

Especially brilliant are Johnson's opening passage—in which he exposes his fundamental assumptions and makes clear his great respect for Shakespeare—and the famous discussion of the classical unities. Between these two passages comes the account of Shakespeare's weaknesses: his failures of morality, looseness of plot, "disproportionate pomp of diction," his occasional coldness, unwieldiness, and lack of subtlety. As W. K. Wimsatt has pointed out in his admirable edition of *Samuel Johnson on Shakespeare* (1960), the faults Johnson finds have to do largely with "the verbal texture" of the plays; when he takes a broad view he is highly discerning of Shakespeare's virtues. His defense of Shakespeare against the charge that violation of the unities is a serious weakness demonstrates Johnson's breadth, originality, and energy in support of a deeply felt critical position.

The text for the following excerpts is from *The Works of Shakespeare*, ed. Samuel Johnson, 8 vols. (London, 1765).

Preface to Shakespeare

That praises are without reason lavished on the dead, and that the

---

1 See Introduction, pp. 37–41.

honours due only to excellence are paid to antiquity, is a complaint likely to be always continued by those, who, being able to add nothing to truth, hope for eminence from the heresies of paradox; or those, who, being forced by disappointment upon consolatory expedients, are willing to hope from posterity what the present age refuses, and flatter themselves that the regard which is yet denied by envy, will be at last bestowed by time.

Antiquity, like every other quality that attracts the notice of mankind, has undoubtedly votaries that reverence it, not from reason, but from prejudice. Some seem to admire indiscriminately whatever has been long preserved, without considering that time has sometimes co-operated with chance; all perhaps are more willing to honour past that present excellence; and the mind contemplates genius through the shades of age, as the eye surveys the sun through artificial opacity. The great contention[2] of criticism is to find the faults of the moderns, and the beauties of the ancients. While an authour is yet living we estimate his powers by his worst performance, and when he is dead we rate them by his best.

To works, however, of which the excellence is not absolute and definite, but gradual and comparative; to works not raised upon principles demonstrative and scientifick, but appealing wholly to observation and experience, no other test can be applied than length of duration and continuance of esteem. What mankind have long possessed they have often examined and compared, and if they persist to value the possession, it is because frequent comparisons have confirmed opinion in its favour. As among the works of nature no man can properly call a river deep or a mountain high, without the knowledge of many mountains and many rivers; so in the productions of genius, nothing can be stiled excellent till it has been compared with other works of the same kind. Demonstration immediately displays its power, and has nothing to hope or fear from the flux of years; but works tentative and experimental must be estimated by their proportion to the general and collective ability of man, as it is discovered in a long succession of endeavours. Of the first building that was raised, it might be with certainty determined that it was round or square, but whether it was spacious or lofty must have been referred to time. The Pythagorean scale of numbers was at once discovered to be perfect;[3] but the poems of *Homer* we yet know not to transcend the common limits

---

2 In the sense of struggle.
3 See Aristotle, *Metaphysics*, I. 5.

of human intelligence, but by remarking, that nation after nation, and century after century, has been able to do little more than transpose his incidents, new name his characters, and paraphrase his sentiments.

The reverence due to writings that have long subsisted arises therefore not from any credulous confidence in the superior wisdom of past ages, or gloomy persuasion of the degeneracy of mankind, but is the consequence of acknowledged and indubitable positions, that what has been longest known has been most considered, and what is most considered is best understood.

The Poet, of whose works I have undertaken the revision, may now begin to assume the dignity of an ancient, and claim the privilege of established fame and prescriptive veneration. He has long outlived his century, the term commonly fixed as the test of literary merit. Whatever advantages he might once derive from personal allusions, local customs, or temporary opinions, have for many years been lost; and every topick of merriment or motive of sorrow, which the modes of artificial life afforded him, now only obscure the scenes which they once illuminated. The effects of favour and competition are at an end; the tradition of his friendships and his enmities has perished; his works support no opinion with arguments, nor supply any faction with invectives; they can neither indulge vanity nor gratify malignity, but are read without any other reason than the desire of pleasure, and are therefore praised only as pleasure is obtained; yet, thus unassisted by interest or passion, they have past through variations of taste and changes of manners, and, as they devolved from one generation to another, have received new honours at every transmission.

But because human judgment, though it be gradually gaining upon certainty, never becomes infallible; and approbation, though long continued, may yet be only the approbation of prejudice or fashion; it is proper to inquire, by what peculiarities of excellence *Shakespeare* has gained and kept the favour of his countrymen.

Nothing can please many, and please long, but just representations of general nature. Particular manners can be known to few, and therefore few only can judge how nearly they are copied. The irregular combinations of fanciful invention may delight a-while, by that novelty of which the common satiety of life sends us all in quest; but the pleasures of sudden wonder are soon exhausted, and the mind can only repose on the stability of truth.

Shakespeare is above all writers, at least above all modern writers, the poet of nature; the poet that holds up to his readers a faithful mirrour of manners and of life. His characters are not modified by the customs of particular places, unpractised by the rest of the world; by the peculiarities of studies or professions, which can operate but upon small numbers; or by the accidents of transient fashions or temporary opinions: they are the genuine progeny of common humanity, such as the world will always supply, and observation will always find. His persons act and speak by the influence of those general passions and principles by which all minds are agitated, and the whole system of life is continued in motion. In the writings of other poets a character is too often an individual; in those of *Shakespeare* it is commonly a species.

It is from this wide extension of design that so much instruction is derived. It is this which fills the plays of *Shakespeare* with practical axioms and domestick wisdom. It was said of *Euripides*, that every verse was a precept;[4] and it may be said of *Shakespeare*, that from his works may be collected a system of civil and oeconomical prudence. Yet his real power is not shewn in the splendour of particular passages, but by the progress of his fable, and the tenour of his dialogue; and he that tries to recommend him by select quotations, will succeed like the pedant in *Hierocles*, who, when he offered his house to sale, carried a brick in his pocket as a specimen.[5]

It will not easily be imagined how much *Shakespeare* excells in accommodating his sentiments to real life, but by comparing him with other authours. It was observed of the ancient schools of declamation, that the more diligently they were frequented, the more was the student disqualified for the world, because he found nothing there which he should ever meet in any other place. The same remark may be applied to every stage but that of *Shakespeare*. The theatre, when it is under any other direction, is peopled by such characters as were never seen, conversing in a language which was never heard, upon topicks which will never arise in the commerce of mankind. But the dialogue of this authour is often so evidently determined by the incident which produces it, and is pursued with so much ease and simplicity, that it seems scarcely to claim the merit of fiction, but to have been gleaned by diligent selection out of common conversation, and common occurrences.

---

4 Cicero, *Epistolae ad Familiares*, XVI. 8.
5 See *Hieroclis Commentarius in Aurea Carmina*, *Asteia* No. 9 (attributed to Hierocles, a neo-Platonic philosopher of the fifth century), ed. Needham (1709), p. 462.

Upon every other stage the universal agent is love, by whose power all good and evil is distributed, and every action quickened or retarded. To bring a lover, a lady and a rival into the fable; to entangle them in contradictory obligations, perplex them with oppositions of interest, and harrass them with violence of desires inconsistent with each other; to make them meet in rapture and part in agony; to fill their mouths with hyperbolical joy and outrageous sorrow; to distress them as nothing human ever was distressed; to deliver them as nothing human ever was delivered, is the business of a modern dramatist. For this probability is violated, life is misrepresented, and language is depraved. But love is only one of many passions, and as it has no great influence upon the sum of life, it has little operation in the dramas of a poet, who caught his ideas from the living world, and exhibited only what he saw before him. He knew, that any other passion, as it was regular or exorbitant, was a cause of happiness or calamity.

Characters thus ample and general were not easily discriminated and preserved, yet perhaps no poet ever kept his personages more distinct from each other. I will not say with *Pope*, that every speech may be assigned to the proper speaker,[6] because many speeches there are which have nothing characteristical; but perhaps, though some may be equally adapted to every person, it will be difficult to find, any that can be properly transferred from the present possessor to another claimant. The choice is right, when there is reason for choice.

Other dramatists can only gain attention by hyperbolical or aggravated characters, by fabulous and unexampled excellence or depravity, as the writers of barbarous romances invigorated the reader by a giant and a dwarf; and he that should form his expectations of human affairs from the play, or from the tale, would be equally deceived. *Shakespeare* has no heroes; his scenes are occupied only by men, who act and speak as the reader thinks that he should himself have spoken or acted on the same occasion: Even where the agency is supernatural the dialogue is level with life. Other writers disguise the most natural passions and most frequent incidents; so that he who contemplates them in the book will not know them in the world; *Shakespeare* approximates the remote, and familiarizes the wonderful; the event which he represents will not happen, but if it were possible, its effects would probably be such as he has as-

---

6 Preface to Pope's edition of Shakespeare (1725), para. 4. (*The Works of Alexander Pope*, eds. Whitwell Elwin and William John Courthope [London, 1886], V. 535.)

signed; and it may be said, that he has not only shewn human nature as it acts in real exigences, but as it would be found in trials, to which it cannot be exposed.

This therefore is the praise of *Shakespeare*, that his drama is the mirrour of life; that he who has mazed his imagination, in following the phantoms which other writers raise up before him, may here be cured of his delirious extasies, by reading human sentiments in human language; by scenes from which a hermit may estimate the transactions of the world, and a confessor predict the progress of the passions.

His adherence to general nature has exposed him to the censure of criticks, who form their judgments upon narrower principles. *Dennis* and *Rhymer*[7] think his *Romans* not sufficiently Roman; and *Voltaire* censures his kings as not completely royal.[8] *Dennis* is offended, that *Menenius*, a senator of *Rome*, should play the buffoon;[9] and *Voltaire* perhaps thinks decency violated when the *Danish* Usurper is represented as a drunkard.[10] But *Shakespeare* always makes nature predominate over accident; and if he preserves the esential character, is not very careful of distinctions super-induced and adventitious. His story requires Romans or kings, but he thinks only on men. He knew that *Rome*, like every other city, had men of all dispositions; and wanting a buffoon, he went into the senate-house for that which the senate-house would certainly have afforded him. He was inclined to shew an usurper and a murderer not only odious but despicable, he therefore added drunkenness to his other qualities, knowing that kings love wine like other men, and that wine exerts its natural power upon kings. These are the petty cavils of petty minds; a poet overlooks the casual distinction of country and condition, as a painter, satisfied with the figure, neglects the drapery.

The censure which he has incurred by mixing comick and tragick scenes, as it extends to all his works, deserves more consideration. Let the fact be first stated, and then examined.

Shakespeare's plays are not in the rigorous and critical sense either tragedies or comedies, but compositions of a distinct kind; exhibiting the

---

7 John Dennis, *Essay on Genius and Writings of Shakespeare* (1712), reprinted in *Critical Works of John Dennis*, 2 vols., ed. E.N. Hooker (1939–1943), II. 56; Thomas Rymer, *A Short View of Tragedy*, in *Critical Works*, ed. Curt A. Zimansky (1965), pp. 164–69.

8 In *L'Appel à toutes les nations d'Europe* (1761); *Oeuvres*, ed. Louis Moland (1877–1885), XXIV. 203.

9 *Essay on Genius and Writings of Shakespeare*, Hooker, II. 5.

10 In *Hamlet*.

real state of sublunary nature, which partakes of good and evil, joy and sorrow, mingled with endless variety of proportion and innumerable modes of combination; and expressing the course of the world, in which the loss of one is the gain of another; in which, at the same time, the reveller is hasting to his wine, and the mourner burying his friend; in which the malignity of one is sometimes defeated by the frolick of another; and many mischiefs and many benefits are done and hindered without design.

Out of this chaos of mingled purposes and casualties the ancient poets, according to the laws which custom had prescribed, selected some the crimes of men, and some their absurdities; some the momentous vicissitudes of life, and some the lighter occurrences; some the terrours of distress, and some the gayeties of prosperity. Thus rose the two modes of imitation, known by the names of *tragedy* and *comedy*, compositions intended to promote different ends by contrary means, and considered as so little allied, that I do not recollect among the *Greeks* or *Romans* a single writer who attempted both.

Shakespeare has united the powers of exciting laughter and sorrow not only in one mind but in one composition. Almost all his plays are divided between serious and ludicrous characters, and, in the successive evolutions of the design, sometimes produce seriousness and sorrow, and sometimes levity and laughter.

That this is a practice contrary to the rules of criticism will be readily allowed; but there is always an appeal open from criticism to nature. The end of writing is to instruct; the end of poetry is to instruct by pleasing. That the mingled drama may convey all the instruction of tragedy or comedy cannot be denied, because it includes both in its alterations of exhibition, and approaches nearer than either to the appearance of life, by shewing how great machinations and slender designs may promote or obviate one another, and the high and the low cooperate in the general system by unavoidable concatenation.

It is objected, that by this change of scenes the passions are interrupted in their progression, and that the principal event, being not advanced by a due gradation of preparatory incidents, wants at last the power to move, which constitutes the perfection of dramatick poetry. This reasoning is so specious, that it is received as true even by those who in daily experience feel it to be false. The interchanges of mingled scenes seldom fail to produce the intended vicissitudes of passion. Fiction cannot move so much, but that the attention may be easily transferred; and

though it must be allowed that pleasing melancholy be sometimes interrupted by unwelcome levity, yet let it be considered likewise, that
melancholy is often not pleasing, and that the disturbance of one man
may be the relief of another; that different auditors have different habitudes; and that, upon the whole, all pleasure consists in variety.

The players, who in their edition divided our authour's works into
comedies, histories, and tragedies, seem not to have distinguished the
three kinds, by any very exact or definite ideas.

An action which ended happily to the principal persons, however
serious or distressful through its intermediate incidents, in their opinion
constituted a comedy. This idea of a comedy continued long amongst
us, and plays were written, which, by changing the catastrophe, were
tragedies to-day and comedies to-morrow.

Tragedy was not in those times a poem of more general dignity or
elevation than comedy; it required only a calamitous conclusion, with
which the common criticism of that age was satisfied, whatever lighter
pleasure it afforded in its progress.

History was a series of actions, with no other than chronological
succession, independent on each other, and without any tendency to
introduce or regulate the conclusion. It is not always very nicely distinguished from tragedy. There is not much nearer approach to unity of
action in the tragedy of *Antony and Cleopatra*, than in the history of
Richard the Second. But a history might be continued through many plays;
as it had no plan, it had no limits.

Through all these denominations of the drama, *Shakespeare*'s mode
of composition is the same; an interchange of seriousness and merriment,
by which the mind is softened at one time, and exhilarated at another.
But whatever be his purpose, whether to gladden or depress, or to conduct the story, without vehemence or emotion, through tracts of easy and
familiar dialogue, he never fails to attain his purpose; as he commands us,
we laugh or mourn, or sit silent with quiet expectation, in tranquillity
without indifference.

When *Shakespeare*'s plan is understood, most of the criticisms of
Rhymer and *Voltaire*[11] vanish away. The play of *Hamlet* is opened, without
impropriety, by two sentinels; *Iago* bellows at *Brabantio*'s window, without injury to the scheme of the play, though in terms which a modern

---

11 See Voltaire, *L'Appel* (Moland, XXIV. 193, 196, 198, 204, 208); and Rymer, *A Short View* (Zimansky, pp. 131–164).

audience would not easily endure; the character of *Polonius* is seasonable and useful; and the Grave-diggers themselves may be heard with applause.

   Shakespeare engaged in dramatick poetry with the world open before him; the rules of the ancients were yet known to few; the publick judgment was unformed; he had no example of such fame as might force him upon imitation, nor criticks of such authority as might restrain his extravagance: He therefore indulged his natural disposition, and his disposition, as *Rhymer* has remarked, led him to comedy.[12] In tragedy he often writes with great appearance of toil and study, what is written at last with little felicity; but in his comick scenes, he seems to produce without labour, what no labour can improve. In tragedy he is always struggling after some occasion to be comick, but in comedy he seems to repose, or to luxuriate, as in a mode of thinking congenial to his nature. In his tragick scenes there is always something wanting, but his comedy often surpasses expectation or desire. His comedy pleases by the thoughts and the language, and his tragedy for the greater part by incident and action. His tragedy seems to be skill, his comedy to be instinct.

   The force of his comick scenes has suffered little diminution from the changes made by a century and a half, in manners or in words. As his personages act upon principles arising from genuine passion, very little modified by particular forms, their pleasures and vexations are communicable to all times and to all places; they are natural, and therefore durable; the adventitious peculiarities of personal habits, are only superficial dies, bright and pleasing for a little while, yet soon fading to a dim tinct, without any remains of former lustre; but the discriminations of true passion are the colours of nature; they pervade the whole mass, and can only perish with the body that exhibits them. The accidental compositions of heterogeneous modes are dissolved by the chance which combined them; but the uniform simplicity of primitive qualities neither admits increase, nor suffers decay. The sand heaped by one flood is scattered by another, but the rock always continues in its place. The stream of time, which is continually washing the dissoluble fabricks of other poets, passes without injury by the adamant of *Shakespeare*.

   If there be, what I believe there is, in every nation, a stile which never becomes obsolete, a certain mode of phraseology so consonant and congenial to the analogy and principles of its respective language as to

---

   12 *A Short View* (Zimansky, p. 169).

remain settled and unaltered; this stile is probably to be sought in the common intercourse of life, among those who speak only to be understood, without ambition of elegance. The polite are always catching modish innovations, and the learned depart from established forms of speech, in hope of finding or making better; those who wish for distinction forsake the vulgar, when the vulgar is right; but there is a conversation above grossness and below refinement, where propriety resides, and where this poet seems to have gathered his comick dialogue. He is therefore more agreeable to the ears of the present age than any other authour equally remote, and among his other excellencies deserves to be studied as one of the original masters of our language.

These observations are to be considered not as unexceptionably constant, but as containing general and predominant truth. *Shakespeare*'s familiar dialogue is affirmed to be smooth and clear, yet not wholly without ruggedness or difficulty; as a country may be eminently fruitful though it has spots unfit for cultivation: His characters are praised as natural, though their sentiments are sometimes forced, and their actions improbable; as the earth upon the whole is spherical, though its surface is varied with protuberances and cavities.

Shakespeare with his excellencies has likewise faults, and faults sufficient to obscure and overwhelm any other merit. I shall shew them in the proportion in which they appear to me, without envious malignity or superstitious veneration. No question can be more innocently discussed than a dead poet's pretensions to renown; and little regard is due to that bigotry which sets candour higher than truth.

His first defect is that to which may be imputed most of the evil in books or in men. He sacrifices virtue to convenience, and is so much more careful to please than to instruct, that he seems to write without any moral purpose. From his writings indeed a system of social duty may be selected, for he that thinks reasonably must think morally; but his precepts and axioms drop casually from him; he makes no just distribution of good or evil, nor is always careful to shew in the virtuous a disapprobation of the wicked; he carries his persons indifferently through right and wrong, and at the close dismisses them without further care, and leaves their examples to operate by chance. This fault the barbarity of his age cannot extenuate; for it is always a writer's duty to make the world better, and justice is a virtue independant on time or place.

The plots are often so loosely formed, that a very slight consideration may improve them, and so carelessly pursued, that he seems not always fully to comprehend his own design. He omits opportunities of instructing or delighting which the train of his story seems to force upon him, and apparently rejects those exhibitions which would be more affecting, for the sake of those which are more easy.

It may be observed, that in many of his plays the latter part is evidently neglected. When he found himself near the end of his work, and, in view of his reward, he shortened the labour, to snatch the profit. He therefore remits his efforts where he should most vigorously exert them, and his catastrophe is improbably produced or imperfectly represented.

He had no regard to distinction of time or place, but gives to one age or nation, without scruple, the customs, institutions, and opinions of another, at the expence not only of likelihood, but of possibility. These faults *Pope* has endeavoured, with more zeal than judgment, to transfer to his imagined interpolators.[13] We need not wonder to find *Hector* quoting *Aristotle*,[14] when we see the loves of *Theseus* and *Hippolyta* combined with the *Gothick* mythology of fairies.[15] *Shakespeare*, indeed, was not the only violator of chronology, for in the same age *Sidney*, who wanted not the advantages of learning, has, in his *Arcadia*,[16] confounded the pastoral with the feudal times, the days of innocence, quiet and security, with those of turbulence, violence and adventure.

In his comick scenes he is seldom very successful when he engages his characters in reciprocations of smartness and contests of sarcasm; their jests are commonly gross, and their pleasantry licentious; neither his gentlemen nor his ladies have much delicacy, nor are sufficiently distinguished from his clowns by any appearance of refined manners. Whether he represented the real conversation of his time is not easy to determine; the reign of *Elizabeth* is commonly supposed to have been a time of stateliness, formality and reserve, yet perhaps the relaxations of that severity were not very elegant. There must, however, have been always some modes of gayety preferable to others, and a writer ought to chuse the best.

In tragedy his performance seems constantly to be worse, as his labour is more. The effusions of passion which exigence forces out are for

---

13 *Preface to Shakespeare* (Elwin and Courthope, V. 544–48).
14 *Troilus and Cressida*, II. ii. 166–67.
15 *A Midsummer Night's Dream*.
16 *Arcadia*, a pastoral romance by Sir Philip Sidney (1554–1586), was published in 1590.

the most part striking and energetick; but whenever he solicits his invention, or strains his faculties, the offspring of his throes is tumour, meanness, tediousness, and obscurity.

In narration he affects a disproportionate pomp of diction and a wearisome train of circumlocution, and tells the incident imperfectly in many words, which might have been more plainly delivered in few. Narration in dramatick poetry is naturally tedious, as it is unanimated and inactive, and obstructs the progress of the action; it should therefore always be rapid, and enlivened by frequent interruption. *Shakespeare* found it an encumbrance, and instead of lightening it by brevity, endeavoured to recommend it by dignity and splendour.

His declamations or set speeches are commonly cold and weak, for his power was the power of nature; when he endeavoured, like other tragick writers, to catch opportunities of amplification, and instead of inquiring what the occasion demanded, to show how much his stores of knowledge could supply, he seldom escapes without the pity or resentment of his reader.

It is incident to him to be now and then entangled with an unwieldy sentiment, which he cannot well express, and will not reject; he struggles with it a while, and if it continues stubborn, comprises it in words such as occur, and leaves it to be disentangled and evolved by those who have more leisure to bestow upon it.

Not that always where the language is intricate the thought is subtle, or the image always great where the line is bulky; the equality of words to things is very often neglected, and trivial sentiments and vulgar ideas disappoint the attention, to which they are recommended by sonorous epithets and swelling figures.

But the admirers of this great poet have never less reason to indulge their hopes of supreme excellence, than when he seems fully resolved to sink them in dejection, and mollify them with tender emotions by the fall of greatness, the danger of innocence, or the crosses of love. He is not long soft and pathetick without some idle conceit, or contemptible equivocation. He no sooner begins to move, than he counteracts himself; and terrour and pity, as they are rising in the mind, are checked and blasted by sudden frigidity.

A quibble[17] is to *Shakespeare*, what luminous vapours are to the traveller; he follows it at all adventures, it is sure to lead him out of his

---

17 A word-play or pun.

way, and sure to engulf him in the mire. It has some malignant power over his mind, and its fascinations are irresistible. Whatever be the dignity or profundity of his disquisition, whether he be enlarging knowledge or exalting affection, whether he be amusing attention with incidents, or enchaining it in suspense, let but a quibble spring up before him, and he leaves his work unfinished. A quibble is the golden apple for which he will always turn aside from his career, or stoop from his elevation. A quibble, poor and barren as it is, gave him such delight, that he was content to purchase it, by the sacrifice of reason, propriety and truth. A quibble was to him the fatal *Cleopatra* for which he lost the world, and was content to lose it.

It will be thought strange, that, in enumerating the defects of this writer, I have not yet mentioned his neglect of the unities; his violation of those laws which have been instituted and established by the joint authority of poets and of criticks.

For his other deviations from the art of writing, I resign him to critical justice, without making any other demand in his favour, than that which must be indulged to all human excellence; that his virtues be rated with his failings: But, from the censure which this irregularity may bring upon him, I shall, with due reverence to that learning which I must oppose, adventure to try how I can defend him.

His histories, being neither tragedies nor comedies, are not subject to any of their laws; nothing more is necessary to all the praise which they expect, than that the changes of action be so prepared as to be understood, that the incidents be various and affecting, and the characters consistent, natural and distinct. No other unity is intended, and therefore none is to be sought.

In his other works he has well enough preserved the unity of action. He has not, indeed, an intrigue regularly perplexed and regularly unravelled; he does not endeavour to hide his design only to discover it, for this is seldom the order of real events, and *Shakespeare* is the poet of nature: But his plan has commonly what *Aristotle* requires, a beginning, a middle, and an end;[18] one event is concatenated with another, and the conclusion follows by easy consequence. There are perhaps some incidents that might be spared, as in other poets there is much talk that only fills up time upon the stage; but the general system makes gradual advances, and the end of the play is the end of expectation.

18 *Poetics*, VII. 3. 26–27.

To the unities of time and place he has shewn no regard, and perhaps a nearer view of the principles on which they stand will diminish their value, and withdraw from them the veneration which, from the time of Corneille,[19] they have very generally received, by discovering that they have given more trouble to the poet, than pleasure to the auditor.

The necessity of observing the unities of time and place arises from the supposed necessity of making the drama credible. The criticks hold it impossible, that an action of months or years can be possibly believed to pass in three hours; or that the spectator can suppose himself to sit in the theatre, while ambassadors go and return between distant kings, while armies are levied and towns besieged, while an exile wanders and returns, or till he whom they saw courting his mistress, shall lament the untimely fall of his son. The mind revolts from evident falsehood, and fiction loses its force when it departs from the resemblance of reality.

From the narrow limitation of time necessarily arises the contraction of place. The spectator, who knows that he saw the first act at *Alexandria*, cannot suppose that he sees the next at *Rome*, at a distance to which not the dragons of *Medea* could, in so short a time, have transported him; he knows with certainty that he has not changed his place; and he knows that place cannot change itself; that what was a house cannot become a plain; that what was *Thebes* can never be *Persepolis*.

Such is the triumphant language with which a critick exults over the misery of an irregular poet, and exults commonly without resistance or reply. It is time therefore to tell him, by the authority of *Shakespeare*, that he assumes, as an unquestionable principle, a position, which, while his breath is forming it into words, his understanding pronounces to be false. It is false, that any representation is mistaken for reality; that any dramatick fable in its materiality was ever credible, or, for a single moment, was ever credited.

The objection arising from the impossibility of passing the first hour at *Alexandria*, and the next at *Rome*, supposes, that when the play opens the spectator really imagines himself at *Alexandria*, and believes that his walk to the theatre has been a voyage to *Egypt*, and that he lives in the days of *Antony* and *Cleopatra*. Surely he that imagines this may imagine more. He that can take the stage at one time for the palace of the *Ptolemies*,

---

19 Pierre Corneille (1606–1684), French dramatist, in 1660 published an edition of Shakespeare's works. For each play he supplied an *Examen;* he also included three *Discours* on the drama. In one of these, and in the *Examens*, he discusses the concept of the unities.

may take it in half an hour for the promontory of *Actium*. Delusion, if delusion be admitted, has no certain limitation; if the spectator can be once persuaded, that his old acquaintance are *Alexander* and *Caesar*, that a room illuminated with candles is the plain of *Pharsalia*, or the bank of *Granicus*, he is in a state of elevation above the reach of reason, or of truth, and from the heights of empyrean poetry, may despise the circumscriptions of terrestrial nature. There is no reason why a mind thus wandering in extasy should count the clock, or why an hour should not be a century in that calenture[20] of the brains that can make the stage a field.

The truth is, that the spectators are always in their senses, and know, from the first act to the last, that the stage is only a stage, and that the players are only players. They come to hear a certain number of lines recited with just gesture and elegant modulation. The lines relate to some action, and an action must be in some place; but the different actions that compleat a story may be in places very remote from each other; and where is the absurdity of allowing that space to represent first *Athens*, and then *Sicily*, which was always known to be neither *Sicily* nor *Athens*, but a modern theatre.

By supposition, as place is introduced, time may be extended; the time required by the fable elapses for the most part between the acts; for, of so much of the action as is represented, the real and poetical duration is the same. If, in the first act, preparations for war against *Mithridates*[21] are represented to be made in *Rome*, the event of the war may, without absurdity, be represented, in the catastrophe, as happening in *Pontus*; we know that there is neither war, nor preparation for war; we know that we are neither in *Rome* nor *Pontus*; that neither *Mithridates* nor *Lucullus*[22] are before us. The drama exhibits successive imitations of successive actions, and why may not the second imitation represent an action that happened years after the first; if it be so connected with it, that nothing but time can be supposed to intervene. Time is, of all modes of existence, most obsequious to the imagination; a lapse of years is as easily conceived as a passage of hours. In contemplation we easily contract the time of real actions, and therefore willingly permit it to be contracted when we only see their imitation.

---

20 A fever formerly thought to affect sailors in the tropics so that they believed the sea a green field and leaped into it.

21 Mithridates VI (c. 135–63 B.C.), Mithridates the Great, king of Pontus in Persia.

22 Roman general (c. 110–c. 58 B.C.) who defeated Mithridates in 73 B.C.

It will be asked, how the drama moves, if it is not credited. It is credited with all the credit due to a drama. It is credited, whenever it moves, as a just picture of a real original; as representing to the auditor what he would himself feel, if he were to do or suffer what is there feigned to be suffered or to be done. The reflection that strikes the heart is not, that the evils before us are real evils, but that they are evils to which we ourselves may be exposed. If there be any fallacy, it is not that we fancy the players, but that we fancy ourselves unhappy for a moment; but we rather lament the possibility than suppose the presence of misery, as a mother weeps over her babe, when she remembers that death may take it from her. The delight of tragedy proceeds from our consciousness of fiction; if we thought murders and treasons real, they would please no more.

Imitations produce pain or pleasure, not because they are mistaken for realities, but because they bring realities to mind. When the imagination is recreated by a painted landscape, the trees are not supposed capable to give us shade, or the fountains coolness; but we consider, how we should be pleased with such fountains playing beside us, and such woods waving over us. We are agitated in reading the history of *Henry* the Fifth, yet no man takes his book for the field of *Agencourt*. A dramatick exhibition is a book recited with concomitants that encrease or diminish its effect. Familiar comedy is often more powerful on the theatre, than in the page; imperial tragedy is always less. The humour of *Petruchio*[23] may be heightened by grimace; but what voice or what gesture can hope to add dignity or force to the soliloquy of *Cato*.[24]

A play read, affects the mind like a play acted. It is therefore evident, that the action is not supposed to be real, and it follows that between the acts a longer or shorter time may be allowed to pass, and that no more account of space or duration is to be taken by the auditor of a drama, than by the reader of a narrative, before whom may pass in an hour the life of a hero, or the revolutions of an empire.

Whether *Shakespeare* knew the unities, and rejected them by design, or deviated from them by happy ignorance, it is, I think, impossible to decide, and useless to enquire. We may reasonably suppose, that, when he rose to notice, he did not want the counsels and admonitions of

---

23 Husband of the termagant Katharina in *Taming of the Shrew*.
24 In Addison's tragedy, *Cato* (1713), V. i. For Edward Young's view of this play, see above, pp. 77–80.

scholars and criticks, and that he at last deliberately persisted in a practice, which he might have begun by chance. As nothing is essential to the fable, but unity of action, and as the unities of time and place arise evidently from false assumptions, and, by circumscribing the extent of the drama, lessen its variety, I cannot think it much to be lamented, that they were not known by him, or not observed: Nor, if such another poet could arise, should I very vehemently reproach him, that his first act passed at *Venice*, and his next in *Cyprus*. Such violations of rules merely positive,[25] become the comprehensive genius of *Shakespeare*, and such censures are suitable to the minute and slender criticism of *Voltaire*:

> *Non usque adeo permiscuit imis*
> *Longus summa dies, ut non, si voce Metelli*
> *Serventur leges, malint a Caesare tolli.*[26]

Yet when I speak thus slightly of dramatick rules, I cannot but recollect how much wit and learning may be produced against me; before such authorities I am afraid to stand, not that I think the present question one of those that are to be decided by mere authority, but because it is to be suspected, that these precepts have not been so easily received but for better reasons than I have yet been able to find. The result of my enquiries, in which it would be ludicrous to boast of impartiality, is, that the unities of time and place are not essential to a just drama, that though they may sometimes conduce to pleasure, they are always to be sacrificed to the nobler beauties of variety and instruction; and that a play, written with nice observation of critical rules, is to be contemplated as an elaborate curiosity, as the product of superfluous and ostentatious art, by which is shewn, rather what is possible, than what is necessary.

He that, without diminution of any other excellence, shall preserve all the unities unbroken, deserves the like applause with the architect, who shall display all the orders of architecture in a citadel, without any deduction from its strength; but the principal beauty of a citadel is to exclude the enemy; and the greatest graces of a play, are to copy nature and instruct life.

Perhaps, what I have here not dogmatically but deliberatively

---

25 Arbitrary, conventional.
26 "The course of time has not wrought such confusion that the laws would not rather be trampled on by Caesar than saved by Metellus" (Lucan, *Pharsalia*, III. 138–40).

written, may recal the principles of the drama to a new examination. I am almost frighted at my own temerity; and when I estimate the fame and the strength of those that maintain the contrary opinion, am ready to sink down in reverential silence; as *Æneas* withdrew from the defence of *Troy*, when he saw *Neptune* shaking the wall, and *Juno* heading the besiegers.[27]

Those whom my arguments cannot persuade to give their approbation to the judgment of *Shakespeare*, will easily, if they consider the condition of his life, make some allowance for his ignorance.

Every man's performances, to be rightly estimated, must be compared with the state of the age in which he lived, and with his own particular opportunities; and though to the reader a book be not worse or better for the circumstances of the authour, yet as there is always a silent reference of human works to human abilities, and as the enquiry, how far man may extend his designs, or how high he may rate his native force, is of far greater dignity than in what rank we shall place any particular performance, curiosity is always busy to discover the instruments, as well as to survey the workmanship, to know how much is to be ascribed to original powers, and how much to casual and adventitious help. The palaces of *Peru* or *Mexico* were certainly mean and incommodious habitations, if compared to the houses of *European* monarchs; yet who could forbear to view them with astonishment, who remembered that they were built without the use of iron?

The *English* nation, in the time of *Shakespeare*, was yet struggling to emerge from barbarity. The philology of *Italy* had been transplanted hither in the reign of *Henry* the Eighth; and the learned languages had been successfully cultivated by *Lilly*, *Linacer*, and *Mere*; by *Pole*, *Cheke*, and *Gardiner*;[28] and afterwards by *Smith*, *Clerk*, *Haddon*, and *Ascham*.[29]

---

27 *Aeneid*, II. 610–14.

28 William Lily (born c. 1468), author of a Latin grammar used by Shakespeare, reputedly the first person to teach Greek in London; Thomas Linacre (c. 1460–1524), Oxford teacher of Greek; Sir Thomas More (1480–1535), author of the Latin *Utopia* (1516); Reginald Pole (1500–1558), a chancellor of Cambridge University; Sir John Cheke (1514–1557), the first professor of Greek at Cambridge; Stephen Gardiner (1483–1555), Bishop of Winchester, another Cambridge chancellor, learned in Greek and Latin.

29 Sir Thomas Smith (c. 1512–1577), regius professor of civil law at Cambridge, author of a treatise on the pronunciation of Greek; John Clerk (d. 1541), Bishop of Bath and Wells; Walter Haddon (1516–1572), also regius professor of law at Cambridge, famed for his skill at Latin composition; Roger Ascham (1515–1568), Latin secretary to Queen Mary, private tutor to Queen Elizabeth, author of *The Schoolmaster* (1571), a book on the teaching of Latin.

Greek was now taught to boys in the principal schools; and those who united elegance with learning, read, with great diligence, the *Italian* and *Spanish* poets. But literature was yet confined to professed scholars, or to men and women of high rank. The publick was gross and dark; and to be able to read and write, was an accomplishment still valued for its rarity.

Nations, like individuals, have their infancy. A people newly awakened to literary curiosity, being yet unacquainted with the true state of things, knows not how to judge of that which is proposed as its resemblance. Whatever is remote from common appearances is always welcome to vulgar, as to childish credulity; and of a country unenlightened by learning, the whole people is the vulgar. The study of those who then aspired to plebeian learning was laid out upon adventures, giants, dragons, and enchantments. *The Death of Arthur* was the favourite volume.[30]

The mind, which has feasted on the luxurious wonders of fiction, has no taste of the insipidity of truth. A play which imitated only the common occurrences of the world, would, upon the admirers of *Palmerin* and *Guy of Warwick*,[31] have made little impression; he that wrote for such an audience was under the necessity of looking round for strange events and fabulous transactions, and that incredibility, by which maturer knowledge is offended, was the chief recommendation of writings, to unskilful curiosity.

Our authour's plots are generally borrowed from novels, and it is reasonable to suppose, that he chose the most popular, such as were read by many, and related by more; for his audience could not have followed him through the intricacies of the drama, had they not held the thread of the story in their hands.

The stories, which we now find only in remoter authours, were in his time accessible and familiar. The fable of *As you like it*, which is supposed to be copied from *Chaucer's* Gamelyn, was a little pamphlet of those times;[32] and old Mr. *Cibber*[33] remembered the tale of *Hamlet* in plain *English* prose, which the criticks have now to seek in *Saxo Grammaticus*.[34]

---

30 Sir Thomas Malory's *Morte d'Arthur* (1485).

31 *Palmerin D'Oliva* and *Palmerin of England*, Spanish prose romances, translated into English in 1588 and 1596; *Guy of Warwick*, English verse romance, written c. 1308, published early in the sixteenth century.

32 *The Tale of Gamelyn*, not in fact by Chaucer, was a source of Thomas Lodge's *Rosalynde* (1590), from which Shakespeare derived the plot of *As You Like It*.

33 Colley Cibber (1671–1757), poet laureate from 1730.

34 Danish historian (c. 1150–1206), author of *Gesta Danorum*, published in Latin in 1514, translated into Danish in 1575.

His *English* histories he took from *English* chronicles and *English* ballads; and as the ancient writers were made known to his countrymen by versions, they supplied him with new subjects; he dilated some of *Plutarch*'s lives into plays, when they had been translated by *North*.[35]

His plots, whether historical or fabulous, are always crouded with incidents, by which the attention of a rude people was more easily caught than by sentiment or argumentation; and such is the power of the marvellous even over those who despise it, that every man finds his mind more strongly seized by the tragedies of *Shakespeare* than of any other writer; others please us by particular speeches, but he always makes us anxious for the event, and has perhaps excelled all but *Homer* in securing the first purpose of a writer, by exciting restless and unquenchable curiosity, and compelling him that reads his work to read it through.

The shows and bustle with which his plays abound have the same original. As knowledge advances, pleasure passes from the eye to the ear, but returns, as it declines, from the ear to the eye. Those to whom our authour's labours were exhibited had more skill in pomps or processions than in poetical language, and perhaps wanted some visible and discriminated events, as comments on the dialogue. He knew how he should most please; and whether his practice is more agreeable to nature, or whether his example has prejudiced the nation, we still find that on our stage something must be done as well as said, and inactive declamation is very coldly heard, however musical or elegant, passionate or sublime.

Voltaire expresses his wonder, that our authour's extravagances are endured by a nation, which has seen the tragedy of *Cato*.[36] Let him be answered, that *Addison* speaks the language of poets, and *Shakespeare*, of men. We find in *Cato* innumerable beauties which enamour us of its authour, but we see nothing that acquaints us with human sentiments or human actions; we place it with the fairest and the noblest progeny which judgment propagates by conjunction with learning, but *Othello* is the vigorous and vivacious offspring of observation impregnated by genius. *Cato* affords a splendid exhibition of artificial and fictitious manners, and delivers just and noble sentiments, in diction easy, elevated and harmonious, but its hopes and fears communicate no vibration to the heart; the composition refers us only to the writer; we pronounce the name of *Cato* but we think on *Addison*.

---

35 Sir Thomas North (c. 1535–c. 1601), whose translation of Plutarch's *Lives of the Noble Grecians and Romans* appeared in 1579.

36 By Addison, referred to above (see note 24). Voltaire's comment is in *L'Appel* (Moland XXIV. 201).

The work of a correct and regular writer is a garden accurately formed and diligently planted, varied with shades, and scented with flowers; the composition of *Shakespeare* is a forest, in which oaks extend their branches, and pines tower in the air, interspersed sometimes with weeds and brambles, and sometimes giving shelter to myrtles and to roses; filling the eye with awful pomp, and gratifying the mind with endless diversity. Other poets display cabinets of precious rarities, minutely finished, wrought into shape, and polished unto brightness. *Shakespeare* opens a mine which contains gold and diamonds in unexhaustible plenty, though clouded by incrustations, debased by impurities, and mingled with mass of meaner minerals.

It has been much disputed, whether *Shakespeare* owed his excellence to his own native force, or whether he had the common helps of scholastick education, the precepts of critical science, and the examples of ancient authours.

There has always prevailed a tradition, that *Shakespeare* wanted learning, that he had no regular education, nor much skill in the dead languages. *Johnson,* his friend, affirms, that *he had small Latin, and no Greek;*[37] who, besides that he had no imaginable temptation to falsehood, wrote at a time when the character and acquisitions of *Shakespeare* were known to multitudes. His evidence ought therefore to decide the controversy, unless some testimony of equal force could be opposed.

Some have imagined, that they have discovered deep learning in many imitations of old writers; but the examples which I have known urged, were drawn from books translated in his time; or were such easy coincidencies of thought, as will happen to all who consider the same subjects; or such remarks on life or axioms of morality as float in conversation, and are transmitted through the world in proverbial sentences.

I have found it remarked, that, in this important sentence, *Go before, I'll follow,* we read a translation of, *I prae, sequar.*[38] I have been told, that when *Caliban,* after a pleasing dream, says, *I cry'd to sleep again,* the authour imitates *Anacreon,*[39] who had, like every other man, the same wish on the same occasion.

---

37 Ben Jonson, verses *To the Memory of my Beloved . . . Mr. William Shakespeare,* prefixed to the First Folio of Shakespeare's plays (1623).

38 Zachary Grey compared this line from *Richard III,* I. i. 143, to Terence, *Andria,* l. 171. See *Critical, Historical, and Explanatory Notes on Shakespeare* (1754), II. 53.

39 *Tempest,* III. ii. 155. Johnson misquotes: the line is, "I cried to dream again." The analogue in Anacreon is from *Songs,* XXXVII. 14, a line which Addison translates " . . . sigh to sleep again." Johnson may have been thinking of his translation.

There are a few passages which may pass for imitations, but so few, that the exception only confirms the rule; he obtained them from accidental quotations, or by oral communication, and as he used what he had, would have used more if he had obtained it.

The *Comedy of Errors* is confessedly taken from the *Menaechmi* of *Plautus*; from the only play of *Plautus* which was then in *English*. What can be more probable, than that he who copied that, would have copied more; but that those which were not translated were inaccessible?

Whether he knew the modern languages is uncertain. That his plays have some *French* scenes proves but little; he might easily procure them to be written, and probably, even though he had known the language in the common degree, he could not have written it without assistance. In the story of *Romeo* and *Juliet* he is observed to have followed the *English* translation, where it deviates from the *Italian*; but this on the other part proves nothing against his knowledge of the original. He was to copy, not what he knew himself, but what was known to his audience.

It is most likely that he had learned *Latin* sufficiently to make him acquainted with construction, but that he never advanced to an easy perusal of the *Roman* authours. Concerning his skill in modern languages, I can find no sufficient ground of determination; but as no imitations of *French* or *Italian* authours have been discovered, though the *Italian* poetry was then high in esteem, I am inclined to believe, that he read little more than *English*, and chose for his fables only such tales as he found translated.

That much knowledge is scattered over his works is very justly observed by *Pope*,[40] but it is often such knowledge as books did not supply. He that will understand *Shakespeare*, must not be content to study him in the closet, he must look for his meaning sometimes among the sports of the field, and sometimes among the manufactures of the shop.

There is however proof enough that he was a very diligent reader, nor was our language then so indigent of books but that he might very liberally indulge his curiosity without excursion into foreign literature. Many of the *Roman* authours were translated, and some of the *Greek*; the reformation had filled the kingdom with theological learning; most of the topicks of human disquisition had found *English* writers; and poetry had been cultivated, not only with diligence, but success. This was a

---

40 *Preface to Shakespeare* (Elwin and Courthope, V. 540).

stock of knowledge sufficient for a mind so capable of appropriating and improving it.

But the greater part of his excellence was the product of his own genius. He found the *English* stage in a state of the utmost rudeness; no essays either in tragedy or comedy had appeared, from which it could be discovered to what degree of delight either one or other might be carried. Neither character nor dialogue were yet understood. *Shakespeare* may be truly said to have introduced them both amongst us, and in some of his happier scenes to have carried them both to the utmost height.

By what gradations of improvement he proceeded, is not easily known; for the chronology of his works is yet unsettled. *Rowe* is of opinion, that *perhaps we are not to look for his beginning, like those of other writers, in his least perfect works; art had so little, and nature so large a share in what he did, that for ought I know*, says he, *the performances of his youth, as they were the the most vigorous, were the best.*[41] But the power of nature is only the power of using to any certain purpose the materials which diligence procures, or opportunity supplies. Nature gives no man knowledge, and when images are collected by study and experience, can only assist in combining or applying them. *Shakespeare*, however favoured by nature, could impart only what he had learned; and as he must increase his ideas, like other mortals, by gradual acquisition, he, like them, grew wiser as he grew older, could display life better, as he knew it more, and instruct with more efficacy, as he was himself more amply instructed.

There is a vigilance of observation and accuracy of distinction which books and precepts cannot confer; from this almost all original and native excellence proceeds. *Shakespeare* must have looked upon mankind with perspicacity, in the highest degree curious and attentive. Other writers borrow their characters from preceding writers, and diversify them only by the accidental appendages of present manners; the dress is a little varied, but the body is the same. Our authour had both matter and form to provide; for except the characters of *Chaucer*, to whom I think he is not much indebted, there were no writers in *English*, and perhaps not many in other modern languages, which shewed life in its native colours.

The contest about the original benevolence or malignity of man had not yet commenced. Speculation had not yet attempted to analyse

---

41 Nicholas Rowe, *Some Account of the Life of Mr. William Shakespeare*, prefixed to his edition of the plays, 1709.

the mind, to trace the passions to their sources, to unfold the seminal principles of vice and virtue, or sound the depths of the heart for the motives of action. All those enquiries, which from that time that human nature became the fashionable study, have been made sometimes with nice discernment, but often with idle subtilty, were yet unattempted. The tales, with which the infancy of learning was satisfied, exhibited only the superficial appearances of action, related the events but omitted the causes, and were formed for such as delighted in wonders rather than in truth. Mankind was not then to be studied in the closet; he that would know the world, was under the necessity of gleaning his own remarks, by mingling as he could in its business and amusements.

Boyle congratulated himself upon his high birth, because it favoured his curiosity, by facilitating his access.[42] *Shakespeare* had no such advantage; he came to *London* a needy adventurer, and lived for a time by very mean employments. Many works of genius and learning have been performed in states of life, that appear very little favourable to thought or to enquiry; so many, that he who considers them is inclined to think that he sees enterprise and perseverance predominating over all external agency, and bidding help and hindrance vanish before them. The genius of *Shakespeare* was not to be depressed by the weight of poverty, nor limited by the narrow conversation to which men in want are inevitably condemned; the incumbrances of his fortune were shaken from his mind, *as dewdrops from a lion's mane.*[43]

Though he had so many difficulties to encounter, and so little assistance to surmount them, he has been able to obtain an exact knowledge of many modes of life, and many casts of native dispositions; to vary them with great multiplicity; to mark them by nice distinctions; and to shew them in full view by proper combinations. In this part of his performances he had none to imitate, but has himself been imitated by all succeeding writers; and it may be doubted, whether from all his successors more maxims of theoretical knowledge, or more rules of practical prudence, can be collected, than he alone has given to his country.

Nor was his attention confined to the actions of men; he was an exact surveyor of the inanimate world; his descriptions have always some peculiarities, gathered by contemplating things as they really exist. It

---

42 Thomas Birch, *Life of the Hon. Robert Boyle* (1744), pp. 18–19.
43 *Troilus and Cressida*, III. iii. 225.

may be observed, that the oldest poets of many nations preserve their reputation, and that the following generations of wit, after a short celebrity, sink into oblivion. The first, whoever they be, must take their sentiments and descriptions immediately from knowledge; the resemblance is therefore just, their descriptions are verified by every eye, and their sentiments acknowledged by every breast. Those whom their fame invites to the same studies, copy partly them, and partly nature, till the books of one age gain such authority, as to stand in the place of nature to another, and imitation, always deviating a little, becomes at last capricious and casual. *Shakespeare*, whether life or nature be his subject, shews plainly, that he has seen with his own eyes; he gives the image which he receives, not weakened or distorted by the intervention of any other mind; the ignorant feel his representations to be just, and the learned see that they are compleat.

Perhaps it would not be easy to find any authour, except *Homer*, who invented so much as *Shakespeare*, who so much advanced the studies which he cultivated, or effused so much novelty upon his age or country. The form, the characters, the language, and the shows of the *English* drama are his. *He seems*, says *Dennis*, *to have been the very original of our* English *tragical harmony, that is, the harmony of blank verse, diversified often by dissyllable and trissyllable terminations. For the diversity distinguishes it from heroick harmony, and by bringing it nearer to common use makes it more proper to gain attention, and more fit for action and dialogue. Such verse we make when we are writing prose; we make such verse in common conversation.*[44]

I know not whether this praise is rigorously just. The dissyllable termination, which the critick rightly appropriates to the drama, is to be found, though, I think, not in *Gorboduc* which is confessedly before our authour; yet in *Hieronnymo*,[45] of which the date is not certain, but which there is reason to believe at least as old as his earliest plays. This however is certain, that he is the first who taught either tragedy or comedy to please, there being no theatrical piece of any older writer, of which the name is known, except to antiquaries and collectors of books, which are sought because they are scarce, and would not have been scarce, had they been much esteemed.

---

44 *Essay on Genius and Writings of Shakespeare* (Hooker, II. 45). Johnson's quotation is not quite accurate.

45 Thomas Kyd, *The Spanish Tragedy, or Hieronimo Is Mad Again* (1592). *Gorboduc*, referred to above, is often called the earliest English tragedy. Written by Thomas Norton and Thomas Sackville, it was first presented in 1562.

To him we must ascribe the praise, unless *Spenser* may divide it with him, of having first discovered to how much smoothness and harmony the *English* language could be softened. He has speeches, perhaps sometimes scenes, which have all the delicacy of *Rowe*,[46] without his effeminacy. He endeavours indeed commonly to strike by the force and vigour of his dialogue, but he never executes his purpose better, than when he tries to sooth by softness.

Yet it must be at last confessed, that as we owe every thing to him, he owes something to us; that, if much of his praise is paid by perception and judgement, much is likewise given by custom and veneration. We fix our eyes upon his graces, and turn them from his deformities, and endure in him what we should in another loath or despise. If we endured without praising, respect for the father of our drama might excuse us; but I have seen, in the book of some modern crick,[47] a collection of anomalies, which shew that he has corrupted language by every mode of depravation, but which his admirer has accumulated as a monument of honour.

He has scenes of undoubted and perpetual excellence, but perhaps not one play, which, if it were now exhibited as the work of a contemporary writer, would be heard to the conclusion. I am indeed far from thinking, that his works were wrought to his own ideas of perfection; when they were such as would satisfy the audience, they satisfied the writer. It is seldom that authours, though more studious of fame than *Shakespeare*, rise much above the standard of their own age; to add a little to what is best will always be sufficient for present praise, and those who find themselves exalted into fame, are willing to credit their encomiasts, and to spare the labour of contending with themselves.

It does not appear, that *Shakespeare* thought his works worthy of posterity, that he levied any ideal tribute upon future times, or had any further prospect, than of present popularity and present profit. When his plays had been acted, his hope was at an end; he solicited no addition of honour from the reader. He therefore made no scruple to repeat the same jests in many dialogues, or to entangle different plots by the same knot of perplexity, which may be at least forgiven him, by those who recollect, that of *Congreve*'s four comedies, two are concluded by a

46 Nicholas Rowe (1674–1718), who in addition to editing Shakespeare, himself wrote several sentimental tragedies, of which the most famous is *The Fair Penitent* (1703).
47 John Upton, *Critical Observations on Shakespeare* (1746).

marriage in a mask,[48] by a deception, which perhaps never happened, and which, whether likely or not, he did not invent.

So careless was this great poet of future fame, that, though he retired to ease and plenty, while he was yet little *declined into the vale of years*,[49] before he could be disgusted with fatigue, or disabled by infirmity, he made no collection of his works, nor desired to rescue those that had been already published from the depravations that obscured them, or secure to the rest a better destiny, by giving them to the world in their genuine state.

Of the plays which bear the name of *Shakespeare* in the late editions, the greater part were not published till about seven years after his death, and the few which appeared in his life are apparently thrust into the world without the care of the authour, and therefore probably without his knowledge.

Of all the publishers, clandestine or professed, their negligence and unskilfulness has by the late revisers been sufficiently shown. The faults of all are indeed numerous and gross, and have not only corrupted many passages perhaps beyond recovery, but have brought others into suspicion, which are only obscured by obsolete phraseology, or by the writer's unskilfulness and affectation. To alter is more easy than to explain, and temerity is a more common quality than diligence. Those who saw that they must employ conjecture to a certain degree, were willing to indulge it a little further. Had the authour published his own works, we should have sat quietly down to disentangle his intricacies, and clear his obscurities; but now we tear what we cannot loose, and eject what we happen not to understand.

The faults are more than could have happened without the concurrence of many causes. The stile of *Shakespeare* was in itself ungrammatical, perplexed and obscure; his works were transcribed for the players by those who may be supposed to have seldom understood them; they were transmitted by copiers equally unskilful, who still multiplied errours; they were perhaps sometimes mutilated by the actors, for the sake of shortening the speeches; and were at last printed without correction of the press.

In this state they remained, not as Dr. *Warburton* supposes,[50] because

---

48 *The Old Bachelor* (1693) and *Love for Love* (1695).
49 *Othello*, III. iii. 265.
50 William Warburton, Preface to *The Works of Shakespear* (1747).

they were unregarded, but because the editor's art was not yet applied
to modern languages, and our ancestors were accustomed to so much
negligence of *English* printers, that they could very patiently endure it.
At last an edition was undertaken by *Rowe;*[51] not because a poet was to
be published by a poet, for *Rowe* seems to have thought very little on
correction or explanation, but that our authour's works might appear
like those of his fraternity, with the appendages of a life and recom-
mendatory preface. *Rowe* has been clamorously blamed for not perform-
ing what he did not undertake, and it is time that justice be done him, by
confessing, that though he seems to have had no thought of corruption
beyond the printer's errours, yet he has made many emendations, if they
were not made before, which his successors have received without
acknowledgement, and which, if they had produced them, would have
filled pages and pages with censures of the stupidity by which the faults
were committed, with displays of the absurdities which they involved,
with ostentatious expositions of the new reading, and self congratulations
on the happiness of discovering it.

The nation had been for many years content enough with Mr.
Rowe's performance, when Mr. *Pope* made them acquainted with the
true state of *Shakespeare*'s text,[52] shewed that it was extremely corrupt,
and gave reason to hope that there were means of reforming it. He
collated the old copies, which none had thought to examine before,
and restored many lines to their integrity; but, by a very compendious
criticism, he rejected whatever he disliked, and thought more of amputation than of cure.

I know not why he is commended by Dr. *Warburton* for distinguishing the genuine from the spurious plays.[53] In this choice he exerted no judgement of his own; the plays which he received, were given
by *Hemings* and *Condel*,[54] the first editors; and those which he rejected,

---

51 *The Works of Mr. William Shakespear*, 6 vols. (1709).

52 *The Works of Shakespear. Collated and Corrected*, 6 vols. (1725).

53 *Preface*, 1747.

54 John Heming (d. 1630) and Henry Condell (d. 1627), actors in many of Shakespeare's plays, co-editors of the First Folio (1623).

though, according to the licentiousness of the press in those times, they were printed during *Shakespeare*'s life, with his name, had been omitted by his friends, and were never added to his works before the edition of 1664, from which they were copied by the later printers.

This was a work which *Pope* seems to have thought unworthy of his abilities, being not able to suppress his contempt of *the dull duty of an editor*.[55] He understood but half his undertaking. The duty of a collator is indeed dull, yet, like other tedious tasks, is very necessary; but an emendatory critick would ill discharge his duty, without qualities very different from dulness. In perusing a corrupted piece, he must have before him all possibilities of meaning, with all possibilities of expression. Such must be his comprehension of thought, and such his copiousness of language. Out of many readings possible, he must be able to select that which best suits with the state, opinions, and modes of language prevailing in every age, and with his authour's particular cast of thought, and turn of expression. Such must be his knowledge, and such his taste. Conjectural criticism demands more than humanity possesses, and he that exercises it with most praise has very frequent need of indulgence. Let us now be told no more of the dull duty of an editor.

Confidence is the common consequence of success. They whose excellence of any kind has been loudly celebrated, are ready to conclude, that their powers are universal. *Pope*'s edition fell below his own expectations, and he was so much offended, when he was found to have left any thing for others to do, that he past the latter part of his life in a state of hostility with verbal criticism.

I have retained all his notes, that no fragment of so great a writer may be lost; his preface, valuable alike for elegance of composition and justness of remark, and containing a general criticism on his authour, so extensive that little can be added, and so exact, that little can be disputed, every editor has an interest to suppress, but that every reader would demand its insertion.

Pope was succeeded by *Theobald*,[56] a man of narrow comprehension and small acquisitions, with no native and intrinsick splendour of genius, with little of the artificial light of learning, but zealous for minute accuracy, and not negligent in pursuing it. He collated the ancient copies, and rectified many errors. A man so anxiously scrupulous might have

---

55 *Preface to Shakespeare* (Elwin and Courthope, V. 548).
56 Lewis Theobald (1688–1744), editor of *The Works of Shakespeare*, 7 vols. (1733).

been expected to do more, but what little he did was commonly right.

In his reports of copies and editions he is not to be trusted, without examination. He speaks sometimes indefinitely of copies, when he has only one. In his enumeration of editions, he mentions the two first folios as of high, and the third folio as of middle authority; but the truth is, that the first is equivalent to all others, and that the rest only deviate from it by the printer's negligence. Whoever has any of the folios has all, excepting those diversities which mere reiteration of editions will produce. I collated them all at the beginning, but afterwards used only the first.

Of his notes I have generally retained those which he retained himself in his second edition, except when they were confuted by subsequent annotators, or were too minute to merit preservation. I have sometimes adopted his restoration of a comma, without inserting the panegyrick in which he celebrates himself for his atchievement. The exuberant excrescence of his diction I have often lopped, his triumphant exultations over *Pope* and *Rowe* I have sometimes suppressed, and his contemptible ostentation I have frequently concealed; but I have in some places shewn him, as he would have shewn himself, for the reader's diversion, that the inflated emptiness of some notes may justify or excuse the contraction of the rest.

Theobald, thus weak and ignorant, thus mean and faithless, thus petulant and ostentatious, by the good luck of having *Pope* for his enemy, has escaped, and escaped alone, with reputation, from this undertaking. So willingly does the world support those who solicite favour, against those who command reverence; and so easily is he praised, whom no man can envy.

Our authour fell then into the hands of Sir *Thomas Hanmer*,[57] the *Oxford* editor, a man, in my opinion, eminently qualified by nature for such studies. He had, what is the first requisite to emendatory criticism, that intuition by which the poet's intention is immediately discovered, and that dexterity of intellect which despatches its work by the easiest means. He had undoubtedly read much; his acquaintance with customs, opinions, and traditions, seems to have been large; and he is often learned without shew. He seldom passes what he does not understand, without an attempt to find or to make a meaning, and sometimes hastily makes what a little more attention would have found. He is solicitous to reduce to grammar, what he could not be sure that his authour intended to be

---

57 Hanmer (1677–1746), editor of *The Works of Shakespear*, 6 vols. (Oxford, 1744).

grammatical. *Shakespeare* regarded more the series of ideas, than of words, and his language, not being designed for the reader's desk, was all that he desired it to be, if it conveyed his meaning to the audience.

Hanmer's care of the metre has been too violently censured. He found the measures reformed in so many passages, by the silent labours of some editors, with the silent acquiescence of the rest, that he thought himself allowed to extend a little further the license, which had already been carried so far without reprehension; and of his corrections in general, it must be confessed, that they are often just and made commonly with the least possible violation of the text.

But, by inserting his emendations, whether invented or borrowed, into the page, without any notice of varying copies, he has appropriated the labour of his predecessors, and made his own edition of little authority. His confidence indeed, both in himself and others, was too great; he supposes all to be right that was done by *Pope* and *Theobald;* he seems not to suspect a critick of fallibility, and it was but reasonable that he should claim what he so liberally granted.

As he never writes without careful enquiry and diligent consideration, I have received all his notes, and believe that every reader will wish for more.

Of the last editor[58] it is more difficult to speak. Respect is due to high place, tenderness to living reputation, and veneration to genius and learning; but he cannot be justly offended at that liberty of which he has himself so frequently given an example, nor very solicitous what is thought of notes, which he ought never to have considered as part of his serious employments, and which, I suppose, since the ardour of composition is remitted, he no longer numbers among his happy effusions.

The original and predominant errour of his commentary, is acquiescence in his first thoughts; that precipitation which is produced by consciousness of quick discernment; and that confidence which presumes to do, by surveying the surface, what labour only can perform, by penetrating the bottom. His notes exhibit sometimes perverse interpretations, and sometimes improbable conjectures; he at one time gives the authour more profundity or meaning, than the sentence admits, and at another discovers absurdities, where the sense is plain to every other reader. But his emendations are likewise often happy and just; and his interpretation of obscure passages learned and sagacious.

---

58 See above, note 50.

Of his notes, I have commonly rejected those, against which the general voice of the publick has exclaimed, or which their own incongruity immediately condemns, and which, I suppose, the authour himself would desire to be forgotten. Of the rest, to part I have given the highest approbation, by inserting the offered reading in the text; part I have left to the judgment of the reader, as doubtful, though specious; and part I have censured without reserve, but I am sure without bitterness of malice, and, I hope, without wantonness of insult.

It is no pleasure to me, in revising my volumes, to observe how much paper is wasted in confutation. Whoever considers the revolutions of learning, and the various questions of greater or less importance, upon which wit and reason have exercised their powers, must lament the unsuccessfulness of enquiry, and the slow advances of truth, when he reflects, that great part of the labour of every writer is only the destruction of those that went before him. The first care of the builder of a new system, is to demolish the fabricks which are standing. The chief desire of him that comments an authour, is to shew how much other commentators have corrupted and obscured him. The opinions prevalent in one age, as truths above the reach of controversy, are confuted and rejected in another, and rise again to reception in remoter times. Thus the human mind is kept in motion without progress. Thus sometimes truth and errour, and sometimes contrarieties of errour, take each others place by reciprocal invasion. The tide of seeming knowledge which is poured over one generation, retires and leaves another naked and barren; the sudden meteors of intelligence which for a while appear to shoot their beams into the regions of obscurity, on a sudden withdraw their lustre, and leave mortals again to grope their way.

These elevations and depressions of renown, and the contradictions to which all improvers of knowledge must for ever be exposed, since they are not escaped by the highest and brightest of mankind, may surely be endured with patience by cricks and annotators, who can rank themselves but as the satellites of their authours. How canst thou beg for life, says *Achilles* to his captive, when thou knowest that thou art now to suffer only what must another day be suffered by *Achilles?*[59]

Dr. *Warburton* had a name sufficient to confer celebrity on those who could exalt themselves into antagonists, and his notes have raised a clamour too loud to be distinct. His chief assailants are the authours of

_____

[59] Achilles to Lycaon, *Iliad*, XXI. 99ff.

the Canons of criticism and of the *Review of* Shakespeare's *text*;[60] of whom
one ridicules his errours with airy petulance, suitable enough to the levity
of the controversy; the other attacks them with gloomy malignity, as if
he were dragging to justice an assassin or incendiary. The one stings like
a fly, sucks a little blood, takes a gay flutter, and returns for more; the
other bites like a viper, and would be glad to leave inflammations and
gangrene behind him. When I think on one, with his confederates, I
remember the danger of *Coriolanus*, who was afraid that *girls with spits,
and boys with stones, should slay him in puny battle*;[61] when the other crosses
my imagination, I remember the prodigy in *Macbeth*,

> *An eagle tow'ring in his pride of place,*
> *Was by a mousing owl hawk'd at and kill'd.*[62]

Let me however do them justice. One is a wit, and one a scholar.
They have both shewn acuteness sufficient in the discovery of faults, and
have both advanced some probable interpretations of obscure passages;
but when they aspire to conjecture and emendation, it appears how falsely
we all estimate our own abilities, and the little which they have been
able to perform might have taught them more candour to the endeavours
of others.

Before Dr. *Warburton*'s edition, *Critical observations on* Shakespeare
had been published by Mr. *Upton*,[63] a man skilled in languages, and
acquainted with books, but who seems to have had no great vigour of
genius or nicety of taste. Many of his explanations are curious and useful,
but he likewise, though he professed to oppose the licentious confidence
of editors, and adhere to the old copies, is unable to restrain the rage of
emendation, though his ardour is ill seconded by his skill. Every cold
empirick, when his heart is expanded by a successful experiment, swells
into a theorist, and the laborious collator at some unlucky moment
frolicks in conjecture.

Critical, historical and explanatory notes have been likewise published
upon *Shakespeare* by Dr. *Grey*,[64] whose diligent perusal of the old *English*

---

60 Thomas Edwards, *Canons of Criticism* (1748); Benjamin Heath, *Revisal of Shakespeare's Text* (1765).
61 *Coriolanus*, IV. iv. 5, slightly misquoted.
62 *Macbeth*, II. iv. 12–13.
63 See note 47 above.
64 See note 38 above.

writers has enabled him to make some useful observations. What he undertook he has well enough performed, but as he neither attempts judicial nor emendatory criticism, he employs rather his memory than his sagacity. It were to be wished that all would endeavour to imitate his modesty who have not been able to surpass his knowledge.

I can say with great sincerity of all my predecessors, what I hope will hereafter be said of me, that not one has left *Shakespeare* without improvement, nor is there one to whom I have not been indebted for assistance and information. Whatever I have taken from them it was my intention to refer to its original authour, and it is certain, that what I have not given to another, I believed when I wrote it to be my own. In some perhaps I have been anticipated; but if I am ever found to encroach upon the remarks of any other commentator, I am willing that the honour, be it more or less, should be transferred to the first claimant, for his right, and his alone, stands above dispute; the second can prove his pretensions only to himself, nor can himself always distinguish invention, with sufficient certainty, from recollection.

They have all been treated by me with candour, which they have not been careful of observing to one another. It is not easy to discover from what cause the acrimony of a scholiast can naturally proceed. The subjects to be discussed by him are of very small importance; they involve neither property nor liberty; nor favour the interest of sect or party. The various readings of copies, and different interpretations of a passage, seem to be questions that might exercise the wit, without engaging the passions. But, whether it be, that *small things make mean men proud*,[65] and vanity catches small occasions; or that all contrariety of opinion, even in those that can defend it no longer, makes proud men angry; there is often found in commentaries a spontaneous strain of invective and contempt, more eager and venomous than is vented by the most furious controvertist in politicks against those whom he is hired to defame.

Perhaps the lightness of the matter may conduce to the vehemence of the agency; when the truth to be investigated is so near to inexistence, as to escape attention, its bulk is to be enlarged by rage and exclamation: That to which all would be indifferent in its original state, may attract notice when the fate of a name is appended to it. A commentator has indeed great temptations to supply by turbulence what he wants of dignity, to beat his little gold to a spacious surface, to work that to foam which no art or diligence can exalt to spirit.

---

65 *2 Henry VI*, IV. i. 106, slightly misquoted.

The notes which I have borrowed or written are either illustrative, by which difficulties are explained; or judicial, by which faults and beauties are remarked; or emendatory, by which depravations are corrected.

The explanations transcribed from others, if I do not subjoin any other interpretation, I suppose commonly to be right, at least I intend by acquiescence to confess, that I have nothing better to propose.

After the labours of all the editors, I found many passages which appeared to me likely to obstruct the greater number of readers, and thought it my duty to facilitate their passage. It is impossible for an expositor not to write too little for some, and too much for others. He can only judge what is necessary by his own experience; and how long soever he may deliberate, will at last explain many lines which the learned will think impossible to be mistaken, and omit many for which the ignorant will want his help. These are censures merely relative, and must be quietly endured. I have endeavoured to be neither superfluously copious, nor scrupulously reserved, and hope that I have made my authour's meaning accessible to many who before were frighted from perusing him, and contributed something to the publick, by diffusing innocent and rational pleasure.

The compleat explanation of an authour not systematick and consequential, but desultory and vagrant, abounding in casual allusions and light hints, is not to be expected from any single scholiast. All personal reflections, when names are suppressed, must be in a few years irrecoverably obliterated; and customs, too minute to attract the notice of law, such as modes of dress, formalities of conversation, rules of visits, disposition of furniture, and practices of ceremony, which naturally find places in familiar dialogue, are so fugitive and unsubstantial, that they are not easily retained or recovered. What can be known, will be collected by chance, from the recesses of obscure and obsolete papers, perused commonly with some other view. Of this knowledge every man has some, and none has much; but when an authour has engaged the publick attention, those who can add any thing to his illustration, communicate their discoveries, and time produces what had eluded diligence.

To time I have been obliged to resign many passages, which, though I did not understand them, will perhaps hereafter be explained, having, I hope, illustrated some, which others have neglected or mistaken, sometimes by short remarks, or marginal directions, such as every editor has added at his will, and often by comments more laborious than the matter will seem to deserve; but that which is most difficult is not always most important, and to an editor nothing is a trifle by which his authour is obscured.

The poetical beauties or defects I have not been very diligent to observe. Some plays have more, and some fewer judicial observations, not in proportion to their difference of merit, but because I gave this part of my design to chance and to caprice. The reader, I believe, is seldom pleased to find his opinion anticipated; it is natural to delight more in what we find or make, than in what we receive. Judgment, like other faculties, is improved by practice, and its advancement is hindered by submission to dictatorial decisions, as the memory grows torpid by the use of a table book. Some initiation is however necessary; of all skill, part is infused by precept, and part is obtained by habit; I have therefore shewn so much as may enable the candidate of criticism to discover the rest.

To the end of most plays, I have added short strictures, containing a general censure of faults, or praise of excellence; in which I know not how much I have concurred with the current opinion; but I have not, by any affectation of singularity, deviated from it. Nothing is minutely and particularly examined, and therefore it is to be supposed, that in the plays which are condemned there is much to be praised, and in these which are praised much to be condemned.

The part of criticism in which the whole succession of editors has laboured with the greatest diligence, which has occasioned the most arrogant ostentation, and excited the keenest acrimony, is the emendation of corrupted passages, to which the publick attention having been first drawn by the violence of the contention between *Pope* and *Theobald*, has been continued by the persecution, which, with a kind of conspiracy, has been since raised against all the publishers of *Shakespeare*.

That many passages have passed in a state of depravation through all the editions is indubitably certain; of these the restoration is only to be attempted by collation of copies or sagacity of conjecture. The collator's province is safe and easy, the conjecturer's perilous and difficult. Yet as the greater part of the plays are extant only in one copy, the peril must not be avoided, nor the difficulty refused.

Of the readings which this emulation of amendment has hitherto produced, some from the labours of every publisher I have advanced into the text; those are to be considered as in my opinion sufficiently supported; some I have rejected without mention, as evidently erroneous; some I have left in the notes without censure or approbation, as resting in equipoise between objection and defence; and some, which seemed specious but not right, I have inserted with a subsequent animadversion.

Having classed the observations of others, I was at last to try what I could substitute for their mistakes, and how I could supply their omissions. I collated such copies as I could procure, and wished for more, but have not found the collectors of these rarities very communicative. Of the editions which chance or kindness put into my hands I have given an enumeration, that I may not be blamed for neglecting what I had not the power to do.

By examining the old copies, I soon found that the later publishers, with all their boasts of diligence, suffered many passages to stand unauthorised, and contented themselves with *Rowe's* regulation of the text, even where they knew it to be arbitrary, and with a little consideration might have found it to be wrong. Some of these alterations are only the ejection of a word for one that appeared to him more elegant or more intelligible. These corruptions I have often silently rectified; for the history of our language, and the true force of our words, can only be preserved, by keeping the text of authours free from adulteration. Others, and those very frequent, smoothed the cadence, or regulated the measure; on these I have not exercised the same rigour; if only a word was transposed, or a particle inserted or omitted, I have sometimes suffered the line to stand; for the inconstancy of the copies is such, as that some liberties may be easily permitted. But this practice I have not suffered to proceed far, having restored the primitive diction wherever it could for any reason be preferred.

The emendations, which comparison of copies supplied, I have inserted in the text; sometimes where the improvement was slight, without notice, and sometimes with an account of the reasons of the change.

Conjecture, though it be sometimes unavoidable, I have not wantonly nor licentiously indulged. It has been my settled principle, that the reading of the ancient books is probably true, and therefore is not to be disturbed for the sake of elegance, perspicuity, or mere improvement of the sense. For though much credit is not due to the fidelity, nor any to the judgment of the first publishers, yet they who had the copy before their eyes were more likely to read it right, than we who read it only by imagination. But it is evident that they have often made strange mistakes by ignorance or negligence, and that therefore something may be properly attempted by criticism, keeping the middle way between presumption and timidity.

Such criticism I have attempted to practise, and where any passage appeared inextricably perplexed, have endeavoured to discover how it may be recalled to sense, with least violence. But my first labour is, always to turn the old text on every side, and try if there be any interstice, through which light can find its way; nor would *Huetius*[66] himself condemn me, as refusing the trouble of research, for the ambition of alteration. In this modest industry I have not been unsuccessful. I have rescued many lines from the violations of temerity, and secured many scenes from the inroads of correction. I have adopted the *Roman* sentiment, that it is more honourable to save a citizen, than to kill an enemy, and have been more careful to protect than to attack.

I have preserved the common distribution of the plays into acts, though I believe it to be in almost all the plays void of authority. Some of those which are divided in the later editions have no division in the first folio, and some that are divided in the folio have no division in the preceding copies. The settled mode of the theatre requires four intervals in the play, but few, if any, of our authour's compositions can be properly distributed in that manner. An act is so much of the drama as passes without intervention of time or change of place. A pause makes a new act. In every real, and therefore in every imitative action, the intervals may be more or fewer, the restriction of five acts being accidental and arbitrary. This *Shakespeare* knew, and this he practised; his plays were written, and at first printed in one unbroken continuity, and ought now to be exhibited with short pauses, interposed as often as the scene is changed, or any considerable time is required to pass. This method would at once quell a thousand absurdities.

In restoring the authour's works to their integrity, I have considered the punctuation as wholly in my power; for what could be their care of colons and commas, who corrupted words and sentences. Whatever could be done by adjusting points[67] is therefore silently performed, in some plays with much diligence, in others with less; it is hard to keep a busy eye steadily fixed upon evanescent atoms, or a discursive mind upon evanescent truth.

The same liberty has been taken with a few particles,[68] or other words of slight effect. I have sometimes inserted or omitted them without

---

66 Pierre Huet, *De Interpretatione* (1661). Huet (1630–1721) was a French churchman and scholar, noted for his classical, Biblical, and scientific learning.

67 I.e., punctuation.

68 Subordinate words, never inflected: prepositions, conjunctions, interjections.

notice. I have done that sometimes, which the other editors have done always, and which indeed the state of the text may sufficiently justify.

The greater part of readers, instead of blaming us for passing trifles, will wonder that on mere trifles so much labour is expended, with such importance of debate, and such solemnity of diction. To these I answer with confidence, that they are judging of an art which they do not understand; yet cannot much reproach them with their ignorance, nor promise that they would become in general, by learning criticism, more useful, happier or wiser.

As I practised conjecture more, I learned to trust it less; and after I had printed a few plays, resolved to insert none of my own readings in the text. Upon this caution I now congratulate myself, for every day encreases my doubt of my emendations.

Since I have confined my imagination to the margin, it must not be considered as very reprehensible, if I have suffered it to play some freaks in its own dominion. There is no danger in conjecture, if it be proposed as conjecture; and while the text remains uninjured, those changes may be safely offered, which are not considered even by him that offers them as necessary or safe.

If my readings are of little value, they have not been ostentatiously displayed or importunately obtruded. I could have written longer notes, for the art of writing notes is not of difficult attainment. The work is performed, first by railing at the stupidity, negligence, ignorance, and asinine tastelessness of the former editors, and shewing, from all that goes before and all that follows, the inelegance and absurdity of the old reading; then by proposing something, which to superficial readers would seem specious, but which the editor rejects with indignation; then by producing the true reading, with a long paraphrase, and concluding with loud acclamations on the discovery, and a sober wish for the advancement and prosperity of genuine criticism.

All this may be done, and perhaps done sometimes without impropriety. But I have always suspected that the reading is right, which requires many words to prove it wrong; and the emendation wrong, that cannot without so much labour appear to be right. The justness of a happy restoration strikes at once, and the moral precept may be well applied to criticism, *quod dubitas ne feceris*.[69]

To dread the shore which he sees spread with wrecks, is natural to the

---

69 "When in doubt, don't do it."

sailor. I had before my eye, so many critical adventures ended in miscarriage, that caution was forced upon me. I encountered in every page Wit struggling with its own sophistry, and Learning confused by the multiplicity of its views. I was forced to censure those whom I admired, and could not but reflect, while I was dispossessing their emendations, how soon the same fate might happen to my own, and how many of the readings which I have corrected may be by some other editor defended and established.

> Criticks, I saw, that other's names efface,
> And fix their own, with labour, in the place;
> Their own, like others, soon their place resign'd,
> Or disappear'd, and left the first behind.

Pope[70]

That a conjectural critick should often be mistaken, cannot be wonderful, either to others or himself, if it be considered, that in his art there is no system, no principal and axiomatical truth that regulates subordinate positions. His chance of errour is renewed at every attempt; an oblique view of the passage, a slight misapprehension of a phrase, a casual inattention to the parts connected, is sufficient to make him not only fail, but fail ridiculously; and when he succeeds best, he produces perhaps but one reading of many probable, and he that suggests another will always be able to dispute his claims.

It is an unhappy state, in which danger is hid under pleasure. The allurements of emendation are scarcely resistible. Conjecture has all the joy and all the pride of invention, and he that has once started a happy change, is too much delighted to consider what objections may rise against it.

Yet conjectural criticism has been of great use in the learned world; nor is it my intention to depreciate a study, that has exercised so many mighty minds, from the revival of learning to our own age, from the Bishop of *Aleria*[71] to English *Bentley*.[72] The criticles on ancient authours have, in the exercise of their sagacity, many assistances, which the editor

---

70 *Temple of Fame*, 37–40, slightly misquoted.
71 Joannes Andreas (1417–c. 1480), librarian to Pope Sixtus IV.
72 Richard Bentley (1662–1742), famous for his textual criticism of Horace and Manilius.

of *Shakespeare* is condemned to want. They are employed upon grammatical and settled languages, whose construction contributes so much to perspicuity, that *Homer* has fewer passages unintelligible than *Chaucer*. The words have not only a known regimen, but invariable quantities, which direct and confine the choice. There are commonly more manuscripts than one; and they do not often conspire in the same mistakes. Yet *Scaliger* could confess to *Salmasius* how little satisfaction his emendations gave him. *Illudunt nobis conjecturae nostrae, quarum nos pudet, posteaquam in meliores codices incidimus.*[73] And *Lipsius* could complain, that criticks were making faults, by trying to remove them, *Ut olim vitiis, ita nunc remediis laboratur.*[74] And indeed, where mere conjecture is to be used, the emendations of *Scaliger* and *Lipsius*, notwithstanding their wonderful sagacity and erudition, are often vague and disputable, like mine or *Theobald's*.

Perhaps I may not be more censured for doing wrong, than for doing little; for raising in the publick expectations, which at last I have not answered. The expectation of ignorance is indefinite, and that of knowledge is often tyrannical. It is hard to satisfy those who know not what to demand, or those who demand by design what they think impossible to be done. I have indeed disappointed no opinion more than my own; yet I have endeavoured to perform my task with no slight solicitude. Not a single passage in the whole work has appeared to me corrupt, which I have not attempted to restore; or obscure, which I have not endeavoured to illustrate. In many I have failed like others; and from many, after all my efforts, I have retreated, and confessed the repulse. I have not passed over, with affected superiority, what is equally difficult to the reader and to myself, but where I could not instruct him, have owned my ignorance. I might easily have accumulated a mass of seeming learning upon easy scenes; but it ought not to be imputed to negligence, that, where nothing was necessary, nothing has been done, or that, where others have said enough, I have said no more.

Notes are often necessary, but they are necessary evils. Let him,

---

73 "Our conjectures makes us look silly; we are ashamed of them after we have come upon better manuscripts." Joseph Justus Scaliger (1540–1609), French philologist and critic, in a letter of July 1608 to Claude de Saumaise (1583–1653), published in Scaliger's *Opuscula Varia antehoc Non Edita* (Paris, 1610), p. 469.

74 Johnson paraphrases the Latin before quoting it. Justus Lipsius (1547–1606), Flemish humanist in *Ad Annales Cornelii Taciti Liber Commentarius sive Notae* (Antwerp, 1581), *Ad. Lectorem*, sig. *5, l. 19.

that is yet unacquainted with the powers of *Shakespeare*, and who desires to feel the highest pleasure that the drama can give, read every play from the first scene to the last, with utter negligence of all his commentators. When his fancy is once on the wing, let it not stoop at correction or explanation. When his attention is strongly engaged, let it disdain alike to turn aside to the name of *Theobald* and of *Pope*. Let him read on through brightness and obscurity, through integrity and corruption; let him preserve his comprehension of the dialogue and his interest in the fable. And when the pleasures of novelty have ceased, let him attempt exactness, and read the commentators.

Particular passages are cleared by notes, but the general effect of the work is weakened. The mind is refrigerated by interruption; the thoughts are diverted from the principal subject; the reader is weary, he suspects not why; and at last throws away the book, which he has too diligently studied.

Parts are not to be examined till the whole has been surveyed; there is a kind of intellectual remoteness necessary for the comprehension of any great work in its full design and its true proportions; a close approach shews the smaller niceties, but the beauty of the whole is discerned no longer.

It is not very grateful to consider how little the succession of editors has added to this authour's power of pleasing. He was read, admired, studied, and imitated, while he was yet deformed with all the improprieties which ignorance and neglect could accumulate upon him; while the reading was yet not rectified, nor his allusions understood; yet then did *Dryden* pronounce

> that *Shakespeare* was the man who, of all modern and perhaps ancient poets had the largest and most comprehensive soul. All the images of nature were still present to him, and he drew them not laboriously, but luckily; When he describes any thing, you more than see it, you feel it too. Those who accuse him to have wanted learning, give him the greater commendation: he was naturally learned: he needed not the spectacles of books to read nature; he looked inwards, and found her there. I cannot say he is every where alike; were he so, I should do him injury to compare him with the greatest of mankind. He is many times flat and insipid; his comick wit degenerating into clenches, his serious swelling into bombast. But he is always great, when some great occasion is presented to him: No man can say, he ever had a fit subject for his wit, and did not then raise himself as high above the rest of poets,

Quantum lenta solent inter viburna cupressi.[75]

It is to be lamented, that such a writer should want a commentary; that his language should become obsolete, or his sentiments obscure. But it is vain to carry wishes beyond the condition of human things; that which must happen to all, has happened to *Shakespeare*, by accident and time; and more than has been suffered by any other writer since the use of types, has been suffered by him through his own negligence of fame, or perhaps by that superiority of mind, which despised its own perform-ances, when it compared them with its powers, and judged those works unworthy to be preserved, which the criticks of following ages were to contend for the fame of restoring and explaining.

Among these candidates of inferiour fame, I am now to stand the judgment of the publick; and wish that I could confidently produce my commentary as equal to the encouragement which I have had the honour of receiving. Every work of this kind is by its nature deficient, and I should feel little solicitude about the sentence, were it to be pronounced only by the skilful and the learned.

---

75 John Dryden, *Essay of Dramatic Poesy* (1668), in *Essays*, ed. W. P. Ker (1926), I. 79–80. The Latin means, "as cypresses do among the bending osiers" (Virgil, *Eclogues*, I. 25).

LIVES OF THE ENGLISH POETS[1]

(1779–1781)

Johnson's interest in the art of biography, as shown by *Rambler* 60 (see above, pp. 109–113), culminated in his writing the lives of fifty English poets. In March 1777 he had agreed with some booksellers to write prefatory lives for an edition of the English poets. The booksellers chose the poets to be included, although Johnson insisted on a few changes. As he worked on the project, it became more and more ambitious; in the final version of the lives, two biographies (Pope and Dryden) are book length; several others are very long, and Johnson's critical judgments often assume far more importance than his presentation of biographical fact.

The *Lives* provided an opportunity for Johnson to record definitively the results of years of meditation on English poetry. It seems certain that he did not reread the poetry he discussed; he simply knew it. Although his biographies are sometimes inaccurate in detail and his critical judgments seem occasionally distorted by prejudice, the work as a whole demonstrates astounding range, sensitivity, wisdom, and economy. Each life includes in varying proportions a biographical account, record of the poet's accomplishment, and critical judgment on that accomplishment. Johnson's critical principles, their depth, their inconsistencies, and their close relationship to his moral convictions, emerge more vividly here than in any other of his works; his personal impress gives interest even to literary figures now long forgotten.

The present text is taken from *Lives of the English Poets*, ed. George Birkbeck Hill, 3 vols. (Oxford, 1905). Used by permission. The sequence of the lives is dictated by the chronology of the poets discussed.

---

1 See Introduction, pp. 37–41.

Johnson's account of Abraham Cowley (1618–1667) was, in his judgment (as reported by Boswell), the best of his biographies because of its discussion, here reprinted, of the metaphysical poets. This part of the *Life* begins immediately after the introductory biographical passages. It places Cowley among his contemporaries and offers interpretations and judgments of seventeenth-century poetry that were long to remain influential. After this general discussion, Johnson supplies many examples of the kind of poetry he is here considering, before moving on to a critical discussion of Cowley's poetry itself.

Life of Cowley

Cowley, like other poets who have written with narrow views and, instead of tracing intellectual pleasure to its natural sources in the mind of man, paid their court to temporary prejudices, has been at one time too much praised and too much neglected at another.

Wit, like all other things subject by their nature to the choice of man, has its changes and fashions, and at different times takes different forms. About the beginning of the seventeenth century appeared a race of writers that may be termed the metaphysical poets, of whom in a criticism on the works of Cowley it is not improper to give some account.

The metaphysical poets were men of learning, and to shew their learning was their whole endeavour; but, unluckily resolving to shew it in rhyme, instead of writing poetry they only wrote verses, and very often such verses as stood the trial of the finger better than of the ear; for the modulation was so imperfect that they were only found to be verses by counting the syllables.

If the father of criticism[2] has rightly denominated poetry τέχνη

---

2 Aristotle. G. B. Hill points out that the phrase Johnson uses does not actually occur in the *Poetics* with regard to poetry, although it is implied in Chapter VIII.

μιμητική, an imitative art, these writers will without great wrong lose their right to the name of poets, for they cannot be said to have imitated any thing: they neither copied nature nor life; neither painted the forms of matter nor represented the operations of intellect.

Those however who deny them to be poets allow them to be wits. Dryden confesses of himself and his contemporaries that they fall below Donne in wit, but maintains that they surpass him in poetry.

If Wit be well described by Pope as being "that which has been often thought, but was never before so well expressed,"[3] they certainly never attained nor ever sought it, for they endeavoured to be singular in their thoughts, and were careless of their diction. But Pope's account of wit is undoubtedly erroneous; he depresses it below its natural dignity, and reduces it from strength of thought to happiness of language.

If by a more noble and more adequate conception that be considered as Wit which is at once natural and new, that which though not obvious is, upon its first production, acknowledged to be just; if it be that, which he that never found it, wonders how he missed; to wit of this kind the metaphysical poets have seldom risen. Their thoughts are often new, but seldom natural; they are not obvious, but neither are they just; and the reader, far from wondering that he missed them, wonders more frequently by what perverseness of industry they were ever found.

But Wit, abstracted from its effects upon the hearer, may be more rigorously and philosophically considered as a kind of *discordia concors*; a combination of dissimilar images, or discovery of occult resemblances in things apparently unlike. Of wit, thus defined, they have more than enough. The most heterogeneous ideas are yoked by violence together; nature and art are ransacked for illustrations, comparisons, and allusions; their learning instructs, and their subtilty surprises; but the reader commonly thinks his improvement dearly bought, and, though he sometimes admires, is seldom pleased.

From this account of their compositions it will be readily inferred that they were not successful in representing or moving the affections. As they were wholly employed on something unexpected and surprising they had no regard to that uniformity of sentiment, which enables us to conceive and to excite the pains and the pleasure of other minds: they never enquired what on any occasion they should have said or done, but

---

3 "*True Wit* is *Nature* to Advantage drest,/What oft was *Thought*, but ne'er so well *Exprest*" (*Essay on Criticism*, 297–98).

wrote rather as beholders than partakers of human nature; as beings looking upon good and evil, impassive and at leisure; as Epicurean deities making remarks on the actions of men and the vicissitudes of life, without interest and without emotion. Their courtship was void of fondness and their lamentation of sorrow. Their wish was only to say what they hoped had been never said before.

Nor was the sublime more within their reach than the pathetick; for they never attempted that comprehension and expanse of thought which at once fills the whole mind, and of which the first effect is sudden astonishment, and the second rational admiration. Sublimity is produced by aggregation, and littleness by dispersion. Great thoughts are always general, and consist in positions not limited by exceptions, and in descriptions not descending to minuteness. It is with great propriety that subtlety, which in its original import means exility[4] of particles, is taken in its metaphorical meaning for nicety of distinction. Those writers who lay on the watch for novelty could have little hope of greatness; for great things cannot have escaped former observation. Their attempts were always analytick: they broke every image into fragments, and could no more represent by their slender conceits and laboured particularities the prospects of nature or the scenes of life, than he who dissects a sun-beam with a prism can exhibit the wide effulgence of a summer noon.

What they wanted however of the sublime they endeavoured to supply by hyperbole; their amplification had no limits: they left not only reason but fancy behind them, and produced combinations of confused magnificence that not only could not be credited, but could not be imagined.

Yet great labour directed by great abilities is never wholly lost: if they frequently threw away their wit upon false conceits, they likewise sometimes struck out unexpected truth: if their conceits were far-fetched, they were often worth the carriage. To write on their plan it was at least necessary to read and think. No man could be born a metaphysical poet, nor assume the dignity of a writer by descriptions copied from descriptions, by imitations borrowed from imitations, by traditional imagery and hereditary similes, by readiness of rhyme and volubility of syllables.

In perusing the works of this race of authors the mind is exercised either by recollection or inquiry; either something already learned is to

---

4 "Thinness, slenderness, meagreness" (*OED*).

be retrieved, or something new is to be examined. If their greatness seldom
elevates their acuteness often surprises; if the imagination is not always
gratified, at least the powers of reflection and comparison are employed;
and in the mass of materials, which ingenious absurdity has thrown together, genuine wit and useful knowledge may be sometimes found,
buried perhaps in grossness of expression, but useful to those who know
their value, and such as, when they are expanded to perspicuity and
polished to elegance, may give lustre to works which have more propriety
though less copiousness of sentiment.

This kind of writing, which was, I believe, borrowed from Marino[5]
and his followers, had been recommended by the example of Donne, a
man of very extensive and various knowledge, and by Jonson, whose
manner resembled that of Donne more in the ruggedness of his lines than
in the cast of his sentiments.

When their reputation was high they had undoubtedly more imitators than time has left behind. Their immediate successors, of whom any
remembrance can be said to remain, were Suckling, Waller, Denham,
Cowley, Cleiveland,[6] and Milton. Denham and Waller sought another
way to fame, by improving the harmony of our numbers. Milton tried
the metaphysick style only in his lines upon Hobson the Carrier.[7] Cowley
adopted it, and excelled his predecessors; having as much sentiment and
more musick. Suckling neither improved versification nor abounded in
conceits. The fashionable style remained chiefly with Cowley: Suckling
could not reach it, and Milton disdained it.

<hr>

5 Giovanni Battisti Marini, or Marino (1569–1625), Italian poet whose work is
characterized by its extravagant "conceits," or fanciful and affected metaphors.
6 Sir John Suckling (1609–1642?), Edmund Waller (1606–1687), Sir John Denham
(1615–1669), John Cleveland (1613–1658). Denham and Waller were admired in the eighteenth century for, respectively, their "strength" and "sweetness." Cleveland produced particularly extravagant examples of the "metaphysical" style.
7 Milton wrote two poems on Hobson, both at the time of the carrier's death in
1631. One ("On the University Carrier") begins, "Here lies old Hobson, Death has broke
his girt,/And here alas, hath laid him in the dirt." The other ("Another on the Same") also
relies heavily on puns and conceits.

LIFE OF MILTON

In Johnson's account of John Milton (1608–1674), the critic displays his religious and political prejudices and sometimes allows them to blind him to Milton's true merits. His condemnation of *Lycidas* (here included) is one of the most famous misjudgments in the history of English criticism. Yet the extended critical account of Milton's poetry, which concludes the long biography, includes lavish praise; its final judgment ("his work is not the greatest of heroick poems, only because it is not the first") is surely as positive as one could ask. Johnson conscientiously mingles praise and blame; in his attack on *Lycidas*, he reveals his general adherence to classical principles in his discussion of the epic and his demand for emotion in literature. The bias which mars his account of Milton's life frequently disappears entirely in his evaluation of the poetry.

Life of Milton

In the examination of Milton's poetical works I shall pay so much regard to time as to begin with his juvenile productions. For his earlier pieces he seems to have had a degree of fondness not very laudable: what he has once written he resolves to preserve, and gives to the publick an unfinished poem, which he broke off because he was "nothing satisfied with what he had done", supposing his readers less nice than himself. These preludes to his future labours are in Italian, Latin, and English. Of the Italian I cannot pretend to speak as a critick, but I have heard them commended by a man well qualified to decide their merit. The Latin pieces are lusciously elegant; but the delight which they afford is rather by the exquisite imitation of the ancient writers, by the purity of the diction, and the harmony of the numbers, than by any power of invention or vigour of sentiment. They are not all of equal value; the elegies excell the odes, and some of the exercises on Gunpowder Treason might have been spared.

The English poems, though they make no promises of *Paradise Lost*, have this evidence of genius, that they have a cast original and unborrowed. But their peculiarity is not excellence: if they differ from verses of others, they differ for the worse; for they are too often distinguished by repulsive harshness; the combinations of words are new, but they are not pleasing; the rhymes and epithets seem to be laboriously sought and violently applied.

That in the early parts of his life he wrote with much care appears from his manuscripts, happily preserved at Cambridge,[1] in which many of his smaller works are found as they were first written, with the subsequent corrections. Such reliques shew how excellence is acquired: what we hope ever to do with ease we may learn first to do with diligence.

Those who admire the beauties of this great poet sometimes force their own judgement into false approbation of his little pieces, and prevail upon themselves to think that admirable which is only singular. All that short compositions can commonly attain is neatness and elegance. Milton never learned the art of doing little things with grace; he overlooked the milder excellence of suavity and softness: he was a "Lion" that had no skill "in dandling the Kid."[2]

One of the poems on which much praise has been bestowed is *Lycidas*; of which the diction is harsh, the rhymes uncertain, and the numbers unpleasing. What beauty there is we must therefore seek in the sentiments and images. It is not to be considered as the effusion of real passion; for passion runs not after remote allusions and obscure opinions. Passion plucks no berries from the myrtle and ivy, nor calls upon Arethuse and Mincius, nor tells of "rough satyrs and fauns with cloven heel." "Where there is leisure for fiction there is little grief."

In this poem there is no nature, for there is no truth; there is no art, for there is nothing new. Its form is that of a pastoral, easy, vulgar, and therefore disgusting:[3] whatever images it can supply are long ago exhausted; and its inherent improbability always forces dissatisfaction on the mind. When Cowley tells of Hervey[4] that they studied together, it is easy to suppose how much he must miss the companion of his labours and the partner of his discoveries; but what image of tenderness can be excited by these lines!

---

1 A volume of Milton manuscripts still exists in Trinity College, Cambridge. It includes original drafts of 10 of the 22 English pieces in the 1645 collection of Milton's English and Latin poems.

2 *Paradise Lost*, IV. 343–44: "Sporting the lion ramp'd, and in his paw/Dandl'd the kid."

3 Offensive to the sensibilities.

4 William Hervey, a friend of Cowley's from Cambridge, about whom he wrote a moving elegy in 1642, five years after *Lycidas*.

> *We drove a field, and both together heard*
> *What time the grey fly winds her sultry horn,*
> *Battening our flocks with the fresh dews of night.*

We know that they never drove a field, and that they had no flocks to batten; and though it be allowed that the representation may be allegorical, the true meaning is so uncertain and remote that it is never sought because it cannot be known when it is found.

Among the flocks and copses and flowers appear the heathen deities, Jove and Phoebus, Neptune and Aeolus, with a long train of mythological imagery, such as a College easily supplies. Nothing can less display knowledge or less exercise invention than to tell how a shepherd has lost his companion and must now feed his flocks alone, without any judge of his skill in piping; and how one god asks another god what is become of Lycidas, and how neither god can tell. He who thus grieves will excite no sympathy; he who thus praises will confer no honour.

This poem has yet a grosser fault. With these trifling fictions are mingled the most awful and sacred truths, such as ought never to be polluted with such irreverent combinations. The shepherd likewise is now a feeder of sheep, and afterwards an ecclesiastical pastor, a superintendent of a Christian flock. Such equivocations are always unskilful; but here they are indecent,[5] and at least approach to impiety, of which, however, I believe the writer not to have been conscious.

Such is the power of reputation justly acquired that its blaze drives away the eye from nice examination. Surely no man could have fancied that he read *Lycidas* with pleasure had he not known its author.

Of the two pieces, *L'Allegro* and *Il Penseroso*, I believe opinion is uniform; every man that reads them, reads them with pleasure. The author's design is not, what Theobald[6] has remarked, merely to shew how objects derived their colours from the mind, by representing the operation of the same things upon the gay and the melancholy temper, or upon the

---

5 I.e., unsuitable.

6 Lewis Theobald, Preface to *The Works of Shakespeare* (1734) pp. xix–xx. William Warburton claimed that he had provided this "observation," which Theobald "did not understand," and that Theobald had made it obscure by contracting it (Letter from Warburton to the Rev. Thomas Birch, November 24, 1737, printed in J. B. Nichols, *Illustrations of Literature*, II. 81).

same man as he is differently disposed; but rather how, among the successive variety of appearances, every disposition of mind takes hold on those by which it may be gratified.

The *chearful* man hears the lark in the morning; the *pensive* man hears the nightingale in the evening. The *chearful* man sees the cock strut, and hears the horn and hounds echo in the wood; then walks "not unseen" to observe the glory of the rising sun or listen to the singing milkmaid, and view the labours of the plowman and the mower; then casts his eyes about him over scenes of smiling plenty, and looks up to the distant tower, the residence of some fair inhabitant: thus he pursues rural gaiety through a day of labour or of play, and delights himself at night with the fanciful narratives of superstitious ignorance.

The *pensive* man at one time walks "unseen" to muse at midnight, and at another hears the sullen curfew. If the weather drives him home he sits in a room lighted only by "glowing embers"; or by a lonely lamp outwatches the North Star to discover the habitation of separate souls, and varies the shades of meditation by contemplating the magnificent or pathetick scenes of tragick and epick poetry. When the morning comes, a morning gloomy with rain and wind, he walks into the dark trackless woods, falls asleep by some murmuring water, and with melancholy enthusiasm expects some dream of prognostication or some musick played by aerial performers.

Both Mirth and Melancholy are solitary, silent inhabitants of the breast that neither receive nor transmit communication; no mention is therefore made of a philosophical friend or a pleasant companion. The seriousness does not arise from any participation of calamity, nor the gaiety from the pleasures of the bottle.

The man of *chearfulness* having exhausted the country tries what "towered cities" will afford, and mingles with scenes of splendor, gay assemblies, and nuptial festivities; but he mingles a mere spectator as, when the learned comedies of Johnson or the wild dramas of Shakespeare are exhibited, he attends the theatre.

The *pensive* man never loses himself in crowds, but walks the cloister or frequents the cathedral. Milton probably had not yet forsaken the Church.

Both his characters delight in musick; but he seems to think that chearful notes would have obtained from Pluto a compleat dismission of

Eurydice, of whom solemn sounds only procured a conditional release.[7]

For the old age of Chearfulness he makes no provision; but Melancholy he conducts with great dignity to the close of life. His Chearfulness is without levity, and his Pensiveness without asperity.

Through these two poems the images are properly selected and nicely distinguished, but the colours of the diction seem not sufficiently discriminated. I know not whether the characters are kept sufficiently apart. No mirth can, indeed, be found in his melancholy; but I am afraid that I always meet some melancholy in his mirth. They are two noble efforts of imagination.

The greatest of his juvenile performances is the *Mask of Comus*, in which may very plainly be discovered the dawn or twilight of *Paradise Lost*. Milton appears to have formed very early that system of diction and mode of verse which his maturer judgement approved, and from which he never endeavoured nor desired to deviate.

Nor does *Comus* afford only a specimen of his language: it exhibits likewise his power of description and his vigour of sentiment, employed in the praise and defence of virtue. A work more truly poetical is rarely found; allusions, images, and descriptive epithets embellish almost every period with lavish decoration. As a series of lines, therefore, it may be considered as worthy of all the admiration with which the votaries have received it.

As a drama it is deficient. The action is not probable. A Masque, in those parts where supernatural intervention is admitted, must indeed be given up to all the freaks of imagination; but so far as the action is merely human it ought to be reasonable, which can hardly be said of the conduct of the two brothers, who, when their sister sinks with fatigue in a pathless wilderness, wander both away in search of berries too far to find their way back, and leave a helpless Lady to all the sadness and danger of solitude. This however is a defect over-balanced by its convenience.

What deserves more reprehension is that the prologue spoken in the wild wood by the attendant Spirit is addressed to the audience; a mode of communication so contrary to the nature of dramatick representation that no precedents can support it.

The discourse of the Spirit is too long, an objection that may be

---

7 Wife of Orpheus, the mythical poet, who after her death visited the underworld and so moved Pluto, its king, with his lyre that he was allowed to take her back to earth, on condition that he not look behind to see that she was following him. He violated this condition, and lost her forever. In *L'Allegro* Milton suggests that mirthful music "would have won the ear/Of Pluto, to have quite set free/His half-regained Eurydice" (ll. 148–50).

made to almost all the following speeches; they have not the spriteliness of a dialogue animated by reciprocal contention, but seem rather declamations deliberately composed and formally repeated on a moral question. The auditor therefore listens as to a lecture, without passion, without anxiety.

The song of Comus has airiness and jollity; but, what may recommend Milton's morals as well as his poetry, the invitations to pleasure are so general that they excite no distinct images of corrupt enjoyment, and take no dangerous hold on the fancy.

The following soliloquies of Comus and the Lady are elegant, but tedious. The song must owe much to the voice, if it ever can delight. At last the Brothers enter, with too much tranquillity; and when they have feared lest their sister should be in danger, and hoped that she is not in danger, the Elder makes a speech in praise of chastity, and the Younger finds how fine it is to be a philosopher.

Then descends the Spirit in form of a shepherd; and the Brother, instead of being in haste to ask his help, praises his singing, and enquires his business in that place. It is remarkable that at this interview the Brother is taken with a short fit of rhyming. The Spirit relates that the Lady is in the power of Comus, the Brother moralises again, and the Spirit makes a long narration, of no use because it is false, and therefore unsuitable to a good Being.

In all these parts the language is poetical and the sentiments are generous, but there is something wanting to allure attention.

The dispute between the Lady and Comus is the most animated and affecting scene of the drama, and wants nothing but a brisker reciprocation of objections and replies, to invite attention and detain it.

The songs are vigorous and full of imagery; but they are harsh in their diction, and not very musical in their numbers.

Throughout the whole the figures are too bold and the language too luxuriant for dialogue: it is a drama in the epick style, inelegantly splendid, and tediously instructive.

The *Sonnets* were written in different parts of Milton's life upon different occasions. They deserve not any particular criticism; for of the best it can only be said that they are not bad, and perhaps only the eighth and the twenty-first are truly entitled to this slender commendation.[8] The fabrick of a sonnet, however adapted to the Italian language, has

---

8 The eighth sonnet begins, "Captain or Colonel, or Knight in arms"; the twenty-first opens, "Cyriack, whose grandsire on the royal bench."

never succeeded in ours, which, having greater variety of termination, requires the rhymes to be often changed.

Those little pieces may be dispatched without much anxiety; a greater work calls for greater care. I am now to examine *Paradise Lost*, a poem which, considered with respect to design, may claim the first place, and with respect to performance the second, among the productions of the human mind.[9]

By the general consent of criticks the first praise of genius is due to the writer of an epick poem, as it requires an assemblage of all the powers which are singly sufficient for other compositions. Poetry is the art of uniting pleasure with truth, by calling imagination to the help of reason. Epick poetry undertakes to teach the most important truths by the most pleasing precepts, and therefore relates some great event in the most affecting manner. History must supply the writer with the rudiments of narration, which he must improve and exalt by a nobler art, must animate by dramatick energy, and diversify by retrospection and anticipation; morality must teach him the exact bounds and different shades of vice and virtue; from policy and the practice of life he has to learn the discriminations of character and the tendency of the passions, either single or combined; and physiology must supply him with illustrations and images. To put these materials to poetical use is required an imagination capable of painting nature and realizing fiction. Nor is he yet a poet till he has attained the whole extension of his language, distinguished all the delicacies of phrase, and all the colours of words, and learned to adjust their different sounds to all the varieties of metrical modulation.

Bossu[10] is of opinion that the poet's first work is to find a *moral*, which his fable is afterwards to illustrate and establish. This seems to have been the process only of Milton: the moral of other poems is incidental and consequent; in Milton's only it is essential and intrinsick. His purpose was the most useful and the most arduous: "to vindicate the ways of God to man"; to shew the reasonableness of religion, and the necessity of obedience to the Divine Law.

To convey this moral there must be a *fable*, a narration artfully constructed so as to excite curiosity and surprise expectation. In this part of his work Milton must be confessed to have equalled every other poet. He has involved in his account of the Fall of Man the events which pre-

---

9 Presumably Johnson would have granted first place to the *Iliad*.
10 René Le Bossu, author of *Treatise of the Epick Poem* (1675; English trans., 1695), which codified a set of "rules" for the epic.

ceded, and those that were to follow it: he has interwoven the whole system of theology with such propriety that every part appears to be necessary, and scarcely any recital is wished shorter for the sake of quickening the progress of the main action.

The subject of an epick poem is naturally an event of great importance. That of Milton is not the destruction of a city, the conduct of a colony, or the foundation of an empire. His subject is the fate of worlds, the revolutions of heaven and of earth; rebellion against the Supreme King raised by the highest order of created beings; the overthrow of their host and the punishment of their crime; the creation of a new race of reasonable creatures; their original happiness and innocence, their forfeiture of immortality, and their restoration to hope and peace.

Great events can be hastened or retarded only by persons of elevated dignity. Before the greatness displayed in Milton's poem all other greatness shrinks away. The weakest of his agents are the highest and noblest of human beings, the original parents of mankind; with whose actions the elements consented; on whose rectitude or deviation of will depended the state of terrestrial nature and the condition of all the future inhabitants of the globe.

Of the other agents in the poem the chief are such as it is irreverence to name on slight occasions. The rest were lower powers;

> *of which the least could wield*
> *Those elements, and arm him with the force*
> *Of all their regions;*[11]

powers which only the controul of Omnipotence restrains from laying creation waste, and filling the vast expanse of space with ruin and confusion. To display the motives and actions of beings thus superiour, so far as human reason can examine them or human imagination represent them, is the task which this mighty poet has undertaken and performed.

In the examination of epick poems much speculation is commonly employed upon the *characters*. The characters in the *Paradise Lost* which admit of examination are those of angels and of man; of angels good and evil, of man in his innocent and sinful state.

Among the angels the virtue of Raphael is mild and placid, of easy condescension and free communication; that of Michael is regal and lofty, and, as may seem, attentive to the dignity of his own nature. Abdiel and

---

11 VI. 221–23, slightly altered.

Gabriel appear occasionally, and act as every incident requires; the solitary fidelity of Abdiel is very amiably painted.

Of the evil angels the characters are more diversified. To Satan, as Addison observes,[12] such sentiments are given as suit "the most exalted and most depraved being." Milton has been censured by Clarke[13] for the impiety which sometimes breaks from Satan's mouth. For there are thoughts, as he justly remarks, which no observation of character can justify, because no good man would willingly permit them to pass, however transiently, through his own mind. To make Satan speak as a rebel, without any such expressions as might taint the reader's imagination, was indeed one of the great difficulties in Milton's undertaking, and I cannot but think that he has extricated himself with great happiness. There is in Satan's speeches little that can give pain to a pious ear. The language of rebellion cannot be the same with that of obedience. The malignity of Satan foams in haughtiness and obstinacy; but his expressions are commonly general, and no otherwise offensive than as they are wicked.

The other chiefs of the celestial rebellion are very judiciously discriminated in the first and second books; and the ferocious character of Moloch appears, both in the battle and the council, with exact consistency.

To Adam and to Eve are given during their innocence such sentiments as innocence can generate and utter. Their love is pure benevolence and mutual veneration; their repasts are without luxury and their diligence without toil. Their addresses to their Maker have little more than the voice of admiration and gratitude. Fruition left them nothing to ask, and Innocence left them nothing to fear.

But with guilt enter distrust and discord, mutual accusation, and stubborn self-defence; they regard each other with alienated minds, and dread their Creator as the avenger of their transgression. At last they seek shelter in his mercy, soften to repentance, and melt in supplication. Both before and after the Fall the superiority of Adam is diligently sustained.

Of the *probable* and the *marvellous*, two parts of a vulgar epick poem which immerge the critick in deep consideration, the *Paradise Lost* requires little to be said. It contains the history of a miracle, of Creation and Redemption; it displays the power and the mercy of the Supreme Being: the probable therefore is marvellous, and the marvellous is probable.

---

12 *Spectator* 303.
13 John Clarke, *Essay Upon Study* (1731), p. 204.

The substance of the narrative is truth; and as truth allows no choice, it is, like necessity, superior to rule. To the accidental or adventitious parts, as to every thing human, some slight exceptions may be made. But the main fabrick is immovably supported.

It is justly remarked by Addison that this poem has, by the nature of its subject, the advantage above all others, that it is universally and perpetually interesting. All mankind will, through all ages, bear the same relation to Adam and to Eve, and must partake of that good and evil which extend to themselves.

Of the *machinery*, so called from Θεός ἀπό μηχανῆς,[14] by which is meant the occasional interposition of supernatural power, another fertile topic of critical remarks, here is no room to speak, because every thing is done under the immediate and visible direction of Heaven; but the rule is so far observed that no part of the action could have been accomplished by any other means.

Of *episodes* I think there are only two, contained in Raphael's relation of the war in heaven and Michael's prophetick account of the changes to happen in this world. Both are closely connected with the great action; one was necessary to Adam as a warning, the other as a consolation.

To the compleatness or *integrity* of the design nothing can be objected; it has distinctly and clearly what Aristotle requires, a beginning, a middle, and an end.[15] These is perhaps no poem of the same length from which so little can be taken without apparent mutilation. Here are no funeral games, nor is there any long description of a shield,[16] The short digressions at the beginning of the third, seventh, and ninth books might doubtless be spared; but superfluities so beautiful who would take away? or who does not wish that the authour of the *Iliad* had gratified succeeding ages with a little knowledge of himself? Perhaps no passages are more frequently or more attentively read than those extrinsick paragraphs; and, since the end of poetry is pleasure, that cannot be unpoetical with which all are pleased.

The questions, whether the action of the poem be strictly *one*, whether the poem can be properly termed *heroick*, and who is the hero, are raised by such readers as draw their principles of judgement rather

---

14 "God from the machine." The phrase alludes to the apparatus used in the ancient theater for the descent of a deity.

15 In the *Poetics*, VII. 3.

16 Funeral games occur in *Iliad*, XXIII, and *Aeneid*, V; descriptions of shields in *Iliad*, XVIII, and *Aeneid*, VIII.

from books than from reason. Milton, though he intituled *Paradise Lost* only a "poem," yet calls it himself "heroick song." Dryden, petulantly and indecently,[17] denies the heroism of Adam because he was overcome; but there is no reason why the hero should not be unfortunate except established practice, since success and virtue do not go necessarily together. Cato is the hero of Lucan, but Lucan's authority will not be suffered by Quintilian to decide.[18] However, if success be necessary, Adam's deceiver was at last crushed; Adam was restored to his Maker's favour, and therefore may securely resume his human rank.

After the scheme and fabrick of the poem must be considered its component parts, the sentiments, and the diction.

The *sentiments*, as expressive of manners or appropriated to characters, are for the greater part unexceptionably just.

Splendid passages containing lessons of morality or precepts of prudence occur seldom. Such is the original formation of this poem that as it admits no human manners till the Fall, it can give little assistance to human conduct. Its end is to raise the thoughts above sublunary cares or pleasures. Yet the praise of that fortitude, with which Abdiel[19] maintained his singularity of virtue against the scorn of multitudes, may be accommodated to all times; and Raphael's reproof of Adam's curiosity after the planetary motions, with the answer returned by Adam,[20] may be confidently opposed to any rule of life which any poet has delivered.

The thoughts which are occasionally called forth in the progress are such as could only be produced by an imagination in the highest degree fervid and active, to which materials were supplied by incessant study and unlimited curiosity. The heat of Milton's mind might be said to sublimate[21] his learning, to throw off into his work the spirit of science, unmingled with its grosser parts.

He had considered creation in its whole extent, and his descriptions are therefore learned. He had accustomed his imagination to unrestrained indulgence, and his conceptions therefore were extensive. The characteristick quality of his poem is sublimity. He sometimes descends to the

---

17 Tastelessly.

18 Cato, hero of Lucan's epic *Pharsalia*, is unsuccessful and dies in the end. Quintilian does not directly discuss this fact, but remarks that Lucan is more suitable for imitation by the orator than the poet (*Institutio Oratoria*, X. 90).

19 See *Paradise Lost*, V. 875ff. The seraph Abdiel resists Satan's temptations: "Among the faithless, faithful only he."

20 *Ibid.*, VIII. 15ff.

21 "To act upon a substance so as to produce a refined product" (*OED*).

elegant, but his element is the great. He can occasionally invest himself with grace; but his natural port is gigantick loftiness. He can please when pleasure is required; but it is his peculiar power to astonish.

He seems to have been well acquainted with his own genius, and to know what it was that Nature had bestowed upon him more bountifully than upon others; the power of displaying the vast, illuminating the splendid, enforcing the awful, darkening the gloomy, and aggravating the dreadful: he therefore chose a subject on which too much could not be said, on which he might tire his fancy without the censure of extravagance.

The appearances of nature and the occurrences of life did not satiate his appetite of greatness. To paint things as they are requires a minute attention, and employs the memory rather than the fancy. Milton's delight was to sport in the wide regions of possibility; reality was a scene too narrow for his mind. He sent his faculties out upon discovery, into worlds where only imagination can travel, and delighted to form new modes of existence, and furnish sentiment and action to superior beings, to trace the counsels of hell, or accompany the choirs of heaven.

But he could not be always in other worlds: he must sometimes revisit earth, and tell of things visible and known. When he cannot raise wonder by the sublimity of his mind he gives delight by its fertility.

Whatever be his subject he never fails to fill the imagination. But his images and descriptions of the scenes or operations of Nature do not seem to be always copied from original form, nor to have the freshness, raciness, and energy of immediate observation. He saw Nature, as Dryden expresses it, "through the spectacles of books";[22] and on most occasions calls learning to his assistance. The garden of Eden brings to his mind the vale of Enna, where Proserpine was gathering flowers.[23] Satan makes his way through fighting elements, like Argo between the Cyanean rocks, or Ulysses between the two *Sicilian* whirlpools, when he shunned Charybdis "on the larboard".[24] The mythological allusions have been justly censured, as not being always used with notice of their vanity; but they

22 Dryden says that Shakespeare "needed not the spectacles of books to read nature" (*Essay on Dramatic Poesy*, first pub. 1668; *Essays*, ed. W.P. Ker [1926], I, 79).

23 *Paradise Lost*, IV. 268ff.

24 Johnson refers to Milton's comparison of Satan (*Ibid.* II. 1016ff.) to Jason's ship Argo when it sought the Golden Fleece (Apollonius, *Argonautica*, II. 528–647) and to Odysseus' struggle to escape between Scylla and Charybdis (*Odyssey*, XII. 73ff.).

contribute variety to the narration, and produce an alternate exercise of the memory and the fancy.

His similes are less numerous and more various than those of his predecessors. But he does not confine himself within the limits of rigorous comparison: his great excellence is amplitude, and he expands the adventitious image beyond the dimensions which the occasion required. Thus, comparing the shield of Satan to the orb of the Moon, he crowds the imagination with the discovery of the telescope and all the wonders which the telescope discovers.[25]

Of his moral sentiments it is hardly praise to affirm that they excel those of all other poets; for this superiority he was indebted to his acquaintance with the sacred writings. The ancient epick poets, wanting the light of Revelation, were very unskilful teachers of virtue: their principal characters may be great, but they are not amiable. The reader may rise from their works with a greater degree of active or passive fortitude, and sometimes of prudence; but he will be able to carry away few precepts of justice, and none of mercy.

From the Italian writers it appears that the advantages of even Christian knowledge may be possessed in vain. Ariosto's pravity[26] is generally known; and, though the *Deliverance of Jerusalem*[27] may be considered as a sacred subject, the poet has been very sparing of moral instruction.

In Milton every line breathes sanctity of thought and purity of manners, except when the train of the narration requires the introduction of the rebellious spirits; and even they are compelled to acknowledge their subjection to God in such a manner as excites reverence and confirms piety.

Of human beings there are but two; but those two are the parents of mankind, venerable before their fall for dignity and innocence, and amiable after it for repentance and submission. In their first state their affection is tender without weakness, and their piety sublime without presumption. When they have sinned they shew how discord begins in mutual frailty, and how it ought to cease in mutual forbearance; how

---

25 *Ibid.*, I. 283ff.

26 Ludovico Ariosto (1471–1533), author of *Orlando Furioso*, an epic treatment of the Roland story—obviously, a secular subject.

27 *Jerusalem Delivered* (1575), by Torquato Tasso (1544–1595), an epic that rivaled Ariosto's in popularity.

confidence of the divine favour is forfeited by sin, and how hope of pardon may be obtained by penitence and prayer. A state of innocence we can only conceive, if indeed in our present misery it be possible to conceive it; but the sentiments and worship proper to a fallen and offending being we have all to learn, as we have all to practise.

The poet whatever be done is always great. Our progenitors in their first state conversed with angels; even when folly and sin had degraded them they had not in their humiliation "the port of mean suitors"; and they rise again to reverential regard when we find that their prayers were heard.

As human passions did not enter the world before the Fall, there is in the *Paradise Lost* little opportunity for the pathetick; but what little there is has not been lost. That passion which is peculiar to rational nature, the anguish arising from the consciousness of transgression and the horrours attending the sense of the Divine Displeasure, are very justly described and forcibly impressed. But the passions are moved only on one occasion; sublimity is the general and prevailing quality in this poem— sublimity variously modified, sometimes descriptive, sometimes argumentative.

The defects and faults of *Paradise Lost*, for faults and defects every work of man must have, it is the business of impartial criticism to discover. As in displaying the excellence of Milton I have not made long quotations, because of selecting beauties there had been no end, I shall in the same general manner mention that which seems to deserve censure; for what Englishman can take delight in transcribing passages, which, if they lessen the reputation of Milton, diminish in some degree the honour of our country?

The generality of my scheme does not admit the frequent notice of verbal inaccuracies which Bentley,[28] perhaps better skilled in grammar than in poetry, has often found, though he sometimes made them, and which he imputed to the obtrusions of a reviser whom the author's blindness obliged him to employ. A supposition rash and groundless, if he thought it true; and vile and pernicious, if, as is said, he in private allowed it to be false.

---

28 Richard Bentley (1662–1742) applied in his edition of Milton (1732) the practices of editorial interpolation and emendation that had distinguished his editions of classical authors, with less happy results.

The plan of *Paradise Lost* has this inconvenience, that it comprises neither human actions nor human manners. The man and woman who act and suffer are in a state which no other man or woman can ever know. The reader finds no transaction in which he can be engaged, beholds no condition in which he can by any effort of imagination place himself; he has, therefore, little natural curiosity or sympathy.

We all, indeed, feel the effects of Adam's disobedience; we all sin like Adam, and like him must all bewail our offences; we have restless and insidious enemies in the fallen angels, and in the blessed spirits we have guardians and friends; in the Redemption of mankind we hope to be included: in the description of heaven and hell we are surely interested, as we are all to reside hereafter either in the regions of horrour or of bliss.

But these truths are too important to be new: they have been taught to our infancy; they have mingled with our solitary thoughts and familiar conversation, and are habitually interwoven with the whole texture of life. Being therefore not new they raise no unaccustomed emotion in the mind: what we knew before we cannot learn; what is not unexpected, cannot surprise.

Of the ideas suggested by these awful scenes, from some we recede with reverence, except when stated hours require their association; and from others we shrink with horrour, or admit them only as salutary inflictions, as counterposes to our interests and passions. Such images rather obstruct the career of fancy than incite it.

Pleasure and terrour are indeed the genuine sources of poetry; but poetical pleasure must be such as human imagination can at least conceive, and poetical terrour such as human strength and fortitude may combat. The good and evil of Eternity are too ponderous for the wings of wit; the mind sinks under them in passive helplessness, content with calm belief and humble adoration.

Known truths however may take a different appearance, and be conveyed to the mind by a new train of intermediate images. This Milton has undertaken, and performed with pregnancy and vigour of mind peculiar to himself. Whoever considers the few radical positions which the Scriptures afforded him will wonder by what energetick operations he expanded them to such extent and ramified them to so much variety, restrained as he was by religious reverence from licentiousness of fiction.

Here is a full display of the united force of study and genius; of a great accumulation of materials, with judgement to digest and fancy to combine them: Milton was able to select from nature or from story, from ancient fable or from modern science, whatever could illustrate or adorn

SAMUEL JOHNSON																																			205

his thoughts. An accumulation of knowledge impregnated his mind, fermented by study and exalted by imagination.

It has been therefore said without an indecent hyperbole by one of his encomiasts, that in reading *Paradise Lost* we read a book of universal knowledge.[29]

But original deficience cannot be supplied. The want of human interest is always felt. *Paradise Lost* is one of the books which the reader admires and lays down, and forgets to take up again. None ever wished it longer than it is. Its perusal is a duty rather than a pleasure. We read Milton for instruction, retire harassed and overburdened, and look elsewhere for recreation; we desert our master, and seek for companions.

Another inconvenience of Milton's design is that it requires the description of what cannot be described, the agency of spirits. He saw that immateriality supplied no images, and that he could not show angels acting but by instruments of action; he therefore invested them with form and matter. This being necessary was therefore defensible; and he should have secured the consistency of his system by keeping immateriality out of sight, and enticing his reader to drop it from his thoughts. But he has unhappily perplexed his poetry with his philosophy. His infernal and celestial powers are sometimes pure spirit and sometimes animated body. When Satan walks with his lance upon the "burning marle" he has a body; when in his passage between hell and the new world he is in danger of sinking in the vacuity and is supported by a gust of rising vapours he has a body; when he animates the toad he seems to be mere spirit that can penetrate matter at pleasure; when he "starts up in his own shape," he has at least a determined form; and when he is brought before Gabriel he has "a spear and a shield," which he had the power of hiding in the toad, though the arms of the contending angels are evidently material.[30]

The vulgar inhabitants of Pandaemonium, being "incorporeal spirits," are "at large though without number"[31] in a limited space, yet in the battle when they were overwhelmed by mountains their armour hurt them, "crushed in upon their substance, now grown gross by sin-

---

29 Perhaps the Latin verses of Dr. Samuel Barrow, beginning, "*Qui legis Amissum Paradisum, grandia magni/Carmina Miltoni, quid nisi cuncta legis?*" ("You who read *Paradise Lost*, the great work by noble Milton, what do you read if not everything?") These are printed in *Paradise Lost*, ed. Thomas Newton, 2 vols. (London, 1770), Preface, p. 87.

30 The references in this paragraph are to I. 296, II. 931–38 (Satan's passage between hell and the new world, in which he is supported by vapors), IV. 800 (Satan animating the toad), IV. 819, and IV. 989.

31 I. 789.

ning."[32] This likewise happened to the uncorrupted angels, who were overthrown "the sooner for their arms, for unarmed they might easily as spirits have evaded by contraction or remove."[33] Even as spirits they are hardly spiritual, for "contraction" and "remove" are images of matter; but if they could have escaped without their armour, they might have escaped from it and left only the empty cover to be battered. Uriel, when he rides on a sun-beam, is material;[34] Satan is material when he is afraid of the prowess of Adam.[35]

The confusion of spirit and matter which pervades the whole narration of the war of heaven fills it with incongruity; and the book in which it is related is, I believe, the favourite of children, and gradually neglected as knowledge is increased.

After the operation of immaterial agents which cannot be explained may be considered that of allegorical persons, which have no real existence. To exalt causes into agents, to invest abstract ideas with form, and animate them with activity has always been the right of poetry. But such airy beings are for the most part suffered only to do their natural office, and retire. Thus Fame tells a tale and Victory hovers over a general or perches on a standard;[36] but Fame and Victory can do no more. To give them any real employment or ascribe to them any material agency is to make them allegorical no longer, but to shock the mind by ascribing effects to non-entity. In the *Prometheus* of Æschylus we see Violence and Strength, and in the *Alcestis* of Euripides we see Death, brought upon the stage, all as active persons of the drama; but no precedents can justify absurdity.

Milton's allegory of Sin and Death is undoubtedly faulty. Sin is indeed the mother of Death, and may be allowed to be the portress of hell; but when they stop the journey of Satan, a journey described as real, and when Death offers him battle, the allegory is broken.[37] That Sin and Death should have shewn the way to hell might have been allowed; but they cannot facilitate the passage by building a bridge, because the

---

32 "Their armor helped their harm, crushed in and bruised/Into their substance pent" (VI. 656–57); "Purest at first, now gross by sinning grown" (VI. 661).
33 VI. 595–97, slightly altered.
34 IV. 555–56.
35 IX. 484–87.
36 Rumor tells a tale in the opening of *2 Henry IV;* Victory sits on helms in Richard III, V. iii. 80.
37 *Paradise Lost*, II. 648ff.

difficulty of Satan's passage is described as real and sensible, and the bridge ought to be only figurative. The hell assigned to the rebellious spirits is described as not less local than the residence of man. It is placed in some distant part of space, separated from the regions of harmony and order by a chaotick waste and an unoccupied vacuity; but Sin and Death worked up a "mole of aggregated soil," cemented with asphaltus;[38] a work too bulky for ideal architects.

This unskilful allegory appears to me one of the greatest faults of the poem; and to this there was no temptation, but the author's opinion of its beauty.

To the conduct of the narrative some objections may be made. Satan is with great expectation brought before Gabriel in Paradise, and is suffered to go away unmolested. The creation of man is represented as the consequence of the vacuity left in heaven by the expulsion of the rebels; yet Satan mentions it as a report "rife in heaven" before his departure.[39]

To find sentiments for the state of innocence was very difficult; and something of anticipation perhaps is now and then discovered. Adam's discourse of dreams[40] seems not to be the speculation of a new-created being. I know not whether his answer to the angel's reproof for curiosity does not want something of propriety: it is the speech of a man acquainted with many other men. Some philosophical notions, especially when the philosophy is false, might have been better omitted. The angel in a comparison speaks of "timorous deer,"[41] before deer were yet timorous, and before Adam could understand the comparison.

Dryden remarks that Milton has some flats among his elevations. This is only to say that all the parts are not equal. In every work one part must be for the sake of others; a palace must have passages, a poem must have transitions. It is no more to be required that wit should always be blazing than that the sun should always stand at noon. In a great work there is a vicissitude of luminous and opaque parts, as there is in the world a succession of day and night. Milton, when he has expatiated in the sky, may be allowed sometimes to revisit earth; for what other author ever soared so high or sustained his flight so long?

---

38 X. 293. It is cemented with "asphaltic slime" (X. 298).
39 I. 650–51.
40 V. 100ff.
41 He speaks of a "timorous flock" (VI. 857).

Milton, being well versed in the Italian poets, appears to have borrowed often from them; and, as every man catches something from his companions, his desire of imitating Ariosto's levity has disgraced his work with the "Paradise of Fools"; a fiction not in itself ill-imagined, but too ludicrous for its place.[42]

His play on words, in which he delights too often; his equivocations, which Bentley endeavours to defend by the example of the ancients[43]; his unnecessary and ungraceful use of terms of art, it is not necessary to mention, because they are easily remarked and generally censured, and at last bear so little proportion to the whole that they scarcely deserve the attention of a critick.

Such are the faults of that wonderful performance *Paradise Lost*; which he who can put in balance with its beauties must be considered not as nice but as dull, as less to be censured for want of candour than pitied for want of sensibility.

Of *Paradise Regained* the general judgement seems now to be right, that it is in many parts elegant, and every-where instructive. It was not to be supposed that the writer of *Paradise Lost* could ever write without great effusions of fancy and exalted precepts of wisdom. The basis of *Paradise Regained* is narrow; a dialogue without action can never please like an union of the narrative and dramatick powers. Had this poem been written, not by Milton but by some imitator, it would have claimed and received universal praise.

If *Paradise Regained* has been too much depreciated, *Sampson Agonistes* has in requital been too much admired. It could only be by long prejudice and the bigotry of learning that Milton could prefer the ancient tragedies with their encumbrance of a chorus to the exhibitions of the French and English stages; and it is only by a blind confidence in the reputation of Milton that a drama can be praised in which the intermediate parts have neither cause nor consequence, neither hasten nor retard the catastrophe.

In this tragedy are however many particular beauties, many just sentiments and striking lines; but it wants that power of attracting attention which a well-connected plan produces.

------

42 *Paradise Lost*, III. 440ff., imitating *Orlando Furioso*, XXXIV. 577–680, which describes a realm where are found "all things vain, and all who in vain things/Built their fond hopes of glory or lasting fame."

43 *Paradise Lost*, ed. Richard Bentley (London, 1732), VI. 615n.

Milton would not have excelled in dramatick writing; he knew human nature only in the gross, and had never studied the shades of character, nor the combinations of concurring or the perplexity of contending passions. He had read much and knew what books could teach; but had mingled little in the world, and was deficient in the knowledge which experience must confer.

Through all his greater works there prevails an uniform peculiarity of *Diction*, a mode and cast of expression which bears little resemblance to that of any former writer, and which is so far removed from common use that an unlearned reader when he first opens his book finds himself surprised by a new language.

This novelty has been, by those who can find nothing wrong in Milton, imputed to his laborious endeavours after words suitable to the grandeur of his ideas. "Our language," says Addison, "sunk under him."[44] But the truth is, that both in prose and verse, he had formed his style by a perverse and pedantick principle. He was desirous to use English words with a foreign idiom. This in all his prose is discovered and condemned, for there judgement operates freely, neither softened by the beauty nor awed by the dignity of his thoughts; but such is the power of his poetry that his call is obeyed without resistance, the reader feels himself in captivity to a higher and a nobler mind, and criticism sinks in admiration.

Motion's style was not modified by his subject: what is shown with greater extent in *Paradise Lost* may be found in *Comus*. One source of his peculiarity was his familiarity with the Tuscan poets: the disposition of his words is, I think, frequently Italian; perhaps sometimes combined with other tongues. Of him, at last, may be said what Jonson says of Spenser, that "he wrote no language," but has formed what Butler calls "a Babylonish Dialect,"[45] in itself harsh and barbarous, but made by exalted genius and extensive. learning the vehicle of so much instruction and so much pleasure that, like other lovers, we find grace in its deformity.

Whatever be the faults of his diction he cannot want the praise of copiousness and variety; he was master of his language in its full extent, and has selected the melodious words with such diligence that from his book alone the Art of English Poetry might be learned.

After his diction something must be said of his versification. "The measure," he says, "is the English heroick verse without rhyme."[46] Of

---

44 *Spectator* 297.
45 *Hudibras*, I. 93.
46 Preface to *Paradise Lost*.

this mode he had many examples among the Italians, and some in his own country. The Earl of Surrey is said to have translated one of Virgil's books without rhyme,[47] and besides our tragedies a few short poems had appeared in blank verse; particularly one tending to reconcile the nation to Raleigh's wild attempt upon Guiana, and probably written by Raleigh himself.[48] These petty performances cannot be supposed to have much influenced Milton, who more probably took his hint from Trisino's *Italia Liberata*;[49] and, finding blank verse easier than rhyme, was desirous of persuading himself that it is better.

"Rhyme," he says, and says truly, "is no necessary adjunct of true poetry."[50] But perhaps of poetry as a mental operation metre or musick is no necessary adjunct; it is however by the musick of metre that poetry has been discriminated in all languages, and in languages melodiously constructed with a due proportion of long and short syllables metre is sufficient. But one language cannot communicate its rules to another; where metre is scanty and imperfect some help is necessary. The musick of the English heroick line strikes the ear so faintly that it is easily lost, unless all the syllables of every line co-operate together; this co-operation can be only obtained by the preservation of every verse unmingled with another as a distinct system of sounds, and this distinctness is obtained and preserved by the artifice of rhyme. The variety of pauses, so much boasted by the lovers of blank verse, changes the measures of an English poet to the periods of a declaimer; and there are only a few skilful and happy readers of Milton who enable their audience to perceive where the lines end or begin. "Blank verse," said an ingenious critick,"[51] seems to be verse only to the eye."

Poetry may subsist without rhyme, but English poetry will not often please; nor can rhyme ever be safely spared but where the subject is able to support itself. Blank verse makes some approach to that which is called the "lapidary style"; has neither the easiness of prose nor the melody

47 Henry Howard, Earl of Surrey (1517–1547) introduced blank verse into English with his translations of the second and fourth books of Virgil's *Aeneid*.

48 *De Guiana Carmen Epicum*, a poem of about 200 lines in blank verse, of which Raleigh is not the author.

49 *Italia Liberata da' Goti* (1548), by Giovanni Georgio Trissino (1478–1550), professedly an imitation of the *Iliad*, unrhymed.

50 "Rhyme being no necessary adjunct or true ornament of poem or good verse. . ." (Preface to *Paradise Lost*).

51 William Locke (1732–1810). The source of the quotation is unknown.

of numbers, and therefore tires by long continuance. Of the Italian writers without rhyme, whom Milton alleges as precedents, not one is popular; what reason could urge in its defence has been confuted by the ear.

But whatever be the advantage of rhyme I cannot prevail on myself to wish that Milton had been a rhymer, for I cannot wish his work to be other than it is; yet like other heroes he is to be admired rather than imitated. He that thinks himself capable of astonishing may write blank verse, but those that hope only to please must condescend to rhyme.

The highest praise of genius is original invention. Milton cannot be said to have contrived the structure of an epick poem, and therefore owes reverence to that vigour and amplitude of mind to which all generations must be indebted for the art of poetical narration, for the texture of the fable, the variation of incidents, the interposition of dialogue, and all the stratagems that surprise and enchain attention. But of all the borrowers from Homer Milton is perhaps the least indebted. He was naturally a thinker for himself, confident of his own abilities and disdainful of help or hindrance; he did not refuse admission to the thoughts or images of his predecessors, but he did not seek them. From his contemporaries he neither courted nor received support; there is in his writings nothing by which the pride of other authors might be gratified or favour gained, no exchange of praise nor solicitation of support. His great works were performed under discountenance and in blindness, but difficulties vanished at his touch; he was born for whatever is arduous; and his work is not the greatest of heroick poems, only because it is not the first.

LIFE OF POMFRET

T he life of Pomfret is a tour de force of economy. In just over three hundred words, Johnson succeeds in writing a biographical and critical account of a minor seventeenth-century poet, an account that offers his customary judicious evaluation and in which he states explicitly one of his most important general dicta ("he who pleases many must have some species of merit"). The *Life* in its entirety is here reprinted.

Life of Pomfret

O f Mr. John Pomfret nothing is known but from a slight and confused account prefixed to his poems by a nameless friend, who relates that he was the son of the Rev. Mr. Pomfret, rector of Luton in Bedfordshire, that he was bred at Cambridge, entered into orders, and was rector of Malden in Bedfordshire, and might have risen in the Church, but that when he applied to Dr. Compton, bishop of London, for institution to a living of considerable value, to which he had been presented,[1] he found a troublesome obstruction raised by a malicious interpretation of some passage in his *Choice*, from which it was inferred that he considered happiness as more likely to be found in the company of a mistress than of a wife.[2]

This reproach was easily obliterated; for it had happened to Pomfret as to almost all other men who plan schemes of life: he had departed from his purpose, and was then married.

The malice of his enemies had however a very fatal consequence;

---

1 He already held two livings.

2 *The Choice*, Pomfret's most famous poem, celebrated the classic theme of the golden mean. The offending passage begins, "Would bounteous Heaven once more indulge, I'd choose/(For who would so much satisfaction lose/As witty nymphs in conversation give)/ Near some obliging modest fair to live." Later in the poem, the poet announces, "I'd have no wife."

the delay constrained his attendance in London, where he caught the small-pox, and died in 1703, in the thirty-sixth year of his age.

He published his poems in 1699; and has been always the favourite of that class of readers, who without vanity or criticism seek only their own amusement.

His *Choice* exhibits a system of life adapted to common notions and equal to common expectations; such a state as affords plenty and tranquillity, without exclusion of intellectual pleasures. Perhaps no composition in our language has been oftener perused than Pomfret's *Choice*.[3]

In his other poems there is an easy volubility; the pleasure of smooth metre is afforded to the ear, and the mind is not oppressed with ponderous or entangled with intricate sentiment. He pleases many, and he who pleases many must have some species of merit.

---

3 It was long regarded as the most widely read of English poems.

Partly because Alexander Pope (1688–1744) was in Johnson's time a subject of lively literary controversy, Johnson devoted particularly meticulous attention to his account of this poet and his works. The biographical section of the *Life of Pope* is especially masterful in its compassionate yet judicious assessment of the ambiguities of Pope's character and career. Many of its "facts" have been discredited, but it provides a memorable portrayal of Pope as a man. The critical portion of the biography, part of which is reprinted here, is equally compelling. Modern commentators have demonstrated that Johnson was, in fact, reacting to specific judgments on Pope offered by other eighteenth-century critics. Perhaps this fact, with its implication that Johnson brought to his work the fervor of the controversialist, helps to account for the vitality of his observations—perceptive, accurate, and finally moving in the famous question, "If Pope be not a poet, where is poetry to be found?"

Life of Pope

Of *The Dunciad* the hint is confessedly taken from Dryden's *Mac Flecknoe,*[1] but the plan is so enlarged and diversified as justly to claim the praise of an original, and affords perhaps the best specimen that has yet appeared of personal satire ludicrously pompous.

That the design was moral, whatever the author might tell either his readers or himself, I am not convinced. The first motive was the desire of revenging the contempt with which Theobald had treated his *Shakespeare,*[2] and regaining the honour which he had lost, by crushing his opponent. Theobald was not of bulk enough to fill a poem, and therefore

---

1 A satiric poem (1682) whose theme is the coronation of a King of Dullness.
2 Lewis Theobald (1688–1744) attacked Pope's edition of Shakespeare (1723) in *Shakespeare Restored; or, A Specimen of the Many Errors as Well Committed as Unamended by Mr. Pope, in His Late Edition of This Poet* (1726). His own edition of Shakespeare appeared in 1733.

it was necessary to find other enemies with other names, at whose expense he might divert the publick.

In this design there was petulance and malignity enough; but I cannot think it very criminal. An author places himself uncalled before the tribunal of criticism, and solicits fame at the hazard of disgrace. Dulness or deformity are not culpable in themselves, but may be very justly reproached when they pretend to the honour of wit or the influence of beauty. If bad writers were to pass without reprehension what should restrain them? "impune dien consumpserit ingens Telephus";[3] and upon bad writers only will censure have much effect. The satire which brought Theobald and Moore[4] into contempt, dropped impotent from Bentley,[5] like the javelin of Priam.[6]

All truth is valuable, and satirical criticism may be considered as useful when it rectifies error and improves judgement: he that refines the publick taste is a publick benefactor.

The beauties of this poem are well known; its chief fault is the grossness of its images. Pope and Swift had an unnatural delight in ideas physically impure, such as every other tongue utters with unwillingness, and of which every ear shrinks from the mention.

But even this fault, offensive as it is, may be forgiven for the excellence of other passages; such as the formation and dissolution of Moore,[7] the account of the Traveller,[8] the misfortune of the Florist,[9] and the crowded thoughts and stately numbers which dignify the concluding paragraph.

The alterations which have been made in *The Dunciad*, not always for the better, require that it should be published, as in the last collection, with all its variations.

The *Essay on Man* was a work of great labour and long considera-

---

3 Juvenal, *Satire*, I. 4–5: "Shall a huge [tragedy about] Telephus take up the whole day unpunished [by my satire]?" Juvenal alludes to the Roman practice of reading one's works aloud to an audience.

4 James Moore, later called James Moore Smythe (1702–1734), coxcomb and minor playwright who was, like Theobald, one of Pope's victims in *The Dunciad*.

5 Alluding to Bentley's mutilation of Milton's text, Pope twice calls him "slashing Bentley" (*Epistle to Dr. Arbuthnot*, 114; *Epistle to Augustus*, 104).

6 See *Aeneid*, II. 544–46, where Priam's javelin fails to pierce the armor of Neoptolemus.

7 *Dunciad*, II. 35–50, 109–20.

8 *Dunciad*, IV. 293–330.

9 *Dunciad*, IV. 403–18.

tion, but certainly not the happiest of Pope's performances. The subject is perhaps not very proper for poetry, and the poet was not sufficiently master of his subject; metaphysical morality was to him a new study, he was proud of his acquisitions, and, supposing himself master of great secrets, was in haste to teach what he had not learned. Thus he tells us, in the first Epistle, that from the nature of the Supreme Being may be deduced an order of beings such as mankind, because Infinite Excellence can do only what is best. He finds out that these beings must be "somewhere," and that "all the question is whether man be in a wrong place." Surely if, according to the poet's Leibnitian[10] reasoning, we may infer that man ought to be only because he is, we may allow that his place is the right place, because he has it. Supreme Wisdom is not less infallible in disposing than in creating. But what is meant by "somewhere" and "place" and "wrong place" it had been vain to ask Pope, who probably had never asked himself.

Having exalted himself into the chair of wisdom he tells us much that every man knows, and much that he does not know himself; that we see but little, and that the order of the universe is beyond our comprehension, an opinion not very uncommon; and that there is a chain of subordinate beings "from infinite to nothing," of which himself and his readers are equally ignorant. But he gives us one comfort which, without his help, he supposes unattainable, in the position "that though we are fools, yet God is wise."

This *Essay* affords an egregious instance of the predominance of genius, the dazzling splendour of imagery, and the seductive powers of eloquence. Never were penury of knowledge and vulgarity of sentiment so happily disguised. The reader feels his mind full, though he learns nothing; and when he meets it in its new array no longer knows the talk of his mother and his nurse. When these wonder-working sounds sink into sense and the doctrine of the *Essay*, disrobed of its ornaments, is left to the powers of its naked excellence, what shall we discover? That we are, in comparison with our Creator, very weak and ignorant; that we do not uphold the chain of existence; and that we could not make one another with more skill than we are made. We may learn yet more: that the arts of human life were copied from the instinctive operations of other animals; that if the world be made for man, it may be said that

---

10 I.e., like the reasoning of the German philosopher Leibnitz (1646–1716) in holding the creation of beings other than itself to be a necessity of the divine nature.

man was made for geese. To these profound principles of natural knowledge are added some moral instructions equally new: that self-interest
well understood will produce social concord; that men are mutual gainers
by mutual benefits; that evil is sometimes balanced by good; that human
advantages are unstable and fallacious, of uncertain duration and doubtful
effect; that our true honour is not to have a great part, but to act it well;
that virtue only is our own; and that happiness is always in our power.

Surely a man of no very comprehensive search may venture to say
that he has heard all this before, but it was never till now recommended
by such a blaze of embellishment or such sweetness of melody. The vigorous contraction of some thoughts, the luxuriant amplification of others,
the incidental illustrations, and sometimes the dignity, sometimes the
softness of the verses, enchain philosophy, suspend criticism, and oppress
judgement by overpowering pleasure.

This is true of many paragraphs; yet if I had undertaken to exemplify Pope's felicity of composition before a rigid critick I should not
select the *Essay on Man*, for it contains more lines unsuccessfully laboured,
more harshness of diction, more thoughts imperfectly expressed, more
levity without elegance, and more heaviness without strength, than will
easily be found in all his other works.

The *Characters of Men and Women*[11] are the product of diligent
speculation upon human life; much labour has been bestowed upon them,
and Pope very seldom laboured in vain. That his excellence may be
properly estimated I recommend a comparison of his *Characters of Women*
with Boileau's *Satire*;[12] it will then be seen with how much more perspicacity female nature is investigated and female excellence selected; and
he surely is no mean writer to whom Boileau shall be found inferior.
The *Characters of Men*, however, are written with more, if not with
deeper, thought, and exhibit many passages exquisitely beautiful. "The
Gem and the Flower"[13] will not easily be equalled. In the women's
part are some defects: the character of Atossa[14] is not so neatly finished as
that of Clodio,[15] and some of the female characters may be found perhaps

---

11 The first and second of Pope's *Epistles to Several Persons*, addressed respectively to
Cobham and to Martha Blount.

12 Nicolas Boileau Despreaux (1636–1711), French poet and critic, whose tenth letter
is also on women.

13 I. 93–100.

14 II. 115–50.

15 I. 179–207. In later editions, "Wharton" (Philip, Duke of Wharton) was substituted
for "Clodio."

more frequently among men; what is said of Philomede was true of Prior.[16]

In the *Epistles to Lord Bathurst* and *Lord Burlington* Dr. Warburton has endeavoured to find a train of thought which was never in the writer's head, and, to support his hypothesis, has printed that first which was published last. In one, the most valuable passage is perhaps the elogy on Good Sense,[17] and in the other the End of the Duke of Buckingham.[18]

The *Epistle to Arbuthnot*, now arbitrarily called the *Prologue to the Satires*, is a performance consisting, as it seems, of many fragments wrought into one design, which by this union of scattered beauties contains more striking paragraphs than could probably have been brought together into an occasional work. As there is no stronger motive to exertion than self-defence, no part has more elegance, spirit, or dignity than the poet's vindication of his own character. The meanest passage is the satire upon Sporus.[19]

Of the two poems which derived their names from the year, and which are called the *Epilogue to the Satires*, it was very justly remarked by Savage that the second was in the whole more strongly conceived and more equally supported, but that it had no single passages equal to the contention in the first for the dignity of Vice and the celebration of the triumph of Corruption.

The *Imitations of Horace* seem to have been written as relaxations of his genius. This employment became his favourite by its facility; the plan was ready to his hand, and nothing was required but to accommodate as he could the sentiments of an old author to recent facts or familiar images; but what is easy is seldom excellent: such imitations cannot give pleasure to common readers. The man of learning may be sometimes surprised and delighted by an unexpected parallel; but the comparison

---

16 "Philomede" appears in II. 83–86:

So Philomedé, lect'ring all mankind
On the soft Passion, and the Taste refin'd,
Th' Address, the Delicacy—stoops at once,
And makes her hearty meal upon a Dunce.

So Prior, who wrote lyrics about an idealized "Chloe," cohabited with "a despicable drab of the lowest species" (Johnson's *Life of Prior;* Hill ed., II. 199).

17 IV. 39–46.
18 III. 299–314.
19 Lines 305–33, where John Hervey, Baron Hervey (1696–1743), one of Walpole's henchmen, is presented as the kept boy Sporus.

requires knowledge of the original, which will likewise often detect strained applications. Between Roman images and English manners there will be an irreconcileable dissimilitude, and the work will be generally uncouth and party-coloured; neither original nor translated, neither ancient nor modern.

Pope had, in proportions very nicely adjusted to each other, all the qualities that constitute genius. He had Invention, by which new trains of events are formed and new scenes of imagery displayed, as in *The Rape of the Lock*, and by which extrinsick and adventitious embellishments and illustrations are connected with a known subject, as in the *Essay on Criticism*; he had Imagination, which strongly impresses on the writer's mind and enables him to convey to the reader the various forms of nature, incidents of life, and energies of passion, as in his *Eloisa*, *Windsor Forest*, and the *Ethick Epistles*; he had Judgement, which selects from life or nature what the present purpose requires, and, by separating the essence of things from its concomitants, often makes the representation more powerful than the reality; and he had colours of language always before him ready to decorate his matter with every grace of elegant expression, as when he accommodates his diction to the wonderful multiplicity of Homer's sentiments and descriptions.

Poetical expression includes sound as well as meaning. "Musick," says Dryden, "is inarticulate poetry"; among the excellences of Pope, therefore, must be mentioned the melody of his metre. By perusing the works of Dryden he discovered the most perfect fabrick of English verse, and habituated himself to that only which he found the best; in consequence of which restraint his poetry has been censured as too uniformly musical, and as glutting the ear with unvaried sweetness. I suspect this objection to be the cant of those who judge by principles rather than perception; and who would even themselves have less pleasure in his works if he had tried to relieve attention by studied discords, or affected to break his lines and vary his pauses.

But though he was thus careful of his versification he did not oppress his powers with superfluous rigour. He seems to have thought with Boileau that the practice of writing might be refined till the difficulty should overbalance the advantage. The construction of his language is not always strictly grammatical; with those rhymes which prescription had conjoined he contented himself, without regard to Swift's remonstrances, though there was no striking consonance; nor was he very careful to vary his terminations or to refuse admission at a small distance to the same rhymes.

To Swift's edict for the exclusion of alexandrines and triplets he paid little regard; he admitted them, but, in the opinion of Fenton,[20] too rarely: he uses them more liberally in his translation than his poems.

He has a few double rhymes, and always, I think, unsuccessfully, except once in *The Rape of the Lock*.

Expletives he very early ejected from his verses; but he now and then admits an epithet rather commodious than important. Each of the six first lines of the *Iliad* might lose two syllables with very little diminution of the meaning, and sometimes, after all his art and labour, one verse seems to be made for the sake of another. In his latter productions the diction is sometimes vitiated by French idioms, with which Bolingbroke had perhaps infected him.

I have been told that the couplet by which he declared his own ear to be most gratified was this:

> Lo, where Mæotis sleeps, and hardly flows
> The freezing Tanais thro' a waste of snows.[21]

But the reason of this preference I cannot discover.

It is remarked by Watts[22] that there is scarcely a happy combination of words or a phrase poetically elegant in the English language which Pope has not inserted into his version of Homer. How he obtained possession of so many beauties of speech it were desirable to know. That he gleaned from authors, obscure as well as eminent, what he thought brilliant or useful, and preserved it all in a regular collection, is not unlikely. When, in his last years, Hall's *Satires*[23] were shewn him he wished that he had seen them sooner.

New sentiments and new images others may produce, but to attempt any further improvement of versification will be dangerous. Art and diligence have now done their best, and what shall be added will be the effort of tedious toil and needless curiosity.

After all this it is surely superfluous to answer the question that has once been asked, Whether Pope was a poet? otherwise than by asking in return, If Pope be not a poet, where is poetry to be found? To circum-

---

20 Elijah Fenton (1683–1730), who with William Broome participated in Pope's translation of the *Odyssey*.

21 *Dunciad*, III. 87–88.

22 Isaac Watts (1674–1748), *The Improvement of the Mind* (1741), Ch. xx, Sect. 36.

23 *Virgidemiae* (1597), by Joseph Hall: six books of satire in rhyming verse.

scribe poetry by a definition will only shew the narrowness of the definer, though a definition which shall exclude Pope will not easily be made. Let us look round upon the present time, and back upon the past; let us enquire to whom the voice of mankind has decreed the wreath of poetry; let their productions be examined and their claims stated, and the pretensions of Pope will be no more disputed. Had he given the world only his version the name of poet must have been allowed him; if the writer of the *Iliad* were to class his successors he would assign a very high place to his translator, without requiring any other evidence of genius.

LIFE OF GRAY

J ohnson's account of the poet Thomas Gray and his work, here reprinted in its entirety, is a good example of the critic's capacity for judicious evaluation. Although he found Gray's odes pretentious and bombastic, he admired much in the churchyard elegy, and his pithy praise of it suggests an important critical principle. In the biographical section of his essay, Johnson also presents a balanced view, praising Gray for his learning and his intellectual integrity without glossing over his prickliness and self-absorption.

Life of Gray

T homas Gray, the son of Mr. Philip Gray, a scrivener[1] of London, was born in Cornhill,[2] November 26, 1716. His grammatical education he received at Eton under the care of Mr. Antrobus, his mother's brother, then assistant to Dr. George,[3] and when he left school, in 1734, entered a pensioner at Peterhouse in Cambridge.

The transition from the school to the college is, to most young scholars, the time from which they date their years of manhood, liberty, and happiness; but Gray seems to have been very little delighted with academical gratifications: he liked at Cambridge neither the mode of life nor the fashion of study, and lived sullenly on to the time when his attendance on lectures was no longer required. As he intended to profess the Common Law he took no degree.

When he had been at Cambridge about five years, Mr. Horace Walpole,[4] whose friendship he had gained at Eton, invited him to travel with him as his companion. They wandered through France into Italy,

---

[1] A professional copyist or writer.

[2] Cornhill Street was one of the principal streets of the City, the central financial district of London. The Gray house (which burned down in 1748) was on the south side of the street.

[3] William George (d. 1756), for seventeen years principal of Eton College.

[4] Walpole (1717–1797), was son of the prime minister Robert Walpole, author, letter writer (see below, pp. 269–77), and antiquary.

and Gray's letters contain a very pleasing account of many parts of their journey. But unequal friendships are easily dissolved: at Florence they quarrelled and parted, and Mr. Walpole is now content to have it told that it was by his fault. If we look, however, without prejudice on the world we shall find that men, whose consciousness of their own merit sets them above the compliances of servility, are apt enough in their association with superiors to watch their own dignity with troublesome and punctilious jealousy, and in the fervour of independance to exact that attention which they refuse to pay. Part they did, whatever was the quarrel, and the rest of their travels was doubtless more unpleasant to them both. Gray continued his journey in a manner suitable to his own little fortune, with only an occasional servant.

He returned to England in September, 1741, and in about two months afterwards buried his father,[5] who had, by an injudicious waste of money upon a new house, so much lessened his fortune that Gray thought himself too poor to study the law. He therefore retired to Cambridge, where he soon after became Bachelor of Civil Law, and where, without liking the place or its inhabitants, or professing to like them, he passed, except a short residence at London, the rest of his life.

About this time he was deprived of Mr. West, the son of a chancellor of Ireland,[6] a friend on whom he appears to have set a high value, and who deserved his esteem by the powers which he shews in his letters, and in the *Ode to May*, which Mr. Mason[7] has preserved, as well as by the sincerity with which, when Gray sent him part of *Agrippina*,[8] a tragedy that he had just begun, he gave an opinion which probably intercepted the progress of the work, and which the judgement of every reader will confirm. It was certainly no loss to the English stage that *Agrippina* was never finished.

In this year (1742) Gray seems first to have applied himself seriously to poetry, for in this year were produced the *Ode to Spring*, his *Prospect of Eton*, and his *Ode to Adversity*. He began likewise a Latin Poem, *De Principiis Cogitandi*.[9]

It may be collected from the narrative of Mr. Mason, that his first ambition was to have excelled in Latin poetry: perhaps it were reasonable

---

5 Who died on November 6, 1741.

6 Richard West (1716–1742), son of Richard West (d. 1726), lord chancellor of Ireland from 1725, author of *Hecuba* (1726), a tragedy.

7 William Mason (1724–1797), himself a poet, was Gray's literary executor and published his *Life and Letters* in 1774.

8 The blank verse tragedy was begun in December 1741. About 175 lines survive; as Johnson suggests, Gray broke it off after West's unfavorable criticism.

9 "Of the Principles of Thinking." Gray called it "a metaphysical poem."

to wish that he had prosecuted his design; for though there is at present some embarrassment[10] in his phrase, and some harshness in his Lyrick numbers, his copiousness of language is such as very few possess, and his lines, even when imperfect, discover a writer whom practice would quickly have made skilful.

He now lived on at Peterhouse, very little solicitous what others did or thought, and cultivated his mind and enlarged his views without any other purpose than of improving and amusing himself; when Mr. Mason, being elected fellow of Pembroke-hall,[11] brought him a companion who was afterwards to be his editor, and whose fondness and fidelity has kindled in him a zeal of admiration, which cannot be reasonably expected from the neutrality of a stranger and the coldness of a critick.

In this retirement he wrote (1747) an ode on *The Death of Mr. Walpole's Cat*, and the year afterwards attempted a poem of more importance, on *Government and Education*, of which the fragments which remain have many excellent lines.

His next production (1750) was his far-famed *Elegy in the Churchyard*,[12] which, finding its way into a Magazine, first, I believe, made him known to the publick.

An invitation from lady Cobham[13] about this time gave occasion to an odd composition called *A Long Story*, which adds little to Gray's character.[14]

Several of his pieces were published (1753), with designs, by Mr. Bentley,[15] and, that they might in some form or other make a book, only one side of each leaf was printed. I believe the poems and the plates recommended each other so well, that the whole impression was soon bought. This year he lost his mother.[16]

Some time afterwards (1756) some young men of the college,

---

10 Excessiveness.

11 Pembroke College, Cambridge, across the street from Peterhouse.

12 Gray sent the poem to Walpole on June 12, 1750. Someone evidently took a copy when Walpole showed it in manuscript; on February 11, 1750–51, Gray wrote Walpole that the editors of *The Magazine of Magazines* were printing it.

13 Wife of Sir Richard Temple, Viscount Cobham. They lived at the Manor House at Stoke Poges, the village to which Gray's mother had moved. With her niece, Harriet Speed, and a friend, Lady Schaub, Lady Cobham called on Gray one day when he was out and left him a note, the provocation for "A Long Story."

14 The poem is a fantastic account of the ladies' visit and of Gray's reaction to it.

15 Richard Bentley (1708–1782) illustrated this edition, which was printed by Walpole on his press at Strawberry Hill.

16 She died on March 11, 1753.

whose chambers were near his, diverted themselves with disturbing him by frequent and troublesome noises, and, as is said, by pranks yet more offensive and contemptuous. This insolence, having endured it a while, he represented to the governors of the society, among whom perhaps he had no friends, and, finding his complaint little regarded, removed himself to Pembroke-hall.

In 1757 he published *The Progress of Poetry* and *The Bard*, two compositions at which the readers of poetry were at first content to gaze in mute amazement.[17] Some that tried them confessed their inability to understand them, though Warburton[18] said that they were understood as well as the works of Milton and Shakespeare, which it is the fashion to admire. Garrick wrote a few lines in their praise.[19] Some hardy champions undertook to rescue them from neglect, and in a short time many were content to be shewn beauties which they could not see.

Gray's reputation was now so high that, after the death of Cibber, he had the honour of refusing the laurel,[20] which was then bestowed on Mr. Whitehead.

His curiosity not long after drew him away from Cambridge to a lodging near the Museum,[21] where he resided near three years, reading and transcribing; and, so far as can be discovered, very little affected by two odes on *Oblivion* and *Obscurity*, in which his Lyrick performances were ridiculed with much contempt and much ingenuity.[22]

When the Professor of Modern History at Cambridge died he was, as he says, "cockered and spirited up," till he asked it of lord Bute,[23] who sent him a civil refusal; and the place was given to Mr. Brocket, the tutor of Sir James Lowther.[24]

---

17 The odes were criticized for their obscurity. See Gray's letter on the subject, below, p. 262.

18 William Warburton (1698–1779), bishop of Gloucester, Pope's literary executor and posthumous editor, also an editor of Shakespeare. For Johnson's view of him, see above, pp. 172–73.

19 David Garrick (1717–1779), famous actor. His poem was published in *The London Chronicle*, October, 1, 1757.

20 I.e., the poet laureateship, which was then bestowed on William Whitehead (1715–1785).

21 The British Museum in Russell Square, London.

22 By George Colman (1732–1794), published in his *Prose on Several Occasions* (1787), but earlier quoted in the *Gentleman's Magazine*, June 1760.

23 John Stuart, Earl of Bute (1713–1792), at this time secretary of state.

24 Lawrence Brockett, of Trinity College, Cambridge. Sir James Lowther (1736–1802), later Earl of Lonsdale, was famous for his skill at electioneering. Lord Bute was his father-in-law.

His constitution was weak, and believing that his health was promoted by exercise and change of place he undertook (1765) a journey into Scotland, of which his account,[25] so far as it extends, is very curious and elegant; for as his comprehension was ample his curiosity extended to all the works of art, all the appearances of nature, and all the monuments of past events. He naturally contracted a friendship with Dr. Beattie,[26] whom he found a poet, a philosopher, and a good man. The Mareschal College at Aberdeen offered him the degree of Doctor of Laws, which, having omitted to take it at Cambridge, he thought it decent to refuse.

What he had formerly solicited in vain was at last given him without solicitation. The Professorship of History became again vacant, and he received (1768) an offer of it from the duke of Grafton.[27] He accepted, and retained it to his death; always designing lectures, but never reading them; uneasy at his neglect of duty, and appeasing his uneasiness with designs of reformation, and with a resolution which he believed himself to have made of resigning the office, if he found himself unable to discharge it.

Ill health made another journey necessary, and he visited (1769) Westmoreland and Cumberland. He that reads his epistolary narration wishes that to travel, and to tell his travels, had been more of his employment; but it is by studying at home that we must obtain the ability of travelling with intelligence and improvement.

His travels and his studies were now near their end. The gout, of which he had sustained many weak attacks, fell upon his stomach, and, yielding to no medicines, produced strong convulsions, which (July 30, 1771) terminated in death.

His character I am willing to adopt, as Mr. Mason has done, from a letter written to my friend Mr. Boswell, by the Rev. Mr. Temple,[28] rector of St. Gluvias in Cornwall; and am as willing as his warmest well-wisher to believe it true.

---

25 In his letters.

26 James Beattie (1735–1803), Scottish poet, professor of moral philosophy and logic at Marischal College.

27 Augustus Henry Fitzroy, Duke of Grafton (1735–1811), at this time prime minister. Richard Stonehewer (c. 1728–1809), a friend of Gray's, was Grafton's private secretary, and recommended the poet for the position.

28 William Johnstone Temple (1739–1796), who had been a law student with Boswell in London in 1762.

Perhaps he was the most learned man in Europe. He was equally acquainted with the elegant and profound parts of science, and that not superficially but thoroughly. He knew every branch of history, both natural and civil; had read all the original historians of England, France, and Italy; and was a great antiquarian. Criticism, metaphysicks, morals, politicks made a principal part of his study; voyages and travels of all sorts were his favourite amusements; and he had a fine taste in painting, prints, architecture, and gardening. With such a fund of knowledge, his conversation must have been equally instructing and entertaining; but he was also a good man, a man of virtue and humanity. There is no character without some speck, some imperfection; and I think the greatest defect in his was an affectation in delicacy, or rather effeminacy, and a visible fastidiousness, or contempt and disdain of his inferiors in science.[29] He also had, in some degree, that weakness which disgusted Voltaire so much in Mr. Congreve.[30] Though he seemed to value others chiefly according to the progress they had made in knowledge, yet he could not bear to be considered himself merely as a man of letters; and though without birth, or fortune, or station, his desire was to be looked upon as a private independent gentleman, who read for his amusement. Perhaps it may be said, What signifies so much knowledge, when it produced so little? Is it worth taking so much pains to leave no memorial but a few poems? But let it be considered that Mr. Gray was, to others, at least innocently employed; to himself, certainly beneficially. His time passed agreeably; he was every day making some new acquisition in science; his mind was enlarged, his heart softened, his virtue strengthened; the world and mankind were shewn to him without a mask; and he was taught to consider every thing as trifling, and unworthy of the attention of a wise man, except the pursuit of knowledge and practice of virtue, in that state wherein God hath placed us.

To this character Mr. Mason has added a more particular account of Gray's skill in zoology. He has remarked that Gray's effeminacy was affected most "before those whom he did not wish to please"; and that he is unjustly charged with making knowledge his sole reason of preference, as he paid his esteem to none whom he did not likewise believe to be good.

---

29 I.e., knowledge.

30 Voltaire reports that when he visited William Congreve (1670–1729), the English dramatist announced that he wished to be considered a gentleman rather than a poet. Voltaire replied that if Congreve had been only a gentleman, he should not have come to visit him. See Voltaire, *Oeuvres*, ed. Louis Moland (1877–1885), XXIV. 116.

What has occurred to me, from the slight inspection of his letters in which my undertaking has engaged me, is that his mind had a large grasp; that his curiosity was unlimited, and his judgement cultivated; that he was a man likely to love much where he loved at all, but that he was fastidious and hard to please. His contempt, however, is often employed, where I hope it will be approved, upon scepticism and infidelity.[31] His short account of Shaftesbury I will insert.[32]

> You say you cannot conceive how lord Shaftesbury came to be a philosopher in vogue; I will tell you: first, he was a lord; secondly, he was as vain as any of his readers; thirdly, men are very prone to believe what they do not understand; fourthly, they will believe any thing at all, provided they are under no obligation to believe it; fifthly, they love to take a new road, even when that road leads no where; sixthly, he was reckoned a fine writer, and seems [seemed] always to mean more than he said. Would you have any more reasons? An interval of above forty years has pretty well destroyed the charm. A dead lord ranks [but] with commoners: vanity is no longer interested in the matter; for a new road is [has] become an old one.

Mr. Mason has added from his own knowledge that though Gray was poor, he was not eager of money, and that out of the little that he had, he was very willing to help the necessitous.

As a writer he had this peculiarity, that he did not write his pieces first rudely, and then correct them, but laboured every line as it arose in the train of composition, and he had a notion not very peculiar, that he could not write but at certain times, or at happy moments; a fantastick foppery,[33] to which my kindness for a man of learning and of virtue wishes him to have been superior.

Gray's poetry is now to be considered, and I hope not to be looked on as an enemy to his name if I confess that I contemplate it with less pleasure than his life.

His *Ode on Spring* has something poetical, both in the language and the thought; but the language is too luxuriant, and the thoughts have nothing new. There has of late arisen a practice of giving to adjectives,

---

31 Lack of religious faith.
32 Anthony Ashley Cooper, Earl of Shaftesbury (1671–1713), moral philosopher.
33 Affectation.

derived from substantives, the termination of participles, such as the *cultured* plain, the *daisied* bank; but I was sorry to see, in the lines of a scholar like Gray, "the *honied* Spring."[34] The morality is natural, but too stale; the conclusion is pretty.

The poem on the Cat[35] was doubtless by its author considered as a trifle, but it is not a happy trifle. In the first stanza "the azure flowers that blow" shew resolutely a rhyme is sometimes made when it cannot easily be found. Selima, the Cat, is called a nymph, with some violence both to language and sense; but there is good use made of it when it is done; for of the two lines,

> *What female heart can gold despise?*
> *What cat's averse to fish?*

the first relates merely to the nymph, and the second only to the cat. The sixth stanza contains a melancholy truth, that "a favourite has no friend," but the last ends in a pointed sentence of no relation to the purpose; if what glistered had been "gold," the cat would not have gone into the water; and, if she had, would not less have been drowned.

The *Prospect of Eton College*[36] suggests nothing to Gray which every beholder does not equally think and feel. His supplication to father Thames, to tell him who drives the hoop or tosses the ball, is useless and puerile. Father Thames has no better means of knowing than himself. His epithet "buxom health" is not elegant; he seems not to understand the word.[37] Gray thought his language more poetical as it was more remote from common use: finding in Dryden "honey redolent of Spring,"[38] an expression that reaches the utmost limits of our language, Gray drove it a little more beyond common apprehension, by making "gales" to be "redolent of joy and youth."

Of the *Ode on Adversity* the hint was at first taken from "O Diva,

---

34 "Ode on the Spring," l. 26.

35 "Ode on the Death of a Favourite Cat, Drowned in a Tub of Gold Fishes." The quotations are from l. 3 (*blow* rhymes with *below*, l. 6), ll. 23–24, and l. 36.

36 "Ode on a Distant Prospect of Eton College." The "supplication to father Thames" is in ll. 21–30.

37 Johnson's own definition is "1. Obedient, obsequious. 2. Gay, lively, brisk. 3. Wanton, jolly." The phrase to which he objects occurs in l. 45.

38 "Of the Pythagorean Philosophy, from Ovid's Metamorphoses, Book XV," l. 110.

gratum quæ regis Antium"[39]; but Gray has excelled his original by the variety of his sentiments and by their moral application. Of this piece, at once poetical and rational, I will not by slight objections violate the dignity.

My process has now brought me to the "Wonderful Wonder of Wonders,"[40] the two Sister Odes;[41] by which, though either vulgar ignorance or common sense at first universally rejected them, many have been since persuaded to think themselves delighted. I am one of those that are willing to be pleased, and therefore would gladly find the meaning of the first stanza of *The Progress of Poetry*.

Gray seems in his rapture to confound the images of "spreading sound" and "running water." A "stream of musick" may be allowed; but where does Musick, however "smooth and strong," after having visited the "verdant vales," "rowl down the steep amain," so as that "rocks and nodding groves rebellow to the roar"? If this be said of Musick, it is nonsense; if it be said of Water, it is nothing to the purpose.

The second stanza, exhibiting Mars's car and Jove's eagle, is unworthy of further notice. Criticism disdains to chase a schoolboy to his common-places.[42]

To the third it may likewise be objected that it is drawn from Mythology, though such as may be more easily assimilated to real life. "Idalia's velvet-green" has something of cant.[43] An epithet or metaphor drawn from Nature ennobles Art; an epithet or metaphor drawn from Art degrades Nature. Gray is too fond of words arbitrarily compounded. "Many-twinkling" was formerly censured as not analogical; we may say *many-spotted*, but scarcely *many-spotting*. This stanza, however, has something pleasing.

Of the second ternary of stanzas the first endeavours to tell something, and would have told it had it not been crossed by Hyperion;[44] the

---

[39] "O goddess, who rules the height of Antium" (Horace, *Odes*, I. xxxv).

[40] A familiar phrase in common speech.

[41] "The Bard" and "The Progress of Poesy," published together by Walpole in 1757.

[42] The account of the "stream of music" is in stanza one of "The Progress of Poesy." Johnson's point here is that the second stanza is highly derivative, from well-known sources.

[43] Johnson's definition: "1. A corrupt dialect used by beggars and vagabonds. 2. A particular form of speaking peculiar to some certain class or body of men. 3. A whining pretension to goodness in formal and affected terms. 4. Barbarous jargon. 5. Auction." Sense 4 is probably the one relevant here. The phrase, "Idalia's velvet-green," is from l. 27. "Many-twinkling," which Johnson objects to below, is in l. 35.

[44] The stanza concerns the ills that afflict mankind; Hyperion appears in its final line.

second describes well enough the universal prevalence of poetry, but I am afraid that the conclusion will not rise from the premises. The caverns of the North and the plains of Chili are not the residences of "Glory" and "generous Shame." But that Poetry and Virtue go always together is an opinion so pleasing that I can forgive him who resolves to think it true.

The third stanza sounds big with Delphi, and Egean, and Ilissus, and Meander, and "hallowed fountain" and "solemn sound"; but in all Gray's odes there is a kind of cumbrous splendour which we wish away. His position is at last false: in the time of Dante and Petrarch, from whom he derives our first school of poetry,[45] Italy was overrun by "tyrant power" and "coward vice"; nor was our state much better when we first borrowed the Italian arts.

Of the third ternary the first gives a mythological birth of Shakespeare. What is said of that mighty genius is true; but it is not said happily: the real effects of this poetical power are put out of sight by the pomp of machinery. Where truth is sufficient to fill the mind, fiction is worse than useless; the counterfeit debases the genuine.

His account of Milton's blindness, if we suppose it caused by study in the formation of his poem, a supposition surely allowable, is poetically true, and happily imagined.[46] But the "car" of Dryden, with his "two coursers," has nothing in it peculiar,[47] it is a car in which any other rider may be placed.

The Bard appears at the first view to be, as Algarotti[48] and others have remarked, an imitation of the prophecy of Nereus.[49] Algarotti thinks it superior to its original, and, if preference depends only on the imagery and animation of the two poems, his judgement is right. There is in *The Bard* more force, more thought, and more variety. But to copy is less than to invent, and the copy has been unhappily produced at a wrong time. The fiction of Horace was to the Romans credible; but its revival disgusts us with apparent and unconquerable falsehood. "Incredulus odi."[50]

To select a singular event, and swell it to a giant's bulk by fabulous

---

45 Lines 79–82.

46 Lines 98–102.

47 The car is not described or characterized, except as "less presumptuous" than Milton's. See ll. 103–105.

48 Francesco, Count Algarotti (1712–1764), Italian writer and connoisseur of art.

49 Horace, *Odes*, I. xv.

50 "Incredulous, I hate" (Horace, *Art of Poetry*, 188).

appendages of spectres and predictions, has little difficulty, for he that forsakes the probable may always find the marvellous. And it has little use: we are affected only as we believe; we are improved only as we find something to be imitated or declined. I do not see that *The Bard* promotes any truth, moral or political.

His stanzas are too long, especially his epodes; the ode is finished before the ear has learned its measures, and consequently before it can receive pleasure from their consonance and recurrence.

Of the first stanza the abrupt beginning has been celebrated;[51] but technical beauties can give praise only to the inventor. It is in the power of any man to rush abruptly upon his subject, that has read the ballad of *Johnny Armstrong,*

Is there ever a man in all Scotland—[52]

The initial resemblances, or alliterations, "ruin," "ruthless," "helm nor hauberk," are below the grandeur of a poem that endeavours at sublimity.

In the second stanza the Bard is well described; but in the third we have the puerilities of obsolete mythology. When we are told that Cadwallo "hush'd the stormy main," and that Modred "made huge Plinlimmon bow his cloud-top'd head,"[53] attention recoils from the repetition of a tale that, even when it was first heard, was heard with scorn.

The "weaving" of the "winding sheet" he borrowed, as he owns, from the northern Bards, but their texture, however, was very properly the work of female powers, as the art of spinning the thread of life in another mythology. Theft is always dangerous; Gray has made weavers of his slaughtered bards by a fiction outrageous and incongruous. They are then called upon to "Weave the warp, and weave the woof," perhaps with no great propriety; for it is by crossing the woof with the warp that men weave the web or piece; and the first line was dearly bought by the admission of its wretched correspondent, "Give ample room and verge enough."[54] He has, however, no other line as bad.

The third stanza of the second ternary is commended, I think, be-

---

51 Mason reports this in his *Life and Letters of Gray,* I. 96.
52 An anonymous Scottish ballad which Johnson admired. He made the same point in conversation about its relation to Gray's poem. See below, p. 562.
53 Lines 29–30, 34.
54 Line 51. Johnson above quotes l. 49.

yond its merit. The personification is indistinct. Thirst and Hunger are not alike, and their features, to make the imagery perfect, should have been discriminated. We are told, in the same stanza, how "towers" are "fed." But I will no longer look for particular faults; yet let it be observed that the ode might have been concluded with an action of better example:[55] but suicide is always to be had without expence of thought.

These odes are marked by glittering accumulations of ungraceful ornaments: they strike, rather than please; the images are magnified by affectation; the language is laboured into harshness. The mind of the writer seems to work with unnatural violence. "Double, double, toil and trouble."[56] He has a kind of strutting dignity, and is tall by walking on tiptoe. His art and his struggle are too visible, and there is too little appearance of ease and nature.

To say that he has no beauties would be unjust: a man like him, of great learning and great industry, could not but produce something valuable. When he pleases least, it can only be said that a good design was ill directed.

His translations of Northern and Welsh Poetry deserve praise: the imagery is preserved, perhaps often improved; but the language is unlike the language of other poets.

In the character of his *Elegy* I rejoice to concur with the common reader; for by the common sense of readers uncorrupted with literary prejudices, after all the refinements of subtilty and the dogmatism of learning, must be finally decided all claim to poetical honours. The *Church-yard* abounds with images which find a mirrour in every mind, and with sentiments to which every bosom returns an echo. The four stanzas beginning "Yet even these bones"[57] are to me original: I have never seen the notions in any other place; yet he that reads them here persuades himself that he has always felt them. Had Gray written often thus it had been vain to blame, and useless to praise him.

---

55 At the end of the poem the bard throws himself from the top of the mountain.
56 *Macbeth*, IV. i. 10.
57 *Elegy Written in a Country Church-yard*, ll. 77ff.

DAVID HUME

(1711–1776)

Born in Edinburgh, David Hume attended the University of Edinburgh; a letter that he wrote to a friend when he was sixteen years old expressed even then his determination to become a philosopher. He was expected to train himself for the law but soon gave up this endeavor and went to France, where he spent several years at La Flêche, the Jesuit college where Descartes studied. When he left France in 1737, he brought with him most of the manuscript of his *Treatise of Human Nature*, published anonymously in 1739. He served briefly as a tutor in the family of the Marquis of Annandale, then as secretary to General St. Clair. His *Philosophical Essays Concerning the Human Understanding* appeared in 1748 and gradually gained a reputation, as did his succeeding essays on politics, aesthetics, and philosophy. He gave up philosophy for history, however, became keeper of the Advocates' Library in Edinburgh, and published a six-volume history of England, which made him wealthy and which was for many years the standard history of the country. He held various minor diplomatic posts, then returned to Edinburgh in 1769, to live there until his death.

Hume is remembered now mainly as a philosopher, the most thorough skeptic of his age. His literary essays are lucid, well organized, concerned with fundamentals. In "On Taste" he treats a vital aesthetic problem with cool faith in the possibility of untangling its intricate components. His essays have the clarity and the power of abstract thought at its best.

Essays Moral, Political, and Literary, 2 vols., eds. Thomas H. Green and T. H. Grose (London, 1875), is the source of the present text.

Biography and Criticism

Burton, John H., *Life and Correspondance of David Hume*, 2 vols., 1846.

Cohen, Ralph, "David Hume's Experimental Method and the Theory of Taste," ELH, XXV (1958), 270–87.

Mossner, Ernest C., *The Forgotten Hume*, 1943.

Pears, D. F., ed., *David Hume: A Symposium*, 1963.

Price, John V., *The Ironic Hume*, 1965.

Smith, Norman K., *The Philosophy of David Hume*, 1941.

Sugg, Redding, Jr., "Hume's Search for the Key with the Leathern Thong," *Journal of Aesthetics and Art Criticism*, XVI (1957), 96–102.

Of the Standard of Taste[1]

(1757)

The great variety of Taste, as well as of opinion, which prevails in the world, is too obvious not to have fallen under every one's observation. Men of the most confined knowledge are able to remark a difference of taste in the narrow circle of their acquaintance, even when the persons have been educated under the same government, and have early imbibed the same prejudices. But those, who can enlarge their view to contemplate distant nations and remote ages, are still more surprized at the great inconsistence and contrariety. We are apt to call *barbarous* whatever departs widely from our own taste and apprehension: But soon find the epithet of reproach retorted on us. And the highest arrogance and self-conceit is at last startled, on observing an equal assurance on all sides, and scruples, amidst such a contest of sentiment, to pronounce positively in its own favour.

As this variety of taste is obvious to the most careless enquirer; so will it be found, on examination, to be still greater in reality than in appearance. The sentiments of men often differ with regard to beauty and deformity of all kinds, even while their general discourse is the same.

---

1 See Introduction, pp. 44-45.

There are certain terms in every language, which import blame, and others praise; and all men, who use the same tongue, must agree in their application of them. Every voice is united in applauding elegance, propriety, simplicity, spirit in writing; and in blaming fustian, affectation, coldness, and a false brilliancy: But when critics come to particulars, this seeming unanimity vanishes; and it is found, that they had affixed a very different meaning to their expressions. In all matters of opinion and science, the case is opposite: The difference among men is there oftener found to lie in generals than in particulars; and to be less in reality than in appearance. An explanation of the terms commonly ends the controversy; and the disputants are surprized to find, that they had been quarrelling, while at bottom they agreed in their judgment.

Those who found morality on sentiment, more than on reason, are inclined to comprehend ethics under the former observation, and to maintain, that, in all questions, which regard conduct and manners, the difference among men is really greater than at first sight it appears. It is indeed obvious, that writers of all nations and all ages concur in applauding justice, humanity, magnanimity, prudence, veracity; and in blaming the opposite qualities. Even poets and other authors, whose compositions are chiefly calculated to please the imagination, are yet found, from HOMER down to FENELON,[2] to inculcate the same moral precepts, and to bestow their applause and blame on the same virtues and vices. This great unanimity is usually ascribed to the influence of plain reason; which, in all these cases, maintains similar sentiments in all men, and prevents those controversies, to which the abstract sciences are so much exposed. So far as the unanimity is real, this account may be admitted as satisfactory: But we must also allow that some part of the seeming harmony in morals may be accounted for from the very nature of language. The word *virtue*, with its equivalent in every tongue, implies praise; as that of *vice* does blame: And no one, without the most obvious and grossest impropriety, could affix reproach to a term, which in general acceptation is understood in a good sense; or bestow applause, where the idiom requires disapprobation. HOMER's general precepts, where he delivers any such, will never be controverted; but it is obvious, that, when he draws particular pictures of manners, and represents heroism in ACHILLES and

---

2 François de Salignac de la Mothe Fénelon (1651–1715), French prelate and author of *Les Aventures de Télémaque*, a moralized account of a young man's education.

prudence in ULYSSES, he intermixes a much greater degree of ferocity in the former, and of cunning and fraud in the latter, than FENELON would admit of. The sage ULYSSES in the GREEK poet seems to delight in lies and fictions, and often employs them without any necessity or even advantage: But his more scrupulous son, in the FRENCH epic writer, exposes himself to the most imminent perils, rather than depart from the most exact line of truth and veracity.

The admirers and followers of the ALCORAN[3] insist on the excellent moral precepts interspersed throughout that wild and absurd performance. But it is to be supposed, that the ARABIC words, which correspond to the ENGLISH, equity, justice, temperance, meekness, charity, were such as, from the constant use of that tongue, must always be taken in a good sense; and it would have argued the greatest ignorance, not of morals, but of language, to have mentioned them with any epithets, besides those of applause and approbation. But would we know, whether the pretended prophet had really attained a just sentiment of morals? Let us attend to his narration; and we shall soon find, that he bestows praise on such instances of treachery, inhumanity, cruelty, revenge, bigotry, as are utterly incompatible with civilized society. No steady rule of right seems there to be attended to; and every action is blamed or praised, so far only as it is beneficial or hurtful to the true believers.

The merit of delivering true general precepts in ethics is indeed very small. Whoever recommends any moral virtues, really does no more than is implied in the terms themselves. That people, who invented the word *charity*, and used it in a good sense, inculcated more clearly and much more efficaciously, the precept, *be charitable*, than any pretended legislator or prophet, who should insert such a *maxim* in his writings. Of all expressions, those, which, together with their other meaning, imply a degree either of blame or approbation, are the least liable to be perverted or mistaken.

It is natural for us to seek a *Standard of Taste*; a rule, by which the various sentiments of men may be reconciled; at least, a decision, afforded, confirming one sentiment, and condemning another.

There is a species of philosophy, which cuts off all hopes of success in such an attempt, and represents the impossibility of ever attaining any standard of taste. The difference, it is said, is very wide between judgment and sentiment. All sentiment is right; because sentiment has a reference to

---

3 The Islamic Koran.

nothing beyond itself, and is always real, wherever a man is conscious of it. But all determinations of the understanding are not right; because they have a reference to something beyond themselves, to wit, real matter of fact; and are not always conformable to that standard. Among a thousand different opinions which different men may entertain of the same subject, there is one, and but one, that is just and true; and the only difficulty is to fix and ascertain it. On the contrary, a thousand different sentiments, excited by the same object, are all right:[Because no sentiment represents what is really in the object. It only marks a certain conformity or relation between the object and the organs or faculties of the mind; and if that conformity did not really exist, the sentiment could never possibly have being. Beauty is no quality in things themselves: It exists merely in the mind which contemplates them; and each mind perceives a different beauty.] One person may even perceive deformity, where another is sensible of beauty; and every individual ought to acquiesce in his own sentiment, without pretending to regulate those of others. To seek the real beauty, or real deformity, is as fruitless an enquiry, as to pretend to ascertain the real sweet or real bitter. According to the disposition of the organs, the same object may be both sweet and bitter; and the proverb has justly determined it to be fruitless to dispute concerning tastes. It is very natural, and even quite necessary, to extend this axiom to mental, as well as bodily taste; and thus common sense, which is so often at variance with philosophy, especially with the sceptical kind, is found, in one instance at least, to agree in pronouncing the same decision.

But though this axiom, by passing into a proverb, seems to have attained the sanction of common sense; there is certainly a species of common sense which opposes it, at least serves to modify and restrain it. Whoever would assert an equality of genius and elegance between OGILBY[4] and MILTON, or BUNYAN and ADDISON, would be thought to defend no less an extravagance, than if he had maintained a mole-hill to be as high as TENERIFFE,[5] or a pond as extensive as the ocean. Though there may be found persons, who give the preference to the former authors; no one pays attention to such a taste; and we pronounce without scruple the sentiment of these pretended critics to be absurd and ridiculous. The principle of the natural equality of tastes is then totally forgot, and while

---

4 John Ogilby (1600–1676) published verse translations of Homer, Virgil, and Aesop.
5 A celebrated montain of 12,172 feet in the island of the same name (one of the Canaries).

we admit it on some occasions, where the objects seem near an equality, it appears an extravagant paradox, or rather a palpable absurdity, where objects so disproportioned are compared together.

It is evident that none of the rules of composition are fixed by reasonings *a priori*, or can be esteemed abstract conclusions of the understanding, from comparing those habitudes and relations of ideas, which are eternal and immutable. Their foundation is the same with that of all the practical sciences, experience; nor are they any thing but general observations, concerning what has been universally found to please in all countries and in all ages. [Many of the beauties of poetry and even of eloquence are founded on falsehood and fiction, on hyperboles, metaphors, and an abuse or perversion of terms from their natural meaning.] To check the sallies of the imagination, and to reduce every expression to geometrical truth and exactness, would be the most contrary to the laws of criticism; because it would produce a work, which, by universal experience, has been found the most insipid and disagreeable. But though poetry can never submit to exact truth, it must be confined by rules of art, discovered to the author either by genius or observation. If some negligent or irregular writers have pleased, they have not pleased by their transgressions of rule or order, but in spite of these transgressions: They have possessed other beauties, which were conformable to just criticism; and the force of these beauties has been able to overpower censure, and give the mind a satisfaction superior to the disgust arising from the blemishes. ARIOSTO[6] pleases; but not by his monstrous and improbable fictions, by his bizarre mixture of the serious and comic styles, by the want of coherence in his stories, or by the continual interruptions of his narration. He charms by the force and clearness of his expression, by the readiness and variety of his inventions, and by his natural pictures of the passions, especially those of the gay and amorous kind: And however his faults may diminish our satisfaction, they are not able entirely to destroy it. Did our pleasure really arise from those parts of his poem, which we denominate faults, this would be no objection to criticism in general: It would only be an objection to those particular rules of criticism, which would establish such circumstances to be faults, and would represent them as universally blameable. If they are found to please, they cannot be faults; let the pleasure, which they produce, be ever so unexpected and unaccountable.

---

6 Ludovico Ariosto (1474–1553), author of *Orlando Furioso*.

But though all the general rules of art are founded only on experience and on the observation of the common sentiments of human
nature, we must not imagine, that, on every occasion, the feelings of men
will be conformable to these rules. Those finer emotions of the mind are
of a very tender and delicate nature, and require the concurrence of many
favourable circumstances to make them play with facility and exactness,
according to their general and established principles. The least exterior
hindrance to such small springs, or the least internal disorder, disturbs
their motion, and confounds the operation of the whole machine. When
we would make an experiment of this nature, and would try the force
of any beauty or deformity, we must choose with care a proper time and
place, and bring the fancy to a suitable situation and disposition. A
perfect serenity of mind, a recollection of thought, a due attention to the
object; if any of these circumstances be wanting, our experiment will be
fallacious, and we shall be unable to judge of the catholic and universal
beauty. The relation, which nature has placed between the form and the
sentiment, will at least be more obscure; and it will require greater accuracy to trace and discern it. We shall be able to ascertain its influence
not so much from the operation of each particular beauty, as from the
durable admiration, which attends those works, that have survived all the
caprices of mode and fashion, all the mistakes of ignorance and envy.

The same HOMER, who pleased at ATHENS and ROME two thousand
years ago, is still admired at PARIS and at LONDON. All the changes of
climate, government, religion, and language, have not been able to
obscure his glory. Authority or prejudice may give a temporary vogue to
a bad poet or orator; but his reputation will never be durable or general.
When his compositions are examined by posterity or by foreigners, the
enchantment is dissipated, and his faults appear in their true colours. On
the contrary, a real genius, the longer his works endure, and the more
wide they are spread, the more sincere is the admiration which he meets
with. Envy and jealousy have too much place in a narrow circle; and even
familiar acquaintance with his person may diminish the applause due to
his performances: But when these obstructions are removed, the beauties,
which are naturally fitted to excite agreeable sentiments, immediately
display their energy; and while the world endures, they maintain their
authority over the minds of men.

It appears then, that, amidst all the variety and caprice of taste,
there are certain general principles of approbation or blame, whose influence a careful eye may trace in all operations of the mind. Some par-

ticular forms or qualities, from the original structure of the internal fabric, are calculated to please, and others to displease; and if they fail of their effect in any particular instance, it is from some apparent defect or imperfection in the organ. A man in a fever would not insist on his palate as able to decide concerning flavours; nor would one, affected with the jaundice, pretend to give a verdict with regard to colours. In each creature, there is a sound and a defective state; and the former alone can be supposed to afford us a true standard of taste and sentiment. If, in the sound state of the organ, there be an entire or a considerable uniformity of sentiment among men, we may thence derive an idea of the perfect beauty; in like manner as the appearance of objects in day-light, to the eye of a man in health, is denominated their true and real colour, even while colour is allowed to be merely a phantasm of the senses.

Many and frequent are the defects in the internal organs, which prevent or weaken the influence of those general principles, on which depends our sentiments of beauty or deformity. Though some objects, by the structure of the mind, be naturally calculated to give pleasure, it is not to be expected, that in every individual the pleasure will be equally felt. Particular incidents and situations occur, which either throw a false light on the objects, or hinder the true from conveying to the imagination the proper sentiment and perception.

One obvious cause, why many feel not the proper sentiment of beauty, is the want of that *delicacy* of imagination, which is requisite to convey a sensibility of those finer emotions. This delicacy every one pretends to: Every one talks of it; and would reduce every kind of taste or sentiment to its standard. But as our intention in this essay is to mingle some light of the understanding with the feelings of sentiment, it will be proper to give a more accurate definition of delicacy, than has hitherto been attempted. And not to draw our philosophy from too profound a source, we shall have recourse to a noted story in DON QUIXOTE.[7]

It is with good reason, says SANCHO to the squire with the great nose, that I pretend to have a judgment in wine: This is a quality hereditary in our family. Two of my kinsmen were once called to give their opinion of a hogshead, which was supposed to be excellent, being old and of a good vintage. One of them tastes it; considers it; and after mature reflection pronounces the wine to be good, were it not for a small taste of leather, which he perceived in it. The other, after using the same pre-

---

7 Part II, Ch. xiii.

cautions, gives also his verdict in favour of the wine; but with the reserve of a taste of iron, which he could easily distinguish. You cannot imagine how much they were both ridiculed for their judgment. But who laughed in the end? On emptying the hogshead, there was found at the bottom, an old key with a leathern thong tied to it.

The great resemblance between mental and bodily taste will easily teach us to apply this story. Though it be certain, that beauty and deformity, more than sweet and bitter, are not qualities in objects, but belong entirely to the sentiment, internal or external; it must be allowed, that there are certain qualities in objects, which are fitted by nature to produce those particular feelings. Now as these qualities may be found in a small degree, or may be mixed and confounded with each other, it often happens, that the taste is not affected with such minute qualities, or is not able to distinguish all the particular flavours, amidst the disorder, in which they are presented. Where the organs are so fine, as to allow nothing to escape them; and at the same time so exact as to perceive every ingredient in the composition: This we call delicacy of taste, whether we employ these terms in the literal or metaphorical sense. Here then the general rules of beauty are of use; being drawn from established models, and from the observation of what pleases or displeases, when presented singly and in a high degree: And if the same qualities, in a continued composition and in a smaller degree, affect not the organs with a sensible delight or uneasiness, we exclude the person from all pretensions to this delicacy. To produce these general rules or avowed patterns of composition is like finding the key with the leathern thong; which justified the verdict of SANCHO's kinsmen, and confounded those pretended judges who had condemned them. Though the hogshead had never been emptied, the taste of the one was still equally delicate, and that of the other equally dull and languid: But it would have been more difficult to have proved the superiority of the former, to the conviction of every by-stander. In like manner, though the beauties of writing had never been methodized, or reduced to general principles; though no excellent models had ever been acknowledged; the different degrees of taste would still have subsisted, and the judgment of one man been preferable to that of another; but it would not have been so easy to silence the bad critic, who might always insist upon his particular sentiment, and refuse to submit to his antagonist. But when we show him an avowed principle of art; when we illustrate this principle by examples, whose operation, from his own particular taste, he acknowledges to be conformable to the principle; when we prove, that the same principle may be applied to the present case, where he did not perceive or feel its influence: He must conclude, upon the whole, that the fault lies in himself, and that he wants the delicacy, which is requisite to make him sensible of every beauty and every blemish, in any composition or discourse.

It is acknowledged to be the perfection of every sense or faculty, to perceive with exactness its most minute objects, and allow nothing to escape its notice and observation. The smaller the objects are, which become sensible to the eye, the finer is that organ, and the more elaborate its make and composition. A good palate is not tried by strong flavours; but by a mixture of small ingredients, where we are still sensible of each part, notwithstanding its minuteness and its confusion with the rest. In like manner, a quick and acute perception of beauty and deformity must be the perfection of our mental taste; nor can a man be satisfied with himself while he suspects, that any excellence or blemish in a discourse has passed him unobserved. In this case, the perfection of the man, and the perfection of the sense or feeling, are found to be united. A very delicate palate, on many occasions, may be a great inconvenience both to a man himself and to his friends: But a delicate taste of wit or beauty must always be a desirable quality; because it is the source of all the finest and most innocent enjoyments, of which human nature is susceptible. In this decision the sentiments of all mankind are agreed. Wherever you can ascertain a delicacy of taste, it is sure to meet with approbation; and the best way of ascertaining it is to appeal to those models and principles, which have been established by the uniform consent and experience of nations and ages.

But though there be naturally a wide difference in point of delicacy between one person and another, nothing tends further to encrease and improve this talent, than *practice* in a particular art, and the frequent survey or contemplation of a particular species of beauty. When objects of any kind are first presented to the eye or imagination, the sentiment, which attends them, is obscure and confused; and the mind is, in a great measure, incapable of pronouncing concerning their merits or defects. The taste cannot perceive the several excellences of the performance; much less distinguish the particular character of each excellency, and ascertain its quality and degree. If it pronounce the whole in general to be beautiful or deformed, it is the utmost that can be expected; and even this judgment, a person, so unpractised, will be apt to deliver with great hesitation and reserve. But allow him to acquire experience in those objects, his feeling becomes more exact and nice: He not only perceives the beauties and defects of each part, but marks the distinguishing species of each quality, and assigns it suitable praise or blame. A clear and distinct sentiment attends him through the whole survey of the objects; and he discerns that very degree and kind of approbation or displeasure, which each part is naturally fitted to produce. The mist dissipates, which seemed formerly to hang over the object: The organ acquires greater perfection in its operations; and can pronounce, without danger of mistake, concerning the merits of every performance. In a word, the same address and dexterity, which practice gives to the execution of any work, is also acquired by the same means, in the judging of it.

So advantageous is practice to the discernment of beauty, that, before we can give judgment on any work of importance, it will even be requisite, that every individual performance be more than once perused by us, and be surveyed in different lights with attention and deliberation. There is a flutter or hurry of thought which attends the first perusal of any piece, and which confounds the genuine sentiment of beauty. The relation of the parts is not discerned: The true characters of style are little distinguished: The several perfections and defects seem wrapped up in a species of confusion, and present themselves indistinctly to the imagination. Not to mention, that there is a species of beauty, which, as it is florid and superficial, pleases at first; but being found incompatible with a just expression either of reason or passion, soon palls upon the taste, and is then rejected with disdain, at least rated at a much lower value.

It is impossible to continue in the practice of contemplating any order of beauty, without being frequently obliged to form *comparisons* between the several species and degrees of excellence, and estimating their proportion to each other. A man, who has had no opportunity of comparing the different kinds of beauty, is indeed totally unqualified to pronounce an opinion with regard to any object presented to him. By comparison alone we fix the epithets of praise or blame, and learn how to assign the due degree of each. The coarsest daubing contains a certain lustre of colours and exactness of imitation, which are so far beauties, and would affect the mind of a peasant or Indian with the highest admiration. The most vulgar ballads are not entirely destitute of harmony or nature; and none but a person, familiarized to superior beauties, would pronounce their numbers harsh, or narration uninteresting. A great inferiority of beauty gives pain to a person conversant in the highest excellence of the kind, and is for that reason pronounced a deformity: As the most finished object, with which we are acquainted, is naturally supposed to have reached the pinnacle of perfection, and to be entitled to the highest applause. One accustomed to see, and examine, and weigh the several performances, admired in different ages and nations, can only rate the merits of a work exhibited to his view, and assign its proper rank among the productions of genius.

But to enable a critic the more fully to execute this undertaking, he must preserve his mind free from all *prejudice,* and allow nothing to enter into his consideration, but the very object which is submitted to his examination. We may observe, that every work of art, in order to produce its due effect on the mind, must be surveyed in a certain point of view, and cannot be fully relished by persons, whose situation, real or imaginary, is not conformable to that which is required by the performance. An orator addresses himself to a particular audience, and must have a regard to their particular genius, interests, opinions, passions, and prejudices; otherwise he hopes in vain to govern their resolutions, and inflame their affections. Should they even have entertained some prepossessions against him, however unreasonable, he must not overlook this disadvantage; but, before he enters upon the subject, must endeavour to conciliate their affection, and acquire their good graces. A critic of a different age or nation, who should peruse this discourse, must have all these circumstances in his eye, and must place himself in the same situation as the audience, in order to form a true judgment of the oration. In like manner, when any work is addressed to the public, though I should have a friendship or enmity with the author, I must depart from this situation; and considering myself as a man in general, forget, if possible, my individual being and my peculiar circumstances. A person influenced by prejudice, complies not with this condition; but obstinately maintains his natural position, without placing himself in that point of view, which the performance supposes. If the work be addressed to persons of a different age or nation, he makes no allowance for their peculiar views and prejudices; but, full of the manners of his own age and country, rashly condemns what seemed admirable in the eyes of those for whom alone the discourse was calculated. If the work be executed for the public, he never sufficiently enlarges his comprehension, or forgets his interest as a friend or enemy, as a rival or commentator. By this means, his sentiments are perverted; nor have the same beauties and blemishes the same influence upon him, as if he had imposed a proper violence on his imagination, and had forgotten himself for a moment. So far his taste evidently departs from the true standard; and of consequence loses all credit and authority.

It is well known, that in all questions, submitted to the understanding, prejudice is destructive of sound judgment, and perverts all operations of the intellectual faculties: It is no less contrary to good taste; nor has it less influence to corrupt our sentiment of beauty. It belongs to *good sense* to check its influence in both cases; and in this respect, as well as in many others, reason, if not an essential part of taste, is at least requisite to the operations of this latter faculty. In all the nobler productions of genius, there is a mutual relation and correspondence of parts; nor can either the beauties or blemishes be perceived by him, whose thought is not capacious enough to comprehend all those parts, and compare them with each other, in order to perceive the consistence and uniformity of the whole. Every work of art has also a certain end or purpose, for which it is calculated; and is to be deemed more or less perfect, as it is more or less fitted to attain this end. The object of eloquence is to persuade, of history to instruct, of poetry to please by means of the passions and the imagination. These ends we must carry constantly in our view, when we peruse any performance; and we must be able to judge how far the means employed are adapted to their respective purposes. Besides, every kind of composition, even the most poetical, is nothing but a chain of propositions and reasonings, not always, indeed, the justest and most exact, but still plausible and specious, however disguised by the colouring of the imagination. The persons introduced in tragedy and epic poetry, must be represented as reasoning, and thinking, and concluding, and acting, suitably to their character and circumstances; and without judgment, as well as taste and invention, a poet can never hope to succeed in so delicate an undertaking. Not to mention, that the same excellence of faculties which contributes to the improvement of reason, the same clearness of conception, the same exactness of distinction, the same vivacity of apprehension, are essential to the operations of true taste, and are its infallible concomitants. It seldom, or never happens, that a man of sense, who has experience in any art, cannot judge of its beauty; and it is no less rare to meet with a man who has a just taste without a sound understanding.

Thus, though the principles of taste be universal, and, nearly, if not entirely the same in all men; yet few are qualified to give judgment on any work of art, or establish their own sentiment as the standard of beauty. The organs of internal sensation are seldom so perfect as to allow the general principles their full play, and produce a feeling correspondent to those principles. They either labour under some defect, or are vitiated by some disorder; and by that means, excite a sentiment, which may be pronounced erroneous. When the critic has no delicacy, he judges without any distinction, and is only affected by the grosser and more palpable qualities of the object: The finer touches pass unnoticed and disregarded. Where he is not aided by practice, his verdict is attended with confusion and hesitation. Where no comparison has been employed, the most frivolous beauties, such as rather merit the name of defects, are the object of his admiration. Where he lies under the influence of prejudice, all his natural sentiments are perverted. Where good sense is wanting, he is not qualified to discern the beauties of design and reasoning, which are the highest and most excellent. Under some or other of these imperfections, the generality of men labour; and hence a true judge in the finer arts is observed, even during the most polished ages, to be so rare a character: Strong sense, united to delicate sentiment, improved by practice, perfected by comparison, and cleared of all prejudice, can alone entitle critics to this valuable character; and the joint verdict of such, wherever they are to be found, is the true standard of taste and beauty.

But where are such critics to be found? By what marks are they to be known? How distinguish them from pretenders? These questions are embarrassing; and seem to throw us back into the same uncertainty, from which, during the course of this essay, we have endeavoured to extricate ourselves.

But if we consider the matter aright, these are questions of fact, not of sentiment. Whether any particular person be endowed with good sense and a delicate imagination, free from prejudice, may often be the subject of dispute, and be liable to great discussion and enquiry: But that such a character is valuable and estimable will be agreed in by all mankind. Where these doubts occur, men can do no more than in other disputable questions, which are submitted to the understanding: They must produce the best arguments, that their invention suggests to them; they must acknowledge a true and decisive standard to exist somewhere, to wit, real existence and matter of fact; and they must have indulgence to such as differ from them in their appeals to this standard. It is sufficient for our present purpose, if we have proved, that the taste of all individuals is not upon an equal footing, and that some men in general, however difficult to be particularly pitched upon, will be acknowledged by universal sentiment to have a preference above others.

But in reality the difficulty of finding, even in particulars, the

standard of taste, is not so great as it is represented. Though in speculation, we may readily avow a certain criterion in science and deny it in
sentiment, the matter is found in practice to be much more hard to ascertain in the former case than in the latter. Theories of abstract philosophy,
systems of profound theology, have prevailed during one age: In a successive period, these have been universally exploded: Their absurdity has
been detected: Other theories and systems have supplied their place,
which again gave place to their successors: And nothing has been experienced more liable to the revolutions of chance and fashion than these
pretended decisions of science. The case is not the same with the beauties
of eloquence and poetry. Just expressions of passion and nature are sure,
after a little time, to gain public applause, which they maintain for ever.
ARISTOTLE, and PLATO, and EPICURUS, and DESCARTES, may successively
yield to each other: But TERENCE and VIRGIL[8] maintain an universal, un-
disputed empire over the minds of men. The abstract philosophy of
CICERO has lost its credit: The vehemence of his oratory is still the object
of our admiration.

Though men of delicate taste be rare, they are easily to be distinguished in society, by the soundness of their understanding and the
superiority of their faculties above the rest of mankind. The ascendant,
which they acquire, gives a prevalence to that lively approbation, with
which they receive any productions of genius, and renders it generally
predominant. Many men, when left to themselves, have but a faint and
dubious perception of beauty, who yet are capable of relishing any fine
stroke, which is pointed out to them. Every convert to the admiration of
the real poet or orator is the cause of some new conversion. And though
prejudices may prevail for a time, they never unite in celebrating any
rival to the true genius, but yield at last to the force of nature and just
sentiment. Thus, though a civilized nation may easily be mistaken in the
choice of their admired philosopher, they never have been found long to
err, in their affection for a favorite epic or tragic author.

But notwithstanding all our endeavours to fix a standard of taste,
and reconcile the discordant apprehensions of men, there still remain two
sources of variation, which are not sufficient indeed to confound all the
boundaries of beauty and deformity, but will often serve to produce a

---

8 The distinction is between philosophers—those cited covering a span in history from
the fifth century B.C. (Plato) to the seventeenth century (Descartes)—and poets: the Roman
playwright Terence (c. 195–c. 158 B.C.) and epic poet Virgil (70–19 B.C.).

difference in the degrees of our approbation or blame. The one is the different humours of particular men; the other, the particular manners and opinions of our age and country. The general principles of taste are uniform in human nature. Where men vary in their judgments, some defect or perversion in the faculties may commonly be remarked; proceeding either from prejudice, from want of practice, or want of delicacy: and there is just reason for approving one taste, and condemning another. But where there is such a diversity in the internal frame or external situation as is entirely blameless on both sides, and leaves no room to give one the preference above the other; in that case a certain degree of diversity in judgment is unavoidable, and we seek in vain for a standard, by which we can reconcile the contrary sentiments.

A young man, whose passions are warm, will be more sensibly touched with amorous and tender images, than a man more advanced in years, who takes pleasure in wise, philosophical reflections concerning the conduct of life and moderation of the passions. At twenty, OVID may be the favourite author; HORACE at forty; and perhaps TACITUS[9] at fifty. Vainly would we, in such cases, endeavour to enter into the sentiments of others, and divest ourselves of those propensities, which are natural to us. We choose our favourite author as we do our friend, from a conformity of humour and disposition. Mirth or passion, sentiment or reflection; whichever of these most predominates in our temper, it gives us a peculiar sympathy with the writer who resembles us.

One person is more pleased with the sublime; another with the tender; a third with raillery. One has a strong sensibility to blemishes, and is extremely studious of correctness: Another has a more lively feeling of beauties, and pardons twenty absurdities and defects for one elevated or pathetic stroke. The ear of this man is entirely turned towards conciseness and energy; that man is delighted with a copious, rich, and harmonious expression. Simplicity is affected by one; ornament by another. Comedy, tragedy, satire, odes, have each its partizans, who prefer that particular species of writing to all others. It is plainly an error in a critic, to confine his approbation to one species or style of writing, and condemn all the rest. But it is almost impossible not to feel a predilection for that which suits our particular turn and disposition. Such preferences

9 Ovid (43 B.C.–A.D. 18), Roman poet noted for his celebration of sexual love (*The Art of Love*); Horace (65–8 B.C.), whose odes, satires, and epistles are more philosophical in tone; Tacitus (born c. A.D. 55), Roman historian.

are innocent and unavoidable, and can never reasonably be the object of dispute, because there is no standard, by which they can be decided.

For a like reason, we are more pleased, in the course of our reading, with pictures and characters, that resemble objects which are found in our own age or country, than with those which describe a different set of customs. It is not without some effort, that we reconcile ourselves to the simplicity of ancient manners, and behold princesses carrying water from the spring, and kings and heroes dressing their own victuals. We may allow in general, that the representation of such manners is no fault in the author, nor deformity in the piece; but we are not so sensibly touched with them. For this reason, comedy is not easily transferred from one age or nation to another. A FRENCHMAN or ENGLISHMAN is not pleased with the ANDRIA of TERENCE, or CLITIA of MACHIAVEL,[10] where the fine lady, upon whom all the play turns, never once appears to the spectators, but is always kept behind the scenes, suitably to the reserved humour of the ancient GREEKS and modern ITALIANS. A man of learning and reflection can make allowance for these peculiarities of manners; but a common audience can never divest themselves so far of their usual ideas and sentiments, as to relish pictures which in no wise resemble them.

But here there occurs a reflection, which may, perhaps, be useful in examining the celebrated controversy concerning ancient and modern learning; where we often find the one side excusing any seeming absurdity in the ancients from the manners of the age, and the other refusing to admit this excuse, or at least, admitting it only as an apology for the author, not for the performance. In my opinion, the proper boundaries in this subject have seldom been fixed between the contending parties. Where any innocent peculiarities of manners are represented, such as those above mentioned, they ought certainly to be admitted; and a man, who is shocked with them, gives an evident proof of false delicacy and refinement. The poet's *monument more durable than brass*,[11] must fall to the ground like common brick or clay, were men to make no allowance for the continual revolutions of manners and customs, and would admit of nothing but what was suitable to the prevailing fashion. Must we throw aside the pictures of our ancestors, because of their ruffs and fardingales? But where the ideas of morality and decency alter from one age to an-

---

10 Comic plays: *Andria* (166 B.C.), or *The Girl from Andros; Clitia* (1525), a prose comedy by Niccolò Machiavelli (1469–1527).

11 A reference to Horace, *Odes*, III. xxx. 1.

other, and where vicious manners are described, without being marked
with the proper characters of blame and disapprobation; this must be allowed to disfigure the poem, and to be a real deformity. I cannot, nor is
it proper I should, enter into such sentiments; and however I may excuse
the poet, on account of the manners of his age, I never can relish the
composition. The want of humanity and of decency, so conspicuous in
the characters drawn by several of the ancient poets, even sometimes by
HOMER and the GREEK tragedians, diminishes considerably the merit of
their noble performances, and gives modern authors an advantage over
them. We are not interested in the fortunes and sentiments of such rough
heroes: We are displeased to find the limits of vice and virtue so much
confounded: And whatever indulgence we may give to the writer on
account of his prejudices, we cannot prevail on ourselves to enter into his
sentiments, or bear an affection to characters, which we plainly discover
to be blameable.

The case is not the same with moral principles, as with speculative
opinions of any kind. These are in continual flux and revolution. The son
embraces a different system from the father. Nay, there scarcely is any
man, who can boast of great constancy and uniformity in this particular.
Whatever speculative errors may be found in the polite writings of any
age or country, they detract but little from the value of those compositions. There needs but a certain turn of thought or imagination to make
us enter into all the opinions, which then prevailed, and relish the sentiments or conclusions derived from them. But a very violent effort is
requisite to change our judgment of manners, and excite sentiments of
approbation or blame, love or hatred, different from those to which the
mind from long custom has been familiarized. And where a man is confident of the rectitude of that moral standard, by which he judges, he is
justly jealous of it, and will not pervert the sentiments of his heart for a
moment, in complaisance to any writer whatsoever.

Of all speculative errors, those, which regard religion, are the most
excusable in compositions of genius; nor is it ever permitted to judge of
the civility or wisdom of any people, or even of single persons, by the
grossness or refinement of their theological principles. The same good
sense, that directs men in the ordinary occurrences of life, is not hearkened
to in religious matters, which are supposed to be placed altogether above
the cognizance of human reason. On this account, all the absurdities of the
pagan system of theology must be overlooked by every critic, who would
pretend to form a just notion of ancient poetry; and our posterity, in their

turn, must have the same indulgence to their fore-fathers. No religious principles can ever be imputed as a fault to any poet, while they remain merely principles, and take not such strong possession of his heart, as to lay him under the imputation of *bigotry* or *superstition*. Where that happens, they confound the sentiments of morality, and alter the natural boundaries of vice and virtue. They are therefore eternal blemishes, according to the principle above mentioned; nor are the prejudices and false opinions of the age sufficient to justify them.

It is essential to the ROMAN catholic religion to inspire a violent hatred of every other worship, and to represent all pagans, mahometans, and heretics as the objects of divine wrath and vengeance. Such sentiments, though they are in reality very blameable, are considered as virtues by the zealots of that communion, and are represented in their tragedies and epic poems as a kind of divine heroism. This bigotry has disfigured two very fine tragedies of the FRENCH theatre, POLIEUCTE and ATHALIA;[12] where an intemperate zeal for particular modes of worship is set off with all the pomp imaginable, and forms the predominant character of the heroes. "What is this," says the sublime JOAD to JOSABET, finding her in discourse with MATHAN, the priest of BAAL, "Does the daughter of DAVID speak to this traitor? Are you not afraid, lest the earth should open and pour forth flames to devour you both? Or lest these holy walls should fall and crush you together? What is his purpose? Why comes that enemy of God hither to poison the air, which we breathe, with his horrid presence?" Such sentiments are received with great applause on the theatre of PARIS; but at LONDON the spectators would be full as much pleased to hear ACHILLES tell AGAMEMNON, that he was a dog in his forehead, and a deer in his heart, or JUPITER threaten JUNO with a sound drubbing, if she will not be quiet.[13]

RELIGIOUS principles are also a blemish in any polite composition, when they rise up to superstition, and intrude themselves into every sentiment, however remote from any connection with religion. It is no excuse for the poet, that the customs of his country had burthened life with so many religious ceremonies and observances, that no part of it was exempt from that yoke. It must for ever be ridiculous in PETRARCH to

---

12 *Polyeucte* (1641–1642) is a tragedy by Pierre Corneille (1606–1684), based on a story of early Christian martyrdom. *Athalie* (1691) is the last tragedy of Jean Racine (1639–1699); it is based on the Biblical story of Athaliah and Joash. The quotation Hume cites below is from this play, III. v. 1–8.

13 See *Iliad*, I. 225; *Iliad*, I. 565–67.

compare his mistress LAURA, to JESUS CHRIST.[14] Nor is it less ridiculous in that agreeable libertine, BOCCACE,[15] very seriously to give thanks to GOD ALMIGHTY and the ladies, for their assistance in defending him against his enemies.

---

[14] In sonnet LXXXI of the series dealing with Laura's death, Francesco Petrarch (1304–1373) compares his mistress to Christ as trampling over death. Another sonnet (XXXIX) declares her divinity; one calls her ambassadress from death to life (LXIII); several (LXVI, LXXVII, LXXVIII) suggest that she is sexually beloved by Christ.

[15] In the "Conclusion of the Author" to the *Decameron* (1471), Boccaccio thanks God and the ladies for bringing him safely to the conclusion of the work he has undertaken.

THOMAS GRAY

(1716–1771)

Thomas Gray, known in his own time as "the most learned man in Europe," is remembered now more as a poet than as a writer of prose. His life was outwardly uneventful. Born in London, the fifth of twelve children, he was the only one who survived infancy. He attended Eton College and Cambridge University, leaving Cambridge without a degree in 1738, and accompanying Horace Walpole on the Grand Tour of Europe. He quarreled with Walpole on the journey and completed it alone (the two were, however, later reconciled); then he returned to Cambridge, where he spent the rest of his life, nominally engaged in the study of law, but actually pursuing literary studies. Having refused the poet laureateship in 1757, Gray became professor of history and modern languages at Cambridge in 1768.

Gray's letters contain his most fully expressive writing. They reveal his fine perception of landscape, his capacity for acute literary criticism, his loyalty in friendship, his sensitivity, his humor, his awareness of nuance. For Gray, as for Cowper, correspondence was a way of enlarging a relatively limited day-to-day experience. He freely discusses his literary and his personal life, dramatizing his values and his personality for us, making the proper diction of poetry seem a living issue, re-creating architecture in such vivid detail that we participate richly in his response to it.

The text for the letters that follow is *Correspondence of Thomas Gray*, 3 vols., eds. P. Toynbee and L. Whibley (Oxford: Clarendon Press, 1935). Used by permission of the Clarendon Press, Oxford.

Biography and Criticism

Cecil, Lord David, *Two Quiet Lives*, 1948.

Golden, Morris, *Thomas Gray*, 1965.

Jones, W. Powell, *Thomas Gray, Scholar*, 1937.

Ketton-Cremer, R. W., "The Poet Who Spoke Out: The Letters of Thomas Gray," *The Familiar Letter in the Eighteenth Century*, pp. 148–64, eds. Anderson, Daghlian, Ehrenpreis, 1966.

———, *Thomas Gray: A Biography*, 1955.

Martin, Roger, *Essai sur Thomas Gray*, 1934.

Starr, Herbert W., *Gray as a Literary Critic*, 1941.

Tillotson, Geoffrey, *Essays in Criticism and Research*, 1942.

The Correspondence[1]
of Thomas Gray

GRAY TO WEST[2]   *London, [8] April, Thursday [1742]*

You are the first who ever made a Muse of a Cough; to me it seems a much more easy task to versify in one's sleep, (that indeed you were of old famous for) than for want of it. Not the wakeful nightingale (when she had a cough) ever sung so sweetly. I give you thanks for your warble, and wish you could sing yourself to rest. These wicked remains of your illness will sure give way to warm weather and gentle exercise; which I hope you will not omit as the season advances. Whatever low spirits and indolence, the effect of them, may advise to the contrary, I pray you add five steps to your walk daily for my sake; by the help of which, in a month's time, I propose to set you on horseback.

I talked of the Dunciad[3] as concluding you had seen it; if you have

---

1 See Introduction, pp. 22–23.

2 Richard West (1716–1742) had been Gray's boyhood friend at Eton. He was a talented and attractive young man; the "cough" to which Gray here refers was to cause West's death on June 1.

3 *The New Dunciad* of 1742, i.e., the fourth book of *The Dunciad*, published in March.

not, do you choose I should get and send it you? I have myself, upon your recommendation, been reading Joseph Andrews. The incidents are ill laid and without invention; but the characters have a great deal of nature, which always pleases even in her lowest shapes. Parson Adams is perfectly well; so is Mrs. Slipslop, and the story of Wilson; and throughout he shews himself well read in Stage-Coaches, Country Squires, Inns, and Inns of Court.[4] His reflections upon high people and low people, and misses and masters, are very good. However the exaltedness of some minds (or rather as I shrewdly suspect their insipidity and want of feeling or observation) may make them insensible to these light things, (I mean such as characterize and paint nature) yet surely they are as weighty and much more useful than your grave discourses upon the mind, the passions, and what not. Now as the paradisaical pleasures of the Mahometans consist in playing upon the flute and lying with Houris,[5] be mine to read eternal new romances of Marivaux[6] and Crebillon.[7]

You are very good in giving yourself the trouble to read and find fault with my long harangues. Your freedom (as you call it) has so little need of apologies, that I should scarce excuse your treating me any otherwise; which, whatever compliment it might be to my vanity, would be making a very ill one to my understanding. As to matter of stile, I have this to say: The language of the age is never the language of poetry; except among the French, whose verse, where the thought or image does not support it, differs in nothing from prose. Our poetry, on the contrary, has a language peculiar to itself; to which almost every one, that has written, has added something by enriching it with foreign idioms and derivatives: Nay sometimes words of their own composition or invention. Shakespeare and Milton have been great creators this way; and no one more licentious than Pope or Dryden, who perpetually borrow expressions from the former. Let me give you some instances from Dryden, whom every body reckons a great master of our poetical tongue.—Full of *museful mopeings*—unlike the *trim* of love—a pleasant *beverage*—a *roundelay* of love—stood silent in his *mood*—with knots and *knares* deformed—his

---

4 The legal societies in London, which had the exclusive right to admit people to the bar.

5 Nymphs of the Mohammedan paradise.

6 Pierre de Marivaux (1688–1763), author of light comedies and novels about lovers.

7 Claude-Prosper-Jolyot de Crébillon (1707–1777), author of *Le Sopha* (1740), an erotic "moral tale."

ireful mood—in proud *array*—his *boon* was granted—and *disarray* and shameful rout—*wayward* but wise—*furbished* for the field—the *foiled dodderd* oaks[8]—*disherited*—*smouldring* flames—*retchless* of laws—*crones* old and ugly—the *beldam* at his side—the *grandam-hag*—*villanize* his Father's fame—But they are infinite: And our language not being a settled thing (like the French) has an undoubted right to words of an hundred years old, provided antiquity have not rendered them unintelligible. In truth, Shakespear's language is one of his principal beauties; and he has no less advantage over your Addisons and Rowes[9] in this, than in those other great excellencies you mention. Every word in him is a picture. Pray put me the following lines into the tongue of our modern Dramatics:

> *But I, that am not shaped for sportive tricks,*
> *Nor made to court an amorous looking-glass:*
> *I, that am rudely stampt, and want love's majesty*
> *To strut before a wanton ambling nymph:*
> *I, that am curtail'd of this fair proportion,*
> *Cheated of feature by dissembling nature,*
> *Deform'd, unfinish'd, sent before my time*
> *Into this breathing world, scarce half made up—*[10]

And what follows. To me they appear untranslatable; and if this be the case, our language is greatly degenerated. However, the affectation of imitating Shakespear may doubtless be carried too far; and is no sort of excuse for sentiments ill-suited, or speeches ill-timed, which I believe is a little the case with me. I guess the most faulty expressions may be these— *silken* son of *dalliance*—*drowsier* pretensions—wrinkled *beldams*—*arched* the hearer's brow and *riveted* his eyes in *fearful extasie.* These are easily altered or omitted: and indeed if the thoughts be wrong or superfluous, there is nothing easier than to leave out the whole. The first ten or twelve lines are, I believe, the best;[11] and as for the rest, I was betrayed into a good

---

8 Gray is mistaken about this quotation. Dryden once refers to "dodder'd Oaks" (*Palamon and Arcite*, III. 905) and twice to "a Doddard Oke" (*Fifth Satire of Persius*, 80; *Ninth Pastoral of Virgil*, 12, with different spelling), but in no instance is there a second modifier. The meaning of *foiled* that Gray has in mind is perhaps the obsolete one, "defiled."

9 I.e., more formal dramatists, like Joseph Addison (1672–1719), author of the classically "correct" tragedy *Cato* (1713), and Nicholas Rowe (1674–1718), who was known for such sentimental tragedies as *The Fair Penitent* (1703) and *Jane Shore* (1714).

10 Shakespeare's *Richard III*, I. i. 14–21.

11 Gray is referring to lines from his own unfinished tragedy, *Agrippina*.

deal of it by Tacitus; only what he has said in five words, I imagine I have
said in fifty lines: Such is the misfortune of imitating the inimitable.
Now, if you are of my opinion, una litura[12] may do the business better
than a dozen; and you need not fear unravelling my web. I am a sort of
spider; and have little else to do but spin it over again, or creep to some
other place and spin there. Alas! for one who has nothing to do but
amuse himself, I believe my amusements are as little amusing as most
folks. But no matter; it makes the hours pass, and is better than ἐν
ἀμαθίᾳ καὶ ἀμγσίᾳ καταβιῶναι.[13]

Adieu.

GRAY TO WHARTON[1]   *Stoke, Sept: 18. 1754.*

Dear S[r]
    I rejoice to find you at last settled to your heart's content, & delight
to hear you talk of *giving your house some Gothic ornaments* already. if
you project any thing, I hope it will be entirely within doors; & don't
let me (when I come gaping into Coleman-street) be directed to the
Gentleman's at the ten Pinnacles, or with the Church-porch at his door.
I am glad you enter into the Spirit of Strawberry-Castle.[2] it has a purity
& propriety of Gothicism in it (with very few exceptions,) that I have
not seen elsewhere. the eating-room & library were not compleated,
when I was there, & I want to know, what effect they have. my L[d]
Radnor's Vagaries[3] (I see) did not keep you from doing justice to his
situation, w[ch] far surpasses every thing near it, & I do not know a more

---

12 "A single blot"—i.e., one erasure.
13 "To pass one's life in a state of ignorance and grossness." The reference is to
Aelian, who explains that the Mytilenaeans punished their revolted allies by forbidding them
to educate their children, it being the heaviest penalty to pass one's life in ignorance (*Various
History*, VII. 15).
1 Dr. Thomas Wharton (1717–1794) was one of Gray's most intimate friends; the
friendship dated from Gray's earliest days in Cambridge. At the time of this letter, having
recently become a fellow of the Royal College of Physicians, Wharton was settling in a new
house in King's Arms Yard, Coleman Street, London.
2 Horace Walpole's famous estate, Strawberry Hill, near Twickenham, which he had
elaborately remodeled into an imitation Gothic castle.
3 John Robartes, Earl of Radnor (c. 1686–1757), whose estate, also fantastically decorated, adjoined Strawberry Hill.

laughing Scene, than that about Twickenham & Richmond. Dr Akenside[4] (I perceive) is no Conjurer in Architecture, especially when he talks of the Ruins of Persepolis, wch are no more Gothic, than they are Chinese. the Egyptian Style (see Dr Pococke,[5] not his discourses, but his prints) was apparently the Mother of ye Greek; & there is such a similitude between the Egyptian, & those Persian Ruins, as gave room to Diodorus[6] to affirm, that the old buildings of Persia were certainly perform'd by Egyptian Artists. as to the other part of his opinion, that the Gothic manner is the Saracen or Moorish, he has a great Authority to support him, that of Sr Christ:^r Wren,[7] & yet (I can not help thinking) is undoubtedly wrong. the Palaces in Spain I never saw but in description, wch gives us little or no Idea of things; but the Doge's Palace at Venice I have seen (wch is in the Arabesque[8] manner) & the houses of Barbary you may see in Dr Shaw's book,[9] not to mention abundance of other eastern Buildings in Turky, Persia, &c: that we have views of, & they seem plainly to be corruptions of the Greek Architecture, broke into little parts indeed, & cover'd with little ornaments, but in a taste very distinguishable from that we call Gothic. there is one thing, that runs thro' the Moorish Buildings, that an Imitator would certainly have been first struck with, & would have tried to copy, & that is the Cupola's, wch cover everything, Baths, Apar[t]ments, & even Kitchens. yet who ever saw a Gothic Cupola? it is a thing plainly of Greek original. I do not see any thing but the slender Spires, that serve for steeples, wch may perhaps be borrowed from the Saracen Minarets on their Mosques.

I was in Northamptonshire, when I received your Letter, but am now returned hither. I have been a Warwick, wch is a place worth seeing. the Town is on an eminence surrounded every way with a fine cultivated Valley, thro' wch the Avon winds, & at the distance of 5 or 6 miles, a

---

4 Mark Akenside (1721–1770), doctor and author of *The Pleasures of the Imagination* (1744), a long, blank-verse poem.

5 Richard Pococke (1704–1765), a famous traveler, whose *Description of the East* (1743–1745), concerned with Egypt and Palestine, contains 178 illustrative plates.

6 Diodorus Siculus, Sicilian historian of the first century B.C., author of a world history in Greek ending with the Gallic Wars.

7 Sir Christopher Wren (1632–1723), the famous English architect, the designer of St. Paul's Cathedral. His opinion that the Gothic style of architecture should properly be called the Saracen style is recorded in a "Memorial to the Bishop of Rochester" (1713), printed by his son in *Parentalia* (1750).

8 I.e., *Arabian*.

9 *Travels, or Observations Relating to Several Parts of Barbary and the Levant* (1738), by Thomas Shaw (1694–1751).

circle of hills well wooded, & with various objects crowning them, that close the Prospect. out of the town on one side of it rises a rock, that might remind one of your rocks at Durham, but that it is not so savage, or so lofty, & that the river, wch washes its foot, is perfectly clear, & so gentle, that its current is hardly visible. upon it stands the Castle, the noble old residence of the Beauchamps & Neville's, & now of Earl Brooke.[10] he has sash'd the great Appartment, that's to be sure, (I can't help these things) & being since told, that square sash-windows were not Gothic, he has put certain whim-wams withinside the glass, wch appearing through are to look like fretwork. then he has scooped out a little Burrough in the massy walls of the place for his little self & his children, wch is hung with Paper & printed Linnen, & carved chimney-pieces, in the exact manner of Berkley-square or Argyle-Buildings. what in short can a Lord do now a days, that is lost in a great old solitary Castle, but sculk about, & get into the first hole he finds, as a Rat would do in like case. a pretty long old stone-bridge leads you into the town with a Mill at the end of it, over wch the rock rises with the Castle upon it with all its battlements & queer ruin'd towers, & on your left hand the Avon strays thro' the Park, whose ancient Elms seem to remember Sr Philip Sidney,[11] (who often walk'd under them) and talk of him to this day. the Beauchamp Earls of Warwick lie under stately Monuments in the Choir of the great Church, & in our Lady's Chappel adjoining to it. there also lie Ambrose Dudley, E: of Warwick; & his Brother, the famous Ld Leicester, with Lettice, his Countess. this Chappel is preserved entire, tho' the Body of the Church was burnt down 60 years ago, & rebuilt by S^r C: Wren. I had heard often of Guy-Cliff two miles from the town, so I walked to see it; & of all improvers commend me to Mr Greathead,[12] its present Owner. he shew'd it me himself, & is literally a fat young Man with a head & face much bigger than they are usually worn. it was naturally a very agreeable rock, whose Cliffs cover'd with large trees hung beetleing over the Avon, wch twists twenty ways in sight of it. there was the Cell of Guy, Earl of Warwick, cut in the living

---

10 Francis Greville, eighth Baron Brooke, in 1746 was made Earl Brooke of Warwick Castle.

11 The Elizabethan poet (1554–1586), famous also as a soldier and a statesman, whose uncle was Ambrose Dudley, Earl of Warwick (1561–1589).

12 Samuel Greathed, whom Walpole also mocked as "that foolish Greathead."

stone, where he died a Hermit[13] (as you may see in a penny History, that
hangs upon the rails in Moorfields) there were his fountains bubbling out
of the Cliff; there was a Chantry founded to his memory in Henry the
6th's time. but behold the Trees are cut down to make room for flowering
shrubs, the rock is cut up, till it is as smooth & as sleek as sattin; the river
has a gravel-walk by its side; the Cell is a Grotta with cockle-shells and
looking-glass; the fountains have an iron-gate before them, and the
Chantry is a Barn, or a little House. even the poorest bits of nature, that
remain, are daily threatned, for he says (& I am sure, when the Great-
heads are once set upon a thing, they will do it) he is determined, it shall
be *all new*. These were his words, & they are Fate. I have also been at
Stow, at Woburn (the Du[ke] of Bedford's), and at Wroxton (L[d] Guilford's) but I defer these Chapt[ers] till we meet. I shall only tell you for your
Comfort, that th[e] part of Northampt:[re], where I have been, is in fruits,
in flowers [& in] corn very near a fortnight behind this part of Bucking-
hamshire, that they have no nightingales, & that the other birds are almost
as silent, as at Durham. it is rich land, but upon a Clay, & in a very bleak,
high, exposed situation. I hope, you have had some warm weather, since
you last complained of the South. I have thoughts of seeing you about
Michaelmas, tho' I shall not stay long in town. I should have been at
Camb:[ge] before now, if the D: of Newc:[le] & his foundation-stone[14]
would have let me, but I want them to have done before I go. I am sorry
M[r] Brown[15] should be the only one, that has stood upon Punctilio's with
me, & would not write first. pray tell him so. Mason[16] is (I believe) in
town, or at Chiswick. [no news of Tuthill]:[17] I wrote a long letter to him
in answer to one he wrote me, but no reply.

Adieu, I am ever Yrs,
TG:

---

13 Chaucer mentions the story of Guy of Warwick in his *Rime of Sir Thopas;* it later
became popular in ballads and prose romances.
14 Plans had been approved for erecting a new front to the university library; the
Duke of Newcastle, chancellor of the university, visited the site on September 16. Gray disliked the Duke and tried to avoid encounters with him.
15 James Brown (1709–1784), a close friend of Gray, was also a fellow of Pembroke,
Gray's college, and eventually (1770–1784) its master. He is referred to again in the postscript
below.
16 William Mason (1724–1797), Gray's friend and later his biographer. A clergyman
by profession, he was also the author of several plays, satires, and poems, many of which
Gray discussed with him in minute detail.
17 Henry Tuthill, a fellow of Pembroke.

Brown call'd here this morning, before I was up, & breakfasted with me.

Addressed: To Dr Thomas Wharton M: D: in Pancras-Lane, near Cheapside London *Postmark:* 20 SE

GRAY TO BEDINGFIELD[1]   *Stoke. Aug: 10. 1757*

Dear S^r

I have order'd Dodsley[2] long since to send you piping hot from the Press four copies of the Bard & his Companion,[3] three of wch I take the liberty to offer to Lady Swinburne,[4] Mrs Bedingfield, & Yourself, and the fourth is intended for Miss Hepburn[5] at Monkridge near Haddington, if there be any such Person, wch I a little doubt. if you remember, you promised to take upon you the trouble of conveying it to her. before this time (I hope) they are come safe to your hands. you are desired to give me your *honest* opinion about the latter part of the Bard, wch you had not seen before, for I know it is weakly in several parts; but it is a mercy, that it ever came to an end at all. there are also six new lines at the end of the 2^d Antistrophe *Fair laughs the Morn* &c: wch my Friends approve & (to say the truth) so do I. you will do me a favour, if you will inform me what the North says either in good or in bad. as to the South, it is too busy & too fastidious to trouble its head about any thing, that has no wit in it. I know, I shall never be admired but in Scotland. by the way I am greatly struck with the Tragedy of Douglas,[6] tho' it has infinite faults. the Author seems to me to have retrieved the true language of the Stage, wch had been lost for these hundred years; & there is one Scene (between Matilda & the old Peasant) so masterly, that it strikes me blind to all the defects in the world.

I will not make you any excuses for my *sulkyness* of late, for in reality I have been ill eversince I left Cambridge. I will not *deprecate* you

---

1 Edward Bedingfield (b. 1730) met Gray at Cambridge in 1755. He was to help Mason with revisions and notes for *Memoirs of the Life and Writings of Mr. Gray.*

2 Robert Dodsley (1703–1764), publisher and bookseller, published Gray's *Odes* after Walpole had printed the first thousand copies on his press at Strawberry Hill.

3 Gray's *Odes* consisted of "The Bard" and "The Progress of Poesy."

4 Mary, the widow of Sir John Swinburne, third Baronet of Capheaton. She was Bedingfield's third cousin.

5 Margaret Hepburn (c. 1720–c. 1760). The circumstances of Gray's meeting with her are unknown.

6 *Douglas* (1756), a highly successful tragedy by John Home, known in his own time as "the Scottish Shakespeare."

with regard to our *Quarrel*, for if any thing escaped me (as you pretend) that seemed *strong*, that is, that hurt you a little, I am not conscious of any such meaning, & you would not have me apologize for mere words, or an ill-contrived expression.

I am highly obliged to you for the two miniatures wch are exceedingly pretty. I shall preserve them with great care, & beg you would kiss (in my name) the fair hand,[7] y^t employs itself so well, & that honour'd me with them. one of the two seems to be from nature: I desire to know whose house it is, & what river runs by it.

Adieu, Dear S^r & believe me
Your Friend & humble Servant
TG:

I am at Mrs Rogers's of Stoke near Windsor Bucks.

GRAY TO WHARTON

Dear Doctor

I feel very ungrateful every day, that I continue silent, & yet I do not write to you: but now the pen is in my hand, and I am in for it. when I left you, in spite of the rain I went out of my way to Richmond, & made a shift to see the Castle, & look down upon the valley, thro' wch the Swale[1] winds: that was all the weather would permitt. at Rippon I visited the Church, which we had neglected before, with some pleasure, & saw the Ure full to its brink & very inclinable to overflow. some faint gleams of sunshine gave me an opportunity of walking over Studley,[2] & descending into the ruins of Fountain's Abbey, wch I examined with attention. I pass'd over the ugly moor of Harrowgate, made a bow to the Queen's-Head,[3] & got late at night to Leedes: here the rain was so

---

7 This may refer to Miss Swinburne, probably a sister-in-law of Bedingfield, who, we learn in a later letter, had sent Gray a "beautiful little Specimen of her art."

1 A river in Yorkshire. Gray had stayed with Wharton at Old Park until late in 1762. On his journey back to Cambridge he made a tour in Yorkshire and Derbyshire, on which he here reports.

2 The villages of Studley Roger and Studley Royal, with Studley Park and the ruins of Fountains Abbey (founded 1132 for Cistercian monks), are about three miles southwest of Ripon.

3 An inn in Harrogate, a fashionable resort celebrated for its medicinal springs.

perverse I could scarce see the Town, much less go to Kirkstall-Abbey,[4] wch was my intention; so I proceeded to Wakefield, & Wentworth Castle.[5] here the Sun again indulged me, & open'd as beautiful a scene of rich & cultivated country, as (I am told) Yorkshire affords. the water is all artificial, but with an air of nature; much wood; a very good house in the Q: Anne style, wch is now new-fronting in a far better taste by the present Earl;[6] many pictures not worth a farthing, & a castle built only for a play-thing on the top of the hill as a point of view, & to command a noble prospect. I went on to Sheffield, liked the situation in a valley by a pretty river's side, surrounded with charming hills: saw the handsome parish-church[7] with the chappel & monuments of the Talbots. then I enter'd the Peak,[8] a countrey beyond comparison uglier than any other I have seen in England, black, tedious, barren, & not mountainous enough to please one with its horrors. this is mitigated, since you were there, by a road like a bowling-green, wch soon brought me to Chatsworth.[9] the house has the air of a Palace, the hills rising on three of its sides shut out the view of its dreary neighbourhood, & are cover'd with wood to their tops: the front opens to the Derwent winding thro' the valley, wch by the art of Mr Brown[10] is now always visible & full to its brim. for heretofore it could not well be seen (but in rainy seasons) from the windows. a handsome bridge is lately thrown over it, & the stables taken away, wch stood full in view between the house & the river. the prospect opens here to a wider tract of country terminated by more distant hills: this scene is yet in its infancy, the objects are thinly scatter'd, & the clumps and plantations lately made: but it promises well in time. within doors the furniture corresponds to the stateliness of the appart-ments, fine tapestry, marble doorcases with fruit, flowers, & foliage, ex-

---

4 Founded in 1152 for Cistercians from Fountains Abbey; located three miles west of Leeds.

5 Wakefield is about thirty miles southwest of York; Wentworth Castle is near Barnsley.

6 William Wentworth, second Earl of Strafford, a close friend of Horace Walpole, who incidentally, valued the pictures in the castle more highly than did Gray.

7 The Church of St. Peter, in Sheffield.

8 A hilly part of Derbyshire, which Gray visited again a few years later.

9 Chatsworth House in Derbyshire, seat of the Duke of Devonshire.

10 "Capability Brown," one of the most famous landscape gardeners of the century, whose real name was Lancelot Brown (1715–1783).

cellently done by Old Cibber's Father,[11] windows of plate-glass in gilded frames, & such a profusion of Gibbons'[12] best carving in wood, viz. Dead-Game, fish, shells, flowers, &c: as I never saw anywhere. the ceilings & staircases all painted by Verrio or Laguerre,[13] in their usual sprawling way, & no other pictures, but in one room 8 or 10 portraits, some of them very good, of James & Charles the first's time. the gardens are small, & in the French style with water-works, particularly a grand Cascade of steps & a *Temple d'eaux*[14] at the head of it. from thence I went to Hardwick.[15] one would think Mary, Queen of Scots, was but just walk'd down into the Park with her Guard for half-an-hour. her Gallery, her room of audience, her antichamber, with the very canopies, chair of state, footstool, Lit-de-repos,[16] Oratory, carpets, & hangings, just as she left them. a little tatter'd indeed, but the more venerable; & all preserved with religious care, & paper'd up in winter. the park & country are just like Hertfordshire. I went by Chesterfield & Mansfield to revisit my old friend the Trent[17] at Nottingham, where I passed 2 or 3 days, & from thence took stage-coach to London.

When I arrived there, I found Professor Turner[18] had been dead above a fortnight, & being cocker'd and spirited up by some Friends (tho' it was rather of the latest) I got my name suggested to L^d B:.[19] you may easily imagine, who undertook it; & indeed he did it with zeal. I received my answer very soon, wch was what you may easily imagine, but join'd with great professions of *his desire to serve me* on any future occasion, & many more fine words, that I pass over, not out of modesty,

---

11 Colley Cibber (1671–1757), poet laureate from 1730, is here referred to as "Old Cibber" to distinguish him from his son, Theophilus. Colley's father, Caius Gabriel Cibber (1630–1700), was a sculptor who had worked at Chatsworth.

12 Grinling Gibbons (1648–1720), a famous wood-carver.

13 Antonio Verrio (c. 1639–1707) and Louis Laguerre (1663–1721) were both noted for their painted decorations of ceilings. Gray here alludes to Pope's "On painted Ceilings you devoutly stare,/Where sprawl the Saints of Verrio or Laguerre" ("Epistle to Burlington," 145–46).

14 Temple of waters.

15 Hardwicke Hall, a seat of the Duke of Devonshire, also in Derbyshire, which Mary Queen of Scots (1542–1587) visited occasionally during her fourteen years in custody at Sheffield Castle.

16 Literally, "bed of repose", i.e., the bed in which she slept.

17 The Trent River.

18 Shallet Turner, who had been regius professor of modern history at Cambridge since 1735.

19 John Stuart, third Earl of Bute, at this time Prime Minister, to whom Sir Henry Erskine had made application, "with zeal," that Gray be given Turner's post.

but for another reason. so you see I have made my fortune, like Sr Fr: Wronghead.[20] this *nothing* is a profound secret, and no one here suspects it even now: today I hear, that Delaval[21] has got it, but we are not yet certain: next to myself I wish'd for him.

You see we have made a peace.[22] I shall be silent about it, because if I say anything antiministerial, you will tell me, you know the reason; & if I approve it, you will tell me, I have expectations still. all I know is, that the D: of Newcastle & Ld Hardwick[23] both say, it is an excellent Peace; & only Mr Pitt[24] calls it inglorious & insidious.

I had a little Gout twice, while I was in Town, wch confined me some time: yet I bespoke your chairs. they are what is call'd *Rout-Chairs*,[25] but as they are to be a little better in shape & materials than ordinary, will come to about 6 9 a chair. I desired your Brother to judge, how he perform'd, & the first, that was made, was to be sent him to see.

My best respects attend Mrs Wharton, who I suppose, receives them in bed. how does she doe? My compliments to Miss.[26] I am ever truly

                                                                                          Yours

Cambridge. Dec: 4. 1762.

Mason is in Yorkshire now, but I miss'd of him.

Addressed: To Dr Wharton M:D: at Old-Park near Durham *Postmark:* YORK

GRAY TO MASON   *London. Nov. 8. 1765*

20 Sir Francis Wronghead is the country squire in "The Provoked Husband," a play by Sir John Vanbrugh and Colley Cibber. He believes—falsely—that he has made his fortune because he has a friend at court. See Act II. i.

21 Edward Hussey Delaval (1729–1814), a distinguished classical scholar and linguist. Although he was a candidate for the professorship at this time (and again in 1768, when Gray was appointed), he did not win it; the new professor was Lawrence Brockett of Trinity College, who had been tutor to Lord Bute's son-in-law.

22 The Preliminaries of Peace with France and Spain had been signed on November 3. The final peace treaty, which ended the Seven Years' War, was not signed until February 1763.

23 Philip Yorke, second Earl of Hardwicke (1720–1796), a Whig statesman; also high-steward of the University of Cambridge.

24 William Pitt (1708–1778), who had resigned as secretary of state in 1761 because of his opposition to the plans for peace; he was at this time not active in the government.

25 So called because of their association with fashionable parties, or *routs*.

26 Wharton's eldest daughter, Mary, aged 14.

Dear Mason

Res est sacra *miser* (says the Poet)[1] but I say, it is the happy Man,
that is the sacred thing; & therefore let the Profane keep their distance:
he is one of Lucretius' Gods,[2] supremely blest in the contemplation of
his own felicity, & what has he to do with Worshippers? this (mind) is
the first reason, why I did not come to York. the second is, that I do not
love confinement, & probably by next summer may be permitted to
touch[3] whom & where & with what I think fit without giving you any
offence. the third & last, & not the least perhaps, is, that the finances
were at so low an ebb, that I could not exactly do what I wish'd, but
was obliged to come the shortest road to Town & recruit them. I do not
justly know what your taste in reasons may be, since you alter'd your
condition; but there is the ingenious, the petulant, & the dull, for you.
any one would have done, for in my conscience I do not believe you
care a half-penny for reasons at present. so God bless ye both, & give ye
all ye wish, when ye are restored to the use of your wishes!

I am return'd from Scotland charm'd with my expedition: it is of
the Highlands I speak: the Lowlands are worth seeing once, but the
Mountains are extatic, & ought to be visited in pilgrimage once a year.
none but those monstrous creatures of God know how to join so much
beauty with so much horror. a fig for your Poets, Painters, Gardiners, &
Clergymen, that have not been among them: their imagination can be
made up of nothing but bowling-greens, flowering shrubs, horse-ponds,
Fleet-ditches, shell-grottoes, & Chinée-rails.[4] then I had so beautiful an
autumn: Italy could hardly produce a nobler scene, or a finer season. and
this so sweetly contrasted with that perfection of nastiness, & total want
of accommodation, that Scotland only can supply. oh! you would have
bless'd yourself. I shall certainly go again. what a pity 'tis I can't draw,
nor describe, nor ride on horseback!

St:r is the busiest creature upon earth, except Mr Fraser:[5] they stand

---

1 "The unfortunate man is a sacred thing" (Seneca, *Epigrams*, IV. 9).

2 The gods, says Lucretius, are far removed from human troubles and need no worship. See *Of the Nature of Things*, II. 646–51. Gray is alluding to Mason's "felicity" in his
recent marriage (September 25, 1765).

3 Gray's letters contain many allusions to the fact that only Mr. Brown, no one else,
was allowed to "touch" Mrs. Mason.

4 Fences of "Chinese" style. Chinese forms and objects ("Chinoiseries") were influential at this time on English landscaping and most other English arts.

5 William Fraser and Stonhewer were now the two under secretaries of state.

pretty tight for all his Royal Highness.[6] have you read (oh no! I had forgot)[7] D[r] Lowth's pamphlet[8] against your Uncle the Bishop? oh how he works him! I hear he will soon be on the same bench.[9] today M[r] Hurd came to see me, but we had not a word of that matter. he is grown pure & plump, just of the proper breadth for a celebrated Town-Preacher. there was D[r] Balguy too: he says, M[rs] Mason is very handsome; so you are his Friend for ever. Ld Newnham[10] (I hear) has ill health of late: it is a nervous case. & have a care! how do your eyes do? the hereditary Prince[11] the morning after he was married, I remember, said to some-body, Sauf le respect que je dois a son Altesse Royale, jamais Princesse n'a eté mieux f—e.[12] can you in conscience mutatis mutandis[13] say the same? I know any body can & will say the same: but can you say it verbo Sacerdotis?[14] Adieu! my respects to the Bride. I would kiss her, but you stand by & pretend, it is not the fashion: tho' I know, they do so at Hull.[15] I am

Ever Yours
TG:

Addressed (by Stonhewer): To The Rev[d] M[r] Mason in the Minster Yard York Free R. Stonhewer *Postmark:* 9 NO

---

6 This cryptic allusion may be to the death of the Duke of Cumberland.

7 Gray's assumption that Mason would not read an attack on Warburton and the reference to Warburton as his "uncle" may be joking allusions to Mason's great respect for Bishop Warburton, who convinced Mason—so the Bishop himself claimed—that he should abandon the writing of poetry when he became a clergyman. This "conviction," however, soon lapsed.

8 Robert Lowth (1710–1787) had published *A Letter to the Author of the "Divine Legation,"* a reply to Bishop Warburton's attack on his dating of the Book of Job and his opinion about the nature of Job's authority.

9 Lowth became a bishop in 1766.

10 Simon, Viscount Nuneham and Lord Harcourt (1714–1777).

11 Charles William Ferdinand, hereditary prince of Brunswick. He had married in 1764 George III's sister Augusta, princess royal.

12 "With all due respect to Her Royal Highness, never has a Princess been better bedded."

13 "Things being changed that have to be changed"—i.e., allowing for the difference in rank.

14 "On the word of a priest"—i.e., word of honor.

15 Mason's bride was from Kingston-upon-Hull.

HORACE WALPOLE,
Fourth Earl of Oxford

(1717–1797)

The fourth son of Sir Robert Walpole, the famous prime minister, Horace Walpole was educated at Eton College and at King's College, Cambridge. He traveled on the continent with the poet Thomas Gray, then became a Member of Parliament, and finally devoted himself largely to his estate at Strawberry Hill, which he made into a Gothic castle. His range of aesthetic, social, intellectual, and political interest was large. On his own press at Strawberry Hill he printed Gray's odes, purportedly classic in form (modeled on Pindar's), and his own Gothic romance, *The Castle of Otranto* (1764): These facts in conjunction suggest the breadth of his taste. He also published various historical works of his own, including *Anecdotes of Painting in England* (1762–1771), a valuable history of English painting. Yet he was very much a man of his own time, as his letters and his *Memoirs* (published only in the nineteenth century) testify.

More than any other famous letter writer of his time, Walpole demonstrates in his correspondence a lively and informed interest in public as well as private affairs. This is partly the interest of a gossip, but also that of a historian. He is conscious of his position as his father's son; his father's enemies remain his. Yet he also has the perspective of an acute external observer. His reports of the large events of his time vitalize history by their keen observation, their sharp and often malicious wit, their unerring sense of the telling detail. Horace Mann, in Venice, was the recipient of much of Walpole's political commentary. The letter here printed evokes the drama of an important and exciting political event, suggesting its human significance.

The source of the present text is *The Yale Edition of Horace Walpole's Correspondence*, ed. W. S. Lewis, Vol. XIX: *Horace Walpole's Correspondence with Sir Horace Mann*, III, eds. W. S. Lewis, Warren Hunting Smith, and George L. Lam (New Haven, Conn.: Yale University Press, 1954). Used by permission of Yale University Press.

Biography and Criticism

Dobson, Austin, *Horace Walpole, A Memoir*, 1927.

Free, William N., "Walpole's Letters: The Art of Being Graceful," *The Familiar Letter in the Eighteenth Century*, pp. 165–185, eds. Anderson, Daghlian, Ehrenpreis, 1966.

Ketton-Cremer, R.W. *Horace Walpole*, 1940.

Kronenberger, Louis, "Horace Walpole's Career," *Encounter*, XXIV (1965), 36–40.

Lewis, Wilmarth S., *Horace Walpole*, 1960.

McAdam, Jr., E. L., "Johnson, Walpole, and Public Order," *Johnson, Boswell and Their Circle*, pp. 93–98, 1965.

Smith, Warren Hunting, ed., *Horace Walpole: Writer, Politician, and Connoisseur*, 1967.

The Correspondence
of Horace Walpole[1]

TO MANN, FRIDAY 1 AUGUST 1746 OS   *Arlington Street, Aug. 1, 1746.*

I am this moment come from the conclusion of the greatest and most melancholy scene I ever yet saw! You will easily guess it was the trials of the rebel Lords.[2] As it was the most interesting sight, it was the most solemn and fine: a coronation is a puppet show, and all the splendour of it, idle; but this sight at once feasted one's eyes and engaged all one's passions. It began last Monday; three parts of Westminster Hall

---

1 See Introduction, p. 24.
2 In 1745 Charles Edward Stuart, the Young Pretender ("Bonnie Prince Charlie"), invaded Scotland from France in an effort to restore the Stuart succession. The "rebel Lords" were tried (July 28–August 1, 1746) for their alliance with him in the unsuccessful attempt.

were enclosed with galleries, and hung with scarlet;[3] and the whole ceremony was conducted with the most awful solemnity and decency, except in the one point of leaving the prisoners at the bar, amidst the idle curiosity of some crowd, and even with the witnesses who had sworn against them; while the Lords adjourned to their own house to consult. No part of the royal family was there, which was a proper regard to the unhappy men who were become their victims. One hundred and thirty-nine lords were present, and made a noble sight on their benches *frequent and full!*[4] The Chancellor[5] was lord high steward; but though a most comely personage with a fine voice, his behaviour was mean, curiously searching for occasion to bow to the minister[6] that is no peer, and constantly applying to the other ministers, in a manner, for their orders; and not even ready at the ceremonial. To the prisoners he was peevish; and instead of keeping up to the humane dignity of the law of England, whose character it is, to point out favour to the criminal, he crossed them, and almost scolded at any offer they made towards defence. I had armed myself with all the resolution I could, with the thought of their crimes and of the danger past, and was assisted by the sight of the Marquis of Lothian in weepers[7] for his son[8] who fell at Culloden—but the first appearance of the prisoners shocked me! Their behaviour melted me! Lord Kilmarnock[9] and Lord Cromartie[10] are both past forty, but look younger. Lord Kilmarnock is tall and slender, with an extreme fine person: his behaviour a most just mixture between dignity and submission; if in anything to be reprehended, a little affected, and his hair too exactly

---

3 The customary decoration when peers were tried for capital offenses.

4 "Then sad in council all the seniors sate,/Frequent and full, assembled to debate" (Pope, *Odyssey*, XXIV. 481–82).

5 "Sir Philip Yorke, Lord Hardwicke" [H.W.]. Lord Hardwicke (1690–1764) was lord chancellor from 1737 to 1756. Walpole retrieved and annotated hundreds of his own letters—for posterity.

6 "Henry Pelham" [H.W.]. Pelham (1696–1754) was at this time chancellor of the exchequer.

7 "A strip of white linen or muslin, formerly worn on the cuff of a man's sleeve" (*OED*).

8 Lord Robert Ker (d. April 16, 1746). The battle of Culloden, at which the Pretender's forces were decisively defeated, marked the end of the rebellion. William Augustus, Duke of Cumberland (1721–1756), leader of the English army, relentlessly pursued the fugitives after the battle; his troops captured the lords whose trial Walpole records.

9 William Boyd, fourth Earl of Kilmarnock (1704–1746); he was beheaded on August 18.

10 George Mackenzie, third Earl of Cromarty (1703–1766), who was sentenced to death but reprieved.

dressed for a man in his situation; but when I say this, it is not to find fault with him, but to show how little fault there was to be found. Lord Cromartie is an indifferent figure, appeared much dejected, and rather sullen: he dropped a few tears the first day, and swooned as soon as he got back to his cell. For Lord Balmerino,[11] he is the most natural brave old fellow I ever saw: the highest intrepidity, even to indifference. At the bar he behaved like a soldier and a man; in the intervals of form, with carelessness and humour. He pressed extremely to have his wife, his pretty Peggy,[12] with him in the Tower; the instant she came to him, he stripped her and went to bed. Lady Cromartie only sees her husband through the grate, not choosing to be shut up with him, as she thinks she can serve him better by her intercession without: she is big with child and very handsome; so are their daughters. When they were to be brought from the Tower in separate coaches, there was some dispute in which the axe must go—old Balmerino cried, "Come, come, put it with me." At the bar, he plays with his fingers upon the axe, while he talks to the gentleman gaoler;[13] and one day somebody coming up to listen, he took the blade and held it like a fan between their faces. During the trial, a little boy was near him, but not tall enough to see; he made room for the child and placed him near himself.

When the trial began, the two Earls pleaded guilty; Balmerino, not guilty, saying he could prove his not being at the taking of the castle of Carlisle,[14] as was laid in the indictment. Then the King's counsel[15] opened, and Serjeant Skinner[16] pronounced the most absurd speech imaginable; and mentioned the Duke of Perth,[17] *who*, said he, *I see by the papers is dead*. Then some witnesses were examined, whom afterwards the old hero shook cordially by the hand. The Lords withdrew to their House, and returning, demanded of the judges, whether, one point not

---

11 Arthur Elphinstone, sixth Lord Balmerino (1688–1746), also beheaded August 18.

12 Margaret Chalmers (c. 1709–1765), wife of Lord Balmerino.

13 Abraham Fowler (fl. 1746–1751), gentleman gaoler, deputy sheriff.

14 The taking of the city and castle of Carlisle (surrendered November 17, 1745) was one of the Young Pretender's great victories.

15 Sir Richard Lloyd.

16 Matthew Skinner (1689–1749), serjeant-at-law (a member of a superior order of barristers, from which common law judges were chosen). He was second counsel for the Crown at this trial.

17 John Drummond, fourth Duke of Perth in the Jacobite peerage, who fought at Culloden for the Pretender; the report of his death at this time was false.

being proved,[18] though all the rest were, the indictment was false? to which they unanimously answered in the negative. Then the Lord High Steward asked the peers severally, whether Lord Balmerino was guilty? All said, *Guilty upon honour!* and then adjourned; the prisoner having begged pardon for giving them so much trouble. While the Lords were withdrawn, the Solicitor-General Murray, (brother of the Pretender's minister)[19] officiously, and insolently, went up to Lord Balmerino, and asked him, how he could give the Lords so much trouble, when his solicitor had informed him that his plea could be of no use to him? Balmerino asked the bystanders who this person was? and being told; he said, "Oh! Mr Murray, I am extremely glad to see you; I have been with several of your relations; the good lady your mother[20] was of great use to us at Perth."—Are not you charmed with this speech? How just it was! As he went away, he said, "They call me Jacobite; I am no more a Jacobite than any that tried me; but if the Great Mogul[21] had set up his standard, I should have followed it, for I could not starve." The worst of his case is, that after the Battle of Dunblain,[22] having a company in the Duke of Argyle's regiment, he deserted with it to the rebels and has since been pardoned.[23] Lord Kilmarnock is a Presbyterian, with four earldoms[24] in him, but so poor since Lord Wilmington's stopping a pension that my father had given him,[25] that he often wanted a dinner. Lord Cromartie was receiver of the rents[26] of the King's second son in Scotland,[27] which, it was understood, he should not account for; and by that means

---

18 The point had to do with the specific date upon which an act of high treason was committed.

19 "Lord Dunbar" [H.W.]. James Murray, first Earl of Dunbar in the Jacobite peerage (c. 1690–1770), a strong supporter of the Old Pretender (the exiled James III). The solicitor-general was William Murray (1704–1793).

20 Marjory Scott (d. 1746), wife of David Murray, fifth Viscount Stormont.

21 The Emperor of Delhi, whose empire at one time included most of Hindustan.

22 The battle of Sheriffmuir (near Dunblane), November 13, 1715, during an earlier Jacobite uprising. The Jacobites were the supporters of the Stuart cause.

23 In 1733.

24 He was Earl of Kilmarnock; his wife was heiress to the Earl of Linlithgow and Callendar on her father's side, and on her mother's, to the Earldom of Errol.

25 While Robert Walpole was prime minister, Lord Kilmarnock received two payments of £150 each, October 14, 1742, and July 6, 1743. Since the latter payments occurred four days after Wilmington's death, Horace Walpole may be wrong in saying that Wilmington stopped the pension.

26 He was sheriff of Cromartyshire, with the duty of collecting the King's rents.

27 This is confusing. The King's second son was the Duke of Cumberland, but Cromarty was not listed as a retainer of the Duke.

had six hundred a year from the government: Lord Ellibank,[28] a very prating impertinent Jacobite, was bound for him in nine thousand pounds, for which the Duke is determined to sue him.[29]

When the peers were going to vote, Lord Foley[30] withdrew, as too well a wisher; Lord Morray,[31] as nephew of Lord Balmerino—and Lord Stair—as I believe, uncle to his great-grandfather.[32] Lord Windsor,[33] very affectedly, said, "I am sorry I must say, *Guilty upon my honour.*" Lord Stamford[34] would not answer to the name of *Henry*, having been christened, *Harry*—what a great way of thinking on such an occasion! I was diverted too with old Norsa, the father of my brother's concubine,[35] an old Jew that kept a tavern; my brother, as auditor of the Exchequer, has a gallery along one whole side of the court; I said, "I really feel for the prisoners!" Old Issachar replied, "Feel for them! Pray, if they had succeeded, what would have become of *all us?*" When my Lady Townshend[36] heard her husband vote, she said, "I always knew *my* Lord was *guilty*, but I never thought he would own it *upon his honour.*" Lord Balmerino said, that one of his reasons for pleading *not guilty*, was, that so many ladies might not be disappointed of their show.

On Wednesday,[37] they were again brought to Westminster Hall to receive sentence; and being asked what they had to say, Lord Kilmarnock with a fine voice read a very fine speech, confessing the extent of his crime, but offering his principles as some alleviation, having his eldest son[38] (his second[39] unluckily was with him) in the Duke's army, *fighting*

28 Patrick Murray, fifth Baron Elibank (1703–1778).

29 Cumberland could not sue Cromarty, because his estates were forfeited to the Crown; he could, however, sue Cromarty's cousin, Lord Elibank, who had apparently endorsed Cromarty's note for £9,000.

30 Thomas Foley, second Baron Foley (c. 1703–1766).

31 James Stuart, eighth Earl of Moray (1708–1767), whose mother was Balmerino's half-sister.

32 Stair's wife and Balmerino's father were first cousins.

33 Probably Herbert Windsor, Viscount Windsor (1707–1758).

34 Harry Grey, fourth Earl of Stamford (1715–1768).

35 Hannah Norsa, mistress of the second Earl of Orford; her father has not been identified.

36 Wife of Charles Townshend, third Viscount Townshend (1700–1764). She was born Etheldreda Harrison (c. 1703–1788).

37 July 30 O.S. (I.e., by the old Julian calendar. The Gregorian calendar was not adopted in England until 1752.)

38 James Boyd (1726–1778).

39 Hon. Charles Boyd (1728–1782), who was with his father on the Jacobite side at the battle of Culloden, after which he fled to the Isle of Arran and then to France.

for the liberties of his country at Culloden, where his unhappy father was in arms to destroy them. He insisted much on his tenderness to the English prisoners, which some deny, and say that he was the man who proposed their being put to death, when General Stapleton[40] urged that *he* was come to fight and not to butcher; and that if they acted any such barbarity, he would leave them with all his men. He very artfully mentioned Vanhoey's letter,[41] and said how much he should scorn to owe his life to such intercession. Lord Cromartie spoke much shorter, and so low that he was not heard but by those who sat very near him; but they prefer his speech to the other. He mentioned his misfortune in having drawn in his eldest son, who is prisoner with him; and concluded with saying, "If no part of this bitter cup must pass from me, not mine, O God, but Thy will be done!" If he had pleaded *not guilty*, there was ready to be produced against him a paper signed with his own hand for putting the English prisoners to death.

Lord Leicester[42] went up to the Duke of Newcastle, and said, "I never heard so great an orator as Lork Kilmarnock; if I was your Grace, I would pardon him and make him *paymaster.*"[43]

That morning a paper had been sent to the lieutenant[44] of the Tower for the prisoners; he gave it to Lord Cornwallis the governor,[45] who carried it to the House of Lords. It was a plea for the prisoners, objecting that the late act[46] for regulating the trials of rebels did not take place till after their crime was committed. The Lords very tenderly and rightly sent this plea to them, of which, as you have seen, the two Earls did not make use, but old Balmerino did, and demanded counsel on it. The High Steward, almost in a passion, told him, that when he had been offered counsel, he did not accept it—do but think on the ridicule of sending them the plea and then denying them counsel on it! The Duke

---

40 Walter Stapleton (d. April 1746), an officer in the French army, in command of the Irish detachments from the French army at Culloden.

41 Abraham Van Hoey (1684–1766), Dutch ambassador at Paris, sent an "impertinent letter," as Walpole describes it, to George Montagu (June 17, 1746), offering to intercede for the rebels.

42 Thomas Coke, Earl of Leicester (1697–1759), a member of Parliament.

43 "Alluding to Mr. Pitt [William Pitt, (1708–1778)], who had lately been preferred to that post from the fear the Ministry had of his abusive eloquence" [H.W.].

44 Lord Cornwallis was lieutenant of the Tower, but Walpole is here referring to Adam Williamson (c. 1676–1747), deputy lieutenant of the Tower.

45 Charles Cornwallis, fifth Baron Cornwallis (1700–1762).

46 The act, passed in 1746, declared that offenders in custody for having participated in the rebellion should be tried.

of Newcastle, who never lets slip an opportunity of being absurd, took it up as a ministerial point[47] in defence of his creature the Chancellor; but Lord Granville[48] moved, according to order, to adjourn to debate in the chamber of Parliament, where the Duke of Bedford[49] and many others spoke warmly for their having counsel; and it was granted. I said *their*, because the plea would have saved them all; and affected nine rebels who had been hanged that very morning; particularly one Morgan,[50] a poetical lawyer. Lord Balmerino asked for Forester[51] and Wilbraham;[52] the latter a very able lawyer in the House of Commons, who, the Chancellor said privately, he was sure would as soon be hanged as plead such a cause.—But he came as counsel today (the third day) when Lord Balmerino gave up his plea as invalid, and submitted, without any speech. The High Steward then made his, very long and very poor, with only one or two good passages: and then pronounced sentence!

Great intercession is made for the two Earls: Duke Hamilton,[53] who has never been at Court, designs to kiss the King's hand and ask Lord Kilmarnock's life. The King is much inclined to some mercy; but the Duke, who has not so much of Caesar after a victory,[54] as in gaining it, is for the utmost severity. It was lately proposed in the City, to present him with the freedom of some company; one of the aldermen said aloud, "Then let it be of the *Butchers'*!" The Scotch and his Royal Highness are not at all guarded in their expressions of each other. When he went to Edinborough, on his pursuit of the rebels, they would not admit his guards, alleging that it was contrary to their privileges; but they rode in, sword in hand; and the Duke, very justly incensed, refused to see any of the magistrates. He came with the utmost expedition to town, in order

---

47 He wished one of the King's Counsel to discuss the matter for the lords, so that they might evaluate the prisoner's point.

48 John Carteret, Earl Granville (1690–1763). From 1742 to 1744, and again very briefly in early 1746, he had been secretary of state for the Northern Department.

49 John Bedford, fourth Duke of Bedford (1710–1771). He was to become secretary of state in 1747.

50 David Morgan, who had been a barrister and was called "the Pretender's counsellor.'

51 Perhaps Walter Forrester (d. 1752) of Hatton Garden, London; he had been a conveyancer, a lawyer specializing in deeds and titles.

52 Randle Wilbraham (c. 1695–1770), a barrister at law of Lincoln's Inn and a member of Parliament.

53 James Hamilton, sixth Duke of Hamilton (1724–1758).

54 Caesar is supposed to have written after Pompey's death "That the chief enjoyment he had of his victory was, in saving every day one or other of his fellow-citizens who had borne arms against him" (Plutarch's *Life of Caesar*, tr. John Langhorne).

for Flanders;[55] but found that the Court of Vienna had already sent Prince Charles thither,[56] without the least notification, at which both King and Duke are greatly offended. When the latter waited on his brother, the Prince carried him into a room, that hangs over the wall of St James's Park, and stood there with his arm about his neck, to charm the gazing mob!

Murray, the Pretender's secretary,[57] has made ample confessions: the Earl of Traquair,[58] and Dr Barry,[59] a physician, are apprehended; and more warrants are out—so much for rebels!—Your friend Lord Sandwich is instantly going ambassador to Holland[60] to pray the Dutch to build more ships—I have received yours of July 19th but you see have no room left, only to say, that I conceive a good idea of my eagle, though the seal is a bad one.[61]

Adieu!

PS.   I have not room to say anything to the Tesi,[62] till next post; but unless she will sing gratis, would advise her to drop this thought.

---

55 Where a campaign was being carried on as part of the continental war between England and France. He did not actually go to Flanders until 1747.

56 An Austrian general, called Prince Charles of Lorraine (1712–1780). He took command of the English troops in the Low Countries.

57 Sir John Murray of Broughton (1718–1777), who had betrayed Lord Lovat.

58 Charles Stewart, fifth Earl of Traquair (d. 1764).

59 Dr. Peter Barry, a London doctor, pardoned in 1747.

60 John Montagu, fourth Earl of Sandwich (1718–1792), who was being sent as minister plenipotentiary to the peace conference at Breda.

61 In his letter of July 19, 1746, Mann asks, "How do you like the enclosed intaglio from the finest eagle in the world?"

62 Vittoria Tesi Tramontini (1700–1775), Italian contralto, who had expressed a desire to sing in England.

SIR JOSHUA REYNOLDS

(1723–1792)

The most famous portrait painter of his time, Sir Joshua Reynolds survives also as a literary figure because of the lucid statement of artistic values in the *Discourses* (1769–1790) he delivered to students at the Royal Academy, of which he was the first president. Born into a scholarly family, Reynolds early manifested artistic talent; he committed himself to the career of painter and spent his young manhood studying and practicing his art. By 1752 he had settled in London, where he painted the portraits of members of the royal family, Dr. Johnson, and the great actor, David Garrick. In 1760 he participated in the first public exhibition of the work of British artists. He was a founder of "The Club," a convivial group which met frequently for extended conversation; Johnson, Burke, Gibbon, and Goldsmith were among its members. By 1790, when he delivered his last discourse, he was almost completely blind. He was buried in St. Paul's Cathedral.

The *Discourses* systematically expound an applied aesthetic for the practicing artist; they also define important critical principles. In the first discourse, Reynolds immediately reveals his high regard for tradition, making it clear that he considers the preservation of tradition to be the highest function of the Royal Academy. Subsequent discourses discuss the validity of established critical principles; insist on the primary aesthetic importance of general, representative forms rather than specific, individual ones; and demonstrate how this principle of generalizations applies to all stages of artistic production. Reynolds evaluates both the "ornamental" and the "grand" style. In the sixth discourse, here reprinted, he elaborates his theory of genius. His essay stands as an eloquent reply to Young (see above, pp. 47–85), exposing the fallacies and weaknesses of Young's simple conviction that "originality" is automatically superior to "imitation." Reynolds's defence of imitation reveals the true creativity of proper use of models. His later discourses concern taste and define various specific rules of art and their application; they examine in detail the great artwork of the past.

In form as well as substance Reynolds's *Discourses* exemplify classic values of discipline, order, balance. They are masterpieces of generalization, constantly insisting on the wide relevance of each individual reference, affirming by their controlled energy the importance and the force of decorum as an artistic principle, and demonstrating the relation between the high values of civilization and those of art.

The source of the present text is *Discourses*, ed. Roger Fry (London: Seeley and Co., 1905). Used by permission of the publishers.

Biography and Criticism

Burke, Joseph, *Hogarth and Reynolds: A Contrast in English Art Theory*, 1943.

Hilles, F. W., *The Literary Career of Sir Joshua Reynolds*, 1936.

———, "Sir Joshua's Prose," *The Age of Johnson*, pp. 49–60, 1949.

Hipple, Jr., Walter J., "General and Particular in the *Discourses* of Sir Joshua Reynolds: A Study in Method," *Journal of Aesthetics and Art Criticism*, XI (1953), 231–247.

Hudson, Derek, *Sir Joshua Reynolds, A Personal Study*, 1958.

Moore, Robert E., "Reynolds and the Art of Characterization," *Studies in Criticism and Aesthetics, 1660–1800*, eds. Howard Anderson and John Shea, 1967.

Thomson, E. N. S., "The *Discourses* of Sir Joshua Reynolds," *PMLA*, XXXII (1917), 339–366.

Waterhouse, Ellis K., *Reynolds*, 1941.

The Sixth Discourse[1]

Delivered to the Students of the Royal Academy, on the Distribution of the Prizes, December 10, 1774

Imitation—Genius begins where rules end—Invention: acquired by being con-

---

1 See Introduction, pp. 41–43.

*versant with the inventions of others—The true method of imitating—Borrowing, how
far allowable—Something to be gathered from every school.*

Gentlemen,

When I have taken the liberty of addressing you on the course and
order of your studies, I never proposed to enter into a minute detail of the
Art. This I have always left to the several professors, who pursue the end
of our institution with the highest honour to themselves, and with the
greatest advantage to the Students.

My purpose in the discourses I have held in the Academy has been
to lay down certain general positions, which seem to me proper for the
formation of a sound taste: principles necessary to guard the pupils against
those errors, into which the sanguine temper common to their time of
life has a tendency to lead them; and which have rendered abortive the
hopes of so many successions of promising young men in all parts of
Europe. I wished also, to intercept and suppress those prejudices which
particularly prevail when the mechanism of painting is come to its perfection; and which, when they do prevail, are certain utterly to destroy
the higher and more valuable parts of this literate and liberal profession.

These two have been my principal purposes; they are still as much
my concern as ever; and if I repeat my own notions on the subject, you
who know how fast mistake and prejudice, when neglected, gain ground
upon truth and reason, will easily excuse me. I only attempt to set the
same thing in the greatest variety of lights.

The subject of this discourse will be IMITATION, as far as a painter is
concerned in it. By imitation, I do not mean imitation in its largest sense,
but simply the following of other masters, and the advantage to be drawn
from the study of their works.

Those who have undertaken to write on our art, and have represented it as a kind of *inspiration*, as a *gift* bestowed upon peculiar
favourites at their birth, seem to insure a much more favourable disposition from their readers, and have a much more captivating and liberal
air, than he who attempts to examine, coldly, whether there are any
means by which this art may be acquired; how the mind may be strengthened and expanded, and what guides will show the way to eminence.

It is very natural for those who are unacquainted with the *cause* of
any thing extraordinary, to be astonished at the effect, and to consider it

as a kind of magic. They, who have never observed the gradation by which art is acquired; who see only what is the full result of long labour and application of an infinite number and infinite variety of acts, are apt to conclude, from their entire inability to do the same at once, that it is not only inaccessible to themselves, but can be done by those only who have some gift of the nature of inspiration bestowed upon them.

The travellers into the East tell us, that when the ignorant inhabitants of those countries are asked concerning the ruins of stately edifices yet remaining amongst them, the melancholy monuments of their former grandeur and long-lost science, they always answer, that they were built by magicians. The untaught mind finds a vast gulf between its own powers, and those works of complicated art, which it is utterly unable to fathom; and it supposes that such a void can be passed only by super-natural powers.

And, as for artists themselves, it is by no means their interest to undeceive such judges, however conscious they may be of the very natural means by which their extraordinary powers were acquired; though our art, being intrinsically imitative, rejects this idea of inspiration, more perhaps than any other.

It is to avoid this plain confession of truth, as it should seem, that this imitation of masters, indeed almost all imitation, which implies a more regular and progressive method of attaining the ends of painting, has ever been particularly inveighed against with great keenness, both by ancient and modern writers.

To derive all from native power, to owe nothing to another, is the praise which men, who do not much think on what they are saying, bestow sometimes upon others, and sometimes on themselves; and their imaginary dignity is naturally heightened by a supercilious censure of the low, the barren, the grovelling, the servile imitator. It would be no wonder if a student, frightened by these terrific and disgraceful epithets, with which the poor imitators are so often loaded, should let fall his pencil in mere despair (conscious as he must be, how much he has been indebted to the labours of others, how little, how very little of his art was born with him); and consider it as hopeless, to set about acquiring by the imitation of any human master, what he is taught to suppose is matter of inspiration from heaven.

Some allowance must be made for what is said in the gaiety of rhetoric. We cannot suppose that any one can really mean to exclude all imitation of others. A position so wild would scarce deserve a serious answer; for it is apparent, if we were forbid to make use of the advantages which our predecessors afford us, the art would be always to begin, and consequently remain always in its infant state; and it is a common observation, that no art was ever invented and carried to perfection at the same time.

But to bring us entirely to reason and sobriety, let it be observed, that a painter must not only be of necessity an imitator of the works of nature, which alone is sufficient to dispel this phantom of inspiration, but he must be as necessarily an imitator of the works of other painters: this appears more humiliating, but is equally true; and no man can be an artist, whatever he may suppose, upon any other terms.

However, those who appear more moderate and reasonable, allow, that our study is to begin by imitation; but maintain that we should no longer use the thoughts of our predecessors, when we are become able to think for ourselves. They hold that imitation is as hurtful to the more advanced student, as it was advantageous to the beginner.

For my own part, I confess, I am not only very much disposed to maintain the absolute necessity of imitation in the first stages of the art; but am of opinion, that the study of other masters, which I here call imitation, may be extended throughout our whole lives, without any danger of the inconveniences with which it is charged, of enfeebling the mind, or preventing us from giving that original air which every work undoubtedly ought always to have.

I am on the contrary persuaded that by imitation only, variety, and even originality of invention, is produced. I will go further; even genius, at least what generally is so called, is the child of imitation. But as this appears to be contrary to the general opinion, I must explain my position before I enforce it.

Genius is supposed to be a power of producing excellences, which are out of the reach of the rules of art; a power which no precepts can teach, and which no industry can acquire.

This opinion of the impossibility of acquiring those beauties, which stamp the work with the character of genius, supposes that it is something more fixed, than in reality it is; and that we always do, and ever did agree in opinion, with respect to what should be considered as the characteristic of genius. But the truth is, that the *degree* of excellence which proclaims *Genius* is different, in different times and different places; and what shows it to be so is, that mankind have often changed their opinion upon this matter.

When the Arts were in their infancy, the power of merely drawing the likeness of any object, was considered as one of its greatest efforts. The common people, ignorant of the principles of art, talk the same language even to this day. But when it was found that every man could be taught to do this, and a great deal more, merely by the observance of certain precepts; the name of Genius then shifted its application, and was given only to him who added the peculiar character of the object he represented; to him who had invention, expression, grace, or dignity; in short, those qualities, or excellences, the power of producing which, could not then be taught by any known and promulgated rules.

We are very sure that the beauty of form, the expression of the passions, the art of composition, even the power of giving a general air of grandeur to a work, is at present very much under the dominion of rules. These excellences were, heretofore, considered merely as the effects of genius; and justly, if genius is not taken for inspiration, but as the effect of close observation and experience.

He who first made any of these observations, and digested them, so as to form an invariable principle for himself to work by, had that merit, but probably no one went very far at once; and generally, the first who gave the hint, did not know how to pursue it steadily and methodically; at least not in the beginning. He himself worked on it, and improved it; others worked more, and improved further; until the secret was discovered, and the practice made as general, as refined practice can be made. How many more principles may be fixed and ascertained, we cannot tell; but as criticism is likely to go hand in hand with the art which is its subject, we may venture to say, that as that art shall advance, its powers will be still more and more fixed by rules.

But by whatever strides criticism may gain ground, we need be under no apprehension, that invention will ever be annihilated, or subdued; or intellectual energy be brought entirely within the restraint of written law. Genius will still have room enough to expatiate, and keep always at the same distance from narrow comprehension and mechanical performance.

What we now call Genius, begins, not where rules, abstractedly taken, end; but where known vulgar and trite rules have no longer any place. It must of necessity be, that even works of Genius, like every other effect, as they must have their cause, must likewise have their rules: it cannot be by chance that excellences are produced with any constancy or any certainty, for this is not the nature of chance; but the rules by which men of extraordinary parts, and such as are called men of Genius, work, are either such as they discover by their own peculiar observations, or of such a nice texture as not easily to admit being expressed in words; especially as artists are not very frequently skilful in that mode of communicating ideas. Unsubstantial, however, as these rules may seem, and difficult as it may be to convey them in writing, they are still seen and felt in the mind of the artist; and he works from them with as much certainty, as if they were embodied, as I may say, upon paper. It is true, these refined principles cannot be always made palpable, like the more gross rules of art; yet it does not follow, but that the mind may be put in such a train, that it shall perceive, by a kind of scientific sense, that propriety, which words, particularly words of unpractised writers, such as we are, can but very feebly suggest.

Invention is one of the great marks of genius; but if we consult experience, we shall find, that it is by being conversant with the inventions of others, that we learn to invent; as by reading the thoughts of others we learn to think.

Whoever has so far formed his taste, as to be able to relish and feel the beauties of the great masters, has gone a great way in his study; for, merely from a consciousness of this relish of the right, the mind swells with an inward pride, and is almost as powerfully affected, as if it had itself produced what it admires. Our hearts, frequently warmed in this manner by the contact of those whom we wish to resemble, will undoubtedly catch something of their way of thinking; and we shall receive in our own bosoms some radiation at least of their fire and splendour. That disposition, which is so strong in children, still continues with us, of catching involuntarily the general air and manner of those with whom we are most conversant; with this difference only, that a young mind is naturally pliable and imitative; but in a more advanced state it grows rigid, and must be warmed and softened, before it will receive a deep impression.

From these considerations, which a little of your own reflection will carry a great way further, it appears of what great consequence it is, that our minds should be habituated to the contemplation of excellence; and that, far from being contented to make such habits the discipline of our youth only, we should, to the last moment of our lives, continue a settled intercourse with all the true examples of grandeur. Their inventions are not only the food of our infancy, but the substance which supplies the fullest maturity of our vigour.

The mind is but a barren soil; a soil which is soon exhausted, and will produce no crop, or only one, unless it be continually fertilized and enriched with foreign matter.

When we have had continually before us the great works of Art to impregnate our minds with kindred ideas, we are then, and not till then, fit to produce something of the same species. We behold all about us with the eyes of those penetrating observers whose works we contemplate; and our minds, accustomed to think the thoughts of the noblest and brightest intellects, are prepared for the discovery and selection of all that is great and noble in nature. The greatest natural genius cannot subsist on its own stock: he who resolves never to ransack any mind but his own, will be soon reduced, from mere barrenness, to the poorest of all imitations; he will be obliged to imitate himself, and to repeat what he has before often repeated. When we know the subject designed by such men, it will never be difficult to guess what kind of work is to be produced.

It is vain for painters or poets to endeavour to invent without materials on which the mind may work, and from which invention must originate. Nothing can come of nothing.

Homer is supposed to be possessed of all the learning of his time; and we are certain that Michel Angelo,[2] and Raffaelle,[3] were equally possessed of all the knowledge in the art which had been discovered in the works of their predecessors.

A mind enriched by an assemblage of all the treasures of ancient and modern art, will be more elevated and fruitful in resources, in proportion to the number of ideas which have been carefully collected and thoroughly digested. There can be no doubt but that he who has the most materials has the greatest means of invention; and if he has not the power of using them, it must proceed from a feebleness of intellect; or from the confused manner in which those collections have been laid up in his mind.

The addition of other men's judgment is so far from weakening our own, as is the opinion of many, that it will fashion and consolidate those ideas of excellence which lay in embryo, feeble, ill-shaped, and confused, but which are finished and put in order by the authority and practice of those whose works may be said to have been consecrated by having stood the test of ages.

---

2 Michelangelo Buonarotti (1474–1563), whom Reynolds described as "the bright luminary from whom painting has borrowed a new lustre,...and from whom all his contemporaries and successors have derived whatever they have possessed of the dignified and majestic."

3 Raphael Sanzio (1483–1520), who imitated his teacher, Perugino, so skillfully that when the two worked on one canvas, it seemed the work of a single hand.

The mind, or genius, has been compared to a spark of fire, which is smothered by a heap of fuel, and prevented from blazing into a flame: This simile, which is made use of by the younger Pliny,[4] may be easily mistaken for argument or proof. But there is no danger of the mind's being over-burthened with knowledge, or the genius extinguished by any addition of images; on the contrary, these acquisitions may as well, perhaps better, be compared, if comparisons signified any thing in reasoning, to the supply of living embers, which will contribute to strengthen the spark, that without the association of more fuel would have died away. The truth is, he whose feebleness is such, as to make other men's thoughts an incumbrance to him, can have no very great strength of mind or genius of his own to be destroyed; so that not much harm will be done at worst.

We may oppose to Pliny the greater authority of Cicero, who is continually enforcing the necessity of this method of study. In his dialogue on Oratory, he makes Crassus say, that one of the first and most important precepts is, to choose a proper model for our imitation. *Hoc sit primum in in præceptis meis, ut demonstremus quem imitemur.*[5]

When I speak of the habitual imitation and continued study of masters, it is not to be understood that I advise any endeavour to copy the exact peculiar colour and complexion of another man's mind; the success of such an attempt must always be like his, who imitates exactly the air, manner, and gestures of him whom he admires. His model may be excellent, but the copy will be ridiculous: this ridicule does not arise from his having imitated, but from his not having chosen the right mode of imitation.

It is necessary and warrantable pride to disdain to walk servilely behind any individual, however elevated his rank. The true and liberal ground of imitation is an open field; where, though he who precedes has had the advantage of starting before you, you may always propose to overtake him: it is enough, however, to pursue his course; you need not tread in his footsteps; and you certainly have a right to outstrip him if you can.

Nor whilst I recommend studying the art from artists, can I be be supposed to mean, that Nature is to be neglected: I take this study in

---

4 Several modern commentators have declared themselves unable to locate this simile; I have had no better luck than they.

5 "Let this then be my first counsel, that we show the student whom to copy" (Cicero, *De Oratore*, II. xxii. 90).

aid, and not in exclusion, of the other. Nature is, and must be the fountain which alone is inexhaustible; and from which all excellences must originally flow.

The great use of studying our predecessors is, to open the mind to shorten our labour, and to give us the result of the selection made by those great minds of what is grand or beautiful in Nature; her rich stores are all spread out before us; but it is an art, and no easy art, to know how or what to choose, and how to attain and secure the object of our choice. Thus the highest beauty of form must be taken from Nature; but it is an art of long deduction and great experience, to know how to find it. We must not content ourselves with merely admiring and relishing; we must enter into the principles on which the work is wrought: these do not swim on the superficies, and consequently are not open to superficial observers.

Art in its perfection is not ostentatious; it lies hid, and works its effect, itself unseen. It is the proper study and labour of an artist to uncover and find out the latent cause of conspicuous beauties, and from thence form principles of his own conduct: such an examination is a continual exertion of the mind; as great, perhaps, as that of the artist whose works he is thus studying.

The sagacious imitator does not content himself with merely remarking what distinguishes the different manner or genius of each master; he enters into the contrivance in the composition how the masses of lights are disposed, the means by which the effect is produced, how artfully some parts are lost in the ground, others boldly relieved, and how all these are mutually altered and interchanged according to the reason and scheme of the work. He admires not the harmony of colouring alone, but examines by what artifice one colour is a foil to its neighbour. He looks close into the tints, examines of what colours they are composed, till he has formed clear and distinct ideas, and has learnt to see in what harmony and good colouring consists. What is learnt in this manner from the works of others, becomes really our own, sinks deep, and is never forgotten; nay, it is by seizing on this clue that we proceed forward, and get further and further in enlarging the principles and in improving the practice of our art.

There can be no doubt, but the art is better learnt from the works themselves, than from the precepts which are formed upon those works; but if it is difficult to choose proper models for imitation, it requires no less circumspection to separate and distinguish what in those models we ought to imitate.

288   *The Sixth Discourse*

I cannot avoid mentioning here, though it is not my intention at present to enter into the art and method of study, an error which students are too apt to fall into. He that is forming himself, must look with great caution and wariness on those peculiarities, or prominent parts, which at first force themselves upon view; and are the marks, or what is commonly called the manner, by which that individual artist is distinguished.

Peculiar marks, I hold to be, generally, if not always, defects; however difficult it may be wholly to escape them.

Peculiarities in the works of art are like those in the human figure: it is by them that we are cognizable, and distinguished one from another, but they are always so many blemishes: which, however, both in real life and in painting, cease to appear deformities, to those who have them continually before their eyes. In the works of art, even the most enlightened mind, when warmed by beauties of the highest kind, will by degrees find a repugnance within him to acknowledge any defects; nay, his enthusiasm will carry him so far, as to transform them into beauties, and objects of imitation.

It must be acknowledged, that a peculiarity of style, either from its novelty or by seeming to proceed from a peculiar turn of mind, often escapes blame; on the contrary, it is sometimes striking and pleasing; but this it is a vain labour to endeavour to imitate; because novelty and peculiarity being its only merit, when it ceases to be new it ceases to have value.

A manner, therefore, being a defect, and every painter, however excellent, having a manner, it seems to follow, that all kinds of faults, as well as beauties, may be learned under the sanction of the greatest authorities. Even the great name of Michel Angelo may be used, to keep in countenance a deficiency, or rather neglect of colouring, and every other ornamental part of the art. If the young student is dry and hard, Poussin[6] is the same. If his work has a careless and unfinished air, he has most of the Venetian school to support him. If he makes no selection of objects, but takes individual nature just as he finds it, he is like Rembrandt.[7] If he is incorrect in the proportions of his figures, Correggio[8] was likewise

---

[6] Nicolas Poussin (1594–1665), French painter of history and landscapes, called "The Raphael of France."

[7] Rembrandt van Rijn (1606–1669), the renowned Dutch painter of history and portraits.

[8] Antonio Allegri da Correggio (1494–1534), highly original Italian painter.

incorrect. If his colours are not blended and united, Rubens[9] was equally
crude. In short, there is no defect that may not be excused, if it is a sufficient
excuse that it can be imputed to considerable artists; but it must be remembered, that it was not by these defects they acquired their reputation;
they have a right to our pardon, but not to our admiration.

However, to imitate peculiarities or mistake defects for beauties, that
man will be most liable, who confines his imitation to one favourite
master; and even though he chooses the best, and is capable of distinguishing the real excellences of his model, it is not by such narrow
practice that a genius or mastery in the art is acquired. A man is as little
likely to form a true idea of the perfection of the art, by studying a single
artist, as he would be to produce a perfectly beautiful figure, by an exact
imitation of any individual living model. And as the painter, by bringing
together in one piece those beauties which are dispersed among a great
variety of individuals, produces a figure more beautiful than can be
found in Nature, so that artist who can unite in himself the excellences
of the various great painters will approach nearer to perfection than any
one of his masters. He who confines himself to the imitation of an individual, as he never proposes to surpass, so he is not likely to equal, the
object of his imitation. He professes only to follow; and he that follows
must necessarily be behind.

We should imitate the conduct of the great artists in the course of
their studies, as well as the works which they produced, when they were
perfectly formed. Raffaelle began by imitating implicitly the manner of
Pietro Perugino,[10] under whom he studied; hence his first works are
scarce to be distinguished from his master's; but soon forming higher and
more extensive views, he imitated the grand outline of Michel Angelo;
he learned the manner of using colours from the works of Leonardo
da Vinci, and Fratre Bartolomeo:[11] to all this he added the contemplation
of all the remains of antiquity that were within his reach, and employed
others to draw for him what was in Greece and distant places. And it
is from his having taken so many models, that he became himself a model
for all succeeding painters, always imitating, and always original.

---

9 Peter Paul Rubens (1577–1640), most famous of Flemish painters, depicted history,
landscape, animals, and people.

10 Italian painter (1446–1523), celebrated for his proficiency in perspective, whose
frescoes in the Sistine Chapel were later covered over by Michelangelo's.

11 Don Bartolomeo della Gatta, abbot of San Clemente, fifteenth-century minia-
turist and painter who may also have contributed to the painting of the Sistine Chapel.

If your ambition, therefore, be to equal Raffaelle you must do as Raffaelle did, take many models, and not even *him* for your guide alone, to the exclusion of others. And yet the number is infinite of those who seem, if one may judge by their style, to have seen no other works but those of their master, or of some favourite, whose *manner* is their first wish, and their last.

I will mention a few that occur to me of this narrow, confined, illiberal, unscientific, and servile kind of imitators. Guido[12] was thus meanly copied by Elizabetta Sirani,[13] and Simone Cantarini;[14] Poussin, by Verdier,[15] and Chéron;[16] Parmegiano, by Jeronimo Mazzuoli.[17] Paolo Veronese,[18] and Iacomo Bassan,[19] had for their imitators their brothers and sons. Pietro da Cortona was followed by Ciro Ferri, and Romanelli;[20] Rubens, by Jacques Jordaens, and Diepenbeke;[21] Guercino,[22] by his own family, the Gennari. Carlo Maratti was imitated by Guiseppe Chiari, and Pietro de Pietri;[23] and Rembrandt, by Bramer, Eeckhout, and Flink.[24]

---

12 Guido Reni (c. 1575–1642), famous in Reynolds' time for his handling of pathetic and devotional subjects.

13 Italian historical painter (1638–1665) who acquired a high reputation through imitating Guido.

14 Simone Cantarini (1612–1648), eminent painter and engraver, a student of Guido's and a noted painter of portraits.

15 Marcel Verdier (1617–1656), French historical painter.

16 Elisabeth Chéron (1648–1711), French poet and painter, successful at portraits and history painting.

17 Girolamo Francesco Mazzola, surnamed Il Parmigiano ("the Parmesan") (1503–1540), an eminent Italian painter, himself a follower of Correggio and Raphael. His most distinguished pupil was Girolamo Bedolo Mazzola (1503–1590), to whom Reynolds refers as "Jeronimo Mazzuoli."

18 Paolo Cagliari, called Veronese (1530–1588), celebrated Italian painter, noted for his richness of imagination. His brothers and sons continued his work, signing their paintings "*Heredes Paoli*" ("Paul's Heirs").

19 Giacomo da Ponte Bassano (1510–1592), well known as a portraitist and painter of historical pictures. His four sons were all distinguished painters.

20 Pietro da Cortona (c. 1600–1669), an eminent Italian painter and architect. Ciro Ferri (1634–1689) and Giovanni Romanelli (1617–1682) were his distinguished pupils.

21 Jakob Jordaens (1594–1678) and Abraham van Diepenbeke (c. 1606–1675) were among the best-known students of Rubens, famous painters in their own right.

22 Giovanni Francesco Barbieri, called Guercino da Cento (1590–1666), a noted Italian painter and a close friend of Guido.

23 Carlo Maratti (1625–1713), the last great painter of the Roman school, in his own time considered one of the best painters in Europe. Giuseppe Chiari (1654–1727) and Pietro Pietri (c. 1665–1716) were his imitators.

24 Leonard Bramer (b. 1596), a Dutch painter who worked mainly in Italy; Anton van den Eeckhout (1656–1695), Flemish painter; and Govaert Flink (1616–1660), imitators of Rembrandt.

All these, to whom may be added a much longer list of painters, whose works, among the ignorant, pass for those of their masters, are justly to be censured for barrenness and servility.

To oppose to this list a few that have adopted a more liberal style of imitation;—Pellegrino Tibaldi[25] Rosso,[26] and Primaticcio,[27] did not coldly imitate, but caught something of the fire that animates the works of Michel Angelo. The Caraccis[28] formed their style from Pellegrino Tibaldi, Correggio, and the Venetian School. Domenichino, Guido, Lanfranco, Albano, Guercino, Cavidone, Schidone, Tiarini,[29] though it is sufficiently apparent that they came from the School of the Caraccis, have yet the appearance of men who extended their views beyond the model that lay before them, and have shown that they had opinions of their own, and thought for themselves after they had made themselves masters of the general principles of their schools.

Le Sueur's[30] first manner resembles very much that of his master, Voüet;[31] but as he soon excelled him, so he differed from him in every part of the art. Carlo Maratti[32] succeeded better than those I have first named, and I think owes his superiority to the extension of his views; beside his master, Andrea Sacchi,[33] he imitated Raffaelle, Guido, and the Caraccis. It is true, there is nothing very captivating in Carlo Maratti; but this proceeded from a want which cannot be completely supplied; that is, want of strength of parts. In this certainly men are not equal; and a man can bring home wares only in proportion to the capital with which he goes to market. Carlo, by diligence, made the most of what he had; but there was undoubtedly a heaviness about him, which extended itself,

25 Pellegrino Pellegrini, also called Tibaldi (1527–c. 1595), Italian painter and architect, took Michelangelo as model but was less extravagant in style.

26 Giovanni Battista del Rosso (1496–1541), born in Florence, studied the works of Michelangelo, and painted mostly in France.

27 Francesco Primaticcio (1490–1570), Italian painter, sculptor, and architect, also painted mainly in France.

28 Agostino Caracci (c. 1558–1602); Annibal Caracci (c. 1560–1609), his brother; Francesco Caracci (1595–1622), another brother; and Antonio Caracci (1583–1618), son of Agostino—all noted Bolognese painters. Ludovico Caracci (1555–1619), a cousin of the brothers, was founder of the Bolognese school.

29 All followers of the Caracci school.

30 Eustache Le Sueur (1617–1655), French religious painter.

31 Simon Vouet (1590–1649), French portrait painter.

32 See note 23, above.

33 Painter of the later Roman school (c. 1600–1661), a follower of Raphael. Poussin and Maratti studied with him.

uniformly, to his invention, expression, his drawing, colouring, and the general effect of his pictures. The truth is, he never equalled any of his patterns[34] in any one thing, and he added little of his own.

But we must not rest contented even in this general study of the moderns; we must trace back the art to its fountain-head; to that source from whence they drew their principal excellences, the monuments of pure antiquity. All the inventions and thoughts of the Ancients, whether conveyed to us in statues, bas-reliefs, intaglios, cameos, or coins, are to be sought after and carefully studied; the genius that hovers over these venerable relics may be called the father modern art.

From the remains of the works of the ancients the modern arts were revived, and it is by their means that they must be restored a second time. However it may mortify our vanity, we must be forced to allow them our masters; and we may venture to prophesy, that when they shall cease to be studied, arts will no longer flourish, and we shall again relapse into barbarism.

The fire of the artist's own genius operating upon these materials which have been thus diligently collected, will enable him to make new combinations, perhaps, superior to what had ever before been in the possession of the art: as in the mixture of the variety of metals, which are said to have been melted and run together at the burning of Corinth, a new, and till then unknown metal was produced, equal in value to any of those that had contributed to its composition. And though a curious refiner should come with his crucibles, analyse and separate its various component parts, yet Corinthian brass would still hold its rank amongst the most beautiful and valuable of metals.

We have hitherto considered the advantages of imitation as it tends to form the taste, and as a practice by which a spark of that genius may be caught, which illumines those noble works that ought always to be present to our thoughts.

We come now to speak of another kind of imitation; the borrowing a particular thought, an action, attitude, or figure, and transplanting it into your own work; this will either come under the charge of plagiarism, or be warrantable, and deserve commendation, according to the address with which it is performed. There is some difference, likewise, whether it is upon the ancients or moderns that these depredations are made. It is generally allowed, that no man need be ashamed of copying the ancients;

---

34 Models.

their works are considered as a magazine of common property, always open to the public, whence every man has a right to take what materials he pleases; and if he has the art of using them, they are supposed to become to all intents and purposes his own property. The collection of the thoughts of the Ancients which Raffaelle made with so much trouble, is a proof of his opinion on this subject. Such collections may be made with much more ease, by means of an art scarce known in this time; I mean that of engraving; by which, at an easy rate, every man may now avail himself of the inventions of antiquity.

It must be acknowledged that the works of the moderns are more the property of their authors. He who borrows an idea from an ancient, or even from a modern artist not his contemporary, and so accommodates it to his own work, that it makes a part of it, with no seam or joining appearing, can hardly be charged with plagiarism; poets practise this kind of borrowing, without reserve. But an artist should not be contented with this only; he should enter into a competition with his original, and endeavour to improve what he is appropriating to his own work. Such imitation is so far from having any thing in it of the servility of plagiarism, that it is a perpetual exercise of the mind, a continual invention. Borrowing or stealing with such art and caution, will have a right to the same lenity as was used by the Lacedemonians; who did not punish theft, but the want of artifice to conceal it.

In order to encourage you to imitation, to the utmost extent, let me add, that very finished artists in the inferior branches of the art, will contribute to furnish the mind and give hints, of which a skilful painter, who is sensible of what he wants, and is in no danger of being infected by the contact of vicious models, will know how to avail himself. He will pick up from dunghills what by a nice chemistry, passing through his own mind, shall be converted into pure gold; and under the rudeness of Gothic essays, he will find original, rational, and even sublime inventions.

The works of Albert Durer,[35] Lucas Van Leyden,[36] the numerous inventions of Tobias Stimmer,[37] and Jost Ammon,[38] afford a rich mass of genuine materials, which, wrought up and polished to elegance, will add copiousness to what, perhaps, without such aid, could have aspired only to justness and propriety.

35 Albrecht Dürer (1471–1528), famous for his woodcuts, paintings, and drawings.
36 Celebrated Dutch painter and engraver (1494–1533), a close friend of Dürer.
37 Swiss painter (1539–1583) whose portraits show the influence of Holbein.
38 A Swiss wood-engraver and painter (1539–1591).

In the luxuriant style of Paul Veronese, in the capricious compositions of Tintoret,[39] he will find something, that will assist his invention, and give points, from which his own imagination shall rise and take flight, when the subject which he treats will with propriety admit of splendid effects.

In every school, whether Venetian, French, or Dutch, he will find either ingenious compositions, extraordinary effects, some peculiar expressions, or some mechanical excellence, well worthy of his attention, and, in some measure, of his imitation. Even in the lower class of the French painters, great beauties are often found, united with great defects. Though Coypel[40] wanted a simplicity of taste, and mistook a presumptuous and assuming air for what is grand and majestic; yet he frequently has good sense and judgment in his manner of telling his stories, great skill in his compositions, and is not without a considerable power of expressing the passions. The modern affectation of grace in his works, as well as in those of Bosch[41] and Watteau,[42] may be said to be separated by a very thin partition, from the more simple and pure grace of Correggio and Parmegiano.

Among the Dutch painters, the correct, firm, and determined pencil, which was employed by Bamboccio[43] and Jean Miel,[44] on vulgar and mean subjects, might, without any change, be employed on the highest; to which, indeed, it seems more properly to belong. The greatest style, if that style is confined to small figures, such as Poussin generally painted, would receive an additional grace by the elegance and precision of pencil so admirable in the works of Teniers[45]; and though the school to which he belonged more particularly excelled in the mechanism of painting;

---

39 Jacopo Robusti, called Il Tintoretto ("little dyer") from his father's trade (1518–1594), a Venetian painter whose work was marked by its dramatic lighting and impressionistic brushwork.

40 Antoine Coypel (1661–1722), French painter and imitator of Poussin, son of Nöel Coypel (1628–1707), also a painter.

41 Hieronymus Bosch (c. 1460–1516), Flemish painter who treated religious subjects in fantastic scenes peopled with diabolical little figures.

42 Antoine Watteau (1684–1721), French painter, famous for his graceful outdoor scenes.

43 Pieter van Laar, called Bamboccio ("cripple") (c. 1613–c. 1674), Dutch genre painter, noted for the humor and naturalness of his scenes.

44 Jan Miel, called Giovanni della Vite (1599–1664), Flemish painter.

45 David Teniers the Elder (1582–1649), Flemish historical, genre, and landscape painter, a pupil of Rubens. His son, David Teniers the Younger (1610–1690), was also a noted painter, his father's pupil.

yet it produced many, who have shown great abilities in expressing what must be ranked above mechanical excellences. In the works of Frank Hals,[46] the portrait-painter may observe the composition of a face, the features well put together, as the painters express it; from whence proceeds that strong-marked character of individual nature, which is so remarkable in his portraits, and is not found in an equal degree in any other painter. If he had joined to this most difficult part of the art, a patience in finishing what he had so correctly planned, he might justly have claimed the place which Vandyck,[47] all things considered, so justly holds as the first of portrait-painters.

Others of the same school have shown great power in expressing the character and passions of those vulgar people which were the subjects of their study and attention. Among these, Jan Steen[48] seems to be one of the most diligent and accurate observers of what passed in those scenes which he frequented, and which were to him an academy. I can easily imagine, that if this extraordinary man had had the good fortune to have been born in Italy, instead of Holland; had he lived in Rome, instead of Leyden, and been blessed with Michel Angelo and Raffaelle for his masters, instead of Brouwer[49] and Van Goyen;[50] the same sagacity and penetration which distinguished so accurately the different characters and expression in his vulgar figures, would, when exerted in the selection and imitation of what was great and elevated in nature, have been equally successful; and he now would have ranged with the great pillars and supporters of our Art.

Men who, although thus bound down by the almost invincible powers of early habits, have still exerted extraordinary abilities within their narrow and confined circle; and have, from the natural vigour of their mind, given a very interesting expression and great force and energy to their works; though they cannot be recommended to be exactly imitated, may yet invite an artist to endeavour to transfer, by a kind of parody, their excellences to his own performances. Whoever has acquired the power of making this use of the Flemish, Venetian, and French

---

46 Dutch painter (c. 1580–1666), noted for his portraits and his studies of base types.

47 Sir Anthony Van Dyck (1599–1641), Flemish artist, strikingly individual in technique, an important painter of portraits.

48 Dutch painter (1626–1679), distinguished by his correctness of drawing and his wide range of subjects.

49 Adrian Brouwer (1608–1640), Dutch painter, apprenticed to Frans Hals, spirited in the design and color of his paintings.

50 Jan van Goyen (1596–1656), Dutch painter of landscapes and marine views.

schools, is a real genius, and has sources of knowledge open to him which were wanting to the great artists who lived in the great age of painting.

To find excellences, however dispersed, to discover beauties, however concealed by the multitude of defects with which they are surrounded, can be the work only of him, who having a mind always alive to his art, has extended his views to all ages and to all schools; and has acquired from that comprehensive mass which he has thus gathered to himself, a well-digested and perfect idea of his art, to which every thing is referred. Like a sovereign judge and arbiter of art, he is possessed of that presiding power which separates and attracts every excellence from every school; selects both from what is great, and what is little; brings home knowledge from the East and from the West, making the universe tributary towards furnishing his mind, and enriching his works with originality and variety of inventions.

Thus I have ventured to give my opinion of what appears to me the true and only method by which an artist makes himself master of his profession; which I hold ought to be one continued course of imitation, that is not to cease but with his life.

Those who, either from their own engagements and hurry of business, or from indolence, or from conceit and vanity, have neglected looking out of themselves, as far as my experience and observation reaches, have from that time, not only ceased to advance, and improve in their performances, but have gone backward. They may be compared to men who have lived upon their principal, till they are reduced to beggary, and left without resources.

I can recommend nothing better therefore, than that you endeavour to infuse into your works what you learn from the contemplation of the works of others. To recommend this has the appearance of needless and superfluous advice; but it has fallen within my own knowledge, that artists, though they were not wanting in a sincere love for their art, though they had great pleasure in seeing good pictures, and were well skilled to distinguish what was excellent or defective in them, yet have gone on in their own manner, without any endeavour to give a little of those beauties, which they admired in others, to their own works. It is difficult to conceive how the present Italian painters, who live in the midst of the treasures of art, should be contented with their own style. They proceed in their commonplace inventions, and never think it worth while to visit the works of those great artists with which they are surrounded.

I remember, several years ago, to have conversed at Rome with an artist of great fame throughout Europe; he was not without a considerable degree of abilities, but those abilities were by no means equal to his own opinion of them. From the reputation he had acquired, he too fondly concluded that he stood in the same rank when compared with his predecessors, as he held with regard to his miserable contemporary rivals. In conversation about some particulars of the works of Raffaelle, he seemed to have, or to affect to have, a very obscure memory of them. He told me that he had not set his foot in the Vatican for fifteen years together; that he had been in treaty to copy a capital picture of Raffaelle, but that the business had gone off, however, if the agreement had held, his copy would have greatly exceeded the original. The merit of this artist, however great we may suppose it, I am sure would have been far greater, and his presumption would have been far less, if he had visited the Vatican, as in reason he ought to have done, at least once every month of his life.

I address myself, Gentlemen, to you who have made some progress in the art, and are to be, for the future, under the guidance of your own judgment and discretion. I consider you as arrived to that period, when you have a right to think for yourselves, and to presume that every man is fallible; to study the masters with a suspicion, that great men are not always exempt from great faults; to criticise, compare, and rank their works in your own estimation, as they approach to, or recede from that standard of perfection which you have formed in your own minds, but which those masters themselves, it must be remembered, have taught you to make, and which you will cease to make with correctness, when you cease to study them. It is their excellences which have taught you their defects.

I would wish you to forget where you are, and who it is that speaks to you, I only direct you to higher models and better advisers. We can teach you here but very little; you are henceforth to be your own teachers. Do this justice, however, to the English Academy; to bear in mind, that in this place you contracted no narrow habits, no false ideas, nothing that could lead you to the imitation of any living master, who may be the fashionable darling of the day. As you have not been taught to flatter us, do not learn to flatter yourselves. We have endeavoured to lead you to the admiration of nothing but what is truly admirable. If you choose inferior patterns, or if you make your own former works your patterns for your latter, it is your own fault.

The purport of this discourse, and, indeed, of most of my other discourses, is, to caution you against that false opinion, but too prevalent among artists, of the imaginary powers of native genius, and its sufficiency in great works. This opinion, according to the temper of mind it meets with, almost always produces, either a vain confidence, or a sluggish despair, both equally fatal to all proficiency.

Study, therefore, the great works of the great masters, for ever. Study, as nearly as you can, in the order, in the manner, and on the principles, on which they studied. Study nature attentively, but always with those masters in your company; consider them as models which you are to imitate, and at the same time as rivals with whom you are to contend.

OLIVER GOLDSMITH

(1728–1774)

Like Edmund Burke, Oliver Goldsmith was of Irish birth. After a tumultuous youth, he completed a medical education and became a practicing physician in Southwark, a metropolitan borough of south London. He had strong literary interests, which led him to the writing of essays and to a friendship with Dr. Johnson (Boswell was critical of him; see below, p. 568). Although he won recognition for his essays and poetry, his financial affairs were always precarious; Johnson sold his novel, *The Vicar of Wakefield* (1766), to save him from imprisonment for debt. He wrote, besides *The Vicar*, plays, essays, poetry, and history, and was successful in all these forms. Buried in the Temple Church, he was honored by a monument in Westminster Abbey.

Goldsmith as a man famously genial and convivial; his geniality emerges, too, in his writing. A strong intelligence controls his prose; although he is capable of gross sentimentality, he can achieve acute discrimination. The relation of thought to feeling is frequently his subject: he values emotion, the capacity to feel, yet recognizes the necessity for discipline; and he recognizes the possibility of keeping emotion in check with emotion—of using comic technique, demanding the response of laughter, to control his tendency to overexploit pathos.

Biography and Criticism

Colum, Padraic, *Oliver Goldsmith*, 1913.

Dobson, Austin, *Life of Oliver Goldsmith*, 1888.

Freeman, William, *Oliver Goldsmith*, 1952.

Gwynn, Stephen, *Oliver Goldsmith*, 1935.

Kirk, Clara, *Oliver Goldsmith*, 1967.

Quintana, Ricardo, "Oliver Goldsmith as a Critic of the Drama," *Studies in English Literature*, V (1965), 435–454.

Reynolds, W. Vaughan, "Goldsmith's Critical Outlook," *Review of English Studies*, XIV (1938), 155–172.

Smith, Hamilton J., *Oliver Goldsmith's Citizen of the world, A Study*, 1926.

Wardle, Ralph M., *Oliver Goldsmith*, 1957.

ENQUIRY INTO THE PRESENT STATE
OF POLITE LEARNING IN EUROPE[1]

(1759)

The *Enquiry* was Goldsmith's first original book. A survey of belles-lettres in Europe, it is moralistic in tone and pessimistic in many of its implications. Goldsmith finds decay in the arts wherever he looks, and he is quick to define its causes. In the chapters here printed, he attacks critics, despite the fact that he was one himself, and bemoans the state of the English theater, where the power of managers is such, he claims, that the people are deprived of the entertainment that should be their due.

The source of the present text is *Collected Works of Oliver Goldsmith*, 5 vols. ed. Arthur Friedman (Oxford: Clarendon Press, 1966). Used by permission of the Clarendon Press, Oxford.

Of Polite Learning in Europe

(1759)

CHAPTER XI

Upon Criticism

But there are still some men, whom fortune has blessed with affluence, to whom the muse pays her morning visit, not like a creditor, but a friend: to this happy few, who have leisure to polish what they write, and liberty to chuse their own subjects, I would direct my advice, which consists in a few words: *Write what you think, regardless of the critics*. To persuade to this, was the chief design of this essay. To break, or at least to loosen those bonds, first put on by caprice, and afterwards drawn hard by fashion, is my wish. I have assumed the critic only to dissuade from criticism.

---

1 See introduction, p. 45.

There is scarce an error of which our present writers are guilty, that does not arise from this source. From this proceeds the affected obscurity of our odes,[2] the tuneless flow of our blank verse, the pompous epithet, laboured diction, and every other deviation from common sense, which procures the poet the applause of the connoisseur; he is praised by all, read by a few, and soon forgotten.

There never was an unbeaten path trodden by the poet, that the critic did not endeavour to reclaim him, by calling his attempt innovation. This might be instanced in Dante, who first followed nature, and was persecuted by the critics as long as he lived. Thus novelty, one of the greatest beauties in poetry, must be avoided, or the connoisseur be displeased. It is one of the chief privileges, however, of genius, to fly from the herd of imitators by some happy singularity; for should he stand still, his heavy pursuers will at length certainly come up, and fairly dispute the victory.

The ingenious Mr. Hogarth[3] used to assert, that every one, except the connoisseur, was a judge of painting. The same may be asserted of writing; the public in general set the whole piece in the proper point of view; the critic lays his eye close to all its minutenesses, and condemns or approves in detail. And this may be the reason why so many writers at present, are apt to appeal from the tribunal of criticism to that of the people.

From a desire in the critic of grafting the spirit of ancient languages upon the English, has proceeded of late several disagreeable instances of pedantry. Among the number, I think we may reckon blank verse. Nothing but the greatest sublimity of subject can render such a measure pleasing; however, we now see it used upon the most trivial occasions; it has particularly found way into our didactic poetry, and is likely to bring that species of composition into disrepute, for which the English are deservedly famous.

Those who are acquainted with writing, know that our language runs almost naturally into blank verse. The writers of our novels, romances, and all of this class, who have no notion of stile, naturally hobble into this unharmonious measure. If rhymes, therefore, be more difficult, for that very reason, I would have our poets write in rhyme. Such a

---

2 Arthur Friedman suggests that Goldsmith may be thinking of Gray. In a review of Gray's *Odes* in September 1757, Goldsmith remarked on their obscurity.

3 William Hogarth (1697–1764), English painter and engraver.

restriction upon the thought of a good poet, often lifts and encreases the vehemence of every sentiment; for fancy, like a fountain, plays highest by diminishing the aperture. But rhymes, it will be said, are a remnant of monkish stupidity, an innovation upon the poetry of the ancients. They are but indifferently acquainted with antiquity, who make the assertion. Rhymes are probably of older date than either the Greek or Latin dactyl and spondé. The Celtic, which is allowed to be the first language spoken in Europe, has ever preserved them, as we may find in the Edda of Iceland, and the Irish carrols still sung among the original inhabitants of that island. Olaus Wormius[4] gives us some of the Teutonic poetry in this way; and Pantoppidan, bishop of Bergen,[5] some of the Norwegian; in short, this jingle of sounds is almost natural to mankind, at least, it is so to our language, if we may judge from many unsuccessful attempts to throw it off.[6]

I should not have employed so much time in opposing this errone-ous innovation, if it were not apt to introduce another in its train: I mean, a disgusting solemnity of manner into our poetry; and as the prose writer has been ever found to follow the poet, it must consequently banish in both, all that agreeable trifling, which, if I may so express it, often de-ceives us into instruction. Dry reasoning, and dull morality, have no force with the wild fantastic libertine. He must be met with smiles, and courted with the allurements of gaiety. He must be taught to believe, that he is in pursuit of pleasure, and be surprized into reformation. The finest sentiment, and the most weighty truth, may put on a pleasing face, and it is even virtuous to jest when serious advice might be disgusting. But instead of this, the most trifling performance among us now, assumes all the didactic stiffness of wisdom. The most diminutive son of fame, or of famine, has his *we* and his *us*, his *firstlys* and his *secondlys* as methodical, as if bound in cow-hide, and closed with clasps of brass. Were these Monthly Reviews and Magazines frothy, pert, or absurd, they might find some pardon; but to be dull and dronish, is an encroachment on the prerogative of a folio.

These pamphlets should be considered as pills to purge melancholly; they should be made up in our splenetic climate, to be taken as physic,

---

4 Wormius (1588–1654), Danish physician, antiquary, and historian.

5 Erik Pontopiddan (1698–1764), bishop of Bergen in Norway, economist, historian, theologian. Goldsmith may be referring to his *Glossarium Norvegicum* (1749).

6 For a contrary opinion on blank verse and rhyme, see Young's *Conjectures*, above, pp. 67–68.

and not so as to be used when we take it. Some such law should be en-acted in the republic of letters, as we find take place in the house of com-mons. As no man there can shew his wisdom, unless first qualified by three hundred pounds a year, so none here should profess gravity, unless his work amounted to three hundred pages.

However, by the power of one single monosyllable, our critics have almost got the victory over humour amongst us. Does the poet paint the absurdities of the vulgar; then he is *low*: does he exaggerate the features of folly, to render it more thoroughly ridiculous, he is then very *low*. In short, they have proscribed the comic or satyrical muse from every walk but high life, which, though abounding in fools as well as the humblest station, is by no means so fruitful in absurdity. Among well-bred fools we may despise much, but have little to laugh at; nature seems to present us with an universal blank of silk, ribbands, smiles and whispers; absurdity is the poet's game, and good breeding is the nice concealment of absurdi-ties. The truth is, the critic generally mistakes humour for wit, which is a very different excellence. Wit raises human nature above its level; humour acts a contrary part, and equally depresses it. To expect exalted humour, is a contradiction in terms; and the critic, by demanding an impossibility from the comic poet, has, in effect, banished new comedies from the stage. But to put the same thought in a different light:

When an unexpected similitude in two objects strikes the imagina-tion; in other words, when a thing is *wittily* expressed, all our pleasure turns into admiration of the artist, who had fancy enough to draw the picture. When a thing is *humourously* described, our burst of laughter proceeds from a very different cause; we compare the absurdity of the character represented with our own, and triumph in our conscious superiority. No natural defect can be a cause of laughter, because it is a misfortune to which ourselves are liable; a defect of this kind, changes the passion into pity or horror; we only laugh at those instances of moral absurdity, to which we are conscious that we ourselves are not liable. For instance, should I describe a man as wanting his nose, there is no humour in this, as it is an accident to which human nature is subject, and may be any man's case: but should I represent this man without his nose, as extremely curious in the choice of his snuff-box, we here see him guilty of an absurdity of which we imagine ourselves can never be guilty, and therefore applaud our own good sense on the comparison. Thus, then, the pleasure we receive from wit, turns on the admiration of another; that we feel from humour, centers in the admiration of ourselves.

The poet, therefore, must place the object he would have the subject of humour in a state of inferiority; in other words, the subject of humour must be low.

The solemnity worn by many of our modern writers is, I fear, often the mask of dulness; for certain it is, it seems to fit every author who pleases to put it on. By the complexion of many of our late publications, one might be apt to cry out with Cicero, *Civem mehercule non puto esse qui his temporibus ridere possit.*[7] On my conscience, I believe we have all forgot to laugh in these days. Such writers probably make no distinction between what is praised, and what is pleasing; between those commendations which the reader pays his own discernment, and those which are the genuine result of his sensations.

As our gentlemen writers have it therefore so much in their power to lead the taste of the times, they may now part with the inflated stile that has for some years been looked upon as fine writing, and which every young writer is now obliged to adopt, if he chuses to be read. They may now dispense with loaded epithet, and dressing up of trifles with dignity. For to use an obvious instance, it is not those who make the greatest noise with their wares in the streets, that have most to sell. Let us, instead of writing finely, try to write naturally. Not hunt after lofty expressions to deliver mean ideas; nor be for ever gaping, when we only mean to deliver a whisper.

CHAPTER XII

Of the Stage

Our Theatre may be regarded as partaking of the shew and decoration of the Italian opera, with the propriety and declamation of French performance. Our stage is more magnificent than any other in Europe, and the people in general fonder of theatrical entertainment. But as our pleasures, as well as more important concerns, are generally managed by party, the stage is subject to its influence. The managers, and all who espouse their side, are for decoration and ornament; the critic, and all who have studied French decorum, are for regularity and declamation. Thus it is almost impossible to please both parties, and the poet, by

---

7 "On my oath, I don't think there is a citizen in existence who can laugh in these days (*Epistles to Friends*, II. iv. 1).

attempting it, finds himself often incapable of pleasing either. If he introduces stage pomp, the critic consigns his performance to the vulgar; if
he indulges in recital, and simplicity, he is accused of insipidity or dry
affectation.

From the nature therefore of our theatre, and the genius of our
country, it is extremely difficult for a dramatic poet to please his audience.
But happy would he be were these the only difficulties he had to encounter; there are many other more dangerous combinations against the
little wit of the age. Our poet's performance must undergo a process
truly chymical before it is presented to the public. It must be tried in the
Review, or the news-paper of the day. At this rate, before it can come to
a private table, it may probably be a mere caput mortuum,[1] and only
proper entertainment for the licenser, manager, or critic himself. But it
may be answered, that we have a sufficient number of plays upon our
theatres already, and therefore there is no need of new ones. But are they
sufficiently good? And is the credit of our age nothing? Must our present
times pass away unnoticed by posterity? We are desirous of leaving them
liberty, wealth, and titles, and we can have no recompence but their
applause. The title of Learned given to an age, is the most glorious applause, and shall this be disregarded? Our reputation among foreigners
will quickly be discontinued, when we discontinue our efforts to deserve
it, and shall we despise their praise? Are our new absurdities, with which
no nation more abounds, to be left unnoticed? Is the pleasure such performances give upon the perusal, to be entirely given up? If these are all
matters of indifference, it then signifies nothing, whether we are to be
entertained with the actor or the poet, with fine sentiments, or painted
canvas, or whether the dancer, or the carpenter, be constituted master
of the ceremonies.

But they are not matters of indifference. Every age produces new
follies and new vices, and one absurdity is often displaced in order to make
room for another. The dramatic poet, however, who should be, and has
often been, a firm champion in the cause of virtue, detects all the new
machinations of vice, levels his satire at the rising structures of folly, or
drives her from behind the retrenchments of fashion. Thus far then, the
poet is useful; but how far the actor, that dear favourite of the public,
may be so, is a question, next to be determined.

As the poet's merit is often not sufficient to introduce his per-

---

1 Death's-head.

formance among the public with proper dignity, he is often obliged to call in the assistance of decoration and dress to contribute to this effect. By this means a performance, which pleases on the stage, often instructs in the closet, and for one who has seen it acted, hundreds will be readers. The actor then is useful, by introducing the works of the poet to the public with becoming splendor; but when these have once become popular, I must confess myself so much a sceptic, as to think it would be more for the interests of virtue, if such performances were read, not acted; made rather our companions in the closet, than on the theatre. While we are readers, every moral sentiment strikes us in all its beauty, but the love scenes are frigid, tawdry, and disgusting. When we are spectators, all the persuasives to vice receive an additional lustre. The love scene is aggravated, the obscenity heightened, the best actors figure in the most debauched characters, while the parts of dull morality, as they are called, are thrown to some mouthing machine, who puts even virtue out of countenance, by his wretched imitation. The principal performers find their interest in chusing such parts as tend to promote, not the benefit of society, but their own reputation; and in using arts which inspire emotions very different from those of morality. How many young men go to the playhouse speculatively in love with the rule of right, but return home actually enamour'd of an actress?

I have often attended to the reflections of the company upon leaving the theatre; one actor had the finest pipe, but the other the most melodious voice; one was a bewitching creature, another a charming devil; and such are generally our acquisitions at the play-house: It brings to my remembrance an old lady, who being passionately fond of a famous preacher, went every Sunday to church, but, struck only with his graceful manner of delivery, disregarded and forgot the truths of his discourse.

But it is needless to mention the incentives to vice which are found at the theatre, or the immorality of some of the performers. Such impeachments, though true, would be regarded as cant, while their exhibitions continue to amuse. I would only infer from hence, that an actor is chiefly useful in introducing new performances upon the stage, since the reader receives more benefit by perusing a well written play in his closet, than by seeing it acted. I would also infer, that to the poet is to be ascribed all the good that attends seeing plays, and to the actor all the harm.

But how is this rule inverted on our theatres at present? Old pieces are revived, and scarce any new ones admitted; the actor is ever in our eye, and the poet seldom permitted to appear; the public are again obliged

to ruminate those hashes of absurdity, which were disgusting to our
ancestors, even in an age of ignorance; and the stage, instead of serving
the people, is made subservient to the interests of an avaricious few.
We must now tamely see the literary honours of our country suppressed
that an actor may dine with elegance; we must tamely sit and see the
celestial muse made a slave to the histrionic Dæmon.

We seem to be pretty much in the situation of travellers at a Scotch
inn, vile entertainment is served up, complained of and sent down, up
comes worse, and that also is changed, and every change makes our
wretched cheer more unsavoury. What must be done? only sit down
contented, cry up all that comes before us, and admire even the absurdities
of Shakespear.

Let the reader suspend his censure; I admire the beauties of this
great father of our stage as much as they deserve, but could wish, for the
honour of our country, and for his honour too, that many of his scenes
were forgotten. A man blind of one eye, should always be painted in
profile. Let the spectator who assists at any of these new revived pieces,
only ask himself, whether he would approve such a performance if written
by a modern poet; if he would not, then his applause proceeds merely
from the sound of a name and an empty veneration for antiquity. In fact,
the revival of those pieces of forced humour, far fetch'd conceit, and unnatural hyperbole, which have been ascribed to Shakespear, is rather
gibbeting than raising a statue to his memory; it is rather a trick of the
actor, who thinks it safest acting in exaggerated characters, and who by
out-stepping nature, chuses to exhibit the ridiculous outré of an harlequin
under the sanction of this venerable name.

What strange vamp'd comedies, farcical tragedies, or what shall I
call them, speaking pantomimes, have we not of late seen. No matter
what the play may be, it is the actor who draws an audience. He throws
life into all; all are in spirits and merry, in at one door and out at another;
the spectator, in a fool's paradise, knows not what all this means till the
last act concludes in matrimony. The piece pleases our critics, because it
talks old English; and it pleases the galleries, because it has fun. True
taste, or even common sense, are out of the question.

But great art must be sometimes used before they can thus impose
upon the public. To this purpose, a prologue written with some spirit
generally precedes the piece, to inform us that it was composed by
Shakespear, or old Ben,[2] or somebody else, who took them for his model.
A face of iron could not have the assurance to avow dislike; the theatre

---

2 I.e., Ben Jonson.

has its partizans who understand the force of combinations, trained up to vociferation, clapping of hands, and clattering of sticks; and tho' a man might have strength sufficient to overcome a lion in single combat, by an army even of mice, he may run the risk of being eaten up marrow-bones and all.

I am not insensible that third nights are disagreeable drawbacks upon the annual profits of the stage;[3] I am confident, it is much more to the manager's advantage to furbish up all the lumber, which the good sense of our ancestors, but for his care, had consign'd to oblivion; it is not with him therefore, but with the public I would expostulate; they have a right to demand respect, and sure those new revived plays are no instances of the manager's deference.

I have been informed, that no new play can be admitted upon our theatre unless the author chuses to wait some years, or to use the phrase in fashion, till it comes to be played in turn. A poet thus can never expect to contract a familiarity with the stage, by which alone he can hope to succeed, nor can the most signal success relieve immediate want. Our Saxon ancestors had but one name for a wit and a witch.[4] I will not dispute the propriety of uniting those characters then; but the man who under the present discouragements ventures to write for the stage now, whatever claim he may have to the appellation of a wit, at least, he has no right to be called a conjuror.

Yet getting a play on even in three or four years, is a privilege reserved only for the happy few who have the arts of courting the manager as well as the muse: who have adulation to please his vanity, powerful patrons to support their merit, or money to indemnify disappointment. The poet must act like our beggars at Christmas, who lay the first shilling on the plate for themselves. Thus all wit is banished from the stage, except it be supported by friends, or fortune, and poets are seldom overburthened with either.

I am not at present writing for a party, but above theatrical connections in every sense of the expression; I have no particular spleen

3 Third nights were benefit performances for the author of the play presented.
4 Friedman cites Sir William Temple ("Of Poetry," *Works* [1720], I. 243–44): "The *Gothic Runers*, to gain and establish the Credit and Admiration of their Rhymes, turned the use of them very much to Incantations and Charms . . . : The Men or Women, who were thought to perform such Wonders or Enchantments, were from *Viises* or *Wises*, the Name of those Verses wherein their Charms were conceived, called *Wizards* or *Witches*." Anglo-Saxon *wita* meant both "a wise man" and "one professing supernatural knowledge."

against the fellow who sweeps the stage with the besom, or the hero
who brushes it with his train. It were a matter of indifference to me,
whether our heroines are in keeping,[5] or our candle-snuffers burn their
fingers, did not such make a great part of public care, and polite conversation. It is not these, but the age I would reproach: the vile complexion of
the times, when those employ our most serious thoughts and seperate us
into parties, whose business is only to amuse our idlest hours. I cannot help
reproaching our meanness in this respect; for our stupidity, and our folly,
will be remembered, when even the attitudes and eye brows of a favourite
actor shall be forgotten.

In the times of Addison and Steele, players were held in greater
contempt than, perhaps, they deserved. Honest Eastcourt, Verbruggen
and Underhill,[6] were extreamly poor, and assumed no airs of insolence.
They were contented with being merry at a city feast, with promoting
the mirth of a set of cheerful companions, and gave their jest for their
reckoning. At that time, it was kind to say something in defence of the
poor good-natured creatures, if it were only to keep them in good
humour; but at present, such encouragements are unnecessary. Our
actors assume all that state off the stage which they do on it; and to use an
expression borrow'd from the Green Room, every one is *up* in his part.
I am sorry to say it, they seem to forget their real characters; more
provoking still, the public seems to forget them too.

Macrobius has preserved a prologue, spoken and written by the
poet Laberius, a Roman knight, whom Caesar forced upon the stage,
written with great elegance and spirit, which shews what opinion the
Romans in general entertained of the profession of an actor.

> *Necessitas cujus cursus transversi impetum, & c.*
>
> *What! no way left to shun th' inglorious stage,*
> *And save from infamy my sinking age.*
> *Scarce half alive, oppress'd with many a year,*
> *What in the name of dotage drives me here?*
> *A time there was, when glory was my guide,*
> *Nor force nor fraud could turn my steps aside,*
> *Unaw'd by pow'r and unappal'd by fear,*
> *With honest thrift I held my honour dear,*

---

5 I.e., are kept as mistresses.
6 Richard Estcourt (1668–1712), John Verbruggen (fl. 1688–1707), and Cave Underhill
(1634–c. 1710) were all actors.

But this vile hour disperses all my store,
And all my hoard of honour is no more.
For ah! too partial to my life's decline,
Cæsar persuades, submission must be mine,
Him I obey, whom heaven itself obeys,
Hopeless of pleasing, yet inclin'd to please.
Here then at once, I welcome every shame,
And cancel at threescore a life of fame;
No more my titles shall my children tell,
The old buffoon will fit my name as well;
This day beyond its term my fate extends,
For life is ended when our honour ends.[7]

From all that has been said upon the state of our theatre, we may easily foresee, whether it is likely to improve or decline; and whether the free-born muse can bear to submit to those restrictions, which avarice or power would impose. For the future, it is somewhat unlikely, that he, whose labours are valuable, or who knows their value, will turn to the stage for either fame or subsistence, when he must at once flatter an actor, and please an audience.

Let no manager impute this to spleen, or disappointment. I only assert the claims of the public, and endeavour to vindicate a profession which has hitherto wanted a defender. A mean or mercenary conduct may continue for some time to triumph over opposition, but it is possible the public will at last be taught to vindicate their privileges. Perhaps, there may come a time, when the poet will be at liberty to encrease the entertainments of the people; but such a period may possibly not arise till our discouragements have banished poetry from the stage.

---

7 *Saturnaliorum*, Book II, Ch. VII.

THE BEE[1]

(1759)

The Bee, a short-lived periodical, made only eight appearances, in the same year as the *Enquiry*. Its essays show far more variety of tone than the more ambitious work. They provide a clear and often amusing view of the contemporary scene, a vivid sense of character, and frequently serious and penetrating reflections on literary or social questions. The two essays here reprinted exemplify Goldsmith's skill at suggesting the serious implications of comic vignettes.

The source of the present text is *Collected Works of Oliver Goldsmith*, 5 vols., ed. Arthur Friedman (Oxford: Clarendon Press, 1966). Used by permission of the Clarendon Press, Oxford.

The Bee

NUMBER II   *Saturday, October 13, 1759*

On Dress

Foreigners observe that there are no ladies in the world more beautiful, or more ill dressed than those of England. Our country-women have been compared to those Pictures, where the face is the work of a Raphael;[2] but the draperies thrown out by some empty pretender, destitute of taste, and unacquainted with design.

If I were a poet, I might observe, on this occasion, that so much beauty set off with all the advantages of dress, would be too powerful an antagonist for the opposite sex, and therefore it was wisely ordered, that our ladies should want taste, lest their admirers should entirely want reason.

But to confess a truth, I do not find they have a greater aversion

---

1 See introduction, pp. 34–35.
2 Italian painter (1483–1520). See Reynolds above, p. 285.

to fine cloaths than the women of any other country whatsoever. I can't fancy that a shopkeeper's wife in Cheapside[3] has a greater tenderness for the fortune of her husband than a citizen's wife in Paris; or that miss in a boarding-school is more an oeconomist in dress than mademoiselle in a nunnery.

Although Paris may be accounted the soil in which almost every fashion takes its rise, its influence is never so general there as with us. They study there the happy method of uniting grace and fashion, and never excuses a woman for being aukwardly dressed, by saying her cloaths are in the mode. A French woman is a perfect architect in dress; she never, with Gothic ignorance, mixes the orders; she never tricks out a squabby[4] Doric shape, with Corinthian[5] finery; or, to speak without metaphor, she conforms to general fashion, only when it happens not to be repugnant to private beauty.

The English ladies, on the contrary, seem to have no other standard of grace but the run of the town. If fashion gives the word, every distinction of beauty, complexion, or stature ceases. Sweeping trains, Prussian bonnets,[6] and trollopees,[7] as like each other, as if cut from the same piece, level all to one standard. The mall, the gardens, and playhouses are filled with ladies in uniform, and their whole appearance shews as little variety or taste as if their cloaths were bespoke[8] by the colonel of a marching regiment, or fancied by the artist who dresses the three battalions of guards.

But not only ladies of every shape and complexion, but of every age too, are possessed of this unaccountable passion for levelling all distinction in dress. The lady of no quality travels fast behind the lady of some quality; and a woman of sixty is as gaudy as her grand-daughter. A friend of mine, a good-natured old man, amused me, the other day, with an account of his journey to the Mall. It seems, in his walk thither, he, for some time, followed a lady who, as he thought by her dress, was a

---

3 Middle-class shopping area in London.

4 Fat, plump.

5 The Corinthian mode was the most ornate of the three Greek architectural modes, hence, the general meaning *elegant, ornate;* in contrast to the Doric mode, the simplest, which produced the general meaning *rude, uncouth.* By a similar process of extension, *Gothic* ("Gothic ignorance," above) came to mean *barbarous, rude.*

6 Bonnets at this time were reaching great sizes, in order to fit over women's elaborate wigs. The precise nature of a Prussian bonnet can no longer be ascertained.

7 Loose dresses.

8 Ordered.

girl of fifteen. It was airy, elegant, and youthful. My old friend had called up all his poetry on this occasion, and fancied twenty Cupids prepared for execution in every folding of her white negligee. He had prepared his imagination for an angel's face; but what was his mortification to find that the imaginary goddess was no other than his cousin Hannah, some years older than himself.

But to give it in his own words, After the transports of our first salute, said he, were over, I could not avoid running my eye over her whole appearance. Her gown was of cambrick,[9] cut short before, in order to discover an high-heeled shoe, which was buckled almost at the toe. Her cap consisted of a few bits of cambrick, and flowers of painted paper stuck on one side of her head. Her bosom, that had felt no hand, but the hand of time, these twenty years, rose, suing to be pressed. I could, indeed, have wished her more than an handkerchief of Paris-net[10] to shade her beauties; for, as Tasso says of the rose-bud, *Quanto si mostra men tanto e piu bella.*[11] A female breast is generally thought more beautiful as it is more sparingly discovered.

As my cousin had not put on all this finery for nothing, she was at that time sallying out to the park, when I had overtaken her. Perceiving, however, that I had on my best wig, she offered, if I would 'squire her there, to send home the footman. Though I trembled for our reception in public, yet I could not, with any civility, refuse; so, to be as gallant as possible, I took her hand in my arm, and thus we marched on together.

When we made our entry at the Park, two antiquated figures, so polite and so tender, soon attracted the eyes of the company. As we made our way among crowds who were out to shew their finery as well as we, wherever we came I perceived we brought good-humour with us. The polite could not forbear smiling, and the vulgar burst out into a horse laugh at our grotesque figures. Cousin Hannah, who was perfectly conscious of the rectitude of her own appearance, attributed all this mirth to the oddity of mine; while I as cordially placed the whole to her account. Thus, from being two of the best-natured creatures alive, before we got half way up the mall, we both began to grow peevish, and, like two mice on a string, endeavoured to revenge the impertinence of the spectators upon each other. "I am amazed, cousin Jeffery," says miss, "that I can

9 A thick, white fabric of flax or linen.
10 A fine mesh material.
11 "The less it shows itself, the more beautiful it is" (*Jerusalem Delivered*, XVI. xiv. 4).

never get you to dress like a Christian. I knew we should have the eyes of the Park upon us, with your great wig so frizzled, and yet so beggarly, and your monstrous muff. I hate those odious muffs." I could have patiently borne a criticism on all the rest of my equipage; but, as I had had always a peculiar veneration for my muff, I could not forbear being piqued a little; and throwing my eyes with a spiteful air on her bosom, "I could heartily wish, madam," replied I, "that, for your sake, my muff was cut into a tippet."[12]

As my cousin, by this time, was grown heartily ashamed of her gentleman usher, and as I was never very fond of any kind of exhibition myself, it was mutually agreed to retire, for a while, to one of the seats, and from that retreat, remark on others as freely as they had remarked on us.

When seated we continued silent for some time, employed in very different speculations. I regarded the whole company now passing in review before me, as drawn out merely for my amusement. For my entertainment the beauty had all that morning been improving her charms, the beau had put on lace, and the young doctor a big wig, merely to please me. But quite different were the sentiments of cousin Hannah; she regarded every well-dressed woman as a victorious rival, hated every face that seemed dressed in good humour, or wore the appearance of greater happiness than her own. I perceived her uneasiness, and attempted to lessen it, by observing that there was no company in the Park to-day. To this she readily assented; "and yet," says she, "it is full enough of scrubs[13] of one kind or another." My smiling at this observation gave her spirits to pursue the bent of her inclination, and now she began to exhibit her skill in secret history, as she found me disposed to listen. "Observe," says she to me, "that old woman in tawdry silk, and dressed out beyond the fashion. That is miss Biddy Evergreen. Miss Biddy, it seems, has money, and as she considers that money was never so scarce as it is now, she seems resolved to keep what she has to herself. She is ugly enough, you see; yet, I assure you, she has refused several offers, to my own knowledge, within this twelvemonth. Let me see, three gentlemen from Ireland who study the law, two waiting captains, her doctor, and a Scotch preacher, who had like to have carried her off. All her time is passed between sickness and finery. Thus she spends the whole week in

---

12 A scarf with hanging ends, which might shield the bosom.
13 People who look lower class and hard working.

a close chamber, with no other company but her monkey, her apothecary, and cat, and comes dressed out to the Park every Sunday, to shew her airs, to get new lovers, to catch a new cold, and to make new work for the doctor.

"There goes Mrs. Roundabout, I mean the fat lady in the lute-string[14] trollopee. Between you and I, she is but a cutler's[15] wife. See how she's dressed as fine as hands and pins can make her, while her two marriageable daughters, like bunters,[16] in stuff gowns, are now taking sixpennyworth of tea at the White-conduit-house.[17] Odious puss, how she waddles along, with her train two yards behind her! She puts me in mind of my lord Bantam's Indian sheep, which are obliged to have their monstrous tails trundled along in a go-cart.[18] For all her airs, it goes to her husband's heart to see four yards of good lutestring wearing against the ground, like one of his knives on a grindstone. To speak my mind, cousin Jeffery, I never liked those tails; for suppose a young fellow should be rude, and the lady should offer to step back in the fright, instead of retiring, she treads upon her train, and falls fairly on her back; and then you know, cousin,—[19] her cloaths may be spoiled."

"Ah! miss Mazzard! I knew we should not miss her in the Park; she in the monstrous Prussian bonnet. Miss, though so very fine, was bred a milliner, and might have had some custom if she had minded her business; but the girl was fond of finery, and instead of dressing her customers, laid out all her goods in adorning herself. Every new gown she put on impaired her credit; she still, however, went on, improving her appearance, and lessening her little fortune, and is now, you see, become a belle and a bankrupt."

My cousin was proceeding in her remarks, which were interrupted by the approach of the very lady she had been so freely describing. Miss had perceived her at a distance, and approached to salute her. I found,

---

14 A plain, stout, lustrous silk.

15 One who makes or deals in cutlery.

16 I.e., the mother is extravagant in dressing herself and stingy in dressing her marriageable daughters, who are made to look like ragpickers, to wear gowns of coarse worsted, and to take cheap refreshment in unfashionable surroundings.

17 An establishment in Islington which advertised itself as "for the Reception of Gentlemen and Ladies, with large Improvements in the Gardens."

18 Broad-tailed sheep, whose tails sometimes weighed thirty pounds, often had to have their tails supported by small boards on wheels.

19 Through the pause represented by the dash, Miss Hannah insinuates a rather different consequence of the lady's falling "on her back."

by the warmth of the two ladies protestations, that they had been long intimate esteemed friends and acquaintance. Both were so pleased at this happy rencounter, that they were resolved not to part for the day. So we all crossed the Park together, and I saw them into a hackney coach at St. James's.

NUMBER III   *Saturday, October 20, 1759*

On the Use of Language

It is usually said by grammarians, that the use of language is to express our wants and desires; but men who know the world hold, and I think with some shew of reason, that he who best knows how to keep his necessities private, is the most likely person to have them redressed; and that the true use of speech is not so much to express our wants as to conceal them.

When we reflect on the manner in which mankind generally confer their favours, there appears something so attractive in riches, that the large heap generally collects from the smaller; and the poor find as much pleasure in encreasing the enormous mass of the rich, as the miser, who owns it, sees happiness in its encrease. Nor is there in this any thing repugnant to the laws of morality. Seneca himself allows, that in conferring benefits, the present should always be suited to the dignity of the receiver.[1] Thus the rich receive large presents, and are thanked for accepting them. Men of middling stations are obliged to be content with presents something less, while the beggar, who may be truly said to want indeed, is well paid if a farthing rewards his warmest solicitations.

Every man who has seen the world, and has had his *ups and downs in life*, as the expression is, must have frequently experienced the truth of this doctrine, and must know that to have much, or to seem to have it, is the only way to have more. Ovid finely compares a man of broken fortune to a falling column; the lower it sinks, the greater is that weight it is obliged to sustain.[2] Thus, when a man's circumstances are such that he has no occasion to borrow, he finds numbers willing to lend him; but, should his wants be such that he sues for a trifle, it is two to one whether he may be trusted with the smallest sum. A certain young fellow whom

---

1 *Of Benefits*, II. XV. 3.
2 *Tristia*, ii. 83–86.

I knew, whenever he had occasion to ask his friend for a guinea, used to prelude his request as if he wanted two hundred, and talked so familiarly of large sums, that none could ever think he wanted a small one. The same gentleman, whenever he wanted credit for a suit of cloaths, always made the proposal in a laced coat;[3] for he found by experience, that if he appeared shabby on these occasions, his taylor had taken an oath against trusting; or what was every whit as bad, his foreman was out of the way, and should not be at home for some time.

There can be no inducement to reveal our wants, except to find pity, and by this means relief; but before a poor man opens his mind in such circumstances, he should first consider whether he is contented to lose the esteem of the person he solicits, and whether he is willing to give up friendship to excite compassion. Pity and friendship are passions incompatible with each other, and it is impossible that both can reside in any breast for the smallest space, without impairing each other. Friendship is made up of esteem and pleasure; pity is composed of sorrow and contempt; the mind may for some time fluctuate between them, but it can never entertain both at once.

In fact, pity, though it may often relieve, is but, at best, a short-lived passion, and seldom affords distress more than transitory assistance: With some it scarce lasts from the first impulse till the hand can be put into the pocket; with others it may continue for twice that space, and on some of extraordinary sensibility, I have seen it operate for half an hour together: but still, last as it may, it generally produces but beggarly effects; and where, from this motive we give five farthings, from others we give pounds: whatever be our feelings from the first impulse of distress, when the same distress solicits a second time, we then feel with diminished sensibility, and like the repetition of an eccho, every stroke becomes weaker, till at last our sensations lose all mixture of sorrow, and degenerate into downright contempt.

These speculations bring to my mind the fate of a very good natured fellow, who is now no more. He was bred in a compting-house, and his father dying just as he was out of his time,[4] left him an handsome fortune, and many friends to advise with. The restraint in which my friend had been brought up, had thrown a gloom upon his temper, which some regarded as prudence, and from such considerations, he had every

---

3 I.e., a coat adorned with lace.
4 Finished with his apprenticeship.

day repeated offers of friendship. Such as had money, were ready to offer him assistance that way; and they who had daughters, frequently, in the warmth of affection, advised him to marry. My friend, however, was in good circumstances; he wanted neither money, friends, nor a wife, and therefore modestly declined their proposals.

Some errors, however, in the management of his affairs, and several losses in trade, soon brought him to a different way of thinking; and he at last considered, that it was his best way to let his friends know that their offers were at length acceptable. His first address was to a scrivener,[5] who had formerly made him frequent offers of money and friendship, at a time when, perhaps, he knew those offers would have been refused. As a man, therefore, confident of not being refused, he requested the use of an hundred guineas for a few days, as he just then had occasion for money. "And pray, Sir," replied the scrivener, "do you want all this money?" "Want it, Sir," says the other, "if I did not want it, I should not have asked it." "I am sorry for that," says the friend; "for those who want money when they borrow, will always want money when they should come to pay. To say the truth, Sir, money is money now; and I believe it is all sunk in the bottom of the sea, for my part; he that has got a little, is a fool if he does not keep what he has got."

Not quite disconcerted by this refusal, our adventurer was resolved to apply to another, whom he knew to be the very best friend he had in the world. The gentleman whom he now addressed, received his proposal with all the affability that could be expected from generous friendship. "Let me see, you want an hundred guineas, and pray, dear Jack, would not fifty answer." "*If you have but fifty to spare, Sir, I must be contented.*" "Fifty to spare, I do not say that, for I believe I have but twenty about me." "*Then I must borrow the other thirty from some other friend.*" "And pray," replied the friend, "would it not be the best way to borrow the whole money from that other friend, and then one note[6] will serve for all, you know. You know, my dear Sir, that you need make no ceremony with me at any time; you know I'm your friend, and when you chuse a bit of dinner or so.—You, Tom, see the gentleman down. You wont forget to dine with us now and then. Your very humble servant."

Distressed, but not discouraged at this treatment, he was at last resolved to find that assistance from love, which he could not have from

---

5 A professional moneylender.
6 I.e., note of hand, promise to pay.

friendship. A young lady, a distant relation by the mother's side, had a fortune in her own hands, and, as she had already made all the advances that her sex's modesty would permit, he made his proposal with confidence. He soon, however, perceived, That *no bankrupt ever found the fair one kind*. She had lately fallen deeply in love with another, who had more money, and the whole neighbourhood thought it would be a match.

Every day now began to strip my poor friend of his former finery; his cloaths flew piece by piece to the pawnbroker's, and he seemed at length equipped in the genuine livery of misfortune. But still he thought himself secure from actual necessity, the numberless invitations he had received to dine, even after his losses, were yet unanswered; he was therefore now resolved to accept of a dinner because he wanted one; and in this manner he actually lived among his friends a whole week without being openly affronted. The last place I saw him in was at a reverend divine's. He had, as he fancied, just nicked[7] the time of dinner, for he came in as the cloth was laying. He took a chair without being desired,[8] and talked for some time without being attended to. He assured the company, that nothing procured so good an appetite as a walk in the Park, where he had been that morning. He went on, and praised the figure of the damask table-cloth; talked of a feast where he had been the day before, but that the vension was over done. But all this procured him no invitation: finding therefore the gentleman of the house insensible to all his fetches,[9] he thought proper, at last, to retire, and mend his appetite by a second walk in the Park.

You then, O ye beggars of my acquaintance, whether in rags or lace; whether in Kent-street or the Mall;[10] whether at the Smyrna or St. Giles's,[11] might I be permitted to advise as a friend, never seem to want the favour which you solicit. Apply to every passion but human pity, for redress: you may find permanent relief from vanity, from self-interest, or from avarice, but from compassion never. The very eloquence of a poor man is disgusting; and that mouth which is opened even by wisdom, is seldom expected to close without the horrors of a petition.

To ward off the gripe of poverty, you must pretend to be a stranger

---

7 Hit on the proper time.
8 Invited.
9 Contrivances, tricks.
10 The Mall, which runs through St. James's Park, was a fashionable part of London, unlike Kent Street (which no longer exists).
11 Coffeehouses.

to her, and she will at least use you with ceremony. If you be caught dining upon a halfpenny porrenger of pease soup and potatoes, praise the wholesomeness of your frugal repast. You may observe, that Dr. Cheyne[12] has prescribed pease broth for the gravel,[13] hint that you are not one of those who are always making a deity of your belly. If, again, you are obliged to wear a flimsy stuff[14] in the midst of winter, be the first to remark that stuffs are very much worn at Paris; or, if there be found some irreparable defects in any part of your equipage, which cannot be concealed by all the arts of sitting cross-legged, coaxing, or derning,[15] say, that neither you nor Sampson Gideon[16] were ever very fond of dress. If you be a philosopher, hint that Plato or Seneca are the taylors you choose to employ; assure the company that man ought to be content with a bare covering, since what now is so much his pride, was formerly his shame. In short, however caught, never give out,[17] but ascribe to the frugality of your disposition what others might be apt to attribute to the narrowness of your circumstances. To be poor, and to seem poor, is a certain method never to rise: pride in the great is hateful, in the wise it is ridiculous; but *beggarly pride* is a rational vanity which I have been taught to applaud and excuse.

---

12 Dr. George Cheyne (1671–1743), famous for his treatises on diet.

13 Kidney stones.

14 I.e., a thin, cheap cloth.

15 Darning.

16 Sampson Gideon (1699–1762), Jewish financier who raised £1,700,000 for the government in 1745 and was famously wealthy.

17 Proclaim, admit.

THE CITIZEN OF THE WORLD[1]

The Chinese, according to eighteenth-century tradition, were a race of philosophers. Governed by reason, they lacked superstition, valued literary achievement, were wisely tolerant. When Goldsmith adopted the disguise of a Chinese visitor to London, he imagined that visitor as truly a "citizen of the world," unlimited by narrow prejudice, capable of seeing clearly and of commenting tellingly on what he saw. In the *Citizen of the World*, he uses his disguise to provide fresh perspective on a great variety of phenomena. The essays here reprinted suggest the range of the series: from literary criticism to social commentary, from a tone of gentle bewilderment to one of energetic assertion, from patriotism (England, it turned out, had much to recommend it in the eyes of a stranger) to skepticism about British traditions and values.

The perspective of a philosophic Chinese gentleman was, of course, for Goldsmith highly artificial. Yet the device enables him to see with genuine originality the world that surrounded him. He provides new insights: Considering the fact that no great poets were known to be writing in England, he suggests that the prose then being written might embody essentially poetic values. He sees the connection between the hypocrisies of prostitution and the hypocrisies of the "lady's man" who dances attendance on women; he sees the real nature of English political freedom; he recognizes the impecuniousness and the prolixity of English authors—both familiar subjects of commentary in his time—but adds a new theory about the value to a nation of having many publications. These essays reveal the energy of his mind, the charm he could project, the range and intensity of his feeling.

The source of the present text is *Collected Works of Oliver Goldsmith*, 5 vols., ed. Arthur Friedman (Oxford: Clarendon Press, 1966). Used by permission of the Clarendon Press, Oxford.

---

1 See Introduction, pp. 33–34.

The Citizen of the World
(1762)

LETTER VIII

[The Chinese deceived by a prostitute, in the streets of London.]

*From Lien Chi Altangi, to Fum Hoam, first president of
the Ceremonial Academy at Pekin, in China.*

How insupportable! oh thou possessor of heavenly wisdom, would be this separation, this immeasurable distance from my friends, were I not able thus to delineate my heart upon paper, and to send thee daily a map of my mind. I am every day better reconciled to the people among whom I reside, and begin to fancy that in time I shall find them more opulent, more charitable, and more hospitable than I at first imagined. I begin to learn somewhat of their manners and customs, and to see reasons for several deviations which they make from us, from whom all other nations derive their politeness as well as their original.

In spite of taste, in spite of prejudice, I now begin to think their women tolerable; I can now look on a languishing blue eye without disgust, and pardon a set of teeth, even though whiter than ivory. I now begin to fancy there is no universal standard for beauty. The truth is, the manners of the ladies in this city are so very open, and so vastly engaging, that I am inclined to pass over the more glaring defects of their persons, since compensated by the more solid, yet latent beauties of the mind; what tho' they want black teeth, or are deprived of the allurements of feet no bigger than their thumbs, yet still they have souls, my friend, such souls, so free, so pressing, so hospitable, and so engaging: I have received more invitations in the streets of London from the sex in one night, than I have met with at Pekin in twelve revolutions of the moon.

Every evening as I return home from my usual solitary excursions, I am met by several of those well disposed daughters of hospitality, at different times and in different streets, richly dressed, and with minds not less noble than their appearance. You know that nature has indulged me

with a person by no means agreeable, yet are they too generous to object
to my homely appearance; they feel no repugnance at my broad face and
flat nose; they perceive me to be a stranger, and that alone is a sufficient
recommendation. They even seem to think it their duty to do the honours
of the country by every act of complaisance in their power. One takes
me under the arm, and in a manner forces me along; another catches me
round the neck, and desires to partake in this office of hospitality; while
a third kinder still, invites me to refresh my spirits with wine. Wine is in
England reserved only for the rich, yet here even wine is given away to
the stranger.

A few nights ago, one of those generous creatures, dressed all in
white, and flaunting like a meteor by my side, forcibly attended me
home to my own apartment. She seemed charmed with the elegance of
the furniture, and the convenience of my situation. And well indeed she
might, for I have hired an apartment for not less than two shillings of
their money every week. But her civility did not rest here; for at parting,
being desirous to know the hour, and perceiving my watch out of order,
she kindly took it to be repaired by a relation of her own, which you
may imagine will save some expence, and she assures me that it will cost
her nothing. I shall have it back in a few days when mended, and am
preparing a proper speech expressive of my gratitude on the occasion:
Celestial excellence, I intend to say, happy I am in having found out,
after many painful adventures, a land of innocence, and a people of humanity; I may rove into other climes, and converse with nations yet
unknown, but where shall I meet a soul of such purity as that which
resides in thy breast! sure thou hast been nurtured by the bill of the Shin
Shin, or suck'd the breasts of the provident Gin Hiung.[2] The melody of
thy voice could rob the Chong Fou of her whelps, or inveigle the Boh
that lives in the midst of the waters. Thy servant shall ever retain a sense
of thy favours; and one day boast of thy virtue, sincerity, and truth
among the daughters of China.

Adieu.

---

2 The "Shin Shin" was apparently a kind of ape; the "Gin Hiung" was a bear. See
J. B. Du Halde, *A Description of the Empire of China and Chinese Tartary*, 2 vols. (1738, 1741),
I. 14. Goldsmith of course uses the names without much regard for the sense. The names in
the next sentence are unidentifiable.

LETTER IX

[The licentiousness of the English, with regard to women. A character of a woman's man.]

From Lien Chi Altangi, to Fum Hoam, first president of
the Ceremonial Academy at Pekin, in China.

I have been deceived; she whom I fancied a daughter of Paradise has proved to be one of the infamous disciples of Han; I have lost a trifle, I have gain'd the consolation of having discovered a deceiver. I once more, therefore, relax into my former indifference with regard to the English ladies, they once more begin to appear disagreeable in my eyes; thus is my whole time passed in forming conclusions which the next minute's experience may probably destroy, the present moment becomes a comment on the past, and I improve rather in humility than wisdom.

Their laws and religion forbid the English to keep more than one woman, I therefore concluded that prostitutes were banished from society; I was deceived, every man here keeps as many wives as he can maintain, the laws are cemented with blood, praised and disregarded. The very Chinese, whose religion allows him two wives, takes not half the liberties of the English in this particular. Their laws may be compared to the books of the Sybils, they are held in great veneration, but seldom read, or seldomer understood; even those who pretend to be their guardians dispute about the meaning of many of them, and confess their ignorance of others. The law therefore which commands them to have but one wife, is strictly observed only by those for whom one is more than sufficient, or by such as have not money to buy two. As for the rest they violate it publicly, and some glory in its violation. They seem to think like the Persians, that they give evident marks of manhood by encreasing their seraglio. A mandarine therefore here generally keeps four wives, a gentleman three, and a stage-player two. As for the magistrates, the country justices and squires, they are employed first in debauching young virgins, and then punishing the transgression.

From such a picture you will be apt to conclude, that he who employs four ladies for his amusement, has four times as much constitution to spare as he who is contented with one; that a Mandarine is much cleverer than a gentleman, and a gentleman than a player, and yet it is quite the reverse; a Mandarine is frequently supported on spindle shanks, appears emaciated by luxury, and is obliged to have recourse to variety, merely from the weakness, not the vigour of his constitution, the number of his wives being the most equivocal symptom of his virility.

Beside the country squire there is also another set of men, whose whole employment consists in corrupting beauty; these the silly part of the fair sex call amiable; the more sensible part of them however give them the title of abominable. You will probably demand what are the talents of a man thus caressed by the majority of the opposite sex; what talents, or what beauty is he possessed of superior to the rest of his fellows. To answer you directly, he has neither talents nor beauty, but then he is possessed of impudence and assiduity. With assiduity and impudence men of all ages, and all figures may commence admirers. I have even been told of some who made professions of expiring for love, when all the world could perceive they were going to die of old age: and what is more surprising still, such batter'd beaus are generally most infamously successful.

A fellow of this kind employs three hours every morning in dressing his head, by which is understood only his hair.

He is a professed admirer, not of any particular lady, but of the whole sex.

He is to suppose every lady has caught cold every night, which gives him an opportunity of calling to see how she does the next morning.

He is upon all occasions to shew himself in very great pain for the ladies; if a lady drops even a pin, he is to fly in order to present it.

He never speaks to a lady without advancing his mouth to her ear, by which he frequently addresses more senses than one.

Upon proper occasions he looks excessively tender. This is performed by laying his hand upon his heart, shutting his eyes, and shewing his teeth.

He is excessively fond of dancing a minuet with the ladies, by which is only meant walking round the floor eight or ten times with his hat on, affecting great gravity, and sometimes looking tenderly on his partner.

He never affronts any man himself, and never resents an affront from another.

He has an infinite variety of small talk upon all occasions, and laughs when he has nothing more to say.

Such is the killing creature who prostrates himself to the sex till he has undone them; all whose submissions are the effects of design, and who to please the ladies almost becomes himself a lady.

LETTER XI

[The benefits of luxury, in making a people more wise and happy.]

*From Lien Chi Altangi, to Fum Hoam, first president of
the Ceremonial Academy at Pekin, in China.*

From such a picture of nature in primeval simplicity, tell me, my much respected friend are you in love with fatigue and solitude. Do you sigh for the severe frugality of the wandering Tartar, or regret being born amidst the luxury and dissimulation of the polite? Rather tell me, has not every kind of life vices peculiarly its own? Is it not a truth, that refined countries have more vices, but those not so terrible, barbarous nations few, and they of the most hideous complexion? Perfidy and fraud are the vices of civilized nations, credulity and violence those of the inhabitants of the desert. Does the luxury of the one produce half the evils of the inhumanity of the other? Certainly those philosophers, who declaim against luxury, have but little understood its benefits; they seem insensible, that to luxury we owe not only the greatest part of our knowledge but even of our virtues.

It may sound fine in the mouth of a declaimer when he talks of subduing our appetites, of teaching every sense to be content with a bare sufficiency, and of supplying only the wants of nature; but is there not more satisfaction in indulging those appetites, if with innocence and safety, than in restraining them? Am not I better pleased in enjoyment than in the sullen satisfaction of thinking that I can live without enjoyment? The more various our artificial necessities, the wider is our circle of pleasure; for all pleasure consists in obviating necessities as they rise; luxury, therefore, as it encreases our wants, encreases our capacity for happiness.

Examine the history of any country remarkable for opulence and wisdom, you will find they would never have been wise had they not been first luxurious; you will find poets, philosophers, and even patriots, marching in luxury's train. The reason is obvious; we then only are curious after knowledge when we find it connected with sensual happiness. The senses ever point out the way, and reflection comments upon the discovery. Inform a native of the desert of Kobe, of the exact measure of the parallax of the moon, he finds no satisfaction at all in the information; he wonders how any could take such pains and lay out such treasures in order to solve so useless a difficulty, but connect it with his happiness, by shewing that it improves navigation, that by such an investigation he may have a warmer coat, a better gun, or a finer knife, and he is instantly in raptures at so great an improvement. In short, we only desire to know what we desire to possess; and whatever we may talk against it, luxury adds the spur to curiosity, and gives us a desire of becoming more wise.

But not our knowledge only, but our virtues are improved by luxury. Observe the brown savage of Thibet,[1] to whom the fruits of the spreading pomegranate supply food, and its branches an habitation. Such a character has few vices I grant, but those he has are of the most hideous nature, rapine and cruelty are scarce crimes in his eye, neither pity nor tenderness, which enoble every virtue, have any place in his heart, he hates his enemies, and kills those he subdues. On the other hand, the polite Chinese and civilized European seem even to love their enemies. I have just now seen an instance where the English have succoured those enemies whom their own countrymen actually refused to relieve.[2]

The greater the luxuries of every country, the more closely, politically speaking, is that country united. Luxury is the child of society alone, the luxurious man stands in need of a thousand different artists to furnish out his happiness; it is more likely, therefore, that he should be a good citizen who is connected by motives of self-interest with so many, than the abstemious man who is united to none.

In whatsoever light therefore we consider luxury, whether as employing a number of hands naturally too feeble for more laborious employment, as finding a variety of occupation for others who might be totally idle, or as furnishing out new inlets to happiness, without encroaching on mutual property, in whatever light we regard it, we shall have reason to stand up in its defence, and the sentiment of Confucius still remains unshaken; *that we should enjoy as many of the luxuries of life as are consistent with our own safety, and the prosperity of others, and that he who finds out a new pleasure is one of the most useful members of society.*[3]

---

1 Tibet.
2 A large public subscription was being raised in England for the relief of distressed French prisoners of war.
3 I have been unable to locate this quotation.

LETTER XXIX

[A description of a club of authors.]

From Lien Chi Altangi, to Fum Hoam, first president of
the Ceremonial Academy at Pekin, in China.

Were we to estimate the learning of the English by the number of books that are every day published among them, perhaps no country, not even China itself could equal them in this particular. I have reckoned not less than twenty-three new books published in one day; which, upon computation, makes eight thousand three hundred and ninety-five in one year. Most of these are not confined to one single science, but embrace the whole circle. History, politics, poetry, mathematics, metaphysics, and the philosophy of nature are all comprized in a manual not larger than that in which our children are taught the letters. If then we suppose the learned of England to read but an eighth part of the works which daily come from the press, (and sure none can pretend to learning upon less easy terms) at this rate every scholar will read a thousand books in one year. From such a calculation you may conjecture what an amazing fund of literature a man must be possessed of, who thus reads three new books every day, not one of which but contains all the good things that ever were said or written.

And yet I know not how it happens, but the English are not in reality so learned as would seem from this calculation. We meet but few who know all arts and sciences to perfection; whether it is that the generality are incapable of such extensive knowledge, or that the authors of those books are not adequate instructors. In China the emperor himself takes cognisance of all the doctors in the kingdom who profess authorship. In England, every man may be an author that can write; for they have by law a liberty not only of saying what they please, but of being also as dull as they please.

Yesterday, I testified my surprize to the man in black,[1] where writers could be found in sufficient number to throw off the books I daily saw crowding from the press. I at first imagined, that their learned seminaries might take this method of instructing the world. But to obviate

---

[1] A character in many of these essays. He professes cynicism and hides his true feelings but is actually generous and compassionate.

this objection, my companion assured me, that the doctors of colleges never wrote, and that some of them had actually forgot their reading: but if you desire, continued he, to see a collection of authors, I fancy I can introduce you this evening to a club, which assembles every Saturday at seven, at the sign of the Broom near Islington,[2] to talk over the business of the last, and the entertainment of the week ensuing. I accepted his invitation, we walked together, and entered the house some time before the usual hour for the company assembling.

My friend took this opportunity of letting me into the characters of the principal members of the club, not even the host excepted, who, it seems, was once an author himself, but preferred by a book-seller to this situation as a reward for his former services.

The first person, said he, of our society, is doctor Nonentity, a metaphysician. Most people think him a profound scholar; but as he seldom speaks, I cannot be positive in that particular; he generally spreads himself before the fire, sucks his pipe, talks little, drinks much, and is reckoned very good company. I'm told he writes indexes to perfection, he makes essays on the origin of evil, philosophical enquiries upon any subject, and draws up an answer to any book upon twenty-four hours warning. You may distinguish him from the rest of the company by his long grey wig, and the blue handkerchief round his neck.

The next to him in merit and esteem is Tim Syllabub, a drole[3] creature; he sometimes shines as a star of the first magnitude among the choice spirits of the age; he is reckoned equally excellent at a rebus,[4] a riddle, a bawdy song, and an hymn for the tabernacle. You'll know him by his shabby finery, his powdered wig, dirty shirt, and broken silk stockings.

After him succeeds Mr. Tibs, a very *useful hand*; he writes receipts for the bite of a mad dog, and throws off an eastern tale to perfection; he understands the *business* of an author as well as any man; for no bookseller alive can cheat him; you may distinguish him by the peculiar clumsiness of his figure and the coarseness of his coat: however, though it be coarse, (as he frequently tells the company) he has paid for it.

Lawyer Squint is the politician of the society; he makes speeches for parliament, writes addresses to his fellow subjects, and letters to noble

---

2 Islington, where he sometimes lived, was a favorite spot of Goldsmith's. Some of the supposed authors in this letter may have been based on real people.

3 I.e., droll.

4 I.e., rebuses, puzzles in which every syllable has a punning application.

commanders; he gives the history of every new play, and finds *seasonable thoughts* upon every occasion—My companion was proceeding in his description, when the host came running in with terror on his countenance to tell us, that the door was beset with bailiffs. If that be the case then, says my companion, we had as good be going; for I am positive we shall not see one of the company this night. Wherefore disappointed we were both obliged to return home, he to enjoy the oddities which compose his character alone, and I to write as usual to my friend the occurrences of the day.

Adieu.

LETTER XL

[The English still have poets, tho' not versifiers.]

*From Lien Chi Altangi, to Fum Hoam, first president of
the Ceremonial Academy at Pekin, in China.*

You have always testified the highest esteem for the English poets, and thought them not inferior to the Greeks, Romans, or even the Chinese in the art. But it is now thought even by the English themselves that the race of their poets is extinct, every day produces some pathetic exclamation upon the decadence of taste and genius. Pegasus, say they, has slipped the bridle from his mouth, and our modern bards attempt to direct his flight by catching him by the tail.

Yet, my Friend, it is only among the ignorant that such discourses prevail, men of true discernment can see several poets still among the English, some of whom equal if not surpass their predecessors. The ignorant term that alone poetry which is couch'd in a certain number of syllables in every line, where a vapid thought is drawn out into a number of verses of equal length, and perhaps pointed with rhymes at the end. But glowing sentiment, striking imagery, concise expression, natural description, and modulated periods are full sufficient entirely to fill up my idea of this art, and make way to every passion.

If my idea of poetry therefore be just, the English are not at present so destitute of poetical merit as they seem to imagine. I can see several poets in disguise among them; men furnished with that strength of soul, sublimity of sentiment, and grandeur of expression, which constitutes the character. Many of the writers of their modern odes, sonnets, tragedies or rebusses, it is true, deserve not the name, tho' they have done nothing but clink rhymes and measure syllables for years together; their Johnson's and Smollet's[1] are truly poets; though for aught I know they never made a single verse in their whole lives.

In every incipient language the poet and the prose writer are very distinct in their qualifications; the poet ever proceeds first, treading unbeaten paths, enriching his native funds, and employed in new adventures. The other follows with more cautious steps, and though slow in his motions, treasures up every useful or pleasing discovery. But when once all the extent and the force of the language is known, the poet then seems to rest from his labour, and is at length overtaken by his assiduous pursuer. Both characters are then blended into one, the historian and orator catch all the poet's fire, and leave him no real mark of distinction except the iteration of numbers regularly returning. Thus in the decline of ancient European learning, Seneca, though he wrote in prose, is as much a poet as Lucan, and Longinus, tho' but a critic, more sublime than Apollonius.[2]

From this then it appears that poetry is not discontinued, but altered among the English at present, the outward form seems different from what it was, but poetry still continues internally the same; the only question remains whether the metric feet used by the good writers of the last age, or the prosaic numbers employed by the good writers of this be preferable. And here the practice of the last age appears to me superior; they submitted to the restraint of numbers and similar sounds; and this restraint instead of diminishing augmented the force of their sentiment and stile. Fancy restrained may be compared to a fountain which plays highest by diminishing the aperture. Of the truth of this maxim in every language, every fine writer is perfectly sensible from his own experience, and yet to explain the reason would be perhaps as difficult as to make a frigid genius profit by the discovery.

There is still another reason in favour of the practice of the last age, to be drawn from the variety of modulation. The musical period in prose

---

1 Tobias George Smollett (1721–1771), author of *Roderick Random* (1748). "Johnson" is, of course, Dr. Johnson, to whom Goldsmith refers not as a poet but as an essayist.

2 Lucius Annaeus Seneca (c. 5 B.C.–A.D. 65), author of moral treatises and epistles; Marcus Annaeus Lucan (38–65), nephew of Seneca, author of the epic poem *Pharsalia*; Longinus, reputed author of the celebrated treatise *On the Sublime*; Apollonius Rhodius (c. 235–c. 194 B.C.), author of the epic poem *Argonautica*.

is confined to a very few changes; the numbers in verse are capable of infinite variation. I speak not now from the practice of their modern verse writers, few of whom have any idea of musical variety, but run on in the same monotonous flow through the whole poem, but rather from the example of their former poets, who were tolerable masters of this variety, and also from a capacity in the language of still admitting various unanticipated music.

Several rules have been drawn up for varying the poetic measure, and critics have elaborately talked of accents and syllables, but good sense and a fine ear which rules can never teach, are what alone can in such a case determine. The rapturous flowings of joy, or the interruptions of indignation, require accents placed entirely different, and a structure consonant to the emotions they would express. Changing passions, and numbers changing with those passions make the whole secret of western as well as eastern poetry. In a word the great faults of the modern professed English poets are, that they seem to want numbers which should vary with the passion, and are more employed in describing to the imagination than striking at the heart.

Adieu.

LETTER L

[An attempt to define what is meant by English liberty.]

From Lien Chi Altangi, to Fum Hoam, first president of the Ceremonial Academy at Pekin, in China.

Ask an Englishman what nation in the world enjoys most freedom, and he immediately answers, his own. Ask him in what that freedom principally consists, and he is instantly silent. This happy pre-eminence does not arise from the people's enjoying a larger share in legislation than elsewhere; for in this particular several states in Europe excel them; nor does it arise from a greater exemption from taxes, for few countries pay more; it does not proceed from their being restrained by fewer laws, for no people are burthened with so many; nor does it particularly consist in the security of their property, for property is pretty well secured in every polite state of Europe.

How then are the English more free (for more free they certainly are) than the people of any other country, or under any other form of government whatever? Their freedom consists in their enjoying all the advantages of democracy with this superior prerogative borrowed from monarchy, *that the severity of their laws may be relaxed without endangering the constitution.*

In a monarchical state, in which the constitution is strongest, the laws may be relaxed without danger; for though the people should be unanimous in the breach of any one in particular, yet still there is an *effective* power superior to the people, capable of enforcing obedience, whenever it may be proper to inculcate the law either towards the support or welfare of the community.

But in all those governments, where laws derive their sanction from the *people alone*, transgressions cannot be overlooked without bringing the constitution into danger. They who transgress the law in such a case, are those who prescribe it, by which means it loses not only its influence but its sanction. In every republic the laws must be strong, because the constitution is feeble: they must resemble an Asiatic husband who is justly jealous, because he knows himself impotent. Thus in Holland, Switzerland, and Genoa new laws are not frequently enacted, but the old ones are observed with unremitting severity. In such republics therefore the people are slaves to laws of their own making, little less than in unmixed monarchies where they are slaves to the will of one subject to frailties like themselves.

In England, from a variety of happy accidents, their constitution is just strong enough, or if you will, monarchical enough, to permit a relaxation of the severity of laws, and yet those laws still to remain sufficiently strong to govern the people. This is the most perfect state of civil liberty, of which we can form any idea; here we see a greater number of laws than in any other country, while the people at the same time obey only such as are *immediately* conducive to the interests of society; several are unnoticed, many unknown; some kept to be revived and enforced upon proper occasions, others left to grow obsolete, even without the necessity of abrogation.

Scarce an Englishman who does not almost every day of his life, offend with impunity against some express law, and for which, in a certain conjuncture of circumstances he would not receive punishment. Gaming houses, preaching at prohibited places, assembled crowds, nocturnal amusements, public shews, and an hundred other instances are forbid and frequented. These prohibitions are useful; though it be prudent in their magistrates, and happy for their people, that they are not enforced, and none but the venal or mercenary attempt to enforce them.

The law in this case, like an indulgent parent, still keeps the rod, though the child is seldom corrected. Were those pardoned offences to rise into enormity, were they likely to obstruct the happiness of society, or endanger the state, it is then that justice would resume her terrors, and punish those faults she had so often overlooked with indulgence. It is to this ductility of the laws that an Englishman owes the freedom he enjoys superior to others in a more popular government; every step therefore the constitution takes towards a Democratic form, every diminution of the regal authority is, in fact a diminution of the subjects freedom; but every attempt to render the government more popular, not only impairs natural liberty, but even will at last, dissolve the political constitution.

Every popular government seems calculated to last only for a time, it grows rigid with age, new laws are multiplying, and the old continue in force, the subjects are oppressed, burthen'd with a multiplicity of legal injunctions, there are none from whom to expect redress, and nothing but a strong convulsion in the state can vindicate them into former liberty; thus the people of Rome, a few great ones excepted, found more real freedom under their Emperors tho' tyrants, than they had experienced in the old age of the common wealth, in which their laws were become numerous and painful, in which new laws were every day enacting and the old ones executed with rigour. They even refused to be reinstated in their former prerogatives, upon an offer made them to this purpose; for they actually found Emperors the only means of softening the rigours of their constitution.

The constitution of England, is at present possessed of the strength of its native oak, and the flexibility of the bending tamarisk, but should the people at any time with a mistaken zeal, pant after an imaginary freedom, and fancy that abridging monarchy was encreasing their privileges, they would be very much mistaken, since every jewel plucked from the crown of majesty would only be made use of as a bribe to corruption; it might enrich the few who shared it among them, but would in fact impoverish the public.

As the Roman senators by slow and imperceptible degrees became masters of the people, yet still flattered them with a shew of freedom, while themselves only were free; so is it possible for a body of men while they stand up for privileges, to grow into an exuberance of power themselves, and the public become actually dependent, while some of its individuals only govern.

If then, my friend, there should in this country, ever be on the throne a King who, thro' good nature or age, should give up the smallest part of his prerogative to the people, if there should come a minister of merit and popularity—But I have room for no more.

LETTER LXXV

[The necessity of amusing each other with new books, insisted upon.]

From Lien Chi Altangi, to Fum Hoam, first president of
the Ceremonial Academy at Pekin, in China.

There are numbers in this city who live by writing new books, and yet there are thousands of volumes in every large library unread and forgotten. This, upon my arrival, was one of these contradictions which I was unable to account for. Is it possible, said I, that there should be any demand for new books, before those already published are read? Can there be so many employed in producing a commodity with which the market is already overstocked; and with goods also better than any of modern manufacture.

What at first view appeared an inconsistence, is a proof at once of this people's wisdom and refinement. Even allowing the works of their ancestors better written than theirs, yet those of the moderns acquire a real value, by being marked with the impression of the times. Antiquity has been in the possession of others, the present is our own; let us first therefore learn to know what belongs to ourselves, and then if we have leisure, cast our reflections back to the reign of *Shouou*, who governed twenty thousand years before the creation of the moon.

The volumes of antiquity like medals, may very well serve to amuse the curious, but the works of the moderns, like the current coin of a kingdom, are much better for immediate use; the former are often prized above their intrinsic value, and kept with care, the latter seldom pass for more than they are worth, and are often subject to the merciless hands of sweating critics, and clipping compilers;[1] the works of antiquity were ever praised, those of the moderns read, the treasures of our ancestors have

---

1 "Sweating" is lightening gold coins by wearing them away through friction; "clipping" mutilates coins by paring their edges.

our esteem, and we boast the passion, those of cotemporary genius engage our heart altho' we blush to own it. The visits we pay the former resemble those we pay the great; the ceremony is troublesome, and yet such as we would not chuse to forego; our acquaintance with modern books, is like sitting with a friend; our pride is not flattered in the interview, but it gives more internal satisfaction.

In proportion as society refines, new books must ever become more necessary. Savage rusticity is reclaimed by oral admonition alone; but the elegant excesses of refinement are best corrected by the still voice of studious enquiry. In a polite age, almost every person becomes a reader, and receives more instruction from the press than the pulpit. The preaching Bonse[2] may instruct the illiterate peasant; but nothing less than the insinuating address of a fine writer can win its way to an heart already relaxed in all the effeminacy of refinement. Books are necessary to correct the vices of the polite, but those vices are ever changing, and the antidote should be changed accordingly; should still be new.

Instead therefore of thinking the number of new publications here too great, I could wish it still greater, as they are the most useful instruments of reformation. Every country must be instructed either by *writers* or *preachers*; but as the number of readers encreases, the number of hearers is proportionably diminished, the writer becomes more useful, and the preaching Bonse less necessary.

Instead, therefore, of complaining that writers are overpaid, when their works procure them a bare subsistence, I should imagine it the duty of a state not only to encourage their numbers, but their industry. A Bonse is rewarded with immense riches for instructing only a few, even of the most ignorant, of the people; and sure the poor scholar should not beg his bread, who is capable of instructing a million!

Of all rewards, I grant, the most pleasing to a man of real merit, is fame; but a polite age, of all times, is that in which scarce any share of merit can acquire it. What numbers of fine writers in the latter empire of Rome, when refinement was carried to the highest pitch, have missed that fame and immortality which they had fondly arrogated to themselves? How many Greek authors, who wrote at that period when Constantinople was the refined mistress of the empire, now rest either not printed, or not read, the libraries of Europe! Those who came first, while either state as yet was barbarous, carried all the reputation away. Authors,

---

2 Usually, "bonze," a term applied by Europeans to the Buddhist clergy of the Orient.

as the age refined, became more numerous, and their numbers destroyed their fame. It is but natural, therefore, for the writer, when conscious that his works will not procure him fame hereafter, to endeavour to make them turn out to his temporal interest here.

Whatever be the motives which induce men to write, whether avarice or fame, the country becomes most wise and happy, in which they most serve for instructors. The countries where sacerdotal instruction alone is permitted, remain in ignorance, superstition, and hopeless slavery. In England where there are as many new books published as in all the rest of Europe together, a spirit of freedom and reason reigns among the people; they have been often known to act like fools, they are generally found to think like men.

The only danger that attends a multiplicity of publications, is that some of them may be calculated to injure, rather than benefit society. But where writers are numerous, they also serve as a check upon each other, and perhaps a literary inquisition is the most terrible punishment that can be conceived, to a literary transgressor.

But to do the English justice, there are but few offenders of this kind, their publications in general aim at mending either the heart, or improving the common weal. The dullest writer talks of virtue, and liberty, and benevolence with esteem; tells his true story, filled with good and wholesome advice; warns against slavery, bribery, or the bite of a mad dog, and dresses up his little useful magazine[3] of knowledge and entertainment, at least with a good intention. The dunces of France, on the other hand, who have less encouragement, are more vicious. Tender hearts, languishing eyes, Leonora in love at thirteen, esctatic transports, stolen blisses, are the frivolous subjects of their frivolous memoirs. In England, if a bawdy blockhead thus breaks in on the community, he sets his whole fraternity in a roar; nor can he escape, even though he should fly to nobility for shelter.

Thus even dunces, my friend, may make themselves useful. But there are others whom nature has blest with talents above the rest of mankind; men capable of thinking with precision, and impressing their thought with rapidity. Beings who diffuse those regards upon mankind, which others contract and settle upon themselves. These deserve every honour from that community of which they are more peculiarly the

---

3 Store, supply.

children, to such I would give my heart, since to them I am indebted for its humanity!

Adieu.

LETTER XC

[The English subject to the spleen.]

From Lien Chi Altangai, to Fum Hoam, first president of the Ceremonial Academy at Pekin, in China.

When the men of this country are once turned of thirty, they regularly retire every year at proper intervals to lie in of the *spleen*.[1] The vulgar unfurnished with the luxurious comforts of the soft cushion, down bed, and easy-chair, are obliged, when the fit is on them, to nurse it up by drinking, idleness, and ill-humour. In such dispositions, unhappy is the foreigner who happens to cross them; his long chin, tarnished coat, or pinched hat, are sure to receive no quarter. If they meet no foreigner however to fight with, they are in such cases generally content with beating each other.

The rich, as they have more sensibility, are operated upon with greater violence by this disorder. Different from the poor, instead of becoming more insolent, they grow totally unfit for opposition. A General here, who would have faced a culverin[2] when well, if the fit be on him, shall hardly find courage to snuff a candle. An Admiral, who could have opposed a broadside without shrinking, shall sit whole days in his chamber mobbed[3] up in double night-caps, shuddering at the intrusive breeze, and distinguishable from his wife only by his black beard and heavy eyebrows.

In the country this disorder mostly attacks the fair sex, in town it is most unfavourable to the men. A Lady, who has pined whole years amidst cooing doves, and complaining nightingales in rural retirement, shall resume all her vivacity in one night at a city gaming-table; her husband who roar'd, hunted, and got drunk at home, shall grow splenetic in town in proportion to his wife's good humour. Upon their arrival in

---

1 Gloominess and irritability, melancholia.
2 A kind of large cannon.
3 Muffled.

London, they exchange their disorders. In consequence of her parties and excursions, he puts on the furred cap and scarlet stomacher, and perfectly resembles an Indian husband, who when his wife is safely delivered, permits her to transact business abroad, while he undergoes all the formality of keeping his bed, and receiving all the condolence in her place.

But those who reside constantly in town, owe this disorder mostly to the influence of the weather. It is impossible to describe what a variety of transmutations an east wind shall produce; it has been known to change a Lady of fashion into a parlour couch; an Alderman into a plate of custards, and a dispenser of justice into a rat trap.[4] Even Philosophers themselves are not exempt from its influence; it has often converted a Poet into a coral and bells, and a patriot Senator into a dumb waiter.

Some days ago I went to visit the man in black, and entered his house with that chearfulness, which the certainty of a favourable reception always inspires. Upon opening the door of his apartment, I found him with the most rueful face imaginable in a morning gown and flannel night-cap, earnestly employed in learning to blow the German flute. Struck with the absurdity of a man in the decline of life, thus blowing away all his constitution and spirits, even without the consolation of being musical; I ventured to ask what could induce him to attempt learning so difficult an instrument so late in life. To this he made no reply, but groaning, and still holding the flute to his lip, continued to gaze at me for some monemts very angrily, and then proceeded to practise his gammut[5] as before. After having produced a variety of the most hideous tones in nature; at last turning to me, he demanded, whether I did not think he had made a surprizing progress in two days? You see, continues he, I have got the Ambusheer[6] already, and as for fingering, my master tells me, I shall have that in a few lessons more. I was so much astonished with this instance of inverted ambition, that I knew not what to reply, but soon discerned the cause of all his absurdities; my friend was under a metamorphosis by the power of spleen, and flute blowing was unluckily become his adventitious passion.

In order therefore to banish his anxiety imperceptibly, by seeming

----

4 Such imaginary transformations were considered characteristic symptoms of spleen. Cf. Pope's account of the Cave of Spleen in *The Rape of the Lock*, IV. 46–54.

5 I.e., gamut, or full range of notes.

6 I.e., *embouchure*, the action of the lips on the mouthpiece in playing a wind instrument.

to indulge it, I began to descant on those gloomy topics by which Philosophers often get rid of their own spleen, by communicating it; the wretchedness of man in this life, the happiness of some wrought out of the miseries of others, the necessity that wretches should expire under punishment, that rogues might enjoy affluence in tranquility; I led him on from the inhumanity of the rich to the ingratitude of the beggar; from the insincerity of refinement to the fierceness of rusticity; and at last had the good fortune to restore him to his usual serenity of temper, by permitting him to expatiate upon all the modes of human misery.

"Some nights ago," says my friend, "sitting alone by my fire; I happened to look into an account of the detection of a set of men called the thieftakers.[7] I read over the many hideous cruelties of those haters of mankind, of their pretended friendship to wretches they meant to betray, of their sending men out to rob and then hanging them. I could not avoid sometimes interrupting the narrative by crying out, *Yet these are men!* As I went on I was informed that they had lived by this practice several years, and had been enriched by the price of blood; *and yet*, cried I, *I have been sent into this world, and am desired to call these men my brothers*; I read that the very man who led the condemned wretch to the gallows, was he who falsely swore his life away; *and yet*, continued I, *that perjurer had just such a nose, such lips, such hands and such eyes as Newton.* I at last came to the account of the wretch that was searched after robbing one of the thieftakers of half a crown. Those of the confederacy knew that he had got but that single half crown in the world; after a long search therefore, which they knew would be fruitless, and taking from him the half crown, which they knew was all he had, one of the gang compassionately cried out, *alas poor creature let him keep all the rest he has got, it will do him service in Newgate, where we are sending him.* This was an instance of such complicated guilt and hypocrisy, that I threw down the book in an agony of rage, and began to think with malice of all the human kind. I sate silent for some minutes, and soon perceiving the ticking of my watch beginning to grow noisy and troublesome, I quickly placed it out of hearing; and strove to resume my serenity. But the watchman soon gave me a second alarm. I had scarcely recovered from this, when my peace was assaulted by the wind at my window; and when that ceased to blow, I listened for

---

7 The profession of thief-takers was to detect and cause the arrest of thieves. They lived by treachery and sometimes encouraged the crimes by which they finally profited, making thieves in order to take them.

death-watches[8] in the wainscot. I now found my whole system discomposed, I strove to find a resource in philosophy and reason; but what could I oppose, or where direct my blow, when I could see no enemy to combat. I saw no misery approaching, nor knew any I had to fear, yet still I was miserable. Morning came, I sought for tranquility in dissipation, sauntered from one place of public resort to another, but found myself disagreeable to my acquaintance, and ridiculous to others. I tried at different times dancing, fencing, and riding, I solved geometrical problems, shaped tobacco-stoppers,[9] wrote verses and cut paper. At last I placed my affections on music, and find, that earnest employment if it cannot cure, at least will palliate every anxiety."

Adieu.

LETTER XCI

[The influence of climate and soil upon the tempers and dispositions of the English.]

*From Lien Chi Altangi, to Fum Hoam, first president of
the Ceremonial Academy at Pekin, in China.*

It is no unpleasing contemplation to consider the influence which soil and climate have upon the disposition of the inhabitants, the animals and vegetables of different countries. That among the brute creation is much more visible than in man, and that in vegetables more than either. In some places those plants which are entirely poisonous at home lose this deleterious quality by being carried abroad; there are serpents in Macedonia so harmless as to be used as play-things for children, and we are told that in some parts of Fez there are lions so very timorous as to be scared away, though coming in herds, by the cries of women.

I know of no country where the influence of climate and soil is more visible than in England, the same hidden cause which gives courage to their dogs and cocks, gives also fierceness to their men. But chiefly this ferocity appears among the vulgar. The polite of every country

---

8 Insects which make a noise like the ticking of a watch, supposed by the superstitious to portend death.

9 Contrivances for pressing down the tobacco in the bowl of a pipe.

pretty nearly resemble each other. But as in simpleing,[1] it is among the uncultivated productions of nature, we are to examine the characteristic differences of climate and soil, so in an estimate of the genius of the people, we must look among the sons of unpolished rusticity. The vulgar English therefore may be easily distinguished from all the rest of the world, by superior pride, impatience, and a peculiar hardiness of soul.

Perhaps no qualities in the world are more susceptible of a fine polish than these, artificial complaisance, and easy deference being superinduced over these, generally forms a great character, something at once elegant and majestic, affable yet sincere. Such in general are the better sort; but they who are left in primitive rudeness are the least disposed for society with others, or comfort internally, of any people under the sun.

The poor indeed of every country are but little prone to treat each other with tenderness, their own miseries are too apt to engross all their pity, and perhaps too they give but little commiseration as they find but little from others. But in England the poor treat each other upon every occasion, with more than savage animosity, and as if they were in a state of open war by nature. In China, if two porters should meet in a narrow street, they would lay down their burthens, make a thousand excuses to each other for the accidental interruption, and beg pardon on their knees; if two men of the same occupation should meet here they would first begin to scold and at last to beat each other. One would think they had miseries enough resulting from penury and labour not to en-crease them by ill-nature among themselves, and subjection to new penalties, but such considerations never weigh with them.

But to recompence this strange absurdity they are in the main generous, brave, and enterprising. They feel the slightest injuries with a degree of ungoverned impatience, but resist the greatest calamities with surprizing fortitude. Those miseries under which any other people in the world would sink, they have often shewed they were capable of enduring; if accidentally cast upon some desolate coast their perseverance is beyond what any other nation is capable of sustaining; if imprisoned for crimes their efforts to escape are greater than among others. The peculiar strength of their prisons, when compared to those elsewhere, argues their hardi-ness; even the strongest prisons I have ever seen in other countries, would be very insufficient to confine the untameable spirit of an Englishman. In

---

[1] Searching for plants and herbs of medicinal use.

short what man dares do in circumstances of danger, an Englishman will. His virtues seem to sleep in the calm, and are called out only to combat the kindred storm.

But the greatest eulogy of this people is the generosity of their miscreants, the tenderness in general of their robbers and highwaymen. Perhaps no people can produce instances of the same kind, where the desperate mix pity with injustice; still shew that they understand a distinction in crimes, and even, in acts of violence, have still some tincture of remaining virtue. In every other country robbery and murder go almost always together, here it seldom happens except upon ill-judged resistance or pursuit. The banditti of other countries are unmerciful to a supreme degree, the highwayman and robber here are generous at least to the public, and pretend even to virtues in their intercourse among each other. Taking therefore my opinion of the English from the virtues and vices practised among the vulgar, they at once present to a stranger all their faults, and keep their virtues up only for the enquiring eye of a philosopher.

Foreigners are generally shocked at their insolence upon first coming among them; they find themselves ridiculed and insulted in every street: they meet with none of those trifling civilities, so frequent elsewhere, which are instances of mutual good will without previous acquaintance; they travel through the country either too ignorant or too obstinate to cultivate a closer acquaintance, meet in every moment something to excite their disgust, and return home to characterise this as the region of spleen, insolence and ill-nature. In short, England would be the last place in the world I would travel to by way of amusement; but the first for instruction. I would chuse to have others for my acquaintance, but Englishmen for my friends.

AN ESSAY ON THE THEATRE;
OR, A COMPARISON BETWEEN
LAUGHING AND SENTIMENTAL COMEDY[1]

In 1768 Goldsmith had produced, at the Covent Garden theater, his first play, *The Good Natur'd Man*, in which he attempted to counteract the sentimental tendencies of the theater of his time by combining sentiment with genuine comedy, mocking the assumption that perfect benevolence must be perfectly admirable. The play was not conspicuously successful, partly because of its real flaws of structure, partly because David Garrick produced at his Drury Lane theater another comedy at the same time (Hugh Kelly's *False Delicacy*) in direct competition with Goldsmith's play. By 1773 he had written another play, *She Stoops to Conquer*. Two and a half months before its first presentation, he published in the first issue of the *Westminster Magazine* (January 1, 1773) an essay on the contemporary theater which suggested the aesthetic principles of his own play.

Goldsmith here states clearly his high valuation of the *vis comica*, the true comic force or energy, and condemns the vapidity of plays that can achieve only an easy sentimental response from their audiences. His sanctions are partly classic: The traditional differentiation of comic and tragic, he points out, was being neglected. But the energy of his writing proclaims his immediate personal conviction that the proper function of comedy is to entertain, his belief that laughter can be a more complex and more significant response than tears.

The source of the present text is *Collected Works of Oliver Goldsmith*, 5 vols., ed. Arthur Friedman (Oxford: Clarendon Press, 1966). Used by permission of the Clarendon Press, Oxford.

An Essay on the Theatre;
or, a Comparison between
Laughing and Sentimental Comedy

(1773)

The Theatre, like all other amusements, has its Fashions and its Prejudices; and when satiated with its excellence, Mankind begin to

---

1 See Introduction, p. 46.

mistake Change for Improvement. For some years, Tragedy was the reigning entertainment; but of late it has entirely given way to Comedy, and our best efforts are now exerted in these lighter kinds of composition. The pompous Train, the swelling Phrase, and the unnatural Rant, are displaced for that natural portrait of Human Folly and Frailty, of which all are judges, because all have sat for the picture.

But as in describing Nature it is presented with a double face, either of mirth or sadness, our modern Writers find themselves at a loss which chiefly to copy from; and it is now debated, Whether the Exhibition of Human Distress is likely to afford the mind more Entertainment than that of Human Absurdity?

Comedy is defined by Aristotle to be a picture of the Frailties of the lower part of Mankind, to distinguish it from Tragedy, which is an exhibition of the Misfortunes of the Great.[2] When Comedy therefore ascends to produce the Characters of Princes or Generals upon the Stage, it is out of its walk, since Low Life and Middle Life are entirely its object. The principal question therefore is, Whether in describing Low or Middle Life, an exhibition of its Follies be not preferable to a detail of its Calamities? Or, in other words, Which deserves the preference? The Weeping Sentimental Comedy, so much in fashion at present, or the Laughing and even Low Comedy, which seems to have been last exhibited by Vanburgh and Cibber?[3]

If we apply to authorities, all the Great Masters in the Dramatic Art have but one opinion. Their rule is, that as Tragedy displays the Calamities of the Great; so Comedy should excite our laughter by ridiculously exhibiting the Follies of the Lower Part of Mankind. Boileau, one of the best modern Critics, asserts, that Comedy will not admit of Tragic Distress.

> *Le Comique, ennemi des soupirs et des pleurs,*
> *N'admet point dans ses vers de tragiques doleurs.*[4]

Nor is this rule without the strongest foundation in Nature, as the distresses of the Mean by no means affect us so strongly as the Calamities of the Great. When Tragedy exhibits to us some Great Man fallen from

---

2 *Poetics*, 1449a.

3 Sir John Vanbrugh (1664–1726); Colley Cibber (1671–1757).

4 "The comic, enemy of sighs and of tears, never admits tragic sorrows into its verse" (*L'Art Poetique*, III. 401–2).

his height, and struggling with want and adversity, we feel his situation in the same manner as we suppose he himself must feel, and our pity is increased in proportion to the height from whence he fell. On the contrary, we do not so strongly sympathize with one born in humbler circumstances, and encountering accidental distress: so that while we melt for Belisarius,[5] we scarce give halfpence to the Beggar who accosts us in the street. The one has our pity; the other our contempt. Distress, therefore, is the proper object of Tragedy, since the Great excite our pity by their fall; but not equally so of Comedy, since the Actors employed in it are originally so mean, that they sink but little by their fall.

Since the first origin of the Stage, Tragedy and Comedy have run in different channels, and never till of late encroached upon the provinces of each other. Terence, who seems to have made the nearest approaches, yet always judiciously stops short before he comes to the downright pathetic; and yet he is even reproached by Cæsar for wanting the *vis comica*.[6] All the other Comic Writers of antiquity aim only at rendering Folly or Vice ridiculous, but never exalt their characters into buskined pomp, or make what Voltaire humourously calls a *Tradesman's Tragedy*.[7]

Yet, notwithstanding this weight of authority, and the universal practice of former ages, a new species of Dramatic Composition has been introduced under the name of *Sentimental* Comedy, in which the virtues of Private Life are exhibited, rather than the Vices exposed; and the Distresses, rather than the Faults of Mankind, make our interest in the piece.[8] These Comedies have had of late great success, perhaps from their novelty, and also from their flattering every man in his favourite foible. In these Plays almost all the Characters are good, and exceedingly generous; they are lavish enough of their *Tin* Money on the Stage, and though they want Humour, have abundance of Sentiment and Feeling. If they happen to have Faults or Foibles, the Spectator is taught not only to pardon, but to applaud them, in consideration of the goodness of their hearts; so that Folly, instead of being ridiculed, is commended, and the

---

5 A great military commander during the reign of Justinian who was accused of conspiring against the emperor. According to tradition his eyes were put out and he became a beggar in the streets of Constantinople.

6 "Comic force."

7 In the article "Art dramatique" (1770) in his *Dictionnaire philosophique*.

8 Goldsmith is referring to the works of such playwrights as Hugh Kelly (1739–1777) and Richard Cumberland (1732–1811), who employed characters of perfect virtue as heroes and heroines and recounted intrigues made more complex by the delicacy and scruples of their participants.

Comedy aims at touching our Passions without the power of being truly
pathetic: in this manner we are likely to lose one great source of Entertainment on the Stage; for while the Comic Poet is invading the province of
the Tragic Muse, he leaves her lovely Sister quite neglected. Of this,
however, he is noway solicitous, as he measures his fame by his profits.

But it will be said, that the Theatre is formed to amuse Mankind,
and that it matters little, if this end be answered, by what means it is
obtained. If Mankind find delight in weeping at Comedy, it would be
cruel to abridge them in that or any other innocent pleasure. If those
Pieces are denied the name of Comedies; yet call them by any other name,
and if they are delightful, they are good. Their success, it will be said, is
a mark of their merit, and it is only abridging our happiness to deny us
an inlet to Amusement.

These objections, however, are rather specious than solid. It is
true, that Amusement is a great object of the Theatre; and it will be allowed, that these Sentimental Pieces do often amuse us: but the question
is, Whether the True Comedy would not amuse us more? The question
is, Whether a Character supported throughout a Piece with its Ridicule
still attending, would not give us more delight than this species of Bastard
Tragedy, which only is applauded because it is new?

A friend of mine who was sitting unmoved at one of these Sentimental Pieces, was asked, how he could be so indifferent. "Why, truly,"
says he, "as the Hero is but a Tradesman, it is indifferent to me whether
he be turned out of his Counting-house on Fish-street Hill, since he will
still have enough left to open shop in St. Giles's."

The other objection is as ill-grounded; for though we should give
these Pieces another name, it will not mend their efficacy. It will continue
a kind of *mulish* production, with all the defects of its opposite parents,
and marked with sterility. If we are permitted to make Comedy weep,
we have an equal right to make Tragedy laugh, and to set down in Blank
Verse the Jests and Repartees of all the Attendants in a Funeral Procession.

But there is one Argument in favour of Sentimental Comedy
which will keep it on the Stage in spite of all that can be said against it.
It is, of all others, the most easily written. Those abilities that can hammer
out a Novel, are fully sufficient for the production of a Sentimental
Comedy. It is only sufficient to raise the Characters a little, to deck out
the Hero with a Ribband, or give the Heroine a Title; then to put an
Insipid Dialogue, without Character or Humour, into their mouths,
give them mighty good hearts, very fine cloaths, furnish a new sett of

Scenes, make a Pathetic Scene or two, with a sprinkling of tender melancholy Conversation through the whole, and there is no doubt but all the Ladies will cry, and all the Gentlemen applaud.

Humour at present seems to be departing from the Stage, and it will soon happen, that our Comic Players will have nothing left for it but a fine Coat and a Song. It depends upon the Audience whether they will actually drive those poor Merry Creatures from the Stage, or sit at a Play as gloomy as at the Tabernacle. It is not easy to recover an art when once lost; and it would be but a just punishment that when, by our being too fastidious, we have banished Humour from the Stage, we should ourselves be deprived of the art of Laughing.

EDMUND BURKE

(1729–1797)

Edmund Burke was in his own time more distinguished as a statesman and orator than as a writer. From his young manhood he involved himself in public affairs. The son of a Dublin attorney, he began the study of law after graduating from Trinity College, Dublin, but neglected his studies and was punished by having his allowance cut off. He participated in stockjobbing operations which ended disastrously in 1769, and was for the rest of his life in financial difficulties. His career in the House of Commons was brilliant; he advocated peace with America, attacked the principles of the French Revolution, was involved in the investigation of the East India Company, and pleaded for the impeachment of Warren Hastings. Pensioned in 1794, after he retired from Parliament, he continued to write, publishing *Letters on a Regicide Peace* the year before his death.

The rhetoric of Burke's written prose reflects the technique of the orator. His political writing is elaborate, carefully structured, passionate yet studied in its manipulation of emotional effect. It is the most powerful presentation ever given to principles that even in our day are fundamental to the maintenance of a philosophical conservatism.

Biography and Criticism

Chapman, Gerald W., *Edmund Burke: The Practical Imagination*, 1967.
Cone, Carl B., *Burke and the Nature of Politics*, 2 vols., 1957–1964.

Copeland, Thomas W., *Our Eminent Friend Burke: Six Essays*, 1949.

Kirk, Russell, *Edmund Burke: A Genius Reconsidered*, 1967.

Magnus, Philip, *Edmund Burke*, 1939.

Osborn, Annie Marion, *Rousseau and Burke: A Study of the Idea of Liberty in Eighteenth-Century Political Thought*, 1940.

Parken, Charles, *The Moral Basis of Burke's Political Thought*, 1956.

Stanlis, Peter J., *Edmund Burke and the Natural Law*, 1958.

SPEECH ON MOVING HIS RESOLUTION
FOR CONCILIATION WITH THE COLONIES[1]

By early 1775, the question of how Great Britain should deal with her American colonies had become pressing. The central issue was whether England had the right to impose taxes on her colonies. Burke was skeptical about this right, although he recognized that special cases might create special necessities. Only one externally imposed tax remained: the duty of threepence per pound on tea imported into America. When the Boston Tea Party dramatized the colonists' opposition to even this tax, the British government began a series of legislative reprisals which brought war ever closer. Burke's Conciliation Speech was a response to one of these penal bills: an act to restrain American commerce and fishery rights. As a practical politician and as a student of history, Burke disapproved of penal measures. His speech, delivered on March 22, 1775, is an eloquent statement of the substance and grounds of his disapproval.

The ideal for which Burke here pleads is the restoration of the "order and repose" of the British Empire. He wishes for peace, for a return of the colonies' confidence in the mother country. Repeatedly he attacks government by abstract principle and calls for measures to fit the immediate situation. He demonstrates, with lavish citation of facts and statistics, that America is worth fighting for; then that the use of force is not the proper means for the desired end. Finally he argues for concilation, with historical examples to support his case, asking Parliament to allow the colonies more control over their financial contributions and insisting once more that the choice before them is between abiding by "a profitable experience, or a mischievous theory."

The present text is that of *The Speech of Edmund Burke, Esq.; on Moving His Resolutions for Conciliation with the Colonies, March 22, 1775* (London, 1775).

Speech on Moving...
for Conciliation with the Colonies

(1775)

I hope, Sir, that, notwithstanding the austerity of the Chair,[2] your good-nature will incline you to some degree of indulgence towards

---

1 See Introduction, pp. 9–12.

2 A formal expression referring to the office of speaker of the house, not to the personality of Sir Fletcher Norton (1716-1789), who then occupied it.

human frailty. You will not think it unnatural, that those who have an object depending,[3] which strongly engages their hopes and fears, should be somewhat inclined to superstition. As I came into the house full of anxiety about the event of my motion, I found to my infinite surprize, that the grand penal Bill, by which we had passed sentence on the trade and sustenance of America, is to be returned to us from the other House[4]. I do confess, I could not help looking on this event as a fortunate omen. I look upon it as a sort of providential favour; by which we are put once more in possession of our deliberative capacity, upon a business so very questionable in its nature, so very uncertain in its issue. By the return of this Bill, which seemed to have taken its flight for ever, we are at this very instant nearly as free to chuse a plan for our American Government, as we were on the first day of the Session. If, Sir, we incline to the side of conciliation, we are not at all embarrassed (unless we please to make ourselves so) by any incongruous mixture of coercion and restraint. We are therefore called upon, as it were by a superior warning voice, again to attend to America; to attend to the whole of it together; and to review the subject with an unusual degree of care and calmness.

Surely it is an awful[5] subject; or there is none so on this side of the grave. When I first had the honour of a seat in this House, the affairs of that Continent pressed themselves upon us, as the most important and most delicate object of parliamentary attention. My little share in this great deliberation oppressed me. I found myself a partaker in a very high trust; and having no sort of reason to rely on the strength of my natural abilities for the proper execution of that trust, I was obliged to take more than common pains, to instruct myself in every thing which relates to our Colonies. I was not less under the necessity of forming some fixed ideas, concerning the general policy of the British Empire. Something of this sort seemed to be indispensable; in order, amidst so vast a fluctuation of passions and opinions, to concenter my thoughts; to ballast my conduct; to preserve me from being blown about by every wind of fashionable doctrine. I really did not think it safe, or manly, to have fresh principles to seek upon every fresh mail which should arrive from America.

---

3 Undetermined, pending.

4 On February 10, 1775, Lord North had proposed a measure to punish the colonies for their opposition to England's attempts to regulate their commerce. The bill would have restricted New England's trade and fishing privileges. It had been returned from the House of Lords with a request that its provisions be enlarged to include other colonies.

5 I.e., awe-inspiring.

At that period, I had the fortune to find myself in perfect concurrence with a large majority in this House. Bowing under that high authority, and penetrated with the sharpness and strength of that early impression, I have continued ever since, without the least deviation, in my original sentiments. Whether this be owing to an obstinate perseverance in error, or to a religious adherence to what appears to me truth and reason, it is in your equity to judge.

Sir, Parliament having an enlarged view of objects, made, during this interval, more frequent changes in their sentiments and their conduct, than could be justified in a particular person upon the contracted scale of private information. But though I do not hazard any thing approaching to a censure on the motives of former parliaments to all those alterations, one fact is undoubted; that under them the state of America has been kept in continual agitation.[6] Every thing administered as remedy to the public complaint, if it did not produce, was at least followed by, an heightening of the distemper; until, by a variety of experiments, that important Country has been brought into her present situation; —a situation, which I will not miscall, which I dare not name; which I scarcely know how to comprehend in the terms of any description.

In this posture, Sir, things stood at the beginning of the session. About that time, a worthy member[7] of great parliamentary experience, who, in the year 1766, filled the chair of the American committee with much ability, took me aside; and, lamenting the present aspect of our politicks, told me, things were come to such a pass, that our former methods of proceeding in the house would be no longer tolerated. That the publick tribunal (never too indulgent to a long and unsuccessful opposition) would now scrutinize our conduct with unusual severity. That the very vicissitudes and shiftings of ministerial measures, instead of convicting their authors of inconstancy and want of system, would be taken as an occasion of charging us with a pre-determined discontent, which nothing could satisfy; whilst we accused every measure of vigour as cruel, and every proposal of lenity as weak and irresolute. The public, he said, would not have patience to see us play the game out with our adversaries: we must produce our hand. It would be expected, that those

---

6 There had been colonial resentment of most of Britain's regulatory measures. Although Burke and his colleague did not yet know this, the battles of Lexington and Concord had actually been fought three weeks before Burke's speech.

7 Mr. Rose Fuller, who on April 19, 1774, had moved the repeal of the tea tax.

who for many years had been active in such affairs should shew, that they had formed some clear and decided idea of the principles of Colony Government; and were capable of drawing out something like a platform of the ground, which might be laid for future and permanent tranquillity.

I felt the truth of what my Hon. Friend represented; but I felt my situation too. His application might have been made with far greater propriety to many other gentlemen. No man was indeed ever better disposed, or worse qualified, for such an undertaking than myself. Though I gave so far into his opinion, that I immediately threw my thoughts into a sort of parliamentary form, I was by no means equally ready to produce them. It generally argues some degree of natural impotence of mind, or some want of knowledge of the world, to hazard Plans of Government, except from a seat of Authority. Propositions are made, not only ineffectually, but somewhat disreputably, when the minds of men are not properly disposed for their reception; and for my part, I am not ambitious of ridicule; not absolutely a candidate for disgrace.

Besides, Sir, to speak the plain truth, I have in general no very exalted opinion of the virtue of Paper Government; [nor of any Politics, in which the plan is to be wholly separated from the execution.] But when I saw, that anger and violence prevailed every day more and more; and that things were hastening towards an incurable alienation of our Colonies; I confess, my caution gave way. I felt this, as one of those few moments in which decorum yields to an higher duty. Public calamity is a mighty leveller; and there are occasions when any, even the slightest, chance of doing good, must be laid hold on, even by the most inconsiderable person.

To restore order and repose to an Empire so great and so distracted as ours, is, merely in the attempt, an undertaking that would ennoble the flights of the highest genius, and obtain pardon for the efforts of the meanest understanding. Struggling a good while with these thoughts, by degrees I felt myself more firm. I derived, at length, some confidence from what in other circumstances usually produces timidity. I grew less anxious, even from the idea of my own insignificance. For, judging of what you are, by what you ought to be, I persuaded myself, that you would not reject a reasonable proposition, because it had nothing but its reason to recommend it. On the other hand, being totally destitute of all shadow of influence, natural or adventitious, I was very sure, that, if my proposition were futile or dangerous; if it were weakly conceived, or improperly timed, there was nothing exterior to it, of power to awe, dazzle, or delude you. You will see it just as it is; and you will treat it just as it deserves.

The proposition is Peace. Not Peace through the medium of War; not Peace to be hunted through the labyrinth of intricate and endless negociations; not Peace to arise out of universal discord, fomented, from principle, in all parts of the Empire; not Peace to depend on the Juridical[8] Determination of perplexing questions; or the precise marking the shadowy boundaries of a complex Government. It is simple Peace; sought in its natural course, and its ordinary haunts.—It is Peace sought in the Spirit of Peace; and laid in principles purely pacific. I propose, by removing the Ground of the difference, and by restoring the *former unsuspecting confidence of the Colonies in the Mother Country*, to give permanent satisfaction to your people; and (far from a scheme of ruling by discord) to reconcile them to each other in the same act, and by the bond of the very same interest, which reconciles them to British Government.

My idea is nothing more. Refined policy ever has been the parent of confusion; and ever will be so, as long as the world endures. Plain good intention, which is as easily discovered at the first view, as fraud is surely detected at last, is, let me say, of no mean force in the Government of Mankind. Genuine Simplicity of heart is an healing and cementing principle. My Plan, therefore, being formed upon the most simple grounds imaginable, may disappoint some people, when they hear it. It has nothing to recommend it to the pruriency of curious ears. There is nothing at all new and captivating in it. It has nothing of the Splendor of the Project, which has been lately laid upon your Table by the Noble Lord in the Blue Ribband.[9] It does not propose to fill your Lobby with squabbling Colony Agents, who will require the interposition of your Mace, at every instant, to keep the peace amongst them. It does not institute a magnificent Auction of Finance, where captivated provinces come to general ransom by bidding against each other, until you knock down the hammer, and determine a proportion of payments, beyond all the powers of Algebra to equalize and settle.

The plan, which I shall presume to suggest, derives, however, one great advantage from the proposition and registry of that Noble Lord's Project. The idea of conciliation is admissible. First, the house, in ac-

8 According to the letter of the law.
9 Lord North (Frederick North, Earl of Guilford, 1732–1792), a member of the House of Commons because his father was still alive and he had not yet succeeded to his title. The blue ribbon is the insignia of the Order of the Garter.

cepting the resolution moved by the Noble Lord, has admitted, not-withstanding the menacing front of our Address, notwithstanding our heavy Bill of Pains and Penalties—that we do not think ourselves pre-cluded from all ideas of free Grace and Bounty.

The house has gone farther; it has declared conciliation admissible, *previous* to any submission on the part of America. It has even shot a good deal beyond that mark, and has admitted, that the complaints of our former mode of exerting the Right of Taxation were not wholly unfounded. That right thus exerted is allowed to have had something reprehensible in it; something unwise, or something grievous: since, in the midst of our heat and resentment, we, of ourselves, have proposed a capital alteration; and, in order to get rid of what seemed so very exceptionable, have instituted a mode that is altogether new; one that is indeed, wholly alien from all the ancient methods and forms of Parlia-ment.

The *principle* of this proceeding is large enough for my purpose. The means proposed by the noble Lord for carrying his ideas into execu-tion, I think indeed, are very indifferently suited to the end; and this I shall endeavour to shew you before I sit down. But, for the present, I take my ground on the admitted principle. I mean to give peace. Peace implies reconciliation; and where there has been a material dispute, reconciliation does in a manner always imply concession on the one part or on the other. In this state of things I make no difficulty in affirming, that the proposal ought to originate from us. Great and acknowledged force is not impaired, either in effect or in opinion, by an unwillingness to exert itself. The superior power may offer peace with honour and with safety. Such an offer from such a power will be attributed to magnanimity. But the concessions of the weak are the concessions of fear. When such a one is disarmed, he is wholly at the mercy of his superior; and he loses for ever that time and those chances, which, as they happen to all men, are the strength and resources of all inferior power.

The capital leading questions on which you must this day decide, are these two. First, whether you ought to concede; and secondly, what your concession ought to be. On the first of these questions we have gained (as I have just taken the liberty of observing to you) some ground. But I am sensible that a good deal more is still to be done. Indeed, Sir, to enable us to determine both on the one and the other of these great questions with a firm and precise judgement, I think it may be necessary to consider distinctly the true nature and the peculiar circumstances of the object which we have before us. Because after all our struggle, whether we will or not, we must govern America, according to that nature, and to those circumstances; and not according to our own imaginations; not according to abstract ideas of right; by no means according to mere general theories of government, the resort to which appears to me, in our present situation, no better than arrant trifling. I shall therefore endeavour, with your leave, to lay before you some of the most material of these circumstances in as full and as clear a manner as I am able to state them.

The first thing that we have to consider with regard to the nature of the object is—the number of people in the Colonies. I have taken for some years a good deal of pains on that point. I can by no calculation justify myself in placing the number below Two Millions of inhabitants of our own European blood and colour; besides at least 500,000 others, who form no inconsiderable part of the strength and opulence of the whole. This, Sir, is, I believe, about the true number. There is no occasion to exaggerate, where plain truth is of so much weight and importance. But whether I put the present numbers too high or too low, is a matter of little moment. Such is the strength with which population shoots in that part of the world, that state the numbers as high as we will, whilst the dispute continues, the exaggeration ends. Whilst we are discussing any given magnitude, they are grown to it. Whilst we spend our time in deliberating on the mode of governing Two Millions, we shall find we have Millions more to manage.⎡Your children do not grow faster from infancy to manhood, than they, spread from families to communities, and from villages to nations.⎤

I put this consideration of the present and the growing numbers in the front of our deliberation; because, Sir, this consideration will make it evident to a blunter discernment than yours, that no partial, narrow, contracted, pinched, occasional system will be at all suitable to such an object. It will shew you, that it is not to be considered as one of those *Minima*[10] which are out of the eye and consideration of the law; not a paltry excrescence of the state; not a mean dependant, who may be neglected with little damage, and provoked with little danger. It will prove, that some degree of care and caution is required in the handling such an object; it will shew, that you ought not, in reason, to trifle with so large a mass of the interests and feelings of the human race. You could

---

10 The smallest possible matters.

at no time do so without guilt; and be assured you will not be able to do it long with impunity.

But the population of this country, the great and growing population, though a very important consideration, will lose much of its weight, if not combined with other circumstances. The commerce of your Colonies is out of all proportion beyond the numbers of the people. This ground of their commerce indeed has been trod some days ago, and with great ability, by a distinguished person, at your bar.[11] This gentleman, after Thirty-five years—it is so long since he first appeared at the same place to plead for the commerce of Great Britain—has come again before you to plead the same cause, without any other effect of time, than, that to the fire of imagination and extent of erudition, which even then marked him as one of the first literary characters of his age, he has added a consummate knowledge in the commercial interest of his country, formed by a long course of enlightened and discriminating experience.

Sir, I should be inexcusable in coming after such a person with any detail; if a great part of the members who now fill the House had not the misfortune to be absent, when he appeared at your bar. Besides, Sir, I propose to take the matter at periods of time somewhat different from his. There is, if I mistake not, a point of view, from whence if you will look at this subject, it is impossible that it should not make an impression upon you.

I have in my hand two accounts; one a comparative state of the export trade of England to its Colonies, as it stood in the year 1704, and as it stood in the year 1772. The other a state of the export trade of this country to its Colonies alone, as it stood in 1772, compared with the whole trade of England to all parts of the world (the Colonies included) in the year 1704. They are from good vouchers; the latter period from the accounts on your table, the earlier from an original manuscript of Davenant,[12] who first established the Inspector General's office, which has been ever since his time so abundant a source of parliamentary information.

The export trade to the Colonies consists of three great branches. The African, which, terminating almost wholly in the Colonies, must be

11 Richard Glover (1712–1785), poet and later barrister, who dabbled in politics. The bar referred to is the oak rail across the entrance to the floor of the House; outsiders wishing to address the House stood there.

12 Charles Davenant (1656–1714), inspector-general of imports and exports, 1705–1714.

put to the account of their commerce; the West Indian; and the North American. All these are so interwoven, that the attempt to separate them, would tear to pieces the contexture of the whole; and if not entirely destroy, would very much depreciate the value of all the parts. I therefore consider these three denominations to be, what in effect they are, one trade.

The trade to the Colonies, taken on the export side, at the beginning of this century, that is, in the year 1704, stood thus:

Exports to North America, and the West Indies, ...	£ 483,265
To Africa, ...	86,665
	569,930

In the year 1772, which I take as a middle year between the highest and lowest of those lately laid on your table, the account was as follows:

To North America, and the West Indies, ...	£4,791,734
To Africa, ...	866,398
To which if you add the export trade from Scotland, which} had in 1704 no existence, ...}	364,000
	6,024,171

From Five Hundred and odd Thousand, it has grown to Six Millions. It has increased no less than twelve-fold. This is the state of the Colony trade, as compared with itself at these two periods, within this century;—and this is matter for meditation. But this is not all. Examine my second account. See how the export trade to the Colonies alone in 1772 stood in the other point of view, that is, as compared to the whole trade of England in 1704.

The whole export trade of England, including that to the} Colonies, in 1704, ...}	£6,509,000
Export to the Colonies alone, in 1772, ...	6,024,000
Difference,	485,000

The trade with America alone is now within less than 500,000£ of being equal to what this great commercial nation, England, carried on at the beginning of this century with the whole world! If I had taken the largest year of those on your table, it would rather have exceeded. But, it will be said, is not this American trade an unnatural protuberance, that has drawn the juices from the rest of the body? The reverse. It is the very food that has nourished every other part into its present magnitude. Our general trade has been greatly augmented; and augmented more or less in almost every part to which it ever extended; but with this material difference; that of the Six Millions which in the beginning of the century constituted the whole mass of our export commerce, the Colony trade was but one twelfth part; it is now (as a part of Sixteen Millions) considerably more than a third of the whole. This is the relative proportion of the importance of the Colonies at these two periods: and all reasoning concerning our mode of treating them must have this proportion as its basis; or it is a reasoning weak, rotten, and sophistical.

Mr. Speaker, I cannot prevail on myself to hurry over this great consideration. It is good for us to be here. We stand where we have an immense view of what is, and what is past. Clouds indeed, and darkness, rest upon the future. Let us however, before we descend from this noble eminence, reflect that this growth of our national prosperity has happened within the short period of the life of man. It has happened within Sixty-eight years. There are those alive whose memory might touch the two extremities. For instance, my Lord Bathurst[13] might remember all the stages of the progress. He was in 1704 of an age, at least to be made to comprehend such things. He was then old enough *acta parentum jam legere, et quæ sit poterit cognoscere virtus*[14]—Suppose, Sir, that the angel of this auspicious youth, foreseeing the many virtues, which made him one of the most amiable, as he is one of the most fortunate men of his age, had opened to him in vision, that, when, in the fourth generation, the third Prince of the House of Brunswick had sat Twelve years on the throne of that nation, which (by the happy issue of moderate and healing councils) was to be made Great Britain, he should see his son, Lord Chancellor of England,[15] turn back the current of hereditary dignity to its fountain, and raise him to an higher rank of Peerage, whilst he enriched the family with a new one—If amidst these bright and happy scenes of domestic honour and prosperity, that angel should have drawn up the curtain, and unfolded the rising glories of his country, and whilst he was gazing with admiration on the then commercial grandeur of England, the Genius

---

13 Allen Bathurst, first Earl Bathurst (1684–1775).

14 "To study the example of his forefathers and to learn what virtue is" (Virgil, *Eclogues*, IV. 26–27, slightly altered).

15 Henry Bathurst, second Earl Bathurst (1714–1794), lord chancellor, 1771–1778; in 1771, created Baron Apsley. At the same time his father became an earl.

should point out to him a little speck, scarce visible in the mass of the national interest, a small seminal principle, rather than a formed body, and should tell him—"Young man, There is America—which at this day serves for little more than to amuse you with stories of savage men, and uncouth manners; yet shall, before you taste of death, shew itself equal to the whole of that commerce which now attracts the envy of the world. Whatever England has been growing to by a progressive increase of improvement, brought in by varieties of people, by succession of civilizing conquests and civilizing settlements in a series of Seventeen Hundred years, you shall see as much added to her by America in the course of a single life!" If this state of his country had been foretold to him, would it not require all the sanguine credulity of youth, and all the fervid glow of enthusiasm, to make him believe it? Fortunate man, he has lived to see it! Fortunate indeed, if he lives to see nothing that shall vary the prospect, and cloud the setting of his day!

Excuse me, Sir, if turning from such thoughts I resume this comparative view once more. You have seen it on a large scale; look at it on a small one. I will point out to your attention a particular instance of it in the single province of Pensylvania. In the year 1704 that province called for 11,459 £ in value of your commodities, native and foreign. This was the whole. What did it demand in 1772? Why nearly Fifty times as much; for in that year the export to Pensylvania was 507,909 £, nearly equal to the export to all the Colonies together in the first period.

I choose, Sir, to enter into these minute and particular details; because generalities, which in all other cases are apt to heighten and raise the subject, have here a tendency to sink it. When we speak of the commerce with our Colonies, fiction lags after truth; invention is unfruitful, and imagination cold and barren.

So far, Sir, as to the importance of the object in the view of its commerce, as concerned in the exports from England. If I were to detail the imports, I could shew how many enjoyments they procure, which deceive[16] the burthen of life; how many materials which invigorate the springs of national industry, and extend and animate every part of our foreign and domestic commerce. This would be a curious subject indeed—but I must prescribe bounds to myself in a matter so vast and various.

I pass therefore to the Colonies in another point of view, their

---

16 Divert from.

agriculture. This they have prosecuted with such a spirit, that besides feeding plentifully their own growing multitude, their annual export of grain, comprehending rice, has some years ago exceeded a Million in value. Of their last harvest, I am persuaded, they will export much more. At the beginning of the century, some of these Colonies imported corn from the mother country. For some time past, the old world has been fed from the new. The scarcity which you have felt would have been a desolating famine; if this child of your old age, with a true filial piety, with a Roman charity, had not put the full breast of its youthful exuberance to the mouth of its exhausted parent.[17]

As to the wealth which the Colonies have drawn from the sea by their fisheries, you had all that matter fully opened at your bar. You surely thought those acquisitions of value; for they seemed even to excite your envy; and yet the spirit, by which that enterprizing employment has been exercised, ought rather, in my opinion, to have raised your esteem and admiration. And pray, Sir, what in the world is equal to it? Pass by the other parts, and look at the manner in which the people of New England have of late carried on the Whale Fishery. Whilst we follow them among the tumbling mountains of ice, and behold them penetrating into the deepest frozen recesses of Hudson's Bay, and Davis's Streights, whilst we are looking for them beneath the Arctic circle, we hear that they have pierced into the opposite region of polar cold, that they are at the Antipodes, and engaged under the frozen serpent of the south. Falkland Island,[18] which seemed too remote and romantick an object for the grasp of national ambition, is but a stage and resting-place in the progress of their victorious industry. Nor is the equinoctial heat more discouraging to them, than the accumulated winter of both the poles. We know that whilst some of them draw the line and strike the harpoon on the coast of Africa, others run the longitude, and pursue their gigantic game along the coast of Brazil. No sea but what is vexed by their fisheries. No climate that is not witness to their toils. Neither the perseverance of Holland, nor the activity of France, nor the dextrous and firm sagacity of English

---

17 Cymon, condemned to starve in prison, was kept alive by his daughter Xanthippe with milk from her breast.

18 Hudson Bay and Davis Strait (an arm of the Atlantic connecting Baffin Bay with the Atlantic) are in the north; the Falkland Islands are in the South Atlantic, east of Patagonia. They had been ceded to England by Spain only in 1771; before that they seemed "too remote . . . an object for . . . national ambition." The "frozen serpent" is the constellation Hydrus, in the extreme south.

enterprize, ever carried this most perilous mode of hardy industry to the extent to which it has been pushed by this recent people; a people who are still, as it were, but in the gristle, and not yet hardened into the bone of manhood. When I contemplate these things; when I know that the Colonies in general owe little or nothing to any care of ours, and that they are not squeezed into this happy form by the constraints of watchful and suspicious government, but that through a wise and salutary neglect, a generous nature has been suffered to take her own way to perfection: when I reflect upon these effects, when I see how profitable they have been to us, I feel all the pride of power sink, and all presumption in the wisdom of human contrivances melt, and die away within me. My rigour relents. I pardon something to the spirit of Liberty.

I am sensible, Sir, that all which I have asserted in my detail, is admitted in the gross; but that quite a different conclusion is drawn from it. America, Gentlemen say, is a noble object. It is an object well worth fighting for. Certainly it is, if fighting a people be the best way of gaining them. Gentlemen in this respect will be led to their choice of means by their complexions and their habits. Those who understand the military art, will of course have some predilection for it. Those who wield the thunder of the state, may have more confidence in the efficacy of arms. But I confess, possibly for want of this knowledge, my opinion is much more in favour of prudent management, than of force; considering force not as an odious, but a feeble instrument, for preserving a people so numerous, so active, so growing, so spirited as this, in a profitable and subordinate connexion with us.

First, Sir, permit me to observe, that the use of force alone is but *temporary*. It may subdue for a moment; but it does not remove the necessity of subduing again: and a nation is not governed, which is perpetually to be conquered.

My next objection is its *uncertainty*. Terror is not always the effect of force; and an armament is not a victory. If you do not succeed, you are without resource; for, conciliation failing, force remains; but, force failing, no further hope of reconciliation is left. Power and authority are sometimes bought by kindness; but they can never be begged as alms, by an impoverished and defeated violence.

A further objection to force is, that you *impair the object* by your very endeavours to preserve it. The thing you fought for, is not the thing which you recover; but depreciated, sunk, wasted, and consumed in the contest. Nothing less will content me, than *whole America*. I do not choose to consume its strength along with our own; because in all parts it is the British strength that I consume. I do not choose to be caught by a foreign enemy at the end of this exhausting conflict; and still less in the midst of it. I may escape; but I can make no insurance against such an event. Let me add, that I do not choose wholly to break the American spirit, because it is the spirit that has made the country.

Lastly, we have no sort of *experience* in favour of force as an instrument in the rule of our Colonies. Their growth and their utility has been owing to methods altogether different. Our ancient indulgence has been said to be pursued to a fault. It may be so. But we know, if feeling is evidence, that our fault was more tolerable than our attempt to mend it; and our sin far more salutary than our penitence.

These, Sir, are my reasons for not entertaining that high opinion of untried force, by which many Gentlemen, for whose sentiments in other particulars I have great respect, seem to be so greatly captivated. But there is still behind a third consideration concerning this object, which serves to determine my opinion on the sort of policy which ought to be pursued in the management of America, even more than its Population and its Commerce, I mean its *Temper and Character*.

In this Character of the Americans, a love of Freedom is the predominating feature, which marks and distinguishes the whole: and as an ardent is always a jealous affection, your Colonies become suspicious, restive, and untractable, whenever they see the least attempt to wrest from them by force, or shuffle from them by chicane,[19] what they think the only advantage worth living for. This fierce spirit of Liberty is stronger in the English Colonies probably than in any other people of the earth; and this from a great variety of powerful causes; which, to understand the true temper of their minds, and the direction which this spirit takes, it will not be amiss to lay open somewhat more largely.

First, the people of the Colonies are descendents of Englishmen. England, Sir, is a nation, which still I hope respects, and formerly adored her freedom. The Colonists emigrated from you, when this part of your character was most predominant; and they took this biass and direction the moment they parted from your hands. They are therefore not only devoted to Liberty, but to Liberty according to English ideas, and on English principles.[Abstract Liberty, like other mere abstractions, is not to be found.]Liberty inheres in some sensible object; and every nation has

---

19 Chicanery, trickery.

formed to itself some favourite point, which by way of eminence becomes the criterion of their happiness. It happened, you know, Sir, that the great contests for freedom in this country were from the earliest times chiefly upon the question of Taxing. Most of the contests in the ancient commonwealths turned primarily on the right of election of magistrates; or on the balance among the several orders of the state. The question of money was not with them so immediate. But in England it was otherwise. On this point of Taxes the ablest pens, and most eloquent tongues have been exercised; the greatest spirits have acted and suffered. In order to give the fullest satisfaction concerning the importance of this point, it was not only necessary for those who in argument defended the excellence of the English constitution, to insist on this privilege of granting money as a dry point of fact, and to prove, that the right had been acknowledged in ancient parchments, and blind[20] usages, to reside in a certain body called an House of Commons. They went much further; they attempted to prove, and they succeeded, that in theory it ought to be so, from the particular nature of a House of Commons, as an immediate representative of the people; whether the old records had delivered this oracle or not. They took infinite pains to inculcate, as a fundamental principle, that, in all monarchies, the people must in effect themselves mediately or immediately possess the power of granting their own money, or no shadow of liberty could subsist. The Colonies draw from you as with their life-blood, these ideas and principles. Their love of liberty, as with you, fixed and attached on this specific point of taxing. Liberty might be safe, or might be endangered in twenty other particulars, without their being much pleased or alarmed. Here they felt its pulse; and as they found that beat, they thought themselves sick or sound. I do not say whether they were right or wrong in applying your general arguments to their own case. It is not easy indeed to make a monopoly of theorems and corollaries. The fact is, that they did thus apply those general arguments; and your mode of governing them, whether through lenity or indolence, through wisdom or mistake, confirmed them in the imagination, that they, as well as you, had an interest in these common principles.

They were further confirmed in this pleasing error by the form of their provincial legislative assemblies. Their governments are popular in an high degree; some are merely popular; in all, the popular representa-

---

20 Obscure.

tive is the most weighty; and this share of the people in their ordinary government never fails to inspire them with lofty sentiments, and with a strong aversion from whatever tends to deprive them of their chief importance.

If any thing were wanting to this necessary operation of the form of government, Religion would have given it a complete effect. Religion, always a principle of energy, in this new people, is no way worn out or impaired; and their mode of professing it is also one main cause of this free spirit. The people are protestants; and of that kind, which is the most adverse to all implicit submission of mind and opinion. This is a persuasion not only favourable to liberty, but built upon it. I do not think, Sir, that the reason of this averseness in the dissenting churches from all that looks like absolute Government is so much to be sought in their religious tenets, as in their history. Every one knows, that the Roman Catholick religion is at least coeval with most of the governments where it prevails; that it has generally gone hand in hand with them; and received great favour and every kind of support from authority. The Church of England too was formed from her cradle under the nursing care of regular government. But the dissenting interests have sprung up in direct opposition to all the ordinary powers of the world; and could justify that opposition only on a strong claim to natural liberty. Their very existence depended on the powerful and unremitted assertion of that claim. All protestantism, even the most cold and passive, is a sort of dissent. [But the religion most prevalent in our Northern Colonies is a refinement on the principle of resistance; it is the dissidence of dissent; and the protestantism of the protestant religion.] This religion, under a variety of denominations, agreeing in nothing but in the communion of the spirit of liberty, is predominant in most of the Northern provinces; where the Church of England, notwithstanding its legal rights, is in reality no more than a sort of private sect, not composing most probably the tenth of the people. The Colonists left England when this spirit was high; and in the emigrants was the highest of all: and even that stream of foreigners, which has been constantly flowing into these Colonies, has, for the greatest part, been composed of dissenters from the establishments of their several countries, and have brought with them a temper and character far from alien to that of the people with whom they mixed.

Sir, I can perceive by their manner, that some Gentlemen object to the latitude of this description; because in the Southern Colonies the Church of England forms a large body, and has a regular establishment.

It is certainly true. There is however a circumstance attending these Colonies, which in my opinion, fully counterbalances this difference, and makes the spirit of liberty still more high and haughty than in those to the Northward. It is that in Virginia and the Carolinas, they have a vast multitude of slaves.[Where this is the case in any part of the world, those who are free, are by far the most proud and jealous of their freedom.] Freedom is to them not only an enjoyment, but a kind of rank and privilege. Not seeing there, that freedom, as in countries where it is a common blessing, and as broad and general as the air, may be united with much abject toil, with great misery, with all the exterior of servitude, Liberty looks amongst them, like something that is more noble and liberal. I do not mean, Sir, to commend the superior morality of this sentiment, which has at least as much pride as virtue in it; but I cannot alter the nature of man. The fact is so; and these people of the Southern Colonies are much more strongly, and with an higher and more stubborn spirit, attached to liberty than those to the Northward.] Such were all the ancient commonwealths; such were our Gothick[21] ancestors; such in our days were the Poles;[22] and such will be all masters of slaves, who are not slaves themselves. In such a people the haughtiness of domination combines with the spirit of freedom, fortifies it, and renders it invincible.

Permit me, Sir, to add another circumstance in our Colonies, which contributes no mean part towards the growth and effect of this untractable spirit. I mean their education. In no country perhaps in the world is the law so general a study. The profession itself is numerous and powerful; and in most provinces it takes the lead. The greater number of the Deputies sent to the Congress were Lawyers. But all who read, and most do read, endeavour to obtain some smattering in that science. I have been told by an eminent Bookseller, that in no branch of his business, after tracts of popular devotion, were so many books as those on the Law exported to the Plantations. The Colonists have now fallen into the way of printing them for their own use. I hear that they have sold nearly as many of Blackstone's Commentaries[23] in America as in England. General Gage[24]

---

21 I.e., our Teutonic forebears.

22 The Czartoryscy family for a half century (c. 1734–1786) led a struggle for constitutional reform in Poland, against the opposition of most of the country's great families and in the face of Russian intrigue designed to keep the country weak.

23 *Commentaries on the Laws of England* (1765–1769) by Sir William Blackstone (1723–1780), still the best general history of English law.

24 Thomas Gage (1721–1787), commander-in-chief in America, 1763–1772.

marks out this disposition very particularly in a letter on your table. He states, that all the people in his government are lawyers, or smatterers in law; and that in Boston they have been enabled, by successful chicane, wholly to evade many parts of one of your capital penal constitutions. The smartness[25] of debate will say, that this knowledge ought to teach them more clearly the rights of legislature, their obligations to obedience, and the penalties of rebellion. All this is mighty well. But my honourable and learned friend on the floor,[26] who condescends to mark what I say for animadversion, will disdain that ground. He has heard as well as I, that when great honours and great emoluments do not win over this knowledge to the service of the state, it is a formidable adversary to government. If the spirit be not tamed and broken by these happy methods, it is stubborn and litigious. *Abeunt studia in mores.*[27] This study renders men acute, inquisitive, dextrous, prompt in attack, ready in defence, full of resources. In other countries, the people, more simple and of a less mercurial cast, judge of an ill principle in government only by an actual grievance; here they anticipate the evil, and judge of the pressure of the grievance by the badness of the principle. They augur misgovern- ✓ ment at a distance; and snuff the approach of tyranny in every tainted breeze.

The last cause of this disobedient spirit in the Colonies is hardly less powerful than the rest, as it is not merely moral, but laid deep in the natural constitution of things. Three thousand miles of ocean lie between you and them. No contrivance can prevent the effect of this distance, in weakening Government. Seas roll, and months pass, between the order and the execution; and the want of a speedy explanation of a single point is enough to defeat an whole system. You have, indeed, winged ministers of vengeance,[28] who carry your bolts in their pounces[29] to the remotest verge of the sea. But there a power steps in, that limits the arrogance of raging passions and furious elements, and says, "So far shalt thou go, and no farther."(Who are you, that should fret and rage, and bite the chains of Nature?)—Nothing worse happens to you, than does to all Nations, who have extensive Empire; and it happens in all the forms into

---

25 Wittiness, acuteness.

26 "The Attorney General" [E.B.]. Edward Thurlow (1731–1806), the attorney general, inflexibly maintained the right of England to exert her full might in America.

27 "Pursuits become habits" (Ovid, *Heroides*, XV. 83).

28 I.e., the ships of the navy.

29 Claws.

which Empire can be thrown. In large bodies, the circulation of power must be less vigorous at the extremities. Nature has said it. The Turk cannot govern Ægypt, and Arabia, and Curdistan, as he governs Thrace; nor has he the same dominion in Crimea and Algiers, which he has at Brusa[30] and Smyrna. Despotism itself is obliged to truck and huckster.[31] The Sultan gets such obedience as he can. He governs with a loose rein, that he may govern at all; and the whole of the force and vigour of his authority in his centre, is derived from a prudent relaxation in all his borders. Spain, in her provinces, is, perhaps, not so well obeyed, as you are in yours. She complies too; she submits; she watches times. This is the immutable condition; the eternal Law, of extensive and detached Empire.

Then, Sir, from these six capital sources; of Descent; of Form of Government; of Religion in the Northern Provinces; of Manners in the Southern; of Education; of the Remoteness of Situation from the First Mover of Government, from all these causes a fierce Spirit of Liberty has grown up. It has grown with the growth of the people in your Colonies, and encreased with the encrease of their wealth; a Spirit, that unhappily meeting with an exercise of Power in England, which, however lawful, is not reconcileable to any ideas of Liberty, much less with theirs, has kindled this flame, that is ready to consume us.

I do not mean to commend either the Spirit in this excess, or the moral causes which produce it. Perhaps a more smooth and accommodating Spirit of Freedom in them would be more acceptable to us. Perhaps ideas of Liberty might be desired, more reconcileable with an arbitrary and boundless authority. Perhaps we might wish the Colonists to be persuaded, that their Liberty is more secure when held in trust for them by us (as their guardians during a perpetual minority) than with any part of it in their own hands. But the question is, not whether their spirit deserves praise or blame;—what, in the name of God, shall we do with it? You have before you the object; such as it is, with all its glories, with all its imperfections on its head. You see the magnitude; the importance; the temper; the habits; the disorders. By all these considerations, we are strongly urged to determine something concerning it. We are called upon to fix some rule and line for our future conduct, which may give a little stability to our politics, and prevent the return of such unhappy delibera-

---

30 Brusa, or Bursa, is a province in northwestern Turkey; Smyrna is a province of western Turkey. Curdistan, or Kurdistan (above), is a mountainous region shared by Turkey, Iraq, and Iran, governed by the Turks alone from the thirteenth to the fifteenth century.
31 Bargain and haggle.

tions as the present. Every such return will bring the matter before us in a still more untractable form. For, what astonishing and incredible things have we not seen already? What monsters have not been generated from this unnatural contention? Whilst every principle of authority and resistance has been pushed, upon both sides, as far as it would go, there is nothing so solid and certain, either in reasoning or in practice, that has been not shaken. Until very lately, all authority in America seemed to be nothing but an emanation from yours. Even the popular part of the Colony Constitution derived all its activity, and its first vital movement, from the pleasure of the Crown. We thought, Sir, that the utmost which the discontented Colonists could do, was to disturb authority; we never dreamt they could of themselves supply it; knowing in general what an operose[32] business it is, to establish a Government absolutely new. But having, for our purposes in this contention, resolved, that none but an obedient Assembly should sit, the humours of the people there, finding all passage through the legal channel stopped, with great violence broke out another way. Some provinces have tried their experiment, as we have tried ours; and theirs has succeeded. They have formed a Government sufficient for its purposes, without the bustle of a Revolution, or the troublesome formality of an Election. Evident necessity, and tacit consent, have done the business in an instant. So well they have done it, that Lord Dunmore[33] (the account is among the fragments on your table) tells you, that the new institution is infinitely better obeyed than the antient Government ever was in its most fortunate periods. Obedience is what makes Government, and not the names by which it is called; not the name of Governor, as formerly, or Committee,[34] as at present. This new Government has originated directly from the people; and was not transmitted through any of the ordinary artificial media of a positive constitution. It was not a manufacture ready formed, and transmitted to them in that condition from England. The evil arising from hence is this; that the Colonists having once found the possibility of enjoying the advantages of order, in the midst of a struggle for Liberty, such struggles will not

---

32 Laborious, tedious.

33 John Murray, fourth Earl of Dunmore (1732–1809), governor of the colony of Virginia, who dissolved the Virginia House of Assembly in March 1773, when it resolved the appointment of a Committee of Correspondence. See next note.

34 The Virginia Committee of Correspondence was established to investigate Britain's legal authority to bring "treasonable individuals" to England for trial; it also organized common action of the colonies against Great Britain.

henceforward seem so terrible to the settled and sober part of mankind, as they had appeared before the trial.

Pursuing the same plan of punishing by the denial of the exercise of Government to still greater lengths, we wholly abrogated the antient Government of Massachuset.[35] We were confident, that the first feeling, if not the very prospect of anarchy, would instantly enforce a compleat submission. The experiment was tried. A new, strange, unexpected face of things appeared. Anarchy is found tolerable. A vast province has now subsisted, and subsisted in a considerable degree of health and vigour, for near a twelvemonth, without Governor, without public Council, without Judges, without executive Magistrates. How long it will continue in this state, or what may arise out of this unheard-of situation, how can the wisest of us conjecture? Our late experience has taught us, that many of those fundamental principles, formerly believed infallible, are either not of the importance they were imagined to be; or that we have not at all adverted to some other far more important, and far more powerful principles, which entirely over-rule those we had considered as omnipotent. I am much against any further experiments, which tend to put to the proof any more of these allowed opinions, which contribute so much to the public tranquillity. In effect, we suffer as much at home, by this loosening of all ties, and this concussion[36] of all established opinions, as we do abroad. For, in order to prove, that the Americans have no right to their Liberties, we are every day endeavouring to subvert the maxims, which preserve the whole Spirit of our own. To prove that the Americans ought not to be free, we are obliged to depreciate the value of Freedom itself; and we never seem to gain a paltry advantage over them in debate, without attacking some of those principles, or deriding some of those feelings, for which our ancestors have shed their blood.

But, Sir, in wishing to put an end to pernicious experiments, I do not mean to preclude the fullest enquiry. Far from it. Far from deciding on a sudden or partial view, I would patiently go round and round the subject, and survey it minutely in every possible aspect. Sir, if I were capable of engaging you to an equal attention, I would state, that, as far as I am capable of discerning, there are but three ways of proceeding relative

---

35 By an "Act for the better regulating the government of the Province of the Massachusets Bay in New England," which provided that the Council was to be appointed by the king, all law officers by the governor, all jurymen by the sheriff; only the Assembly could be elected.

36 Violent agitation.

to this stubborn Spirit, which prevails in your Colonies, and disturbs your Government. These are—To change that Spirit, as inconvenient, by removing the Causes. To prosecute it as criminal. Or, to comply with it ✓ as necessary. I would not be guilty of an imperfect enumeration; I can think of but these three. Another has indeed been started, that of giving up the Colonies; but it met so slight a reception, that I do not think myself obliged to dwell a great while upon it. It is nothing but a little sally of anger; like the frowardness of peevish children; who, when they cannot get all they would have, are resolved to take nothing.

The first of these plans, to change the Spirit as inconvenient, by removing the causes, I think is the most like a systematick proceeding. It is radical in its principle; but it is attended with great difficulties, some of them little short, as I conceive, of impossibilities. This will appear by examining into the Plans which have been proposed.

As the growing population in the Colonies is evidently one cause of their resistance, it was last session mentioned in both Houses, by men of weight, and received not without applause, that, in order to check this evil, it would be proper for the crown to make no further grants of land. But to this scheme, there are two objections. The first, that there is already so much unsettled land in private hands, as to afford room for an immense future population, although the crown not only withheld its grants, but annihilated its soil. If this be the case, then the only effect of this avarice of desolation, this hoarding of a royal wilderness, would be to raise the value of the possessions in the hands of the great private monopolists, without any adequate check to the growing and alarming mischief of population.

But, if you stopped your grants, what would be the consequence? The people would occupy without grants. They have already so occupied in many places. You cannot station garrisons in every part of these deserts. If you drive the people from one place, they will carry on their annual Tillage, and remove with their flocks and herds to another. Many of the people in the back settlements are already little attached to particular situations. Already they have topped the Apalachian mountains. From thence they behold before them an immense plain, one vast, rich, level meadow; a square of five hundred miles. Over this they would wander, without a possibility of restraint; they would change their manners with the habits of their life; would soon forget a government, by which they were disowned; would become Hordes of English Tartars; and, pouring down upon your unfortified frontiers a fierce and irresistible cavalry, become masters of your Governors and your Counsellors, your collectors and comptrollers, and of all the Slaves that adhered to them. Such would, and, in no long time, must be, the effect of attempting to forbid as a crime, and to suppress as an evil, the Command and Blessing of Providence, "Encrease and Multiply."[37] Such would be the happy result of an endeavour to keep as a lair of wild beasts, that earth, which God, by an express Charter, has given to the children of men. Far different, and surely much wiser, has been our policy hitherto. Hitherto we have invited our people by every kind of bounty, to fixed establishments. We have invited the husbandman, to look to authority for his title. We have taught him piously to believe in the mysterious virtue of wax and parchment.[38] We have thrown each tract of land, as it was peopled, into districts; that the ruling power should never be wholly out of sight. We have settled all we could; and we have carefully attended every settlement with government.

Adhering, Sir, as I do, to this policy, as well as for the reasons I have just given, I think this new project of hedging-in population to be neither prudent nor practicable.

To impoverish the Colonies in general, and in particular to arrest the noble course of their marine enterprizes, would be a more easy task. I freely confess it. We have shewn a disposition to a system of this kind; a disposition even to continue the restraint after the offence; looking on ourselves as rivals to our Colonies, and persuaded that of course we must gain all that they shall lose. Much mischief we may certainly do. The power inadequate to all other things is often more than sufficient for this. I do not look on the direct and immediate power of the Colonies to resist our violence, as very formidable. In this, however, I may be mistaken. But when I consider, that we have Colonies for no purpose but to be serviceable to us, it seems to my poor understanding a little preposterous, to make them unserviceable, in order to keep them obedient. It is, in truth, nothing more than the old, and, as I thought, exploded problem of tyranny, which proposes to beggar its subjects into submission. But, remember, when you have compleated your system of impoverishment, that Nature still proceeds in her ordinary course; that discontent will encrease with misery; and that there are critical moments in the fortune

---

37 Cf. Genesis 1:22: "Be fruitful, and multiply"; Exodus 1:7: "And the children of Israel . . . increased abundantly, and multiplied."

38 E.g., of title deeds.

of all states, when they, who are too weak to contribute to your prosperity, may be strong enough to complete your ruin. *Spoliatis arma supersunt.*[39]

The temper and character which prevail in our Colonies, are, I am afraid, unalterable by any human art. We cannot, I fear, falsify the pedigree of this fierce people, and persuade them that they are not sprung from a nation, in whose veins the blood of freedom circulates. The language in which they would hear you tell them this tale, would detect the imposition; your speech would betray you. An Englishman is the unfittest person on earth, to argue another Englishman into slavery.

I think it is nearly as little in our power to change their republican Religion, as their free descent; or to substitute the Roman-Catholick, as a penalty; or the Church of England, as an improvement. The mode of inquisition and dragooning,[40] is going out of fashion in the old world; and I should not confide much to their efficacy in the new. The education of the Americans is also on the same unalterable bottom[41] with their religion. You cannot persuade them to burn their books of curious science; to banish their lawyers from their courts of law; or to quench the lights of their assemblies, by refusing to choose those persons who are best read in their privileges. It would be no less impracticable to think of wholly annihilating the popular assemblies, in which these lawyers sit. The army, by which we must govern in their place, would be far more chargeable[42] to us; not quite so effectual; and perhaps, in the end, full as difficult to be kept in obedience.

With regard to the high aristocratick spirit of Virginia and the southern Colonies, it has been proposed, I know, to reduce it, by declaring a general enfranchisement of their slaves. This project has had its advocates and panegyrists; yet I never could argue myself into any opinion of it. Slaves are often much attached to their masters. A general wild offer of liberty, would not always be accepted. History furnishes few instances of it. It is sometimes as hard to persuade slaves to be free, as it is to compel freemen to be slaves; and in this auspicious scheme, we should have both these pleasing tasks on our hands at once. But when we talk of enfranchisement, do we not perceive that the American master may en-

---

[39] "Plundered though they be, they still have their weapons" (Juvenal, *Satires*, VIII. 124).

[40] Despotic rule by armed force.

[41] Foundation.

[42] Expensive.

franchise too; and arm servile hands in defence of freedom? A measure to which other people have had recourse more than once, and not without success, in a desperate situation of their affairs.

Slaves as these unfortunate black people are, and dull as all men are from slavery, must they not a little suspect the offer of freedom from that very nation which has sold them to their present masters? From that nation, one of whose causes of quarrel with those masters, is their refusal to deal any more in that inhuman traffick?[43] An offer of freedom from England, would come rather oddly, shipped to them in an African vessel, which is refused an entry into the ports of Virginia or Carolina, with a cargo of three hundred Angola negroes. It would be curious to see the Guinea captain attempting at the same instant to publish his proclamation of liberty, and to advertise his sale of slaves.

But let us suppose all these moral difficulties got over. The Ocean remains. You cannot pump this dry; and as long as it continues in its present bed, so long all the causes which weaken authority by distance will continue. "Ye gods, annihilate but space and time, and make two lovers happy!"[44]—was a pious and passionate prayer;—but just as reasonable, as many of the serious wishes of very grave and solemn politicians.

If then, Sir, it seems almost desperate to think of any alternative course, for changing the moral causes (and not quite easy to remove the natural), which produce prejudices irreconcileable to the late exercise of our authority; but that the spirit infallibly will continue; and, continuing, will produce such effects, as now embarrass us; the second mode under consideration is, to prosecute that spirit in its overt acts, as *criminal*.

At this proposition, I must pause a moment. The thing seems a great deal too big for my ideas of jurisprudence. It should seem, to my way of conceiving such matters, that there is a very wide difference in reason and policy, between the mode of proceeding on the irregular conduct of scattered individuals, or even of bands of men, who disturb order within the state, and the civil dissensions which may, from time to time, on great questions, agitate the several communities which compose a great Empire. It looks to me to be narrow and pedantic, to apply the ordinary ideas of criminal justice to this great public contest. I do not

---

43 Opposition to slavery had been marked as the colonies became increasingly pre-occupied by the question of freedom. By the time Burke spoke, Connecticut and Rhode Island had forbidden the slave trade, and an effort by Massachusetts to outlaw it had been vetoed by the governor.

44 Alexander Pope, *Martinus Scriblerus on the Art of Sinking in Poetry* (1728), Ch. XI.

know the method of drawing up an indictment against an whole people. I cannot insult and ridicule the feelings of Millions of my fellow-creatures, as Sir Edward Coke[45] insulted one excellent individual (Sir Walter Rawleigh) at the bar. I am not ripe to pass sentence on the gravest public bodies, entrusted with magistracies of great authority and dignity, and charged with the safety of their fellow-citizens, upon the very same title that I am. I really think, that for wise men, this is not judicious; for sober men, not decent; for minds tinctured with humanity, not mild and merciful.

Perhaps, Sir, I am mistaken in my idea of an Empire, as distinguished from a single State or Kingdom. But my idea of it is this; that an Empire is the aggregate of many States, under one common head; whether this head be a monarch, or a presiding republic. It does, in such constitutions, frequently happen (and nothing but the dismal, cold, dead uniformity of servitude can prevent its happening) that the subordinate parts have many local privileges and immunities. Between these privileges, and the supreme common authority, the line may be extremely nice. Of course disputes, often too, very bitter disputes, and much ill blood, will arise. But though every privilege is an exemption (in the case) from the ordinary exercise of the supreme authority, it is no denial of it. The claim of a privilege seems rather, *ex vi termini*,[46] to imply a superior power. For to talk of the privileges of a State or of a person, who has no superior, is hardly any better than speaking nonsense. Now, in such unfortunate quarrels, among the component parts of a great political union of communities, I can scarcely conceive any thing more compleatly imprudent, than for the Head of the Empire to insist, that, if any privilege is pleaded against his will, or his acts, that his whole authority is denied; instantly to proclaim rebellion, to beat to arms, and to put the offending provinces under the ban. Will not this, Sir, very soon teach the provinces to make no distinctions on their part? Will it not teach them that the Government, against which a claim of Liberty is tantamont to high-treason, is a Government to which submission is equivalent to slavery? It may not always be quite convenient to impress dependent communities with such an idea.

We are, indeed, in all disputes with the Colonies, by the necessity

45 Notorious judge and attorney general (1552–1634), who displayed great rancor at the trial of Sir Walter Raleigh (1603).
46 "From the very meaning of the term."

of things, the judge. It is true, Sir. But, I confess, that the character of judge in my own cause, is a thing that frightens me. Instead of filling me with pride, I am exceedingly humbled by it. I cannot proceed with a stern, assured, judicial confidence, until I find myself in something more like a judicial character. I must have these hesitations as long as I am compelled to recollect, that, in my little reading upon such contests as these, the sense of mankind has, at least, as often decided against the superior as the subordinate power. Sir, let me add too, that the opinion of my having some abstract right in my favour, would not put me much at my ease in passing sentence; unless I could be sure, that there were no rights which, in their exercise under certain circumstances, were not the most odious of all wrongs, and the most vexatious of all injustice. Sir, these considerations have great weight with me, when I find things so circumstanced; that I see the same party, at once a civil litigant against me in a point of right; and a culprit before me, while I sit as a criminal judge, on acts of his, whose moral quality is to be decided upon the merits of that very litigation. Men are every now and then put, by the complexity of human affairs, into strange situations; but Justice is the same, let the Judge be in what situation he will.

There is, Sir, also a circumstance which convinces me, that this mode of criminal proceeding is not (at least in the present stage of our contest) altogether expedient; which is nothing less than the conduct of those very persons who have seemed to adopt that mode, by lately declaring a rebellion in Massachuset's Bay, as they had formerly addressed to have Traitors brought hither under an act of Henry the Eighth, for Trial.[47] For though rebellion is declared, it is not proceeded against as such; nor have any steps been taken towards the apprehension or conviction of any individual offender, either on our late or our former address; but modes of public coercion have been adopted, and such as have much more resemblance to a sort of qualified hostility towards an independant power than the punishment of rebellious subjects. All this seems rather inconsistent; but it shews how difficult it is to apply these juridical ideas to our present case.

In this situation, let us seriously and coolly ponder. What is it we have got by all our menaces, which have been many and ferocious?

---

[47] During the reign of Henry VIII, before the existence of the American colonies, an act was passed providing for the trial in England of treason committed outside the realm. In 1769 Parliament decided that this act should be applied to the colonies.

What advantage have we derived from the penal laws we have passed, and which, for the time, have been severe and numerous? What advances have we made towards our object, by the sending of a force, which, by land and sea, is no contemptible strength? Has the disorder abated? Nothing less.—When I see things in this situation, after such confident hopes, bold promises, and active exertions, I cannot, for my life, avoid a suspicion, that the plan itself is not correctly right.

If then the removal of the causes of this Spirit of American Liberty be, for the greater part, or rather entirely, impracticable; if the ideas of Criminal Process be inapplicable, or, if applicable, are in the highest degree inexpedient, what way yet remains? No way is open, but the third and last—to comply with the American Spirit as necessary; or, if you please, to submit to it, as a necessary Evil.

If we adopt this mode; if we mean to conciliate and concede; let us see of what nature the concession ought to be? To ascertain the nature of our concession, we must look at their complaint. The Colonies complain, that they have not the characteristic Mark and Seal of British Freedom. They complain, that they are taxed in a Parliament, in which they are not represented. If you mean to satisfy them at all, you must satisfy them with regard to this complaint. If you mean to please any people, you must give them the boon which they ask; not what you may think better for them, but of a kind totally different. Such an act may be a wise regulation, but it is no concession: whereas our present theme is the mode of giving satisfaction.

Sir, I think you must perceive, that I am resolved this day to have nothing at all to do with the question of the right of taxation. Some gentlemen startle—but it is true: I put it totally out of the question. It is less than nothing in my consideration. I do not indeed wonder, nor will you, Sir, that gentlemen of profound learning are fond of displaying it on this profound subject. But my consideration is narrow, confined, and wholly limited to the Policy of the question. I do not examine, whether the giving away a man's money be a power excepted and reserved out of the general trust of Government; and how far all mankind, in all forms of Polity, are intitled to an exercise of that Right by the Charter of Nature. Or whether, on the contrary, a Right of Taxation is necessarily involved in the general principle of Legislation, and inseparable from the ordinary Supreme Power? These are deep questions, where great names militate against each other; where reason is perplexed; and an appeal to authorities only thickens the confusion. For high and reverend authorities

No Abstract Liberty

lift up their heads on both sides; and there is no sure footing in the middle. This point is the *great Serbonian bog, betwixt Damiata and Mount Casius old, where armies whole have sunk.*[48] I do not intend to be overwhelmed in that bog, though in such respectable company. The question with me is, not whether you have a right to render your people miserable; but whether it is not your interest to make them happy? It is not, what a lawyer tells me, I *may* do; but what humanity, reason, and justice, tells me, I ought to do. Is a politic act the worse for being a generous one? Is no concession proper, but that which is made from your want of right to keep what you grant? Or does it lessen the grace or dignity of relaxing in the exercise of an odious claim, because you have your evidence-room full of Titles, and your magazines stuffed with arms to enforce them? What signify all those titles, and all those arms? Of what avail are they, when the reason of the thing tells me, that the assertion of my title is the loss of my suit; and that I could do nothing but wound myself by the use of my own weapons?

Such is stedfastly my opinion of the absolute necessity of keeping up the concord of this empire by a Unity of Spirit, though in a diversity of operations, that, if I were sure the Colonists had, at their leaving this country, sealed a regular compact of servitude; that they had solemnly abjured all the rights of citizens; that they had made a vow to renounce all Ideas of Liberty for them and their posterity, to all generations; yet I should hold myself obliged to conform to the temper I found universally prevalent in my own day, and to govern two million of men, impatient of Servitude, on the principles of Freedom. I am not determining a point of law; I am restoring tranquillity; and the general character and situation of a people must determine what sort of government is fitted for them. That point nothing else can or ought to determine.

My idea therefore, without considering whether we yield as matter of right, or grant as matter of favour, is *to admit the people of our Colonies into an interest in the constitution*; and, by recording that admission in the Journals of Parliament, to give them as strong an assurance as the nature of the thing will admit, that we mean for ever to adhere to that solemn declaration of systematic indulgence.

Some years ago, the repeal of a revenue act, upon its understood principle, might have served to shew, that we intended an unconditional abatement of the exercise of a Taxing Power. Such a measure was then

---

48 *Paradise Lost*, II. 592–94.

sufficient to remove all suspicion; and to give perfect content. But unfortunate events, since that time, may make something further necessary; and not more necessary for the satisfaction of the Colonies, than for the dignity and consistency of our own future proceedings.

I have taken a very incorrect measure of the disposition of the House, if this proposal in itself would be received with dislike. I think, Sir, we have few American Financiers. But our misfortune is, we are too acute; we are too exquisite[49] in our conjectures of the future, for men oppressed with such great and present evils. The more moderate among the opposers of Parliamentary Concession freely confess, that they hope no good from Taxation; but they apprehend the Colonists have further views; and if this point were conceded, they would instantly attack the Trade-laws. These Gentlemen are convinced, that this was the intention from the beginning; and the quarrel of the Americans with Taxation was no more than a cloke and cover to this design. Such has been the language even of a Gentleman of real moderation, and of a natural temper well adjusted to fair and equal Government.[50] I am, however, Sir, not a little surprized at this kind of discourse, whenever I hear it; and I am the more surprized, on account of the arguments which I constantly find in company with it, and which are often urged from the same mouths, and on the same day.

For instance, when we alledge, that it is against reason to tax a people under so many restraints in trade as the Americans, the Noble Lord in the blue ribband shall tell you, that the restraints on trade are futile and useless; of no advantage to us, and of no burthen to those on whom they are imposed; that the trade to America is not secured by the acts of navigation,[51] but by the natural and irresistible advantage of a commercial preference.

Such is the merit of the trade laws in this posture of the debate. But when strong internal circumstances are urged against the taxes; when the scheme is dissected; when experience and the nature of things are brought to prove, and do prove, the utter impossibility of obtaining an effective revenue from the Colonies; when these things are pressed, or rather press themselves, so as to drive the advocates of Colony taxes to a clear admission of the futility of the scheme; then, Sir, the sleeping

---

49 Apprehensive.
50 George Rice (1724–1779), a supporter of Lord North, one of many who suspected that America was seeking independence.
51 I.e., the many acts restricting the colonies' trade.

trade laws revive from their trance; and this useless taxation is to be kept sacred, not for its own sake, but as a counterguard and security of the laws of trade.

Then, Sir, you keep up revenue laws which are mischievous, in order to preserve trade laws that are useless. Such is the wisdom of our plan in both its members. They are separately given up as of no value; and yet one is always to be defended for the sake of the other. But I cannot agree with the Noble Lord, nor with the pamphlet from whence he seems to have borrowed these ideas, concerning the inutility of the trade laws. For without idolizing them, I am sure they are still, in many ways, of great use to us; and in former times, they have been of the greatest. They do confine, and they do greatly narrow, the market for the Americans. But my perfect conviction of this, does not help me in the least to discern how the revenue laws form any security whatsoever to the commercial regulations; or that these commercial regulations are the true ground of the quarrel; or, that the giving way in any one instance of authority, is to lose all that may remain unconceded.

One fact is clear and indisputable. The public and avowed origin of this quarrel, was on taxation. This quarrel has indeed brought on new disputes on new questions; but certainly the least bitter, and the fewest of all, on the trade laws. To judge which of the two be the real radical cause of quarrel, we have to see whether the commercial dispute did, in order of time, precede the dispute on taxation? There is not a shadow of evidence for it. Next, to enable us to judge whether at this moment a dislike to the Trade Laws be the real cause of quarrel, it is absolutely necessary to put the taxes out of the question by a repeal. See how the Americans act in this position, and then you will be able to discern correctly what is the true object of the controversy, or whether any controversy at all will remain? Unless you consent to remove this cause of difference, it is impossible, with decency, to assert that the dispute is not upon what it is avowed to be. And I would, Sir, recommend to your serious consideration, whether it be prudent to form a rule for punishing people, not on their own acts, but on your conjectures? Surely it is preposterous at the very best. It is not justifying your anger, by their misconduct; but it is converting your ill-will into their delinquency.

But the Colonies will go further.—Alas! alas! when will this speculating against fact and reason end? What will quiet these panick fears which we entertain of the hostile effect of a conciliatory conduct? Is it true, that no case can exist, in which it is proper for the sovereign to accede to the desires of his discontented subjects? Is there any thing peculiar in this case, to make a rule for itself? Is all authority of course lost, when it is not pushed to the extreme? Is it a certain maxim, that, the fewer causes of dissatisfaction are left by government, the more the subject will be inclined to resist and rebel?

All these objections being in fact no more than suspicions, conjectures, divinations; formed in defiance of fact and experience; they did not, Sir, discourage me from entertaining the idea of a conciliatory concession, founded on the principles which I have just stated.

In forming a plan for this purpose, I endeavoured to put myself in that frame of mind, which was the most natural, and the most reasonable; and which was certainly the most probable means of securing me from all error. I set out with a perfect distrust of my own abilities; a total renunciation of every speculation of my own; and with a profound reverence for the wisdom of our ancestors, who have left us the inheritance of so happy a constitution, and so flourishing an empire, and what is a thousand times more valuable, the treasury of the maxims and principles which formed the one, and obtained the other.

During the reigns of the kings of Spain of the Austrian family, whenever they were at a loss in the Spanish councils, it was common for their statesmen to say, that they ought to consult the genius of Philip the Second.[52] The genius of Philip the Second might mislead them; and the issue of their affairs shewed, that they had not chosen the most perfect standard. But, Sir, I am sure that I shall not be misled, when, in a case of constitutional difficulty, I consult the genius of the English constitution. Consulting at that oracle (it was with all due humility and piety) I found four capital examples in a similar case before me: those of Ireland, Wales, Chester, and Durham.

Ireland, before the English conquest, though never governed by a despotick power, had no Parliament. How far the English Parliament itself was at that time modelled according to the present form, is disputed among antiquarians. But we have all the reason in the world to be assured, that a form of Parliament, such as England then enjoyed, she instantly communicated to Ireland; and we are equally sure that almost every successive improvement in constitutional liberty, as fast as it was made here, was transmitted thither. The feudal Baronage, and the feudal Knighthood, the roots of our primitive constitution, were early transplanted into that soil; and grew and flourished there. Magna Charta, if it did not give

---

52 Philip II of Spain (1527–1598), although he was notoriously cruel, won many military successes.

us originally the House of Commons, gave us at least an House of Commons of weight and consequence. But your ancestors did not churlishly sit down alone to the feast of Magna Charta. Ireland was made immediately a partaker. This benefit of English laws and liberties, I confess, was not at first extended to *all* Ireland. Mark the consequence. English authority and English liberties, had exactly the same boundaries. Your standard could never be advanced an inch before your privileges. Sir John Davis[53] shews beyond a doubt, that the refusal of a general communication of these rights, was the true cause why Ireland was five hundred years in subduing; and after the vain projects of a Military Government, attempted in the reign of Queen Elizabeth, it was soon discovered, that nothing could make that country English, in civility[54] and allegiance, but your laws and your forms of legislature. It was not English arms, but the English constitution, that conquered Ireland. From that time, Ireland has ever had a general Parliament, as she had before a partial Parliament. You changed the people; you altered the religion; but you never touched the form or the vital substance of free government in that kingdom. You deposed kings; you restored them; you altered the succession to theirs, as well as to your own crown; but you never altered their constitution; the principle of which was respected by usurpation; restored with the restoration of Monarchy, and established, I trust, for ever, by the glorious Revolution. This has made Ireland the great and flourishing kingdom that it is; and from a disgrace and a burthen intolerable to this nation, has rendered her a principal part of our strength and ornament. This country cannot be said to have ever formally taxed her. The irregular things done in the confusion of mighty troubles, and on the hinge of great revolutions, even if all were done that is said to have been done, form no example. If they have any effect in argument, they make an exception to prove the rule. None of your own liberties could stand a moment, if the casual deviations from them, at such times, were suffered to be used as proofs of their nullity. By the lucrative amount of such casual breaches in the constitution, judge what the stated and fixed rule of supply has been in that Kingdom. Your Irish pensioners would starve, if they had no other fund to live on than taxes granted by English authority. Turn your eyes to those popular grants from whence all your

---

53 Sir John Davies (1569–1626), attorney general for Ireland and speaker of the first Irish House of Commons.
54 Civilization.

great supplies are come; and learn to respect that only source of publick wealth in the British empire.

My next example is Wales. This country was said to be reduced by Henry the Third.[55] It was said more truly to be so by Edward the First.[56] But though then conquered, it was not looked upon as any part of the realm of England. Its old constitution, whatever that might have been, was destroyed; and no good one was substituted in its place. The care of that tract was put into the hands of Lords Marchers[57]—a form of Government of a very singular kind; a strange heterogeneous monster, something between Hostility and Government; perhaps it has a sort of resemblance, according to the modes of those times, to that of commander in chief at present, to whom all civil power is granted as secondary. The manners of the Welsh nation, followed the Genius of the Government: The people were ferocious, restive, savage, and uncultivated; sometimes composed, never pacified. Wales within itself, was in perpetual disorder; and it kept the frontier of England in perpetual alarm. Benefits from it to the state, there were none. Wales was only known to England, by incursion and invasion.

Sir, during that state of things, Parliament was not idle. They attempted to subdue the fierce spirit of the Welsh by all sorts of rigorous laws. They prohibited by statute the sending all sorts of arms into Wales, as you prohibit by proclamation (with something more of doubt on the legality) the sending arms to America. They disarmed the Welsh by statute, as you attempted (but still with more question on the legality) to disarm New England by an instruction. They made an act to drag offenders from Wales into England for trial, as you have done (but with more hardship) with regard to America. By another act, where one of the parties was an Englishman, they ordained, that his trial should be always by English. They made acts to restrain trade, as you do; and they prevented the Welsh from the use of fairs and markets, as you do the Americans from fisheries and foreign ports. In short, when the statute-book was not quite so much swelled as it is now, you find no less than fifteen acts of penal regulation on the subject of Wales.

---

55 Henry III (1207–1272) conducted several campaigns against the Welsh, most successfully in 1245.

56 Eldest son of Henry III (1239–1307), who forced on the Welsh the English system of local government and finally defeated them.

57 Lords of the marches or frontiers, authorized by the early English kings to rule as much territory as they could seize and hold.

Here we rub our hands—A fine body of precedents for the authority of Parliament and the use of it!—I admit it fully; and pray add likewise to these precedents, that all the while, Wales rid[58] this kingdom like an *incubus*; that it was an unprofitable and oppressive burthen; and that an Englishman travelling in that country, could not go six yards from the high road without being murdered.

J The march of the human mind is slow. Sir, it was not, until after Two Hundred years, discovered, that by an eternal law, Providence had decreed vexation to violence; and poverty to rapine. Your ancestors did however at length open their eyes to the ill husbandry of injustice. They found that the tyranny of a free people could of all tyrannies the least be endured; and that laws made against an whole nation were not the most effectual methods for securing its obedience. Accordingly, in the Twenty-seventh year of Henry VIII.[59] the course was entirely altered. With a preamble stating the entire and perfect rights of the crown of England, it gave to the Welsh all the rights and privileges of English subjects. A political order was established; the military power gave way to the civil; the marches were turned into counties. But that a nation should have a right to English liberties, and yet no share at all in the fundamental security of these liberties, the grant of their own property, seemed a thing so incongruous; that Eight years after, that is, in the Thirty-fifth of that reign, a complete and not ill proportioned representation by counties and boroughs was bestowed upon Wales, by act of Parliament. From that moment, as by a charm, the tumults subsided; obedience was restored; peace, order, and civilization, followed in the train of liberty—When the day-star of the English constitution had arisen in their hearts, all was harmony within and without—

> *Simul alba nautis*
> *Stella refulsit,*
> *Defluit saxis agitatus humor:*
> *Concidunt venti, fugiúntque nubes:*
> *Et minax (quòd sic voluere) ponto*
> *Unda recumbit.*[60]

---

58 Rode. *Incubus* is a nightmare, an oppressive burden.
59 I.e., 1536.
60 "Their clear star shines for the sailors, the stormy seas flow back down the rocks, the winds subside, the clouds flee, and because they have so willed, the threatening wave falls to rest upon the deep" (Horace, *Odes*, I. xii. 27–32).

The very same year the county palatine of Chester[61] received the same relief from its oppressions, and the same remedy to its disorders. Before this time Chester was little less distempered than Wales. The inhabitants, without rights themselves, were the fittest to destroy the rights of others; and from thence Richard II. drew the standing army of Archers, with which for a time he oppressed England. The people of Chester applied to Parliament in a petition penned as I shall read to you:

> To the King our Sovereign Lord, in most humble wise shewn unto your Excellent Majesty, the inhabitants of your Grace's county palatine of Chester; That where the said county palatine of Chester is and hath been always hitherto exempt, excluded and separated out and from your high court of parliament, to have any knights and burgesses within the said court; by reason whereof the said inhabitants have hitherto sustained manifold disherisons, losses and damages, as well in their lands, goods, and bodies, as in the good, civil, and politick governance and maintenance of the commonwealth of their said country: (2.) And for as much as the said inhabitants have always hitherto been bound by the acts and statutes made and ordained by your said highness, and your most noble progenitors, by authority of the said court, as far forth as other counties, cities, and boroughs have been, that have had their knights and burgesses within your said court of parliament, and yet have had neither knight ne burgess there for the said county palatine; the said inhabitants, for lack thereof, have been oftentimes touched and grieved with acts and statutes made within the said court, as well derogatory unto the most antient jurisdictions, liberties, and privileges of your said county palatine, as prejudicial unto the common wealth, quietness, rest, and peace of your grace's most bounden subjects inhabiting within the same.

What did Parliament with this audacious address?—reject it as a libel? Treat it as an affront to government? Spurn it as a derogation from the rights of legislature? Did they toss it over the table? Did they burn it by the hands of the common hangman?—They took the petition of grievance, all rugged as it was, without softening or temperament, unpurged of the original bitterness and indignation of complaint; they made it the very preamble to their act of redress; and consecrated its principle to all ages in the sanctuary of legislation.

Here is my third example. It was attended with the success of the two former. Chester, civilized as well as Wales, has demonstrated that

---

61 A northern county of England, bounded on the northwest by the Irish Sea.

✓ [freedom and not servitude is the cure of anarchy; as religion, and not atheism, is the true remedy for superstition.) Sir, this pattern of Chester was followed in the reign of Charles II. with regard to the county palatine of Durham, which is my fourth example. This county had long lain out of the pale of free legislation. So scrupulously was the example of Chester followed, that the style of the preamble is nearly the same with that of the Chester act; and without affecting the abstract extent of the authority of Parliament, it recognizes the equity of not suffering any considerable district in which the British subjects may act as a body, to be taxed without their own voice in the grant.

Now if the doctrines of policy contained in these preambles, and the force of these examples in the acts of Parliament, avail any thing, what can be said against applying them with regard to America? Are not the people of America as much Englishmen as the Welsh? The preamble of the act of Henry VIII. says, the Welsh speak a language no way resembling that of his Majesty's English subjects. Are the Americans not as numerous? If we may trust the learned and accurate Judge Barrington's account of North Wales,[62] and take that as a standard to measure the rest, there is no comparison. The people cannot amount to above 200,000; not a tenth part of the number in the Colonies. Is America in rebellion? Wales was hardly ever free from it. Have you attempted to govern America by penal statutes? You made Fifteen for Wales. But your legislative authority is perfect with regard to America; was it less perfect in Wales, Chester, and Durham? But America is virtually represented. What! does the electric force of virtual representation more easily pass over the Atlantic, than pervade Wales, which lies in your neighbourhood; or than Chester and Durham surrounded by abundance of representation that is actual and palpable? But, Sir, your ancestors thought this sort of virtual representation, however ample, to be totally insufficient for the freedom of the inhabitants of territories that are so near, and comparatively so inconsiderable. How then can I think it sufficient for those which are infinitely greater, and infinitely more remote?

You will now, Sir, perhaps imagine, that I am on the point of proposing to you a scheme for a representation of the Colonies in Parliament. Perhaps I might be inclined to entertain some such thought; but

---

62 Daines Barrington (1727–1800), a lawyer, was justice of three Welsh counties. He wrote several papers on natural history, customs, and manners, many of which are collected in his *Miscellanies* (1781).

a great flood stops me in my course. *Opposuit natura*[63]—I cannot remove the eternal barriers of the creation. The thing in that mode, I do not know to be possible. [As I meddle with no theory, I do not absolutely assert the impracticability of such a representation.] But I do not see my way to it; and those who have been more confident, have not been more successful. However, the arm of public benevolence is not shortened; and there are often several means to the same end. What nature has disjoined in one way, wisdom may unite in another. When we cannot give the benefit as we would wish, let us not refuse it altogether. If we cannot give the principal, let us find a substitute. But how? Where? What substitute?

Fortunately I am not obliged for the ways and means of this substitute to tax my own unproductive invention. I am not even obliged to go to the rich treasury of the fertile framers of imaginary commonwealths; not to the Republick of Plato, not to the Utopia of More; not to the Oceana of Harrington.[64] It is before me—It is at my feet, *and the rude swain treads daily on it with his clouted shoon.*[65] I only wish you to recognize, for the theory, the ancient constitutional policy of this kingdom with regard to representation, as that policy has been declared in acts of parliament; and, as to the practice, to return to that mode which an uniform experience has marked out to you, as best; and in which you walked with security, advantage, and honour, until the year 1763.[66]

My resolutions therefore mean to establish the equity and justice of a taxation of America, by *grant*, and not by *imposition*. To mark the *legal competency* of the Colony assemblies for the support of their government in peace, and for public aids in time of war. To acknowledge that this legal competency has had *a dutiful and beneficial exercise*; and that experience has shewn the *benefit of their grants*, and the *futility of parliamentary taxation as a method of supply*.

These solid truths compose six fundamental propositions. There are three more resolutions corollary to these. If you admit the first set, you can hardly reject the others. But if you admit the first, I shall be far from

---

63 "Nature opposes it" (Juvenal, *Satires*, X. 152).
64 Accounts of ideal commonwealths from the fourth century B.C., the sixteenth century (*Utopia*, 1516), and the seventeenth century (*Oceana*, 1656, by James Harrington, 1611–1677).
65 John Milton, *Comus*, 634–35, slightly misquoted.
66 When George Grenville, then secretary of state for the northern department, abandoned the policy of "salutary neglect" and began restricting the colonies.

sollicitous whether you accept or refuse the last. I think these six massive pillars will be of strength sufficient to support the temple of British concord. I have no more doubt than I entertain of my existence, that, if you admitted these, you would command an immediate peace; and with but tolerable future management, a lasting obedience in America. I am not arrogant in this confident assurance. The propositions are all mere matters of fact; and if they are such facts as draw irresistible conclusions even in the stating, this is the power of truth, and not any management of mine.

Sir, I shall open the whole plan to you together, with such observations on the motions as may tend to illustrate them where they may want explanation. The first is a resolution—

> That the Colonies and Plantations of Great Britain in North America, consisting of Fourteen separate Governments, and containing Two Millions and upwards of free inhabitants, have not had the liberty and privilege of electing and sending any Knights and Burgesses, or others to represent them in the high Court of Parliament.

—This is a plain matter of fact, necessary to be laid down, and (excepting the description) it is laid down in the language of the constitution; it is taken nearly *verbatim* from acts of Parliament.

The second is like unto the first—

> That the said Colonies and Plantations have been liable to, and bounden by, several subsidies, payments, rates, and taxes, given and granted by Parliament, though the said Colonies and Plantations have not their Knights and Burgesses, in the said high Court of Parliament, of their own election, to represent the condition of their country; by lack whereof they have been oftentimes touched and grieved by subsidies given, granted, and assented to, in the said court, in a manner prejudicial to the common wealth, quietness, rest, and peace, of the subjects inhabiting within the same.

Is this description too hot, or too cold, too strong, or too weak? Does it arrogate too much to the supreme legislature? Does it lean too much to the claims of the people? If it runs into any of these errors, the fault is not mine. It is the language of your own ancient acts of Parliament. *Non meus hic sermo, sed quæ præcepit Ofellus, rusticus, abnormis sapiens.*[67]

---

[67] "Now this is no talk of mine, but is the teaching of Ofellus, a peasant, wise after a fashion of his own" (Horace, *Satires*, II. ii. 2–3).

It is the genuine produce of the ancient rustick, manly, home-bred sense of this country—I did not dare to rub off a particle of the venerable rust that rather adorns and preserves, than destroys the metal. It would be a profanation to touch with a tool the stones which construct the sacred altar of peace. I would not violate with modern polish the ingenuous and noble roughness of these truly constitutional materials. Above all things, I was resolved not to be guilty of tampering, the odious vice of restless and unstable minds. I put my foot in the tracks of our forefathers; where I can neither wander nor stumble. Determining to fix articles of peace, I was resolved to use nothing else than the form of sound words; to let others abound in their own sense; and carefully to abstain from all expressions of my own. What the law has said, I say. In all things else I am silent. I have no organ but for her words. This, if it be not ingenious, I am sure is safe.

There are indeed words expressive of grievance in this second resolution, which those who are resolved always to be in the right, will deny to contain matter of fact, as applied to the present case; although Parliament thought them true, with regard to the counties of Chester and Durham. They will deny that the Americans were ever "touched and grieved" with the taxes. If they consider nothing in taxes but their weight as pecuniary impositions, there might be some pretence for this denial. But men may be sorely touched and deeply grieved in their privileges, as well as in their purses. Men may lose little in property by the act which takes away all their freedom. When a man is robbed of a trifle on the highway, it is not the Two-pence lost that constitutes the capital outrage. This is not confined to privileges. Even ancient indulgences withdrawn, without offence on the part of those who enjoyed such favours, operate as grievances. But were the Americans then not touched and grieved by the taxes, in some measure, merely as taxes? If so, why were they almost all, either wholly repealed or exceedingly reduced? Were they not touched and grieved, even by the regulating Duties of the Sixth of George II?[68] Else why were the duties first reduced to one Third in 1764, and afterwards to a Third of that Third in the year 1766? Were they not touched and grieved by the Stamp Act? I shall say they were, until that tax is revived. Were they not touched and grieved by the duties of 1767, which were likewise repealed, and which, Lord

---

[68] I.e., the sixth act passed in the reign of George II.

Hillsborough[69] tells you (for the ministry) were laid contrary to the true principle of commerce? Is not the assurance given by that noble person to the Colonies of a resolution to lay no more taxes on them, an admission that taxes would touch and grieve them? Is not the resolution of the noble Lord in the blue ribband, now standing on your Journals, the strongest of all proofs that parliamentary subsidies really touched and grieved them? Else, why all these changes, modifications, repeals, assurances, and resolutions?

The next proposition is—

> That, from the distance of the said Colonies, and from other circumstances, no method hath hitherto been devised for procuring a representation in Parliament for the said Colonies.

This is an assertion of a fact. I go no further on the paper; though in my private judgement, an useful representation is impossible; I am sure it is not desired by them; nor ought it perhaps by us; but I abstain from opinions.

The fourth resolution is—

> That each of the said Colonies hath within itself a body, chosen in part, or in the whole, by the freemen, freeholders, or other free inhabitants thereof, commonly called the General Assembly, or General Court, with powers legally to raise, levy, and assess, according to the several usage of such Colonies, duties and taxes towards defraying all sorts of public services.

This competence in the Colony assemblies is certain. It is proved by the whole tenour of their acts of supply in all the assemblies, in which the constant style of granting is, "an aid to his Majesty"; and acts granting to the Crown have regularly for near a century passed the public offices without dispute. Those who have been pleased paradoxically to deny this right, holding that none but the British parliament can grant to the Crown, are wished to look to what is done, not only in the Colonies, but in Ireland, in one uniform unbroken tenour every session. Sir, I am surprized, that this doctrine should come from some of the law servants of the Crown. I say, that if the Crown could be responsible, his Majesty—

---

69 Wills Hill, Earl of Hillsborough (1718–1793), at this time colonial secretary. He had written to America an assurance that the ministry would levy no further taxes on the colonies and that it would remove the duties on glass, paper, and colors, as duties contrary to the true principles of commerce.

but certainly the ministers, and even these law officers themselves, through whose hands the acts pass, biennially in Ireland, or annually in the Colonies, are in an habitual course of committing impeachable offences. What habitual offenders have been all Presidents of the Council, all Secretaries of State, all First Lords of Trade, all Attornies and all Sollicitors General! However, they are safe; as no one impeaches them; and there is no ground of charge against them, except in their own unfounded theories.

The fifth resolution is also a resolution of fact—

> That the said General Assemblies, General Courts, or other bodies legally qualified as aforesaid, have at sundry times freely granted several large subsidies and public aids for his Majesty's service, according to their abilities, when required thereto by letter from one of his Majesty's principal Secretaries of State; and that their right to grant the same, and their chearfulness and sufficiency in the said grants, have been at sundry times acknowledged by Parliament.

To say nothing of their great expences in the Indian wars; and not to take their exertion in foreign ones, so high as the supplies in the year 1695; not to go back to their public contributions in the year 1710; I shall begin to travel only where the Journals give me light; resolving to deal in nothing but fact, authenticated by parliamentary record; and to build myself wholly on that solid basis.

On the 4th of April 1748, a Committee of this House came to the following Resolution:

> RESOLVED,
> That it is the opinion of this Committee, *that it is just and reasonable* that the several Provinces and Colonies of Massachuset's Bay, New Hampshire, Connecticut, and Rhode Island, be reimbursed the expences they have been at in taking and securing to the crown of Great Britain, the Island of Cape Breton, and its dependencies.

These expences were immense for such Colonies. They were above 200,000*l.* sterling; money first raised and advanced on their public credit.

On the 28th of January 1756, a message from the King came to us, to this effect—

> His Majesty, being sensible of the zeal and vigour with which his faithful subjects of certain Colonies in North America have exerted themselves in defence of His Majesty's just rights and possessions, recommends it to this

House to take the same into their consideration, and to enable His Majesty to give them such assistance as may be a *proper reward and encouragement.*

On the 3d of February 1756, the House came to a suitable resolution, expressed in words nearly the same as those of the message: but with the further addition, that the money then voted was as an *encouragement* to the Colonies to exert themselves with vigour. It will not be necessary to go through all the testimonies which your own records have given to the truth of my resolutions. I will only refer you to the places in the Journals:

Vol. XXVII.—16th and 19th May 1757.
Vol. XXVIII.—June 1st, 1758—April 26th and 30th, 1759—March 26th and 31st, and April 28th, 1760—Jan. 9th and 20th, 1761.
Vol. XXIX.—Jan. 22d and 26th, 1762—March 14th and 17th, 1763.

Sir, here is the repeated acknowledgement of Parliament, that the Colonies not only gave, but gave to satiety. This nation has formally acknowledged two things; first, that the Colonies had gone beyond their abilities, Parliament having thought it necessary to reimburse them; secondly, that they had acted legally and laudably in their grants of money, and their maintenance of troops, since the compensation is expressly given as reward and encouragement. Reward is not bestowed for acts that are unlawful; and encouragement is not held out to things that deserve reprehension. My resolution therefore does nothing more than collect into one proposition, what is scattered through your Journals. I give you nothing but your own; and you cannot refuse in the gross, what you have so often acknowledged in detail. The admission of this, which will be so honourable to them and to you, will, indeed, be mortal to all the miserable stories, by which the passions of the misguided people have been engaged in an unhappy system. The people heard, indeed, from the beginning of these disputes, one thing continually dinned in their ears, that reason and justice demanded, that the Americans, who paid no Taxes, should be compelled to contribute. How did that fact of their paying nothing, stand, when the Taxing System began? When Mr. Grenville[70] began to form his system of American Revenue, he stated in this House, that the Colonies were then in debt two millions six hundred thousand pounds sterling money; and was of opinion they

---

70 George Grenville (1712–1770). See note 66, above.

would discharge that debt in four years. On this state, those untaxed people were actually subject to the payment of taxes to the amount of six hundred and fifty thousand a year. In fact, however, Mr. Grenville was mistaken. The funds given for sinking the debt did not prove quite so ample as both the Colonies and he expected. The calculation was too sanguine: the reduction was not compleated till some years after, and at different times in different Colonies. However, the Taxes after the war, continued too great to bear any addition, with prudence or propriety; and when the burthens imposed in consequence of former requisitions were discharged, our tone became too high to resort again to requisition. No Colony since that time, ever has had any requisition whatsoever made to it.

We see the sense of the Crown, and the sense of Parliament, on the productive nature of a *Revenue by Grant*. Now search the same Journals for the produce of the *Revenue by Imposition*—Where is it?—let us know the volume and the page?—what is the gross, what is the nett produce?—to what service is it applied?—how have you appropriated its surplus?—What, can none of the many skilful Index-makers, that we are now employing, find any trace of it?—Well, let them and that rest together.—But are the Journals, which say nothing of the Revenue, as silent on the discontent?—Oh no! a child may find it. It is the melancholy burthen and blot of every page.

I think then I am, from those Journals, justified in the sixth and last resolution which is—

> That it hath been found by experience, that the manner of granting the said supplies and aids, by the said General Assemblies, hath been more agreeable to the said Colonies, and more beneficial, and conducive to the public service, than the mode of giving and granting aids in Parliament, to be raised and paid in the said Colonies.

This makes the whole of the fundamental part of the plan. The conclusion is irresistible. You cannot say, that you were driven by any necessity, to an exercise of the utmost Rights of Legislature. You cannot assert, that you took on yourselves the task of imposing Colony Taxes, from the want of another legal body, that is competent to the purpose of supplying the Exigencies of the State without wounding the prejudices of the people. Neither is it true that the body so qualified, and having that competence, had neglected the duty.

The question now, on all this accumulated matter, is;—whether

you will chuse to abide by a profitable experience, or a mischievous
theory; [whether you chuse to build on imagination or fact;] whether
you prefer enjoyment or hope; satisfaction in your subjects, or discontent?

If these propositions are accepted, every thing which has been
made to enforce a contrary system, must, I take it for granted, fall along
with it. On that ground, I have drawn the following resolution, which,
when it comes to be moved, will naturally be divided in a proper manner:

> That it may be proper to repeal an act, made in the seventh year of the
> reign of his present Majesty, intituled, An act for granting certain duties in
> the British Colonies and Plantations in America; for allowing a drawback
> of the duties of customs upon the exportation from this Kingdom, of coffee
> and cocoa-nuts of the produce of the said Colonies or Plantations; for
> discontinuing the drawbacks payable on China Earthen-ware exported to
> America; and for more effectually preventing the clandestine running
> of goods in the said Colonies and Plantations.—And that it may be proper
> to repeal an act, made in the fourteenth year of the reign of his present
> Majesty, intituled, An act to discontinue, in such manner, and for such
> time, as are therein mentioned, the landing and discharging, lading or
> shipping, of goods, wares, and merchandize, at the town and within the
> harbour of Boston, in the Province of Massachuset's Bay, in North Amer-
> ica.—And that it may be proper to repeal an act, made in the fourteenth
> year of the reign of his present Majesty, intituled, An act for the impartial
> administration of justice, in the cases of persons questioned for any acts
> done by them, in the execution of the law, or for the suppression of riots
> and tumults, in the province of Massachuset's Bay in New England—And
> that it may be proper to repeal an act, made in the fourteenth year of the
> reign of his present Majesty, intituled, An act for the better regulating the
> Government of the province of the Massachuset's Bay in New England.—
> And also that it may be proper to explain and amend an act, made in the
> thirty-fifth year of the reign of King Henry the Eighth, intituled, An act for
> the Trial of Treasons committed out of the King's Dominions.

I wish, Sir, to repeal the Boston Port Bill, because (independently
of the dangerous precedent of suspending the rights of the subject during
the King's pleasure) it was passed, as I apprehend, with less regularity, and
on more partial principles, than it ought. The corporation of Boston was
not heard, before it was condemned. Other towns, full as guilty as she
was, have not had their ports blocked up. Even the Restraining Bill of the
present Session does not go to the length of the Boston Port Act. The
same ideas of prudence, which induced you not to extend equal punish-

ment to equal guilt, even when you were punishing, induce me, who mean not to chastise, but to reconcile, to be satisfied with the punishment already partially inflicted.

Ideas of prudence, and accommodation to circumstances, prevent you from taking away the Charters of Connecticut and Rhode-island, as you have taken away that of Massachuset's Colony, though the Crown has far less power in the two former provinces that it enjoyed in the latter; and though the abuses have been full as great, and as flagrant, in the exempted as in the punished. The same reasons of prudence and accommodation have weight with me in restoring the Charter of Massachuset's Bay. Besides, Sir, the Act which changes the Charter of Massachuset's is in many particulars so exceptionable, that, if I did not wish absolutely to repeal, I would by all means desire to alter it; as several of its provisions tend to the subversion of all public and private justice. Such, among others, is the power in the Governor to change the sheriff at his pleasure; and to make a new returning officer for every special cause. It is shameful to behold such a regulation standing among English Laws.

The act for bringing persons accused of committing murder under the orders of Government to England for Trial, is but temporary. That act has calculated the probable duration of our quarrel with the Colonies; and is accommodated to that supposed duration. I would hasten the happy moment of reconciliation; and therefore must, on my principle, get rid of that most justly obnoxious act.

The act of Henry the Eighth, for the Trial of Treasons, I do not mean to take away, but to confine it to its proper bounds and original intention; to make it expressly for Trial of Treasons (and the greatest Treasons may be committed) in places where the jurisdiction of the Crown does not extend.

Having guarded the privileges of Local Legislature, I would next secure to the Colonies a fair and unbiassed Judicature; for which purpose, Sir, I propose the following resolution:

> That, from the time when the General Assembly or General Court of any Colony or Plantation in North America, shall have appointed by act of Assembly, duly confirmed, a settled salary to the offices of the Chief Justice and other Judges of the Superior Court, it may be proper, that the said Chief Justice and other Judges of the Superior Courts of such Colony, shall hold his and their office and offices during their good behaviour; and shall not be removed therefrom, but when the said removal shall be adjudged by his Majesty in Council, upon a hearing on complaint from the

General Assembly, or on a complaint from the Governor, or Council, or the House of Representatives severally, of the Colony in which the said Chief Justice and other Judges have exercised the said offices.

The next resolution relates to the Courts of Admiralty. It is this.

That it may be proper to regulate the Courts of Admiralty, or Vice Admiralty, authorized by the 15th Chap. of the 4th of George the Third, in such a manner as to make the same more commodious to those who sue, or are sued in the said Courts, and to provide for the more decent maintenance of the Judges in the same.

These Courts I do not wish to take away; they are in themselves proper establishments. This Court is one of the capital securities of the Act of Navigation. The extent of its jurisdiction, indeed, has been encreased; but this is altogether as proper, and is, indeed, on many accounts, more eligible, where new powers were wanted, than a Court absolutely new. But Courts incommodiously situated, in effect, deny justice; and a Court, partaking in the fruits of its own condemnation, is a robber. The congress complain, and complain justly, of this grievance.

These are the three consequential propositions. I have thought of two or three more; but they come rather too near detail, and to the province of executive Government, which I wish Parliament always to superintend, never to assume. If the first six are granted, congruity will carry the latter three. If not, the things that remain unrepealed, will be, I hope, rather unseemly incumbrances on the building, than very materially detrimental to its strength and stability.

Here, Sir, I should close; but that I plainly perceive some objections remain, which I ought, if possible, to remove. The first will be, that, in resorting to the doctrine of our ancestors, as contained in the preamble to the Chester act, I prove too much; that the grievance from a want of representation, stated in that preamble goes to the whole of Legislation as well as to Taxation. And that the Colonies grounding themselves upon that doctrine, will apply it to all parts of Legislative Authority.

To this objection, with all possible deference and humility, and wishing as little as any man living to impair the smallest particle of our supreme authority, I answer, that *the words are the words of Parliament, and not mine*; and, that all false and inconclusive inferences, drawn from them, are not mine; for I heartily disclaim any such inference. I have chosen the words of an act of Parliament, which Mr. Grenville, surely a tolerably zealous and very judicious advocate for the sovereignty of Parliament, formerly moved to have read at your table, in confirmation of his tenets. It is true that Lord Chatham[71] considered these preambles as declaring strongly in favour of his opinions. He was a no less powerful advocate for the privileges of the Americans. Ought I not from hence to presume, that these preambles are as favourable as possible to both, when properly understood; favourable both to the rights of Parliament, and to the privilege of the dependencies of this crown? But, Sir, the object of grievance in my resolution, I have not taken from the Chester, but from the Durham act, which confines the hardship of want of representation, to the case of subsidies; and which therefore falls in exactly with the case of the Colonies. But whether the unrepresented counties were *de jure*, or *de facto*,[72] bound, the preambles do not accurately distinguish; nor indeed was it necessary; for, whether *de jure*, or *de facto*, the Legislature thought the exercise of the power of taxing, as of right, or as of fact without right, equally a grievance and equally oppressive.

I do not know, that the Colonies have, in any general way, or in any cool hour, gone much beyond the demand of immunity in relation to taxes. It is not fair to judge of the temper or dispositions of any man, or any set of men, when they are composed and at rest, from their conduct, or their expressions, in a state of disturbance and irritation. It is besides a very great mistake to imagine, that mankind follow up practically, any speculative principle either of government, or of freedom, as far as it will go in argument and logical illation.[73] We Englishmen, stop very short of the principles upon which we support any given part of our constitution; or even the whole of it together. I could easily, if I had not already tired you, give you very striking and convincing instances of it. This is nothing but what is natural and proper. All government, indeed every human benefit and enjoyment, every virtue, and every prudent act, is founded on compromise and barter. We balance inconveniencies; we give and take; we remit some rights, that we may enjoy others; and, we chuse rather to be happy citizens, than subtle disputants. As we must give away some natural liberty, to enjoy civil advantages; so we must sacrifice some civil liberties, for the advantages to be derived from the communion and fellowship of a great empire. But

71 William Pitt, Earl of Chatham (1708–1778), urged conciliation of the colonies, then any policy short of granting independence.
72 "By right" or "by fact."
73 The action of drawing a conclusion from premises.

in all fair dealings the thing bought, must bear some proportion to the purchase paid. None will barter away the immediate jewel of his soul. Though a great house is apt to make slaves haughty, yet it is purchasing a part of the artificial importance of a great empire too dear, to pay for it all essential rights, and all the intrinsic dignity of human nature. None of us who would not risque his life, rather than fall under a government purely arbitrary. But, although there are some amongst us who think our constitution wants many improvements, to make it a complete system of liberty, perhaps none who are of that opinion, would think it right to aim at such improvement, by disturbing his country, and risquing every thing that is dear to him. In every arduous enterprize, we consider what we are to lose, as well as what we are to gain; and the more and better stake of liberty every people possess, the less they will hazard in a vain attempt to make it more. These are *the cords of man*.[74] Man acts from adequate motives relative to his interest; and not on metaphysical speculations. Aristotle, the great master of reasoning, cautions us, and with great weight and propriety, against this species of delusive geometrical accuracy in moral arguments, as the most fallacious of all sophistry.

The Americans will have no interest contrary to the grandeur and glory of England, when they are not oppressed by the weight of it; and they will rather be inclined to respect the acts of a superintending legislature; when they see them the acts of that power, which is itself the security, not the rival, of their secondary importance. In this assurance, my mind most perfectly acquiesces; and I confess, I feel not the least alarm, from the discontents which are to arise, from putting people at their ease; nor do I apprehend the destruction of this empire, from giving, by an act of free grace and indulgence, to two millions of my fellow citizens, some share of those rights, upon which I have always been taught to value myself.

It is said indeed, that this power of granting vested in American assemblies, would dissolve the unity of the empire; which was preserved, entire, although Wales, and Chester, and Durham, were added to it. Truly, Mr. Speaker, I do not know what this unity means; nor has it ever been heard of, that I know, in the constitutional policy of this country. The very idea of subordination of parts, excludes this notion of simple and undivided unity. England is the head; but she is not the head and the members too. Ireland has ever had from the beginning a separate,

---

74 Hosea 6: 4.

but not an independent, legislature; which, far from distracting, promoted the union of the whole. Every thing was sweetly and harmoniously disposed through both Islands for the conservation of English dominion, and the communication of English liberties. I do not see that the same principles might not be carried into twenty Islands, and with the same good effect. This is my model with regard to America, as far as the internal circumstances of the two countries are the same. I know no other unity of this empire, than I can draw from its example during these periods, when it seemed to my poor understanding more united than it is now, or than it is likely to be by the present methods.

But since I speak of these methods, I recollect, Mr. Speaker, almost too late, that I promised, before I finished, to say something of the proposition of the Noble Lord on the floor, which has been so lately received, and stands on your Journals. I must be deeply concerned, whenever it is my misfortune to continue a difference with the majority of this house. But as the reasons for that difference are my apology for thus troubling you, suffer me to state them in a very few words. I shall compress them into as small a body as I possibly can, having already debated that matter at large, when the question was before the committee.

First, then, I cannot admit that proposition of a ransom by auction;—because it is a meer project. It is a thing new; unheard of; supported by no experience; justified by no analogy; without example of our ancestors, or root in the constitution. It is neither regular parliamentary taxation, nor Colony grant. *Experimentum in corpore vili*,[75] is a good rule, which will ever make me adverse to any trial of experiments on what is certainly the most valuable of all subjects; the peace of this Empire.

Secondly, it is an experiment which must be fatal in the end to our constitution. For what is it but a scheme for taxing the Colonies in the antichamber of the Noble Lord and his successors? To settle the quotas and proportions in this house, is clearly impossible. You, Sir, may flatter yourself, you shall sit a state auctioneer with your hammer in our hand, and knock down to each Colony as it bids. But to settle (on the plan laid down by the Noble Lord) the true proportional payment for four or five and twenty governments, according to the absolute and the relative wealth of each, and according to the British proportion of wealth and burthen, is a wild and chimerical notion. This new taxation must therefore come in by the back-door of the constitution. Each quota

---

75 "Experiment on a worthless object."

must be brought to this House ready formed; you can neither add nor alter. You must register it. You can do nothing further. For on what grounds can you deliberate either before or after the proposition? You cannot hear the counsel for all these Provinces, quarrelling each on its own quantity of payment, and its proportion to others. If you should attempt it, the Committee of Provincial Ways and Means, or by whatever other name it will delight to be called, must swallow up all the time of Parliament.

Thirdly, it does not give satisfaction to the complaint of the Colonies They complain, that they are taxed without their consent; you answer, that you will fix the sum at which they shall be taxed. That is, you give them the very grievance for the remedy. You tell them indeed, that you will leave the mode to themselves. I really beg pardon: it gives me pain to mention it; but you must be sensible that you will not perform this part of the compact. For, suppose the Colonies were to lay the duties which furnished their Contingent, upon the importation of your manufactures; you know you would never suffer such a tax to be laid. You know too, that you would not suffer many other modes of taxation. So that, when you come to explain yourself, it will be found, that you will neither leave to themselves the quantum nor the mode; nor indeed any thing. The whole is delusion from one end to the other.

Fourthly, this method of ransom by auction, unless it be *universally* accepted, will plunge you into great and inextricable difficulties. In what year of our Lord are the proportions of payments to be settled? To say nothing of the impossibility that Colony agents should have general powers of taxing the Colonies at their discretion; consider, I implore you, that the communication by special messages, and orders between these agents and their constituents on each variation of the case, when the parties come to contend together, and to dispute on their relative proportions, will be a matter of delay, perplexity, and confusion, that never can have an end.

If all the Colonies do not appear at the outcry, what is the condition of those assemblies, who offer, by themselves or their agents, to tax themselves up to your ideas of their proportion? The refractory Colonies, who refuse all composition,[76] will remain taxed only to your old impositions; which, however grievous in principle, are trifling as to production. The obedient Colonies in this scheme are heavily taxed; the refractory

---

76 Compromise, agreement.

remain unburthened. What will you do? Will you lay new and heavier taxes by Parliament on the disobedient? Pray consider in what way you can do it? You are perfectly convinced that in the way of taxing, you can do nothing but at the ports. Now suppose it is Virginia that refuses to appear at your auction, while Maryland and North Carolina bid handsomely for their ransom, and are taxed to your quota? How will you put these Colonies on a par? Will you tax the tobacco of Virginia? If you do, you give its death-wound to your English revenue at home, and to one of the very greatest articles of your own foreign trade. If you tax the import of that rebellious Colony, what do you tax but your own manufactures, or the goods of some other obedient, and already well-taxed Colony? Who has said one word on this labyrinth of detail, which bewilders you more and more as you enter into it? Who has presented, who can present you, with a clue, to lead you out of it? I think Sir, it is impossible, that you should not recollect that the Colony bounds are so implicated in one another (you know it by your other experiments in the Bill for prohibiting the New-England fishery) that you can lay no possible restraints on almost any of them which may not be presently eluded, if you do not confound the innocent with the guilty, and burthen those whom upon every principle, you ought to exonerate. He must be grosly ignorant of America, who thinks, that, without falling into this confusion of all rules of equity and policy, you can restrain any single Colony, especially Virginia and Maryland, the central, and most important of them all.

Let it also be considered, that, either in the present confusion you settle a permanent contingent, which will and must be trifling; and then you have no effectual revenue: or you change the quota at every exigency; and then on every new repartition you will have a new quarrel.

Reflect besides, that when you have fixed a quota for every Colony, you have not provided for prompt and punctual payment. Suppose one, two, five, ten years arrears. You cannot issue a treasury extent[77] against the failing Colony. You must make new Boston port bills, new restraining laws, new Acts for dragging men to England for trial. You must send out new fleets, new armies. All is to begin again. From this day forward the Empire is never to know an hour's tranquillity. An intestine fire will be kept alive in the bowels of the Colonies, which one time or other must consume this whole empire. I allow indeed that the empire of Germany

---

77 A writ issued against the body, land, and goods of a Crown debtor.

raises her revenue and her troops by quotas and contingents; but the revenue of the empire, and the army of the empire, is the worst revenue, and the worst army, in the world.

Instead of a standing revenue, you will therefore have a perpetual quarrel. Indeed the noble Lord, who proposed this project of a ransom by auction, seemed himself to be of that opinion. His project was rather designed for breaking the union of the Colonies, than for establishing a Revenue. He confessed, he apprehended that his proposal would not be to *their taste*. I say, this scheme of disunion seems to be at the bottom of the project; for I will not suspect that the noble Lord meant nothing but merely to delude the nation by an airy phantom which he never intended to realize. But whatever his views may be; as I propose the peace and union of the Colonies as the very foundation of my plan, it cannot accord with one whose foundation is perpetual discord.

Compare the two. This I offer to give you is plain and simple. The other full of perplexed and intricate mazes. This is mild; that harsh. This is found by experience effectual for its purposes; the other is a new project. This is universal; the other calculated for certain Colonies only. This is immediate in its conciliatory operation; the other remote, contingent, full of hazard. Mine is what becomes the dignity of a ruling people; gratuitous, unconditional, and not held out as matter of bargain and sale. I have done my duty in proposing it to you. I have indeed tired you by a long discourse; but this is the misfortune of those to whose influence nothing will be conceded, and who must win every inch of their ground by argument. You have heard me with goodness. May you decide with wisdom! For my part, I feel my mind greatly disburthened, by what I have done to-day. I have been the less fearful of trying your patience, because on this subject I mean to spare it altogether in future. I have this comfort, that in every stage of the American affairs, I have steadily opposed the measures that have produced the confusion, and may bring on the destruction, of this empire. I now go so far as to risque a proposal of my own. If I cannot give peace to my country; I give it to my conscience.

But what (says the Financier) is peace to us without money? Your plan gives us no Revenue. No! But it does—For it secures to the subject the power of REFUSAL; the first of all Revenues. Experience is a cheat, and fact a liar, if this power in the subject of proportioning his grant, or of not granting at all, has not been found the richest mine of Revenue ever discovered by the skill or by the fortune of man. It does not indeed vote you £152,750 : 11 : 2¾ths. nor any other paltry limited sum.—But it gives the strong box itself, the fund, the bank, from whence only revenues can arise amongst a people sensible of freedom: *Posita luditur arca.*[78] Cannot you in England; cannot you at this time of day; cannot you, an House of Commons, trust to the principle which has raised so mighty a revenue, and accumulated a debt of near 140 millions in this country? Is this principle to be true in England, and false every where else? Is it not true in Ireland? Has it not hitherto been true in the Colonies? Why should you presume that, in any country, a body duly constituted for any function, will neglect to perform its duty, and abdicate its trust? Such a presumption would go against all government in all modes. But, in truth, this dread of penury of supply, from a free assembly, has no foundation in nature. For first observe, that, besides the desire which all men have naturally of supporting the honour of their own government; that sense of dignity, and that security to property, which ever attends freedom, has a tendency to increase the stock of the free community. Most may be taken where most is accumulated. And what is the soil or climate where experience has not uniformly proved, that the voluntary flow of heaped-up plenty, bursting from the weight of its own rich luxuriance, has ever run with a more copious stream of revenue, than could be squeezed from the dry husks of oppressed indigence, by the straining of all the politick machinery in the world.

Next we know, that parties must ever exist in a free country. We know too, that the emulations of such parties, their contradictions, their reciprocal necessities, their hopes, and their fears, must send them all in their turns to him that holds the balance of the state. The parties are the Gamesters; but Government keeps the table, and is sure to be the winner in the end. When this game is played, I really think it is more to be feared, that the people will be exhausted, than that Government will not be supplied. Whereas, whatever is got by acts of absolute power ill obeyed, because odious, or by contracts ill kept, because constrained; will be narrow, feeble, uncertain, and precarious. *"Ease would retract vows made in pain, as violent and void."*[79]

I, for one, protest against compounding our demands: I declare against compounding, for a poor limited sum, the immense, ever-growing, eternal Debt, which is due to generous Government from

---

78 "The treasure chest itself is staked on the game" (Juvenal, *Satires*, I. 90).
79 *Paradise Lost*, IV. 96–97, slightly altered.

protected Freedom. And so may I speed in the great object I propose to
you, as I think it would not only be an act of injustice, but would be the
worst œconomy in the world, to compel the Colonies to a sum certain,
either in the way of ransom, or in the way of compulsory compact.

But to clear up my ideas on this subject—a revenue from America
transmitted hither—do not delude yourselves—you never can receive
it—No, not a shilling. We have experience that from remote countries
it is not to be expected. If, when you attempted to extract revenue from
Bengal, you were obliged to return in loan what you had taken in imposition; what can you expect from North America? for certainly, if ever
there was a country qualified to produce wealth, it is India; or an institution fit for the transmission, it is the East-India company. America has
none of these aptitudes. If America gives you taxable objects, on which
you lay your duties here, and gives you, at the same time, a surplus by
a foreign sale of her commodities to pay the duties on these objects which
you tax at home, she has performed her part to the British revenue. But
with regard to her own internal establishments; she may, I doubt not she
will, contribute in moderation. I say in moderation; for she ought not to
be permitted to exhaust herself. She ought to be reserved to a war; the
weight of which, with the enemies that we are most likely to have, must
be considerable in her quarter of the globe. There she may serve you,
and serve you essentially.

For that service, for all service, whether of revenue, trade, or
empire, my trust is in her interest in the British constitution. My hold of
the Colonies is in the close affection which grows from common names,
from kindred blood, from similar privileges, and equal protection. These
are ties, which, though light as air, are as strong as links of iron. Let the
Colonies always keep the idea of their civil rights associated with your
Government;—they will cling and grapple to you; and no force under
heaven will be of power to tear them from their allegiance. But let it be
once understood, that your Government may be one thing, and their
Privileges another; that these two things may exist without any mutual
relation; the cement is gone; the cohesion is loosened; and every thing
hastens to decay and dissolution. As long as you have the wisdom to keep
the sovereign authority of this country as the sanctuary of liberty, the
sacred temple consecrated to our common faith, wherever the chosen
race and sons of England worship freedom, they will turn their faces
towards you. The more they multiply, the more friends you will have;
the more ardently they love liberty, the more perfect will be their obedi-

ence. Slavery they can have any where. It is a weed that grows in every soil. They may have it from Spain, they may have it from Prussia. But until you become lost to all feeling of your true interest and your natural dignity, freedom they can have from none but you. This is the commodity of price, of which you have the monopoly. This is the true act of navigation, which binds to you the commerce of the Colonies, and through them secures to you the wealth of the world. Deny them this participation of freedom, and you break that sole bond, which originally made, and must still preserve, the unity of the empire. Do not entertain so weak an imagination, as that your registers and your bonds, your affidavits and your sufferances, your cockets and your clearances,[80] are what form the great securities of your commerce. Do not dream that your letters of office, and your instructions, and your suspending clauses, are the things that hold together the great contexture of this mysterious whole. These things do not make your government. Dead instruments, passive tools as they are, it is the spirit of English communion that gives all their life and efficacy to them. It is the spirit of the English constitution, which, infused through the mighty mass, pervades, feeds, unites, invigorates, vivifies, every part of the empire, even down to the minutest member.

Is it not the same virtue which does every thing for us here in England? Do you imagine then, that it is the land tax act which raises your revenue? that it is the annual vote in the committee of supply, which gives you your army? or that it is the Mutiny Bill which inspires it with bravery and discipline? No! surely no! It is the love of the people; it is their attachment to their government from the sense of the deep stake they have in such a glorious institution, which gives you your army and your navy, and infuses into both that liberal obedience, without which your army would be a base rabble, and your navy nothing but rotten timber.

All this, I know well enough, will sound wild and chimerical to the profane herd of those vulgar and mechanical politicians, who have no place among us; a sort of people who think that nothing exists but what is gross and material; and who therefore, far from being qualified to be directors of the great movement of empire, are not fit to turn a wheel in the machine. But to men truly initiated and rightly taught, these ruling and master principles, which, in the opinion of such men as I have

---

80 "Cockets" are receipts for payment of duties; "clearances" are sailing papers granted to merchantmen; "sufferances" (above) are permits for the shipment of dutiable goods.

mentioned, have no substantial existence, are in truth every thing, and all in all. Magnanimity in politicks is not seldom the truest wisdom; and a great empire and little minds go ill together. If we are conscious of our situation, and glow with zeal to fill our place as becomes our station and ourselves, we ought to auspicate[81] all our public proceedings on America, with the old warning of the church, *Sursum corda!*[82] We ought to elevate our minds to the greatness of that trust to which the order of Providence has called us. By adverting to the dignity of this high calling, our ancestors have turned a savage wilderness into a glorious empire; and have made the most extensive, and the only honourable conquests; not by destroying, but by promoting, the wealth, the number, the happiness, of the human race. Let us get an American revenue as we have got an American empire. English privileges h ve made it all that it is; English privileges alone will make it all it can be. In full confidence of this unalterable truth, I now (*quod felix faustumque sit*)[83]—lay the first stone of the Temple of Peace; and I move you,

> That the Colonies and Plantations of Great Britain in North America, consisting of Fourteen separate governments, and containing Two Millions and upwards of free inhabitants, have not had the liberty and privilege of electing and sending any Knights and Burgesses, or others, to represent them in the high Court of Parliament.

Upon this Resolution, the previous question was put, and carried;—for the previous question 270,—against it 78.

As the Propositions were opened separately in the body of the Speech, the Reader perhaps may wish to see the whole of them together, in the form in which they were moved for.[84]

MOVED,
That the Colonies and Plantations of Great-Britain in North-America, consisting of Fourteen separate Governments, and containing two Millions and upwards of Free Inhabitants, have not had the liberty and privilege of electing and sending any Knights and Burgesses, or others, to represent them in the High Court of Parliament.

---

81 Favorably introduce.
82 "Let us lift up our heart" (Lamentations 3: 41, in the Vulgate).
83 "And may the outcome be happy and successful!" (Old Roman invocation.)
84 This is Burke's summary; it appears in the printed but of course not the spoken form of the speech. His motions were all defeated; by an amendment from the floor, the words in italics in the second proposition were left out when it came to a vote.

That the said Colonies and Plantations have been made liable to, and bounden by, several subsidies, payments, rates, and taxes, given and granted by Parliament; though the said Colonies and Plantations have not their Knights and Burgesses, in the said High Court of Parliament, of their own election, to represent the condition of their country; *by lack whereof, they have been often times touched and grieved by subsidies given, granted, and assented to, in the said Court, in a manner prejudicial to the common wealth, quietness, rest, and peace, of the subjects inhabiting within the same.*

That, from the distance of the said Colonies, and from other circumstances, no method hath hitherto been devised for procuring a Representation in Parliament for the said Colonies.

That each of the said Colonies hath within itself a Body, chosen, in part or in the whole, by the Freemen, Freeholders, or other Free Inhabitants thereof, commonly called the General Assembly, or General Court; with powers legally to raise, levy, and assess, according to the several usage of such Colonies, duties and taxes towards defraying all sorts of public services.

That the said General Assemblies, General Courts, or other bodies, legally qualified as aforesaid, have at sundry times freely granted several large subsidies and public aids for his Majesty's service, according to their abilities, when required thereto by letter from one of his Majesty's Principal Secretaries of State; and that their right to grant the same, and their chearfulness and sufficiency in the said grants, have been at sundry times acknowledged by Parliament.

That it hath been found by experience, that the manner of granting the said supplies and aids, by the said General Assemblies, hath been more agreeable to the inhabitants of the said Colonies, and more beneficial and conducive to the public service, than the mode of giving and granting aids and subsidies in Parliament to be raised and paid in the said Colonies.

That it may be proper to repeal an act made in the 7th year of the reign of his present Majesty, intituled, An Act for granting certain duties in the British Colonies and Plantations in America; for allowing a draw-back of the duties of Customs, upon the exportation from this kingdom, of coffee and cocoa-nuts, of the produce of the said Colonies or Plantations; for discontinuing the draw-backs payable on china earthen ware exported to America; and for more effectually preventing the clandestine running of goods in the said Colonies and Plantations.

That it may be proper to repeal an Act, made in the 14th year of the reign of his present Majesty, intituled, An Act to discontinue, in such manner, and for such time, as are therein mentioned, the landing and discharging, lading or shipping of goods, wares, and merchandize, at the Town, and within the Harbour, of Boston, in the province of Massachuset's Bay, in North America.

That it may be proper to repeal an Act made in the 14th year of the reign of his present Majesty, intituled, An Act for the impartial administration of justice, in cases of persons questioned for any acts done by them in the execution of the law, or for the suppression of riots and tumults, in the province of Massachuset's Bay in New England.

That it is proper to repeal an Act, made in the 14th year of the reign of his present Majesty, intituled, An Act for the better regulating the government of the province of the Massachuset's Bay in New England.

That it is proper to explain and amend an Act made in the 35th year of the reign of King Henry VIII, intituled, An Act for the trial of treasons committed out of the King's dominions.

That, from the time when the General Assembly, or General Court, of any Colony or Plantation, in North America, shall have appointed, by act of Assembly duly confirmed, a settled salary to the offices of the Chief Justice and Judges of the superior courts, it may be proper that the said Chief Justice and other Judges of the superior courts of such Colony shall hold his and their office and offices during their good behaviour; and shall not be removed therefrom, but when the said removal shall be adjudged by his Majesty in Council, upon a hearing on complaint from the General Assembly, or on a complaint from the Governor, or Council, or the house of representatives, severally, of the Colony in which the said Chief Justice and other Judges have exercised the said office.

That it may be proper to regulate the Courts of Admiralty, or Vice-admiralty, authorized by the 15th chapter of the 4th of George III, in such a manner, as to make the same more commodious to those who sue, or are sued, in the said courts; *and to provide for the more decent maintenance of the Judges of the same.*

REFLECTIONS
ON THE REVOLUTION IN FRANCE[1]

(1790)

In the 1770's Burke had understood and sympathized with the cause of the
American colonists; in the 1780's he had to come to terms with a revolution in
France. The principles supporting this revolution, he believed, were sinister. In
Reflections on the Revolution in France (1790) he expounded his most fundamental
political beliefs, revealing his faith in the British Constitution and his horror at
the anarchy displayed by the French revolutionists and implicit in their theory.
He rests his case on facts, on the reports of eyewitnesses, and on the evidence of
history; he concludes that no one aware of the facts could approve a theory that
produced such chaos and destruction. Again, experience is for him the ultimate
test. The power of his abstract philosophic statement derives from its basis on
a vivid sense of reality, made compelling for his readers on every page.

The immediate pretext for the *Reflections* was a sermon given by Richard
Price to the Society for Commemorating the Revolution in Great Britain. Price
insisted on analogies between the French Revolution and the English Revolution
of 1688; Burke begins his argument by examining and refuting these analogies.
Then, in the selection here reprinted, he investigates the rights of kings and of
people, expounds the nature of liberty, and looks at the French legislative system.
He offers a detailed comparison of the English and French Constitutions before
turning to specific criticism of the acts of the French National Assembly; finally
he declares his own disinterestedness, his devotion to the cause of liberty, and his
belief—implicit throughout his work—that the British Constitution offers the
best possible model to nations desiring to improve their government.

The present text is from Edumnd Burke, *Reflections on the Revolution in
France*, ed. William B. Todd (New York: Holt, Rinehart, and Winston, 1959).
Used by permission.

---

[1] See Introduction, pp. 12–15.

Reflections
on the Revolution in France

Kings, in one sense, are undoubtedly the servants of the people, because their power has no other rational end than that of the general advantage; but it is not true that they are, in the ordinary sense (by our constitution, at least) any thing like servants; the essence of whose situation is to obey the commands of some other, and to be removeable at pleasure. But the king of Great Britain obeys no other person; all other persons are individually, and collectively too, under him, and owe to him a legal obedience. The law, which knows neither to flatter nor to insult, calls this high magistrate, not our servant, as this humble Divine[2] calls him, but *"our sovereign Lord the King"*; and we, on our parts, have learned to speak only the primitive language of the law, and not the confused jargon of their Babylonian pulpits.

As he is not to obey us, but as we are to obey the law in him, our constitution has made no sort of provision towards rendering him, as a servant, in any degree responsible. Our constitution knows nothing of a magistrate like the *Justicia* of Arragon[3]; nor of any court legally appointed, nor of any process legally settled for submitting the king to the responsibility belonging to all servants. In this he is not distinguished from the commons and the lords; who, in their several public capacities, can never be called to an account for their conduct; although the Revolution Society[4] chooses to assert, in direct opposition to one of the wisest and most beautiful parts of our constitution, that "a king is no more than the first servant of the public, created by it, *and responsible to it.*"

Ill would our ancestors at the Revolution have deserved their fame

---

2 On November 4, 1789, at the meeting house in the Old Jewry, Richard Price, dissenting minister and philosopher (1723–1791), delivered to the Society for Commemorating the Revolution in Great Britain "A Discourse on the Love of Our Country," to which Burke here alludes.

3 The chief magistrate of Spanish Aragon, who had enormous power and was independent of the king.

4 A society which met every November 4 to celebrate the anniversary of the landing in England of William of Orange in the "bloodless revolution" of 1688, by which James II was deposed. This society maintained that the principles of the French Revolution were the fulfillment of those of the English Revolution of 1688.

for wisdom, if they had found no security for their freedom, but in rendering their government feeble in its operations, and precarious in its tenure; if they had been able to contrive no better remedy against arbitrary power than civil confusion. Let these gentlemen state who that *representative* public is to whom they will affirm the king, as a servant, to be responsible. It will be then time enough for me to produce to them the positive statute law which affirms that he is not.

The ceremony of cashiering kings, of which these gentlemen talk so much at their ease, can rarely, if ever, be performed without force. It then becomes a case of war, and not of constitution. Laws are commanded to hold their tongues amongst arms; and tribunals fall to the ground with the peace they are no longer able to uphold. The Revolution of 1688 was obtained by a just war, in the only case in which any war, and much more a civil war, can be just. "Justa bella quibus *necessaria*."[5] The question of dethroning, or, if these gentlemen like the phrase better, "cashiering kings," will always be, as it has always been, an extraordinary question of state, and wholly out of the law; a question (like all other questions of state) of dispositions, and of means, and of probable consequences, rather than of positive rights. As it was not made for common abuses, so it is not to be agitated by common minds. The speculative line of demarcation, where obedience ought to end, and resistance must begin, is faint, obscure, and not easily definable. It is not a single act, or a single event, which determines it. Governments must be abused and deranged indeed, before it can be thought of; and the prospect of the future must be as bad as the experience of the past. When things are in that lamentable condition, the nature of the disease is to indicate the remedy to those whom nature has qualified to administer in extremities this critical, ambiguous, bitter portion to a distempered state. Times and occasions, and provocations, will teach their own lessons. The wise will determine from the gravity of the case; the irritable from sensibility to oppression; the high-minded from disdain and indignation at abusive power in unworthy hands; the brave and bold from the love of honourable danger in a generous cause: but, with or without right, a revolution will be the very last resource of the thinking and the good.

The third head of right, asserted by the pulpit of the Old Jewry, namely, the "right to form a government for ourselves," has, at least, as little countenance from any thing done at the Revolution, either in

5 Loosely, "the only just war is a necessary war."

precedent or principle, as the two first of their claims. The Revolution
was made to preserve our *antient* indisputable laws and liberties, and that
antient constitution of government which is our only security for law
and liberty. If you are desirous of knowing the spirit of our constitution,
and the policy which predominated in that great period which has secured
it to this hour, pray look for both in our histories, in our records, in
our acts of parliament, and journals of parliament, and not in the sermons
of the Old Jewry, and the after-dinner toasts of the Revolution Society.—
In the former you will find other ideas and another language. Such a
claim is as ill-suited to our temper and wishes as it is unsupported by any
appearance of authority. The very idea of the fabrication of a new
government, is enough to fill us with disgust and horror. We wished at
the period of the Revolution, and do now wish, to derive all we possess as
an inheritance from our forefathers. Upon that body and stock of inheritance
we have taken care not to inoculate any cyon alien to the nature of the
original plant. [All the reformations we have hitherto made, have proceeded upon the principle of reference to antiquity; and I hope, nay I am
persuaded, that all those which possibly may be made hereafter, will be
carefully formed upon analogical precedent, authority, and example.]

   Our oldest reformation is that of Magna Charta. You will see that
Sir Edward Coke, that great oracle of our law, and indeed all the great
men who follow him, to Blackstone,[6] are industrious to prove the pedigree of our liberties. They endeavour to prove, that the antient charter,
the Magna Charta of King John, was connected with another positive
charter from Henry I. and that both the one and the other were nothing
more than a re-affirmance of the still more antient standing law of the
kingdom. [In the matter of fact, for the greater part, these authors appear
to be in the right; perhaps not always: but if the lawyers mistake in some
particulars, it proves my position still the more strongly; because it
demonstrates the powerful prepossession towards antiquity, with which
the minds of all our lawyers and legislators, and of all the people whom
they wish to influence, have been always filled; and the stationary policy
of this kingdom in considering their most sacred rights and franchises as
an *inheritance.*

------

   6 Sir Edward Coke (1552–1634) was a great authority on English law, author of *Coke
Upon Littleton*, the first part of the *Institutes of the Laws of England*. Sir William Blackstone
(1723–1780), a celebrated jurist, published *Commentaries on the Laws of England*. Burke's own
footnote reads, "See Blackstone's Magna Charta, printed at Oxford, 1759."

In the famous law of the 3d of Charles I. called the *Petition of Right*,[7] the parliament says to the king, "Your subjects have *inherited* this freedom," claiming their franchises not on abstract principles "as the rights of men," but as the rights of Englishmen, and as a patrimony derived from their forefathers. Selden,[8] and the other profoundly learned men, who drew this petition of right, were as well acquainted, at least, with all the general theories concerning the "rights of men," as any of the discoursers in our pulpits, or on your tribune;[9] full as well as Dr. Price, or as the Abbé Sieyes.[10] But, for reasons worthy of that practical wisdom which superseded their theoretic science, they preferred this positive, recorded, *hereditary* title to all which can be dear to the man and the citizen, to that vague speculative right, which exposed their sure inheritance to be scrambled for and torn to pieces by every wild litigious spirit.

The same policy pervades all the laws which have since been made for the preservation of our liberties. In the 1st of William and Mary, in the famous statute, called the Declaration of Right,[11] the two houses utter not a syllable of "a right to frame a government for themselves." You will see, that their whole care was to secure the religion, laws, and liberties, that had been long possessed, and had been lately endangered. "Taking into their most serious consideration the *best* means for making such an establishment, that their religion, laws, and liberties, might not be in danger of being again subverted," they auspicate all their proceedings, by stating as some of those *best* means, "in the *first place*" to do "as their *ancestors in like case have usually* done for vindicating their *antient* rights and liberties, to *declare*";—and then they pray the king and queen, "that it may be *declared* and enacted, that *all and singular* the rights and liberties *asserted and declared* are the true *antient* and indubitable rights and liberties of the people of this kingdom."

---

7 A demand by Parliament to Charles I (May 28, 1628) for the rights of subjects. It provided that no freeman should be taxed without an act of Parliament, that no freeman should be imprisoned contrary to the laws of the land, that soldiers and sailors should not be billeted in private houses, and that commissions for punishment by martial law should be revoked.

8 John Selden (1584–1654), English jurist, helped in the formulation of the bill to secure the liberties of the subject that Burke refers to as the petition of right.

9 In the sense of "rostrum" or "pulpit."

10 Richard Price (see note 2, above) supported the cause of American liberty; Emmanuel Joseph, Comte Sieyès, called Abbé Sieyès (1748–1836), French politician, was an eminent supporter of the French Revolution.

11 A recapitulation of the grievances of Parliament against the government of James II, later reformulated as the Bill of Rights.

You will observe, that from Magna Charta to the Declaration of Right, it has been the uniform policy of our constitution to claim and assert our liberties, as an *entailed inheritance* derived to us from our fore-fathers, and to be transmitted to our posterity; as an estate specially belonging to the people of this kingdom without any reference whatever to any other more general or prior right. By this means our constitution preserves an unity in so great a diversity of its parts. We have an inherit-able crown; an inheritable peerage; and an house of commons and a people inheriting privileges, franchises, and liberties, from a long line of ancestors.

This policy appears to me to be the result of profound reflection; or rather the happy effect of following nature, which is wisdom without reflection, and above it. A spirit of innovation is generally the result of a selfish temper and confined views. People will not look forward to posterity, who never look backward to their ancestors. Besides, the people of England well know, that the idea of inheritance furnishes a sure prin-ciple of conservation, and a sure principle of transmission; without at all excluding a principle of improvement. It leaves acquisition free; but it secures what it acquires. Whatever advantages are obtained by a state proceeding on these maxims, are locked fast as in a sort of family settle-ment; grasped as in a kind of mortmain for ever. By a constitutional policy, working after the pattern of nature, we receive, we hold, we transmit our government and our privileges, in the same manner in which we enjoy and transmit our property and our lives. The institutions of policy, the goods of fortune, the gifts of Providence, are handed down, to us and from us, in the same course and order. Our political system is placed in a just correspondence and symmetry with the order of the world, and with the mode of existence decreed to a permanent body composed of transitory parts; wherein, by the disposition of a stupendous wisdom, moulding together the great mysterious incorporation of the human race, the whole, at one time, is never old, or middle-aged, or young, but in a condition of unchangeable constancy, moves on through the varied tenour of perpetual decay, fall, renovation, and progression. Thus, by preserving the method of nature in the conduct of the state, in what we improve we are never wholly new; in what we retain we are never wholly obsolete. By adhering in this manner and on those principles to our forefathers, we are guided not by the superstition of antiquarians, but by the spirit of philosophic analogy. In this choice of inheritance we have given to our frame of polity the image of a relation in blood; binding up the constitution of our country with our dearest domestic ties; adopting our fundamental laws into the bosom of our family affections; keeping inseparable, and cherishing with the warmth of all their combined and mutually reflected charities, our state, our hearths, our sepulchres, and our altars.

Through the same plan of a conformity to nature in our artificial institutions, and by calling in the aid of her unerring and powerful instincts, to fortify the fallible and feeble contrivances of our reason, we have derived several other, and those no small benefits, from considering our liberties in the light of an inheritance. Always acting as if in the presence of canonized forefathers, the spirit of freedom, leading in itself to misrule and excess, is tempered with an awful gravity. This idea of a liberal descent inspires us with a sense of habitual native dignity, which prevents that upstart insolence almost inevitably adhering to and disgracing those who are the first acquirers of any distinction. By this means our liberty becomes a noble freedom. It carries an imposing and majestic aspect. It has a pedigree and illustrating ancestors. It has its bearings and its ensigns armorial. It has its gallery of portraits; its monumental inscriptions; its records, evidences, and titles. We procure reverence to our civil institutions on the principle upon which nature teaches us to revere individual men; on account of their age; and on account of those from whom they are descended. All your sophisters cannot produce any thing better adapted to preserve a rational and manly freedom than the course that we have pursued, who have chosen our nature rather than our speculations, our breasts rather than our inventions, for the great conservatories and magazines of our rights and privileges.

You might, if you pleased, have profited of our example, and have given to your recovered freedom a correspondent dignity. Your privileges, though discontinued, were not lost to memory. Your constitution, it is true, whilst you were out of possession, suffered waste and dilapidation; but you possessed in some parts the walls, and in all the foundations of a noble and venerable castle. You might have repaired those walls; you might have built on those old foundations. Your constitution was suspended before it was perfected; but you had the elements of a constitution very nearly as good as could be wished. In your old states you possessed that variety of parts corresponding with the various descriptions of which your community was happily composed; you had all that combination, and all that opposition of interests, you had that action and counteraction which, in the natural and in the political world, from the reciprocal struggle of discordant powers, draws out the harmony of the universe. These opposed and conflicting interests, which you considered as so great a blemish in your old and in our present constitution, interpose a salutary check to all precipitate resolutions; They render deliberations a matter not of choice, but of necessity; they make all change a subject of *compromise*, which naturally begets moderation; they produce *temperaments*,[12] preventing the sore evil of harsh, crude, unqualified reformations; and rendering all the headlong exertions of arbitrary power, in the few or in the many, for ever impracticable. Through that diversity of members and interests, general liberty had as many securities as there were separate views in the several orders; whilst by pressing down the whole by the weight of a real monarchy, the separate parts would have been prevented from warping and starting from their allotted places.

You had all these advantages in your antient states; but you chose to act as if you had never been moulded into civil society, and had every thing to begin anew. You began ill, because you began by despising every thing that belonged to you. You set up your trade without a capital. If the last generations of your country appeared without much lustre in your eyes, you might have passed them by, and derived your claims from a more early race of ancestors. Under a pious predilection for those ancestors, your imaginations would have realized in them a standard of virtue and wisdom, beyond the vulgar practice of the hour: and you would have risen with the example to whose imitation you aspired. Respecting your forefathers, you would have been taught to respect yourselves. You would not have chosen to consider the French as a people of yesterday, as a nation of low-born servile wretches until the emancipating year of 1789. In order to furnish, at the expence of your honour, an excuse to your apologists here for several enormities of yours, you would not have been content to be represented as a gang of Maroon[13] slaves, suddenly broke loose from the house of bondage, and therefore to be pardoned for your abuse of the liberty to which you were not accustomed and ill fitted. Would it not, my worthy friend,[14] have been wiser to have you thought, what I, for one, always thought you, a generous and gallant nation, long misled to your disadvantage by your high

---

12 Mixtures (where one element is qualified by another).

13 Fugitive slaves. The word is said to be a corruption of Spanish *cimarron*, "wild" or "untamed."

14 Pierre-Gaëton Dupont, the "gentleman in Paris" to whom Burke addressed the *Reflections*.

and romantic sentiments of fidelity, honour, and loyalty; that events had
been unfavourable to you, but that you were not enslaved through any
illiberal or servile disposition; that in your most devoted submission,
you were actuated by a principle of public spirit, and that it was your
country you worshipped, in the person of your king? Had you made it to
be understood, that in the delusion of this amiable error you had gone
further than your wise ancestors; that you were resolved to resume your
ancient privileges, whilst you preserved the spirit of your ancient and
your recent loyalty and honour; or, if diffident of yourselves, and not
clearly discerning the almost obliterated constitution of your ancestors,
you had looked to your neighbours in this land, who had kept alive the
ancient principles and models of the old common law of Europe melio-
rated and adapted to its present state—by following wise examples you
would have given new examples of wisdom to the world. You would
have rendered the cause of liberty venerable in the eyes of every worthy
mind in every nation. You would have shamed despotism from the earth,
by shewing that freedom was not only reconcileable, but as, when well
disciplined it is, auxiliary to law. You would have had an unoppressive
but a productive revenue. You would have had a flourishing commerce
to feed it. You would have had a free constitution; a potent monarchy;
a disciplined army; a reformed and venerated clergy; a mitigated but
spirited nobility, to lead your virtue, not to overlay it; you would have
had a liberal order of commons, to emulate and to recruit that nobility;
you would have had a protected, satisfied, laborious, and obedient people,
taught to seek and to recognize the happiness that is to be found by virtue
in all conditions; in which consists the true moral equality of mankind,
and not in that monstrous fiction,[15] which, by inspiring false ideas and
vain expectations into men destined to travel in the obscure walk of
laborious life, serves only to aggravate and imbitter that real inequality,
which it never can remove; and which the order of civil life establishes
as much for the benefit of those whom it must leave in an humble state,
as those whom it is able to exalt to a condition more splendid, but not
more happy. You had a smooth and easy career of felicity and glory laid
open to you, beyond any thing recorded in the history of the world;
but you have shewn that difficulty is good for man.

Compute your gains: see what is got by those extravagant and
presumptuous speculations which have taught your leaders to despise

---

15 That all men are equal.

all their predecessors, and all their contemporaries, and even to despise themselves, until the moment in which they became truly despicable. By following those false lights, France has bought undignified calamities at a higher price than any nation has purchased the most unequivocal blessings! France has bought poverty by crime! France has not sacrificed her virtue to her interest; but she has abandoned her interest, that she might prostitute her virtue. All other nations have begun the fabric of a new government, or the reformation of an old, by establishing originally, or by enforcing with greater exactness some rites or other of religion. All other people have laid the foundations of civil freedom in severer manners, and a system of a more austere and masculine morality. France, when she let loose the reins of regal authority, doubled the licence, of a ferocious dissoluteness in manners, and of an insolent irreligion in opinions and practices; and has extended through all ranks of life, as if she were communicating some privilege, or laying open some secluded benefit, all the unhappy corruptions that usually were the disease of wealth and power. This is one of the new principles of equality in France.

France, by the perfidy of her leaders, has utterly disgraced the tone of lenient[16] council in the cabinets of princes, and disarmed it of its most potent topics. She has sanctified the dark suspicious maxims of tyrannous distrust; and taught kings to tremble at (what will hereafter be called) the delusive plausibilities, of moral politicians. Sovereigns will consider those who advise them to place an unlimited confidence in their people, as subverters of their thrones; as traitors who aim at their destruction, by leading their easy good-nature, under specious pretences, to admit combinations of bold and faithless men into a participation of their power. This alone (if there were nothing else) is an irreparable calamity to you and to mankind. Remember that your parliament of Paris told your king, that in calling the states together, he had nothing to fear but the prodigal excess of their zeal in providing for the support of the throne. It is right that these men should hide their heads. It is right that they should bear their part in the ruin which their counsel has brought on their sovereign and their country. Such sanguine declarations tend to lull authority asleep; to encourage it rashly to engage in perilous adventures of untried policy; to neglect those provisions, preparations, and precautions, which distinguish benevolence from imbecillity; and without which no man can answer for the salutary effect of any abstract

---

16 Tolerant, soothing.

plan of government or of freedom. For want of these, they have seen the medicine of the state corrupted into its poison. They have seen the French rebel against a mild and lawful monarch, with more fury, outrage, and insult, than ever any people has been known to rise against the most illegal usurper, or the most sanguinary tyrant. Their resistance was made to concession; their revolt was from protection; their blow was aimed at an hand holding out graces, favours, and immunities.

This was unnatural. The rest is in order. They have found their punishment in their success. Laws overturned; tribunals subverted; industry without vigour; commerce expiring; the revenue unpaid, yet the people impoverished; a church pillaged, and a state not relieved; civil and military anarchy made the constitution of the kingdom; every thing human and divine sacrificed to the idol of public credit, and national bankruptcy the consequence; and to crown all, the paper securities of new, precarious, tottering power, the discredited paper securities[17] of impoverished fraud, and beggared rapine, held out as a currency for the support of an empire, in lieu of the two great recognized species[18] that represent the lasting conventional credit of mankind, which disappeared and hid themselves in the earth from whence they came, when the principle of property, whose creatures and representatives they are, was systematically subverted.

Were all these dreadful things necessary? were they the inevitable results of the desperate struggle of determined patriots, compelled to wade through blood and tumult, to the quiet shore of a tranquil and prosperous liberty? No! nothing like it. The fresh ruins of France, which shock our feelings wherever we can turn our eyes, are not the devastation of civil war; they are the sad but instructive monuments of rash and ignorant counsel in time of profound peace. They are the display of inconsiderate and presumptuous, because unresisted and irresistible authority. The persons who have thus squandered away the precious treasure of their crimes, the persons who have made this prodigal and wild waste of public evils (the last stake reserved for the ultimate ransom of the state) have met in their progress with little, or rather with no opposition at all. Their whole march was more like a triumphal procession

---

17 The *assignats*, notes issued on the security of church and crown lands which the government had seized and sold. The notes soon depreciated in value, mainly because too many were issued.

18 Coinages: i.e., gold and silver. Many people buried or hid their gold and valuables as disorder increased.

than the progress of a war. Their pioneers have gone before them, and demolished and laid every thing level at their feet. Not one drop of *their* blood have they shed in the cause of the country they have ruined. They have made no sacrifices to their projects of greater consequence than their shoe-buckles, whilst they were imprisoning their king, murdering their fellow citizens, and bathing in tears, and plunging in poverty and distress, thousands of worthy men and worthy families. Their cruelty has not even been the base result of fear. It has been the effect of their sense of perfect safety, in authorizing treasons, robberies, rapes, assassinations, slaughters, and burnings throughout their harrassed land. But the cause of all was plain from the beginning.

This unforced choice, this fond election of evil, would appear perfectly unaccountable, if we did not consider the composition of the National Assembly; I do not mean its formal constitution, which, as it now stands, is exceptionable enough, but the materials of which in a great measure it is composed, which is of ten thousand times greater consequence than all the formalities in the world. If we were to know nothing of this Assembly but by its title and function, no colours could paint to the imagination any thing more venerable. In that light the mind of an enquirer, subdued by such an awful image as that of the virtue and wisdom of a whole people collected into a focus, would pause and hesitate in condemning things even of the very worst aspect. Instead of blameable, they would appear only mysterious. But no name, no power, no function, no artificial institution whatsoever, can make the men of whom any system of authority is composed, any other than God, and nature, and education, and their habits of life have made them. Capacities beyond these the people have not to give. Virtue and wisdom may be the objects of their choice; but their choice confers neither the one nor the other on those upon whom they lay their ordaining hands. They have not the engagement of nature, they have not the promise of revelation for any such powers.

After I had read over the list of the persons and descriptions elected into the *Tiers Etat*,[19] nothing which they afterwards did could appear astonishing. Among them, indeed, I saw some of known rank; some of shining talents; but of any practical experience in the state, not one man was to be found. The best were only men of theory. But whatever the

---

19 The "third estate," representatives of the common people. The National Assembly, as Burke later explains, consisted of 300 nobles, 300 clergymen, and 600 from the third estate.

distinguished few may have been, it is the substance and mass of the body which constitutes its character, and must finally determine its direction. In all bodies, those who will lead, must also, in a considerable degree, follow. They must conform their propositions to the taste, talent, and disposition of those whom they wish to conduct: therefore, if an Assembly is viciously or feebly composed in a very great part of it, nothing but such a supreme degree of virtue as very rarely appears in the world, and for that reason cannot enter into calculation, will prevent the men of talents disseminated through it from becoming only the expert instruments of absurd projects! If what is the more likely event, instead of that unusual degree of virtue, they should be actuated by sinister ambition and a lust of meretricious glory, then the feeble part of the Assembly, to whom at first they conform, becomes in its turn the dupe and instrument of their designs. In this political traffick the leaders will be obliged to bow to the ignorance of their followers, and the followers to become subservient to the worst designs of their leaders.

To secure any degree of sobriety in the propositions made by the leaders in any public assembly, they ought to respect, in some degree perhaps to fear, those whom they conduct. To be led any otherwise than blindly, the followers must be qualified, if not for actors, at least for judges; they must also be judges of natural weight and authority. Nothing can secure a steady and moderate conduct in such assemblies, but that the body of them should be respectably composed, in point of condition in life, of permanent property, of education, and of such habits as enlarge and liberalize the understanding.

In the calling of the states general of France, the first thing which struck me, was a great departure from the antient course. I found the representation for the Third Estate composed of six hundred persons. They were equal in number to the representatives of both the other orders. If the orders were to act separately, the number would not, beyond the consideration of the expence, be of much moment. But when it became apparent that the three orders were to be melted down into one, the policy and necessary effect of this numerous representation became obvious. A very small desertion from either of the other two orders must throw the power of both into the hands of the third. In fact, the whole power of the state was soon resolved into that body. Its due composition became therefore of infinitely the greater importance.

Judge, sir, of my surprize, when I found that a very great proportion of the Assembly (a majority, I believe, of the members who attended)

was composed of practitioners in the law. It was composed not of distinguished magistrates, who had given pledges to their country of their
science, prudence, and integrity; not of leading advocates, the glory of
the bar; not of renowned professors in universities;—but for the far
greater part, as it must in such a number, of the inferior, unlearned,
mechanical, merely instrumental members of the profession. There were
distinguished exceptions; but the general composition was of obscure
provincial advocates, of stewards of petty local jurisdictions, country
attornies, notaries, and the whole train of the ministers of municipal
litigation, the fomentors and conductors of the petty war of village vexation. From the moment I read the list I saw distinctly, and very nearly as
it has happened, all that was to follow.

The degree of estimation in which any profession is held becomes
the standard of the estimation in which the professors hold themselves.
Whatever the personal merits of many individual lawyers might have
been, and in many it was undoubtedly very considerable, in that military
kingdom, no part of the profession had been much regarded, except the
highest of all, who often united to their professional offices great family
splendour, and were invested with great power and authority. These
certainly were highly respected, and even with no small degree of awe.
The next rank was not much esteemed; the mechanical part was in a
very low degree of repute.

Whenever the supreme authority is invested in a body so composed,
it must evidently produce the consequences of supreme authority placed
in the hands of men not taught habitually to respect themselves; who had
no previous fortune in character at stake; who could not be expected to
bear with moderation, or to conduct with discretion, a power which they
themselves, more than any others, must be surprized to find in their
hands. Who could flatter himself that these men, suddenly, and, as it
were, by enchantment, snatched from the humblest rank of subordination, would not be intoxicated with their unprepared greatness? Who
could conceive, that men who are habitually meddling, daring, subtle,
active, of litigious dispositions and unquiet minds, would easily fall
back into their old condition of obscure contention, and laborious, low,
unprofitable chicane? Who could doubt but that, at any expence to the
state, of which they understood nothing, they must pursue their private
interests, which they understood but too well? It was not an event depending on chance or contingency. It was inevitable; it was necessary;
it was planted in the nature of things. They must *join* (if their capacity did

not permit them to *lead*) in any project which could procure to them a *litigious constitution;* which could lay open to them those innumerable lucrative jobs which follow in the train of all great convulsions and revolutions in the state, and particularly in all great and violent permutations of property. Was it to be expected that they would attend to the stability of property, whose existence had always depended upon whatever rendered property questionable, ambiguous, and insecure? Their objects would be enlarged with their elevation, but their disposition and habits, and mode of accomplishing their designs, must remain the same.

Well! but these men were to be tempered and restrained by other descriptions, of more sober minds, and more enlarged understandings. Were they then to be awed by the super-eminent authority and awful dignity of an handful of country clowns who have seats in that Assembly, some of whom are said not to be able to read and write? and by not a greater number of traders, who, though somewhat more instructed, and more conspicuous in the order of society, had never known any thing beyond their counting-house? No! both these descriptions were more formed to be overborne and swayed by the intrigues and artifices of lawyers, than to become their counterpoise. With such a dangerous disproportion, the whole must needs be governed by them. To the faculty of law was joined a pretty considerable proportion of the faculty of medicine. This faculty had not, any more than that of the law, possessed in France its just estimation. Its professors therefore must have the qualities of men not habituated to sentiments of dignity. But supposing they had ranked as they ought to do, and as with us they do actually, the sides of sick beds are not the academies for forming statesmen and legislators. Then came the dealers in stocks and funds, who must be eager, at any expence, to change their ideal paper wealth for the more solid substance of land. To these were joined men of other descriptions, from whom as little knowledge of or attention to the interests of a great state was to be expected, and as little regard to the stability of any institution; men formed to be instruments, not controls. Such in general was the composition of the *Tiers Etat* in the National Assembly; in which was scarcely to be perceived the slightest traces of what we call the natural landed interest of the country.

We know that the British house of commons, without shutting its doors to any merit in any class, is by the sure operation of adequate causes, filled with every thing illustrious in rank, in descent, in hereditary and in acquired opulence, in cultivated talents, in military, civil, naval, and politic distinction, that the country can afford. But supposing, what hardly can be supposed as a case, that the house of commons should be composed in the same manner with the Tiers Etat in France, would this dominion of chicane be borne with patience, or even conceived without horror? God forbid I should insinuate any thing derogatory to that profession, which is another priesthood, administering the rites of sacred justice. But whilst I revere men in the functions which belong to them, and would do, as much as one man can do, to prevent their exclusion from any, I cannot, to flatter them, give the lye to nature. They are good and useful in the composition; they must be mischievous if they preponderate so as virtually to become the whole. Their very excellence in their peculiar functions may be far from a qualification for others. It cannot escape observation, that when men are too much confined to professional and faculty habits, and as it were, inveterate in the recurrent employment of that narrow circle, they are rather disabled than qualified for whatever depends on the knowledge of mankind, on experience in mixed affairs, on a comprehensive connected view of the various complicated external and internal interests which go to the formation of that multifarious thing called a state.

After all, if the house of commons were to have an wholly professional and faculty composition, what is the power of the house of commons, circumscribed and shut in by the immoveable barriers of laws, usages, positive rules of doctrine and practice, counterpoized by the house of lords, and every moment of its existence at the discretion of the crown to continue, prorogue, or dissolve us? The power of the house of commons, direct or indirect, is indeed great; and long may it be able to preserve its greatness, and the spirit belonging to true greatness, at the full; and it will do so, as long as it can keep the breakers of law in India from becoming the makers of law for England. The power, however, of the house of commons, when least diminished, is as a drop of water in the ocean, compared to that residing in a settled majority of your National Assembly. That Assembly, since the destruction of the orders, has no fundamental law, no strict convention, no respected usage to restrain it. Instead of finding themselves obliged to conform to a fixed constitution, they have a power to make a constitution which shall conform to their designs. Nothing in heaven or upon earth can serve as a control on them. What ought to be the heads, the hearts, the dispositions, that are qualified, or that dare, not only to make laws under a fixed constitution, but at one heat to strike out a totally new constitution for a great kingdom, and in every part of it, from the monarch on the throne to the vestry of a parish? But—"*fools rush in where angels fear to tread.*"[20] In such a state of unbounded power, for undefined and undefinable purposes, the evil of a moral and almost physical inaptitude of the man to the function must be the greatest we can conceive to happen in the management of human affairs. . . .

---

20 Alexander Pope, *Essay on Criticism*, 625.

LETTER TO A NOBLE LORD[1]

In 1794 Burke retired from the House of Commons; his interest now focused on his son, Richard, who in July 1794, was also elected to the House. The next month Richard died of tuberculosis, and his father never recovered from the blow. He believed that Richard's life had been sacrificed to him; the youth had devoted himself to an attempt to straighten out his father's finances. Moreover, Edmund Burke was in acute financial distress. William Pitt, the prime minister, promised him that a grateful country would provide security for his old age; on the strength of these promises Burke in 1794 borrowed £4,500 from his friend William Wentworth, Earl Fitzwilliam (1748–1833). In late August 1794, the King granted Burke a Civil List pension of £1,200 a year; a larger annuity was to follow by Parliamentary grant. Burke's enemies filled Parliament, however, and Pitt decided not to ask for a further pension. Finally, in 1795, the Crown granted two further annuities totaling £2,500. Burke, hurt by the failure of Parliament to provide for him, was forced by his debts to accept the Crown pension. On November 13, 1795, the Duke of Bedford and the Earl of Lauderdale implied in the House of Lords that Burke had been bought by the Crown and that he had betrayed his own principles. *Letter to a Noble Lord* (1796) is his reply to their attack.

Although Burke refers to himself in the *Letter* as a "desolate old man," the work throbs with energy; it is perhaps his most forceful piece of rhetoric. After the opening sections, here reprinted, Burke continues to review his contributions to the welfare of his country, declaring once more his fundamental commitment to liberty and to order. His defence against a personal attack becomes a declaration of principle as he rebukes the Duke of Bedford for the venality and corruption of his own family and demonstrates the weakness and dangers of the principles of the French Revolution.

The present text is that of *A Letter from the Right Honourable Edmund Burke to A Noble Lord* (London, 1796).

---

1 See Introduction, pp. 14–16.

Letter to a Noble Lord

(1796)

My Lord,[2]

I could hardly flatter myself with the hope, that so very early in the season I should have to acknowledge obligations to the Duke of Bedford and to the Earl of Lauderdale. These noble persons have lost no time in conferring upon me, that sort of honour, which it is alone within their competence, and which it is certainly most congenial to their nature and their manners to bestow.

To be ill spoken of, in whatever language they speak, by the zealots of the new sect in philosophy and politicks, of which these noble persons think so charitably, and of which others think so justly, to me, is no matter of uneasiness or surprise. To have incurred the displeasure of the Duke of Orleans[3] or the Duke of Bedford, to fall under the censure of Citizen Brissot[4] or of his friend the Earl of Lauderdale, I ought to consider as proofs, not the least satisfactory, that I have produced some part of the effect I proposed by my endeavours.[5] I have laboured hard to earn, what the noble Lords are generous enough to pay. Personal offence I have given them none. The part they take against me is from zeal to the cause. It is well! It is perfectly well! I have to do homage to their justice. I have to thank the Bedfords and the Lauderdales for having so faithfully and so fully acquitted towards me whatever arrear of debt was left undischarged by the Priestleys and the Paines.[6]

---

2 This letter is addressed to William Wentworth, Earl Fitzwilliam, who had loaned Burke money on the expectation that he would receive a pension. On November 13, 1795, after Burke had been awarded his pension, the Duke of Bedford and the Earl of Lauderdale implied in the House of Lords that Burke had been bought by the Crown and had betrayed his own policy of public economy. Since he had borrowed money on his expectations, Burke could not refuse the pension, but he refuted his attackers in this letter.

3 Louis Philippe Joseph, Duc d'Orléans (1747–1793), was noted for his revolutionary ideas; he joined the Third Estate (composed of commoners) at the beginning of the French Revolution.

4 Jean Pierre Brissot de Warville (1754–1793) was the master spirit of the Girondist Party after the Revolution. He was a member of the French National Assembly from 1791.

5 I.e., his constant attacks on revolutionary principles and their adherents.

6 Thomas Paine (1737–1809) wrote *The Rights of Man* (1790), a reply to Burke's *Reflections on the Revolution in France*. Joseph Priestley (1733–1804), a theologian and scientist noted for his revolutionary sympathies, also attacked Burke.

Some, perhaps, may think them executors in their own wrong: I at least have nothing to complain of. They have gone beyond the demands of justice. They have been (a little perhaps beyond their intention) favourable to me. They have been the means of bringing out, by their invectives, the handsome things which Lord Grenville[7] has had the goodness and condescension to say in my behalf. Retired as I am from the world, and from all its affairs and all its pleasures, I confess it does kindle, in my nearly extinguished feelings, a very vivid satisfaction to be so attacked and so commended. It is soothing to my wounded mind, to be commended by an able, vigorous, and well informed statesman, and at the very moment when he stands forth with a manliness and resolution, worthy of himself and of his cause, for the preservation of the person and government of our Sovereign, and therein for the security of the laws, the liberties, the morals, and the lives of his people. To be in any fair way connected with such things, is indeed a distinction. No philosophy can make me above it: no melancholy can depress me so low, as to make me wholly insensible to such an honour.

Why will they not let me remain in obscurity and inaction? Are they apprehensive, that if an atom of me remains, the sect has something to fear? Must I be annihilated, lest, like old *John Zisca's*,[8] my skin might be made into a drum, to animate Europe to eternal battle, against a tyranny that threatens to overwhelm all Europe, and all the human race?

My Lord, it is a subject of aweful meditation. Before this of France, the annals of all time have not furnished an instance of a *compleat* revolution. That revolution seems to have extended even to the constitution of the mind of man. It has this of wonderful in it, that it resembles what Lord Verulam[9] says of the operations of nature: It was perfect, not only in all its elements and principles, but in all its members and its organs from the very beginning. The moral scheme of France furnishes the only pattern ever known, which they who admire will *instantly* resemble. It is indeed an inexhaustible repertory of one kind of examples. In my wretched condition, though hardly to be classed with the living, I am not safe

---

7 William Wyndham Grenville, Lord Grenville (1759–1834), was at this time secretary for foreign affairs. He had defended Burke against attacks for venality in the House of Lords dispute of 1795.

8 John Ziska (c. 1360–1424) was a Bohemian general; he had a high reputation as a patriot and a champion of liberty and equality. Before dying of the plague, he is supposed to have ordered a drum made of his skin, because the sound of it would intimidate his enemies.

9 I.e., Francis Bacon (1561–1626), philosopher.

from them. They have tygers to fall upon animated strength. They have hyenas to prey upon carcasses. The national menagerie is collected by the first physiologists of the time; and it is defective in no description of savage nature. They pursue, even such as me, into the obscurest retreats, and haul them before their revolutionary tribunals. Neither sex, nor age— not the sanctuary of the tomb is sacred to them. They have so determined a hatred to all privileged orders, that they deny even to the departed, the sad immunities of the grave. They are not wholly without an object. Their turpitude purveys to their malice; and they unplumb the dead for bullets to assassinate the living. If all revolutionists were not proof against all caution, I should recommend it to their consideration, that no persons were ever known in history, either sacred or profane, to vex the sepulchre, and by their sorceries, to call up the prophetic dead, with any other event, than the prediction of their own disastrous fate.—"Leave me, oh leave me to repose!"[10]

In one thing I can excuse the Duke of Bedford for his attack upon me and my mortuary pension. He cannot readily comprehend the transaction he condemns. What I have obtained was the fruit of no bargain; the production of no intrigue; the result of no compromise; the effect of no solicitation. The first suggestion of it never came from me, mediately or immediately, to his Majesty or any of his Ministers. It was long known that the instant my engagements would permit it, and before the heaviest of all calamities had for ever condemned me to obscurity and sorrow, I had resolved on a total retreat. I had executed that design. I was entirely out of the way of serving or of hurting any statesman, or any party, when the Ministers so generously and so nobly carried into effect the spontaneous bounty of the Crown. Both descriptions have acted as became them. When I could no longer serve them, the Ministers have considered my situation. When I could no longer hurt them, the revolutionists have trampled on my infirmity. My gratitude, I trust, is equal to the manner in which the benefit was conferred. It came to me indeed, at a time of life, and in a state of mind and body, in which no circumstance of fortune could afford me any real pleasure. But this was no fault in the Royal Donor, or in his Ministers, who were pleased, in acknowledging the merits of an invalid servant of the publick, to assuage the sorrows of a desolate old man.

---

10 The refrain of Thomas Gray's poem, *The Descent of Odin;* it is spoken by a dead prophetess, who resents being raised from the grave.

It would ill become me to boast of any thing. It would as ill become me, thus called upon, to depreciate the value of a long life, spent with un-exampled toil in the service of my country. Since the total body of my services, on account of the industry which was shewn in them, and the fairness of my intentions, have obtained the acceptance of my Sovereign, it would be absurd in me to range myself on the side of the Duke of Bed-ford and the Corresponding Society, or, as far as in me lies, to permit a dispute on the rate at which the authority appointed by *our* Constitution to estimate such things, has been pleased to set them.

Loose libels ought to be passed by in silence and contempt. By me they have been so always. I knew that as long as I remained in publick, I should live down the calumnies of malice, and the judgments of ignorance. If I happened to be now and then in the wrong, as who is not, like all other men, I must bear the consequence of my faults and my mistakes. The libels of the present day, are just of the same stuff as the libels of the past. But they derive an importance from the rank of the persons they come from, and the gravity of the place where they were uttered. In some way or other I ought to take some notice of them. To assert myself thus traduced is not vanity or arrogance. It is a demand of justice; it is a demon-stration of gratitude. If I am unworthy, the Ministers are worse than prodigal. On that hypothesis, I perfectly agree with the Duke of Bedford.

For whatever I have been (I am now no more) I put myself on my country. I ought to be allowed a reasonable freedom, because I stand upon my deliverance; and no culprit ought to plead in irons. Even in the ut-most latitude of defensive liberty, I wish to preserve all possible decorum. Whatever it may be in the eyes of these noble persons themselves, to me, their situation calls for the most profound respect. If I should happen to trespass a little, which I trust I shall not, let it always be supposed, that a confusion of characters may produce mistakes; that in the masquerades of the grand carnival of our age, whimsical adventures happen; odd things are said and pass off. If I should fail a single point in the high respect I owe to those illustrious persons, I cannot be supposed to mean the Duke of Bedford and the Earl of Lauderdale of the House of Peers, but the Duke of Bedford and the Earl of Lauderdale of Palace Yard;—The Dukes and Earls of Brentford.[11] There they are on the pavement; there they seem to come nearer to my humble level; and, virtually at least, to have waved their high privilege.

---

11 The two kings of Brentford are absurd characters who enter hand in hand in *The Rehearsal* (1672), a farce attributed to George Villiers, second Duke of Buckingham.

Making this protestation, I refuse all revolutionary tribunals, where men have been put to death for no other reason, than that they had obtained favours from the Crown. I claim, not the letter, but the spirit of the old English law, that is, to be tried by my peers. I decline his Grace's jurisdiction as a judge. I challenge the Duke of Bedford as a juror to pass upon the value of my services. Whatever his natural parts may be, I cannot recognize in his few and idle years, the competence to judge of my long and laborious life. If I can help it, he shall not be on the inquest of my *quantum meruit*.[12] Poor rich man! He can hardly know any thing of publick industry in its exertions, or can estimate its compensations when its work is done. I have no doubt of his Grace's readiness in all the calculations of vulgar arithmetick; but I shrewdly suspect, that he is very little studied in the theory of moral proportions; and has never learned the Rule of Three[13] in the arithmetick of policy and state.

His Grace thinks I have obtained too much. I answer, that my exertions, whatever they have been, were such as no hopes of pecuniary reward could possibly excite; and no pecuniary compensation can possibly reward them. Between money and such services, if done by abler men than I am, there is no common principle of comparison: they are quantities incommensurable. Money is made for the comfort and convenience of animal life. It cannot be a reward for what, mere animal life must indeed sustain, but never can inspire. With submission to his Grace, I have not had more than sufficient. As to any noble use, I trust I know how to employ, as well as he, a much greater fortune than he possesses. In a more confined application, I certainly stand in need of every kind of relief and easement much more than he does. When I say I have not received more than I deserve, is this the language I hold to Majesty? No! Far, very far, from it! Before that presence, I claim no merit at all. Every thing towards me is favour, and bounty. One style to a gracious benefactor; another to a proud and insulting foe.

His Grace is pleased to aggravate my guilt, by charging my acceptance of his Majesty's grant as a departure from my ideas, and the spirit of my conduct with regard to œconomy. If it be, my ideas of œconomy were false and ill founded. But they are the Duke of Bedford's

---

12 "How much did he deserve?"
13 The rule of three is a method of finding a fourth number from three given numbers, so that the third number is in the same proportion to the fourth as the first is to the second. Burke means that the Duke has never learned the most elementary principles of statesmanship.

ideas of œconomy I have contradicted, and not my own. If he means to allude to certain bills brought in by me on a message from the throne in 1782, I tell him, that there is nothing in my conduct that can contradict either the letter or the spirit of those acts.[14]—Does he mean the pay-office act? I take it for granted he does not. The act to which he alludes is, I suppose, the establishment act. I greatly doubt whether his Grace has ever read the one or the other. The first of these systems cost me, with every assistance which my then situation gave me, pains incredible. I found an opinion common through all the offices, and general in the publick at large, that it would prove impossible to reform and methodize the office of Paymaster General. I undertook it, however; and I succeeded in my undertaking. Whether the military service, or whether the general œconomy of our finances have profited by that act, I leave to those who are acquainted with the army, and with the treasury, to judge.

An opinion full as general prevailed also at the same time, that nothing could be done for the regulation of the civil-list establishment. The very attempt to introduce method into it, and any limitations to its services, was held absurd. I had not seen the man, who so much as suggested one œconomical principle, or an œconomical expedient, upon that subject. Nothing but coarse amputation, or coarser taxation, were then talked of, both of them without design, combination, or the least shadow of principle. Blind and headlong zeal, or factious fury, were the whole contribution brought by the most noisy on that occasion, towards the satisfaction of the publick, or the relief of the Crown.

Let me tell my youthful Censor, that the necessities of that time required something very different from what others then suggested, or what his Grace now conceives. Let me inform him, that it was one of the most critical periods in our annals.

Astronomers have supposed, that if a certain comet, whose path intersected the ecliptick, had met the earth in some (I forget what) sign, it would have whirled us along with it, in its excentrick course, into God knows what regions of heat and cold. Had the portentous comet of the rights of man, (which "from its horrid hair shakes pestilence, and war,"[15] and "with fear of change perplexes Monarchs"[16]) had that comet crossed

---

14 When Burke took office as paymaster-general in 1782, he first instituted a complete reform of his own department (the "pay-office act"), then proposed a plan of economic reform (the "establishment act") which reduced the government's patronage in sinecures.

15 *Paradise Lost*, II. 710–11.

16 *Paradise Lost*, I. 598–99.

upon us in that internal state of England, nothing human could have prevented our being irresistibly hurried, out of the highway of heaven, into all the vices, crimes, horrours and miseries of the French revolution.

Happily, France was not then jacobinized. Her hostility was at a good distance. We had a limb cut off; but we preserved the body: We lost our Colonies; but we kept our Constitution. There was, indeed, much intestine heat; there was a dreadful fermentation. Wild and savage insurrection quitted the woods, and prowled about our streets in the name of reform.[17] Such was the distemper of the publick mind, that there was no madman, in his maddest ideas, and maddest projects, who might not count upon numbers to support his principles and execute his designs.

Many of the changes, by a great misnomer called parliamentary reforms, went, not in the intention of all the professors and supporters of them, undoubtedly, but went in their certain, and, in my opinion, not very remote effect, home to the utter destruction of the Constitution of this kingdom. Had they taken place, not France, but England, would have had the honour of leading up the death-dance of Democratick Revolution. Other projects, exactly coincident in time with those, struck at the very existence of the kingdom under any constitution. There are who remember the blind fury of some, and the lamentable helplessness of others; here, a torpid confusion, from a panic fear of the danger; there, the same inaction from a stupid insensibility to it; here, well-wishers to the mischief; there, indifferent lookers-on. At the same time, a sort of National Convention,[18] dubious in its nature, and perilous in its example, nosed Parliament in the very seat of its authority; sat with a sort of superintendance over it; and little less than dictated to it, not only laws, but the very form and essence of Legislature itself. In Ireland things ran in a still more eccentrick course.[19] Government was unnerved, confounded, and in a manner suspended. Its equipoise was totally gone. I do not mean to speak

---

17 Burke is alluding to the Gordon Riots in London (1780), caused by the efforts of Burke and others to repeal or lighten the laws penalizing Irish Catholics.

18 The Protestant Association of England, headed by Lord George Gordon, presented Parliament with a petition demanding the repeal of the Catholic Relief Act. A mob of 60,000 gathered outside the House when the petition was presented, to besiege Parliament and press acceptance of the petition.

19 In Ireland, masses of armed volunteers, gathered originally for local defence, exerted strong political pressure. The example of America caused a rising spirit of discontent and a cry for legislative independence. The ordinary procedures of government were paralyzed.

disrespectfully of Lord North.[20] He was a man of admirable parts; of general knowledge; of a versatile understanding fitted for every sort of business; of infinite wit and pleasantry; of a delightful temper; and with a mind most perfectly disinterested. But it would be only to degrade myself by a weak adulation, and not to honour the memory of a great man, to deny that he wanted something of the vigilance, and spirit of command, that the time required. Indeed, a darkness, next to the fog of this awful day, loured over the whole region. For a little time the helm appeared abandoned—

> *Ipse diem noctemque negat discernere cælo*
> *Nec meminisse viæ mediâ Palinurus in undâ.*[21]

At that time I was connected with men of high place in the community. They loved Liberty as much as the Duke of Bedford can do; and they understood it at least as well. Perhaps their politicks, as usual, took a tincture from their character, and they cultivated what they loved. The Liberty they pursued was a Liberty inseparable from order, from virtue, from morals, and from religion, and was neither hypocritically nor fanatically followed. They did not wish, that Liberty, in itself, one of the first of blessings, should in its perversion become the greatest curse which could fall upon mankind. To preserve the Constitution entire, and practically equal to all the great ends of its formation, not in one single part, but in all its parts, was to them the first object. Popularity and power they regarded alike. These were with them only different means of obtaining that object; and had no preference over each other in their minds, but as one or the other might afford a surer or a less certain prospect of arriving at that end. It is some consolation to me in the chearless gloom, which darkens the evening of my life, that with them I commenced my political career, and never for a moment, in reality, nor in appearance, for any length of time, was separated from their good wishes and good opinion.

By what accident it matters not, nor upon what desert, but just then, and in the midst of that hunt of obloquy, which ever has pursued me with a full cry through life, I had obtained a very considerable degree of publick confidence. I know well enough how equivocal a test this kind

---

20 Frederick North, later Earl of Guildford (1733–1792), was prime minister at this time.

21 "Even Palinurus avows that he knows not day from night in the sky nor remembers the way amid the waters" (*Aeneid*, III. 201–02). Palinurus was Aeneas's helmsman.

of popular opinion forms of the merit that obtained it. I am no stranger to the insecurity of its tenure. I do not boast of it. It is mentioned, to shew, not how highly I prize the thing, but my right to value the use I made of it. I endeavoured to turn that short-lived advantage to myself into a permanent benefit to my Country. Far am I from detracting from the merit of some Gentlemen, out of office or in it, on that occasion. No!—It is not my way to refuse a full and heaped measure of justice to the aids that I receive. I have, through life, been willing to give every thing to others; and to reserve nothing for myself, but the inward conscience, that I had omitted no pains, to discover, to animate, to discipline, to direct the abilities of the Country for its service, and to place them in the best light to improve their age, or to adorn it. This conscience I have. I have never suppressed any man; never checked him for a moment in his course, by any jealousy, or by any policy. I was always ready, to the height of my means (and they were always infinitely below my desires) to forward those abilities which overpowered my own. He is an ill-furnished undertaker, who has no machinery but his own hands to work with. Poor in my own faculties, I ever thought myself rich in theirs. In that period of difficulty and danger, more especially, I consulted, and sincerely co-operated with men of all parties, who seemed disposed to the same ends, or to any main part of them. Nothing, to prevent disorder, was omitted: when it appeared, nothing to subdue it, was left uncounselled, nor unexecuted, as far as I could prevail. At the time I speak of, and having a momentary lead, so aided and so encouraged, and as a feeble instrument in a mighty hand—I do not say, I saved my Country; I am sure I did my Country important service. There were few, indeed, that did not at that time acknowledge it, and that time was thirteen years ago. It was but one voice, that no man in the kingdom better deserved an honourable provision should be made for him.

So much for my general conduct through the whole of the portentous crisis from 1780 to 1782, and the general sense then entertained of that conduct by my country. But my character, as a reformer, in the particular instances which the Duke of Bedford refers to, is so connected in principle with my opinions on the hideous changes, which have since barbarized France, and spreading thence, threaten the political and moral order of the whole world, that it seems to demand something of a more detailed discussion.

My œconomical reforms were not, as his Grace may think, the suppression of a paltry pension or employment, more or less. Œconomy in my plans was, as it ought to be, secondary, subordinate, instrumental. I acted on state principles. I found a great distemper in the commonwealth; and, according to the nature of the evil and of the object, I treated it. The malady was deep; it was complicated, in the causes and in the symptoms. Throughout it was full of contraindicants.[22] On one hand Government, daily growing more invidious for an apparent increase of the means of strength, was every day growing more contemptible by real weakness. Nor was this dissolution confined to Government commonly so called. It extended to Parliament; which was losing not a little in its dignity and estimation, by an opinion of its not acting on worthy motives. On the other hand, the desires of the People, (partly natural and partly infused into them by art) appeared in so wild and inconsiderate a manner, with regard to the œconomical object (for I set aside for a moment the dreadful tampering with the body of the Constitution itself) that if their petitions had literally been complied with, the State would have been convulsed; and a gate would have been opened, through which all property might be sacked and ravaged. Nothing could have saved the Publick from the mischiefs of the false reform but its absurdity; which would soon have brought itself, and with it all real reform, into discredit. This would have left a rankling wound in the hearts of the people who would know they had failed in the accomplishment of their wishes, but who, like the rest of mankind in all ages, would impute the blame to any thing rather than to their own proceedings. But there were then persons in the world, who nourished complaint; and would have been thoroughly disappointed if the people were ever satisfied. I was not of that humour. I wished that they *should* be satisfied. It was my aim to give to the People the substance of what I knew they desired, and what I thought was right whether they desired it or not, before it had been modified for them into senseless petitions. I knew that there is a manifest marked distinction, which ill men, with ill designs, or weak men incapable of any design, will constantly be confounding, that is, a marked distinction between Change and Reformation. The former alters the substance of the objects themselves; and gets rid of all their essential good, as well as of all the accidental evil annexed to them. Change is novelty; and whether it is to operate any one of the effects of reformation at all, or whether it may not contradict the very principle upon which reformation is desired, cannot be certainly known beforehand. Reform is, not a change in the substance, or in the primary

---

22 Indications that make a particular treatment inadvisable.

modification of the object, but a direct application of a remedy to the grievance complained of. So far as that is removed, all is sure. It stops there; and if it fails, the substance which underwent the operation, at the very worst, is but where it was.

All this, in effect, I think, but am not sure, I have said elsewhere. It cannot at this time be too often repeated; line upon line; precept upon precept; until it comes into the currency of a proverb. *To innovate is not to reform.* The French revolutionists complained of every thing; they refused to reform any thing; and they left nothing, no, nothing at all *unchanged.* The consequences are *before* us,—not in remote history; not in future prognostication: they are about us; they are upon us. They shake the publick security; they menace private enjoyment. They dwarf the growth of the young; they break the quiet of the old. If we travel, they stop our way. They infest us in town; they pursue us to the country. Our business is interrupted; our repose is troubled; our pleasures are saddened; our very studies are poisoned and perverted, and knowledge is rendered worse than ignorance, by the enormous evils of this dreadful innovation. The revolution harpies of France, sprung from night and hell, or from that chaotick anarchy, which generates equivocally "all monstrous, all prodigious things,"[23] cuckoo-like, adulterously lay their eggs, and brood over, and hatch them in the nest of every neighbouring State. These obscene harpies, who deck themselves, in I know not what divine attributes, but who in reality are foul and ravenous birds of prey (both mothers and daughters) flutter over our heads, and souse down upon our tables, and leave nothing unrent, unrifled, unravaged, or unpolluted with the slime of their filthy offal.[24]

If his Grace can contemplate the result of this compleat innovation,

---

23 *Paradise Lost*, II. 625.
24 "Tristius haud illis monstrum, nec sævior ulla
Pestis, & ira Deûm Stygiis sese extulit undis.
Virginei volucrum vultus; fædissima ventris
Proluvies; uncæque manus; & pallida semper
Ora fame—

Here the Poet breaks the line, because he (and that He is Virgil) had not verse or language to describe that monster even as he had conceived her. Had he lived to our time, he would have been more overpowered with the reality than he was with the imagination. Virgil only knew the horror of the times before him. Had he lived to see the Revolutionists and Constitutionalists of France, he would have had more horrid and disgusting features of his harpies to describe, and more frequent failures in the attempt to describe them." (E.B.)
The lines Burke quotes may be translated, "No monster more baneful than these, no

or, as some friends of his will call it *reform*, in the whole body of its solidity and compound mass, at which, as Hamlet says, the face of Heaven glows with horrour and indignation,[25] and which, in truth, makes every reflecting mind, and every feeling heart, perfectly thought-sick, without a thorough abhorrence of every thing they say, and every thing they do, I am amazed at the morbid strength, or the natural infirmity of his mind.

---

fiercer plague or wrath of the gods ever rose from the Stygian waves. Maiden faces have these birds, foulest filth they drop, clawed hands are theirs, and faces ever gaunt with hunger" (*Aeneid*, III. 214–18; tr. H. Rushton Fairclough).

25   Heaven's face does glow
O'er this solidity and compound mass
With heated visage, as against the doom
        (*Hamlet*, III. iv. 49–51)

WILLIAM COWPER

(1731–1800)

The attacks of acute melancholia which troubled William Cowper's later years began in his young manhood; his first bout of insanity and his first attempted suicide resulted from his apprehension, as a young barrister, over the prospect of facing an oral examination for a clerkship in the House of Lords. He was confined for two years in a private asylum; during this period his evangelical religious fervor increased. Moving to Huntingdon in 1765, he became a boarder in the home of Morley Unwin; Mary Unwin, who was widowed soon after, was his companion, although the two were not lovers, for the rest of his life. They moved to Olney in 1767, where he came under the influence of the evangelical preacher John Newton, with whom he composed the *Olney Hymns*. Cowper became engaged to Mrs. Unwin, but another attack of insanity prevented the marriage. He continued to live a quiet life, writing original poetry and translations in the intervals between his fits of insanity, but becoming increasingly depressed, particularly after Mrs. Unwin's death in 1796.

Cowper's poetry is noted for its sensitivity to nature and for the fine sensibility it displays. The same qualities are apparent in his letters. In those that follow he demonstrates his interest in the drama of his own sensibility, recording the shifts of his psychic state and dwelling with something close to pride on his capacity for despair; but he also illustrates his capacity for taking joy in such simple matters as the flowers of his garden or his domestic animals. We find him explaining his craft with a poet's intensity; projecting his warmth and playfulness, particularly in letters to his cousin, Lady Hesketh; giving brief attention to the country's political affairs; but making it clear that the concerns of village life—who is ill, who pays visits, who has a hunting accident—really involve him more. He writes of the details of an apparently commonplace life with freshness and delicacy of perception; and despite his neurotic self-absorption, he displays subtle awareness of and responsiveness to the psychic needs of others.

The text for the letters here printed is *The Correspondence of William Cowper*, 4 vols., ed. Thomas Wright (London, 1904).

Biography and Criticism

Cagle, William R., "Cowper's Letters: Mirror to the Man," *The Familiar Letter in the Eighteenth Century*, eds. Anderson, Daghlian, Ehrenpreis, pp. 210–23 1966.

Cecil, Lord David, *The Stricken Deer*, 1930.

Hartley, Lodwick C., *William Cowper, Humanitarian*, 1938.

Irvine, Lyn L., *Ten Letter Writers*, 1932.

Nicholson, Norman, *William Cowper*, 1951.

Quinlan, Maurice J., *William Cowper, A Critical Life*, 1953.

Ryskamp, Charles, *William Cowper of the Inner Temple, Esq.: A Study of His Life and Works to the Year 1768*, 1959.

Thomas, Gilbert, *William Cowper and the Eighteenth Century*, 1948.

Correspondence of William Cowper[1]

TO THE REV. WILLIAM BULL[2]   *Oct. 27, 1782.*

Mon Aimable et Tres Cher Ami,—

It is not in the power of chaises or chariots to carry you where my affections will not follow you; if I heard that you were gone to finish your days in the Moon, I should not love you the less; but should contemplate the place of your abode, as often as it appeared in the heavens, and say—Farewell, my friend, for ever! Lost, but not forgotten! Live happy in thy lantern, and smoke the remainder of thy pipes in peace! Thou art rid of Earth, at least of all its cares, and so far can I rejoice in thy removal; and as to the cares that are to be found in the Moon, I am resolved to suppose them lighter than those below; heavier they can hardly be.

I have never since I saw you failed to inquire of all the few that were likely to inform me, whether you were sick or abroad, for I have long wondered at your long silence and your long absence. I believe it was Mr. Jones[3] who told me that you were gone from home. I suppose, therefore, that you have been at Ramsgate,[4] and upon that condition I excuse you; but you should have remembered, my friend, that people do not go to the seaside to bring back with them pains in the bowels and such weakness and lassitude as you complain of. You ought to have returned ten years younger, with your nerves well braced and your spirits at the top of the weather glass. Come to us, however, and Mrs. Unwin shall add her attentions and her skill to those of Mrs. Bull; and we will give you broth to heal your bowels, and toasted rhubarb to strengthen them, and send you back as brisk and as cheerful as we wish you to be always. Both your advice[5] and your manner of giving it are gentle and friendly, and like yourself. I thank you for them, and do not refuse your counsel

---

1 See Introduction, pp. 21–22.

2 Bull (1738–1814) was the Independent minister of Newport Pagnell, near Cowper's home at Olney. He became a close friend of Cowper, whom he visited frequently, although Cowper would seldom undertake the five-mile return visit. Cowper frequently joked about his pipe smoking (see below).

3 The Reverend Thomas Jones, of Clifton, one mile east of Olney.

4 A resort on the Isle of Thanet, Kent.

5 Bull had recommended prayer as a remedy for despair.

because it is not good, or because I dislike it, but because it is not for me; there is not a man upon earth that might not be the better for it, myself only excepted. Prove to me that I have a right to pray, and I will pray without ceasing; yes, and praise too, even in the belly of this hell, compared with which Jonah's was a palace, a temple of the living God. But let me add, there is no encouragement in the Scriptures so comprehensive as to include my case, nor any consolation so effectual as to reach it. I do not relate it to you, because you could not believe it; you would agree with me if you could. And yet the sin by which I am excluded from the privileges I once enjoyed, you would account no sin,[6] you would even tell me that it was a duty. This is strange;—you will think me mad,—but I am not mad, most noble Festus,[7] I am only in despair, and those powers of mind which I possess are only permitted to me for my amusement at some times, and to acuminate[8] and enhance my misery at others. I have not even asked a blessing upon my food these ten years, nor do I expect that I shall ever ask it again. Yet I love you, and such as you, and determine to enjoy your friendship while I can:—it will not be long, we must soon part for ever.

Madame Guyon[9] is finished, but not quite transcribed. Mrs. Unwin, who has lately been much indisposed, unites her love to you with mine, and we both wish to be affectionately remembered to Mrs. Bull and the young gentleman.[10]

—Yours, my friend,
Wm. Cowper

TO THE REV. WILLIAM UNWIN[1]					*Nov. 18, 1782.*

My Dear William,—

On the part of the poor, and on our part, be pleased to make ac-

---

6 Cowper long believed that he had committed "the unforgivable sin." In 1773 he had a dream in which he heard a voice saying, "*Actum est de te, periisti*" ("It is all over with thee; thou hast perished"). He attempted to commit suicide; when the attempt failed, he believed that he had displeased God and was forever damned. The "sin" he here refers to may be that of failing in his suicide attempt.

7 Festus was the Roman officer before whom Paul was arraigned by the Jews; he behaved with great honor. See Acts 24–26.

8 Sharpen.

9 Jeanne Marie Bouvier de la Motte Guyon (1648–1717), French mystic, thirty-seven of whose poems Cowper translated at Bull's suggestion.

10 Bull's son.

1 William Unwin, a clergyman at Stock, Essex, was the son of Mary Unwin, Cowper's companion.

knowledgments, such as the occasion calls for, to our beneficent friend
Mr. Smith.[2] I call him ours, because having experienced his kindness to
myself in a former instance, and in the present his disinterested readiness
to succour the distressed, my ambition will be satisfied with nothing less.
He may depend upon the strictest secrecy; no creature shall hear him
mentioned, either now or hereafter, as the person from whom we have
received this bounty. But when I speak of him, or hear him spoken of by
others, which sometimes happens, I shall not forget what is due to so rare
a character. I wish, and your mother wishes it too, that he could sometimes take us in his way to Nottingham; he will find us happy to receive
a person whom we must needs account it an honour to know. We shall
exercise our best discretion in the disposal of the money; but in this town,
where the Gospel has been preached so many years, where the people
have been favoured so long with laborious and conscientious ministers,
it is not an easy thing to find those who make no profession of religion at
all, and are yet proper objects of charity. The profane are so profane, so
drunken, dissolute, and in every respect worthless, that to make them
partakers of his bounty would be to abuse it. We promise, however, that
none shall touch it but such as are miserably poor, yet at the same time
industrious and honest, two characters frequently united here, where the
most watchful and unremitting labour will hardly procure them bread.
We make none but the cheapest laces, and the price of them is fallen almost to nothing.

Thanks are due to yourself likewise, and are hereby accordingly
rendered, for waiving your claim in behalf of your own parishioners.
You are always with them, and they are always, at least some of them,
the better for your residence among them. Olney is a populous place,
inhabited chiefly by the half-starved and the ragged of the earth, and it is
not possible for our small party and small ability to extend their operations so far as to be much felt among such numbers. Accept, therefore,
your share of their gratitude, and be convinced that when they pray for a
blessing upon those who have relieved their wants, He that answers that
prayer, and when He answers it, will remember His servant as Stock.

---

2 Unwin had introduced Cowper to Robert Smith (later Lord Carrington) (1752–
1838), a wealthy Nottingham banker, who had sent a considerable sum of money for Cowper
to administer as he thought best for the poor of Olney.

I little thought when I was writing the history of John Gilpin,[3] that he would appear in print—I intended to laugh, and to make two or three others laugh, of whom you were one. But now all the world laughs, at least if they have the same relish for a tale ridiculous in itself, and quaintly told, as we have.—Well—they do not always laugh so innocently, or at so small an expense—for in a world like this, abounding with subjects for satire, and with satirical wits to mark them, a laugh that hurts nobody has at least the grace of novelty to recommend it. Swift's darling motto was, *Vive la bagatelle*[4]—a good wish for a philosopher of his complexion, the greater part of whose wisdom, whencesoever it came, most certainly came not from above. *La bagatelle* has no enemy in me, though it has neither so warm a friend, nor so able a one, as it had in him. If I trifle, and merely trifle, it is because I am reduced to it by necessity—a melancholy, that nothing else so effectually disperses, engages me sometimes in the arduous task of being merry by force. And, strange as it may seem, the most ludicrous lines I ever wrote have been written in the saddest mood, and, but for that saddest mood, perhaps had never been written at all. To say truth, it would be but a shocking vagary, should the mariners on board a ship buffeted by a terrible storm, employ themselves in fiddling and dancing; yet sometimes much such a part act I.

Your mother is delighted with your purchase,[5] and esteems it an excellent bargain; the 13s. 6d. included in Mr. Smith's draft she sinks in the same purpose, and gives it to the poor. On so laudable an occasion we are not willing to be inactive.

I hear from Mrs. Newton,[6] that some great persons have spoken with great approbation of a certain book.[7] Who they are, and what they

---

3 Lady Austen (born Ann Richardson, the widow of Sir Robert Austen, Baronet), Cowper's close friend, had told him the story of a draper named John Gilpin, whose horse ran away with him. Cowper, who had been depressed, was amused by the tale and immediately wrote out a first draft of *John Gilpin*, which was to become one of his best-known poems. It was first published, anonymously, in the *Public Advertiser* (1782).

4 "Hurrah for trifles."

5 Presumably Unwin has sent part or all of the purchases Cowper requested in a letter of November 4: "Your Mother wishes you to buy her twelve yards of Silk for a gown..10 yards and a qu^r. of yard wide Irish cloth..2 yards of Satten of any colour" (ms. in British Museum). I am indebted for this reference to Charles Ryskamp.

6 Wife of John Newton, the Evangelical clergyman who made Cowper his disciple.

7 Cowper's first volume of poetry (*Poems*) had been published this year. The reviews had been generally favorable.

have said, I am to be told in a future letter. The Monthly Reviewers in the meantime have satisfied me well enough.

—Yours, my dear William,
W. C.

TO THE REV. JOHN NEWTON[1]   *Sept. 18, 1784.*

My Dear Friend,—

Following your good example, I lay before me a sheet of my largest paper. It was this moment fair and unblemished, but I have begun to blot it, and having begun, am not likely to cease till I have spoiled it. I have sent you many a sheet that in my judgment of it has been very unworthy of your acceptance, but my conscience was in some measure satisfied by reflecting, that if it were good for nothing, at the same time it cost you nothing, except the trouble of reading it. But the case is altered now. You must pay a solid price for frothy matter, and though I do not absolutely pick your pocket, yet you lose your money, and, as the saying is, are never the wiser; a saying literally fulfilled to the reader of my epistles.

My greenhouse is never so pleasant as when we are just upon the point of being turned out of it. The gentleness of the autumnal suns, and the calmness of this latter season, make it a much more agreeable retreat than we ever find it in summer; when, the winds being generally brisk, we cannot cool it by admitting a sufficient quantity of air, without being at the same time incommoded by it. But now I sit with all the windows and the door wide open, and am regaled with the scent of every flower in a garden as full of flowers as I have known how to make it. We keep no bees, but if I lived in a hive I should hardly hear more of their music. All the bees in the neighbourhood resort to a bed of mignonette, opposite to the window, and pay me for the honey they get out of it by a hum, which, though rather monotonous, is as agreeable to my ear as the whistling of my linnets. All the sounds that nature utters are delightful— at least in this country. I should not perhaps find the roaring of lions in Africa, or of bears in Russia, very pleasing; but I know no beast in England whose voice I do not account musical, save and except always the

---

1 Newton (1725–1807) was of great importance in Cowper's life. An Evangelical clergyman, rector of Olney when Cowper moved there, he collaborated with the poet on the Olney Hymns. In 1780 he had moved to a parish in London.

braying of an ass. The notes of all our birds and fowls please me, without one exception. I should not, indeed, think of keeping a goose in a cage, that I might hang him up in the parlour for the sake of his melody, but a goose upon a common, or in a farm-yard, is no bad performer; and as to insects, if the black beetle, and beetles indeed of all hues, will keep out of my way, I have no objection to any of the rest; on the contrary, in whatever key they sing, from the gnat's fine treble, to the bass of the humble bee, I admire them all. Seriously, however, it strikes me as a very observable instance of providential kindness to man, that such an exact accord has been contrived between his ear, and the sounds with which, at least in a rural situation, it is almost every moment visited. All the world is sensible of the uncomfortable effect that certain sounds have upon the nerves, and consequently upon the spirits:—and if a sinful world had been filled with such as would have curdled the blood, and have made the sense of hearing a perpetual inconvenience, I do not know that we should have had a right to complain. But now the fields, the woods, the gardens, have each their concert, and the ear of man is for ever regaled by creatures who seem only to please themselves. Even the ears that are deaf to the Gospel are continually entertained, though without knowing it, by sounds for which they are solely indebted to its author. There is somewhere in infinite space a world that does not roll within the precincts of mercy, and as it is reasonable, and even scriptural, to suppose that there is music in Heaven, in those dismal regions perhaps the reverse of it is found; tones so dismal, as to make woe itself more insupportable, and to acuminate even despair. But my paper admonishes me in good time to draw the reins, and to check the descent of my fancy into deeps, with which she is but too familiar.

Our best love attends you both, with yours, *Sum ut semper, tui studiosissimus,*[2]

W. C.

TO THE REV. WILLIAM UNWIN   *Oct. 10, 1784.*

My Dear William,—

I send you four quires of verse,[1] which having sent, I shall dismiss

---

2 "I am as always, your most affectionate...."
1 From *The Task*, Cowper's long, blank-verse poem about the virtues of country life,

from my thoughts, and think no more of, till I see them in print. I have not after all found time or industry enough to give the last hand to the points.[2] I believe, however, they are not very erroneous, though in so long a work, and in a work that requires nicety in this particular, some inaccuracies will escape. Where you find any, you will oblige me by correcting them.

In some passages, especially in the second book, you will observe me very satirical. Writing on such subjects I could not be otherwise. I can write nothing without aiming at least at usefulness: it were beneath my years to do it, and still more dishonourable to my religion. I know that a reformation of such abuses as I have censured is not to be expected from the efforts of a poet; but to contemplate the world, its follies, its vices, its indifference to duty, and its strenuous attachment to what is evil, and not to reprehend, were to approve it. From this charge at least I shall be clear, for I have neither tacitly nor expressly flattered either its characters or its customs. I have paid one, and only one compliment, which was so justly due, that I did not know how to withhold it, especially having so fair an occasion;—I forget myself, there is another in the first book to Mr. Throckmorton,[3]—but the compliment I mean is to Mr. Smith.[4] It is however so managed, that nobody but himself can make the application, and you, to whom I disclose the secret; a delicacy on my part, which so much delicacy on his obliged me to the observance of.

What there is of a religious cast in the volume I have thrown towards the end of it, for two reasons; first, that I might not revolt the reader at his entrance,—and secondly, that my best impressions might be made last. Were I to write as many volumes as Lope de Vega,[5] or Voltaire, not one of them would be without this tincture. If the world like it not, so much the worse for them. I make all the concessions I can, that I may please them, but I will not please them at the expense of conscience.

My descriptions are all from nature: not one of them second-handed. My delineations of the heart are from my own experience: not

---

in which he incorporated many of his ideas and observations about life in general. A quire is twenty-four sheets of paper.

2 The punctuation.

3 *The Task*, I. 262–65: a compliment to John Courtney Throckmorton, Cowper's neighbor at Weston Underwood, for sparing his chestnuts as shade trees.

4 *The Task*, IV. 427–28: praise of Robert Smith, the banker (see letter to Unwin, November 18, 1782, note 2).

5 Lope Felix De Vega Carpio (1562–1635), Spanish dramatist and poet, wrote more than 520 plays.

one of them borrowed from books, or in the least degree conjectural. In my numbers, which I have varied as much as I could (for blank verse without variety of numbers is no better than bladder and string), I have imitated nobody, though sometimes perhaps there may be an apparent resemblance; because at the same time that I would not imitate, I have not affectedly differed.

If the work cannot boast a regular plan (in which respect however I do not think it altogether indefensible), it may yet boast, that the reflections are naturally suggested always by the preceding passage, and that except the fifth book, which is rather of a political aspect, the whole has one tendency: to discountenance the modern enthusiasm after a London life, and to recommend rural ease and leisure, as friendly to the cause of piety and virtue.

If it pleases you, I shall be happy, and collect from your pleasure in it an omen of its general acceptance.

—Yours, my dear friend,
W. C.

Your mother's love. She wishes that you would buy her a second-hand cream-pot, small, either kit,[6] jug, or ewer of silver.

I shall be glad of an immediate line to apprise me of its safe arrival.

TO LADY HESKETH[1]								*Oct. 12, 1785*

My Dear Cousin,—

It is no new thing with you to give pleasure; but I will venture to say, that you do not often give more than you gave me this morning. When I came down to breakfast, and found upon the table a letter franked by my uncle, and when opening that frank I found that it contained a letter from you, I said within myself—"This is just as it should be. We are all grown young again, and the days that I thought I should see no

---

6 A tuh-shaped vessel for carrying milk.

1 Lady Hesketh was Cowper's first cousin, the daughter of Ashley Cowper. Born Harriet Cowper, a friendly companion of Cowper in his early days in London, she had married Sir Thomas Hesketh, who had died in 1778. She had been out of touch with Cowper for seventeen years, but renewed her correspondence with him when the publication of *The Task* made him a considerable popular success.

more, are actually returned." You perceive, therefore, that you judged well when you conjectured, that a line from you would not be disagreeable to me. It could not be otherwise than, as in fact it proved, a most agreeable surprise, for I can truly boast of an affection for you, that neither years, nor interrupted intercourse, have at all abated. I need only recollect how much I valued you once, and with how much cause, immediately to feel a revival of the same value: if that can be said to revive, which at the most has only been dormant for want of employment, but I slander it when I say that it has slept. A thousand times have I recollected a thousand scenes, in which our two selves have formed the whole of the drama, with the greatest pleasure; at times, too, when I had no reason to suppose that I should ever hear from you again. I have laughed with you at the *Arabian Nights' Entertainments*, which afforded us, as you well know, a fund of merriment that deserves never to be forgot. I have walked with you to Netley Abbey, and have scrambled with you over hedges in every direction, and many other feats we have performed together, upon the field of my remembrance, and all within these few years. Should I say within this twelvemonth, I should not transgress the truth. The hours that I have spent with you were among the pleasantest of my former days, and are therefore chronicled in my mind so deeply, as to feel no erasure. Neither do I forget my poor friend, Sir Thomas.[2] I should remember him, indeed, at any rate, on account of his personal kindness to myself; but the last testimony that he gave of his regard for you endears him to me still more. With his uncommon understanding (for with many peculiarities he had more sense than any of his acquaintance), and with his generous sensibilities, it was hardly possible that he should not distinguish you as he has done. As it was the last, so it was the best proof, that he could give, of a judgment that never deceived him, when he would allow himself leisure to consult it.

You say that you have often heard of me: that puzzles me. I cannot imagine from what quarter, but it is no matter. I must tell you, however, my cousin, that your information has been a little defective. That I am happy in my situation is true; I live, and have lived these twenty years, with Mrs. Unwin, to whose affectionate care of me, during the far greater part of that time, it is, under Providence, owing that I live at all. But I do not account myself happy in having been for thirteen of those years in a state of mind that has made all that care and attention necessary; an at-

---

2 Lady Hesketh's dead husband.

tention, and a care, that have injured her health, and which, had she not
been uncommonly supported, must have brought her to the grave. But
I will pass to another subject; it would be cruel to particularise only to
give pain, neither would I by any means give a sable hue to the first letter
of a correspondence so unexpectedly renewed.

I am delighted with what you tell me of my uncle's good health.
To enjoy any measure of cheerfulness at so late a day is much; but to have
that late day enlivened with the vivacity of youth, is much more, and in
these postdiluvian times a rarity indeed. Happy, for the most part, are
parents who have daughters. Daughters are not apt to outlive their natural
affections, which a son has generally survived, even before his boyish
years are expired. I rejoice particularly in my uncle's felicity, who has
three female descendants from his little person, who leave him nothing to
wish for upon that head.

My dear cousin, dejection of spirits, which, I suppose, may have
prevented many a man from becoming an author, made me one. I find
constant employment necessary, and therefore take care to be constantly
employed. Manual occupations do not engage the mind sufficiently, as I
know by experience, having tried many. But composition, especially of
verse, absorbs it wholly. I write, therefore, generally three hours in a
morning, and in an evening I transcribe. I read also, but less than I write,
for I must have bodily exercise, and therefore never pass a day without it.

You ask me where I have been this summer. I answer, at Olney.
Should you ask me where I spent the last seventeen summers, I should still
answer, at Olney. Ay, and the winters also; I have seldom left it, and except when I attended my brother in his last illness, never I believe a fortnight together.

Adieu, my beloved cousin, I shall not always be thus nimble in
reply, but shall always have great pleasure in answering you when I can.

—Yours, my dear friend, and cousin,
W. C.

TO LADY HESKETH   *The Lodge, Nov. 3, 1787*

Suffer not thyself, my dearest coz., to be seduced from thy purpose.
There are those among thy friends and kindred who being covetous of thy
company will endeavour to keep thee near them, and the better to effect

their machinations, will possess thee, if they can, with many megrims[1] concerning the roads and the season of the year. But heed them not. They only do what I should do myself were I in their predicament, who certainly should not fail, for my own sake, to represent your intended journey as an enterprise rather to be admired than approved—more bold than prudent. The turnpike, as you well know, will facilitate your progress every inch of the way till you come to Sherrington, and from Sherrington hither you will find the way equally safe, though undoubtedly a little rough. Rough it was when you were here, such it is still, but not rougher than then, nor will it be so. The reason is this—that the soil being naturally a rock is very little, or rather not at all, affected by the season, for as thou well knowest, no showers will melt a stone. The distance also from Sherrington toll-gate to our door is but four miles and a quarter. The only reason why I do not recommend the back road rather than this, is because it is apt to be heavy; in other respects it deserves the preference, for it is just as safe as the other, and from the turning at Gayhurst, is shorter than that by a mile and a half. The Throcks[2] travel them both continually, and so do all the chaises and coaches in the country, and I never heard of an accident to any of them in all the twenty years that I have lived in it. Mr. and Mrs. Throck., understanding that you are a little apprehensive on this subject, begged me yesterday evening to tell you that *they* will send their servant to meet you at Newport, who will direct your *cocher*[3] to all the best and most commodious quarters. As to the season of the year, I grant that it is November. It would be but folly to deny it. But what then?— Does not the sun shine in November? One would imagine that it did not, or would not, were we to listen only to the suggestions of certain persons. But, my dear, the matter is far otherwise; nay it is even just the reverse: for he not only shines, but with such splendour too, that I write at this moment in a room heated by his beams, and with the curtain at my side let down on purpose to abate their fervour. Then let November have its just praise, and let not my cousin fear to find the country pleasant even now. I have said it in verse, and I think it in prose, that as it is at all times preferable to the town, so it is especially preferable in winter, provided I

---

1 Fanciful worries.
2 Mr. and Mrs. John Courtney Throckmorton, Cowper's neighbors at Weston Underwood. The poet's compliment to Mr. Throckmorton in *The Task* is mentioned above, letter of October 10, 1784 (p. 449).
3 Driver.

mean that you have gravel to walk upon, of which there is no scarcity at Weston.

Coming home from my walk yesterday I met Mr. Throck., on his return from Gayhurst. I was glad that I had so good an opportunity to inform myself concerning Mrs. Wrighte.[4] His account of her was in some respects favourable, but upon the whole not flattering. She eats, it is true, and knows those about her; but she almost keeps her bed, is torpid, and inattentive to all that passes, and can hardly be prevailed with to speak, unless constrained to it. Dr. Kerr professes himself perfectly master of her case, but I have more than once heard some wonder expressed that they have not called in other assistance. The present is an unfortunate period in that family: three or four days since, Mr. Wrighte had a terrible fall from his horse. He was fox-hunting; and in Yardley Chase, the hounds chose to follow the deer. He rode violently to whip them off, when his horse plunged into a slough, pitched him over his head, and fell upon him. The softness of the ground saved him, but he was much hurt in both shoulders, and is now suffering by a fit of the gout, which the fall has brought upon him. Mr. Throck. and Mrs. Throck.'s brother, who is now at the hall, happened to see him thrown, and very humanely assisted him to mount again, which without their help he could never have done. The rest of the company were too much fox-hunters to trouble themselves at all about him.

Many thanks, my dear cousin, both on Mrs. Unwin's part and mine for the gown you have purchased for her. She is even now proud of it, and will be prouder still when she shall put it on. I shall be glad of the paper; not that I am in immediate want, but it is good to be provided. I shall put the fourteenth *Iliad*[5] into Mrs. Throck.'s hands in a day or two; I am at present only employed by blots and obliterations in making it more difficult for her to decipher.

Adieu, my dear. Our best love, and best wishes are always with you.

—Yours affectionately,
Wm. Cowper

---

4 Mr. and Mrs. Wrighte were friends of Cowper's from the nearby village of Gayhurst. Mrs. Wrighte had been seriously ill, with an unspecified disease, described in an earlier letter as "a terrible malady."

5 From late 1784 to 1787 Cowper had been working on a blank-verse translation of the *Iliad*, partly because he was dissatisfied with Pope's. It was published, along with his translation of the *Odyssey*, in 1791.

I hear of three prints lately published. Two of Crazy Kate,[6] and one of the Lacemaker[7] in "Truth." Mr. Wm. Throckmorton has said that he will send them to me.

I rejoice that we have peace, at least a respite from war. But you do well to suspect the French of a double meaning, or even of a treble one if that be possible. I believe they mean nothing so little, as to be honest.

TO LADY HESKETH   *The Lodge, Nov. 10, 1787*

The parliament, my dearest cousin, prorogued continually, is a meteor dancing before my eyes, promising me my wish only to disappoint me, and none but the king and his ministers can tell when you and I shall come together. I hope, however, that the period, though so often postponed, is not far distant, and that once more I shall behold you, and experience your power to make winter gay and sprightly.

I have never forgotten (I never say forgot) to tell you the reason why Mr. Bull[1] did not fulfil his engagement to call on you on his return from the West. It was owing to an accident that happened to one of those legs of his. At Exmouth he chose to wallow in the sea and made use of a bathing machine[2] for that purpose. It has a ladder, as you know, attached to its tail. On the lowermost step of that ladder he stood, when it broke under him. He fell of course, and with his knee on the point of a large nail which pierced it almost to the depth of two inches. The consequence was that when he reached London he could think of nothing but getting home as fast as possible. The wound has been healed some time but is occasionally still painful, so that he is not without apprehensions that it may open again, which, considering that he is somewhat gross in his habit,[3] is not impossible. But I have just sent to invite him to dine with us on Monday.

I have a kitten, my dear, the drollest of all creatures that ever wore a cat's skin. Her gambols are not to be described, and would be incredible

---

6 In Book I of *The Task*, Cowper tells the story of Crazy Kate, a girl who went mad for love of a sailor who had gone to sea and died.

7 In Cowper's "Truth" (pub. 1782), the peasant lacemaker is an idealized figure, "Content, though mean; and cheerful, if not gay." Like Crazy Kate, she was a popular fictional character; the existence of the prints Cowper refers to testify to her popularity.

1 See note 2, letter of October 27, 1782, p. 443.

2 A small bathhouse on wheels, driven into the water so that bathers might bathe in their bathing costumes unobserved.

3 I.e., stout of body.

if they could. She tumbles head over heels several times together, she lays her cheek to the ground and presents her rump at you with an air of most supreme disdain, from this posture she rises to dance on her hind feet, an exercise that she performs with all the grace imaginable, and she closes these various exhibitions with a loud smack of her lips, which, for want of greater propriety of expression, we call spitting. But though all cats spit, no cat ever produced such a sound as she does. In point of size she is likely to be a kitten always, being extremely small of her age, but time I suppose, that spoils everything, will make her also a cat. You will see her I hope before that melancholy period shall arrive, for no wisdom that she may gain by experience and reflection hereafter, will compensate the loss of her present hilarity. She is dressed in a tortoise-shell suit, and I know that you will delight in her.

Mrs. Throckmorton carries us to-morrow in her chaise to Chicheley.

Mr. Chester has been often here, and Mrs. Chester,[4] as I told you, once; and we are glad and obliged to our neighbours for an opportunity to return their visits, at once so convenient and inviting. The event, however, must be supposed to depend on elements, at least on the state of the atmosphere, which is turbulent beyond measure. Yesterday it thundered, last night it lightened, and at three this morning I saw the sky as red as a city in flames could have made it. I have a leech in a bottle, my dear, that foretells all these prodigies and convulsions of nature: no, not as you will naturally conjecture by articulate utterance of oracular notices, but by a variety of gesticulations, which here I have not room to give an account of. Suffice it to say, that no change of weather surprises him, and that in point of the earliest and most accurate intelligence, he is worth all the barometers in the world. None of them all indeed can make the least pretence to foretell thunder—a species of capacity of which he has given the most unequivocal evidence. I gave but sixpence for him, which is a groat more than the market price, though he is in fact, or rather would be, if leeches were not found in every ditch, an invaluable acquisition.

Mrs. Throck. *sola* dined with us last Tuesday. She invited herself; the particular reason of her so doing was that her husband and brother dined at Horton.[5] The next day we dined at the Hall.[6]

Mrs. Wrighte's is still considered as a melancholy case, though we

---

4 The Chesters were residents of the nearby village of Chicheley.
5 A village five miles from Olney.
6 I.e., the Throckmortons' residence.

learn this evening that she has twice or thrice taken airing in the chaise, and must therefore I suppose be better. Pray, my dear, add to what I have already desired you to bring with you, a roll or two of green wax candle[7] to go upon a spindle, spindle, spindle. I repeat it three times, having more than once experienced how apt that circumstance is to escape the memory. I have no room for any other addition than that of our best love, and to assure you how truly I am ever yours,

Wm. Cowper

TO SAMUEL ROSE[1]   *Weston, Dec. 13, 1787*

Dear Sir,—

Unless my memory deceives me, I forewarned you that I should prove a very unpunctual correspondent. The work that lies before me engages unavoidably my whole attention. The length of it, the spirit of it, and the exactness that is requisite to its due performance, are so many most interesting subjects of consideration to me, who find that my best attempts are only introductory to others, and that what to-day I suppose finished, to-morrow I must begin again. Thus it fares with a translator of Homer. To exhibit the majesty of such a poet in a modern language is a task that no man can estimate the difficulty of till he attempts it. To paraphrase him loosely, to hang him with trappings that do not belong to him, all this is comparatively easy. But to represent him with only his own ornaments, and still to preserve his dignity, is a labour that, if I hope in any measure to achieve it, I am sensible can only be achieved by the most assiduous and most unremitting attention. Our studies, however different in themselves, in respect of the means by which they are to be successfully carried on, bear some resemblance to each other. A perseverance that

---

7 In the eighteenth century long lengths of wax taper were often coiled on a vertical shaft (or spindle, as Cowper calls it), so that pieces of it could be cut off as needed. "Green" probably refers to the freshness rather than the color of the candle; tallow, the most common wax of the time, grows brittle with age and coils better when new. I am indebted for this information to Ralph Hodgkinson, Director of Craft Demonstrations at Old Sturbridge Village.

1 Rose, then a student at Glasgow, had stopped by Weston, where Cowper was then living, in January, to declare his admiration of Cowper as a poet. When Cowper recovered from his attack of insanity in 1787 he initiated a correspondence with the young man, who became a close friend. Rose later became a London solicitor.

nothing can discourage, a minuteness of observation that suffers nothing to escape, and a determination not to be seduced from the straight line that lies before us, by any images with which fancy may present us, are essentials that should be common to us both. There are perhaps few arduous undertakings that are not in fact more arduous than we at first supposed them. As we proceed, difficulties increase upon us, but our hopes gather strength also, and we conquer difficulties which, could we have foreseen them, we should never have had the boldness to encounter. May this be your experience, as I doubt not that it will. You possess by nature all that is necessary to success in the profession that you have chosen. What remains is in your own power. They say of poets that they must be born such: so must mathematicians, so must great generals, and so must lawyers, and so indeed must men of all denominations, or it is not possible that they should excel. But with whatever faculties we are born, and to whatever studies our genius may direct us, studies they must still be. I am persuaded that Milton did not write his *Paradise Lost,* nor Homer his *Iliad,* nor Newton his *Principia,* without immense labour. Nature gave them a bias to their respective pursuits, and that strong propensity, I suppose, is what we mean by genius. The rest they gave themselves. "*Macte esto,*"[2] therefore, have no fears for the issue!

I have had a second kind letter from your friend Mr.———, which I have just answered. I must not I find hope to see him here, at least I must not much expect it. He has a family that does not permit him to fly southward. I have also a notion, that we three could spend a few days comfortably together, especially in a country like this, abounding in scenes with which I am sure you would both be delighted. Having lived till lately at some distance from the spot that I now inhabit, and having never been master of any sort of vehicle whatever, it is but just now that I begin myself to be acquainted with the beauties of our situation. To you I may hope, one time or other, to show them, and shall be happy to do it, when an opportunity offers.

—Yours, most affectionately,
W. C.

---

2 "Be blessed" (Martial, *Epigrams,* IV. xiii. 2).

EDWARD GIBBON

(1737–1794)

Notorious as a freethinker after the publication of his *Decline and Fall*, Edward Gibbon in his youth was briefly a Catholic convert. He had been intellectually precocious and physically feeble throughout his childhood. At the age of fifteen he entered Oxford, but a year later went to Lausanne, where a Calvinist minister was expected to cure him of his Catholicism. The cure worked, Gibbon learned French, courted a Swiss girl, became interested in Latin literature. His father refused him permission to marry, so he returned docilely to England and committed himself to scholarly pursuits. The idea of recounting the decline of Rome occurred to him in 1764, on a trip to Italy, where, as he explains in his autobiography, he heard barefoot friars singing in the ruins of the capitol. The first volume of the history appeared in 1776, a great success despite the furor over its deprecating remarks about Christianity. Gibbon became a member of Parliament, but in 1783 he returned to Lausanne, where he finished volumes five and six of the *Decline and Fall*. The last three volumes were published in 1788; Adam Smith said, "They place the author at the very head of the literary tribe in Europe."

Biography and Criticism

Bond, Harold L., *The Literary Art of Edward Gibbon*, 1960.
Curtis, Lewis P., "Gibbon's Paradise Lost," *The Age of Johnson: Essays Presented to*

Chauncey Brewster Tinker, pp. 73–90, 1949.

Keast, William R., "The Element of Art in Gibbon's *History*," *ELH*, XXIII (1956), 153–62.

Low, David M., *Edward Gibbon, 1737–1794*, 1937.

Swain, Joseph Ward, *Edward Gibbon the Historian*, 1966.

Tillyard, E. M. W., *The English Epic and Its Background*, Ch. XI, "Gibbon," 510–27, 1954.

Wedgwood, C. V., *Edward Gibbon*, 1955.

THE HISTORY OF THE
DECLINE AND FALL OF THE ROMAN EMPIRE[1]

(1776–1788)

Carl Becker has remarked of *The Decline and Fall* that it is "something more than a history, a memorial oration: Gibbon is commemorating the death of ancient civilization" (*The Heavenly City of the Eighteenth-century Philosophers* [New Haven, Conn.: Yale University Press, 1932], p. 118). The height of civilization had existed in Rome, and it had vanished; Gibbon, recording in minute detail the process through which it decayed, at once celebrated its grandeur and provided a melancholy warning for his own contemporaries, once more engaged in the struggle to preserve the high values of civilization. Various great figures emerge, then disappear in the course of the epic account. Gibbon tells his story with immense narrative skill, with full awareness of its dramatic and poetic as well as its moral and historical values. The first three volumes take the narrative to the extinction of the empire of the west. They begin with a great period of Roman stability, looking forward and backward from that, and end with the deposition of Augustulus (476), the last emperor of the west. In the fourth volume, Gibbon concentrates on the great Emperors Theodoric and Justinian; in the rest of the work he considers, in more summary fashion, the decline of the eastern empire.

Christianity was for Gibbon one of many causes of Rome's destruction. He thinks of religion in terms of its later developments, as associated with superstition and fanaticism, and it is by no means the only undermining force he discovers: others include luxury and despotism, barbarians, decline of moral values, civil wars, too ambitious conquests. Not until he gets to the rise and conversion of Constantine does he introduce the subject of Christianity; then he presents a devastating portrayal of its faults and corruptions. The chapter here reprinted is another such presentation; once more Gibbon emphasizes fanaticism and the loss of perspective it implies. Christianity, as he understands it, was historically the enemy of reason; and the fall of Rome was perhaps most importantly the fall of reason. This fact helps to account for the tragic grandeur and moral weight of Gibbon's account. Reason and freedom were the central values he wished to preserve; his account of their destruction, like Pope's *Dunciad*, was intended to provide a terrible lesson for his contemporaries; it teaches us the same lesson.

---

1 See introduction, pp. 16–20.

The literary distinction of Gibbon's history is the product of the awareness, discipline, and detachment of his mind. He makes sense of a chaos of details;
he judges with authority and with irony. The elaborate balance of his prose derives from his constant effort to achieve a balanced—and therefore presumably
accurate—view of the world.

The text for the following chapter is *The History of the Decline and Fall of
the Roman Empire*, 6 vols. (London, 1776–1788).

The History of the
Decline and Fall of the Roman Empire
(1776–1788)

CHAPTER XXXVII

*Origin, Progress, and Effects of the Monastic Life.—Conversion of the Barbarians
to Christianity and Arianism—Persecution of the Vandals in Africa.—Extinction of
Arianism among the Barbarians.*

The indissoluble connection of civil and ecclesiastical affairs, has
compelled, and encouraged, me to relate the progress, the persecutions,
the establishment, the divisions, the final triumph, and the gradual corruption of Christianity. I have purposely delayed the consideration of two
religious events, interesting in the study of human nature, and important
in the decline and fall of the Roman empire. (I) The institution of the
monastic life; and, (II) The conversion of the northern Barbarians.

I. Prosperity and peace introduced the distinction of the *vulgar* and
the *Ascetic Christians*. The loose and imperfect practice of religion satisfied
the conscience of the multitude. The prince or magistrate, the soldier or
merchant, reconciled their fervent zeal, and implicit faith, with the exercise of their profession, the pursuit of their interest, and the indulgence of
their passions: but the Ascetics who obeyed and abused the rigid precepts
of the gospel, were inspired by the savage enthusiasm, which represents
man as a criminal, and God as a tyrant. They seriously renounced the
business, and the pleasures, of the age; abjured the use of wine, of flesh,
and of marriage; chastised their body, mortified their affections, and embraced a life of misery, as the price of eternal happiness. In the reign of

Constantine, the Ascetics fled from a profane and degenerate world, to perpetual solitude, or religious society. Like the first Christians of Jerusalem, they resigned the use, or the property,[2] of their temporal possessions; established regular communities of the same sex, and a similar disposition; and assumed the names of *Hermits*, *Monks*, and *Anachorets*, expressive of their lonely retreat in a natural or artificial desert. They soon acquired the respect of the world, which they despised; and the loudest applause was bestowed on this DIVINE PHILOSOPHY, which surpassed, without the aid of science or reason, the laborious virtues of the Grecian schools. The monks might indeed contend with the Stoics, in the contempt of fortune, of pain, and of death: the Pythagorean silence and submission[3] were revived in their servile discipline; and they disdained, as firmly as the Cynics[4] themselves, all the forms and decencies of civil society. But the votaries of this Divine Philosophy aspired to imitate a purer and more perfect model. They trod in the footsteps of the prophets, who had retired to the desert; and they restored the devout and contemplative life, which had been instituted by the Essenians, in Palestine and Egypt. The philosophic eye of Pliny[5] had surveyed with astonishment a solitary people, who dwelt among the palm-trees near the Dead Sea; who subsisted without money, who were propagated without women; and who derived from the disgust and repentance of mankind, a perpetual supply of voluntary associates.

Egypt, the fruitful parent of superstition, afforded the first example of the monastic life. Antony,[6] an illiterate youth of the lower parts of Thebais, distributed his patrimony, deserted his family and native home, and executed his *monastic* penance with original and intrepid fanaticism. After a long and painful noviciate, among the tombs, and in a ruined tower, he boldly advanced into the desert three days journey to the eastward of the Nile; discovered a lonely spot, which possessed the advantages of shade and water, and fixed his last residence on mount Colzim near the Red Sea; where an ancient monastery still preserves the name and memory of the saint. The curious devotion of the Christians pursued him to the

---

2 I.e., ownership.

3 Disciples of Pythagoras, pre-Socratic Greek philosopher, were vowed to silence and worshipped their leader as a demigod.

4 Devotees of a school of Greek philosophy (founded by a disciple of Socrates) which repudiated pleasure and society in favor of abstinence and self-sufficiency.

5 Caius Plinius Secundus (23–79), *Natural History*, V. 15.

6 St. Anthony (251–c. 350), one of the Egyptian Fathers of the Church and reputed founder of monasticism, who established a monastery near Faioom, c. 305.

desert; and when he was obliged to appear at Alexandria, in the face of mankind,[7] he supported his fame with discretion and dignity. He enjoyed the friendship of Athanasius,[8] whose doctrine he approved; and the Egyptian peasant respectfully declined a respectful invitation from the emperor Constantine. The venerable patriarch (for Antony attained the age of one hundred and five years) beheld the numerous progeny which had been formed by his example and his lessons. The prolific colonies of monks multiplied with rapid increase on the sands of Libya, upon the rocks of Thebais, and in the cities of the Nile. To the south of Alexandria, the mountain, and adjacent desert, of Nitria, was peopled by five thousand anachorets; and the traveller may still investigate the ruins of fifty monasteries, which were planted in that barren soil, by the disciples of Antony. In the Upper Thebais, the vacant Island of Tabenne[9] was occupied by Pachomius,[10] and fourteen hundred of his brethren. That holy abbot successively founded nine monasteries of men, and one of women; and the festival of Easter sometimes collected fifty thousand religious persons, who followed his *angelic* rule of discipline. The stately and populous city of Oxyrinchus, the seat of Christian orthodoxy, had devoted the temples, the public edifices, and even the ramparts, to pious and charitable uses; and the bishop, who might preach in twelve churches, computed ten thousand females, and twenty thousand males, of the monastic profession. The Egyptians, who gloried in this marvellous revolution, were disposed to hope, and to believe, that the number of the monks was equal to the remainder of the people; and posterity might repeat the saying, which had formerly been applied to the sacred animals of the same country, That, in Egypt, it was less difficult to find a god, than a man.

Athanasius introduced into Rome the knowledge and practice of the monastic life; and a school of this new philosophy was opened by the disciples of Antony, who accompanied their primate to the holy threshold of the Vatican. The strange and savage appearance of these Egyptians excited, at first, horror and contempt, and, at length, applause and zealous imitation. The senators, and more especially the matrons, transformed

---

7 He came to Alexandria to testify against Arianism (see note 41, below).

8 St. Athanasius (c. 296–373), a Greek Father of the Church, considered a leader of the orthodox party, which held that Christ was of one substance with God, not a subordinate divinity.

9 "Tabenne is a small island in the Nile, in the diocese of Tentyra or Dendera, between the modern town of Girge and the ruins of ancient Thebes." [E.G.]

10 An Egyptian ascetic (d. c. 348), reputedly the founder of regular monastic communities.

their palaces and villas into religious houses; and the narrow institution of *six* Vestals,[11] was eclipsed by the frequent monasteries, which were seated on the ruins of ancient temples, and in the midst of the Roman Forum. Inflamed by the example of Antony, a Syrian youth, whose name was Hilarion,[12] fixed his dreary abode on a sandy beach, between the sea and a morass, about seven miles from Gaza. The austere penance, in which he persisted forty-eight years, diffused a similar enthusiasm; and the holy man was followed by a train of two or three thousand anachorets, whenever he visited the innumerable monasteries of Palestine. The fame of Basil[13] is immortal in the monastic history of the East. With a mind, that had tasted the learning and eloquence of Athens; with an ambition, scarcely to be satisfied by the archbishopric of Caesarea, Basil retired to a savage solitude in Pontus; and deigned, for a while, to give laws to the spiritual colonies which he profusely scattered along the coast of the Black Sea. In the West, Martin of Tours, a soldier, an hermit, a bishop, and a saint, established the monasteries of Gaul; two thousand of his disciples followed him to the grave; and his eloquent historian[14] challenges the deserts of Thebais, to produce, in a more favourable climate, a champion of equal virtue. The progress of the monks was not less rapid, or universal, than that of Christianity itself. Every province, and, at last, every city, of the empire, was filled with their increasing multitudes; and the bleak and barren isles, from Lerins to Lipari, that arise out of the Tuscan sea, were chosen by the anachorets, for the place of their voluntary exile. An easy and perpetual intercourse by sea and land connected the provinces of the Roman world; and the life of Hilarion displays the facility with which an indigent hermit of Palestine might traverse Egypt, embark for Sicily, escape to Epirus, and finally settle in the island of

---

11 Virgins consecrated to the Roman goddess Vesta and to the perpetual watching of the sacred fire.

12 "See the Life of Hilarion, by St. Jerom. . . . The stories of Paul, Hilarion, and Malchus, by the same author, are admirably told; and the only defect of these pleasing compositions is the want of truth and common sense." [E.G.] St. Hilarion (c. 292–c. 372) was a noted ascetic who gained a wide reputation for his austerities.

13 "His original retreat was in a small village on the banks of the Iris, not far from Neo-Caesarea. The ten or twelve years of his monastic life were disturbed by long and frequent avocations. Some critics have disputed the authenticity of his Ascetic rules; but the external evidence is weighty, and they can only prove, that it is the work of a real or affected enthusiast." [E.G.] St. Basil (c. 329–379) had studied law and rhetoric before he retired to the cloister. He later became Bishop of Caesarea.

14 Sulpicius Severus (c. 363–c. 410), who wrote St. Martin's life in Latin.

Cyprus.[15] The Latin Christians embraced the religious institutions of Rome. The pilgrims, who visited Jerusalem, eagerly copied, in the most distant climates of the earth, the faithful model of the monastic life. The disciples of Antony spread themselves beyond the tropic over the Christian empire of Æthiopia. The monastery of Banchor, in Flintshire, which contained above two thousand brethren, dispersed a numerous colony among the Barbarians of Ireland; and Iona, one of the Hebrides, which was planted by the Irish monks, diffused over the northern regions a doubtful ray of science and superstition.[16]

These unhappy exiles from social life, were impelled by the dark and implacable genius of superstition. Their mutual resolution was supported by the example of millions, of either sex, of every age, and of every rank; and each proselyte, who entered the gates of a monastery, was persuaded, that he trod the steep and thorny path of eternal happiness.[17] But the operation of these religious motives was variously determined by the temper and situation of mankind. Reason might subdue, or passion might suspend, their influence: but they acted most forcibly on the infirm minds of children and females; they were strengthened by secret remorse, or accidental misfortune; and they might derive some aid from the temporal considerations of vanity or interest. It was naturally supposed, that the pious and humble monks, who had renounced the world, to accomplish the work of their salvation, were the best qualified for the spiritual government of the Christians. The reluctant hermit was

---

15 "When Hilarion sailed from Paraetonium to Cape Pachynus, he offered to pay his passage with a book of the Gospels. Posthumian, a Gallic monk, who had visited Egypt, found a merchant-ship bound from Alexandria to Marseilles, and performed the voyage in thirty days. . . . Athanasius, who addressed his Life of St. Antony to the foreign monks, was obliged to hasten the composition, that it might be ready for the sailing of the fleets." [E.G.]

16 "This small, though not barren spot, Iona, Hy, or Columbkill, only two miles in length, and one mile in breadth, has been distinguished, (1) By the monastery of St. Columba, founded A.D. 566; whose abbot exercised an extraordinary jurisdiction over the bishops of Caledonia, (2) By a *classic* library, which afforded some hopes of an entire Livy; and, (3) By the tombs of sixty kings, Scots, Irish and Norwegians; who reposed in holy ground." [E.G.]

17 "Chrysostom (in the first tome of the Benedictine edition) has consecrated three books to the praise and defence of the monastic life. He is encouraged by the example of the ark, to presume that none but the elect (the monks) can possibly be saved. . . . Elsewhere indeed he becomes more merciful. . . . and allows different degrees of glory like the sun, moon, and stars. In his lively comparison of a king and a monk. . . . he supposes (what is hardly fair), that the king will be more sparingly rewarded, and more rigorously punished." [E.G.]

torn from his cell, and seated, amidst the acclamations of the people, on the episcopal throne: the monasteries of Egypt, of Gaul, and of the East, supplied a regular succession of saints and bishops; and ambition soon discovered the secret road which led to the possession of wealth and honours. The popular monks, whose reputation was connected with the fame and success of the order, assiduously laboured to multiply the number of their fellow-captives. They insinuated themselves into noble and opulent families; and the specious arts of flattery and seduction were employed to secure those proselytes, who might bestow wealth or dignity on the monastic profession. The indignant father bewailed the loss, perhaps of an only son: the credulous maid was betrayed by vanity to violate the laws of nature, and the matron aspired to imaginary perfection, by renouncing the virtues of domestic life. Paula yielded to the persuasive eloquence of Jerom;[18] and the profane title of mother-in-law of God, tempted that illustrious widow, to consecrate the virginity of her daughter Eustochium. By the advice, and in the company, of her spiritual guide, Paula abandoned Rome and her infant son; retired to the holy village of Bethlem; founded an hospital and four monasteries; and acquired, by her alms and pennance, an eminent and conspicuous station in the catholic church. Such rare and illustrious penitents were celebrated as the glory and example of their age; but the monasteries were filled by a crowd of obscure and abject plebeians, who gained in the cloyster much more than they had sacrificed in the world. Peasants, slaves, and mechanics, might escape from poverty and contempt, to a safe and honourable profession; whose apparent hardships were mitigated by custom, by popular applause, and by the secret relaxation of discipline. The subjects of Rome, whose persons and fortunes were made responsible for unequal and exorbitant tributes, retired from the oppression of the Imperial government; and the pusillanimous youth preferred the pennance of a monastic, to the dangers of a military, life. The affrighted provincials, of every rank, who fled before the Barbarians, found shelter and subsistence; whole legions were buried in these religious sanctuaries; and the same cause, which

---

18 "Jerom's devout ladies form a very considerable portion of his works: the particular treatise, which he styles the Epitaph of Paula . . . is an elaborate and extravagant panegyric. The exordium is ridiculously turgid: 'If all the members of my body were changed into tongues, and if all my limbs resounded with a human voice, yet should I be incapable,' &c." [E.G.] St. Paula (347–404), a Roman lady noted for her ascetic piety, was one of St. Jerome's most famous disciples.

relieved the distress of individuals, impaired the strength and fortitude of the empire.[19]

The monastic profession of the ancients was an act of voluntary devotion. The inconstant fanatic was threatened with the eternal vengeance of the God whom he deserted: but the doors of the monastery were still open for repentance. Those monks, whose conscience was fortified by reason or passion, were at liberty to resume the character of men and citizens; and even the spouses of Christ might accept the legal embraces of an earthly lover. The examples of scandal, and the progress of superstition, suggested the propriety of more forcible restraints. After a sufficient trial, the fidelity of the novice was secured by a solemn and perpetual vow; and his irrevocable engagement was ratified by the laws of the church and state. A guilty fugitive was pursued, arrested, and restored to his perpetual prison; and the interposition of the magistrate oppressed the freedom and merit, which had alleviated, in some degree, the abject slavery of the monastic discipline. The actions of a monk, his words, and even his thoughts, were determined by an inflexible rule,[20] or a capricious superior: the slightest offences were corrected by disgrace or confinement, extraordinary fasts or bloody flagellation; and disobedience, murmur, or delay, were ranked in the catalogue of the most heinous sins.[21] A blind submission to the commands of the abbot, however absurd, or even criminal, they might seem, was the ruling principle, the first virtue of the Egyptian monks; and their patience was frequently exercised by the most extravagant trials. They were directed to remove an enormous rock; assiduously to water a barren staff, that was planted in the ground, till, at the end of three years, it should vegetate and blossom like a tree; to walk into a fiery furnace; or to cast their infant into a deep pond: and several saints, or madmen, have been immortalized in monastic story, by

---

19 "See a very sensible preface of Lucas Holstenius to the Codex Regularum. The emperors attempted to support the obligation of public and private duties; but the feeble dykes were swept away by the torrent of superstition; and Justinian surpassed the most sanguine wishes of the monks." [E.G.]

20 "The ancient Codex Regularum, collected by Benedict Anianinus, the reformer of the monks in the beginning of the ninth century, and published in the seventeenth by Lucas Holstenius, contains thirty different rules for men and women. Of these, seven were composed in Egypt, one in the East, one in Cappadocia, one in Italy, one in Africa, four in Spain, eight in Gaul, or France, and one in England." [E.G.]

21 "The rule of Columbanus, so prevalent in the West, inflicts one hundred lashes for very slight offences. . . . Before the time of Charlemagne, the abbots indulged themselves in multilating their monks, or putting out their eyes; a punishment much less cruel than the tremendous *vade in pace* (the subterraneous dungeon, or sepulchre), which was afterwards invented." [E.G.]

their thoughtless, and fearless, obedience. The freedom of the mind, the source of every generous and rational sentiment, was destroyed by the habits of credulity and submission; and the monk, contracting the vices of a slave, devoutly followed the faith and passions of his ecclesiastical tyrant. The peace of the eastern church was invaded by a swarm of fanatics, incapable of fear, or reason, or humanity; and the Imperial troops acknowledged, without shame, that they were much less apprehensive of an encounter with the fiercest Barbarians.

Superstition has often framed and consecrated the fantastic garments of the monks: but their apparent singularity sometimes proceeds from their uniform attachment to a simple and primitive model, which the revolutions of fashion have made ridiculous in the eyes of mankind. The father of the Benedictines expressly disclaims all idea of choice, or merit; and soberly exhorts his disciples to adopt the coarse and convenient dress of the countries which they may inhabit. The monastic habits of the ancients varied with the climate, and their mode of life; and they assumed, with the same indifference, the sheep-skin of the Egyptian peasants, or the cloak of the Grecian philosophers. They allowed themselves the use of linen in Egypt, where it was a cheap and domestic manufacture; but in the West, they rejected such an expensive article of foreign luxury. It was the practice of the monks either to cut or shave their hair; they wrapped their heads in a cowl, to escape the sight of profane objects; their legs and feet were naked, except in the extreme cold of winter and their slow and feeble steps were supported by a long staff. The aspect of a genuine anachoret was horrid and disgusting: every sensation that is offensive to man, was thought acceptable to God; and the angelic rule of Tabenne condemned the salutary custom of bathing the limbs in water, and of anointing them with oil. The austere monks slept on the ground, on a hard mat, or a rough blanket; and the same bundle of palm-leaves served them as a seat in the day, and a pillow in the night. Their original cells were low narrow huts, built of the slightest materials; which formed, by the regular distribution of the streets, a large and populous village, inclosing, within the common wall, a church, an hospital, perhaps a library, some necessary offices, a garden, and a fountain or reservoir of fresh water. Thirty or forty brethren composed a family of separate discipline and diet; and the great monasteries of Egypt consisted of thirty or forty families.

Pleasure and guilt are synonymous terms in the language of the monks: and they had discovered, by experience, that rigid fasts, and abstemious diet, are the most effectual preservatives against the impure desires of the flesh. The rules of abstinence, which they imposed, or practised, were not uniform or perpetual: the cheerful festival of the Pentecost was balanced by the extraordinary mortification of Lent; the fervour of new monasteries was insensibly relaxed; and the voracious appetite of the Gauls could not imitate the patient, and temperate, virtue of the Egyptians. The disciples of Anthony and Pachomius were satisfied with their daily pittance,[22] of twelve ounces of bread, or rather biscuit, which they divided into two frugal repasts, of the afternoon, and of the evening. It was esteemed a merit, and almost a duty, to abstain from the boiled vegetables, which were provided for the refectory; but the extraordinary bounty of the abbot sometimes indulged them with the luxury of cheese, fruit, sallad, and the small dried fish of the Nile. A more ample latitude of sea and river fish was gradually allowed or assumed: but the use of flesh was long confined to the sick or travellers; and when it gradually prevailed in the less rigid monasteries of Europe, a singular distinction was introduced;[23] as if birds, whether wild or domestic, had been less profane than the grosser animals of the field. Water was the pure and innocent beveridge of the primitive monks; and the founder of the Benedictines regrets the daily portion of half a pint of wine, which had been extorted from him by the intemperance of the age. Such an allowance might be easily supplied by the vineyards of Italy; and his victorious disciples, who passed the Alps, the Rhine, and the Baltic, required, in the place of wine, an adequate compensation of strong beer or cyder.

The candidate who aspired to the virtue of evangelical poverty, abjured, at his first entrance into a regular community, the idea, and even the name, of all separate, or exclusive, possession.[24] The brethren were supported by their manual labour; and the duty of labour was strenuously recommended as a pennance, as an exercise, and as the most laudable means of securing their daily subsistence. The garden, and fields, which the industry of the monks had often rescued from the forest or the morass,

---

22 " 'Those who drink only water, and have no nutritious liquor, ought, at least, to have a pound and a half (*twenty-four ounces*) of bread every day.' State of Prisons, p. 40, by Mr. Howard." [E.G.] John Howard (1726–1790), from whom Gibbon quotes, was a celebrated English philanthropist who initiated important reforms in prison conditions.

23 Poultry was declared to be legitimate food for "meatless" meals.

24 "Such expressions as *my* book, *my* cloak, *my* shoes, . . . were not less severely prohibited among the Western monks. . . . and the Rule of Columbanus punished them with six lashes. The ironical author of the *Ordres Monastiques* [Pierre Hélyot, *Histoire des ordres monastiques*, an important source for Gibbon], who laughs at the foolish nicety of modern convents, seems ignorant that the ancients were equally absurd." [E.G.]

were diligently cultivated by their hands. They performed, without reluctance, the menial offices of slaves and domestics; and the several trades that were necessary to provide their habits, their utensils, and their lodging, were exercised within the precincts of the great monasteries. The monastic studies have tended, for the most part, to darken, rather than to dispel, the cloud of superstition. Yet the curiosity or zeal of some learned solitaries has cultivated the ecclesiastical, and even the profane, sciences: and posterity must gratefully acknowledge, that the monuments of Greek and Roman literature have been preserved and multiplied by their indefatigable pens. But the more humble industry of the monks, especially in Egypt, was contented with the silent, sedentary, occupation, of making wooden sandals, or of twisting the leaves of the palm-tree into mats and baskets. The superfluous stock, which was not consumed in domestic use, supplied, by trade, the wants of the community: the boats of Tabenne, and the other monasteries of Thebais, descended the Nile as far as Alexandria; and, in a Christian market, the sanctity of the workmen might enhance the intrinsic value of the work.

But the necessity of manual labour was insensibly superseded. The novice was tempted to bestow his fortune on the saints, in whose society he was resolved to spend the remainder of his life; and the pernicious indulgence of the laws permitted him to receive, for their use, any future accessions of legacy or inheritance. Melania[25] contributed her plate, three hundred pounds weight of silver; and Paula contracted an immense debt, for the relief of their favourite monks; who kindly imparted the merits of their prayers and pennance to a rich and liberal sinner. Time continually increased, and accidents could seldom diminish, the estates of the popular monasteries, which spread over the adjacent country and cities: and, in the first century of their institution, the infidel Zosimus[26] has maliciously observed, that, for the benefit of the poor, the Christian monks had reduced a great part of mankind to a state of beggary. As long as they maintained their original fervour, they approved themselves, however, the faithful and benevolent stewards of the charity, which was entrusted to their care. But their discipline was corrupted by prosperity: they gradually assumed the pride of wealth, and at last indulged the

25 St. Melania (383–439) was very wealthy; she sold her estates in Spain and Gaul and distributed the proceeds to the poor. Of Roman birth, she fled the Goths with her husband and went to Africa and later to Bethlehem.

26 Greek historian of the fifth century, a pagan, author of a *History of the Roman Empire Down to 410* A.D.

luxury of expence. Their public luxury might be excused by the magnificence of religious worship, and the decent motive of erecting durable habitations for an immortal society. But every age of the church has accused the licentiousness of the degenerate monks; who no longer remembered the object of their institution, embraced the vain and sensual pleasures of the world, which they had renounced,[27] and scandalously abused the riches which had been acquired by the austere virtues of their founders.[28] Their natural descent, from such painful and dangerous virtue, to the common vices of humanity, will not, perhaps, excite much grief or indignation in the mind of a philosopher.

The lives of the primitive monks were consumed in penance and solitude; undisturbed by the various occupations which fill the time, and exercise the faculties, of reasonable, active, and social beings. Whenever they were permitted to step beyond the precincts of the monastery, two jealous companions were the mutual guards and spies of each other's actions; and, after their return, they were condemned to forget, or, at least, to suppress, whatever they had seen or heard in the world. Strangers, who professed the orthodox faith, were hospitably entertained in a separate apartment; but their dangerous conversation was restricted to some chosen elders of approved discretion and fidelity. Except in their presence, the monastic slave might not receive the visits of his friends or kindred; and it was deemed highly meritorious, if he afflicted a tender sister, or an aged parent, by the obstinate refusal of a word or look.[29] The monks themselves passed their lives, without personal attachments, among a crowd, which had been formed by accident, and was detained, in the same prison, by force or prejudice. Recluse fanatics have few ideas or sentiments to communicate: a special licence of the abbot regulated the time and duration of their familiar visits; and, at their silent meals, they were enveloped in their cowls, inaccessible, and almost invisible, to each

---

27 "The sixth general council . . . restrains women from passing the night in a male, or men in a female, monastery. The seventh general council . . . prohibits the erection of double or promiscuous monasteries of both sexes; but it appears from Balsamon, that the prohibition was not effectual." [E.G.]

28 "I have somewhere heard or read the frank confession of a Benedictine abbot: 'My vow of poverty has given me an hundred thousand crowns a year; my vow of obedience has raised me to the rank of a sovereign prince.'—I forget the consequences of his vow of chastity." [E.G.]

29 "Pior, an Egyptian monk, allowed his sister to see him; but he shut his eyes during the whole visit . . . . Many such examples might be added." [E.G.]

other. Study is the resource of solitude: but education had not prepared and qualified for any liberal studies the mechanics and peasants, who filled the monastic communities. They might work: but the vanity of spiritual perfection was tempted to disdain the exercise of manual labour; and the industry must be faint and languid, which is not excited by the sense of personal interest.

According to their faith and zeal, they might employ the day, which they passed in their cells, either in vocal or mental prayer: they assembled in the evening, and they were awakened in the night, for the public worship of the monastery. The precise moment was determined by the stars, which are seldom clouded in the serene sky of Egypt; and a rustic horn, or trumpet, the signal of devotion, twice interrupted the vast silence of the desert. Even sleep, the last refuge of the unhappy, was rigorously measured: the vacant hours of the monk heavily rolled along, without business or pleasure; and, before the close of each day, he had repeatedly accused the tedious progress of the Sun.[30] In this comfortless state, superstition still pursued and tormented her wretched votaries.[31] The repose which they had sought in the cloister was disturbed by tardy repentance, profane doubts, and guilty desires; and, while they considered each natural impulse as an unpardonable sin, they perpetually trembled on the edge of a flaming and bottomless abyss. From the painful struggles of disease and despair, these unhappy victims were sometimes relieved by madness or death; and, in the sixth century, an hospital was founded at Jerusalem for a small portion of the austere penitents, who were deprived of their senses. Their visions, before they attained this extreme and acknowledged term of frenzy, have afforded ample materials of supernatural history. It was their firm persuasion, that the air, which they breathed, was peopled with invisible enemies; with innumerable dæmons, who watched every occasion, and assumed every form, to terrify, and above all to tempt, their unguarded virtue. The imagination, and even the senses, were deceived by the illusions of distempered fanaticism; and the hermit, whose midnight prayer was oppressed by

---

30 "Cassian, from his own experience, describes the *acedia*, or listlessness of mind and body, to which a monk was exposed, when he sighed to find himself alone." [E.G.]

31 "The temptations and sufferings of Stagirius were communicated by that unfortunate youth to his friend St. Chrysostom .... Something similar introduces the life of every saint; and the famous Inigo, or Ignatius, the founder of the Jesuits, ... may serve as a memorable example." [E.G.]

involuntary slumber, might easily confound the phantoms of horror or delight, which had occupied his sleeping, and his waking dreams.[32]

The monks were divided into two classes: the *Cœnobites*, who lived under a common, and regular, discipline; and the *Anachorets*, who indulged their unsocial, independent, fanaticism. The most devout, or the most ambitious, of the spiritual brethren, renounced the convent, as they had renounced the world. The fervent monasteries of Egypt, Palestine, and Syria, were surrounded by a *Laura*,[33] a distant circle of solitary cells; and the extravagant penance of the Hermits was stimulated by applause and emulation. They sunk under the painful weight of crosses and chains; and their emaciated limbs were confined by collars, bracelets, gauntlets, and greaves, of massy, and rigid, iron. All superfluous incumbrance of dress they contemptuously cast away; and some savage saints of both sexes have been admired, whose naked bodies were only covered by their long hair. They aspired to reduce themselves to the rude and miserable state in which the human brute is scarcely distinguished above his kindred animals: and a numerous sect of Anachorets derived their name from their humble practice of grazing in the fields of Mesopotamia with the common herd. They often usurped the den of some wild beast whom they affected to resemble; they buried themselves in some gloomy cavern, which art or nature had scooped out of the rock; and the marble quarries of Thebais are still inscribed with the monuments of their penance. The most perfect Hermits are supposed to have passed many days without food, many nights without sleep, and many years without speaking; and glorious was the *man* (I abuse that name) who contrived any cell, or seat, of a peculiar construction, which might expose him, in the most inconvenient posture, to the inclemency of the seasons.

Among these heroes of the monastic life, the name and genius of Simeon Stylites have been immortalized by the singular invention of an aerial pennance. At the age of thirteen, the young Syrian deserted the profession of a shepherd, and threw himself into an austere monastery. After a long and painful noviciate, in which Simeon was repeatedly saved from pious suicide, he established his residence on a mountain, about thiry or forty miles to the East of Antioch. Within the space of a *mandra*, or circle of stones, to which he had attached himself by a ponderous chain,

---

[32] "See the seventh and eighth Collations of Cassian, who gravely examines why the dæmons were grown less active and numerous, since the time of St. Antony. Rosweyde's copious index to the Vitae Patrum will point out a variety of infernal scenes. The devils were most formidable in a female shape." [E.G.]

[33] The name comes from a Greek word for *lane* or *alley*.

he ascended a column, which was successively raised from the height of nine, to that of sixty, feet, from the ground.[34] In this last, and lofty, station, the Syrian Anachoret resisted the heat of thirty summers, and the cold of as many winters. Habit and exercise instructed him to maintain his dangerous situation without fear or giddiness, and successively to assume the different postures of devotion. He sometimes prayed in an erect attitude, with his out-stretched arms, in the figure of a cross; but his most familiar practice was that of bending his meagre skeleton from the forehead to the feet: and a curious spectator, after numbering twelve hundred and forty-four repetitions, at length desisted from the endless account. The progress of an ulcer in his thigh[35] might shorten, but it could not disturb, this *celestial* life; and the patient Hermit expired, without descending from his column. A prince, who should capriciously inflict such tortures, would be deemed a tyrant; but it would surpass the power of a tyrant, to impose a long and miserable existence on the reluctant victims of his cruelty. This voluntary martyrdom must have gradually destroyed the sensibility both of the mind and body; nor can it be presumed that the fanatics, who torment themselves, are susceptible of any lively affection for the rest of mankind. A cruel unfeeling temper has distinguished the monks of every age and country: their stern indifference, which is seldom mollified by personal friendship, is inflamed by religious hatred; and their merciless zeal has strenuously administered the holy office of the Inquisition.

The monastic saints, who excite only the contempt and pity of a philosopher, were respected, and almost adored, by the prince and people. Successive crowds of pilgrims from Gaul and India saluted the divine pillar of Simeon: the tribes of Saracens disputed in arms the honour of his benediction; the queens of Arabia and Persia gratefully confessed his supernatural virtue; and the angelic Hermit was consulted by the younger Theodosius,[36] in the most important concerns of the church and state. His remains were transported from the mountain of Telenissa, by a solemn procession of the patriarch, the master-general of the East, six bishops,

---

34 "The narrow circumference of two cubits, or three feet, which Evagrius assigns for the summit of the column, is inconsistent with reason, with facts, and with the rules of architecture. The people who saw it from below might be easily deceived." [E.G.]

35 "I must not conceal a piece of ancient scandal concerning the origin of this ulcer. It has been reported that the Devil, assuming an angelic form, invited him to ascend, like Elijah, into a fiery chariot. The saint too hastily raised his foot, and Satan seized the moment of inflicting this chastisement on his vanity." [E.G.]

36 Emperor Theodosius II (401–450).

twenty-one counts or tribunes, and six thousand soldiers; and Antioch revered his bones, as her glorious ornament and impregnable defence. The fame of the apostles and martyrs was gradually eclipsed by these recent and popular Anachorets; the Christian world fell prostrate before their shrines; and the miracles ascribed to their relics exceeded, at least in number and duration, the spiritual exploits of their lives. But the golden legend of their lives was embellished by the artful credulity of their interested brethren; and a believing age was easily persuaded, that the slightest caprice of an Egyptian or a Syrian monk, had been sufficient to interrupt the eternal laws of the universe. The favourites of Heaven were accustomed to cure inveterate diseases with a touch, a word, or a distant message; and to expel the most obstinate dæmons from the souls, or bodies, which they possessed. They familiarly accosted, or imperiously commanded, the lions and serpents of the desert; infused vegetation into a sapless trunk; suspended iron on the surface of the water; passed the Nile on the back of a crocodile, and refreshed themselves in a fiery furnace. These extravagant tales, which display the fiction, without the genius, of poetry, have seriously affected the reason, the faith, and the morals, of the Christians. Their credulity debased and vitiated the faculties of the mind: they corrupted the evidence of history; and superstition gradually extinguished the hostile light of philosophy and science. Every mode of religious worship which had been practised by the saints, every mysterious doctrine which they believed, was fortified by the sanction of divine revelation, and all the manly virtues were oppressed by the servile and pusillanimous reign of the monks. If it be possible to measure the interval, between the philosophic writings of Cicero and the sacred legend of Theodoret,[37] between the character of Cato and that of Simeon, we may appreciate the memorable revolution which was accomplished in the Roman empire within a period of five hundred years.

II. The progress of Christianity has been marked by two glorious and decisive victories: over the learned and luxurious citizens of the Roman empire; and over the warlike Barbarians of Scythia and Germany, who subverted the empire, and embraced the religion, of the Romans. The Goths were the foremost of these savage proselytes; and the nation was indebted for its conversion to a countryman, or, at least, to a subject, worthy to be ranked among the inventors of useful arts, who have

---

37 Theodoret (c. 390–457) wrote an early *History of the Church*, undependable in chronology and of little real historical importance.

deserved the remembrance and gratitude of posterity. A great number of Roman provincials had been led away into captivity by the Gothic bands, who ravaged Asia in the time of Gallienus:[38] and of these captives, many were Christians, and several belonged to the ecclesiastical order. Those involuntary missionaries, dispersed as slaves in the villages of Dacia, successively laboured for the salvation of their masters. The seeds, which they planted of the evangelic doctrine, were gradually propagated; and, before the end of a century, the pious work was atchieved by the labours of Ulphilas,[39] whose ancestors had been transported beyond the Danube from a small town of Cappadocia.

Ulphilas, the bishop and apostle of the Goths, acquired their love and reverence by his blameless life and indefatigable zeal; and they received, with implicit confidence, the doctrines of truth and virtue, which he preached and practised. He executed the arduous task of translating the Scriptures into their native tongue, a dialect of the German, or Teutonic, language; but he prudently suppressed the four books of Kings, as they might tend to irritate the fierce and sanguinary spirit of the Barbarians. The rude, imperfect, idiom of soldiers and shepherds, so ill-qualified to communicate any spiritual ideas, was improved and modulated by his genius; and Ulphilas, before he could frame his version, was obliged to compose a new alphabet of twenty-four letters; four of which he invented, to express the peculiar sounds that were unknown to the Greek, and Latin, pronunciation. But the prosperous state of the Gothic church was soon afflicted by war and intestine discord, and the chieftains were divided by religion as well as by interest. Fritigern,[40] the friend of the Romans, became the proselyte of Ulphilas; while the haughty soul of Athanaric disdained the yoke of the empire, and of the Gospel. The faith of the new converts was tried by the persecution which he excited. A waggon, bearing aloft the shapeless image, of Thor, perhaps, or of Woden was conducted in solemn procession through the streets of the camp; and the rebels, who refused to worship the God of their fathers, were immediately burnt, with their tents and families. The character of Ulphilas recommended him to the esteem of the Eastern court, where he twice appeared as the minister of peace; he pleaded the cause of the distressed

---

38 Roman emperor (c. 233–268), whose frontiers were invaded by barbarian armies.

39 Celebrated Gothic scholar and writer (c. 318–c. 388), who became bishop of the Arian Goths living between Mt. Haemus and the Danube.

40 King of the Visigoths (died c. 392); Athanaric, below, was chief of a Visigoth tribe (d. 381).

Goths, who implored the protection of Valens[41]; and the name of *Moses* was applied to this spiritual guide, who conducted his people, through the deep waters of the Danube, to the Land of Promise. The devout shepherds who were attached to his person, and tractable to his voice, acquiesced in their settlement, at the foot of the Maesian mountains, in a country of woodlands and pastures, which supported their flocks and herds, and enabled them to purchase the corn and wine of the more plentiful provinces. These harmless Barbarians multiplied, in obscure peace, and the profession of Christianity.

Their fiercer brethren, the formidable Visigoths, universally adopted the religion of the Romans, with whom they maintained a perpetual intercourse, of war, of friendship, or of conquest. In their long and victorious march from the Danube to the Atlantic ocean, they converted their allies; they educated the rising generation; and the devotion which reigned in the camp of Alaric, or the court of Thoulouse, might edify, or disgrace, the palaces of Rome and Constantinople. During the same period, Christianity was embraced by almost all the Barbarians, who established their kingdoms on the ruins of the Western empire; the Burgundians in Gaul, the Suevi in Spain, the Vandals in Africa, the Ostrogoths in Pannonia, and the various bands of Mercenaries, that raised Odoacer to the throne of Italy. The Franks and the Saxons still persevered in the errors of Paganism; but the Franks obtained the monarchy of Gaul by their submission to the example of Clovis;[42] and the Saxon conquerors of Britain were reclaimed from their savage superstition by the missionaries of Rome. These Barbarian proselytes displayed an ardent and successful zeal in the propagation of the faith. The Merovingian kings, and their successors, Charlemagne and the Othos,[43] extended, by their laws and victories, the dominion of the cross. England produced the apostle of Germany[44]; and the evangelic light was gradually diffused from the neighbourhood of the Rhine, to the nations of the Elbe, the Vistula, and the Baltic.

The different motives which influenced the reason, or the passions, of the Barbarian converts, cannot easily be ascertained. They were often

---

[41] Flavius Valens (c. 328–378), emperor of the east.

[42] Clovis (c. 466–511), king of the Franks, was educated as a pagan but converted to Christianity after his marriage to Clotilda, a Christian princess.

[43] Otho I, II, and III—successive emperors of Germany in the tenth century.

[44] Boniface, archbishop of Mayence (c. 680–755), who in 718 was appointed by Gregory II as missionary for the Germans east of the Rhine.

capricious and accidental; a dream, an omen, the report of a miracle, the example of some priest, or hero, the charms of a believing wife, and above all, the fortunate event of a prayer, or vow, which, in a moment of danger, they had addressed to the God of the Christians. The early prejudices of education were insensibly erazed by the habits of frequent and familiar society; the moral precepts of the Gospel were protected by the extravagant virtues of the monks; and a spiritual theology was supported by the visible power of relics, and the pomp of religious worship. But the rational and ingenious mode of persuasion, which a Saxon bishop[45] suggested to a popular saint, might sometimes be employed by the missionaries, who laboured for the conversion of infidels. "Admit," says the sagacious disputant,

> whatever they are pleased to assert of the fabulous, and carnal, genealogy of their gods and goddesses, who are propagated from each other. From this principle deduce their imperfect nature, and human infirmities, the assurance they were *born*, and the probability that they will *die*. At what time, by what means, from what cause, were the eldest of the gods or goddesses produced? Do they still continue, or have they ceased, to progate? If they have ceased, summon your antagonists to declare the reason of this strange alteration. If they still continue, the number of the gods must become infinite; shall we not risk, by the indiscreet worship of some impotent deity, to excite the resentment of his jealous superior? The visible heavens and earth, the whole system of the universe, which may be conceived by the mind, is it created or eternal? If created, how, or where, could the gods themselves exist before the creation? If eternal, how could they assume the empire of an independent and pre-existing world? Urge these arguments with temper and moderation; insinuate, at seasonable intervals, the truth, and beauty, of the Christian revelation; and endeavour to make the unbelievers ashamed, without making them angry.

This metaphysical reasoning, too refined perhaps for the Barbarians of Germany, was fortified by the grosser weight of authority and popular consent. The advantage of temporal prosperity had deserted the Pagan cause, and passed over to the service of Christianity. The Romans themselves, the most powerful and enlightened nation of the globe, had renounced their ancient superstition; and, if the ruin of their empire seemed to accuse the efficacy of the new faith, the disgrace was already retrieved by the conversion of the victorious Goths. The valiant and fortunate

---

45 Identified by Gibbon as "Daniel, the 1st bishop of Winchester."

Barbarians, who subdued the provinces of the West, successively received, and reflected, the same edifying example. Before the age of Charlemagne, the Christian nations of Europe might exult in the exclusive possession of the temperate climates, of the fertile lands, which produced corn, wine, and oil; while the savage idolaters, and their helpless idols, were confined to the extremities of the earth, the dark and frozen regions of the North.

Christianity, which opened the gates of Heaven to the Barbarians, introduced an important change in their moral and political condition. They received, at the same time, the use of letters, so essential to a religion whose doctrines are contained in a sacred book; and while they studied the divine truth, their minds were insensibly enlarged by the distant view of history, of nature, of the arts, and of society. The version of the Scriptures into their native tongue, which had facilitated their conversion, must excite, among their clergy, some curiosity to read the original text, to understand the sacred liturgy of the church, and to examine, in the writings of the fathers, the chain of ecclesiastical tradition. These spiritual gifts were preserved in the Greek and Latin languages, which concealed the inestimable monuments of ancient learning. The immortal productions of Virgil, Cicero, and Livy, which were accessible to the Christian Barbarians, maintained a silent intercourse between the reign of Augustus, and the times of Clovis and Charlemagne. The emulation of mankind was encouraged by the remembrance of a more perfect state; and the flame of science was secretly kept alive, to warm and enlighten the mature age of the Western world. In the most corrupt state of Christianity, the Barbarians might learn justice from the *law*, and mercy from the *gospel:* and if the knowledge of their duty was insufficient to guide their actions, or to regulate their passions; they were sometimes restrained by conscience, and frequently punished by remorse. But the direct authority of religion was less effectual, than the holy communion which united them with their Christian brethren in spiritual friendship. The influence of these sentiments contributed to secure their fidelity in the service, or the alliance, of the Romans, to alleviate the horrors of war, to moderate the insolence of conquest, and to preserve, in the downfall of the empire, a permanent respect for the name and institutions of Rome. In the days of Paganism, the priests of Gaul and Germany reigned over the people, and controuled the jurisdiction of the magistrates; and the zealous proselytes transferred an equal, or more ample, measure of devout obedience, to the pontiffs of the Christian faith. The sacred character of the bishops was supported by their temporal possessions; they obtained an honourable seat in the legislative assemblies of soldiers and freemen; and it was their interest, as well as their duty, to mollify, by peaceful counsels, the fierce spirit of the Barbarians. The perpetual correspondence of the Latin clergy, the frequent pilgrimages to Rome and Jerusalem, and the growing authority of the Popes, cemented the union of the Christian republic: and gradually produced the similar manners, and common jurisprudence, which have distinguished, from the rest of mankind, the independent, and even hostile, nations of modern Europe.

But the operation of these causes was checked and retarded by the unfortunate accident, which infused a deadly poison into the cup of Salvation. Whatever might be the early sentiments of Ulphilas, his connections with the empire and the church were formed during the reign of Arianism.[46] The apostle of the Goths subscribed the creed of Rimini;[47] professed with freedom, and perhaps with sincerity, that the SON was not equal, or consubstantial to the FATHER;[48] communicated these errors to the clergy and people; and infected the Barbaric world with an heresy, which the great Theodosius[49] proscribed and extinguished among the Romans. The temper and understanding of the new proselytes were not adapted to metaphysical subtleties; but they strenuously maintained, what they had piously received, as the pure and genuine doctrines of Christianity. The advantage of preaching and expounding the Scriptures in the Teutonic language, promoted the apostolic labours of Ulphilas, and his successors; and they ordained a competent number of bishops and presbyters, for the instruction of the kindred tribes. The Ostrogoths, the Burgundians, the Suevi, and the Vandals, who had listened to the eloquence of the Latin clergy, preferred the more intelligible lessons of their domestic teachers; and Arianism was adopted as the national faith of the warlike converts, who were seated on the ruins of the Western empire. This irreconcilable

46 A heresy which won strong support in the Eastern churches during the fourth century. It declared that God is absolutely alone, that Christ is a created being (hence not fully God), and that in the Incarnation the Logos assumed a body but not a human soul, so that jesus Christ was neither truly God nor truly man.

47 An Arianizing creed signed by a group of orthodox bishops who had at first resisted the pressure of the Arian heresy.

48 "The opinions of Ulphilas and the Goths inclined to Semi-Arianism, since they would not say that the Son was a *creature*, although they held communion with those who maintained that heresy. Their apostle represented the whole controversy as a question of trifling moment, which had been raised by the passions of the clergy." [E.G.]

49 Emperor Theodosius the Great (346–395).

difference of religion was a perpetual source of jealousy and hatred; and the reproach of *Barbarian* was embittered by the more odious epithet of *Heretic*. The heroes of the North, who had submitted, with some reluctance, to believe that all their ancestors were in Hell;[50] were astonished and exasperated to learn, that they themselves had only changed the mode of their eternal condemnation: Instead of the smooth applause, which Christian kings are accustomed to expect from their loyal prelates, the orthodox bishops and their clergy were in a state of opposition to the Arian courts; and their indiscreet opposition frequently became criminal, and might sometimes be dangerous. The pulpit, that safe and sacred organ of sedition, resounded with the names of Pharaoh and Holofernes;[51] the public discontent was inflamed by the hope or promise of a glorious deliverance; and the seditious saints were tempted to promote the accomplishment of their own predictions. Notwithstanding these provocations, the Catholics of Gaul, Spain, and Italy, enjoyed, under the reign of the Arians, the free, and peaceful, exercise of their religion. Their haughty masters respected the zeal of a numerous people, resolved to die at the foot of their altars; and the example of their devout constancy was admired and imitated by the Barbarians themselves. The conquerors evaded, however, the disgraceful reproach, or confession, of fear, by attributing their toleration to the liberal motives of reason and humanity; and while they affected the language, they imperceptibly imbibed the spirit, of genuine Christianity.

The peace of the church was sometimes interrupted. The Catholics were indiscreet, the Barbarians were impatient; and the partial acts of severity or injustice which had been recommended by the Arian clergy, were exaggerated by the orthodox writers. The guilt of persecution may be imputed to Euric, king of the Visigoths; who suspended the exercise of ecclesiastical, or at least, of episcopal, functions; and punished the popular bishops of Aquitain with imprisonment, exile, and confiscation. But the cruel and absurd enterprise of subduing the minds of a whole people, was undertaken by the Vandals alone. Genseric[52] himself, in his

---

50 "Radbod, king of the Frisons, was so much scandalized by this rash declaration of a missionary, that he drew back his foot after he had entered the baptismal font." [E.G.]

51 I.e., Old Testament tyrants. The preachers were suggesting an analogy between their rulers and these figures of the past.

52 Genseric (c. 406–477), famous king of the Vandals, was himself an Arian. He was notably fierce in war; Gibbon refers to him as "monarch of the sea" because his powerful fleet was a great scourge to the Romans.

early youth, had renounced the orthodox communion; and the apostate could neither grant, nor expect, a sincere forgiveness. He was exasperated to find, that the Africans, who had fled before him in the field, still presumed to dispute his will in synods and churches; and his ferocious mind was incapable of fear, or of compassion. His Catholic subjects were oppressed by intolerant laws, and arbitrary punishments. The language of Genseric was furious, and formidable; the knowledge of his intentions might justify the most unfavourable interpretation of his actions; and the Arians were reproached with the frequent executions, which stained the palace, and the dominions, of the tyrant. Arms and ambition were, however, the ruling passions of the monarch of the sea. But Hunneric,[53] his inglorious son, who seemed to inherit only his vices, tormented the Catholics with the same unrelenting fury, which had been fatal to his brother, his nephews, and the friends and favourites of his father: and, even to the Arian patriarch, who was inhumanly burnt alive in the midst of Carthage. The religious war was preceded and prepared by an insidious truce; persecution was made the serious and important business of the Vandal court; and the loathsome disease, which hastened the death of Hunneric, revenged the injuries, without contributing to the deliverance, of the church. The throne of Africa was successively filled by the two nephews of Hunneric; by Gundamund, who reigned about twelve, and by Thrasimund, who governed the nation above twenty-seven, years. Their administration was hostile and oppressive to the orthodox party. Gundamund appeared to emulate, or even to surpass, the cruelty of his uncle; and, if at length he relented, if he recalled the bishops, and restored the freedom of Athanasian worship, a præmature death intercepted the benefits of his tardy clemency. His brother, Thrasimund, was the greatest and most accomplished of the Vandal kings, whom he excelled in beauty, prudence, and magnanimity of soul. But this magnanimous character was degraded by his intolerant zeal and deceitful clemency. Instead of threats and tortures, he employed the gentle, but efficacious, powers of seduction. Wealth, dignity, and the royal favour, were the liberal rewards of apostasy; the Catholics, who had violated the laws, might purchase their pardon by the renunciation of their faith; and whenever Thrasimund meditated any rigorous measure, he patiently waited till the indiscretion of his adversaries furnished him with a specious opportunity. Bigotry was his last sentiment in the hour of death: and he exacted from his successor

---

53 Genseric's eldest son, who ruled 477–484.

a solemn oath, that he would never tolerate the sectaries of Athanasius. But his successor, Hilderic, the gentle son of the savage Hunneric, preferred the duties of humanity and justice, to the vain obligation of an impious oath; and his accession was gloriously marked by the restoration of peace and universal freedom. The throne of that virtuous, though feeble monarch, was usurped by his cousin Gelimer, a zealous Arian: but the Vandal kingdom, before he could enjoy or abuse his power, was subverted by the arms of Belisarius;[54] and the orthodox party retaliated the injuries which they had endured.

The passionate declamations of the Catholics, the sole historians of this persecution, cannot afford any distinct series of causes and events; any impartial view of characters, or counsels; but the most remarkable circumstances, that deserve either credit or notice, may be referred to the following heads: (I) In the original law, which is still extant, Hunneric expressly declares, and the declaration appears to be correct, that he had faithfully transcribed the regulations and penalties of the Imperial edicts; against the heretical congregations, the clergy, and the people, who dissented from the established religion. If the rights of conscience had been understood, the Catholics must have condemned their past conduct, or acquiesced in their actual sufferings. But they still persisted to refuse the indulgence which they claimed. While they trembled under the lash of persecution, they praised the *laudable* severity of Hunneric himself, who burnt or banished great numbers of Manichaeans;[55] and they rejected, with horror, the ignominious compromise, that the disciples of Arius, and of Athanasius, should enjoy a reciprocal and similar toleration in the territories of the Romans, and in those of the Vandals. (II) The practice of a conference, which the Catholics had so frequently used to insult and punish their obstinate antagonists, was retorted against themselves. At the command of Hunneric, four hundred and sixty-six orthodox bishops assembled at Carthage; but when they were admitted into the hall of audience, they had the mortification of beholding the Arian Cirila[56] exalted on the patriarchal throne. The disputants were separated, after the mutual and ordinary reproaches of noise and silence, of delay and pre-

---

54 A famous Byzantine general (c. 505–565) who in 533 and 534 won decisive victories over the Vandals and captured Gelimer.

55 The Manichaeans believed that a cosmic conflict existed between the good forces of light and the bad forces of darkness and that man's duty is to aid the good.

56 St. Cyril (412–444), an arrogant controversialist, was archbishop of Alexandria. He was excommunicated in 437.

cipitation, of military force and of popular clamour. One martyr and one confessor were selected among the Catholic bishops; twenty-eight escaped by flight, and eighty-eight by conformity; forty-six were sent into Corsica to cut timber for the royal navy; and three hundred and two were banished to the different parts of Africa, exposed to the insults of their enemies, and carefully deprived of all the temporal and spiritual comforts of life. The hardships of ten years exile must have reduced their numbers; and if they had complied with the law of Thrasimund, which prohibited any episcopal consecrations, the orthodox church of Africa must have expired with the lives of its actual members. They disobeyed; and their disobedience was punished by a second exile of two hundred and twenty bishops into Sardinia; where they languished fifteen years, till the accession of the gracious Hilderic. The two islands were judiciously chosen by the malice of their Arian tyrants. Seneca, from his own experience, has deplored and exaggerated the miserable state of Corsica,[57] and the plenty of Sardinia was overbalanced by the unwholesome quality of the air. (III) The zeal of Genseric, and his successors, for the conversion of the Catholics, must have rendered them still more jealous to guard the purity of the Vandal faith. Before the churches were finally shut, it was a crime to appear in a Barbarian dress; and those who presumed to neglect the royal mandate, were rudely dragged backwards by their long hair. The Palatine officers, who refused to profess the religion of their prince, were ignominiously stripped of their honours, and employments; banished to Sardinia and Sicily; or condemned to the servile labours of slaves and peasants in the fields of Utica. In the districts which had been peculiarly allotted to the Vandals, the exercise of the Catholic worship was more strictly prohibited; and severe penalties were denounced against the guilt, both of the missionary, and the proselyte. By these arts, the faith of the Barbarians was preserved, and their zeal was inflamed: they discharged, with devout fury, the office of spies, informers, or executioners; and whenever their cavalry took the field, it was the favourite amusement of the march, to defile the churches, and to insult the clergy of the adverse faction. (IV) The citizens who had been educated in the luxury of the Roman province, were delivered, with exquisite cruelty, to the Moors of

---

57 "See the base and insipid epigrams of the Stoic, who could not support exile with more fortitude than Ovid. Corsica might not produce corn, wine, or oil; but it could not be destitute of grass, water, and even fire." [E.G.] Seneca the Younger (c. 5 B.C.–A.D. 65), Roman Stoic, famous for his moral epistles and treatises, was for eight years (41–49) banished to Corsica by the Emperor Claudius because of his intimacy with Julia, Claudius' niece.

the desert. A venerable train of bishops, presbyters, and deacons, with a faithful crowd of four thousand and ninety-six persons, whose guilt is not precisely ascertained, were torn from their native homes, by the command of Hunneric. During the night they were confined, like a herd of cattle, amidst their own ordure: during the day they pursued their march over the burning sands; and if they fainted under the heat and fatigue, they were goaded, or dragged along, till they expired in the hands of their tormentors. These unhappy exiles, when they reached the Moorish huts, might excite the compassion of a people, whose native humanity was neither improved by reason, nor corrupted by fanaticism: but if they escaped the dangers, they were condemned to share the distress, of a savage life. (V) It is incumbent on the authors of persecution previously to reflect, whether they are determined to support it in the last extreme. They excite the flame which they strive to extinguish; and it soon becomes necessary to chastise the contumacy, as well as the crime, of the offender. The fine, which he is unable or unwilling, to discharge, exposes his person to the severity of the law; and his contempt of lighter penalties suggests the use and propriety of capital punishment. Through the veil of fiction and declamation, we may clearly perceive, that the Catholics, more especially under the reign of Hunneric, endured the most cruel and ignominious treatment. Respectable citizens, noble matrons, and consecrated virgins, were stripped naked, and raised in the air by pullies, with a weight suspended at their feet. In this painful attitude their naked bodies were torn with scourges, or burnt in the most tender parts with red-hot plates of iron. The amputation of the ears, the nose, the tongue, and the right-hand, was inflicted by the Arians; and although the precise number cannot be defined, it is evident that many persons, among whom a bishop and a proconsul may be named, were entitled to the crown of martyrdom. The same honour has been ascribed to the memory of count Sebastian, who professed the Nicene creed with unshaken constancy; and Genseric might detest, as an heretic, the brave and ambitious fugitive whom he dreaded as a rival. (VI) A new mode of conversion, which might subdue the feeble, and alarm the timorous, was employed by the Arian ministers. They imposed, by fraud or violence, the rites of baptism; and punished the apostacy of the Catholics, if they disclaimed this odious and profane ceremony, which scandalously violated the freedom of the will, and the unity of the sacrament. The hostile sects had formerly allowed the validity of each other's baptism; and the innovation, so fiercely maintained by the Vandals, can be imputed only to the example and advice of the Donatists.[58] (VII) The Arian clergy surpassed, in religious cruelty, the king and his Vandals; but they were incapable of cultivating the spiritual vineyard, which they were so desirous to possess. A patriarch[59] might seat himself on the throne of Carthage; some bishops, in the principal cities, might usurp the place of their rivals; but the smallness of their numbers, and their ignorance of the Latin language,[60] disqualified the Barbarians for the ecclesiastical ministry of a great church; and the Africans, after the loss of their orthodox pastors, were deprived of the public exercise of Christianity. (VIII) The emperors were the natural protectors of the Homoousian doctrine:[61] and the faithful people of Africa, both as Romans and as Catholics, preferred their lawful sovereignty to the usurpation of the Barbarous heretics. During an interval of peace and friendship, Hunneric restored the cathedral of Carthage; at the intercession of Zeno, who reigned in the East, and of Placidia, the daughter and relict[62] of emperors, and the sister of the queen of the Vandals. But this decent regard was of short duration; and the haughty tyrant displayed his contempt for the religion of the Empire, by studiously arranging the bloody images of persecution, in all the principal streets through which the Roman ambassador must pass in his way to the palace. An oath was required from the bishops, who were assembled at Carthage, that they would support the succession of his son Hilderic, and that they would renounce all foreign or *transmarine* correspondence. This engagement, consistent as it should seem, with their moral and religious duties, was refused by the more sagacious members of the assembly. Their refusal, faintly coloured by the pretence that it is unlawful for a Christian to swear, must provoke the suspicions of a jealous tyrant.

The Catholics, oppressed by royal and military force, were far superior to their adversaries in numbers and learning. With the same

---

58 The Donatists, believing that the validity of the sacraments depends on the spiritual state of the minister, forced all who joined their group to be rebaptized.

59 "*Primate* was more properly the title of the bishop of Carthage: but the name of *patriarch* was given by the sects and nations to their principal ecclesiastic." [E.G.]

60 "The patriarch Cyrila himself publicly declared, that he did not understand Latin . . . ; and he might converse with tolerable ease, without being capable of disputing or preaching in that language. His Vandal clergy were still more ignorant; and small confidence could be placed in the Africans who had conformed." [E.G.]

61 The orthodox doctrine of the Nicene Creed, holding that the Son of God is of the same essence or substance as the Father.

62 Widow.

weapons which the Greek[63] and Latin fathers had already provided for the
Arian controversy, they repeatedly silenced, or vanquished, the fierce and
illiterate successors of Ulphilas. The consciousness of their own superiority
might have raised them above the arts, and passions, of religious warfare.
Yet, instead of assuming such honourable pride, the orthodox theologians
were tempted, by the assurance of impunity, to compose fictions, which
must be stigmatized with the epithets of fraud and forgery. They ascribed
their own polemical works to the most venerable names of Christian antiquity: the characters of Athanasius and Augustin were aukwardly per-
sonated by Vigilius and his disciples;[64] and the famous creed, which so
clearly expounds the mysteries of the Trinity and the Incarnation, is
deduced, with strong probability, from this African school.[65] Even the
Scriptures themselves were profaned by their rash and sacrilegious hands.
The memorable text, which asserts the unity of the THREE who bear witness in heaven,[66] is condemned by the universal silence of the orthodox
fathers, ancient versions, and authentic manuscripts. It was first alleged by
the Catholic bishops whom Hunneric summoned to the conference of
Carthage. An allegorical interpretation, in the form, perhaps, of a marginal
note, invaded the text of the Latin Bibles, which were renewed and corrected in a dark period of ten centuries.[67] After the invention of printing,

---

63 "Fulgentius, bishop of Ruspae, in the Byzacene province, was of a senatorial
family, and had received a liberal education. He could repeat all Homer and Menander before
he was allowed to study Latin, his native tongue. . . . Many African bishops might understand Greek, and many Greek theologians were translated into Latin." [E.G.]

64 "Compare the two prefaces to the Dialogue of Vigilius of Thapsus. . . . He might
amuse his learned reader with an innocent fiction; but the subject was too grave, and the
Africans were too ignorant." [E.G.] Vigilius, an orthodox African bishop, wrote several
works which he tried to pass as productions of Athanasius, Augustine, and other church
fathers.

65 "The P. Quesnel started this opinion, which has been favourably received. But the
three following truths, however surprising they may seem, are *now* universally acknowledged. . . . (1) St. Athanasius is not the author of the creed which is so frequently read in our
churches. (2) It does not appear to have existed, within a century after his death. (3) It was
originally composed in the Latin tongue, and consequently, in the Western provinces.
Gennadius, patriarch of Constantinople, was so much amazed by this extraordinary composition, that he frankly pronounced it to be the work of a drunken man." [E.G.] Pasquier
Quesnel was a French Jansenist (1634–1719) who wrote extensively on theology.

66 The text is 1 John 5: 7, which Gibbon rightly declared spurious. In the King James
Bible it reads, "For there are those that beare record in heaven, the Father, the Word, and the
holy Ghost: and the three are one." The New English Bible has eliminated the verse.

67 "In the eleventh and twelfth centuries, the Bibles were corrected by Lanfranc,
archbishop of Canterbury, and by Nicolas, cardinal and librarian of the Roman church,
secundum orthodoxam fidem. . . . Notwithstanding these corrections, the passage is still
wanting in twenty-five Latin MSS., . . . the oldest and the fairest; two qualities seldom united,

the editors of the Greek Testament yielded to their own prejudices, or those of the times; and the pious fraud, which was embraced with equal zeal at Rome and at Geneva,[68] has been infinitely multiplied in every country and every language of modern Europe.

The example of fraud must excite suspicion; and the specious miracles by which the African Catholics have defended the truth and justice of their cause, may be ascribed, with more reason, to their own industry, than to the visible protection of Heaven. Yet the historian, who views this religious conflict with an impartial eye, may condescend to mention *one* preternatural event, which will edify the devout, and surprise the incredulous. Tipasa, a maritime colony of Mauritania, sixteen miles to the east of Cæsarea, had been distinguished, in every age, by the orthodox zeal of its inhabitants. They had braved the fury of the Donatists; they resisted, or eluded, the tyranny of the Arians. The town was deserted on the approach of an heretical bishop: most of the inhabitants who could procure ships passed over to the coast of Spain; and the unhappy remnant, refusing all communion with the usurper, still presumed to hold their pious, but illegal, assemblies. Their disobedience exasperated the cruelty of Hunneric. A military count was dispatched from Carthage to Tipasa: he collected the Catholics in the Forum, and, in the presence of the whole province, deprived the guilty of their right-hands and their tongues. But the holy confessors continued to speak without tongues; and this miracle is attested by Victor, an African bishop, who published an history of the persecution within two years after the event. "If any one," says Victor, "should doubt of the truth, let him repair to Constantinople, and listen to the clear and perfect language of Restitutus, the sub-deacon, one of these glorious sufferers, who is now lodged in the palace of the emperor Zeno, and is respected by the devout empress." At Constantinople we are astonished to find a cool, a learned, an unexceptionable witness, without interest, and without passion. Æneas of Gaza, a Platonic philosopher, has accurately described his own observations on these African sufferers.

> I saw them myself: I heard them speak: I diligently enquired by what means such an articulate voice could be formed without any organ of speech: I used my eyes to examine the report of my ears: I opened their

---

except in manuscripts." [E.G.] Gibbon means, of course, that age and beauty rarely coexist. The Latin phrase means, "according to orthodox faith."

68 I.e., by Catholics and Protestants alike.

mouth, and saw that the whole tongue had been completely torn away by the roots; an operation which the physicians generally suppose to be mortal.

The testimony of Æneas of Gaza might be confirmed by the superfluous evidence of the emperor Justinian, in a perpetual edict; of count Marcellinus, in his Chronicle of the times; and of pope Gregory the First, who had resided at Constantinople, as the minister of the Roman pontiff.[69] They all lived within the compass of a century; and they all appeal to their personal knowledge, or the public notoriety, for the truth of a miracle, which was repeated in several instances, displayed on the greatest theatre of the world, and submitted, during a series of years, to the calm examination of the senses. This supernatural gift of the African confessors, who spoke without tongues, will command the assent of those, and of those only, who already believe, that their language was pure and orthodox. But the stubborn mind of an infidel is guarded by secret, incurable, suspicion; and the Arian, or Socinian,[70] who has seriously rejected the doctrine of the Trinity, will not be shaken by the most plausible evidence of an Athanasian miracle.

The Vandals and the Ostrogoths persevered in the profession of Arianism till the final ruin of the kingdoms which they had founded in Africa and Italy. The Barbarians of Gaul submitted to the orthodox dominion of the Franks; and Spain was restored to the Catholic church by the voluntary conversion of the Visigoths.

This salutary revolution was hastened by the example of a royal martyr, whom our calmer reason may style an ungrateful rebel. Leovigild, the Gothic monarch of Spain, deserved the respect of his enemies, and the love of his subjects: the Catholics enjoyed a free toleration, and his Arian synods attempted, without much success, to reconcile their scruples by abolishing the unpopular rite of a *second* baptism. His eldest son Hermenegild, who was invested by his father with the royal diadem, and the fair principality of Boetica, contracted an honourable and orthodox alliance with a Merovingian princess, the daughter of Sigebert king of Austrasia, and of the famous Brunechild. The beauteous Ingundis, who was no more than thirteen years of age, was received, beloved, and per-

---

69 After citing these witnesses in a footnote, Gibbon adds, "None of these witnesses have specified the number of the confessors, which is fixed at sixty in an old menology. . . . Two of them lost their speech by fornication; but the miracle is enhanced by the singular instance of a boy who had *never* spoken before his tongue was cut out."

70 The Socinians denied the divinity of Christ, the doctrine of the Trinity, and the natural depravity of man.

secuted, in the Arian court of Toledo; and her religious constancy was alternately assaulted with blandishments and violence by Goisvintha, the Gothic queen, who abused the double claim of maternal authority.[71] Incensed by her resistance, Goisvintha seized the Catholic princess by her long hair, inhumanly dashed her against the ground, kicked her till she was covered with blood, and at last gave orders that she should be stripped, and thrown into a bason, or fish-pond. Love and honour might excite Hermenegild to resent this injurious treatment of his bride; and he was gradually persuaded, that Ingundis suffered for the cause of divine truth. Her tender complaints, and the weighty arguments of Leander, archbishop of Seville, accomplished his conversion; and the heir of the Gothic monarchy was initiated in the Nicene faith by the solemn rites of confirmation. The rash youth, inflamed by zeal, and perhaps by ambition, was tempted to violate the duties of a son, and a subject; and the Catholics of Spain, although they could not complain of persecution, applauded his pious rebellion against an heretical father. The civil war was protracted by the long and obstinate sieges of Merida, Cordova, and Seville, which had strenuously espoused the party of Hermenegild. He invited the orthodox Barbarians, the Suevi, and the Franks, to the destruction of his native land: he solicited the dangerous aid of the Romans, who possessed Africa, and a part of the Spanish coast; and his holy ambassador, the archbishop Leander, effectually negociated in person with the Byzantine court. But the hopes of the Catholics were crushed by the active diligence of a monarch who commanded the troops and treasures of Spain; and the guilty Hermenegild, after his vain attempts to resist or to escape, was compelled to surrender himself into the hands of an incensed father. Leovigild was still mindful of that sacred character; and the rebel, despoiled of the regal ornaments, was still permitted, in a decent exile, to profess the Catholic religion. His repeated and unsuccessful treasons at length provoked the indignation of the Gothic king; and the sentence of death, which he pronounced with apparent reluctance, was privately executed in the tower of Seville. The inflexible constancy with which he refused to accept the Arian communion, as the price of his safety, may excuse the honours that have been paid to the memory of St. Hermenegild. His wife and infant son were detained by the Romans in ignominious

---

71 "Goisvintha successively married two kings of the Visigoths: Athanagild, to whom she bore Brunechild, the mother of Ingundis; and Leovigild, whose two sons, Hermenegild and Recared, were the issue of a former marriage." [E.G.] She was thus both Ingundis's grandmother and her stepmother-in-law, and so had a "double claim of maternal authority."

captivity: and this domestic misfortune tarnished the glories of Leovigild, and embittered the last moments of his life.

His son and successor, Recared, the first Catholic king of Spain, had imbibed the faith of his unfortunate brother, which he supported with more prudence and success. Instead of revolting against his father, Recared patiently expected the hour of his death. Instead of condemning his memory, he piously supposed, that the dying monarch had abjured the errors of Arianism, and recommended to his son the conversion of the Gothic nation. To accomplish that salutary end, Recared convened an assembly of the Arian clergy and nobles, declared himself a Catholic, and exhorted them to imitate the example of their prince. The laborious interpretation of doubtful texts, or the curious pursuit of metaphysical arguments, would have excited an endless controversy; and the monarch discreetly proposed to his illiterate audience, two substantial and visible arguments, the testimony of Earth, and of Heaven. The *Earth* had submitted to the Nicene synod: the Romans, the Barbarians, and the inhabitants of Spain, unanimously professed the same orthodox creed; and the Visigoths resisted, almost alone, the consent of the Christian world. A superstitious age was prepared to reverence, as the testimony of *Heaven*, the preternatural cures, which were performed by the skill or virtue of the Catholic clergy; the baptismal fonts of Osset in Boetica,[72] which were spontaneously replenished each year, on the vigil of Easter;[73] and the miraculous shrine of St. Martin of Tours, which had already converted the Suevic prince and people of Gallicia. The Catholic king encountered some difficulties on this important change of the national religion. A conspiracy, secretly fomented by the queen-dowager, was formed against his life; and two counts excited a dangerous revolt in the Narbonnese Gaul. But Recared disarmed the conspirators, defeated the rebels, and executed severe justice; which the Arians, in their turn, might brand with the reproach of persecution. Eight bishops, whose names betray their Barbaric origin, abjured their errors; and all the books of Arian theology were reduced to ashes, with the house in which they had been purposely collected. The whole body of the Visigoths and Suevi were allured or driven into the pale of the Catholic communion; the faith, at least of the rising generation, was fervent and sincere; and the devout liberality of the

---

72 "Osset, or Julia Constantia, was opposite to Seville, on the northern side of the Boetis." [E.G.]

73 "This miracle was skilfully performed. An Arian king sealed the doors, and dug a deep trench round the church, without being able to intercept the Easter supply of baptismal water." [E.G.]

Barbarians enriched the churches and monasteries of Spain. Seventy bishops, assembled in the council of Toledo, received the submission of their conquerors; and the zeal of the Spaniards improved the Nicene creed, by declaring the procession of the Holy Ghost, from the Son, as well as from the Father; a weighty point of doctrine, which produced, long afterwards, the schism of the Greek and Latin churches. The royal proselyte immediately saluted and consulted pope Gregory, surnamed the Great, a learned and holy prelate, whose reign was distinguished by the conversion of heretics and infidels. The ambassadors of Recared respectfully offered on the threshold of the Vatican his rich presents of gold and gems: they accepted, as a lucrative exchange, the hairs of St. John the Baptist; a cross, which inclosed a small piece of the true wood; and a key, that contained some particles of iron which had been scraped from the chains of St. Peter.

The same Gregory, the spiritual conqueror of Britain, encouraged the pious Theodelinda, queen of the Lombards, to propagate the Nicene faith among the victorious savages, whose recent Christianity was polluted by the Arian heresy. Her devout labours still left room for the industry and success of future missionaries; and many cities of Italy were still disputed by hostile bishops. But the cause of Arianism was gradually suppressed by the weight of truth, of interest, and of example; and the controversy, which Egypt had derived from the Platonic school, was terminated, after a war of three hundred years, by the final conversion of the Lombards of Italy.

The first missionaries who preached the gospel to the Barbarians, appealed to the evidence of reason, and claimed the benefit of toleration. But no sooner had they established their spiritual dominion, than they exhorted the Christian kings to extirpate, without mercy, the remains of Roman or Barbaric superstition. The successors of Clovis inflicted one hundred lashes on the peasants who refused to destroy their idols; the crime of sacrificing to the dæmons was punished by the Anglo-Saxon laws with the heavier penalties of imprisonment and confiscation; and even the wise Alfred adopted, as an indispensable duty, the extreme rigour of the Mosaic institutions. But the punishment, and the crime, were gradually abolished among a Christian people: the theological disputes of the schools were suspended by propitious ignorance; and the intolerant spirit, which could find neither idolaters nor heretics, was reduced to the persecution of the Jews. That exiled nation had founded some synagogues in the cities of Gaul; but Spain, since the time of Hadrian, was filled with their numerous colonies. The wealth which they accumulated by trade, and the management of the finances, invited the pious avarice of their masters; and they might be oppressed without danger, as they had lost the use, and even the remembrance, of arms. Sisebut, a Gothic king, who reigned in the beginning of the seventh century, proceeded at once to the last extremes of persecution. Ninety thousand Jews were compelled to receive the sacrament of baptism; the fortunes of the obstinate infidels were confiscated, their bodies were tortured; and it seems doubtful whether they were permitted to abandon their native country. The excessive zeal of the Catholic king was moderated, even by the clergy of Spain, who solemnly pronounced an inconsistent sentence: *that* the sacraments should not be forcibly imposed; but *that* the Jews who had been baptized should be constrained, for the honour of the church, to persevere in the external practice of a religion which they disbelieved, and detested. Their frequent relapses provoked one of the successors of Sisebut to banish the whole nation from his dominions; and a council of Toledo published a decree, that every Gothic king should swear to maintain this salutary edict. But the tyrants were unwilling to dismiss the victims, whom they delighted to torture, or to deprive themselves of the industrious slaves, over whom they might exercise a lucrative oppression. The Jews still continued in Spain, under the weight of the civil and ecclesiastical laws, which in the same country have been faithfully transcribed in the Code of the Inquisition. The Gothic kings and bishops at length discovered, that injuries will produce hatred, and that hatred will find the opportunity of revenge. A nation, the secret or professed enemies of Christianity, still multiplied in servitude, and distress; and the intrigues of the Jews promoted the rapid success of the Arabian conquerors.

As soon as the Barbarians withdrew their powerful support, the unpopular heresy of Arius sunk into contempt and oblivion. But the Greeks still retained their subtle and loquacious disposition: the establishment of an obscure doctrine suggested new questions, and new disputes; and it was always in the power of an ambitious prelate, or a fanatic monk, to violate the peace of the church, and, perhaps, of the empire. The historian of the empire may overlook those disputes which were confined to the obscurity of schools and synods. The Manichæans, who laboured to reconcile the religions of Christ and of Zoroaster,[74] had secretly introduced themselves into the provinces: but these foreign sectaries were in-

---

[74] Founder of a religion that told of a cosmic struggle between a Spirit of Good and a Spirit of Evil.

volved in the common disgrace of the Gnostics,[75] and the Imperial laws were executed by the public hatred. The rational opinions of the Pelagians[76] were propagated from Britain to Rome, Africa, and Palestine, and silently expired in a superstitious age. But the East was distracted by the Nestorian and Eutychian controversies;[77] which attempted to explain the mystery of the incarnation, and hastened the ruin of Christianity in her native land. These controversies were first agitated under the reign of the younger Theodosius:[78] but their important consequences extend far beyond the limits of the present volume. The metaphysical chain of argument, the contests of ecclesiastical ambition, and their political influence on the decline of the Byzantine empire, may afford an interesting and instructive series of history, from the general councils of Ephesus and Chalcedon,[79] to the conquest of the East by the successors of Mahomet.

---

75 Members of sects which claimed superior knowledge of spiritual matters and which explained the world as having been created by emanations from the Godhead.

76 The Pelagian heresy held that man took the fundamental steps toward salvation by his own efforts, without the assistance of divine grace.

77 Nestorius occasioned a schism by refusing to call the Virgin Mary "the mother of God." Eutychus, a strong opponent of Nestorius, taught that Christ had only one nature, the divine.

78 See above, note 36.

79 The Council of Ephesus took place in 431; the Council of Chalcedon was in 451. Both were occasions for the promulgation of church doctrine.

THE AUTOBIOGRAPHIES
OF EDWARD GIBBON[1]

(1796)

Gibbon wrote six different accounts of his own life. They vary in length and completeness; only one takes his history as far as 1789, five years before his death. The last and most polished of the memoirs brings his life only to 1753. First published in a confused and expurgated form by Gibbon's friend Lord Sheffield in 1796, they were in the nineteenth century re-edited from the manuscripts in more accurate form. The passage here reprinted in its entirety is Memoir E, dated by Gibbon as having been written in 1791. Although it is stylistically sketchy in some places, it provides the historian's fullest account of his own career and offers some insight into his way of considering his life as a whole.

One striking aspect of Gibbon's autobiographical technique is his attention only to private matters. Although he lived in a time of stirring national events, he seldom refers to them: only when reference is necessary to illustrate his own situation does he consider public matters. This is essentially an intellectual autobiography, a record of an individual mind's growth and development.

The present text is from *The Autobiographies of Edward Gibbon*, ed. John Murray (London, 1896).

My Own Life

My family is ancient and honourable in the county of Kent. As early as the year 1326 the Gibbons, who still bear the same arms as myself,[2]

---

1 See introduction, pp. 30–32.

2 "*A Lyon, rampant, gardant, between three Schallops*. Blue-mantle tells a whimsical story of Edmond Gibbon, who changed the three schallops of his arms into three ogresses, or female monsters, the emblems of three cousins with whom he had a law-suit (p. 161)." [E.G.] "*Schallops*," are scallop shells. "Blue-mantle" was John Gibbon (1629–1719), the brother of the historian's great-grandfather. He held the title of Blue-mantle Poursuivant at Arms in the College of Heralds (a "poursuivant" is an attendant of a herald; "Blue-mantle" refers to the traditional costume of the office) and published *Introduction ad Latinam Blazoniam* (1682), a treatise on heraldry whose distinction was its introduction of Latin terms.

were possessed of lands in the parish of Rolvenden, and their successive
alliances connect them with many worthy names of the English gentry.
About the beginning of the last century, a younger branch appears to have
migrated from the country to the city. My grandfather, Edward Gibbon,
was Commissioner of the Customs (1710–1714), and a Director of the
South Sea Company. In the calamitous year twenty, he was stripped of
his apparent fortune (£106,543 5s. 6d.) by an arbitrary vote of the house of
commons, which reduced him to an allowance of ten thousand pounds;[3]
yet such were his dexterity and diligence, that he died, sixteen years afterwards, in very affluent circumstances. My father, Edward Gibbon (born
in 1707), enjoyed the advantages of education and travel, and successively
represented in Parliament the borough of Petersfield (1734) and the town
of Southampton (1740). In the opposition to Sir Robert Walpole and the
Pelhams[4] he was connected with the Tories—shall I say the Jacobites?
With them he gave many a vote, with them he drank many a bottle. But
the prejudices of youth were gradually corrected by time, temper, and
good sense.

I was born at his house at Putney, in Surry, the eldest child of his
marriage, a marriage of inclination, with Judith Porten.[5] My five brothers
and my sister all died in their infancy, and the premature decease of my
mother (1746) left her fond husband a disconsolate widower. Some years
afterwards (1755) he was married to his second wife, Mrs. Dorothea
Patten,[6] whose tender friendship has often made me forget that I had
scarcely known the blessing of a mother.

---

3 "See the whole course of these iniquitous proceedings in Rapin and Tindal's History
of England (vol. iv. pt. ii. pp. 629–644, folio Edition). The offence of the South Sea Directors
was not defined in law; their guilt was not proved, in fact: they were refused the common
right of being heard by their council against a bill of pains and penalties, and their fate was
decided by hasty and passionate votes on the character and fortune of each individual. It may
be added, as a last aggravation, that the legal existence of the Parliament which condemned
them is extemely questionable." [E.G.] The South Sea Company had assumed the national debt
in return for annual government payments and for certain trade monopolies. The resultant
speculation in shares involved many fraudulent schemes, and in 1720 the company collapsed.
The history Gibbon refers to is *The History of England*, by M. Rapin de Thoras, continued by
N. Tindal, M. A., Vol. IV (1747).
4 Robert Walpole, Earl of Orford (1676–1745), prime minister (1721–1742). Henry
Pelham (1696–1754) and his brother Thomas Pelham-Holles, Duke of Newcastle (1693–
1768), were Whig prime ministers after Walpole.
5 She was the daughter of James Porten, a merchant whose credit was failing at the
time of the marriage (1736). Both families opposed the match.
6 Mrs. Patten (c. 1715–1796), daughter of David and Elizabeth Patten. Gibbon confesses, "I was disposed to hate the rival of my mother and the enemy of her son."

From my birth to the age of fifteen, my puny constitution was afflicted with almost every species of disease and weakness; and I owe my life to the maternal tenderness of my aunt, Mrs. Catherine Porten, at whose name I feel a tear of gratitude trickling down my cheek. My first domestic tutor was Mr. John Kirkby, the author of an English Grammar and the Philosophical Romance of Automathes.[7] But my progress at Kingston and Westminster Schools was too often interrupted by my returns of illness; and the want of public discipline was imperfectly supplied by private instruction. It is fashionable for the *man* to envy and regret the happiness of the *boy*, but I never could understand the happiness of servitude; and my want of agility and strength disqualified me for the joyous play of my equals. The long hours of confinement to my chamber or my couch were soothed, however, by an early and eager love of reading. Some books of fiction, Pope's Homer and the Arabian Nights, were the first food of my mind; but I soon began to devour, with indiscriminate appetite, the history, chronology, and geography of the ancient and modern world.

At an unripe age I was matriculated as a Gentleman-commoner at Magdalen College, in the University of Oxford, where I lost fourteen valuable months of my youth. The reader will ascribe this loss to my own incapacity, or to the vices of that ancient institution.

Without a master or a guide, I unfortunately stumbled on some books of Popish controversy; nor is it a matter of reproach that a boy should have believed that he believed, etc. I was seduced like Chillingworth and Bayle,[8] and, like them, my growing reason soon broke through the toils of sophistry and superstition.

Most fortunately my father was persuaded to fix my exile and

---

7 "A self-taught Youth who discovers Religion and Science in a desert island, is indeed a Romance. The characters of a Philosopher and a Bigot are blended in my old tutor; but the story of Automathes (London, 1745, in 12mo) is agreably told. The original idea is borrowed, however, from the life of Hai Ebu Yokdhan, composed in the twelfth century by Abû Jaafar Ebn Tophail, and translated from Arabic into Latin by Dr. Pocock (Oxon, 1700, in 4to, secundâ edit.)." [E.G.]

8 "When these masters of argument were seduced by Popery, the Frenchman was near twenty-two, the Englishman above twenty-eight years of age. In their retrograde motion, the logic of Chillingworth paused on the last verge of Christianity; the genius of Bayle pervaded the boundless regions of Scepticism." [E.G.] William Chillingsworth (1602–1644), English theologian, became a Catholic convert but was reconverted, and in 1638, took orders in the Church of England. He argued for the individual's right to personal interpretation of the Bible. Pierre Bayle (1647–1706) moved from Catholicism to extreme rationalism.

education at Lausanne, in Switzerland, under the care of Mr. Pavillard,[9] a Calvinist Minister. I would praise his virtue above his learning, his learning above his genius: yet a pupil might imbibe from his lessons the love, the method, and the rudiments of science, and I shall always esteem that worthy man as the first father of my mind.

At the end of five years I was recalled home—of five years which my voluntary and rational diligence had profitably employed. It was at Lausanne that I acquired the perfect knowledge and use of the French language; that I read almost all the Latin Classics in prose and verse; that I made some progress in Greek litterature; and that I finished a regular course of Philosophy and Mathematics. It was there that my taste and reason were expanded; that I formed the habits of being pleased (I will not say of pleasing) in good company; and that I eradicated the prejudices which would have ripened in the Atmosphere of an English Cloyster. A tour of Switzerland enlarged my views of Nature and man: I enjoyed the singular amusement of seeing Voltaire an actor in his own tragedies;[10] and, before the age of twenty, I solicited and sustained a learned correspondence with several professors in foreign universities. I should blush if the season of youth had passed away without love or friendship. My connection with Mr. George Deyverdun,[11] a young gentleman of Lausanne, has been terminated only by the death of my friend. A lover's wishes reluctantly yielded to filial duty; time and absence produced their effect; but my choice has been justified by the virtues of Mademoiselle C———(now Madame N———) in the most humble and the most splendid fortune.[12]

On my return home I was indulged with a decent allowance of money and liberty; and the two following years were unequally divided

---

9 M. Daniel Pavillard (1704–1775), pastor and professor of history, secured Gibbon's reconversion to Protestantism by December 1754.

10 "Voltaire had lately escaped from the dangers of Royal friendship, and now began, at the age of threescore, to enjoy his freedom and fortune." [E.G.] François Marie Arouet de Voltaire (1694–1778), French philosopher, wrote many tragedies in the classical style; *Zaïre* (1732) is probably the best known. For his views on Shakespearean tragedy, see Johnson's *Preface*, above, pp. 147, 161.

11 Georges Deyverdun (1754–1789) pursued a desultory literary career; for a time, as a result of Gibbon's influence, he was a clerk in the office of the English secretary of state.

12 Suzanne Curchod (1737–1794), daughter of a country minister, was the object of Gibbon's devotion. His father's opposition to his proposed marriage to a foreigner caused the young man to renounce her; she married Jacques Necker (1732–1804), Swiss banker, who became director of the treasury and director general of finances in France. Mme. Necker remained Gibbon's friend to the end of his life.

between a short visit to London, and a long calm residence in my father's house at Buriton, near Petersfield, in Hampshire. For rural sports and agriculture I had no taste; and all the hours that I could steal from family duties were deliciously passed in a library, which soon became my own. By practise and study I recovered the purity of my native tongue; and the English, Greek, and Latin Classics were the best companions of my solitude. My pen was seldom idle, and I began to write for the public eye as well as for my own.

From these studies I was called away by the sound of the militia drum, by the embodying of the South Battalion of the Hampshire, in which I had rashly accepted a Captain's commission, and in which I was afterwards promoted to the rank of Major and Lieutenant Colonel-Commandant. At the first outset I was dazzled and fired by the play of arms, the exercise, the march, and the camp, and my present acquaintance will smile when I assure them that I was once a very tolerable officer. I read Homer in my tent, I compared the theory of ancient with the practise of modern tactics; and the Captain of Grenadiers (they may again smile) has not been useless to the historian of the Roman Empire. By degrees our mimic Bellona[13] unveiled her naked deformity, and before our final dissolution I had long sighed for my release.

In the midst of this military life, I published my *Essai sur l'étude de la Litterature*,[14] which was extorted from me by my father's authority, and the advice of Dr. Maty[15] and Mr. Mallet,[16] after it had slept two or three years in my desk. The vanity of being the first English author in the French language might perhaps be excused; but, in sober truth, I wrote, as I thought, in the most familiar idiom. The journals of Paris and Holland have praised the style and spirit, the learning and judgement,

---

13 Roman goddess of war.

14 Published in 1761, the book champions the study of ancient literature as a proper exercise for the intellect.

15 "The eighteen volumes of the *Journal Britannique*, which he sustained six years (1750–1755), almost alone had displayed the moderation and taste of Dr. Maty. A flattering epistle which he prefixed to my Essay is so cautiously worded, that, in case of a defeat, he might have excused his indulgence to a *young English gentleman*." [E. G.] Dr. Matthew Maty (1718–1776), physician and writer, principal librarian of the British Museum, from 1750–1755 publisher of *Journal Britannique*, which reviewed English publications in French.

16 "The author of a Life of Bacon (which has been rated above its value), of some forgotten poems and plays, and of the pathetic ballad of William and Margaret. An enemy, and a stern enemy (Johnson's Lives of the Poets), acknowledges that Mallet's conversation was elegant and easy." [E.G.] David Mallet (c. 1705–1765); his *Life of Francis Bacon* was published in 1740.

of this juvenile performance, with which, at the distance of thirty years, I am not absolutely displeased. But in England my Essay was slowly circulated, little read, and soon forgotten; till the fame of the historian enhanced the price of the remaining copies, which I refused to multiply by a new edition. After this first experiment, I meditated some historical composition. Many subjects were examined and rejected: an *history of the freedom and victories of the Swiss* was the theme on which I dwelt with the longest pleasure, and which I abandoned with the most reluctance.[17]

The hour of peace and national triumph was propitious to my design of visiting the continent. The arts and public buildings, the libraries and theatres of Paris, might have occupied more than four months the curiosity of a stranger. But the favourable reception of my Essay, and some weighty recommendations, introduced me into the societies of Helvetius, of the Baron d'Holbach, of Mr. de Foncemagne, of Madame Geoffrin, and of Madame du Bocage.[18] At these elegant Symposia, to which I was wellcome, without invitation, almost every day of the week, I saw and heard the most eminent of the wits, scholars, and philosophers of France; and it was amusing, as well as instructive, to compare the writings with the characters of the men.

In my second voluntary visit I was received at Lausanne as a native, who, after a long absence, returns to his friends, his family, and his country. The simple charms of Nature and society detained me at the foot of the Alps till the ensuing spring; and I justified my delay by the useful study of the Italian and Roman antiquities.

The pilgrimage of Italy, which I now accomplished, had long been the object of my curious devotion. The passage of Mount Cenis,[19] the regular streets of Turin, the Gothic cathedral of Milan, the scenery of the

---

17 "By the assistance of Mr. Deyverdun I obtained many extracts and translations from the German originals of Tschudi, Stetler, Schilling, Lauffer, Leu, etc.; but I soon found, on a tryal, that these materials were insufficient. An historian should command the language, the libraries, and the archives of the country of which he presumes to write." [E.G.] Aegidius Tschudi (1505–1572), Swiss historian; Michael Stettler (1580–1642) and Diebold Schilling (d. 1509), historians of Berne; Jacob Lauffer (1688–1734), author of a *History of the Swiss*; Hans Jacob Lew (1689–1768), compiler of *Universal Swiss Lexicon* (1747–1763), a collection of materials for Swiss history.

18 Claude Helvétius (1715–1771) and Paul Henri, Baron d'Holbach (1723–1789), French philosophers; Etienne de Foncemagne (1694–1774), historian and controversialist; Marie Thérèse Geoffrin (1699–1777), widow of a French colonel: she presided over a famous literary salon; Marie du Boccage (1710–1802), poet and social leader.

19 Alpine pass, 6,835 feet high, on the French-Italian border.

Boromean Islands,[20] the marble palaces of Genoa, the beauties of Florence, the wonders of Rome, the curiosities of Naples, the galleries of Bologna, the singular aspect of Venice, the amphitheatre of Verona, and the Palladian[21] architecture of Vicenza, are still present to my imagination. I read the Tuscan writers on the banks of the Arno; but my conversation was with the dead rather than the living, and the whole college of Cardinals was of less value in my eyes than the transfiguration of Raphael,[22] the Apollo of the Vatican,[23] or the massy greatness of the Coliseum. It was at Rome, on the fifteenth of October, 1764, as I sat musing amidst the ruins of the Capitol, while the barefooted fryars were singing Vespers in the temple of Jupiter, that the idea of writing the decline and fall of the City first started to my mind. After Rome has kindled and satisfied the enthusiasm of the Classic pilgrim, his curiosity for all meaner objects insensibly subsides. My father was impatient, and I returned home by the way of Lyons and Paris, enriched with a new stock of images and ideas, which I could never have acquired in the solitude of the Closet.

After this various and delightful excursion, I again settled, in the dull division of my English year, between London and Buriton. But in the militia I had been used to command, in my travels I was free from controul. The most gentle authority will sometimes frown without reason, the most chearful obedience will sometimes murmur without cause; and, at the age of thirty, I felt the natural wish of being master in my own house. The love of study secured me against the tediousness of an idle life, but I sometimes regretted that I had not consulted my interest and independence by the timely choice of a lucrative profession.

The greatest part of the seven years which elapsed after my return home was seriously employed in preparing the materials of my Roman history, of whose nature and extent at first I had a very inadequate idea. (i) From the Augustan age to the fall of the western Empire, I studied, almost always with my pen in my hand, the original records, both Greek and Latin, both Ecclesiastical and profane. I have never denied or dissembled my obligations to modern glasses, more especially to the in-

---

20 Islands in Lago Maggiore in the Alpine foothills of northern Italy and southern Switzerland.

21 So named from Andria Palladio (1508–1580), whose romanizing architectural principles were much admired and followed by Gibbon's contemporaries.

22 "Transfiguration," a painting by Raphael (1483–1520) in the church of San Pietro in Montorio, Rome.

23 Probably the famous statue of the Apollo Belvedere, although Gibbon may mean the Apollo Musagetes, attributed to Scopas, also in the Vatican.

comparable microscope of Tillemont;[24] but as it was my privilege to
think with my own reason, so it was my duty to see with my own eyes.
(ii) In the Italian history of the middle ages, Muratori and Pagi,[25] Sigonius
and Maffei,[26] were my faithful and assiduous guides; and I grasped the
ruins of Rome in the fourteenth century, without suspecting that the
distant object would fly before me to the end of a sixth quarto.

Yet in the progress of my work I was often diverted by the amusements of the World, and the avocations of old and new books; of the
ancient Classics of Greece and Rome, of the annual publications of France
and England. During this period I twice gave my thoughts, without
giving my name, to the public. I joyned with my friend Mr. Deyverdun,
who resided several years in England: we published two volumes of a
litterary Journal or review, *Memories Litteraires de la Grande Bretagne*, for
the years 1767 and 1768; but in this social work I am not ambitious of
ascertaining my peculiar property. In the year 1770 I sent to the press
some *Critical Observations on the Sixth Book of the Æneid*. This anonymous
pamphlet was pointed against Bishop Warburton, who demonstrates
that the descent of Æneas to the shades is an Allegory of his initiation to
the Eleusinian mysteries. The love of Virgil, the hatred of a Dictator,[27]
and the example of Lowth,[28] awakened me to arms. The coldness of the

---

24 Sébastien le Nain de Tillemont (1637–1698), French historian, author of *Mémoires
pour servir à l'histoire ecclésiastique des six premiers siècles* (1693–1712). The "microscope" is
figurative: Tillemont was noted for the exactitude and precision with which he examined
available facts.
25 Ludovico Muratori (1672–1750), Italian priest, who edited collections of historical
documents; Antoine Pagi (1624–1721), French historian and editor.
26 Carolus Sigonius (c. 1524–1584), Italian humanist, writer on Greek and Roman
antiquities; Francesco Scipione Maffei (1675–1755), Italian poet, archaeologist, and littérateur.
27 "Our litterary Sylla was encompassed with a guard of flatterers and slaves ready to
execute every sentence of proscription which his arrogance had pronounced. The assassina-
tion of Jortin by Dr. Hurd, now Bishop of Worcester (see the Delicacy of Friendship), is a base
and malignant act, which cannot be erazed by time or expiated by *secret* pennance." [E.G.]
"Sylla" (Roman dictator, who lived 138–78 B.C.) refers to William Warburton (1698–1779),
author of *The Divine Legation of Moses Demonstrated* (1738–1788), an antideistic interpretation
of the fact that no mention of a future state of reward or punishment occurs in Mosaic texts.
Dr. John Jortin (1698–1770), in *On the State of the Dead as Described by Homer and Virgil* (1755),
attacked Warburton's theories and was thereupon attacked himself by Richard Hurd (1720–
1808), Warburton's protégé, in *On the Delicacy of Friendship* (1755).
28 "See a letter from a late Professor in the University of Oxford (1766, fourth
Edition). The public adjudged the prize to the chaste and temperate spirit of Dr. Lowth
(since Bishop of London), who had been furiously attacked by Warburton and his blood-
hounds. As long as the dispute is connected with the taste and knowledge of Hebrew poetry,
the Oxford professor fights on his own ground. But his argument is often weak; and how
can it be strong, when he pleads the cause of bigotry and persecution?" [E.G.] Robert Lowth

public has been amply compensated by the esteem of Heyne,[29] of Hayley,[30] and of Parr;[31] but the acrimony of my style has been justly blamed by the Professor of Gottingen.[32] Warburton was *not* an object of contempt.

At the time of my father's decease I was upwards of thirty-three years of age, the ordinary term of an human generation. My grief was sincere for the loss of an affectionate parent, an agreeable companion, and a worthy man. But the ample fortune which my grandfather had left was deeply impaired, and would have been gradually consumed by the easy and generous nature of his son.[33] I revere the memory of my father, his errors I forgive, nor can I repent of the important sacrifices which were chearfully offered by filial piety. Domestic command, the free distribution of time and place, and a more liberal measure of expence, were the immediate consequences of my new situation; but two years rolled away before I could disentangle myself from the web of rural œconomy, and adopt a mode of life agreeable to my wishes. From Buriton Mrs. Gibbon[34] withdrew to Bath; while I removed myself and my books into my new house in Bentinck Street, Cavendish Square, in which I continued to reside near eleven years. The clear untainted remains

---

(1710–1787), author of *Lectures on Hebrew Poetry* (delivered 1741, published in Latin 1753), had a dispute with Warburton over the use made of the Book of Job in support of a chronolgical argument in Lowth's lectures. He answered Warburton's attack, contained in the sixth book of the *Divine Legation*, with his own *Letter to the Author of the Divine Legation* (1765), to which Gibbon refers in his note.

29 Christian Gottlob Heyne (1729–1812), a distinguished philologist and Virgilian scholar.

30 William Hayley (1745–1820), popular poet, author of verse *Essays on Painting, History and Epic Poetry*; those on history were inscribed to Gibbon.

31 Samuel Parr (1745–1825), schoolmaster and clergyman, constantly involved in literary quarrels.

32 I.e., Professor Heyne.

33 In his Hampshire retirement, my father might seem to enjoy the state of primitive happiness—"Beatus ille qui procul negotiis, etc." But, alas! he was not "solutus omni foenore," and without such freedom there can be no content." [E.G.] The full quotation is,

> Beatus ille, qui procul negotiis,
> Ut prisca gens mortalium,
> Paterna rura bubus exercet suis,
> Solutus omni faenore.

> Horace, *Epodes*, II 1.

"Happy the man who far from schemes of business, like the early generations of mankind, plows and plows again his ancestral land with his own oxen, with no yoke of usury on his neck."

34 I.e., his father's widow.

of my patrimony have been always sufficient to support the rank of a Gentleman, and to satisfy the desires of a philosopher.

I had now attained the solid comforts of life—a convenient well-furnished house, a domestic table, half a dozen chosen servants, my own carriage, and all those decent luxuries whose value is the more sensibly felt the longer they are enjoyed. These advantages were crowned by the first of earthly blessings, independence. I was the absolute master of my hours and actions; nor was I deceived in the hope that the establishment of my library in town would allow me to divide the day between study and society. Each year the circle of my acquaintance, the number of my dead and living companions, was enlarged. To a lover of books the shops and sales in London present irresistible temptations, and the manufacture of my history required a various and growing stock of materials. The Militia, my travels, the House of Commons, the fame of an author, contributed to multiply my connections. I was chosen a member of the fashionable clubs; and before I left England there were few persons of any eminence in the litterary or political World to whom I was a stranger.[35] By my own choice I passed in town the greatest part of the year; but whenever I was desirous of breathing the air of the Country, I possessed an hospitable retreat at Sheffield Place, in Sussex, in the family of Mr. Holroyd, a valuable friend, whose character, under the name of Lord Sheffield, has since been more conspicuous to the public.[36]

No sooner was I settled in my house and library than I undertook the composition of the first Volume of my history. At the outset all was dark and doubtful—even the title of the work, the true æra of the decline and fall of the Empire, the limits of the Introduction, the division of the chapters, and the order of the narrative; and I was often tempted to cast away the labour of seven years. The style of an author should be the image of his mind, but the choice and command of language is the fruit of exercise; many experiments were made before I could hit the middle tone between a dull Chronicle and a Rhetorical declamation; three times did I compose the first chapter, and twice the second and third, before I was

---

35 "It would most assuredly be in my power to amuse the reader with a gallery of portraits and a collection of anecdotes; but I have always condemned the practise of transforming a private memorial into a vehicle of satire and praise." [E.G.]

36 John Baker Holroyd, Lord Sheffield (1735–1821), became about this time Gibbon's constant adviser. He later managed the historian's financial affairs and after Gibbon's death edited his *Miscellaneous Works* in five volumes (1815; an earlier version, in two volumes, appeared in 1796).

tolerably satisfied with their effect. In the remainder of the way I advanced
with a more equal and easy pace; but the fifteenth and sixteenth Chapters
have been reduced, by three successive revisals, from a large Volume to
their present size, and they might still be compressed without any loss of
facts or sentiments. An opposite fault may be imputed to the concise and
superficial narrative of the first reigns from Commodus to Alexander,[37]
a fault of which I have never heard except from Mr. Hume[38] in his last
journey to London. Such an oracle might have been consulted and obeyed
with rational devotion; but I was soon disgusted with the modest practise
of reading the manuscript to my friends. Of such friends some will praise
from politeness, and some will criticise from vanity. The author himself
is the best Judge of his own performances; none has so deeply meditated
on the subject, none is so sincerely interested in the event.

By the friendship of Mr. (now Lord) Eliot, who had married my
first cousin,[39] I was returned at the general election for the borough of
Leskeard. I took my seat at the beginning of the memorable contest
between Great Britain and America; and supported, with many a sincere
and *silent* vote, the rights, though not perhaps the interests, of the mother-
country. After a fleeting illusive[40] hope, prudence condemned me to
acquiesce in the humble station of a mute. I was not armed by Nature or
education with the intrepid energy of mind and voice—

Vincentem strepitus, et natum rebus agendis.[41]

timidity was fortified by pride, and even the success of my pen discouraged
the tryal of my voice. But I assisted at the debates of a free assembly,
which agitated the most important questions, of peace and war, of Justice
and Policy: I listened to the attack and defence of eloquence and reason;
I had a near prospect of the characters, views, and passions of the first
men of the age. The eight sessions that I sat in Parliament were a school of

---

37 Commodus was Roman emperor, A.D. 180–192; Alexander Severus ruled from
222 to 235.
38 David Hume (1711–1776), Scottish philosopher and historian (see above, p. 234).
His *History of England* (1754–1762) was particularly admired for its prose style.
39 "Catherine Elliston, whose mother, Catherine Gibbon, was my grandfather's
second daughter." [E.G.] Lord Eliot was Edward Eliot (1727–1804), in 1784 first Baron Eliot
of St. Germans.
40 Illusory.
41 "Able to drown the clamors of the pit, and by nature fit for action" (Horace,
Art of Poetry, 82).

civil prudence, the first and most essential virtue of an historian.

The volume of my history, which had been somewhat delayed by the novelty and tumult of a first session, was now ready for the press. After the perilous adventure had been declined by my timid friend Mr. Elmsley,[42] I agreed, on very easy terms, with Mr. Thomas Cadell,[43] a respectable bookseller, and Mr. William Strahan,[44] an eminent printer; and they undertook the care and risk of the publication, which derived more credit from the name of the shop than from that of the author. The last revisal of the proofs was submitted to my vigilance; and many blemishes of style, which had been invisible in the manuscript, were discovered and corrected in the printed sheet. So moderate were our hopes, that the original impression had been stinted to five hundred, till the number was doubled by the prophetic taste of Mr. Strahan. During this awful interval I was neither elated by the ambition of fame, nor depressed by the apprehension of contempt. My diligence and accuracy were attested by my own conscience. History is the most popular species of writing, since it can adapt itself to the highest or the lowest capacity. I had chosen an illustrious subject; Rome is familiar to the schoolboy and the statesman, and my narrative was deduced from the last period of Classical reading. I had likewise flattered myself that an age of light and liberty would receive, without scandal, an enquiry into the *human* causes of the progress and establishment of Christianity.

I am at a loss how to describe the success of the work without betraying the vanity of the writer. The first impression was exhausted in a few days; a second and third edition were scarcely adequate to the demand, and the bookseller's property was twice invaded by the pyrates of Dublin. My book was on every table, and almost on every toilette; the historian was crowned by the taste or fashion of the day; nor was the general voice disturbed by the barking of any profane critic. The favour of mankind is most freely bestowed on a new acquaintance of any original merit, and the mutual surprize of the public and their favourite is productive of those warm sensibilities which, at a second meeting, can no longer be rekindled. If I listened to the music of praise, I was more seriously satisfied

---

42 Peter Elmsley (1736–1802), bookseller, to whom Gibbon left fifty pounds in his will. Gibbon died at his house.

43 Thomas Cadell (1742–1802), London publisher who printed the works of Johnson and the historian Robertson (see below, note 45) as well as those of Gibbon.

44 William Strahan (1715–1785), printer and publisher, Cadell's partner.

with the approbation of my Judges. The candour of Dr. Robertson[45] embraced his disciple; a letter from Mr. Hume overpaid the labour of ten years; but I have never presumed to accept a place in the triumvirate of British historians.

My second excursion to Paris was determined by the pressing invitation of Mr. and Madame Necker,[46] who had visited England in the preceding summer. On my arrival I found Mr. Necker, Director-general of the finances, in the first bloom of power and popularity; his private fortune enabled him to support a liberal establishment; and his wife, whose talents and virtues I had long admired, was admirably qualified to preside in the conversation of her table and drawing-room. As their friend, I was introduced to the best company of both sexes; to the foreign ministers of all nations, and to the first names and characters of France, who distinguished me by such marks of civility and kindness as gratitude will not suffer me to forget, and modesty will not allow me to enumerate. The fashionable suppers often broke into the morning hours; yet I occasionally consulted the Royal Library, and that of the Abbey of St. Germain; and in the free use of their books at home I had always reason to praise the liberality of those institutions. The society of men of letters I neither courted nor declined; but I was happy in the acquaintance of Mr. de Buffon,[47] who united with a sublime Genius the most amiable simplicity of mind and manners. At the table of my old friend, Mr. de Foncemagne,[48] I was involved in a dispute with the Abbé de Mably,[49] and his jealous irascible spirit revenged itself on a work which he was incapable of reading in the original.

Near two years had elapsed between the publication of my first and the commencement of my second Volume; and the causes must be assigned of this long delay. (1) After a short holyday I indulged my curiosity in some studies of a very different nature; a course of Anatomy which was demonstrated by Dr. Hunter,[50] and some lessons of Chemistry

---

45 William Robertson (1721–1793), Scottish historian, author of *History of Scotland During the Reigns of Queen Mary and of King James VI* (1759) and *History of America* (1777). He and Hume were the most famous living British historians.

46 See note 12, above.

47 Georges Leclerc, Comte de Buffon (1707–1788), famous French naturalist.

48 See note 18, above.

49 Gabriel Bonnot, Abbé de Mably (1709–1785), historical writer, author of *Observations on the Romans* (1751).

50 John Hunter (1728–1793), surgeon and anatomist, whose lectures on surgery began in 1773.

which were delivered by Mr. Higgins:[51] the principles of these sciences, and a taste for books of Natural history, contributed to multiply my ideas and images, and the Anatomist or Chemist may sometimes track me in their own snow.[52] (2) I dived perhaps too deeply into the mud of the Arian controversy[53]; and many days of reading, thinking, and writing were consumed in the pursuit of a phantom. (3) It is difficult to arrange with order and perspicuity the various transactions of the age of Constantine;[54] and so much was I displeased with the first Essay, that I committed to the flames above fifty sheets. (4) The six months of Paris and pleasure must be deducted from the account. But when I resumed my task I felt my improvement. I was now master of my style and subject; and while the measure of my daily performance was enlarged, I discovered less reason to cancel or correct. It has always been my practise to cast a long paragraph in a single mould, to try it by my ear, to deposit it in my memory, but to suspend the action of the pen till I had given the last polish to my work. Shall I add that I never found my mind more vigorous or my composition more happy than in the winter hurry of society and Parliament?

Had I believed that the majority of English readers were so fondly attached even to the name and shadow of Christianity, had I foreseen that the pious, the timid, and the prudent would feel, or affect to feel, with such exquisite sensibility, I might perhaps have softened the two invidious Chapters,[55] which would create many enemies and conciliate few friends. But the shaft was shot, the alarm was sounded, and I could only rejoyce that if the voice of our priests was clamorous and bitter, their hands were disarmed of the powers of persecution. I adhered to the wise resolution of trusting myself and my writings to the candour of the Public, till Mr. Davies[56] of Oxford presumed to attack, not the faith,

---

51 Bryan Higgins (c. 1737–1820), physician and chemist; in 1774 he established a school of chemistry in Soho.

52 I.e., find signs of my having been in their world through my use of imagery or references drawn from their professions.

53 The Arian controversy arose from the heretical teaching of the Libyan theologian Arius (c. 256–336), who argued that Christ was neither eternal nor equal with the Father.

54 Constantine (c. 274–337) ruled as emperor of the west (312–324), and as sole emperor for the rest of his life.

55 Chapters XV and XVI, accounts of the growth and corruption of the early church, were widely interpreted as attacks on Christianity.

56 Henry Edwards Davies (1756–1784), whose *Examination of the Fifteenth and Sixteenth Chapters of Mr. Gibbon's History* was published shortly after he received his B.A. from Oxford in 1778.

but the good faith, of the historian. My *Vindication*,[57] expressive of less anger than contempt, amused for a moment the busy and idle metropolis; and the most rational part of the Laity, and even of the Clergy, appears to have been satisfied of my innocence and accuracy. My antagonists, however, were rewarded in this World: poor Chelsum[58] was indeed neglected, and I dare not boast the making Dr. Watson[59] a Bishop;[60] but I enjoyed the pleasure of giving a Royal pension to Mr. Davies,[61] and of collating Dr. Apthorpe[62] to an Archiepiscopal living. Their success encouraged the zeal of Taylor[63] the Arian[64] and Milner the Methodist,[65] with many others whom it would be difficult to remember and tedious to rehearse: the list of my adversaries was graced with the more respectable names of Dr. Priestley,[66] Sir David Dalrymple,[67] and Dr. White,[68] and

---

57 "*A Vindication of some passages in the fifteenth and sixteenth chapters of the History of the Decline and Fall of the Roman Empire, by the Author: London*, 1779, *in octavo*—for I would not print it in quarto, lest it should be bound and preserved with the History itself." [E.G.]

58 James Chelsum (1740–1801) wrote *Remarks on Mr. Gibbon's History* (1772 and 1778) and *Reply to Gibbon's Vindication* (1779).

59 Richard Watson (1737–1816), professor of chemistry and regius professor of divinity in Cambridge University, was in 1782 created Bishop of Llandaf. He wrote *An Apology for Christianity, in a Series of Letters to Edward Gibbon* (1776).

60 "Dr. Watson, now Bishop of Llandaff, is a prelate of a large mind and liberal spirit. I should be happy to think that his apology for Christianity had contributed, though at my expence, to clear his Theological character. He has amply repaid the obligation by the amusement and instruction which I have received from the five Volumes of his Chemical Essays. It is a great pity that an agreeable and useful science should not yet be reduced to state of *fixity*." [E.G.]

61 See note 56, above.

62 East Apthorp (1732–1816), a native of Boston, Mass., was in 1790 appointed Prebend of Finsbury. He wrote *Letters on the Prevalence of Christianity* (1778). To *collate* is to bestow a benefice upon.

63 Henry Taylor (d. 1785), rector of Crawley, vicar of Portsmouth, author of *Thoughts on the Nature of the Grand Apostacy, with Reflections on the Fifteenth Chapter of Mr. Gibbon's History* (1781–1782).

64 "The stupendous title, *Thoughts on the Causes of the Grand Apostacy*, at first agitated my nerves, till I discovered that it was the apostacy of the whole Church since the Council of Nice, from Mr. Taylor's private Religion. His book is a strange mixture of *high* enthusiasm, and *low* buffoonery, and the *Millennium* is a fundamental article of his creed." [E.G.]

65 Joseph Milner (1744–1797), headmaster of Hull Grammar School, later vicar of Holy Trinity, Hull; author of *Gibbon's Account of Christianity Considered* (1781) and of many other works.

66 Joseph Priestley (1733–1804), English theologian and scientist, author of *History of the Corruptions of Christianity* (1782).

67 Scottish judge (1726–1792), author of *An Inquiry into the Secondary Causes which Mr. Gibbon Has Assigned for the Rapid Growth of Christianity* (1786).

68 Joseph White (1746–1814), Laudian professor of Arabic and regius professor of Hebrew at Oxford, who alluded slightingly to Gibbon in his *Sermons Containing View of Christianity and Mahometanism* (1784).

every polemic of either University discharged his sermon or pamphlet
against the impenetrable silence of the Roman historian. Let me frankly
own that I was startled at the first vollies of this Ecclesiastical ordnance;
but as soon as I found that this empty noise was mischievous only in
the intention, my fear was converted to indignation, and every feeling
of indignation or curiosity has long since subsided in pure and placid
indifference.

The prosecution of my history was soon afterwards checked by
another controversy of a very different kind. At the request of the
Chancellor[69] and of Lord Weymouth,[70] then Secretary of State, I vindi-
cated against the French manifesto the justice of the British arms. The
whole correspondence of Lord Stormont,[71] our late Ambassador at
Paris, was submitted to my inspection, and the *Memoire Justificatif*, which
I composed in French, was first approved by the Cabinet Ministers, and
then delivered as a state paper to the Courts of Europe. The style and
manner are praised by Beaumarchais[72] himself, who, in his private quarrel,
attempted a reply; but he flatters me by ascribing the *Memoire* to Lord
Stormont, and the grossness of his invective betrays the loss of temper
and of wit.

Among the honourable connections which I had formed, I may
justly be proud of the friendship of Mr. Wedderburne,[73] at that time
Attorney-General, who now illustrates the title of Lord Loughborough,
and the office of Chief Justice of the Common pleas. By his strong recommendation, and the favourable disposition of Lord North,[74] I was appointed one of the Lords Commissioners of trade and plantations, and my
private income was enlarged by a clear addition of between seven and
eight hundred pounds a year. The fancy of an hostile Orator may paint
in the strong colours of ridicule "the perpetual virtual adjournment and

---

69 Frederick North, Baron North (1732–1792), prime minister 1770–1782.
70 Thomas Thynne, Viscount Weymouth and Marquis of Bath (1734–1796), statesman, secretary of the southern department from 1775 and of the northern department as
well in 1779; he resigned both offices that year.
71 David Murray, Viscount Stormont and Earl of Mansfield (c. 1728–1796), ambassador at Vienna and at Paris. Gibbon's *Mémoire Justificatif* (1778) was an attack on a French
manifesto justifying French aid to the American colonies.
72 Pierre Augustin Caron de Beaumarchais (1732–1799), French polemic and dramatic
writer, much involved in the cause of American independence. He sent a fleet to the support
of the colonists at his own expense.
73 Alexander Wedderburn, Baron Loughborough (1733–1805), attorney general in
1778, chief justice of common pleas, 1780–1793.
74 See note 69, above.

the unbroken sitting vacation of the board of trade";[75] but it must be allowed that our duty was not intolerably severe, and that I enjoyed many days and weeks of repose without being called away from my library to the office. My acceptance of a place provoked some of the Leaders of opposition, with whom I lived in habits of intimacy, and I was most unjustly accused of deserting a party in which I had never been enlisted.[76]

The aspect of the next Session of parliament was stormy and perilous: County meetings, petitions, and committees of correspondence announced the public discontent; and instead of voting with a triumphant majority, the friends of government were often exposed to a struggle and sometimes to a defeat. The house of Commons adopted Mr. Dunning's motion, "that the influence of the Crown had encreased, was encreasing, and ought to be diminished";[77] and Mr. Burke's bill of reform was framed with skill, introduced with eloquence, and supported by numbers. Our late president, the American Secretary of State, very narrowly escaped the sentence of proscription,[78] but the unfortunate board of trade was abolished in the committee by a small majority (207 to 199) of eight votes.[79] The storm, however, blew over for a time. A large defection of Country Gentlemen eluded the sanguine hopes of the patriots; the Lords of trade were revived; administration recovered their strength and spirit; and the flames of London, which were kindled by a mischievous madman, admonished all thinking men of the danger of an appeal to the people.[80] In the præmature dissolution which followed this Session of parliament I lost my seat. Mr. Eliot[81] was now deeply engaged in the measures of opposition, and the Electors of Leskeard are commonly of the same opinion as Mr. Eliot.

---

75 Edmund Burke, "Speech on . . . A Plan for . . . the Economical Reformation of the Civil and Other Establishments," February 11, 1780, in Bohn Edition of *The Works of Burke*, II. 115.

76 Gibbon had objected to certain actions of the administration and had expressed his admiration for some members of the opposition. In general, though, he concurred in the acts of the government throughout the American Revolution.

77 John Dunning, Baron Ashburton (1731–1783), member of Parliament for Calne, whose famous resolution was passed in 1780.

78 In the vote (March 9, 1780) on the first clause of Burke's Establishment Bill, the office of third secretary of state (secretary of state for the colonies) was saved by seven votes.

79 On March 13, as a result of further votes on Burke's bill, the Board of Trade was abolished.

80 Lord George Gordon (1750–1793) in 1770 led a mob of petitioners against a parliamentary bill for relief of Roman Catholics. Riots and fires ensued.

81 See note 39, above. Mr. Eliot controlled the borough of Liskeard, in Cornwall; Gibbon had not followed his political lead about the war in America.

In this interval of my Senatorial life, I published the second and third Volumes of the decline and fall. My Ecclesiastical history still breathed the same spirit of freedom; but Protestant zeal is more indifferent to the characters and controversies of the fourth and fifth Centuries; my obstinate silence had damped the ardour of the polemics; Dr. Watson,[82] the most candid of my adversaries, assured me that he had no thoughts of renewing the attack, and my impartial balance of the virtues and vices of Julian[83] was generally praised. This truce was interrupted only by some animadversions of the Catholics of Italy,[84] and by some angry letters from Mr. Travis,[85] who made me personally responsible for condemning with the best Critics the spurious text of the three heavenly Witnesses.[86] The bigotted advocate of Popes and monks may be turned over even to the bigots of Oxford, and the wretched Travis still howls under the lash of the merciless Porson.[87] But I perceived, and without surprize, the coldness and even prejudice of the town; nor could a whisper escape my ear that, in the judgement of many readers, my continuation was much inferior to the original attempt. An author who cannot ascend will always appear to sink: envy was now prepared for my reception, and the zeal of my religious was fortified by the malice

---

82 See note 59, above.

83 Julianus Flavius Claudius, called Julian the Apostate (331–363), Roman emperor (355–363).

84 Five letters from an anonymous Italian divine, attacking Gibbon, were published with the fifth and seventh volumes of the Italian translation of *The Decline and Fall* (Pisa, 1779–1786).

85 "The brutal insolence of his challenge can only be excused by the absence of learning, judgement, and humanity; and to that excuse he has the fairest or foulest title. Compared with Archdeacon Travis, Chelsum and Davies assume the character of respectable enemies." [E.G.] George Travis (1740–1797), archdeacon of Chester, author of *Letters to Edward Gibbon* (1784). For Davies and Chelsum, see notes 56 and 58, above.

86 The dispute between Gibbon and Travis concerned the authenticity of 1 John, 5: 7, a verse which Gibbon rightly declared to be spurious. In the King James Bible it reads, "For there are those that beare record in heaven, the Father, the Word, and the holy Ghost: and the three are one." The New English Bible has eliminated the verse.

87 "I consider Mr. Porson's answer to Archdeacon Travis as the most acute and accurate piece of criticism which has appeared since the days of Bentley. His strictures are founded in argument, enriched with learning, and enlivened with wit, and his adversary neither deserves nor finds any quarter at his hands. The evidence of the three heavenly witnesses would now be rejected in any court of Justice; but prejudice is blind, authority is deaf, and our vulgar Bibles will ever be polluted by this spurious text, "Sedet æternumque sedebit." The more learned Ecclesiastics will, indeed, have the secret satisfaction of reprobating in the Closet what they read in the Church." [E.G.] Richard Porson (1759–1808), a great Greek scholar, defended Gibbon's position in *Letters to Archdeacon Travis* (1790). The Latin quotation in Gibbon's note is from Virgil, *Aeneid*, VI. 617: "It lasts and will forever last."

of my political enemies. I was, however, encouraged by some domestic and foreign testimonies of applause, and the second and third volumes insensibly rose in sale and reputation to a level with the first. But the public is seldom wrong; and I am inclined to believe that, especially in the beginning, they are more prolix and less entertaining than the first: my efforts had not been relaxed by success, and I had rather deviated into the opposite fault of minute and superfluous diligence. On the continent my name and writings were slowly diffused; a French translation of the first volume had disappointed the booksellers of Paris, and a passage in the third was construed as a personal reflection on the reigning Monarch.[88]

Before I could apply for a seat at the general Election, the list was already full; but Lord North's promise was sincere, his recommendation was effectual, and I was soon chosen on a vacancy for the borough of Lymington, in Hampshire. In the first Session of the new parliament, administration stood their ground; their final overthrow was reserved for the second. The American War had once been the favourite of the Country; the pride of England was irritated by the resistance of her Colonies; and the executive power was driven by national clamour into the most vigorous and coercive measures. But the length of a fruitless contest, the loss of armies, the accumulation of debt and taxes, and the hostile confederacy of France, Spain, and Holland, indisposed the public to the American War and the persons by whom it was conducted.[89] The representatives of the people followed at a slow distance the changes of their opinion, and the ministers who refused to bend were broken by the tempest. As soon as Lord North had lost, or was about to lose, a majority in the house of Commons, he surrendered his office, and retired to a private station,[90] with the tranquil assurance of a clear conscience and a chearful temper; the old fabric was dissolved, and the posts of Government were occupied by the victorious and veteran troops of opposition. The Lords of Trade were not immediately dismissed; but the board itself

---

88 Louis XVI (1754–1793) of France thought that Gibbon had compared him to Arcadius (383–408), emperor of the east from 395, a weak prince controlled by his empress, and to his brother Honorius (384–423), emperor of the west from 395, also a weak and vicious man. In Gibbon's note he refuses to "disclaim the allusion, [or] examine the likeness."

89 France entered the war against Great Britain in 1778, joined by Spain in 1779 and by the Netherlands in 1780.

90 Lord North (see note 69) had wished to withdraw from office as England's military reverses in the American war continued. He resigned when the increasing demand for peace reduced his majority.

was abolished by Mr. Burke's bill,[91] which decency compelled the patriots to revive, and I was stripped of a convenient salary after I had enjoyed it about three years.

So flexible is the title of my history, that the final æra might be fixed at my own choice, and I long hesitated whether I should be content with the three Volumes, the fall of the Western Empire, which fullfilled my first engagement with the public. In this interval of suspense, near a twelvemonth, I returned by a natural impulse to the Greek authors of antiquity. In my library in Bentinck street, at my summer lodgings at Brighthelmstone, at a country house which I hired at Hampton Court, I read with new pleasure the Iliad and Odyssey, the histories of Herodotus, Thucydides, and Xenophon, a large portion of the tragic and comic theatre of Athens, and many interesting dialogues of the Socratic school. Yet in the luxury of freedom I began to wish for the daily task, the active pursuit which gave a value to every book, and an object to every enquiry: the preface of a new edition announced my design, and I dropt without reluctance from the age of Plato to that of Justinian.[92] The original texts of Procopius and Agathias[93] supplied the events, and even the characters, of his reign; but a laborious winter was devoted to the Codes, the Pandects,[94] and the modern interpreters before I presumed to form an abstract of the Civil law. My skill was improved by practise, my diligence perhaps was quickened by the loss of office, and, except the last chapter, I had finished my fourth Volume before I sought a retreat on the banks of the Leman lake.[95]

It is not the purpose of this narrative to expatiate on the public or secret history of the times—the schism which followed the death of the Marquis of Rockingham,[96] the appointment of the Earl of Shelburne,

---

91 Burke's Establishment Act (1782) for the reform of civil service abolished 134 offices in the king's household and the ministry.

92 The Greek philosopher Plato lived in the fifth century B.C.; Justinian, one of the most celebrated emperors of the east, ruled from A.D. 527 to 565.

93 Procopius (c. 495–c. 565), Byzantine historian, wrote a *History of His Own Times;* Agathias Asianus (died c. 580), Greek historian, began but never finished a history of his own time.

94 *Codes*, the systematic collection of statutes ordered by Justinian; *Pandects*, a compendium in fifty books of Roman civil law, made by order of Justinian.

95 In Switzerland.

96 Charles Watson Wentworth, Marquis of Rockingham (1730–1782), succeeded Lord North as prime minister but died less than four months after taking office.

the resignation of Mr. Fox, and his famous coalition with Lord North.[97] But I may affirm with some degree of assurance that in their political conflict those great antagonists had never felt any personal animosity to each other; that their reconciliation was easy and sincere; and that their friendship has never been clouded by the shadow of suspicion or jealousy. The most violent or venal of their respective followers embraced this fair occasion of revolt; but their alliance still commanded a majority in the House of Commons: the peace was censured; Lord Shelburne resigned, and the two friends knelt on the same cushion to take the oath of Secretary of State. From a principle of gratitude I adhered to the coalition; my vote was counted in the day of battle, but I was overlooked in the division of the spoil. There were many claimants more deserving and importunate than myself: the board of trade could not be restored; and while the list of places was curtailed, the number of candidates was doubled. An easy dismission to a secure seat at the board of customs or excise was promised on the first vacancy; but the chance was distant and doubtful, nor could I solicit with much ardour an ignoble servitude which would have robbed me of the most valuable of my studious hours.[98] At the same time, the tumult of London and the attendance on Parliament were grown more irksome, and without some additional income I could not long or prudently maintain the style of expence to which I was accustomed.

From my early acquaintance with Lausanne I had always cherished a secret wish that the school of my youth might become the retreat of my declining age. A moderate fortune would secure the blessings of ease, leisure, and independence: the country, the people, the manners, the language, were congenial to my taste; and I might indulge the hope of passing some years in the domestic society of a friend. After travelling with several English, Mr. Deyverdun was now settled at home in a pleasant habitation, the gift of his deceased aunt: we had long been separated, we had long been silent; yet in my first letter I exposed with the most perfect confidence my situation, my sentiments and my designs. His

---

97 William Petty, Earl of Shelburne (1737–1805), was secretary of state in Rockingham's ministry and succeeded him as prime minister; Charles James Fox (1749–1806) was foreign secretary under Rockingham but resigned at his death. By the coalition between him and Lord North, Lord Shelburne's ministry was forced to resign in 1783, and Fox and North became joint secretaries of state.

98 Gibbon also competed unsuccessfully at this time for the office of secretary to the embassy at Paris.

immediate answer was a warm and joyful acceptance: the picture of our future life provoked my impatience; and the terms of arrangement were short and simple, as he possessed the property and I undertook the expence of our common house. Before I could break my English chain, it was incumbent on me to struggle with the feelings of my heart, the indolence of my temper, and the opinion of the World, which unanimously condemned this voluntary banishment. In the disposal of my effects, the library, a sacred deposit, was alone excepted: as my postchaise moved over Westminster bridge, I bid a long farewell to the "fumum, et opes, strepitumque Romæ."[99] My journey by the direct road through France was not attended with any accident, and I arrived at Lausanne near twenty years after my second departure. Within less than three months the Coalition struck on some hidden rocks; had I remained aboard I should have perished in the general shipwreck.[100]

Since my establishment at Lausanne more than seven years have elapsed, and if every day has not been equally soft and serene, not a day, not a moment has occurred in which I have repented of my choice. During my absence, a long portion of human life, many changes had happened: my elder acquaintance had left the stage; virgins were ripened into matrons, and children were grown to the age of manhood. But the same manners were transmitted from one generation to another: my friend alone was an inestimable treasure; my name was not totally forgotten, and all were ambitious to welcome the arrival of a stranger, and the return of a fellow-citizen. The first winter was given to a general embrace, without any nice discrimination of persons and characters: after a more regular settlement, a more accurate survey, I discovered three solid and permanent benefits of my new situation. (1) My personal freedom had been somewhat impaired by the house of commons and the board of trade; but I was now delivered from the chain of duty and dependence, from the hopes and fears of political adventure: my sober mind was no longer intoxicated by the fumes of party, and I rejoyced in my escape as often as I read of the midnight debates which preceded the dissolution of Parliament. (2) My English œconomy had been that of a solitary batchelor who might afford some occasional dinners. In Switzerland I enjoyed at every meal, at every hour, the free and pleasant conver-

---

99 "The smoke and the grandeur and the noise of Rome" (Horace, *Odes*, III. 29. 12).
100 By December 1783, the coalition government was dissolved, to be succeeded by the ministry of William Pitt (1759–1806).

sation of the friend of my youth; and my daily table was always provided for the reception of one or two extraordinary guests. Our importance in society is less a positive than a relative weight: in London I was lost in the crowd; I ranked with the first families of Lausanne, and my style of prudent expence enabled me to maintain a fair balance of reciprocal civilities. (3) Instead of a small house between a street and a stableyard, I began to occupy a spacious and convenient mansion, connected on the north side with the City, and open on the south to a beautiful and boundless horizon. A garden of four acres had been laid out by the taste of Mr. Deyverdun; from the garden a rich scenery of meadows and vineyards descends to the Leman lake, and the prospect far beyond the lake is crowned by the stupendous mountains of Savoy. My books and my acquaintance had been first united in London; but this happy position of my library in town *and* country was finally reserved for Lausanne. Possessed of every comfort in this triple alliance, I could not be tempted to change my habitation with the changes of the seasons.

My friends had been kindly apprehensive that I should not be able to exist in a Swiss town at the foot of the Alps, after so long conversing with the first men of the first cities of the World. Such lofty connections may attract the curious and gratify the vain, but I am too modest or too proud to rate my own value by that of my associates; and whatsoever may be the fame of learning or genius, experience has shewn me that the cheaper qualifications of politeness and good sense are of more useful currency in the commerce of life. By many conversation is esteemed as a theatre or a school; but after the morning has been occupied by the labours of the library, I wish to unbend rather than to exercise my mind, and in the interval between tea and super I am far from disdaining the innocent amusement of a game at cards. Lausanne is peopled by a numerous gentry, whose companionable idleness is seldom disturbed by the pursuits of avarice or ambition; the women, though confined to a domestic education, are endowed for the most part with more taste and knowledge than their husbands or brothers; but the decent freedom of both sexes is equally remote from the extremes of simplicity and refinement. I shall add, as a misfortune rather than a merit, that the situation and beauty of the Pays de Vaud,[101] the long habits of the English, the medical reputation of Dr. Tissot,[102] and the fashion of viewing the

101 The Swiss canton immediately north of Lake Leman; Lausanne is its capital.
102 Simon André Tissot (1728–1797), celebrated Swiss physician, lived at Lausanne.

mountains and *glaciers*, have opened us on all sides to the incursions of foreigners. The visits of Mr. and Madame Necker,[103] of Prince Henry of Prussia,[104] and of Mr. Fox[105] may form some pleasing exceptions; but, in general, Lausanne has appeared most agreeable in my eyes when we have been abandoned to our own society.

My transmigration from London to Lausanne could not be effected without interrupting the course of my historical labours. The hurry of my departure, the joy of my arrival, the delay of my tools, suspended their progress, and a full twelvemonth was lost before I could resume the thread of regular and daily industry. A number of books, most requisite and least common, had been præviously selected; the Academical library of Lausanne, which I could use as my own, contains at least the fathers and councils, and I have derived some occasional succour from the public collections of Bern and Geneva. The fourth volume was soon terminated by an abstract of the controversies of the Incarnation, which the learned Dr. Prideaux was apprehensive of exposing to profane eyes.[106] In the fifth and sixth Volumes the revolutions of the Empire and the World are most rapid, various, and instructive; and the Greek or Roman historians are checked by the hostile narratives of the Barbarians of the East and West. It was not till after many designs and many tryals that I preferred, as I still prefer, the method of grouping my picture by nations, and the

---

103 "I saw them frequently in the summer of 1784, at a country house near Lausanne, where Mr. Necker composed his treatise of the administration of the Finances. I have since (in October, 1790) visited them in their present residence, the castle and barony of Copet, near Geneva. Of the merits and measures of that Statesman various opinions may be entertained, but all impartial men must agree in their esteem of his integrity and patriotism." [E.G.]

104 Prince Henry (1726–1802) was a brother of Frederick the Great. He visited in Lausanne in August 1784.

105 "In his tour of Switzerland (September, 1788), Mr. Fox gave me two days of free and private society. He seemed to feel and even to envy the happiness of my situation; while I admired the powers of a superior man, as they are blended in his attractive character, with the softness and simplicity of a child. Perhaps no human being was ever more perfectly exempt from the taint of malevolence, vanity, or falsehood." [E.G.] For Fox's identity, see note 97, above.

106 "It had been the original design of the learned Dean Prideaux to write the history of the ruin of the Eastern Church. In this work it would have been necessary not only to unravel all those controversies which the Christians made about the Hypostatical Union, but also to unfold all the niceties and subtile notions which each sect did hold concerning it. The pious historian was apprehensive of exposing that incomprehensible Mystery to the cavils and objections of unbelievers, and he durst not, considering the nature of this book, venture it abroad in so wanton and lewd an age (see Preface to the Life of Mahomet, p. xxi.)." [E.G.] Humphrey Prideaux (1648–1724), Dean of Norwich, published his *Life of Mahomet* in 1697.

seeming neglect of Chronological order is surely compensated by the superior merits of interest and perspicuity. The style of the first Volume is, in my opinion, somewhat crude and elaborate; in the second and third it is ripened into ease, correctness, and numbers; but in the three last I may have been seduced by the facility of my pen, and the constant habit of speaking one language and writing another may have infused some mixture of Gallic idioms. Happily for my eyes, I have always closed my studies with the day, and commonly with the morning, and a long but temperate labour has been accomplished without fatiguing either the mind or body. But when I computed the remainder of my time and my task, it was apparent that, according to the season of publication, the delay of a month would be productive of that of a year. I was now straining for the goal, and in the last winter many evenings were borrowed from the social pleasures of Lausanne. I could now wish that a pause, an interval, had been allowed for a serious revisal.

I have presumed to mark the moment of conception; I shall now commemorate the hour of my final deliverance. It was on the day, or rather the night, of the 27th of June, 1787, between the hours of eleven and twelve, that I wrote the last lines of the last page in a summer-house in my garden. After laying down my pen I took several turns in a *berceau*, or covered walk of Acacias, which commands a prospect of the country, the lake, and the mountains. The air was temperate, the sky was serene, the silver orb of the moon was reflected from the waters, and all Nature was silent. I will not dissemble the first emotions of joy on the recovery of my freedom, and perhaps the establishment of my fame. But my pride was soon humbled, and a sober melancholy was spread over my mind by the idea that I had taken my everlasting leave of an old and agreeable companion, and that, whatsoever might be the future date of my history, the life of the historian must be short and precarious. I will add two facts which have seldom occurred in the composition of six, or at least of five, quartos. (1) My first rough manuscript, without any intermediate copy, has been sent to the press.[107] (2) Not a sheet has been seen by any human eyes except those of the Author and the printer; the faults and the merits are exclusively my own.

---

107 "I cannot help recollecting a much more extraordinary fact, which is affirmed of himself by Rétif de la Bretonne, a voluminous and original writer of French novels. He laboured, and may still labour, in the humble office of Corrector to a printing-house. But this office enabled him to transport an entire volume from his mind to the press; and his work was given to the public without ever having been written with a pen." [E.G.] Nicolas Rétif de la Bretonne lived from 1734 to 1806.

After a quiet residence of four years, during which I had never moved ten miles from Lausanne, it was not without some reluctance and terror that I undertook, in a journey of two hundred leagues, to cross the mountains and the sea. Yet this formidable adventure was atchieved without danger or fatigue, and at the end of a fortnight I found myself in Lord Sheffield's house and library, safe, happy, and at home. The character of my friend (Mr. Holroyd) had recommended him to a seat in Parliament for Coventry, the command of a regiment of light Dragoons, and an Irish peerage. The sense and spirit of his political writings have decided the public opinion on the great questions of our commercial intercourse with America[108] and Ireland.[109] He fell (in 1784) with the unpopular coalition, but his merit has been acknowledged at the last general election (1790) by the honourable invitation and free choice of the city of Bristol. During the whole time of my residence in England, I was entertained at Sheffield place and in Downing Street by his hospitable kindness, and the most pleasant period was that which I passed in the domestic society of the family. In the larger circle of the Metropolis, I observed the country and the inhabitants with the knowledge and without the prejudices of an Englishman; but I rejoyced in the apparent encrease of wealth and prosperity which might be fairly divided between the spirit of the nation and the wisdom of the minister. All party resentment was now lost in oblivion; since I was no man's rival, no man was my enemy: I felt the dignity of independence, and as I asked no more, I was satisfied with the general civilities of the World. The house in London which I frequented with the most pleasure and assiduity was that of Lord North: after the loss of power and of sight, he was still happy in himself and his friends, and my public tribute of gratitude and esteem could no longer be suspected of any interested motive. Before my departure from England I assisted at the august spectacle of Mr. Hastings's tryal in Westminster hall: I shall

108 "*Observations on the commerce of the American states, by John Lord Sheffield: the sixth edition, London*, 1784, *in octavo*. Their sale was diffusive, their effect beneficial. The Navigation act, the Palladium of Britain, was defended, and perhaps saved, by his pen; and he proves, by the weight of fact and argument, that the mother-country may survive and flourish after the loss of America. My friend has never cultivated the arts of composition, but his materials are copious and correct, and he leaves on his paper the clear impression of an active and vigorous mind." [E.G.] For Lord Sheffield's identity, see note 36, above.

109 "*Observations on the trade, manufactures, and present state of Ireland, by John Lord Sheffield: the third edition, London*, 1784, *in octavo*. Their useful aim was to guide the industry, to correct the prejudices, and to asswage the passions of a country which seemed to forget that she could only be free and prosperous by a friendly connection with Great Britain. The concluding observations are expressed with so much ease and spirit, that they may be read by those who are the least interested in the subject." [E.G.]

not absolve or condemn the Governor of India, but Mr. Sheridan's eloquence demanded my applause; nor could I hear without emotion the personal compliment[110] which he paid me in the presence of the British nation.[111]

As the publication of my three last volumes was the principal object, so it was the first care of my English journey. The prævious arrangements with the bookseller and the printer were settled in my passage through London, and the proofs which I returned more correct were transmitted every post from the press to Sheffield Place. The length of the operation and the leisure of the country allowed some time to review my manuscript: several rare and useful books, the Assises de Jerusalem, Ramusius de bello C. Pano., the Greek Acts of the Synod of Florence, the Statuta Urbis Romæ,[112] etc., were procured, and I introduced in their proper places the supplements which they afforded. The impression of the fourth volume had consumed three months; our common interest required that we should move with a quicker pace, and Mr. Strahan fullfilled his engagement, which few printers could sustain, of delivering every week three thousand copies of nine sheets. The day of publication was, however, delayed, that it might coincide with the fifty-first anniversary of my own birthday: the double festival was celebrated by a chearful litterary dinner at Cadell's house, and I seemed to blush while they read an elegant compliment from Mr. Hayley,[113] whose poetical talent had more than once been employed in the praise of his friend. As most of the former purchasers were naturally

---

110 Warren Hastings (1732–1818), first governor-general of India, was in 1787 impeached for his violent extortion of money from the Indian nobility. He was acquitted in 1795. Richard Brinsley Sheridan (1751–1816), the Irish dramatist, attacked Hastings in a famous speech at the trial, during which he referred to "the luminous page of Gibbon." In private he is supposed to have explained that he meant *voluminous.*

111 "From this display of Genius, which blazed four successive days, I shall stoop to a very mechanical circumstance. As I was waiting in the Manager's box, I had the curiosity to enquire of the short-hand writer how many words a ready and rapid Orator might pronounce in an hour. From 7000 to 7500 was his answer. The medium of 7200 will afford one hundred and twenty words in a minute, and two words in each second. But this computation will only apply to the English language" [E.G.]

112 *Assises et Usages du Royaume de Jérusalem,* by Jean d'Ibelin (d. 1270); Geoffroy de Villehardouin (c. 1165–c. 1213), *History of the Conquest of Constantinople,* tr. into Latin with additions by Paulo Ramusius (1532–1600), pub. 1609; the Greek Acts are records of the Council of Florence, which began in 1438 and temporarily united the Greek and Roman churches; the Statuta are statutes of the city of Rome.

113 For Hayley, see note 30, above. The poet contributed a seven-stanza poem for

desirous of compleating their sets, the sale of the quarto edition was quick and easy; and an octavo size was printed, to satisfy, at a cheaper rate, the public demand. The conclusion of my work appears to have diffused a strong sensation; it was generally read and variously judged. The style has been exposed to much Academical criticism; a religious clamour was revived; and the reproach of indecency has been loudly echoed by the rigid censors of morals.[114] Yet, upon the whole, the history of the decline and fall seems to have struck a root both at home and abroad, and may, perhaps, an hundred years hence, still continue to be abused. The French, Italian, and German translations have been executed with various success; but instead of patronizing, I should willingly suppress such imperfect copies which injure the character while they propagate the name of the author. [The Irish pyrates are at once my friends and my enemies,] but I cannot be displeased with the two numerous and correct impressions of the English original, which have been published for the use of the Continent at Basil in Switzerland. The conquests of our language and litterature are not confined to Europe alone; and the writer who succeeds in London is speedily read on the banks of the Delaware and the Ganges.

In the preface of the fourth Volume, while I gloried in the name of an Englishman, I announced my approaching return to the neighbourhood of the lake of Lausanne. This last tryal confirmed my assurance that I had wisely chosen for my own happiness; nor did I once, in a year's visit, entertain a wish of settling in my native country. Britain is the free and fortunate island, but where is the spot in which I could unite the comforts and beauties of my establishment at Lausanne? The tumult of London astonished my eyes and ears; the amusements of public places were no longer adequate to the trouble; the clubs and assemblies were filled with new faces and young men; and our best society, our long and

---

the occasion. Its penultimate stanza reads,

> Science for Thee a Newton rais'd;
> For thy renown a Shakespeare blaz'd,
> Lord of the drama's sphere!
> In different fields to equal praise
> See History now thy GIBBON raise
> To shine without a peer!

114 Gibbon found this reproach incomprehensible because, as he pointed out, the charge of indecency was leveled at him merely for painting the manners of the times; moreover, he had carefully left "all licentious passages . . . in the obscurity of a learned language."

late dinners, would soon have been prejudicial to my health. Without any share in the political wheel, I must be idle and insignificant; yet the most splendid temptations would not have enlisted me a second time in the servitude of parliament or office. At Tunbridge, some weeks after the publication of my history, I tore myself from the embraces of Lord and Lady Sheffield, and, with a young Swiss friend[115] whom I had introduced to the English world, I pursued the road of Dover and Lausanne. My habitation was embellished in my absence, and the last division of books which followed my steps encreased my chosen library to the number of six or seven thousand volumes. My Seraglio[116] was ample, my choice was free, my appetite was keen. After a full repast on Homer and Aristophanes, I involved myself in the philosophic maze of the writings of Plato, of which the dramatic is perhaps more interesting than the argumentative part; but I stept aside into every path of enquiry which reading or reflection accidentally opened.

Alas! the joy of my return and my studious ardour were soon damped by the melancholy state of my friend, Mr. Deyverdun. His health and spirits had long suffered a gradual decline; a succession of Apoplectic fits announced his dissolution, and before he expired, those who loved him could not wish for the continuance of his life. The voice of reason might congratulate his deliverance, but the feelings of Nature and friendship could be subdued only by time: his amiable character was still alive in my remembrance; each room, each walk, was imprinted with our common footsteps, and I should blush at my own philosophy if a long interval of study had not preceded and followed the death of my friend. By his last will he left me the option of purchasing his house and garden, or of possessing them during my life on the payment either of a stipulated price, or of an easy retribution to his kinsman and heir. I should probably have been tempted by the Dæmon of property, if some legal difficulties had not been started against my title. A contest would have been vexatious, doubtful, and invidious; and the heir most gratefully subscribed an agreement which rendered my life-possession more perfect, and his future condition more advantageous. The certainty of my tenure has allowed me to lay out a considerable sum in improvements and alterations; they have been executed with skill and taste, and few men

---

115 M. Wilhelm de Severy (1767–1838), son of Charriere and Catherine de Severy of Lausanne. Gibbon was much attached to the family, to which he refers again below, p. 525.

116 A seraglio is a harem; Gibbon uses the term metaphorically to refer to his books.

of letters, perhaps, in Europe, are so desirably lodged as myself. But I feel, and with the decline of years I shall more painfully feel, that I am alone in paradise. Among the circle of my acquaintance at Lausanne, I have gradually acquired the solid and tender friendship of a respectable family: the four persons of whom it is composed are all endowed with the virtues best adapted to their age and situation; and I am encouraged to love the parents as a brother, and the children as a father. Every day we seek and find the opportunities of meeting, yet even this valuable connection cannot supply the loss of domestic society.

Within the last two or three years our tranquillity has been clouded by the disorders of France: many families of Lausanne were alarmed and affected by the terrors of an impending bankruptcy; but the revolution or rather the dissolution of the Kingdom,[117] has been heard and felt in the adjacent lands. A swarm of emigrants of both sexes, who escaped from the public ruin, has been attracted by the vicinity, the manners, and the language of Lausanne, and our narrow habitations in town and country are now occupied by the first names and titles of the departed Monarchy. These noble fugitives are entitled to our pity; they may claim our esteem, but they cannot, in the present state of their mind and fortune, much contribute to our amusement. Instead of looking down as calm and idle spectators, on the theatre of Europe, our domestic harmony is somewhat embittered by the infusion of party spirit; our ladies and gentlemen assume the character of self-taught politicians, and the sober dictates of wisdom and experience are silenced by the clamours of the triumphant *Democrates*. The fanatic missionaries of sedition have scattered the seeds of discontent in our cities and villages, which had flourished above two hundred and fifty years without fearing the approach of war, or feeling the weight of government. Many individuals, and some communities, appear to be infected with the French disease, the wild theories of equal and boundless freedom: but I trust that the body of the people will be faithful to their sovereign and themselves; and I am satisfied that the failure or success of a revolt would equally terminate in the ruin of the country. While the Aristocracy of Bern protects the happiness, it is superfluous to enquire whether it is founded in the rights of man: the œconomy of the state is liberally supplied with-

---

117 "I beg leave to subscribe my assent to Mr. Burke's creed on the Revolution of France. I admire his eloquence, I approve his politics, I adore his Chivalry, and I can almost excuse his reverence for Church establishments." [E.G.]

out the aid of taxes;[118] and the magistrates *must* reign with prudence and equity, since they are unarmed in the midst of an armed nation. For myself (may the omen be averted) I can only declare that the first stroke of a rebel drum would be the signal of my immediate departure.

When I contemplate the common lot of mortality, I must acknowledge that I have drawn a high prize in the lottery of life. The far greater part of the globe is overspread with barbarism or slavery; in the civilized world the most numerous class is condemned to ignorance and poverty, and the double fortune of my birth in a free and enlightened country, in an honourable and wealthy family, is the lucky chance of an unit against millions. The general probability is about three to one that a new-born infant will not live to compleat his fiftieth year. I have now passed that age, and may fairly estimate the present value of my existence in the threefold division of mind, body, and estate.

(i) The first indispensable requisite of happiness is a clear conscience, unsullied by the reproach or remembrance of an unworthy action.

>   Hic murus aheneus esto
>   Nil conscire sibi, nullâ pallescere culpâ.[119]

I am endowed with a chearful temper, a moderate sensibility, and a natural disposition to repose rather than to action: some mischievous appetites and habits have perhaps been corrected by philosophy or time. The love of study, a passion which derives fresh vigour from enjoyment, supplies each day, each hour, with a perpetual source of independent and rational pleasure, and I am not sensible of any decay of the mental faculties. The original soil has been highly improved by labour and manure; but it may be questioned whether some flowers of fancy, some grateful errors, have not been eradicated with the weeds of prejudice. (ii) Since I have escaped from the long perils of my childhood, the serious advice of a physician has seldom been requisite. "The madness of superfluous health" I have never known; but my tender constitution has been fortified by time; the play of the animal machine still continues to be easy and regular, and the inestimable gift of the sound and peaceful slumbers of infancy

---

118 "The revenue of Bern (I except some small duties) is derived from Church lands, tythes, feudal rights, and interest of money. The Republic has near 500,000 pounds sterling in the English funds, and the amount of their treasure is unknown to the Citizens themselves." [E.G.]

119 "Be this your wall of brass, to have no guilty secrets, no wrong-doing that makes you turn pale" (Horace, *Epistles*, I. i. 59–60).

may be imputed both to the mind and body. About the age of forty I was first afflicted with the gout, which in the space of fourteen years has made seven or eight different attacks; their duration, though not their intensity, appears to encrease, and after each fit I rise and walk with less strength and agility than before. But the gout has hitherto been confined to my feet and knees; the pain is never intolerable; I am surrounded by all the comforts that art and attendance can bestow; my sedentary life is amused with books and company, and in each step of my convalescence I pass through a progress of agreable sensations. (iii) I have already described the merits of my society and situation; but these enjoyments would be tasteless and bitter, if their possession were not assured by an annual and adequate supply. By the painful method of amputation, my father's debts have been compleatly discharged; the labour of my pen, the sale of lands, the inheritance of a maiden aunt (Mrs. Hester Gibbon), have improved my property, and it will be exonerated on some melancholy day from the payment of Mrs. Gibbon's jointure. According to the scale of Switzerland I am a rich man; and I am indeed rich, since my income is superior to my expence, and my expence is equal to my wishes. My friend Lord Sheffield has kindly relieved me from the cares to which my taste and temper are most adverse: the œconomy of my house is settled without avarice or profusion; at stated periods all my bills are regularly paid, and in the course of my life I have never been reduced to appear, either as plaintiff or defendant, in a court of Justice. Shall I add that, since the failure of my first wishes, I have never entertained any serious thoughts of a matrimonial connection?

I am disgusted with the affectation of men of letters, who complain that they have renounced a substance for a shadow, and that their fame, (which sometimes is no insupportable weight) affords a poor compensation for envy, censure, and persecution.[120] My own experience, at least, has taught me a very different lesson: twenty happy years have been animated by the labour of my history; and its success has given me a name, a rank, a character, in the World, to which I should not otherwise

---

120 "Mr. d'Alembert relates that, as he was walking in the gardens of Sans-souci with the King of Prussia, Frederic said to him, 'Do you see that old woman, a poor weeder, asleep on that Sunny bank? She is probably a more happy Being than either of us.' The King and the Philosopher may speak for themselves; for my part, I do not envy the old woman." [E.G.] Jean le Rond d'Alembert (1717–1783) was an eminent philosopher and a friend of Frederick II of Prussia (Frederick the Great, 1712–1786), who in 1754 granted him an annual pension of 1,200 francs.

have been entitled. The freedom of my writings has, indeed, provoked an implacable tribe; but as I was safe from the stings, I was soon accustomed to the buzzing of the hornets: my nerves are not tremblingly alive: and my litterary temper is so happily framed, that I am less sensible of pain than pleasure. The rational pride of an author may be offended rather than flattered by vague indiscriminate praise; but he cannot, he should not, be indifferent to the fair testimonies of private and public esteem. Even his social sympathy may be gratified by the idea that, now in the present hour, he is imparting some degree of amusement or knowledge to *his friends* in a distant land; that one day his mind will be familiar to the grandchildren of those who are yet unborn. I cannot boast of the friendship or favour of princes; the patronage of English litterature has long since been devolved on our booksellers, and the measure of their liberality is the least ambiguous test of our common success. Perhaps the golden mediocrity[121] of my fortune has contributed to fortify my application: few books of merit and importance have been composed either in a garret or a palace. A Gentleman, possessed of leisure and competency, may be encouraged by the assurance of an honourable reward; but wretched is the writer, and wretched will be the work, where daily diligence is stimulated by daily hunger.

The present is a fleeting moment: the past is no more; and our prospect of futurity is dark and doubtful. This day may *possibly* be my last; but the laws of probability, so true in general, so fallacious in particular, still allow me about fifteen years, and I shall soon enter into the period which, as the most agreable of his long life, was selected by the judgement and experience of the sage Fontenelle.[122] His choice is approved by the eloquent historian of Nature, who fixes our moral happiness to the mature season, in which our passions are supposed to be calmed, our duties fullfilled, our ambition satisfied, our fame and fortune established on a solid basis.[123] I am far more inclined to embrace than to dispute this comfortable doctrine: I will not suppose any præmature decay of the mind or body; but I must reluctantly observe that two causes, the abbreviation of time and the failure of hope, will always tinge with a

---

121 In the classic sense: the condition of being in the mean between extremes.

122 I have been unable to locate his comment. Bernard le Bovier de Fontenelle, French interpreter of the new sciences of the seventeenth century, who lived to be a hundred years old (1657–1757).

123 "See Buffon, p. 413. In private conversation, that great and amiable man added the weight of his own experience; and this autumnal felicity might be exemplified in the lives of Voltaire, Hume, and many other men of letters." [E.G.]

browner shade the evening of life. (1) The proportion of a part to the whole is the only standard by which we can measure the length of our existence. At the age of twenty, one year is a tenth, perhaps, of the time which has elapsed within our consciousness and memory; at the age of fifty it is no more than a fortieth, and this relative value continues to decrease till the last sands are shaken by the hand of death. This reasoning may seem metaphysical, but on a tryal it will be found satisfactory and just. (2) The warm desires, the long expectations of youth, are founded on the ignorance of themselves and of the World: they are gradually damped by time and experience, by disappointment or possession; and after the middle season the crowd must be content to remain at the foot of the mountain, while the few who have climbed the summit aspire to descend or expect to fall. In old age, the consolation of hope is reserved for the tenderness of parents, who commence a new life in their children; the faith of enthusiasts who sing Hallelujahs above the clouds,[124] and the vanity of authors who presume the immortality of their name and writings.

Lausanne, March 2, 1791.

---

124 "This cœlestial hope is confined to a small number of the Elect, and we must deduct: (1) All the *mere* philosophers, who can only speculate about the immortality of the soul. (2) All the *earthly* Christians, who repeat without thought or feeling the words of their Catechism. (3) All the *gloomy* fanatics, who are more strongly affected by the fear of Hell, than by the hopes of Heaven. 'Strait is the way and narrow is the gate, and *few* there be who find it.'" [E.G.]

JAMES BOSWELL

(1740–1795)

James Boswell, long renowned as the biographer of Samuel Johnson, has only in the twentieth century acquired an important reputation for his other writing. Born in Scotland, he was trained for the law; he soon evidenced a powerful appetite for personal distinction and a longing to move in distinguished society. He met Dr. Johnson during an early trip to London, where he thought of pursuing an army career, and immediately begain taking notes on the great man's conversation. During a long trip to the continent (he studied law in Utrecht) he met other important men of his day, but his relationship with Johnson remained central in his life. He practiced law in Edinburgh, frequently visiting London; in 1769 he married his cousin, Margaret Montgomerie. His *Life* of Johnson, published in 1791, was an immediate success.

The honesty of Boswell's writing—even when he presents a dramatized view of himself or of others, it seems the product of personal conviction—is one of its principal charms. In his biographical and autobiographical prose he manifests an eye and an ear for the telling detail; he brings to life himself and his contemporaries and makes his own time real and relevant to twentieth-century readers.

Editions

Boswell's journals are being published in a Yale edition of which several volumes have already appeared, including *Boswell's London Journal*, 1762–1763, ed. Frederick A. Pottle, 1950; and *Boswell's Journal of a Tour to the Hebrides with Samuel Johnson, LL. D.*, 1773, rev. eds. F. A. Pottle and C. H. Bennett, 1961.

Biography and Criticism

Brady, Frank., *Boswell's Political Career*, 1965.

Bronson, B. H., *Johnson, Agonistes* 1946.

Fussell, Paul, Jr., "The Force of Literary Memory in Boswell's *London Journal*," *Studies in Literature*, II (1962), 351–57.

Kiley, Frederick S., "Boswell's Literary Art in the *London Journal*," *College English*, XXIII (1962), 629–32.

Lustig, Irma S., "Boswell's Literary Criticism in *The Life of Johnson*," *Studies in English Literature*, VI (1966), 529–41.

Molin, Sven Eric, "Boswell's Account of the Johnson–Wilkes Meeting," *Studies in English Literature*, III (1963), 307–22.

Pottle, Frederick A., "Boswell Revalued," *Literary Views: Critical and Historical Essays*, pp. 79–91, ed. Carroll Camden (1964).

———, "James Boswell, Journalist," *The Age of Johnson: Essays Presented to C. B. Tinker*, pp. 15–26, 1949.

———, *James Boswell, The Earlier Years*, 1966.

Ross, Ian, "Boswell in Search of a Father? or a Subject?" *Review of English Literature*, V, i (1964), 19–34.

BOSWELL'S LONDON JOURNAL[1]

The story of the rediscovery of Boswell's journals is one of the great scholarly dramas of the twentieth century. Not until 1949 was the huge mass of newly discovered Boswell papers transferred to Yale and made available to scholars. Some papers had been stuffed away in croquet boxes, escritoires, attics, and closets of Malahide Castle in Ireland, where a great granddaughter of Boswell's had lived; only in the 1920's did scholars learn of their existence. Others were found in Fettercairn House in Scotland, property of a descendant of Sir William Forbes, one of Boswell's literary executors. The *London Journal*, a portion of the newly discovered material, was a surprise best seller in the United States, and its popularity remains striking; it has been issued in several paperback editions.

Modern readers respond readily to the verve and frankness of Boswell's self-portrayal, to his agonizings, his triumphs, and his falls. The selection here reprinted begins with the opening of the *Journal*. The young man (he was 22) had long dreamed of a life in London which would be the antithesis of his narrow existence under the eye of a strict father in Scotland. After much effort and repeated quarrels with his father, he had won permission to go to the city in search of a commission in the Foot Guards, which would assure him the glamorous metropolitan life he desired. His father wished him to study law; the trip to London was an effort at self-assertion and freedom. The early passages of the *Journal* record a typical psychic pattern in their alternation between triumphant, ambitious optimism and fearful despair. They display Boswell's zest for life, but also his recurrent sense of inadequacy to life's demands. In the rest of the *Journal*, Boswell's absorbing narrative describes his meeting and developing friendship with Dr. Johnson, his diminishing hopes of patronage and commission, his amorous adventures, and his eventual decision to return to the profession his father had chosen for him.

The present text is from *Boswell's London Journal*, 1762–1763, edited by F. A. Pottle. Copyright 1950, Yale University. Used by permission of McGraw-Hill Book Company.

---

1 See Introduction, pp. 25–27.

Boswell's London Journal

(1762)

The ancient philosopher certainly gave a wise counsel when he said, "Know thyself." For surely this knowledge is of all the most important. I might enlarge upon this. But grave and serious declamation is not what I intend at present. A man cannot know himself better than by attending to the feelings of his heart and to his external actions, from which he may with tolerable certainty judge "what manner of person he is."[2] I have therefore determined to keep a daily journal in which I shall set down my various sentiments and my various conduct, which will be not only useful but very agreeable. It will give me a habit of application and improve me in expression; and knowing that I am to record my transactions will make me more careful to do well. Or if I should go wrong, it will assist me in resolutions of doing better. I shall here put down my thoughts on different subjects at different times, the whims that may seize me and the sallies of my luxuriant imagination. I shall mark the anecdotes and the stories that I hear, the instructive or amusing conversations that I am present at, and the various adventures that I may have.

I was observing to my friend Erskine[3] that a plan of this kind was dangerous, as a man might in the openness of his heart say many things and discover many facts that might do him great harm if the journal should fall into the hands of my enemies. Against which there is no perfect security. "Indeed," said he, "I hope there is no danger at all; for I fancy you will not set down your robberies on the highway, or the murders that you commit. As to other things there can be no harm." I laughed heartily at my friend's observation, which was so far true. I shall be upon my guard to mention nothing that can do harm. Truth shall ever be

---

2 James 1:24.

3 Lt. Andrew Erskine (1740–1793), whom Boswell had met in 1761. The younger son of the Earl of Kellie, Erskine was a poetaster who had been much published. He and Boswell had a rather self-conscious correspondence.

observed, and these things (if there should be any such) that require the gloss of falsehood shall be passed by in silence. At the same time I may relate things under borrowed names with safety that would do much mischief if particularly known.

In this way I shall preserve many things that would otherwise be lost in oblivion. I shall find daily employment for myself, which will save me from indolence and help to keep off the spleen, and I shall lay up a store of entertainment for my after life. Very often we have more pleasure in reflecting on agreeable scenes that we have been in than we had from the scenes themselves. I shall regularly record the business or rather the pleasure of every day. I shall not study much correctness, lest the labour of it should make me lay it aside altogether. I hope it will be of use to my worthy friend Johnston, and that while he laments my personal absence, this journal may in some measure supply that defect and make him happy.[4]

Monday 15 November

Elated with the thoughts of my journey to London, I got up. I called upon my friend Johnston, but found he was not come from the country, which vexed me a little, as I wished to bid him cordially adieu. However, I excused him to myself, and as Cairnie[5] told me that people never took leave in France, I made the thing sit pretty easy. I had a long serious conversation with my father and mother. They were very kind to me. I felt parental affection was very strong towards me; and I felt a very warm filial regard for them. The scene of being a son setting out from home for the wide world and the idea of being my own master, pleased me much. I parted with my brother Davy, leaving him my best advices to be diligent at his business as a banker and to make rich and be happy.

At ten I got into my chaise, and away I went. As I passed the Cross, the cadies and the chairmen bowed and seemed to say, "GOD prosper long our noble Boswell." I rattled down the High Street in high elevation of spirits, bowed and smiled to acquaintances, and took up my partner at Boyd's Close. He was a Mr. Stewart, eldest son to Ardsheal, who

---

4 John Johnston of Grange was perhaps Boswell's closest friend at this time. He was a minor solicitor in Edinburgh, of no particular distinction. Boswell wrote his journal with Johnston in mind and sent him weekly installments by mail.

5 Dr. John Cairnie of Edinburgh.

was forfeited in the year 1746.[6] He had made four voyages to the East Indies, and was now going out first mate. I made the chaise stop at the foot of the Canongate; asked pardon of Mr. Stewart for a minute; walked to the Abbey of Holyroodhouse, went round the Piazzas, bowed thrice: once to the Palace itself, once to the crown of Scotland above the gate in front, and once to the venerable old Chapel.[7] I next stood in the court before the Palace, and bowed thrice to Arthur Seat, that lofty romantic mountain on which I have so often strayed in my days of youth, indulged meditation and felt the raptures of a soul filled with ideas of the magnificence of GOD and his creation. Having thus gratified my agreeable whim and superstitious humour, I felt a warm glow of satisfaction. Indeed, I have a strong turn to what the cool part of mankind have named superstition. But this proceeds from my genius for poetry, which ascribes many fanciful properties to everything. This I have great pleasure from; as I have now by experience and reflection gained the command of it so far that I can keep it within just bounds by the power of reason, without losing the agreeable feeling and play to the imagination which it bestows. I am surely much happier in this way than if I just considered Holyroodhouse as so much stone and lime which has been put together in a certain way, and Arthur Seat as so much earth and rock raised above the neighbouring plains.

We then pursued our journey. I found my companion a jolly honest plain fellow. I set out with a determined resolution against *shaving*, that is to say, playing upon people;[8] and therefore I talked sensibly and roughly. We did very well till we passed Old Camus, when one of the wheels of our chaise was so much broke that it was of no use. The driver proposed that we should mount the horses and ride to Berwick. But this I would by no means agree to; and as my partner let me be the principal man and take the direction of our journey, I made the chaise be dragged on to Ayton, where we waited till the driver rode to Berwick and brought us a chaise. Never did I pass three hours more unhappily. We were set down in a cold ale-house in a little dirty village. We had a beefsteak ill-dressed and had nothing to drink but thick muddy beer. We were

---

6 I.e., his estate had been forfeited because of his active part in the Jacobite uprising of 1745.

7 Boswell is here paying obeisance to monuments associated with Scottish history and tradition. He was intensely and romantically patriotic.

8 Boswell had been a member of a frivolous group called the Soaping Club, from the idiom, "let every man soap his own beard," meaning "do what you will."

both out of humour so that we could not speak. We tried to sleep but in vain. We only got a drowsy headache. We were scorched by the fire on the one hand and shivering with frost on the other. At last our chaise came, and we got to Berwick about twelve at night. We had a slice of hard dry toast, a bowl of warm negus,[9] and went comfortable to bed.

Tuesday 16 November

We set off at six; breakfasted at Alnwick, where we had with us a Captain Elliot of the East Indies, and were hearty. Stewart and I began now to be acquainted and to talk about the Peace[10] and voyages and ways of living. We had a safe day, and got at night to Durham.

Wednesday 17 November

We had a very good day of it, and got at night to Doncaster.

Thursday 18 November

We chatted a good deal. Stewart told me that some blacks in India were attacking their boat in order to plunder it, and that he shot two with his own hand. In the afternoon between Stamford and Stilton there was a young unruly horse in the chaise which run away with the driver, and jumping to one side of the road, we were overturned. We got a pretty severe rap. Stewart's head and my arm were somewhat hurt. However, we got up and pursued our way. During our two last stages this night, which we travelled in the dark, I was a good deal afraid of robbers. A great many horrid ideas filled my mind. There is no passion so distressing as fear, which gives us great pain and makes us appear contemptible in our own eyes to the last degree. However, I affected resolution, and as each of us carried a loaded pistol in his hand, we were pretty secure. We got at night to Biggleswade.

Friday 19 November

It was very cold. Stewart was as effeminate as I. I asked him how he, who shivered if a pane of glass was broke in a post-chaise, could

---

9 Sherry sweetened and flavored with lemon and spices.

10 The Seven Year's War was drawing to an end; hostilities had ceased, although the actual treaty was not signed until February 10, 1763.

bear the severe hardship of a sea life. He gave me to understand that
necessity made anything be endured. Indeed this is very true. For when
the mind knows that it cannot help itself by struggling, it quietly and
patiently submits to whatever load is laid upon it. When we came upon
Highgate hill and had a view of London, I was all life and joy. I repeated
Cato's soliloquy on the immortality of the soul,[11] and my soul bounded
forth to a certain prospect of happy futurity. I sung all manner of songs,
and began to make one about an amorous meeting with a pretty girl, the
burthen of which was as follows:

> She gave me this, I gave her that;
> And tell me, had she not tit for tat?

I gave three huzzas, and we went briskly in.

I got from Digges[12] a list of the best houses on the road, and also
a direction to a good inn at London. I therefore made the boy drive me
to Mr. Hayward's, at the Black Lion, Water Lane, Fleet Street. The noise,
the crowd, the glare of shops and signs agreeably confused me. I was
rather more wildly struck than when I first came to London. My companion could not understand my feelings. He considered London just as
a place where he was to receive orders from the East India Company.
We now parted, with saying that we had agreed well and been happy,
and that we should keep up the acquaintance. I then had a bit of dinner,
got myself shaved and cleaned, and had my landlord, a civil jolly man,
to take a glass of wine with me. I was all in a flutter at having at last got
to the place which I was so madly fond of, and being restrained, had
formed so many wild schemes to get back to. I had recourse to philosophy,
and so rendered myself calm.

I immediately went to my friend Douglas's,[13] surgeon in Pall
Mall, a kind-hearted, plain, sensible man, where I was cordially received.
His wife is a good-humoured woman, and is that sort of character
which is often met with in England: very lively without much wit. Her
fault is speaking too much, which often tires people. He was my great
adviser as to everything; and in the mean time insisted that I should have
a bed in his house till I got a lodging to my mind. I agreed to come there

---

11 From Addison's famous tragedy, *Cato* (1713), V. i. 1–41.
12 West Digges, leading man in an Edinburgh theatrical company.
13 Boswell had met him in 1760.

next day. I went to Covent Garden—*Every Man in His Humour*.[14] Wood-ward[15] played Bobadil finely. He entertained me much. It was fine after the fatigues of my journey to find myself snug in a theatre, my body warm and my mind elegantly amused. I went to my inn, had some negus, and went comfortably to bed.

Saturday 20 November

I got into a hackney-coach with my baggage and drove to Douglas's. We calculated my expenses, and I found that to live would require great economy. However, I was upon honour to do my best. I strolled about all the forenoon calling for different people, but found nobody in. I went and saw a collection of wild beasts. I felt myself bold, easy, and happy. Only I had a kind of uneasiness from feeling no amazing difference between my existence now and at Edinburgh. I dined at Douglas's; sat in all the afternoon and wrote letters.

Sunday 21 November

I got up well and enjoyed my good situation. I had a handsome dining-room and bed-chamber, just in Pall Mall, the finest part of the town; I was in pursuit of my commission,[16] which I was vastly fond of; and I had money enough to live like a gentleman.

I went to Mayfair Chapel and heard prayers and an excellent sermon from the Book of Job on the comforts of piety. I was in a fine frame. And I thought that GOD really designed us to be happy. I shall certainly be a religious old man. I was much so in youth. I have now and then flashes of devotion, and it will one day burn with a steady flame.

I waited on Mr. George Lewis Scott,[17] who was very kind and polite to me, and on the Laird of Macfarlane,[18] with whom I was a good deal diverted. He was keenly interested in the reigning contests between

---

14 By Ben Jonson. Bobadil is a coward who tries to win a reputation as a gentleman by boasts about his fencing.

15 Henry Woodward (1714–1777), an important comic actor.

16 Boswell had come to London to get a commission in the Foot Guards; he had planned to make a career as an army officer.

17 Scott was a brilliant mathematician, at the time one of the commissioners of excise. He was a friend of Boswell's father, Lord Auchinleck.

18 His wife was Andrew Erskine's sister.

Scots and English. He talked much against the Union. He said we were perfect underlings; that our riches were carried out of the country; that no town but Glasgow had any advantage of trade by it, and that many others were hurt by it.

I dined with Dr. Pringle,[19] where were Mr. Murdoch, the publisher, or rather the editor, of Thomson;[20] Mr. Symmer, a travelling governor,[21] and some more, all Scotch. I found the Doctor in the way of discouraging me, which as from my father's friend I took patiently and intended to get the better of. The conversation was on indifferent common topics; the Peace, Lord Bute,[22] footmen, and cookery.

I went to Douglas's and drank tea. I next went and called in Southampton Street, Strand, for Miss Sally Forrester, my first love, who lived at the Blue Periwig. I found that the people of the house were broke and dead, and could hear nothing of her. I also called for Miss Jeany Wells in Barrack Street, Soho, but found that she was fled, they knew not whither, and had been ruined with extravagance. Good heaven, thought I, what an amazing change in two years! I saw in the year 1760 these young ladies in all the glow of beauty and admiration; and now they are utterly erased or worse. I then called on Love, and saw him and Mrs. Love and Billy.[23] I eat a tart there. He showed me a pantomime, called *The Witches*, of his.

Since I came up, I have begun to acquire a composed genteel character very different from a rattling uncultivated one which for some time past I have been fond of. I have discovered that we may be in some degree whatever character we choose. Besides, practice forms a man to anything. I was now happy to find myself cool, easy, and serene.

Monday 22 November

I strolled about all day looking for lodgings. At night I went to Drury Lane and saw Garrick play Scrub and the Farmer returned, and

---

19 John Pringle, physician general to the army, also a friend of Lord Auchinleck.

20 Patrick Murdoch (d. 1774), editor of James Thomson (1700–1748), author of *The Seasons*.

21 Robert Symmer, F.R.S., had made his living by accompanying young gentlemen abroad as a tutor or "travelling governor."

22 John Stuart, Earl of Bute (1713–1792), was at the time prime minister.

23 James Dance, former manager of the theatre at Edinburgh, had taken "Love" as a stage name. He was an old friend of Boswell and was now member of the Drury Lane company. His son Billy was at this time seven years old.

Love play Boniface, which brought the Cannongate full in my head.[24]
I was exceedingly well entertained.

Tuesday 23 November

I went into the City and called for George Home, Lord Kames's
son.[25] As Lord Eglinton[26] had used me neglectfully, and as I considered
him as not to be depended upon, I determined to keep clear of him as a
patron, but to like him as a companion; and if he offered to do me any
service, good and well, but I should ask no assistance from him. I called
thrice, but he was out. This day I received a formal card of invitation to
dine with him. I went, and was warmly received. Finding myself with
him in the very dining-room where in my days of youthful fire I had
been so happy, melted me much. Mylne the architect[27] dined with us.
We talked on a rude and on a polished state of society. I kept up a *retenue*[28]
and spoke only when I was sure that I was right. I drank tea. I parted
from him on a very good footing.

Wednesday 24 November

I called on Dodsley, and found that although he had refused to
take the hazard of publishing my *Cub*, that it had sold well, and that
there was thirteen shillings of profit, which I made him pay me down.[29]
Never did I set so high a value on a sum. I was much in spirits. I still went
about seeking lodgings, but could find none that would answer. At
night I called on Pringle. He was sour. Indeed, he is a good deal so,
although a sensible learned man, a good philosopher, and an excellent
physician. By the cheerful ease of my address I made him smile and be
very kind to me. I consulted him about all my plans. I began to find that

---

24 David Garrick (1717–1779), the greatest actor of his time, was manager of the
Drury Lane Theatre. "Scrub" and "Boniface" are parts in George Farquhar's comedy,
The Beaux' Stratagem. Garrick himself was author of the farce, *The Farmer's Return from
London*. The Edinburgh Theatre was located in the Canongate.
25 Henry Home, Lord Kames, the famous critic (1696–1782), was a judge and a
colleague of Boswell's father. He had been very kind to Boswell.
26 Archibald Montgomerie, Earl of Eglinton (1726–1796), a bachelor and something
of a rake. He was a close friend of Lord Bute.
27 Robert Mylne, a Scotsman, was building Blackfriars Bridge.
28 Caution, self-control.
29 Boswell had written a doggerel poem, *The Cub at Newmarket*, which had been
published by the noted booksellers Robert and James Dodsley—at Boswell's expense.

£200 a year was very little. I left him before twelve. I began to tire much
of Mrs. Douglas, she spoke so much. And I was rather somewhat low-
spirited.

Thursday 25 November

I had been in a bad situation during the night for I dreamt that
Johnston did not care for me. That he came to see me set off on a long
journey, and that he seemed dissipated and tired, and left me before I
got away. I lay abed very gloomy. I thought London did me no good.
I rather disliked it; and I thought of going back to Endinburgh immediately. In short, I was most miserable.

I got up and breakfasted. I got a card from Lord Eglinton asking
me to the House of Lords. I accordingly went and heard the King make
his speech.[30] It was a very noble thing. I here beheld the King of Great
Britain on his throne with the crown on his head addressing both the
Lords and the Commons. His Majesty spoke better than any man I ever
heard: with dignity, delicacy, and ease. I admired him. I wished much
to be acquainted with him.

I went to Love's and drank tea. I had now been some time in town
without female sport. I determined to have nothing to do with whores,
as my health was of great consequence to me. I went to a girl with whom
I had an intrigue at Edinburgh, but my affection cooling, I had left her.
I knew she was come up. I waited on her and tried to obtain my former
favours, but in vain. She would by no means listen.[31] I was really unhappy
for want of women. I thought it hard to be in such a place without them.
I picked up a girl in the Strand; went into a court with intention to enjoy
her in armour.[32] But she had none. I toyed with her. She wondered at
my size, and said if I ever took a girl's maidenhead, I would make her
squeak. I gave her a shilling, and had command enough of myself to go
without touching her. I afterwards trembled at the danger I had escaped.
I resolved to wait cheerfully till I got some safe girl or was liked by some
woman of fashion.

I went to Lord Eglinton's; John Ross Mackye[33] was there. We had

---

30 This was a speech opening the session of Parliament.
31 This "girl" turns out to have been Mrs. Love.
32 I.e., wearing a prophylactic sheath.
33 A Scots M.P.

a little bit of supper, and I was easy. I have never yet mentioned General Douglas,[34] whom I found to be a plain, civil man. I learnt that the Duke of Queensberry was not to be in town till Sunday, so that till then I could know nothing certain of my commission.

1763   Saturday 1 January

Dialogue at Child's

1 *Citizen.*	Pray, Sir, have you read Mr. Warton's *Essay on the Life and Writings of Pope?*[35] He will not allow him to be a poet. He says he had good sense and good versification, but wants the warm imagination and brilliancy of expression that constitute the true poetical genius. He tries him by a rule prescribed by Longinus, which is to take the words out of their metrical order and then see if they have the sparks of poetry.[36] Don't you remember this?
2 *Citizen.*	I don't agree with him.
1 *Citizen.*	Nor I, neither. He is fond of Thomson.[37] He says he has great force.
2 *Citizen.*	He has great faults.
1 *Citizen.*	Ay, but great force, too.
2 *Citizen.*	I have eat beefsteaks with him.
3 *Citizen.*	So have I.

I received for a suit of old clothes 11s., which came to me in good time. I went to Louisa[38] at one. "Madam, I have been thinking seriously." "Well, Sir, I hope you are of my way of thinking." "I hope, Madam, you are of mine. I have considered this matter most seriously. The week is now elapsed, and I hope you will not be so cruel as to keep me in misery." (I then began to take some liberties.) "Nay, Sir—now—but do consider—" "Ah, Madam!" "Nay, but you are an encroaching creature!"

---

34 Lieutenant-General Archibald Douglas was a relative of the Duke of Queensberry. Boswell had been told that the General could help him to a commission.

35 Joseph Warton, *Essay on the Writings and Genius of Pope*, Vol. I (1756), which claimed that Pope was a "correct" poet, not a genius.

36 *A Treatise Concerning Sublimity*, Sect. XL, where the author suggests that rearrangement of the words in a line of Euripides will indicate clearly "that Euripides is a poet of composition rather than of intellect."

37 James Thomson (1700–1748), author of *The Seasons* (1746), which Warton admired.

38 Louisa was Mrs. Lewis, an actress about whom little is known. Boswell first mentions her on December 14, 1762, as "a handsome actress . . . whom I was a little acquainted with." He had been courting her since.

(Upon this I advanced to the greatest freedom by a sweet elevation of the charming petticoat.) "Good heaven, Sir!" "Madam, I cannot help it. I adore you. Do you like me?" (She answered me with a warm kiss, and pressing me to her bosom, sighed, "O Mr. Boswell!") "But, my dear Madam! Permit me, I beseech you." "Lord, Sir, the people may come in." "How then can I be happy? What time? Do tell me." "Why, Sir, on Sunday afternoon my landlady, of whom I am most afraid, goes to church, so you may come here a little after three." "Madam, I thank you a thousand times." "Now, Sir, I have but one favour to ask of you. Whenever you cease to regard me, pray don't use me ill, nor treat me coldly. But inform me by a letter or any other way that it is over." "Pray, Madam, don't talk of such a thing. Indeed, we cannot answer for our affections. But you may depend on my behaving with civility and politeness."

I drank tea at Lady Betty's.[39] The Dempsters[40] were there. Jocularity and loud mirth went round. After the elegant scene of gallantry which I had just been solacing my romantic imagination with, and after the high-relished ideas with which my fancy had been heated, I could consider the common style of company and conversation but as low and insipid. But the Fife tongue and the Niddry's Wynd address were quite hideous.[41] After the tender respect with which I had been treated by the adorable Louisa I could not brook the not-ill-meant though coarse gibes of this *hamely*[42] company. I was hurt, but seemed easy. I left them at nine o'clock and went home.

Sunday 2 January

I had George Home[43] at breakfast with me. He is a good honest fellow and applies well to his business as a merchant. He had seen me all giddiness at his father's, and was astonished to find me settled on so prudent a plan. As I have made it a rule to dine every Sunday at home, and have got my landlady to give us regularly on that day a piece of good

---

39 Lady Betty Macfarlane, sister of Boswell's close friend Andrew Erskine. See note 3.

40 George Dempster (1732–1818), a Scots lawyer and member of parliament, and his sister Jeanie.

41 Niddry's Wynd, an alley in Edinburgh. The Musical Society of Edinburgh held its concerts there. Since this was an organization with socially prominent members, "Niddry's Wynd address" probably means "Edinburgh society manners."

42 Scotch form of *homely*, meaning "plain, simple, unsophisticated."

43 Son of Henry Home, Lord Kames. See note 25.

roast beef with a warm apple-pie, I was a little difficulted[44] today, as our time of dining is three o'clock, just my hour of assignation. However, I got dinner to be at two, and at three I hastened to my charmer.

Here a little speculation on the human mind may well come in. For here was I, a young man full of vigour and vivacity, the favourite lover of a handsome actress and going to enjoy the full possession of my warmest wishes. And yet melancholy threw a cloud over my mind. I could relish nothing. I felt dispirited and languid. I approached Louisa with a kind of an uneasy tremor. I sat down. I toyed with her. Yet I was not inspired by Venus. I felt rather a delicate sensation of love than a violent amorous inclination for her. I was very miserable. I thought myself feeble as a gallant, although I had experienced the reverse many a time. Louisa knew not my powers. She might imagine me impotent. I sweated almost with anxiety, which made me worse. She behaved extremely well; did not seem to remember the occasion of our meeting at all. I told her I was very dull. Said she, "People cannot always command their spirits." The time of church was almost elapsed when I began to feel that I was still a man. I fanned the flame by pressing her alabaster breasts and kissing her delicious lips. I then barred the door of her dining-room, led her all fluttering into her bedchamber, and was just making a triumphal entry when we heard her landlady coming up. "O Fortune why did it happen thus?" would have been the exclamation of a Roman bard. We were stopped most suddenly and cruelly from the fruition of each other. She ran out and stopped the landlady from coming up. Then returned to me in the dining-room. We fell into each other's arms, sighing and panting, "O dear, how hard this is." "O Madam, see what you can contrive for me." "Lord, Sir, I am so frightened."

Her brother then came in. I recollected that I had been at no place of worship today. I begged pardon for a little and went to Covent Garden Church, where there is evening service between five and six. I heard a few prayers and then returned and drank tea. She entertained us with her adventures when travelling through the country. Some of them were excellent. I told her she might make a novel. She said if I would put them together that she would give me material. I went home at seven. I was unhappy at being prevented from the completion of my wishes, and yet I thought that I had saved my credit for prowess, that

44 Impeded, embarrassed.

I might through anxiety have not acted a vigorous part; and that we might contrive a meeting where I could love with ease and freedom.

Monday 3 January

I begged Louisa to invent some method by which we might meet in security. I insisted that she should go and pass the night with me somewhere. She begged time to think of it.

Webster[45] and I dined at Gould's.[46] The Colonel was not at home, being upon guard. A Mrs. Douglas was there, lady to Captain Douglas of the Guards, a mighty pretty, agreeable creature. She asked me how long I had been from Scotland. If my name was Mr. *James* Boswell, and if I remembered her at Moffat.[47] She said if I did not recollect her name then, she would not tell me. "Madam," said I, "did it not begin with M?" She said it did. She proved to be a Miss Mackay with whom I was deeply in love at thirteen, a passion which Mr. Joseph Fergusson, then my tutor, ridiculed most roughly by setting his teeth together and giving hard thumps on the knees of his breeches. However, I certainly at that time felt all the pleasing anguish of a genuine flame. I told Mrs. Gould, "This, Madam, is a lady whom I was most desperately in love with." "Sir," said Mrs. Douglas, "I never knew it." "No, Madam, I never declared my hopeless passion." I diverted them by expatiating on this affair, and we were very cheerful. She hoped to see me, she said, at her house. Webster appeared in a poor light today. He seemed very young. He was lively, but it was the liveliness of a boy.

Tuesday 4 January

Louisa told me that she would go with me to pass the night when she was sure that she would not be wanted at the playhouse next day; and she mentioned Saturday as most convenient, being followed by Sunday, on which nothing is done. "But, Sir," said she, "may not this be attended with expense? I hope you'll excuse me." There was something so kind and so delicate in this hint that it charmed me. "No, Madam, it cannot be a great expense, and I can save on other articles to have money for this."

---

45 Captain James Webster, Boswell's first cousin.

46 Lieutenant-Colonel Nathaniel Gould, whose wife was Boswell's second cousin.

47 A small town near the Annan River in southern Scotland, about thirty miles southeast of the Auchinleck estate, Boswell's family home.

I recollected that when I was in London two years ago I had left a guinea with Mr. Meighan, a Roman-Catholic bookseller in Drury Lane, of which I had some change to receive.[48] I went to him and got 5s. and 6d., which gave me no small consolation. Elated with this new acquisition of pecuniary property, I instantly resolved to eat, drink, and be merry. I therefore hied me to a beer-house; called for some bread and cheese and a pint of porter.[49]

Close by the fire sat an old man whose countenance was furrowed with distress. He said his name was Michael Cholmondeley, that he was a day-labourer but out of work, that he had laid out a penny for some beer, and had picked up a bit of bread in the street which he was eating with it. I immediately ordered such a portion of victuals and drink for him as I took for myself. He then told me he was a sad dog in his youth, run off from his friends to London, wrought here some time, and at last, wanting money, he had sold himself for a slave to the Plantations for seven years. "Upon my word," said I, "you are a most extraordinary genius. How much did you get?" CHOLMONDELEY. "Twenty pounds." BOSWELL. "And pray, what sort of a life had you there?" CHOLMONDELEY. "O, Sir, a very good life. We had plenty of meat and drink, and wrought but five hours a day." He said he then came back, and afterwards made voyages in lighters[50] both to France and Spain. Poor creature! He had got falls and was sorely bruised, and often, even in severe weather, has been obliged to lie in the streets. I paid for his meal and gave him a penny. Why such a wretched being subsists is to me a strange thing. But I am a weak creature. I submit to GOD's will, I hope to know the reason of it some time.

I then bethought me of a place to which Louisa and I might safely go. I went to my good friend Hayward's[51] at the Black Lion, told him that I had married, and that I and my wife, who was to be in town on Saturday, would sleep in his house till I got a lodging for her. The King of Prussia says in one of his poems that gallantry comprises every vice.[52]

---

48 He may have left a deposit for books to be sent to him.

49 A dark, bitter beer.

50 A lighter is usually a flat-bottomed barge, used for unloading ships and for transporting goods in a harbor.

51 Mr. Hayward's inn had been recommended to Boswell by his actor friend, West Digges.

52 Professor Pottle suggests "*Epitre VIII, A Chasot (Sur la modération dans l'amour)*, though no lines in that poem correspond exactly to Boswell's paraphrase."

That of lying it certainly does, without which intrigue can never be carried on. But as the proverb says, in love and war all is fair. I who am a lover and hope to be a soldier think so. In this instance we could not be admitted to any decent house except as man and wife. Indeed, we are so if union of hearts be the principal requisite. We are so, at least for a time. How cleverly this can be done here. In Scotland it is impossible. We should be married with a vengeance.[53] I went home and dined. I thought my slender diet weakened me. I resolved to live hearty and be stout. This afternoon I became very low-spirited. I sat in close. I hated all things. I almost hated London. O miserable absurdity! I could see nothing in a good light. I just submitted and hoped to get the better of this.

Wednesday 5 January

I was agreeably surprised at breakfast with the arrival of my brother John in good health and spirits, although he had been for three months lately in a most terrible way. I walked with him in the Park. He talked sensibly and well.[54]

I then went to Lady Betty's. I was rather in the low-spirited humour still. She was by herself. I talked of my schemes. I owned my unsettled views, which indeed are only so at times, as I have preserved almost an uninterrupted constancy to the Guards. She asked me to dine. I told her I now had money to support me till Friday, was not obliged by a dinner, and therefore would come. I went and had some elegant conversation with Louisa; told her all was fixed for Saturday. She sweetly acquiesced. I like her better and better every day.

I was very hearty at dinner, but was too ridiculous. This is what I ought most to guard against. People in company applaud a man for it very much, but behind his back hold him very cheap. I have a strange knack at inventing odd phrases. We were talking of Mr. Garrick's power of making plays run. "Ay," said I, "he never takes a calf by the tail but he makes it run." This we made a common byword of. I had this morning sent a letter to Lord Eglinton as follows:

---

53 In Scotland a marriageable couple who acknowledged themselves man and wife before two witnesses were legally married. It was necessary, however, for the persons involved to have a true intention of marriage.

54 John Boswell, a lieutenant in the Thirty-first Regiment of Foot, had been suffering from mental illness. He had periodic fits of insanity for the rest of his life.

MY LORD:—Your Lordship's card, which came safe, was received by me with different feelings.[55] At first I talked very cavalierly: "Upon my word, the man has brought himself well off." But on a second perusal and a discovery of the poignant ridicule, I was obliged to acknowledge that you had used me as Mr. Moodie did the Devil: *left me no the likeness o' a cat.*[56] However, I contrive to get an indirect compliment by being the cause (as Falstaff says) of something so clever. You know we have often disputed whether or not I am a poet. I have sent you an ode. Lord Elibank[57] thought it good. I think so too.

As we were at dinner I got his answer as follows:

DEAR JAMIE,—I received your note, and am very glad you are got right again. I like your ode much. There was no need of that to convince me you had genius. I wish I was as sure of your judgment of men and things. I know you think yourself as well acquainted with both as Mr. Moodie's elders think him with GOD and the Devil. I agree you are upon a par, but I differ from the chosen ones. Yours,

E———.

Pray sup with me tonight. I have a choice spirit or two. Bring the *Captain* with you. We'll rub him up, and shall have leave to laugh at him for not knowing the world. Lady Macfarlane's brother, I mean.

This was really so good that they all agreed I should go, which the Captain complied with; so we sent our compliments, and we would wait on him. We then resumed our free jollity. I said I was happy. Indeed, after my gloom yesterday, it was a great odds. "But," said Lady Betty, "his weakness is that he would prefer Mrs. Gould's to this." "Indeed," said I. "I like your company much. But then I want to be among English people and to acquire the language." They laughed at that. I declaimed on the felicity of London. But they were cold and could not understand me. They reasoned plainly like people in the common road of life, and I like a man of fancy and whim. Indeed, it will not bear reasoning. But I can hear the rude attacks of people on my notions, and pursue them

55 Boswell had indicated his displeasure that Lord Eglinton (see note 26) communicated with him through a secretary. Lord Eglinton replied with a cutting note heavily laden with irony, returning Boswell "a great many thanks for being so good as to teach him good breeding." The letter printed here is Boswell's response.
56 Probably an anecdote about the Reverend Alexander Moodie of Riccarton, whom Burns immortalized in *The Holy Fair.*
57 Patrick Murray, fifth Baron Elibank (1703–1778), whom Boswell earlier described as "a man of great genius, great knowledge, and much whim." No copy of this ode has been preserved.

with complacency and satisfaction. Indeed, as to the happiness of life, it is neither in this thing nor that thing. It is in everything. Reason is not the sole guide. Inclination must chiefly direct us; and in this, one man's inclination is just as good as another's. For my own part, I shall always endeavour to be as happy as I can.

I represented Michael Cholmondeley's case and got three shillings for him. I drank tea with my landlord.

At nine Erskine and I went to Lord Eglinton's. His choice spirits were Lord Advocate,[58] Sir James Macdonald,[59] and Captain Johnstone of the Navy,[60] son to Sir James. Erskine and I were most amazingly bashful and stupid. The conversation was all about the banks of Scotland; a method to burn ships at a distance, as by burning glasses; and other topics out of our way entirely. In short, we appeared to horrid disadvantage. Let never people form a character of a man from being a night in his company, especially a man of wit. George Selwyn,[61] one of the brightest geniuses in England, of whom more good sayings are recorded than anybody, is often the dullest fellow that can be seen. He was a droll dog when at Oxford, and kept up a most earnest and grave correspondence with a reverend bishop on a point of controversial divinity: whether, after receiving the Communion before Confirmation, he was in a reprobate state or in a state of grace. He kept up the disguise of mystical religion long, and tormented the worthy prelate with his many grievous doubts. The letters he has by him. He was at last expelled the University for a piece of gross profanity, giving the sacrament to a dog. He did it literally, to a degree of craziness. He cut his arm and made the dog drink his blood, saying, "This is my blood, &c."[62]

Lord Eglinton and Sir James disputed about vanity. Sir James said it always made a man disagreeable. My Lord said vanity did not, because a vain man in order to be flattered always pays you great court. But a proud man despises you. The vain man piques himself on some qualities which you must know and admire. The proud man piques himself on

---

58 Thomas Miller, the lord advocate of Scotland, a title equivalent to attorney general in England.

59 Eglinton's nephew, an extraordinarily learned young man, still an Oxford undergraduate.

60 George Johnstone (1730–1787), later commodore, in 1763 governor of West Florida.

61 George Selwyn (1719–1791), wit and politician, noted for his escapades.

62 Pottle reports that the more probable version of the episode is that Selwyn was rusticated for using a chalice at a wine party.

being quite above you; so the lower he can thrust you, the higher he is himself; and of all things a purse-proud man is the most terrible. Sir James mentioned a disagreeable pride of understanding, which I thought very applicable to himself. My Lord mentioned poetry. Sir James said it was just personification, animating every object and every feeling, and that measure was not necessary. Erskine agreed with him. I maintained that personification was only one requisite in poetry, and that measure was absolutely necessary, without which it ceased to be poetry and must be denominated some other work of the imagination. That indeed it might be called poetical, as it partook of the nature of poetry. This was all the show that I made tonight in the way of speech. But my Lord produced me in writing, saying he had got a new poem (which was my *Ode to Ambition*). I asked him when he got it. He said it was lying in the pocket of a coat that he wore last year. Sir James read it aloud. He praised it upon the whole. He said the author wanted correctness, which is the least fault in a poet. He said these lines,

> *When Fancy from its bud scarce peep'd,*
> *And Life's sweet matins rung,*

were poor. But I think them two beautiful allusions. So speaks the author.

There was a simile which Captain Johnstone said was what the French call *une simile*[63] *avec une longue queue,* a simile with a long tail. Sir James said, "The author of this does not want either poetical imagination or ambition." Such a scene would have disconcerted some people. But I sat by with the most unconcerned ease. My Lord took me by the hand. "I hope we are very good friends." "My Lord, I hope we never were otherwise."

We stayed till near three. I was really uneasy going home. Robberies in the street are now very frequent. The night air, too, is very bad for the health, and always hurts me. I resolved to be determined against suppers, and always to be at home early, in spite of every temptation.

Thursday 6 January

My brother breakfasted with me. This was Twelfth-day, on which a great deal of jollity goes on in England, at the eating of the Twelfth-cake

---

63 Pottle points out that there is no French word *simile* and that "Boswell's French at this time was very imperfect."

all sugared over.[64] I called at Gould's. Mrs. Gould chid me for not being oftener there, and said jestingly that if she did not see me more, she would write to my father that I was idle. I then walked into the City. I took a whim that between St. Paul's and the Exchange and back again, taking the different sides of the street, I would eat a penny Twelfth-cake at every shop where I could get it. This I performed most faithfully.

I then dined comfortably at Dolly's Beefsteak-house. I regretted much my not being acquainted in some good opulent City family where I might participate in the hearty sociality over the ancient ceremony of the Twelfth-cake. I hope to have this snug advantage by this time next year.

I drank tea at Dempster's. Erskine and Lady Anne were there. We laughed a good deal.

Friday 7 January

Captain Maxwell[65] and my brother breakfasted with me. I then waited on Louisa. She informed me that Saturday could not be the hoped-for time to bestow perfect felicity upon me. "Not," said she, "that I have changed my mind. But it cannot be." In short, I understood that Nature's periodical effects on the human, or more properly female, constitution forbade it. I was a little uneasy at this, though it could not be helped. It kept me longer anxious till my ability was known. I have, together with my vivacity and good-humour, a great anxiety of temper which often renders me uneasy. My grandfather had it in a very strong degree.

I dined at Dr. Pringle's,[66] where was a Scotch company, none of whom were of much note. We had however a kind of cordiality of conversation that did very well. I drank tea at Douglas's, and then, though very indolent, went home and dressed, and went to the private party at Lady Northumberland's.[67] I was not there last Friday, and as my Lady knows I have nothing very important to take me up, it would look ill not to be often there, since she has been so kind as to ask me there.

Indeed, as I do not play, I am at a disadvantage, as people get much

---

64 An ornamented cake used in Twelfth-night festivities, with a bean or a coin introduced to determine the "king" or "queen" of the feast.

65 Captain William Maxwell of Dalswinton, Boswell's cousin.

66 See note 19.

67 Elizabeth Seymour Percy, Countess of Northumberland, famous for her entertainments at Northumberland House.

easier acquainted when set round a card-table and mixing a little chat while the cards are dealt. But I am under a promise to Sheridan[68] not to play for five years. He relieved me from game distress when he was at Edinburgh by lending me five guineas. Happy is it for me that I am thus tied up; for with my warmth and impetuosity of temper, I might go to the greatest lengths and soon involve myself in ruin and misery. There is no setting bounds to gaming when one engages keenly in it; and it is more genteel to say you never play than to refuse playing for whatever sums the company choose. The acquaintances made in this way are very slight. One made by a man who does not play is worth a hundred of them. Because in the one case it is only for the respect due to his money that he is known. In the other it is for the respect due to himself. This night I was badly off, I being the only person in the room who was not engaged at play. So that I was a little awkward and uneasy.

---

[68] Thomas Sheridan (1719–1788), Irish actor and teacher of elocution, father of the famous playwright, Richard Brinsley Sheridan. Boswell had attended his lectures on English elocution.

LIFE OF SAMUEL JOHNSON, LL.D.[1]

(1791)

Boswell labored for many years to produce what is surely the most famous biography in English. His own Advertisement to the first edition suggests that he was awe-inspired at what he had accomplished: "The stretch of mind and prompt assiduity by which so many conversations were preserved, I myself, at some distance of time, contemplate with wonder." He claims for his work absolute accuracy, and boasts of the trouble to which he has gone to ascertain facts. And he states his belief—and his satisfaction in that belief—"that by recording so considerable a portion of the wisdom and wit 'of the brightest ornament of the eighteenth century,' I have largely provided for the instruction and entertainment of mankind."

Although Boswell's self-estimates, in his moments of vanity, usually exceed any judgment of him that could be made by an outside observer, he has not overstated the claim to attention he has earned by this biography. Modern readers, too, wonder at the vivid reality of the thousands of conversations here recorded and continue to be instructed and entertained by this detailed, vigorous, altogether human account of a great man in action, his idiosyncrasies, his weaknesses, his triumphs. Boswell makes his subject at once lovable and awe-inspiring, and absolutely real. He individualizes even the most minor character on his crowded stage by his unerring eye for the definitive detail. He shapes his narrative with consummate skill; the publication of the journals, which provided raw material for the biography, reveals more sharply than ever the artifice with which he selected and formed the individual stories he tells. Never has another biography seemed so fully a work of art.

Johnson was fifty-four years old in 1763, when Boswell met him. His account of that meeting follows. The excerpt of the *Life* dealing with the year 1769 is particularly rich in specimens of Johnson's conversation; Boswell considered "the peculiar value" of his work to be "the quantity that it contains of Johnson's conversation; which is universally acknowledged to have been eminently instructive and entertaining." Any sample of it is likely to prove Boswell's point.

The present text is from *Boswell's Life of Johnson*, ed. G. B. Hill, revised and

---

1 See Introduction, pp. 27–30.

enlarged by L. F. Powell, 6 vols. (Oxford: Clarendon Press, 1934). Used by permission of the Clarendon Press, Oxford.

Life of Samuel Johnson L.L.D.

(1791)

[*May 16, 1763*]

    At last, on Monday the 16th of May, when I was sitting in Mr. Davies's[2] back-parlour, after having drunk tea with him and Mrs. Davies, Johnson unexpectedly came into the shop; and Mr. Davies having perceived him through the glass-door in the room in which we were sitting, advancing towards us,—he announced his aweful approach to me, somewhat in the manner of an actor in the part of Horatio, when he addresses Hamlet on the appearance of his father's ghost, "Look, my Lord, it comes."[3] I found that I had a very perfect idea of Johnson's figure, from the portrait of him painted by Sir Joshua Reynolds[4] soon after he had published his Dictionary, in the attitude of sitting in his easy chair in deep meditation, which was the first picture his friend did for him, which Sir Joshua very kindly presented to me, and from which an engraving has been made for this work. Mr. Davies mentioned my name, and respectfully introduced me to him. I was much agitated; and recollecting his prejudice against the Scotch, of which I had heard much, I said to Davies, "Don't tell where I come from."—"From Scotland," cried Davies, roguishly. "Mr. Johnson, (said I) I do indeed come from Scotland, but I cannot help it." I am willing to flatter myself that I meant this as light pleasantry to sooth and conciliate him, and not as an humiliating abasement at the expence of my country. But however that might be, this speech was somewhat unlucky; for with that quickness of wit for which he was so remarkable, he seized the expression "come from Scotland," which I used in the sense of being of that country; and, as if I had said that I had come away from it, or left it, retorted, "That, Sir, I find, is

---

2 Thomas Davies (c. 1712–1785), bookseller and author, whose bookshop was at 8 Russell Street, Covent Garden.

3 *Hamlet*, I. iv. 38.

4 For Reynolds, see above, pp. 278–79.

what a very great many of your countrymen cannot help." This stroke
stunned me a good deal; and when we had sat down, I felt myself not
a little embarrassed, and apprehensive of what might come next. He
then addressed himself to Davies: "What do you think of Garrick?[5] He
has refused me an order for the play for Miss Williams,[6] because he knows
the house will be full, and that an order would be worth three shillings."
Eager to take any opening to get into conversation with him, I ventured
to say, "O, Sir, I cannot think Mr. Garrick would grudge such a trifle
to you." "Sir, (said he, with a stern look,) I have known David Garrick
longer than you have done: and I know no right you have to talk to
me on the subject." Perhaps I deserved this check; for it was rather
presumptuous in me, an entire stranger, to express any doubt of the
justice of his animadversion upon his old acquaintance and pupil. I now
felt myself much mortified, and began to think that the hope which I had
long indulged of obtaining his acquaintance was blasted. And, in truth,
had not my ardour been uncommonly strong, and my resolution
uncommonly persevering, so rough a reception might have deterred
me for ever from making any further attempts. Fortunately, however,
I remained upon the field not wholly discomfited; and was soon rewarded by hearing some of his conversation, of which I preserved the
following short minute, without marking the questions and observations
by which it was produced.

"People (he remarked) may be taken in once, who imagine that an
authour is greater in private life than other men. Uncommon parts[7]
require uncommon opportunities for their exertion."

"In barbarous society, superiority of parts is of real consequence.
Great strength or great wisdom is of much value to an individual. But in
more polished times there are people to do every thing for money; and
then there are a number of other superiorities, such as those of birth and
fortune, and rank, that dissipate men's attention, and leave no extraordinary share of respect for personal and intellectual superiority. This is
wisely ordered by Providence, to preserve some equality among mankind."

"Sir, this book ('The Elements of Criticism[8],' which he had taken

---

5 David Garrick (1717–1779), the famous actor.
6 Anna Williams (1706–1783), Dr. Johnson's friend and member of his household.
She had been blind since about 1740.
7 Abilities.
8 Published 1762, by Henry Home, Lord Kames (1696–1782), Scots judge and author.

up,) is a pretty essay, and deserves to be held in some estimation, though much of it is chimerical."

Speaking of one who with more than ordinary boldness attacked publick measures and the royal family,[9] he said,

"I think he is safe from the law, but he is an abusive scoundrel; and instead of applying to my Lord Chief Justice to punish him, I would send half a dozen footmen and have him well ducked."

"The notion of liberty amuses the people of England, and helps to keep off the *tædium vitæ*.[10] When a butcher tells you that *his heart bleeds for his country*, he has, in fact, no uneasy feeling."

"Sheridan will not succeed at Bath with his oratory. Ridicule has gone down before him, and, I doubt, Derrick is his enemy."[11]

"Derrick may do very well, as long as he can outrun his character; but the moment his character gets up with him, it is all over."

It is, however, but just to record, that some years afterwards, when I reminded him of this sarcasm, he said, "Well, but Derrick has now got a character that he need not run away from."

I was highly pleased with the extraordinary vigour of his conversation, and regretted that I was drawn away from it by an engagement at another place. I had, for a part of the evening, been left alone with him, and had ventured to make an observation now and then, which he received very civilly; so that I was satisfied that though there was a roughness in his manner, there was no ill-nature in his disposition. Davies followed me to the door, and when I complained to him a little of the hard blows which the great man had given me, he kindly took upon him to console me by saying, "Don't be uneasy. I can see he likes you very well."

A few days afterwards I called on Davies, and asked him if he thought I might take the liberty of waiting on Mr. Johnson at his Chambers in the Temple. He said I certainly might, and that Mr. Johnson would take it as a compliment. So upon Tuesday the 24th of May, after having been enlivened by the witty sallies of Messieurs Thornton, Wilkes, Churchill and Lloyd,[12] with whom I had passed the morning, I boldly

---

9 John Wilkes (1727–1797), whose periodical *The North-Briton* violently attacked government policies.

10 "Weariness of life."

11 Thomas Sheridan (1719–1788)—father of the playwright Richard Brinsley Sheridan, actor and lecturer on elocution,—was, according to Boswell's note, "then reading lectures upon Oratory at Bath." Samuel Derrick (1724–1769) was master of the ceremonies at Bath.

12 Bonnell Thornton (1724–1768), miscellaneous writer; Charles Churchill (1731–

repaired to Johnson. His Chambers were on the first floor of No. 1, Inner-Temple-lane, and I entered them with an impression given me by the Reverend Dr. Blair,[13] of Edinburgh, who had been introduced to him not long before, and described his having "found the Giant in his den"; an expression, which, when I came to be pretty well acquainted with Johnson, I repeated to him, and he was diverted at this picturesque account of himself. Dr. Blair had been presented to him by Dr. James Fordyce.[14] At this time the controversy concerning the pieces published by Mr. James Macpherson, as translations of Ossian,[15] was at its height. Johnson had all along denied their authenticity; and, what was still more provoking to their admirers, maintained that they had no merit. The subject having been introduced by Dr. Fordyce, Dr. Blair, relying on the internal evidence of their antiquity, asked Dr. Johnson whether he thought any man of a modern age could have written such poems? Johnson replied, "Yes, Sir, many men, many women, and many children." Johnson, at this time, did not know that Dr. Blair had just published a Dissertation, not only defending their authenticity, but seriously ranking them with the poems of Homer and Virgil; and when he was afterwards informed of this circumstance, he expressed some displeasure at Dr. Fordyce's having suggested the topick, and said, "I am not sorry that they got thus much for their pains. Sir, it was like leading one to talk of a book, when the authour is concealed behind the door."

He received me very courteously; but, it must be confessed, that his apartment, and furniture, and morning dress, were sufficiently uncouth. His brown suit of cloaths looked very rusty; he had on a little old shrivelled unpowdered wig, which was too small for his head; his shirt-neck and knees of his breeches were loose; his black worsted stockings ill drawn up; and he had a pair of unbuckled shoes by way of slippers. But all these slovenly particularities were forgotten the moment that he began to talk. Some gentlemen, whom I do not recollect, were sitting with

---

1764), satiric poet; Robert Lloyd (1733–1764), poet, who had been a schoolfellow of Churchill. For Wilkes, see above, note 9.

13 Dr. Hugh Blair (1718–1800), clergyman and critic. Blair had encouraged Macpherson in his "translations" of Ossian (see below, note 15) and then defended their authenticity in his *Critical Dissertation on the Poems of Ossian* (1763).

14 Fordyce (1720–1796), Presbyterian divine.

15 James Macpherson (1736–1796) adapted and invented tales from the Gaelic tradition (*Fignal*, 1762; *Temora*, 1763) and published them as translations of ancient manuscripts. Ossian was the supposed author of these works.

him; and when they went away, I also rose; but he said to me, "Nay, don't go."—"Sir, (said I,) I am afraid that I intrude upon you. It is benevolent to allow me to sit and hear you." He seemed pleased with this compliment, which I sincerely paid him, and answered, "Sir, I am obliged to any man who visits me."—I have preserved the following short minute of what passed this day.

"Madness frequently discovers itself merely by unnecessary deviation from the usual modes of the world. My poor friend Smart[16] shewed the disturbance of his mind, by falling upon his knees, and saying his prayers in the street, or in any other unusual place. Now although, rationally speaking, it is greater madness not to pray at all, than to pray as Smart did, I am afraid there are so many who do not pray, that their understanding is not called in question."

Concerning this unfortunate poet, Christopher Smart, who was confined in a mad-house, he had, at another time, the following conversation with Dr. Burney.[17]—BURNEY. "How does poor Smart do, Sir; is he likely to recover?"JOHNSON. "It seems as if his mind had ceased to struggle with the disease; for he grows fat upon it." BURNEY. "Perhaps, Sir, that may be from want of exercise." JOHNSON. "No, Sir; he has partly as much exercise as he used to have, for he digs in the garden. Indeed, before his confinement, he used for exercise to walk to the ale-house; but he was *carried* back again. I did not think he ought to be shut up. His infirmities were not noxious to society. He insisted on people praying with him; and I'd as lief pray with Kit Smart as any one else. Another charge was, that he did not love clean linen; and I have no passion for it."

Johnson continued. "Mankind have a great aversion to intellectual labour; but even supposing knowledge to be easily attainable, more people would be content to be ignorant than would take even a little trouble to acquire it."

"The morality of an action depends on the motive from which we act. If I fling half a crown to a beggar with intention to break his head, and he picks it up and buys victuals with it, the physical effect is good; but, with respect to me, the action is very wrong. So, religious exercises, if not performed with an intention to please GOD, avail us

16 Christopher Smart (1722–1771), author of A *Song to David* (1763).
17 Dr. Charles Burney (1726–1814), musician and author, father of the novelist, Frances Burney.

nothing. As our Saviour says of those who perform them from other motives, 'Verily they have their reward.' "[18]

"The Christian religion has very strong evidences. It, indeed, appears in some degree strange to reason; but in History we have undoubted facts, against which, in reasoning *à priori*, we have more arguments than we have for them; but then, testimony has great weight, and casts the balance. I would recommend to every man whose faith is yet unsettled, Grotius,—Dr. Pearson,—and Dr. Clarke."[19]

Talking of Garrick,[20] he said, "He is the first man in the world for sprightly conversation."

When I rose a second time he again pressed me to stay, which I did.

He told me, that he generally went abroad at four in the afternoon, and seldom came home till two in the morning. I took the liberty to ask if he did not think it wrong to live thus, and not make more use of his great talents. He owned it was a bad habit. On reviewing, at the distance of many years, my journal of this period, I wonder how, at my first visit, I ventured to talk to him so freely, and that he bore it with so much indulgence.

Before we parted, he was so good as to promise to favour me with his company one evening at my lodgings; and, as I took my leave, shook me cordially by the hand. It is almost needless to add, that I felt no little elation at having now so happily established an acquaintance of which I had been so long ambitious.

My readers will, I trust, excuse me for being thus minutely circumstantial, when it is considered that the acquaintance of Dr. Johnson was to me a most valuable acquisition, and laid the foundation of whatever instruction and entertainment they may receive from my collections concerning the great subject of the work which they are now perusing.

I did not visit him again till Monday, June 13, at which time I recollect no part of his conversation, except that when I told him I had been to see Johnson ride upon three horses,[21] he said, "Such a man, Sir, should be encouraged; for his performances shew the extent of the human powers in one instance, and thus tend to raise our opinion of the faculties

18 Matthew 6:16.

19 Hugo Grotius (1583–1645), Dutch statesman and jurist, author of *De veritate religionis Christi*, which Johnson had read in his youth; Dr. John Pearson (1613–1686), bishop of Chester; Dr. Samuel Clarke (1675–1729), author of *A Discourse Concerning the Being and Attributes of God* (1705–1706).

20 See note 5, above.

21 This Johnson is not otherwise identified; G. B. Hill cites a letter by Walpole referring to the same equestrian feat.

of man. He shews what may be attained by persevering application; so that every man may hope, that by giving as much application, although perhaps he may never ride three horses at a time, or dance upon a wire, yet he may be equally expert in whatever profession he has chosen to pursue."

He again shook me by the hand at parting, and asked me why I did not come oftener to him. Trusting that I was now in his good graces, I answered, that he had not given me much encouragement, and reminded him of the check I had received from him at our first interview. "Poh, poh! (said he, with a complacent smile,) never mind these things. Come to me as often as you can. I shall be glad to see you."

I had learnt that his place of frequent resort was the Mitre tavern in Fleet-street, where he loved to sit up late, and I begged I might be allowed to pass an evening with him there soon, which he promised I should. A few days afterwards I met him near Temple-bar, about one o'clock in the morning, and asked if he would then go to the Mitre. "Sir, (said he) it is too late; they won't let us in. But I'll go with you another night with all my heart."

A revolution of some importance in my plan of life had just taken place; for instead of procuring a commission in the foot-guards, which was my own inclination, I had, in compliance with my father's wishes, agreed to study the law, and was soon to set out for Utrecht, to hear the lectures of an excellent Civilian in that University, and then to proceed on my travels. Though very desirous of obtaining Dr. Johnson's advice and instructions on the mode of pursuing my studies, I was at this time so occupied, shall I call it? or so dissipated, by the amusements of London, that our next meeting was not till Saturday, June 25, when happening to dine at Clifton's eating-house, in Butcher-row,[22] I was surprized to perceive Johnson come in and take his seat at another table. The mode of dining, or rather being fed, at such houses in London, is well known to many to be particularly unsocial, as there is no Ordinary, or united company, but each person has his own mess, and is under no obligation to hold any intercourse with any one. A liberal and full-minded man, however, who loves to talk, will break through this churlish and unsocial restraint. Johnson and an Irish gentlemen got into a dispute concerning the cause of some part of mankind being black. "Why, Sir, (said Johnson,)

---

[22] A row of tenements in the Strand which received its name from the butchers' shambles on the south side.

it has been accounted for in three ways: either by supposing that they are the posterity of Ham, who was cursed; or that GOD at first created two kinds of men, one black and another white; or that by the heat of the sun the skin is scorched, and so acquires a sooty hue. This matter has been much canvassed among naturalists, but has never been brought to any certain issue." What the Irishman said is totally obliterated from my mind; but I remember that he became very warm and intemperate in his expressions; upon which Johnson rose, and quietly walked away. When he had retired, his antagonist took his revenge, as he thought, by saying, "He has a most ungainly figure, and an affectation of pomposity, unworthy of a man of genius."

Johnson had not observed that I was in the room. I followed him, however, and he agreed to meet me in the evening at the Mitre. I called on him, and we went thither at nine. We had a good supper, and port wine, of which he then sometimes drank a bottle. The orthodox high-church sound of the MITRE,—the figure and manner of the celebrated SAMUEL JOHNSON,—the extraordinary power and precision of his conversation, and the pride arising from finding myself admitted as his companion, produced a variety of sensations, and a pleasing elevation of mind beyond what I had ever before experienced. I find in my journal the following minute of our conversation, which, though it will give but a very faint notion of what passed, is, in some degree, a valuable record; and it will be curious in this view, as shewing how habitual to his mind were some opinions which appear in his works.

"Colley Cibber,[23] Sir, was by no means a blockhead; but by arrogating to himself too much, he was in danger of losing that degree of estimation to which he was entitled. His friends gave out that he *intended* his birth-day Odes should be bad: but that was not the case, Sir; for he kept them many months by him, and a few years before he died he shewed me one of them, with great solicitude to render it as perfect as might be, and I made some corrections, to which he was not very willing to submit. I remember the following couplet in allusion to the King and himself:

Perch'd on the eagle's soaring wing,
The lowly linnet loves to sing.

Sir, he had heard something of the fabulous tale of the wren sitting upon the eagle's wing, and he had applied it to a linnet. Cibber's familiar style,

---

23 Colley Cibber (1671–1757), poet laureate from 1730.

however, was better than that which Whitehead[24] has assumed. *Grand* nonsense is insupportable. Whitehead is but a little man to inscribe dramatick verses to players."

I did not presume to controvert this censure, which was tinctured with his prejudice against players; but I could not help thinking that a dramatick poet might with propriety pay a compliment to an eminent performer, as Whitehead has very happily done in his verses to Mr. Garrick.

"Sir, I do not think Gray[25] a first-rate poet. He has not a bold imagination, nor much command of words. The obscurity in which he has involved himself will not persuade us that he is sublime. His Elegy in a Church-yard has a happy selection of images, but I don't like what are called his great things. His Ode which begins

> *Ruin seize thee, ruthless King,*
> *Confusion on thy banners wait!*[26]

has been celebrated for its abruptness, and plunging into the subject all at once. But such arts as these have no merit, unless when they are original. We admire them only once; and this abruptness has nothing new in it. We have had it often before. Nay, we have it in the old song of Johnny Armstrong:[27]

> *Is there ever a man in all Scotland*
> *From the highest estate to the lowest degree, &c.*

And then, Sir,

> *Yes, there is a man in Westmoreland,*
> *And Johnny Armstrong they do him call.*

There, now, you plunge at once into the subject. You have no previous narration to lead you to it.—The two next lines in that Ode are, I think, very good:

> *Though fann'd by conquest's crimson wing,*
> *They mock the air with idle state.*

---

24 William Whitehead (1715–1785) succeeded Cibber as poet laureate.
25 Thomas Gray (1716–1771). See above, p. 254.
26 *The Bard* (1757).
27 Johnson made the same comparison in his *Life of Gray*. See above, p. 232.

Here let it be observed, that although his opinion of Gray's poetry was widely different from mine, and I believe from that of most men of taste, by whom it is with justice highly admired, there is certainly much absurdity in the clamour which has been raised, as if he had been culpably injurious to the merit of that bard, and had been actuated by envy. Alas! ye little short-sighted criticks, could JOHNSON be envious of the talents of any of his contemporaries? That his opinion on this subject was what in private and in publick he uniformly expressed, regardless of what others might think, we may wonder, and perhaps regret; but it is shallow and unjust to charge him with expressing what he did not think.

Finding him in a placid humour, and wishing to avail myself of the opportunity which I fortunately had of consulting a sage, to hear whose wisdom, I conceived in the ardour of youthful imagination, that men filled with a noble enthusiasm for intellectual improvement would gladly have resorted from distant lands;—I opened my mind to him ingenuously, and gave him a little sketch of my life, to which he was pleased to listen with great attention.

I acknowledged, that though educated very strictly in the principles of religion, I had for some time been misled into a certain degree of infidelity; but that I was come now to a better way of thinking, and was fully satisfied of the truth of the Christian revelation, though I was not clear as to every point considered to be orthodox. Being at all times a curious examiner of the human mind, and pleased with an undisguised display of what had passed in it, he called to me with warmth, "Give me your hand; I have taken a liking to you." He then began to descant upon the force of testimony, and the little we could know of final causes; so that the objections of, why was it so? or why was it not so? ought not to disturb us: adding, that he himself had at one period been guilty of a temporary neglect of religion, but that it was not the result of argument, but mere absence of thought.

After having given credit to reports of his bigotry, I was agreeably surprized when he expressed the following very liberal sentiment, which has the additional value of obviating an objection to our holy religion, founded upon the discordant tenets of Christians themselves: "For my part, Sir, I think all Christians, whether Papists or Protestants, agree in the essential articles, and that their differences are trivial, and rather political than religious."

We talked of belief in ghosts. He said, "Sir, I make a distinction between what a man may experience by the mere strength of his imagination, and what imagination cannot possibly produce. Thus, suppose I should think that I saw a form, and heard a voice cry 'Johnson, you are a very wicked fellow, and unless you repent you will certainly be punished'; my own unworthiness is so deeply impressed upon my mind, that I might *imagine* I thus saw and heard, and therefore I should not believe that an external communication had been made to me. But if a form should appear, and a voice should tell me that a particular man had died at a particular place, and a particular hour, a fact which I had no apprehension of, nor any means of knowing, and this fact, with all its circumstances, should afterwards be unquestionably proved, I should, in that case, be persuaded that I had supernatural intelligence imparted to me."

Here it is proper, once for all, to give a true and fair statement of Johnson's way of thinking upon the question, whether departed spirits are ever permitted to appear in this world, or in any way to operate upon human life. He has been ignorantly misrepresented as weakly credulous upon that subject; and, therefore, though I feel an inclination to disdain and treat with silent contempt so foolish a notion concerning my illustrious friend, yet as I find it has gained ground, it is necessary to refute it. The real fact then is, that Johnson had a very philosophical mind, and such a rational respect for testimony, as to make him submit his understanding to what was authentically proved, though he could not comprehend why it was so. Being thus disposed, he was willing to inquire into the truth of any relation of supernatural agency, a general belief of which has prevailed in all nations and ages. But so far was he from being the dupe of implicit faith, that he examined the matter with a jealous attention, and no man was more ready to refute its falsehood when he had discovered it. Churchill, in his poem entitled "The Ghost," availed himself of the absurd credulity imputed to Johnson, and drew a caricature of him under the name of "POMPOSO,"[28] representing him as one of the believers of the story of a Ghost in Cock-lane, which, in the year 1762, had gained very general credit in London. Many of my readers, I am convinced, are to this hour under an impression that Johnson was thus foolishly deceived. It will therefore surprise them a good deal when they are informed upon undoubted authority, that Johnson was one of those by whom the imposture was detected. The story had become so popular, that he thought it should be investigated; and in this research

---

28 *The Ghost*, a satiric attack on Johnson, was published in 1762–1763.

he was assisted by the Reverend Dr. Douglas,[29] now Bishop of Salisbury, the great detecter of impostures; who informs me, that after the gentlemen who went and examined into the evidence were satisfied of its falsity, Johnson wrote in their presence an account of it, which was published in the newspapers and Gentleman's Magazine, and undeceived the world.

Our conversation proceeded. "Sir, (said he) I am a friend to subordination, as most conducive to the happiness of society. There is a reciprocal pleasure in governing and being governed."

"Dr. Goldsmith is one of the first men we now have as an authour, and he is a very worthy man too. He has been loose in his principles, but he is coming right."

I mentioned Mallet's tragedy of "ELVIRA,"[30] which had been acted the preceding winter at Drury-lane, and that the Honourable Andrew Erskine, Mr. Dempster,[31] and myself, had joined in writing a pamphlet, entitled "Critical Strictures" against it. That the mildness of Dempster's disposition had, however, relented; and he had candidly said, "We have hardly a right to abuse this tragedy; for bad as it is, how vain should either of us be to write one not near so good." JOHNSON. "Why no, Sir; this is not just reasoning. You *may* abuse a tragedy, though you cannot write one. You may scold a carpenter who has made you a bad table, though you cannot make a table. It is not your trade to make tables."

When I talked to him of the paternal estate to which I was heir, he said, "Sir, let me tell you, that to be a Scotch landlord, where you have a number of families dependent upon you, and attached to you, is, perhaps, as high a situation as humanity can arrive at. A merchant upon the 'Change of London, with a hundred thousand pounds, is nothing: an English Duke, with an immense fortune, is nothing: he has no tenants who consider themselves as under his patriarchal care, and who will follow him to the field upon any emergency."

His notion of the dignity of a Scotch landlord had been formed upon what he had heard of the Highland Chiefs; for it is long since a lowland landlord has been so curtailed in his feudal authority, that he has little more influence over his tenants than an English landlord; and of late

29 Dr. John Douglas (1721–1807), whom Goldsmith described in *Retaliation* as "The scourge of impostors, the terror of quacks."
30 By David Mallet (c. 1705–1765), poet, playwright, and biographer.
31 Andrew Erskine (1740–1793) was a close friend of Boswell; George Dempster (1732–1818), though older than the other two, participated with them in many of their attempts at literature and at wit.

years most of the Highland Chiefs have destroyed, by means too well known, the princely power which they once enjoyed.[32]

He proceeded: "Your going abroad, Sir, and breaking off idle habits, may be of great importance to you. I would go where there are courts and learned men. There is a good deal of Spain that has not been perambulated.[33] I would have you go thither. A man of inferiour talents to yours may furnish us with useful observations upon that country." His supposing me, at that period of life, capable of writing an account of my travels that would deserve to be read, elated me not a little.

I appeal to every impartial reader whether this faithful detail of his frankness, complacency, and kindness to a young man, a stranger and a Scotchman, does not refute the unjust opinion of the harshness of his general demeanour. His occasional reproofs of folly, impudence, or impiety, and even the sudden sallies of his constitutional irritability of temper, which have been preserved for the poignancy of their wit, have produced that opinion among those who have not considered that such instances, though collected by Mrs. Piozzi[34] into a small volume, and read over in a few hours, were, in fact, scattered through a long series of years; years, in which his time was chiefly spent in instructing and delighting mankind by his writings and conversation, in acts of piety to GOD, and good-will to men.

I complained to him that I had not yet acquired much knowledge, and asked his advice as to my studies. He said, "Don't talk of study now. I will give you a plan; but it will require some time to consider of it." "It is very good in you (I replied,) to allow me to be with you thus. Had it been foretold to me some years ago that I should pass an evening with with the authour of the RAMBLER, how should I have exulted!" What I then expressed, was sincerely from the heart. He was satisfied that it was, and cordially answered, "Sir, I am glad we have met. I hope we shall pass many evenings and mornings too, together." We finished a couple of bottles of port, and sat till between one and two in the morning.

He wrote this year in the Critical Review the account of "Telemachus, a Mask," by the Reverend George Graham, of Eton College.[35]

---

32 Both Johnson and Boswell talk elsewhere of how the chiefs are degenerating into "rapacious landlords."
33 Traveled through.
34 Hester Lynch Thrale, later Mrs. Piozzi (1741–1821), Johnson's close friend until her second marriage.
35 George Graham (d. 1767), assistant master at Eton.

The subject of this beautiful poem was particularly interesting to Johnson, who had much experience of "the conflict of opposite principles," which he describes as, "The contention between pleasure and virtue, a struggle which will always be continued while the present system of nature shall subsist: nor can history or poetry exhibit more than pleasure triumphing over virtue, and virtue subjugating pleasure."

As Dr. Oliver Goldsmith will frequently appear in this narrative, I shall endeavour to make my readers in some degree acquainted with his singular character. He was a native of Ireland, and a contemporary with Mr. Burke,[36] at Trinity College, Dublin, but did not then give much promise of future celebrity. He, however, observed to Mr. Malone,[37] that "though he made no great figure in mathematicks, which was a study in much repute there, he could turn an Ode of Horace into English better then any of them." He afterwards studied physick[38] at Edinburgh, and upon the Continent; and I have been informed, was enabled to pursue his travels on foot, partly by demanding at Universities to enter the lists as a disputant, by which, according to the custom of many of them, he was entitled to the premium of a crown, when luckily for him his challenge was not accepted; so that, as I once observed to Dr. Johnson, he *disputed* his passage through Europe. He then came to England, and was employed successively in the capacities of an usher to an academy, a corrector of the press, a reviewer, and a writer for a news-paper. He had sagacity enough to cultivate assiduously the acquaintance of Johnson, and his faculties were gradually enlarged by the contemplation of such a model. To me and many others it appeared that he studiously copied the manner of Johnson, though, indeed, upon a smaller scale.

At this time I think he had published nothing with his name, though it was pretty generally known that *one Dr. Goldsmith* was the authour of "An Enquiry into the present State of polite Learning in Europe," and of "The Citizen of the World,"[39] a series of letters supposed to be written from London by a Chinese. No man had the art of displaying with more advantage as a writer, whatever literary acquisitions he made. "*Nihil quod tetigit non ornavit.*"[40] His mind resembled a fertile, but thin soil.

---

36 Edmund Burke (1729–1797). See above, p. 350.
37 Edmond Malone (1741–1812), critic and editor who read the manuscript of Boswell's *Life* and made suggestions for revision. He was a close friend of Johnson.
38 Medicine.
39 For selections from both works, see above, pp. 301–11, 322–44.
40 "Nothing that he touched did he fail to ornament." From Johnson's epitaph on Goldsmith in Westminster Abbey.

There was a quick, but not a strong vegetation, of whatever chanced to be thrown upon it. No deep root could be struck. The oak of the forest did not grow there; but the elegant shrubbery and the fragrant parterre[41] appeared in gay succession. It has been generally circulated and believed that he was a mere fool in conversation; but, in truth, this has been greatly exaggerated. He had, no doubt, a more than common share of that hurry of ideas which we often find in his countrymen, and which sometimes produces a laughable confusion in expressing them. He was very much what the French call *un etourdi*,[42] and from vanity and an eager desire of being conspicuous wherever he was, he frequently talked carelessly without knowledge of the subject, or even without thought. His person was short, his countenance coarse and vulgar, his deportment that of a scholar awkwardly affecting the easy gentleman. Those who were in any way distinguished, excited envy in him to so ridiculous an excess, that the instances of it are hardly credible. When accompanying two beautiful young ladies[43] with their mother on a tour in France, he was seriously angry that more attention was paid to them than to him; and once at the exhibition of the *Fantoccini*[44] in London, when those who sat next him observed with what dexterity a puppet was made to toss a pike, he could not bear that it should have such praise, and exclaimed with some warmth, "Pshaw! I can do it better myself."

He, I am afraid, had no settled system of any sort, so that his conduct must not be strictly scrutinised; but his affections were social and generous, and when he had money he gave it away very liberally. His desire of imaginary consequence predominated over his attention to truth. When he began to rise into notice, he said he had a brother who was Dean of Durham, a fiction so easily detected, that it is wonderful how he should have been so inconsiderate[45] as to hazard it. He boasted to me at this time of the power of his pen in commanding money, which I believe was true in a certain degree, though in the instance he gave he was by no means correct. He told me that he had sold a novel for four hundred pounds. This was his "Vicar of Wakefield." But Johnson informed me, that he had made the bargain for Goldsmith, and the price was sixty

---

41 "A level space in a garden occupied by flower-beds ornamentally arranged" (*OED*).

42 A madcap or romp.

43 Miss Catherine (d. 1798) and Miss Mary Horneck (c. 1750–1840).

44 Italian puppets.

45 Imprudent, indiscreet.

pounds. "And, Sir, (said he,) a sufficient price too, when it was sold; for then the fame of Goldsmith had not been elevated, as it afterwards was, by his "Traveller";[46] and the bookseller had such faint hopes of profit by his bargain, that he kept the manuscript by him a long time, and did not publish it till after the "Traveller" had appeared. Then, to be sure, it was accidentally worth more money."

Mrs. Piozzi and Sir John Hawkins[47] have strangely mis-stated the history of Goldsmith's situation and Johnson's friendly interference, when this novel was sold. I shall give it authentically from Johnson's own exact narration: "I received one morning a message from poor Goldsmith that he was in great distress, and, as it was not in his power to come to me, begging that I would come to him as soon as possible. I sent him a guinea, and promised to come to him directly. I accordingly went as soon as I was drest, and found that his landlady had arrested him for his rent, at which he was in a violent passion. I perceived that he had already changed my guinea, and had got a bottle of Madeira and a glass before him. I put the cork into the bottle, desired he would be calm, and began to talk to him of the means by which he might be extricated. He then told me that he had a novel ready for the press, which he produced to me. I looked into it, and saw its merit; told the landlady I should soon return, and having gone to a bookseller, sold it for sixty pounds. I brought Goldsmith the money, and he discharged his rent, not without rating[48] his landlady in a high tone for having used him so ill."

My next meeting with Johnson was on Friday the 1st of July, when he and I and Dr. Goldsmith supped together at the Mitre. I was before this time pretty well acquainted with Goldsmith, who was one of the brightest ornaments of the Johnsonian school. Goldsmith's respectful attachment to Johnson was then at its height; for his own literary reputation had not yet distinguished him so much as to excite a vain desire of competition with his great Master. He had increased my admiration of the goodness of Johnson's heart, by incidental remarks in the course of conversation, such as, when I mentioned Mr. Levet,[49] whom he entertained under his roof, "He is poor and honest, which is recommendation

---

46 A long poem in couplets, published in 1764, the first work to appear under Goldsmith's name.

47 Sir John Hawkins (1719–1789) wrote a competing *Life of Johnson* (1787).

48 Berating.

49 Robert Levet (1705–1782), an obscure doctor, was Johnson's intimate and long a member of his household. He was notoriously awkward and uncouth.

enough to Johnson"; and when I wondered that he was very kind to a man of whom I had heard a very bad character, "He is now become miserable, and that insures the protection of Johnson."

Goldsmith attempted this evening to maintain, I suppose from an affectation of paradox, "that knowledge was not desirable on its own account, for it often was a source of unhappiness." JOHNSON. "Why, Sir, that knowledge may in some cases produce unhappiness, I allow. But, upon the whole, knowledge, *per se*, is certainly an object which every man would wish to attain, although, perhaps, he may not take the trouble necessary for attaining it."

Dr. John Campbell,[50] the celebrated political and biographical writer, being mentioned, Johnson said, "Campbell is a man of much knowledge, and has a good share of imagination. His 'Hermippus Redivivus' is very entertaining, as an account of the Hermetick philosophy, and as furnishing a curious history of the extravagancies of the human mind. If it were merely imaginary, it would be nothing at all. Campbell is not always rigidly careful of truth in his conversation; but I do not believe there is any thing of this carelessness in his books. Campbell is a good man, a pious man. I am afraid he has not been in the inside of a church for many years; but he never passes a church without pulling off his hat. This shews that he has good principles. I used to go pretty often to Campbell's on a Sunday evening, till I began to consider that the shoals of Scotchmen who flocked about him might probably say, when any thing of mine was well done, 'Ay, ay, he has learnt this of CAW-MELL!' "

He talked very contemptuously of Churchill's poetry, observing, that "it had a temporary currency, only from its audacity of abuse, and being filled with living names, and that it would sink into oblivion." I ventured to hint that he was not quite a fair judge, as Churchill had attacked him violently. JOHNSON. "Nay, Sir, I am a very fair judge. He did not attack me violently till he found I did not like his poetry; and his attack on me shall not prevent me from continuing to say what I think of him, from an apprehension that it may be ascribed to resentment. No, Sir, I called the fellow a blockhead at first, and I will call him a blockhead still. However, I will acknowledge that I have a better opinion of him now, than I once had; for he has shewn more fertility than I ex-

50 Campbell (1708–1775), miscellaneous writer, author of *Hermippus Redivivus, or the Sage's Triumph over Old Age and the Grave* (1744).

pected. To be sure, he is a tree that cannot produce good fruit: he only bears crabs. But, Sir, a tree that produces a great many crabs is better than a tree which produces only a few."

In this depreciation of Churchill's poetry I could not agree with him. It is very true that the greatest part of it is upon the topicks of the day, on which account, as it brought him great fame and profit at the time, it must proportionally slide out of the publick attention as other occasional objects succeed. But Churchill had extraordinary vigour both of thought and expression. His portraits of the players will ever be valuable to the true lovers of the drama; and his strong caricatures of several eminent men of his age, will not be forgotten by the curious. Let me add, that there are in his works many passages which are of a general nature; and his "Prophecy of Famine"[51] is a poem of no ordinary merit. It is, indeed, falsely injurious to Scotland; but therefore may be allowed a greater share of invention.

Bonnell Thornton had just published a burlesque "Ode on St. Cecilia's day, adapted to the ancient British musick, viz. the salt-box, the jew's-harp, the marrow-bones and cleaver, the humstrum or hurdy-gurdy, &c." Johnson praised its humour, and seemed much diverted with it. He repeated the following passage:

> *In strains more exalted the salt-box shall join,*
> *And clattering and battering and clapping combine;*
> *With a rap and a tap, while the hollow side sounds,*
> *Up and down leaps the flap, and with rattling rebounds.*

I mentioned the periodical paper called "THE CONNOISSEUR".[52] He said it wanted matter.—No doubt it has not the deep thinking of Johnson's writings. But surely it has just views of the surface of life, and a very sprightly manner. His opinion of THE WORLD[53] was not much higher than of the Connoisseur.

Let me here apologize for the imperfect manner in which I am obliged to exhibit Johnson's conversation at this period. In the early part of my acquaintance with him, I was so wrapt in admiration of his extraordinary colloquial talents, and so little accustomed to his peculiar

---

51 The poem (1763) centrally attacked the Scots.

52 Published by Bonnell Thornton (see note 12, above) and George Colman (1732–1794).

53 Another periodical, edited by Edward Moore (1712–1757) from 1753 to 1756.

mode of expression, that I found it extremely difficult to recollect and record his conversation with its genuine vigour and vivacity. In progress of time, when my mind was, as it were, *strongly impregnated with the Johnsonian æther*, I could, with much more facility and exactness, carry in my memory and commit to paper the exuberant variety of his wisdom and wit.

At this time *Miss* Williams, as she was then called, though she did not reside with him in the Temple under his roof, but had lodgings in Bolt-court, Fleet-street, had so much of his attention, that he every night drank tea with her before he went home, however late it might be, and she always sat up for him. This, it may be fairly conjectured, was not alone a proof of his regard for *her*, but of his own unwillingness to go into solitude, before that unseasonable hour at which he had habituated himself to expect the oblivion of repose. Dr. Goldsmith, being a privileged man, went with him this night, strutting away, and calling to me with an air of superiority, like that of an esoterick over an exoterick disciple of a sage of antiquity, "I go to Miss Williams." I confess, I then envied him this mighty privilege, of which he seemed so proud; but it was not long before I obtained the same mark of distinction.

On Tuesday the 5th of July, I again visited Johnson. He told me he had looked into the poems of a pretty voluminous writer, Mr. (now Dr.) John Ogilvie,[54] one of the Presbyterian ministers of Scotland, which had lately come out, but could find no thinking in them. BOSWELL. "Is there not imagination in them, Sir?" JOHNSON. "Why, Sir, there is in them what *was* imagination, but it is no more imagination in *him*, than sound is sound in the echo. And his diction too is not his own. We have long ago seen *white-robed innocence*, and *flower-bespangled meads*."

Talking of London, he observed, "Sir, if you wish to have a just notion of the magnitude of this city, you must not be satisfied with seeing its great streets and squares, but must survey the innumerable little lanes and courts. It is not in the showy evolutions of buildings, but in the multiplicity of human habitations which are crouded together, that the wonderful immensity of London consists."—I have often amused myself with thinking how different a place London is to different people. They, whose narrow minds are contracted to the consideration of some one particular pursuit, view it only through that medium. A politician thinks of it

---

54 John Ogilvie (1733–1813), Presbyterian divine and poet, whose *Poems on Several Subjects* had recently been published.

merely as the seat of government in its different departments; a grazier, as a vast market for cattle; a mercantile man, as a place where a prodigious deal of business is done upon 'Change; a dramatick enthusiast, as the grand scene of theatrical entertainments; a man of pleasure, as an assemblage of taverns, and the great emporium for ladies of easy virtue. But the intellectual man is struck with it, as comprehending the whole of human life in all its variety, the contemplation of which is inexhaustible.

On Wednesday, July 6, he was engaged to sup with me at my lodgings in Downing-street, Westminster. But on the preceding night my landlord having behaved very rudely to me and some company who were with me, I had resolved not to remain another night in his house. I was exceedingly uneasy at the aukward appearance I supposed I should make to Johnson and the other gentlemen whom I had invited, not being able to receive them at home, and being obliged to order supper at the Mitre. I went to Johnson in the morning, and talked of it as of a serious distress. He laughed, and said, "Consider, Sir, how insignificant this will appear a twelvemonth hence."—Were this consideration to be applied to most of the little vexatious incidents of life, by which our quiet is too often disturbed, it would prevent many painful sensations. I have tried it frequently, with good effect. "There is nothing (continued he) in this mighty misfortune; nay, we shall be better at the Mitre." I told him that I had been at Sir John Fielding's[55] office, complaining of my landlord, and had been informed, that though I had taken my lodgings for a year, I might, upon proof of his bad behaviour, quit them when I pleased, without being under an obligation to pay rent for any longer time than while I possessed them. The fertility of Johnson's mind could shew itself even upon so small a matter as this. "Why, Sir, (said he,) I suppose this must be the law, since you have been told so in Bow-street. But, if your landlord could hold you to your bargain, and the lodgings should be yours for a year, you may certainly use them as you think fit. So, Sir, you may quarter two life-guardmen upon him; or you may send the greatest scoundrel you can find into your apartments; or you may say that you want to make some experiments in natural philosophy, and may burn a large quantity of assafœtida in his house."

I had as my guests this evening at the Mitre tavern, Dr. Johnson, Dr. Goldsmith, Mr. Thomas Davies, Mr. Eccles, an Irish gentleman, for whose agreeable company I was obliged to Mr. Davies, and the Reverend

---

55 Sir John Fielding (d. 1780), Bow Street magistrate.

Mr. John Ogilvie, who was desirous of being in company with my illustrious friend, while I, in my turn, was proud to have the honour of shewing one of my countrymen upon what easy terms Johnson permitted me to live with him.

Goldsmith, as usual, endeavoured, with too much eagerness, to *shine*, and disputed very warmly with Johnson against the well-known maxim of the British constitution, "the King can do no wrong"; affirming, that "what was morally false could not be politically true; and as the King might, in the exercise of his regal power, command and cause the doing of what was wrong, it certainly might be said, in sense and in reason, that he could do wrong." JOHNSON. "Sir, you are to consider, that in our constitution, according to its true principles, the King is the head; he is supreme; he is above every thing, and there is no power by which he can be tried. Therefore it is, Sir, that we hold the King can do no wrong; that whatever may happen to be wrong in government may not be above our reach, by being ascribed to Majesty. Redress is always to be had against oppression, by punishing the immediate agents. The King, though he should command, cannot force a Judge to condemn a man unjustly; therefore it is the Judge whom we prosecute and punish. Political institutions are formed upon the consideration of what will most frequently tend to the good of the whole, although now and then exceptions may occur. Thus it is better in general that a nation should have a supreme legislative power, although it may at times be abused. And then, Sir, there is this consideration, that *if the abuse be enormous, Nature will rise up, and claiming her original rights, overturn a corrupt political system.*" I mark this animated sentence with peculiar pleasure, as a noble instance of that truly dignified spirit of freedom which ever glowed in his heart, though he was charged with slavish tenets by superficial observers; because he was at all times indignant against that false patriotism, that pretended love of freedom, that unruly restlessness, which is inconsistent with the stable authority of any good government.

This generous sentiment, which he uttered with great fervour, struck me exceedingly, and stirred my blood to that pitch of fancied resistance, the possibility of which I am glad to keep in mind, but to which I trust I never shall be forced.

"Great abilities (said he) are not requisite for an Historian; for in historical composition, all the greatest powers of the human mind are quiescent. He has facts ready to his hand; so there is no exercise of invention. Imagination is not required in any high degree; only about as much as is used in the lower kinds of poetry. Some penetration, accuracy, and colouring will fit a man for the task, if he can give the application which is necessary."

"Bayle's Dictionary[56] is a very useful work for those to consult who love the biographical part of literature, which is what I love most."

Talking of the eminent writers in Queen Anne's reign, he observed, "I think Dr. Arbuthnot[57] the first man among them. He was the most universal genius, being an excellent physician, a man of deep learning, and a man of much humour. Mr. Addison was, to be sure, a great man; his learning was not profound; but his morality, his humour, and his elegance of writing, set him very high."

Mr. Ogilvie was unlucky enough to choose for the topick of his conversation the praises of his native country. He began with saying, that there was very rich land round Edinburgh. Goldsmith, who had studied physick there, contradicted this very untruly, with a sneering laugh. Disconcerted a little by this, Mr. Ogilvie then took new ground, where, I suppose, he thought himself perfectly safe; for he observed, that Scotland had a great many noble wild prospects. JOHNSON. "I believe, Sir, you have a great many. Norway, too, has noble wild prospects; and Lapland is remarkable for prodigious noble wild prospects. But, Sir, let me tell you, the noblest prospect which a Scotchman ever sees, is the high road that leads him to England!" This unexpected and pointed sally produced a roar of applause. After all, however, those, who admire the rude grandeur of Nature, cannot deny it to Caledonia.

On Saturday, July 9, I found Johnson surrounded with a numerous levee, but have not preserved any part of his conversation. On the 14th we had another evening by ourselves at the Mitre. It happening to be a very rainy night, I made some common-place observations on the relaxation of nerves and depression of spirits which such weather occasioned; adding, however, that it was good for the vegetable creation. Johnson, who, as we have already seen, denied that the temperature of the air had any influence on the human frame, answered, with a smile of ridicule, "Why yes, Sir, it is good for vegetables, and for the animals who eat those vegetables, and for the animals who eat those animals." This ob-

---

56 Pierre Bayle (1647–1706), *Dictionnaire historique et critique* (1697).
57 Dr. John Arbuthnot (1667–1735), physician to Queen Anne, friend of Pope and Swift, author of *History of John Bull* (1712), and collaborator in the *Memoirs of Martinus Scriblerus* (1741).

servation of his aptly enough introduced a good supper; and I soon forgot, in Johnson's company, the influence of a moist atmosphere.

Feeling myself now quite at ease as his companion, though I had all possible reverence for him, I expressed a regret that I could not be so easy with my father, though he was not much older than Johnson, and certainly however respectable had not more learning and greater abilities to depress me. I asked him the reason of this. JOHNSON. "Why, Sir, I am a man of the world. I live in the world, and I take, in some degree, the colour of the world as it moves along. Your father is a Judge in a remote part of the island, and all his notions are taken from the old world. Besides, Sir, there must always be a struggle between a father and son, while one aims at power and the other at independence." I said, I was afraid my father would force me to be a lawyer. JOHNSON. "Sir, you need not be afraid of his forcing you to be a laborious practising lawyer; that is not in his power. For as the proverb says, 'One man may lead a horse to the water, but twenty cannot make him drink.' He may be displeased that you are not what he wishes you to be; but that displeasure will not go far. If he insists only on your having as much law as is necessary for a man of property, and then endeavours to get you into Parliament, he is quite in the right."

He enlarged very convincingly upon the excellence of rhyme over blank verse in English poetry. I mentioned to him that Dr. Adam Smith,[58] in his lectures upon composition, when I studied under him in the College of Glasgow, had maintained the same opinion strenuously, and I repeated some of his arguments. JOHNSON. "Sir, I was once in company with Smith, and we did not take to each other; but had I known that he loved rhyme as much as you tell me he does, I should have HUGGED him."

Talking of those who denied the truth of Christianity, he said, "It is always easy to be on the negative side. If a man were now to deny that there is salt upon the table, you could not reduce him to an absurdity. Come, let us try this a little further. I deny that Canada is taken, and I can support my denial by pretty good arguments. The French are a much more numerous people than we; and it is not likely that they would allow us to take it. 'But the ministry have assured us, in all the formality of the Gazette, that it is taken.'—Very true. But the ministry have put us to an enormous expence by the war in America, and it is their interest to persuade us that we have got something for our money.—'But the fact is

---

58 Adam Smith (1723–1790), political economist, later with Johnson a member of The Club.

confirmed by thousands of men who were at the taking of it.'—Ay, but these men have still more interest in deceiving us. They don't want that you should think the French have beat them, but that they have beat the French. Now suppose you should go over and find that it is really taken, that would only satisfy yourself; for when you come home we will not believe you. We will say, you have been bribed.—Yet, Sir, notwithstanding all these plausible objections, we have no doubt that Canada is really ours. Such is the weight of common testimony. How much stronger are the evidences of the Christian religion?"

"Idleness is a disease which must be combated; but I would not advise a rigid adherence to a particular plan of study. I myself have never persisted in any plan for two days together. A man ought to read just as inclination leads him; for what he reads as a task will do him little good. A young man should read five hours in a day, and so may acquire a great deal of knowledge."

To a man of vigorous intellect and ardent curiosity like his own, reading without a regular plan may be beneficial; though even such a man must submit to it, if he would attain a full understanding of any of the sciences.

To such a degree of unrestrained frankness had he now accustomed me, that in the course of this evening I talked of the numerous reflections which had been thrown out against him on account of his having accepted a pension from his present Majesty. "Why, Sir, (said he, with a hearty laugh,) it is a mighty foolish noise that they make. I have accepted of a pension as a reward which has been thought due to my literary merit; and now that I have this pension, I am the same man in every respect that I have ever been; I retain the same principles. It is true, that I cannot now curse (smiling) the House of Hanover; nor would it be decent for me to drink King James's health in the wine that King George gives me money to pay for. But, Sir, I think that the pleasure of cursing the House of Hanover, and drinking King James's health, are amply overbalanced by three hundred pounds a year."

There was here, most certainly, an affectation of more Jacobitism than he really had; and indeed an intention of admitting, for the moment, in a much greater extent than it really existed, the charge of disaffection imputed to him by the world, merely for the purpose of shewing how dexterously he could repel an attack, even though he were placed in the most disadvantageous position; for I have heard him declare, that if holding up his right hand would have secured victory at Culloden to Prince Charles's army, he was not sure he would have held it up; so little confidence had he in the right claimed by the house of Stuart, and so fearful was he of the consequences of another revolution on the throne of Great-Britain; and Mr. Topham Beauclerk[59] assured me, he had heard him say this before he had his pension. At another time he said to Mr. Langton, "Nothing has ever offered, that has made it worth my while to consider the question fully." He, however, also said to the same gentleman, talking of King James the Second, "It was become impossible for him to reign any longer in this country." He no doubt had an early attachment to the House of Stuart; but his zeal had cooled as his reason strengthened. Indeed I heard him once say, that "after the death of a violent Whig, with whom he used to contend with great eagerness, he felt his Toryism much abated." I suppose he meant Mr. Walmsley.[60]

Yet there is no doubt that at earlier periods he was wont often to exercise both his pleasantry and ingenuity in talking Jacobitism. My much respected friend, Dr. Douglas, now Bishop of Salisbury,[61] has favoured me with the following admirable instance from his Lordship's own recollection. One day when dining at old Mr. Langton's, where Miss Roberts, his niece, was one of the company, Johnson, with his usual complacent attention to the fair sex, took her by the hand and said, "My dear, I hope you are a Jacobite." Old Mr. Langton, who, though a high and steady Tory, was attached to the present Royal Family, seemed offended, and asked Johnson, with great warmth, what he could mean by putting such a question to his niece? "Why, Sir, (said Johnson) I meant no offence to your niece, I meant her a great compliment. A Jacobite, Sir, believes in the divine right of Kings. He that believes in the divine right of Kings believes in a Divinity. A Jacobite believes in the divine right of Bishops. He that believes in the divine right of Bishops believes in the divine authority of the Christian religion. Therefore, Sir, a Jacobite is neither an Atheist nor a Deist. That cannot be said of a Whig; for *Whiggism is a negation of all principle.*"

He advised me, when abroad, to be as much as I could with the Professors in the Universities, and with the Clergy; for from their conversation I might expect the best accounts of every thing in whatever country I should be, with the additional advantage of keeping my learning alive.

59 Topham Beauclerk (1739–1780), Johnson's friend, noted for his wide learning and his witty conversation.
60 Gilbert Walmesley (1680–1751), registrar of the Ecclesiastical Court, Lichfield.
61 See above, note 29.

It will be observed, that when giving me advice as to my travels, Dr. Johnson did not dwell upon cities, and palaces, and pictures, and shows, and Arcadian scenes. He was of Lord Essex's opinion, who advises his kinsman Roger Earl of Rutland, "rather to go an hundred miles to speak with one wise man, than five miles to see a fair town."[62]

I described to him an impudent fellow[63] from Scotland, who affected to be a savage, and railed at all established systems. JOHNSON. "There is nothing surprizing in this, Sir. He wants to make himself conspicuous. He would tumble in a hogstye, as long as you looked at him and called to him to come out. But let him alone, never mind him, and he'll soon give it over."

I added, that the same person maintained that there was no distinction between virtue and vice. JOHNSON. "Why, Sir, if the fellow does not think as he speaks, he is lying; and I see not what honour he can propose to himself from having the character of a lyar. But if he does really think that there is no distinction between virtue and vice, why, Sir, when he leaves our houses, let us count our spoons."

Sir David Dalrymple,[64] now one of the Judges of Scotland by the title of Lord Hailes, had contributed much to increase my high opinion of Johnson, on account of his writings, long before I attained to a personal acquaintance with him; I, in return, had informed Johnson of Sir David's eminent character for learning and religion; and Johnson was so much pleased, that at one of our evening meetings he gave him for his toast. I at this time kept up a very frequent correspondence with Sir David; and I read to Dr. Johnson to-night the following passage from the letter which I had last received from him:

It gives me pleasure to think that you have obtained the friendship of Mr. Samuel Johnson. He is one of the best moral writers which England has produced. At the same time, I envy you the free and undisguised converse with such a man. May I beg you to present my best respects to him, and to assure him of the veneration which I entertain for the authour of the Rambler and of Rasselas? Let me recommend this last work to you; with

---

62 *Letter to Rutland on Travel* (1596). This work is contained in a volume entitled *Profitable Instructions; describing what special observations are to be taken by travellers* . . . By . . . Robert, late Earl of Essex, Sir Philip Sidney, and Secretary Davison (1633).

63 James Macpherson. See note 15, above.

64 Sir David Dalrymple (1726–1792), one of Boswell's models as a learned lawyer, a man of style, a literary figure, and a devout Christian.

the Rambler you certainly are acquainted. In Rasselas you will see a tender-hearted operator, who probes the wound only to heal it. Swift, on the contrary, mangles human nature. He cuts and slashes, as if he took pleasure in the operation, like the tyrant who said, *Ita feri ut se sentiat emori.*[65]

Johnson seemed to be much gratified by this just and well-turned compliment.

He recommended to me to keep a journal of my life, full and unreserved. He said it would be a very good exercise, and would yield me great satisfaction when the particulars were faded from my remembrance. I was uncommonly fortunate in having had a previous coincidence of opinion with him upon this subject, for I had kept such a journal for some time; and it was no small pleasure to me to have this to tell him, and to receive his approbation. He counselled me to keep it private, and said I might surely have a friend who would burn it in case of my death. From this habit I have been enabled to give the world so many anecdotes, which would otherwise have been lost to posterity. I mentioned that I was afraid I put into my journal too many little incidents. JOHNSON. "There is nothing, Sir, too little for so little a creature as man. It is by studying little things that we attain the great art of having as little misery and as much happiness as possible."

Next morning Mr. Dempster happened to call on me, and was so much struck even with the imperfect account which I gave him of Dr. Johnson's conversation, that to his honour be it recorded, when I complained that drinking port and sitting up late with him, affected my nerves for some time after, he said, "One had better be palsied at eighteen, than not keep company with such a man."

On Tuesday, July 18, I found tall Sir Thomas Robinson[66] sitting with Johnson. Sir Thomas said, that the King of Prussia valued himself upon three things;—upon being a hero, a musician, and an authour. JOHNSON. "Pretty well, Sir, for one man. As to his being an authour, I have not looked at his poetry; but his prose is poor stuff. He writes just as you might suppose Voltaire's footboy to do, who has been his amanuensis. He has such parts as the valet might have, and about as much of the colouring of the style as might be got by transcribing his works." When I

---

65 "Strike so that he may feel that he is dying" (Suetonius, *Lives of the Caesars, Caligula*, xxx).

66 Sir Thomas Robinson (c. 1700–1777), called "tall" because of his height and to distinguish him from Sir Thomas Robinson, Lord Grantham (1695–1770).

was at Ferney, I repeated this to Voltaire,[67] in order to reconcile him somewhat to Johnson, whom he, in affecting the English mode of expression, had previously characterised as "a superstitious dog"; but after hearing such a criticism on Frederick the Great, with whom he was then on bad terms, he exclaimed, "An honest fellow!"

But I think the criticism much too severe; for the "Memoirs of the House of Brandenburgh" are written as well as many works of that kind. His poetry, for the style of which he himself makes a frank apology, *"Jargonnant un François barbare,"*[68] though fraught with pernicious ravings of infidelity, has, in many places, great animation, and in some a pathetick tenderness.

Upon this contemptuous animadversion on the King of Prussia, I observed to Johnson, "It would seem then, Sir, that much less parts are necessary to make a King, than to make an Authour; for the King of Prussia is confessedly the greatest King now in Europe, yet you think he makes a very poor figure as an Authour."

Mr. Levet this day shewed me Dr. Johnson's library, which was contained in two garrets over his Chambers, where Lintot, son of the celebrated bookseller of that name,[69] had formerly his warehouse. I found a number of good books, but very dusty and in great confusion. The floor was strewed with manuscript leaves, in Johnson's own handwriting, which I beheld with a degree of veneration, supposing they perhaps might contain portions of the Rambler, or of Rasselas. I observed an apparatus for chymical experiments, of which Johnson was all his life very fond. The place seemed to be very favourable for retirement and meditation. Johnson told me, that he went up thither without mentioning it to his servant, when he wanted to study, secure from interruption; for he would not allow his servant to say he was not at home when he really was. "A servant's strict regard for truth, (said he) must be weakened by such a practice. A philosopher may know that it is merely a form of denial; but few servants are such nice distinguishers. If I accustom a servant to tell a lie for *me*, have I not reason to apprehend that he will tell many lies for *himself*?" I am, however, satisfied that every servant,

---

67 In 1764 Boswell visited Voltaire at Ferney in France; he spent two days with the philosopher.

68 "Chattering a barbarous French." *François* was an eighteenth-century form of *Français*.

69 Henry Lintot (1703–1758), like his more celebrated father Bernard (1675–1736) was a bookseller.

of any degree of intelligence, understands saying his master is not at home, not at all as the affirmation of a fact, but as customary words, intimating that his master wishes not to be seen; so that there can be no bad effect from it.

Mr. Temple, now vicar of St. Gluvias, Cornwall,[70] who had been my intimate friend for many years, had at this time chambers in Farrar's-buildings, at the bottom of Inner Temple-lane, which he kindly lent me upon my quitting my lodgings, he being to return to Trinity Hall, Cambridge. I found them particularly convenient for me, as they were so near Dr. Johnson's.

On Wednesday, July 20, Dr. Johnson, Mr. Dempster, and my uncle Dr. Boswell,[71] who happened to be now in London, supped with me at these Chambers. JOHNSON. "Pity is not natural to man. Children are always cruel. Savages are always cruel. Pity is acquired and improved by the cultivation of reason. We may have uneasy sensations from seeing a creature in distress, without pity; for we have not pity unless we wish to relieve them. When I am on my way to dine with a friend, and finding it late, have bid the coachman make haste, if I happen to attend when he whips his horses, I may feel unpleasantly that the animals are put to pain, but I do not wish him to desist. No, Sir, I wish him to drive on."

Mr. Alexander Donaldson, bookseller of Edinburgh, had for some time opened a shop in London, and sold his cheap editions of the most popular English books, in defiance of the supposed common-law right of *Literary Property*. Johnson, though he concurred in the opinion which was afterwards sanctioned by a judgement of the House of Lords,[72] that there was no such right, was at this time very angry that the Booksellers of London, for whom he uniformly professed much regard, should suffer from an invasion of what they had ever considered to be secure: and he was loud and violent against Mr. Donaldson. "He is a fellow who takes advantage of the law to injure his brethren; for, notwithstanding that the statute secures only fourteen years of exclusive right, it has always been understood by *the trade*, that he, who buys the copy-right of a book from the authour, obtains a perpetual property; and upon that belief, numberless bargains are made to transfer that property after the expiration

---

70 The Rev. William Johnstone Temple (1739–1796), essayist and Boswell's intimate friend.

71 Dr. John Boswell (1707–1780).

72 The House of Lords ruled in 1774 that the common law right of literary property had been removed by the Copyright Act of 1709 and a statutory right substituted for it.

of the statutory term. Now Donaldson, I say, takes advantage here, of people who have really an equitable title from usage; and if we consider how few of the books, of which they buy the property, succeed so well as to bring profit, we should be of opinion that the term of fourteen years is too short; it should be sixty years." DEMPSTER. "Donaldson, Sir, is anxious for the encouragement of literature. He reduces the price of books, so that poor students may buy them." JOHNSON, (laughing.) "Well, Sir, allowing that to be his motive, he is no better than Robin Hood, who robbed the rich in order to give to the poor."

It is remarkable, that when the great question concerning Literary Property came to be ultimately tried before the supreme tribunal of this country, in consequence of the very spirited exertions of Mr. Donaldson, Dr. Johnson was zealous against a perpetuity; but he thought that the term of the exclusive right of authours should be considerably enlarged. He was then for granting a hundred years.

The conversation now turned upon Mr. David Hume's[73] style. JOHNSON. "Why, Sir, his style is not English; the structure of his sentences is French. Now the French structure and the English structure may, in the nature of things, be equally good. But if you allow that the English language is established, he is wrong. My name might originally have been Nicholson, as well as Johnson; but were you to call me Nicholson now, you would call me very absurdly."

Rousseau's treatise on the inequality of mankind[74] was at this time a fashionable topick. It gave rise to an observation by Mr. Dempster, that the advantages of fortune and rank were nothing to a wise man, who ought to value only merit. JOHNSON. "If man were a savage, living in the woods by himself, this might be true; but in civilized society we all depend upon each other, and our happiness is very much owing to the good opinion of mankind. Now, Sir, in civilized society, external advantages make us more respected. A man with a good coat upon his back meets with a better reception than he who has a bad one. Sir, you may analyse this, and say what is there in it? But that will avail you nothing, for it is a part of a general system. Pound St. Paul's church into atoms, and consider any single atom; it is, to be sure, good for nothing: but, put all these atoms together, and you have St. Paul's church. So it is with human felicity, which is made up of many ingredients, each of

---

73 For Hume (1711–1776), see above, p. 234.
74 *Discours sur l'origine et les fondemens de l'inégalité parmi les hommes* (1755).

which may be shewn to be very insignificant. In civilized society, personal merit will not serve you so much as money will. Sir, you may make the experiment. Go into the street, and give one man a lecture on morality, and another a shilling, and see which will respect you most. If you wish only to support nature, Sir William Petty[75] fixes your allowance at three pounds a year; but as times are much altered, let us call it six pounds. This sum will fill your belly, shelter you from the weather, and even get you a strong lasting coat, supposing it to be made of good bull's hide. Now, Sir, all beyond this is artificial, and is desired in order to obtain a greater degree of respect from our fellow-creatures. And, Sir, if six hundred pounds a year procure a man more consequence, and, of course, more happiness than six pounds a year, the same proportion will hold as to six thousand, and so on as far as opulence can be carried. Perhaps he who has a large fortune may not be so happy as he who has a small one; but that must proceed from other causes than from his having the large fortune: for, *cæteris paribus*,[76] he who is rich in a civilized society, must be happier than he who is poor; as riches, if properly used, (and it is a man's own fault if they are not,) must be productive of the highest advantages. Money, to be sure, of itself is of no use; for its only use is to part with it. Rousseau, and all those who deal in paradoxes, are led away by a childish desire of novelty. When I was a boy, I used always to choose the wrong side of a debate, because most ingenious things, that is to say, most new things, could be said upon it. Sir, there is nothing for which you may not muster up more plausible arguments, than those which are urged against wealth and other external advantages. Why now, there is stealing; why should it be thought a crime? When we consider by what unjust methods property has been often acquired, and that what was unjustly got it must be unjust to keep, where is the harm in one man's taking the property of another from him? Besides, Sir, when we consider the bad use that many people make of their property, and how much better use the thief may make of it, it may be defended as a very allowable practice. Yet, Sir, the experience of mankind has discovered stealing to be so very bad a thing, that they make no scruple to hang a man for it. When I was running about this town a very poor fellow, I was a great arguer for the advantages of poverty; but I was, at the same time, very sorry to be poor. Sir, all the arguments which are brought to represent

---

75 Sir William Petty (1623–1687), political economist.
76 "Other things being equal."

poverty as no evil, shew it to be evidently a great evil. You never find people labouring to convince you that you may live very happily upon a plentiful fortune.—So you hear people talking how miserable a King must be; and yet they all wish to be in his place."

It was suggested that Kings must be unhappy, because they are deprived of the greatest of all satisfactions, easy and unreserved society. JOHNSON. "That is an ill-founded notion. Being a King does not exclude a man from such society. Great Kings have always been social. The King of Prussia, the only great King at present, is very social. Charles the Second, the last King of England who was a man of parts, was social; and our Henrys and Edwards were all social."

Mr. Dempster having endeavoured to maintain that intrinsick merit *ought* to make the only distinction amongst mankind. JOHNSON. "Why, Sir, mankind have found that this cannot be. How shall we determine the proportion of intrinsick merit? Were that to be the only distinction amongst mankind, we should soon quarrel about the degrees of it. Were all distinctions abolished, the strongest would not long acquiesce, but would endeavour to obtain a superiority by their bodily strength. But, Sir, as subordination is very necessary for society, and contentions for superiority very dangerous, mankind, that is to say, all civilised nations, have settled it upon a plain invariable principle. A man is born to hereditary rank; or his being appointed to certain offices, gives him a certain rank. Subordination tends greatly to human happiness. Were we all upon an equality, we should have no other enjoyment than mere animal pleasure."

I said, I considered distinction of rank to be of so much importance in civilised society, that if I were asked on the same day to dine with the first Duke in England, and with the first man in Britain for genius, I should hesitate which to prefer. JOHNSON. "To be sure, Sir, if you were to dine only once, and it were never to be known where you dined, you would choose rather to dine with the first man for genius; but to gain most respect, you should dine with the first Duke in England. For nine people in ten that you meet with, would have a higher opinion of you for having dined with a Duke; and the great genius himself would receive you better, because you had been with the great Duke."

He took care to guard himself against any possible suspicion that his settled principles of reverence for rank and respect for wealth were at all owing to mean or interested motives; for he asserted his own independence as a literary man. "No man (said he) who ever lived by literature, has lived more independently than I have done." He said he had taken longer time than he needed to have done in composing his Dictionary. He received our compliments upon that great work with complacency, and told us that the Academy *della Crusca*[77] could scarcely believe that it was done by one man.

Next morning I found him alone, and have preserved the following fragments of his conversation. Of a gentleman who was mentioned, he said, "I have not met with any man for a long time who has given me such general displeasure. He is totally unfixed in his principles, and wants to puzzle other people." I said, his principles had been poisoned by a noted infidel writer, but that he was, nevertheless, a benevolent good man. JOHNSON. "We can have no dependance upon that instinctive, that constitutional goodness which is not founded upon principle. I grant you that such a man may be a very amiable member of society. I can conceive him placed in such a situation that he is not much tempted to deviate from what is right; and as every man prefers virtue, when there is not some strong incitement to transgress its precepts, I can conceive him doing nothing wrong. But if such a man stood in need of money, I should not like to trust him; and I should certainly not trust him with young ladies, for *there* there is always temptation. Hume, and other sceptical innovators, are vain men, and will gratify themselves at any expence. Truth will not afford sufficient food to their vanity; so they have betaken themselves to errour. Truth, Sir, is a cow that will yield such people no more milk, and so they are gone to milk the bull. If I could have allowed myself to gratify my vanity at the expence of truth, what fame might I have acquired. Every thing which Hume has advanced against Christianity had passed through my mind long before he wrote. Always remember this, that after a system is well settled upon positive evidence, a few partial objections ought not to shake it. The human mind is so limited, that it cannot take in all the parts of a subject, so that there may be objections raised against any thing. There are objections against a *plenum*, and objections against a *vacuum*; yet one of them must certainly be true."

I mentioned Hume's argument against the belief of miracles, that it is more probable that the witnesses to the truth of them are mistaken, or speak falsely, than that the miracles should be true. JOHNSON. "Why, Sir, the great difficulty of proving miracles should make us very cautious in

---

77 The Accademia della Crusca was founded in Florence in the sixteenth century as a guardian of linguistic purity.

believing them. But let us consider; although GOD has made Nature to operate by certain fixed laws, yet it is not unreasonable to think that he may suspend those laws, in order to establish a system highly advantageous to mankind. Now the Christian religion is a most beneficial system, as it gives us light and certainty where we were before in darkness and doubt. The miracles which prove it are attested by men who had no interest in deceiving us; but who, on the contrary, were told that they should suffer persecution, and did actually lay down their lives in confirmation of the truth of the facts which they asserted. Indeed, for some centuries the heathens did not pretend to deny the miracles; but said they were performed by the aid of evil spirits. This is a circumstance of great weight. Then, Sir, when we take the proofs derived from prophecies which have been so exactly fulfilled, we have most satisfactory evidence. Supposing a miracle possible, as to which, in my opinion, there can be no doubt, we have as strong evidence for the miracles in support of Christianity, as the nature of the thing admits."

At night, Mr. Johnson and I supped in a private room at the Turk's Head coffee-house, in the Strand. "I encourage this house (said he); for the mistress of it is a good civil woman, and has not much business."

"Sir, I love the acquaintance of young people; because, in the first place, I don't like to think myself growing old. In the next place, young acquaintances must last longest, if they do last; and then, Sir, young men have more virtue than old men; they have more generous sentiments in every respect. I love the young dogs of this age; they have more wit and humour and knowledge of life than we had; but then the dogs are not so good scholars. Sir, in my early years I read very hard. It is a sad reflection, but a true one, that I knew almost as much at eighteen as I do now. My judgement, to be sure, was not so good; but, I had all the facts. I remember very well, when I was at Oxford, an old gentleman said to me, 'Young man, ply your book diligently now, and acquire a stock of knowledge; for when years come upon you, you will find that poring upon books will be but an irksome task.' "

This account of his reading, given by himself in plain words, sufficiently confirms what I have already advanced upon the disputed question as to his application. It reconciles any seeming inconsistency in his way of talking upon it at different times; and shews that idleness and reading hard were with him relative terms, the import of which, as used by him, must be gathered from a comparison with what scholars of different degrees of ardour and assiduity have been known to do. And let it be remembered, that he was now talking spontaneously, and expressing his genuine sentiments; whereas at other times he might be induced from his spirit of contradiction, or more properly from his love of argumentative contest, to speak lightly of his own application to study. It is pleasing to consider that the old gentleman's gloomy prophecy as to the irksomeness of books to men of an advanced age, which is too often fulfilled, was so far from being verified in Johnson, that his ardour for literature never failed, and his last writings had more ease and vivacity than any of his earlier productions.

He mentioned to me now, for the first time, that he had been distrest by melancholy, and for that reason had been obliged to fly from study and meditation, to the dissipating variety of life. Against melancholy he recommended constant occupation of mind, a great deal of exercise, moderation in eating and drinking, and especially to shun drinking at night. He said melancholy people were apt to fly to intemperance for relief, but that it sunk them much deeper in misery. He observed, that labouring men who work hard, and live sparingly, are seldom or never troubled with low spirits.

He again insisted on the duty of maintaining subordination of rank. "Sir, I would no more deprive a nobleman of his respect, than of his money. I consider myself as acting a part in the great system of society, and I do to others as I would have them to do to me. I would behave to a nobleman as I should expect he would behave to me, were I a nobleman and he Sam. Johnson. Sir, there is one Mrs. Macaulay[78] in this town, a great republican. One day when I was at her house, I put on a very grave countenance, and said to her, 'Madam, I am now become a convert to your way of thinking. I am convinced that all mankind are upon an equal footing; and to give you an unquestionable proof, Madam, that I am in earnest, here is a very sensible, civil, well-behaved fellow-citizen, your footman; I desire that he may be allowed to sit down and dine with us.' I thus, Sir, shewed her the absurdity of the levelling doctrine. She has never liked me since. Sir, your levellers wish to level *down* as far as themselves; but they cannot bear levelling *up* to themselves. They would all have some people under them; why not then have some people above them?" I mentioned a certain authour who disgusted me by his forwardness, and by shewing no deference to noblemen into whose company he was admitted. JOHNSON. "Suppose a shoemaker should claim an equality

---

[78] Mrs. Catharine Macaulay (1731–1791), historian and political controversialist.

with him, as he does with a Lord; how he would stare. 'Why, Sir, do
you stare? (says the shoemaker,) I do great service to society. 'Tis true,
I am paid for doing it; but so are you, Sir: and I am sorry to say it, paid
better than I am, for doing something not so necessary. For mankind
could do better without your books, than without my shoes.' Thus, Sir,
there would be a perpetual struggle for precedence, were there no fixed
invariable rules for the distinction of rank, which creates no jealousy, as
it is allowed to be accidental."

[*October 16, 1769*]

    He honoured me with his company at dinner on the 16th of
October, at my lodgings in Old Bond-street, with Sir Joshua Reynolds,
Mr. Garrick, Dr. Goldsmith, Mr. Murphy, Mr. Bickerstaff, and Mr.
Thomas Davies.[79] Garrick played round him with a fond vivacity, taking
hold of the breasts of his coat, and, looking up in his face with a lively
archness, complimented him on the good health which he seemed then
to enjoy; while the sage, shaking his head, beheld him with a gentle
complacency. One of the company not being come at the appointed
hour, I proposed, as usual upon such occasions, to order dinner to be
served; adding, "Ought six people to be kept waiting for one?" "Why,
yes, (answered Johnson, with a delicate humanity,) if the one will suffer
more by your sitting down, than the six will do by waiting." Goldsmith,
to divert the tedious minutes, strutted about, bragging of his dress, and
I believe was seriously vain of it, for his mind was wonderfully prone to
such impressions. "Come, come, (said Garrick,) talk no more of that.
You are, perhaps, the worst—eh, eh!"—Goldsmith was eagerly attempting to interrupt him, when Garrick went on, laughing ironically, "Nay,
you will always *look* like a gentleman; but I am talking of being well or
ill *drest*." "Well, let me tell you, (said Goldsmith,) when my tailor brought
home my bloom-coloured[80] coat, he said, 'Sir, I have a favour to beg
of you. When any body asks you who made your clothes, be pleased to
mention John Filby, at the Harrow, in Water-lane.' " JOHNSON. "Why,
Sir, that was because he knew the strange colour would attract crouds to
gaze at it, and thus they might hear of him, and see how well he could
make a coat even of so absurd a colour."

---

79 Arthur Murphy (1727–1805), journalist, actor, and comic playwright; Isaac
Bickerstaffe (c. 1735–c. 1812), author of comic operas and farces. For Davies, see above,
note 2.
    80 Probably crimson.

After dinner our conversation first turned upon Pope. Johnson said, his characters of men were admirably drawn, those of women not so well.[81] He repeated to us, in his forcible melodious manner, the concluding lines of the Dunciad.[82] While he was talking loudly in praise of those lines, one of the company ventured to say, "Too fine for such a poem:—a poem on what?" JOHNSON, (with a disdainful look,) "Why, on *dunces*. It was worth while being a dunce then. Ah, Sir, hadst *thou* lived in those days! It is not worth while being a dunce now, when there are no wits." Bickerstaff observed, as a peculiar circumstance, that Pope's fame was higher when he was alive than it was then. Johnson said, his Pastorals were poor things, though the versification was fine. He told us, with high satisfaction, the anecdote of Pope's inquiring who was the authour of his "London,"[83] and saying, he will be soon *détérre*.[84] He observed, that in Dryden's poetry there were passages drawn from a profundity which Pope could never reach. He repeated some fine lines on love, by the former, (which I have now forgotten,) and gave great applause to the character of Zimri.[85] Goldsmith said, that Pope's character of Addison[86] shewed a deep knowledge of the human heart. Johnson said, that the description of the temple, in 'The Mourning Bride,'[87] was the finest poetical passage he had ever read; he recollected none in Shakspeare equal to it. —"But, (said Garrick, all alarmed for 'the god of his idolatry,'[88]) we know not the extent and variety of his powers. We are to suppose there are such passages in his works. Shakspeare must not suffer from the badness of our memories." Johnson, diverted by this enthusiastick jealousy, went on with greater ardour: "No, Sir; Congreve has *nature*"; (smiling on the tragick eagerness of Garrick;) but composing himself, he added, "Sir, this is not comparing Congreve on the whole, with Shakspeare on the whole; but only maintaining that Congreve has one finer passage than any

---

81 Epistle I, "To Richard Temple, Viscount Cobham," deals with "the Knowledge and Characters of Men"; Epistle II, "To a Lady," is subtitled, "Of the Characters of Women."
82 Bk. IV, 627–40, the account of the process by which "*Art* after *Art* goes out, and all is Night."
83 Published anonymously by Johnson in 1738.
84 Discovered.
85 *Absalom and Achitophel*, 544–68. Zimri was George Villiers, Duke of Buckingham.
86 *Epistle to Arbuthnot*, 193–214.
87 By William Congreve (1670–1729), published in 1697. The passage Johnson refers to is II. i. 48–59.
88 "Swear by thy gracious self,/Which is the god of my idolatry" (*Romeo and Juliet*, II. ii. 113–14.

that can be found in Shakspeare. Sir, a man may have no more than ten guineas in the world, but he may have those ten guineas in one piece; and so may have a finer piece than a man who has ten thousand pounds: but then he has only one ten-guinea piece.—What I mean is, that you can shew me no passage where there is simply a description of material objects, without any intermixture of moral notions, which produces such an effect." Mr. Murphy mentioned Shakspeare's description of the night before the battle of Agincourt;[89] but it was observed, it had *men* in it. Mr. Davies suggested the speech of Juliet, in which she figures herself awaking in the tomb of her ancestors.[90] Some one mentioned the description of Dover Cliff.[91] JOHNSON. "No, Sir; it should be all precipice,—all vacuum. The crows impede your fall. The diminished appearance of the boats, and other circumstances, are all very good description; but do not impress the mind at once with the horrible idea of immense height. The impression is divided; you pass on by computation, from one stage of the tremendous space to another. Had the girl in 'The Mourning Bride' said, she could not cast her shoe to the top of one of the pillars in the temple, it would not have aided the idea, but weakened it."

Talking of a Barrister who had a bad utterance, some one, (to rouse Johnson,) wickedly said, that he was unfortunate in not having been taught oratory by Sheridan.[92] JOHNSON. "Nay, Sir, if he had been taught by Sheridan, he would have cleared the room." GARRICK. "Sheridan has too much vanity to be a good man." We shall now see Johnson's mode of *defending* a man; taking him into his own hands, and discriminating. JOHNSON. "No, Sir. There is, to be sure, in Sheridan, something to re-prehend, and every thing to laugh at; but, Sir, he is not a bad man. No, Sir; were mankind to be divided into good and bad, he would stand considerably within the ranks of good. And, Sir, it must be allowed that Sheridan excels in plain declamation, though he can exhibit no character."

I should, perhaps, have suppressed this disquisition concerning a person of whose merit and worth I think with respect, had he not attacked Johnson so outrageously in his Life of Swift, and, at the same time, treated

---

89 *Henry V*, Act IV, Prologue.
90 *Romeo and Juliet*, IV. iii. 31–55.
91 *King Lear*, IV. vi. 11–24.
92 When the Earl of Bute, who had also pensioned Johnson, awarded Thomas Sheridan (see note 10, above) a pension for his project of a pronouncing dictionary, Johnson was affronted, and Sheridan severed relations after hearing a sarcastic comment of his.

us his admirers as a set of pigmies.[93] He who has provoked the lash of wit, cannot complain that he smarts from it.

Mrs. Montagu,[94] a lady distinguished for having written an Essay on Shakspeare, being mentioned;—REYNOLDS. "I think that essay does her honour." JOHNSON. "Yes, Sir; it does *her* honour, but it would do nobody else honour. I have, indeed, not read it all. But when I take up the end of a web, and find it packthread,[95] I do not expect, by looking further, to find embroidery. Sir, I will venture to say, there is not one sentence of true criticism in her book." GARRICK. "But, Sir, surely it shews how much Voltaire[96] has mistaken Shakspeare, which nobody else has done." JOHNSON. "Sir, nobody else has thought it worth while. And what merit is there in that? You may as well praise a schoolmaster for whipping a boy who has construed ill. No, Sir, there is no real criticism in it: none shewing the beauty of thought, as formed on the workings of the human heart."

The admirers of this Essay may be offended at the slighting manner in which Johnson spoke of it; but let it be remembered, that he gave his honest opinion, unbiassed by any prejudice, or any proud jealousy of a woman intruding herself into the chair of criticism; for Sir Joshua Reynolds has told me, that when the Essay first came out, and it was not known who had written it, Johnson wondered how Sir Joshua could like it. At this time Sir Joshua himself had received no information concerning the authour, except being assured by one of our most eminent literati, that it was clear its authour did not know the Greek tragedies in the original. One day at Sir Joshua's table, when it was related that Mrs. Montagu, in an excess of compliment to the authour of a modern tragedy, had exclaimed, "I tremble for Shakspeare"; Johnson said, "When Shakspeare has got————[97] for his rival, and Mrs. Montagu for his defender, he is in a poor state indeed."

Johnson proceeded: 'The Scotchman[98] has taken the right method

---

93 He characterized Johnson as "A writer of gigantick fame in these days of little men." *Life of Swift* (1784).

94 Elizabeth Montagu (1720–1800) defended Shakespeare against Voltaire in her *Essay on the Writings and Genius of Shakespeare* (1769).

95 Stout thread of twine for sewing or tying up packs or bundles.

96 François Marie Arouet de Voltaire (1694–1778) declared Shakespeare to be a buffoon in the article on *"Art Dramatique"* in his *Dictionnaire Philosophique* (1765). In the article on *"Gout"* ("Taste") he claimed that Corneille was superior to Shakespeare.

97 Robert Jephson (1736–1803), dramatist and poet.

98 Lord Kames. See Johnson's earlier reaction, above, pp. 555–56.

in his 'Elements of Criticism.' I do not mean that he has taught us any thing; but he has told us old things in a new way." MURPHY. "He seems to have read a great deal of French criticism, and wants to make it his own; as if he had been for years anatomising the heart of man, and peeping into every cranny of it." GOLDSMITH. "It is easier to write that book, than to read it." JOHNSON. "We have an example of true criticism in Burke's 'Essay on the Sublime and Beautiful';[99] and, if I recollect, there is also Du Bos;[100] and Bouhours,[101] who shews all beauty to depend on truth. There is no great merit in telling how many plays have ghosts in them, and how this ghost is better than that. You must shew how terrour is impressed on the human heart.—In the description of night in Macbeth,[102] the beetle and the bat detract from the general idea of darkness,—inspissated[103] gloom."

Politicks being mentioned, he said, "This petitioning[104] is a new mode of distressing government, and a mighty easy one. I will undertake to get petitions either against quarter-guineas or half-guineas, with the help of a little hot wine. There must be no yielding to encourage this. The object is not important enough. We are not to blow up half a dozen palaces, because one cottage is burning."

The conversation then took another turn. JOHNSON. "It is amazing what ignorance of certain points one sometimes finds in men of eminence. A wit about town, who wrote Latin bawdy verses, asked me, how it happened that England and Scotland, which were once two kingdoms, were now one:—and Sir Fletcher Norton[105] did not seem to know that there were such publications as the Reviews."[106]

"The ballad of Hardyknute[107] has no great merit, if it be really

---

99 Published by Edmund Burke in 1759.

100 Jean Baptiste Dubos (1670–1742), author of *Réflexions Critiques sur La Poesie et sur La Peinture* (1719).

101 Dominique Bouhours (1628–1702), author of *La Manière de bien penser sur les ouvrages d'esprit* (1687).

102 III. ii. 40–44.

103 Condensed.

104 Numerous petitions were presented to the King during this year, on trivial and important subjects.

105 Norton (1716–1789) was afterwards speaker of the House of Commons. In 1782 he was created Baron Grantley.

106 The *Monthly Review* (1749–1845) and the *Critical Review* (1756–1817) were at this time highly influential in their critical opinions.

107 First printed in 1719, as an ancient poem; actually written by Elizabeth Halket, Lady Wardlaw (d. 1727).

ancient. People talk of nature. But mere obvious nature may be exhibited
with very little power of mind."

On Thursday, October 19, I passed the evening with him at his
house. He advised me to complete a Dictionary of words peculiar to
Scotland, of which I shewed him a specimen. "Sir, (said he), Ray has
made a collection of north-country words.[108] By collecting those of your
country, you will do a useful thing towards the history of the language."
He bade me also go on with collections which I was making upon the
antiquities of Scotland. "Make a large book; a folio." BOSWELL. "But of
what use will it be, Sir?" JOHNSON. "Never mind the use; do it."

I complained that he had not mentioned Garrick in his Preface to
Shakspeare; and asked him if he did not admire him. JOHNSON. "Yes, as
'a poor player, who frets and struts his hour upon the stage';—as a
shadow."[109] BOSWELL. "But has he not brought Shakspeare into notice?"
JOHNSON. "Sir, to allow that, would be to lampoon the age. Many of
Shakspeare's plays are the worse for being acted: Macbeth, for instance."
BOSWELL. "What, Sir, is gained by decoration and action? Indeed, I do
wish that you had mentioned Garrick." JOHNSON. "My dear Sir, had
I mentioned him, I must have mentioned many more: Mrs. Pritchard,
Mrs. Cibber,[110]—nay, and Mr. Cibber[111] too; he too altered Shakspeare."
BOSWELL. "You have read his apology, Sir?" JOHNSON. "Yes, it is very
entertaining. But as for Cibber himself, taking from his conversation all
that he ought not to have said, he was a poor creature. I remember when
he brought me one of his Odes to have my opinion of it, I could not bear
such nonsense, and would not let him read it to the end; so little respect
had I for *that great man!* (laughing.) Yet I remember Richardson[112]
wondering that I could treat him with familiarity."

I mentioned to him that I had seen the execution of several convicts
at Tyburn, two days before, and that none of them seemed to be under

108 John Ray, *A Collection of English Words Not Generally Used* (1674).

109 "Life's but a walking shadow, a poor player/That struts and frets his hour upon
the stage" (*Macbeth*, V. v. 24–25).

110 Hannah Pritchard (1711–1768) and Charlotte Cibber Charke (d. 1760?), daughter
of Colley Cibber, were well-known actresses. Mrs. Pritchard played many Shakspearean
roles; Mrs. Charke was notorious for her assumption of the male part of Roderigo in *Othello.*

111 Colley Cibber (1671–1757), actor, playwright, poet laureate, altered Shakespeare
by rewriting him: his *Richard III* (1700), for example, an adaptation of the Shakespearean
play, was acted in place of the original for several decades. His *Apology* (1740) was an autobiography and self-justification.

112 The novelist Samuel Richardson (1689–1761).

any concern. JOHNSON. "Most of them, Sir, have never thought at all." BOSWELL. "But is not the fear of death natural to man?" JOHNSON. "So much so, Sir, that the whole of life is but keeping away the thoughts of it." He then, in a low and earnest tone, talked of his meditating upon the aweful hour of his own dissolution, and in what manner he should conduct himself upon that occasion: "I know not (said he,) whether I should wish to have a friend by me, or have it all between GOD and myself."

Talking of our feeling for the distresses of others;—JOHNSON. "Why, Sir, there is much noise made about it, but it is greatly exaggerated. No, Sir, we have a certain degree of feeling to prompt us to do good: more than that, Providence does not intend. It would be misery to no purpose." BOSWELL. "But suppose now, Sir, that one of your intimate friends were apprehended for an offence for which he might be hanged." JOHNSON. "I should do what I could to bail him, and give him any other assistance; but if he were once fairly hanged, I should not suffer." BOSWELL. "Would you eat your dinner that day, Sir?" JOHNSON. "Yes, Sir; and eat it as if he were eating it with me. Why, there's Baretti,[113] who is to be tried for his life to-morrow, friends have risen up for him on every side; yet if he should be hanged, none of them will eat a slice of plumb-pudding the less. Sir, that sympathetick feeling goes a very little way in depressing the mind."

I told him that I had dined lately at Foote's,[114] who shewed me a letter which he had received from Tom Davies, telling him that he had not been able to sleep from the concern which he felt on account of *"This sad affair of Baretti,"* begging of him to try if he could suggest any thing that might be of service; and, at the same time, recommending to him an industrious young man who kept a pickle-shop. JOHNSON. "Ay, Sir, here you have a specimen of human sympathy; a friend hanged, and a cucumber pickled. We know not whether Baretti or the pickle-man has kept Davies from sleep; nor does he know himself. And as to his not sleeping, Sir; Tom Davies is a very great man; Tom has been upon the stage, and knows how to do those things: I have not been upon the stage, and cannot do those things." BOSWELL. "I have often blamed myself, Sir, for not feeling for others as sensibly as many say they do." JOHNSON.

113 Joseph Baretti (1719–1789) had been accosted by a prostitute whom he drove away with a blow. Three bullies then attacked him; he fled in fear but, being pursued, stabbed two of them with a knife he carried.
114 Samuel Foote (1720–1777) was a writer of satiric comedies. He was noted for his gift of mimicry, which Boswell refers to below, and often devised plays to display this talent.

"Sir, don't be duped by them any more. You will find these very feeling people are not very ready to do you good. They *pay* you by *feeling*."

BOSWELL. "Foote has a great deal of humour?" JOHNSON. "Yes, Sir." BOSWELL. "He has a singular talent of exhibiting character." JOHNSON. "Sir, it is not a talent; it is a vice; it is what others abstain from. It is not comedy, which exhibits the character of a species, as that of a miser gathered from many misers: it is farce, which exhibits individuals." BOSWELL. "Did not he think of exhibiting you, Sir?" JOHNSON. "Sir, fear restrained him; he knew I would have broken his bones. I would have saved him the trouble of cutting off a leg; I would not have left him a leg to cut off."[115] BOSWELL. "Pray, Sir, is not Foote an infidel?" JOHNSON. "I do not know, Sir, that the fellow is an infidel; but if he be an infidel, he is an infidel as a dog is an infidel; that is to say, he has never thought upon the subject." BOSWELL. "I suppose, Sir, he has thought superficially, and seized the first notions which occurred to his mind." JOHNSON. "Why then, Sir, still he is like a dog, that snatches the piece next him. Did you never observe that dogs have not the power of comparing? A dog will take a small bit of meat as readily as a large, when both are before him."

"Buchanan (he observed,) has fewer *centos*[116] than any modern Latin poet. He not only had great knowledge of the Latin language, but was a great poetical genius. Both the Scaligers[117] praise him."

He again talked of the passage in Congreve with high commendation, and said, "Shakspeare never has six lines together without a fault. Perhaps you may find seven: but this does not refute my general assertion. If I come to an orchard, and say there's no fruit here, and then comes a poring man, who finds two apples and three pears, and tells me, 'Sir, you are mistaken, I have found both apples and pears,' I should laugh at him: what would that be to the purpose?"

BOSWELL. "What do you think of Dr. Young's 'Night Thoughts,'[118] Sir?" JOHNSON. "Why, Sir, there are very fine things in them." BOSWELL. "Is there not less religion in the nation now, Sir, than there was formerly?"

---

115 In 1766 Foote lost a leg through a practical joke which involved his being mounted on a spirited horse.

116 "*Cento*. A composition formed by joining scraps from other authours" (Johnson's *Dictionary*). George Buchanan (1506–1582) was a poet and scholar.

117 Julius Caesar Scaliger (1484–1558), Italian philologist and critic, author of *Poetics* (1561), which helped to establish important neoclassic principles; and his son Joseph Justus Scaliger (1540–1609), renowned for his learning in mathematics, philosophy, and criticism.

118 See pp. 47–48 for Edward Young. His *The Complaint: or Night Thoughts on Life, Death, and Immortality* (1742) was an immensely popular poem.

JOHNSON. "I don't know, Sir, that there is." BOSWELL. "For instance, there used to be a chaplain in every great family, which we do not find now." JOHNSON. "Neither do you find may of the state servants[119] which great families used formerly to have. There is a change of modes in the whole department of life."

Next day, October 20, he appeared, for the only time I suppose in his life, as a witness in a Court of Justice, being called to give evidence to the character of Mr. Baretti, who having stabbed a man in the street, was arraigned at the Old Bailey for murder. Never did such a constellation of genius enlighten the aweful Sessions-House, emphatically called JUSTICE HALL; Mr. Burke, Mr. Garrick, Mr. Beauclerk,[120] and Dr. Johnson: and undoubtedly their favourable testimony had due weight with the Court and Jury. Johnson gave his evidence in a slow, deliberate, and distinct manner, which was uncommonly impressive. It is well known that Mr. Baretti was acquitted.

On the 26th of October, we dined together at the Mitre tavern. I found fault with Foote for indulging his talent of ridicule at the expence of his visitors, which I colloquially termed making fools of his company. JOHNSON. "Why, Sir, when you go to see Foote, you do not go to see a saint: you go to see a man who will be entertained at your house, and then bring you on a publick stage; who will entertain you at his house, for the very purpose of bringing you on a publick stage. Sir, he does not make fools of his company; they whom he exposes are fools already: he only brings them into action."

Talking of trade, he observed, "It is a mistaken notion that a vast deal of money is brought into a nation by trade. It is not so. Commodities come from commodities; but trade produces no capital accession of wealth. However, though there should be little profit in money, there is a considerable profit in pleasure, as it gives to one nation the productions of another; as we have wines and fruits, and many other foreign articles, brought to us." BOSWELL. "Yes, Sir, and there is a profit in pleasure, by its furnishing occupation to such numbers of mankind." JOHNSON. "Why, Sir, you cannot call that pleasure to which all are averse, and which none begin but with the hope of leaving off; a thing which men dislike before they have tried it, and when they have tried it." BOSWELL. "But, Sir, the mind must be employed, and we grow weary when idle."

---

119 I.e., servants employed on state occasions.
120 For Topham Beauclerk, see above, note 59.

JOHNSON. "That is, Sir, because, others being busy, we want company; but if we were all idle, there would be no growing weary; we should all entertain one another. There is, indeed, this in trade:—it gives men an opportunity of improving their situation. If there were no trade, many who are poor would always remain poor. But no man loves labour for itself." BOSWELL. "Yes, Sir, I know a person who does. He is a very laborious Judge, and he loves the labour."[121] JOHNSON. "Sir, that is because he loves respect and distinction. Could he have them without labour, he would like it less." BOSWELL. "He tells me he likes it for itself."—"Why, Sir, he fancies so, because he is not accustomed to abstract."

We went home to his house to tea. Mrs. Williams[122] made it with sufficient dexterity, notwithstanding her blindness, though her manner of satisfying herself that the cups were full enough appeared to me a little aukward; for I fancied she put her finger down a certain way, till she felt the tea touch it. In my first elation at being allowed the privilege of attending Dr. Johnson at his late visits to this lady, which was like being *é secretioribus consiliis*,[123] I willingly drank cup after cup, as if it had been the Heliconian spring.[124] But as the charm of novelty went off, I grew more fastidious; and besides, I discovered that she was of a peevish temper.

There was a pretty large circle this evening. Dr. Johnson was in very good humour, lively, and ready to talk upon all subjects. Mr. Fergusson,[125] the self-taught philosopher, told him of a new-invented machine which went without horses: a man who sat in it turned a handle, which worked a spring that drove it forward. "Then, Sir, (said Johnson,) what is gained is, the man has his choice whether he will move himself alone, or himself and the machine too." Dominicetti[126] being mentioned, he would not allow him any merit. "There is nothing in all this boasted system. No, Sir; medicated baths can be no better than warm water: their only effect can be that of tepid moisture." One of the company took the other side, maintaining that medicines of various sorts, and some too of most

---

121 Boswell is referring to his father, Lord Auchinleck.

122 For Anna Williams see above, note 6.

123 "A member of the inner cabinet."

124 A spring sacred to the Muses.

125 James Ferguson (1710–1775), the son of a day laborer, taught himself to read and early displayed signs of mechanical genius. He became a well-known astronomer and inventor.

126 Bartholomew de Dominiceti was an Italian quack who came to England in 1753, settling in Cheyne Walk, Chelsea, in 1765, to offer baths and sweating chambers as remedies for various ailments.

powerful effect, are introduced into the human frame by the medium of the pores; and, therefore, when warm water is impregnated with saluti-ferous[127] substances, it may produce great effects as a bath. This appeared to me very satisfactory. Johnson did not answer it; but talking for victory, and determined to be master of the field, he had recourse to the device which Goldsmith imputed to him in the witty words of one of Cibber's comedies: "There is no arguing with Johnson; for when his pistol misses fire, he knocks you down with the butt end of it."[128] He turned to the gentleman, "Well, Sir, go to Dominicetti, and get thyself fumigated; but be sure that the steam be directed to thy *head*, for *that* is the *peccant part*."[129] This produced a triumphant roar of laughter from the motley assembly of philosophers, printers, and dependents, male and female.

I know not how so whimsical a thought came into my mind, but I asked, "If, Sir, you were shut up in a castle, and a new-born child with you, what would you do?" JOHNSON. "Why, Sir, I should not much like my company." BOSWELL. "But would you take the trouble of rearing it?" He seemed, as may well be supposed, unwilling to pursue the subject: but upon my persevering in my question, replied, "Why yes, Sir, I would; but I must have all conveniencies. If I had no garden, I would make a shed on the roof, and take it there for fresh air. I should feed it, and wash it much, and with warm water to please it, not with cold water to give it pain." BOSWELL. "But, Sir, does not heat relax?" JOHNSON. "Sir, you are not to imagine the water is to be very hot. I would not *coddle*[130] the child. No, Sir, the hardy method of treating children does no good. I'll take you five children from London, who shall cuff five Highland children. Sir, a man bred in London will carry a burthen, or run, or wrestle, as well as a man brought up in the hardiest manner in the country." BOSWELL. "Good living, I suppose, makes the Londoners strong." JOHNSON. "Why, Sir, I don't know that it does. Our chairmen from Ireland, who are as strong men as any, have been brought up upon potatoes. Quantity makes up for quality." BOSWELL. "Would you teach this child that I have furnished you with, any thing?" JOHNSON. "No, I should not be apt to teach it." BOSWELL. "Would not you have a pleasure in teaching it?"

---

127 Salutary, promoting health.

128 *The Refusal* (1721), I. i.: "What! now your Fire's gone, you would knock me down with the Butt-end, would you?"

129 A reference to Pope, *Essay on Man*, II. 143-44: "Imagination plies her dang'rous art,/And pours it all upon the peccant part."

130 I.e., as an egg is coddled: boiled gently. According to the NED, the meaning, "to treat as an invalid, to nurse overmuch," originated only in 1815.

JOHNSON. "No, Sir, I should *not* have a pleasure in teaching it." BOSWELL. "Have you not a pleasure in teaching men?—*There* I have you. You have the same pleasure in teaching men, that I should have in teaching children." JOHNSON. "Why, something about that."

BOSWELL. "Do you think, Sir, that what is called natural affection is born with us? It seems to me to be the effect of habit, or of gratitude for kindness. No child has it for a parent whom it has not seen." JOHNSON. "Why, Sir, I think there is an instinctive natural affection in parents towards their children."

Russia being mentioned as likely to become a great empire, by the rapid increase of population:—JOHNSON. "Why, Sir, I see no prospect of their propagating more. They can have no more children than they can get. I know of no way to make them breed more than they do. It is not from reason and prudence that people marry, but from inclination. A man is poor; he thinks ,'I cannot be worse, and so I'll e'en take Peggy.'" BOSWELL. "But have not nations been more populous at one period than another?" JOHNSON. "Yes, Sir; but that has been owing to the people being less thinned at one period than another, whether by emigrations, war, or pestilence, not by their being more or less prolifick. Births at all times bear the same proportion to the same number of people." BOSWELL. "But, to consider the state of our own country;—does not throwing a number of farms into one hand hurt population?" JOHNSON. "Why no, Sir; the same quantity of food being produced, will be consumed by the same number of mouths, though the people may be disposed of in different ways. We see, if corn be dear, and butchers' meat cheap, the farmers all apply themselves to the raising of corn, till it becomes plentiful and cheap, and then butchers' meat becomes dear; so that an equality is always preserved. No, Sir, let fanciful men do as they will, depend upon it, it is difficult to disturb the system of life." BOSWELL. "But, Sir, is it not a very bad thing for landlords to oppress their tenants, by raising their rents?" JOHNSON. "Very bad. But, Sir, it never can have any general influence; it may distress some individuals. For, consider this: landlords cannot do without tenants. Now tenants will not give more for land, than land is worth. If they can make more of their money by keeping a shop, or any other way, they'll do it, and so oblige landlords to let land come back to a reasonable rent, in order that they may get tenants. Land, in England, is an article of commerce. A tenant who pays his landlord his rent, thinks himself no more obliged to him than you think yourself obliged to a man in whose shop you buy a piece of goods. He knows the landlord does not let him have his land for less than he can get from others, in the same manner as the shopkeeper sells his goods. No shop-keeper sells a yard of ribband for sixpence when seven-pence is the current price." BOSWELL. "But, Sir, is it not better that tenants should be depend-ent on landlords?" JOHNSON. "Why, Sir, as there are many more tenants than landlords, perhaps, strictly speaking, we should wish not. But if you please you may let your lands cheap, and so get the value, part in money and part in homage. I should agree with you in that." BOSWELL. "So, Sir, you laugh at schemes of political improvement." JOHNSON. "Why, Sir, most schemes of political improvement are very laughable things."

He observed, "Providence has wisely ordered that the more nu-merous men are, the more difficult it is for them to agree in any thing, and so they are governed. There is no doubt, that if the poor should reason, 'We'll be the poor no longer, we'll make the rich take their turn,' they could easily do it, were it not that they can't agree. So the common soldiers, though so much more numerous than their officers, are governed by them for the same reason."

He said, "Mankind have a strong attachment to the habitations to which they have been accustomed. You see the inhabitants of Norway do not with one consent quit it, and go to some part of America, where there is a mild climate, and where they may have the same produce from land, with the tenth part of the labour. No, Sir; their affection for their old dwellings, and the terrour of a general change, keep them at home. Thus, we see many of the finest spots in the world thinly inhabited, and many rugged spots well inhabited."

"The London Chronicle," which was the only news-paper he constantly took in, being brought, the office of reading it aloud was assigned to me. I was diverted by his impatience. He made me pass over so many parts of it, that my task was very easy. He would not suffer one of the petitions to the King about the Middlesex election to be read.[131]

I had hired a Bohemian as my servant[132] while I remained in London, and being much pleased with him, I asked Dr. Johnson whether his

---

131 John Wilkes had been elected a member of Parliament for Middlesex in March 1768. Before Parliament met he had been imprisoned for his political agitation; in February 1769, he was declared incapable of being elected. In three succeeding elections he won over-whelming majorities (twice he was elected without opposition), but his election was declared void and his opponent, who had received a fourth as many votes as Wilkes, was declared elected. Johnson believed this procedure to be justified.

132 Joseph Ritter, who later accompanied Boswell on his tour of the Hebrides.

being a Roman Catholick should prevent my taking him with me to Scotland. JOHNSON. "Why no, Sir. If *he* has no objection, you can have none." BOSWELL. "So, Sir, you are no great enemy to the Roman Catholick religion." JOHNSON. "No more, Sir, than to the Presbyterian religion." BOSWELL. "You are joking." JOHNSON. "No, Sir, I really think so. Nay, Sir, of the two, I prefer the Popish." BOSWELL. "How so, Sir?" JOHNSON. "Why, Sir, the Presbyterians have no church, no apostolical ordination." BOSWELL. "And do you think that absolutely essential, Sir?" JOHNSON. "Why, Sir, as it was an apostolical institution, I think it is dangerous to be without it. And, Sir, the Presbyterians have no publick worship: they have no form of prayer in which they know they are to join. They go to hear a man pray, and are to judge whether they will join with him." BOSWELL. "But, Sir, their doctrine is the same with that of the Church of England. Their confession of faith, and the thirty-nine articles, contain the same points, even the doctrine of predestination." JOHNSON. "Why yes, Sir; predestination was a part of the clamour of the times, so it is mentioned in our articles, but with as little positiveness as could be." BOSWELL. "Is it necessary, Sir, to believe all the thirty-nine articles?" JOHNSON. "Why, Sir, that is a question which has been much agitated. Some have thought it necessary that they should all be believed; others have considered them to be only articles of peace, that is to say, you are not to preach against them." BOSWELL. "It appears to me, Sir, that predestination, or what is equivalent to it, cannot be avoided, if we hold an universal prescience in the Deity." JOHNSON. "Why, Sir, does not GOD every day see things going on without preventing them?" BOSWELL. "True, Sir; but if a thing be *certainly* foreseen, it must be fixed, and cannot happen otherwise; and if we apply this consideration to the human mind, there is no free will, nor do I see how prayer can be of any avail." He mentioned Dr. Clarke, and Bishop Bramhall on Liberty and Necessity, and bid me read South's Sermons on Prayer;[133] but avoided the question which has excruciated philosophers and divines, beyond any other. I did not press it further, when I perceived that he was displeased, and shrunk from any abridgement of an attribute usually ascribed to the Divinity, however irreconcileable in its full extent with the grand system of moral government. His supposed orthodoxy here cramped the vigorous

---

133 For Clarke, see note 19. above. Dr. John Bramhall (1594–1663), archbishop of Armagh, wrote *A Defence of the True Liberty of Human Actions* (1655); Dr. Robert South (1634–1716) was a prolific writer of sermons: e.g. *Sermons Preached Upon Several Occasions* (1679).

powers of his understanding. He was confined by a chain which early imagination and long habit made him think massy and strong, but which, had he ventured to try, he could at once have snapt asunder.

I proceeded: "What do you think, Sir, of Purgatory, as believed by the Roman Catholicks?" JOHNSON. "Why, Sir, it is a very harmless doctrine. They are of opinion that the generality of mankind are neither so obstinately wicked as to deserve ever-lasting punishment, nor so good as to merit being admitted into the society of blessed spirits; and therefore that GOD is graciously pleased to allow of a middle state, where they may be purified by certain degrees of suffering. You see, Sir, there is nothing unreasonable in this." BOSWELL. "But then, Sir, their masses for the dead?" JOHNSON. "Why, Sir, if it be once established that there are souls in purgatory, it is as proper to pray for *them*, as for our brethren of mankind who are yet in this life." BOSWELL. "The idolatry of the Mass?"—JOHNSON. "Sir, there is no idolatry in the Mass. They believe GOD to be there, and they adore him." BOSWELL. "The worship of Saints?"—JOHNSON. "Sir, they do not worship saints; they invoke them; they only ask their prayers. I am talking all this time of the *doctrines* of the Church of Rome. I grant you that in *practice*, Purgatory is made a lucrative imposition, and that the people do become idolatrous as they recommend themselves to the tutelary protection of particular saints. I think their giving the sacrament only in one kind is criminal, because it is contrary to the express institution of CHRIST, and I wonder how the Council of Trent[134] admitted it." BOSWELL. "Confession?"—JOHNSON. "Why, I don't know but that is a good thing. The scripture says, "Confess your faults one to another;"[135] and the priests confess as well as the laity. Then it must be considered that their absolution is only upon repentance, and often upon penance also. You think your sins may be forgiven without penance, upon repentance alone."

I thus ventured to mention all the common objections against the Roman Catholick Church, that I might hear so great a man upon them. What he said is here accurately recorded. But it is not improbable that if one had taken the other side, he might have reasoned differently.

I must however mention, that he had a respect for "*the old religion*,"

---

134 The Council of Trent (1545–1547, 1551–1552, 1562–1563) was the nineteenth ecumenical council of the Catholic Church and the chief instrument of religious reform, setting the pattern for modern Catholicism.
135 *James* 5:16.

as the mild Melancthon[136] called that of the Roman Catholick Church, even while he was exerting himself for its reformation in some particulars. Sir William Scott[137] informs me, that he heard Johnson say, "A man who is converted from Protestantism to Popery, may be sincere: he parts with nothing: he is only superadding to what he already had. But a convert from Popery to Protestantism, gives up so much of what he has held as sacred as any thing that he retains; there is so much *laceration of mind* in such a conversion, that it can hardly be sincere and lasting." The truth of this reflection may be confirmed by many and eminent instances, some of which will occur to most of my readers.

When we were alone, I introduced the subject of death, and endeavoured to maintain that the fear of it might be got over. I told him that David Hume said to me, he was no more uneasy to think he should *not be* after this life, than that he *had not been* before he began to exist. JOHNSON. "Sir, if he really thinks so, his perceptions are disturbed; he is mad: if he does not think so, he lies. He may tell you, he holds his finger in the flame of a candle, without feeling pain; would you believe him? When he dies, he at least gives up all he has." BOSWELL. "Foote, Sir, told me, that when he was very ill he was not afraid to die." JOHNSON. "It is not true, Sir. Hold a pistol to Foote's breast, or to Hume's breast, and threaten to kill them, and you'll see how they behave." BOSWELL. "But may we not fortify our minds for the approach of death?"—Here I am sensible I was in the wrong, to bring before his view what he ever looked upon with horrour; for although when in a celestial frame, in his "Vanity of human Wishes," he has supposed death to be "kind Nature's signal for retreat," from this state of being to "a happier seat,"[138] his thoughts upon this aweful change were in general full of dismal apprehensions. His mind resembled the vast amphitheatre, the Colisæum at Rome. In the centre stood his judgement, which, like a mighty gladiator, combated those apprehensions that, like the wild beasts of the *Arena*, were all around in cells, ready to be let out upon him. After a conflict, he drove them back into their dens; but not killing them, they were still assailing him. To my question, whether we might not fortify our minds for the approach of death, he answered, in a passion, "No, Sir, let it alone. It matters

---

136 Philip Melancthon (1497–1560), German reformer, the chief figure after Luther in the Lutheran Reformation.

137 Sir William Scott, later Baron Stowell (1745–1836), maritime and international lawyer, a close friend of Johnson and a member of The Club.

138 Lines 363–64.

JAMES BOSWELL

not how a man dies, but how he lives. The act of dying is not of importance, it lasts so short a time." He added, (with an earnest look,) "A man knows it must be so, and submits. It will do him no good to whine."

I attempted to continue the conversation. He was so provoked, that he said, "Give us no more of this"; and was thrown into such a state of agitation, that he expressed himself in a way that alarmed and distressed me; shewed an impatience that I should leave him, and when I was going away, called to me sternly, "Don't let us meet to-morrow."

I went home exceedingly uneasy. All the harsh observations which I had ever heard made upon his character, crowded into my mind; and I seemed to myself like the man who had put his head into the lion's mouth a great many times with perfect safety, but at last had it bit off.

Next morning I sent him a note, stating, that I might have been in the wrong, but it was not intentionally; he was therefore, I could not help thinking, too severe upon me. That notwithstanding our agreement not to meet that day, I would call on him in my way to the city, and stay five minutes by my watch. "You are, (said I,) in my mind, since last night, surrounded with cloud and storm. Let me have a glimpse of sunshine, and go about my affairs in serenity and chearfulness."

Upon entering his study, I was glad that he was not alone, which would have made our meeting more awkward. There were with him, Mr. Steevens[139] and Mr. Tyers,[140] both of whom I now saw for the first time. My note had, on his own reflection, softened him, for he received me very complacently; so that I unexpectedly found myself at ease, and joined in the conversation.

He said, the criticks had done too much honour to Sir Richard Blackmore,[141] by writing so much against him. That in his "Creation" he had been helped by various wits, a line by Philips[142] and a line by Tickell;[143] so that by their aid, and that of others, the poem had been made out.

---

139 George Steevens (1736–1800), like Johnson an editor of Shakespeare, was a friend of Johnson who later supplied him with anecdotes for the *Lives of the Poets*.
140 Thomas Tyers (1726–1787), later described by Boswell as one who "ran about the world with a pleasant carelessness, amusing every body by his desultory conversation."
141 Sir Richard Blackmore (d. 1729), a doctor and a prolific bad poet, author of *Creation* (1712), a versified argument attempting to support religion on grounds of natural reason.
142 Ambrose Philips (1674–1749).
143 Thomas Tickell (1686–1740).

I defended Blackmore's supposed lines, which have been ridiculed as absolute nonsense:

A painted vest Prince Voltiger had on,
Which from a naked Pict his grandsire won.[144]

I maintained it to be a poetical conceit. A Pict being painted, if he is slain in battle, and a vest is made of his skin, it is a painted vest won from him, though he was naked.

Johnson spoke unfavourably of a certain pretty voluminous authour, saying, "He used to write anonymous books, and then other books commending those books, in which there was something of rascality."

I whispered him, "Well, Sir, you are now in good humour." JOHNSON. "Yes, Sir." I was going to leave him, and had got as far as the staircase. He stopped me, and smiling, said, "Get you gone *in*"; a curious mode of inviting me to stay, which I accordingly did for some time longer.

This little incidental quarrel and reconciliation, which, perhaps, I may be thought to have detailed too minutely, must be esteemed as one of many proofs which his friends had, that though he might be charged with *bad humour* at times, he was always a *good-natured* man; and I have heard Sir Joshua Reynolds, a nice and delicate observer of manners, particularly remark, that when upon any occasion Johnson had been rough to any person in company, he took the first opportunity of reconciliation, by drinking to him, or addressing his discourse to him; but if he found his dignified indirect overtures sullenly neglected, he was quite indifferent, and considered himself as having done all that he ought to do, and the other as now in the wrong.

---

144 Boswell's note explains that the lines are in fact by the Hon. Edward Howard (fl. 1669), that they were written in a less ridiculous form and altered by "some wag."

Seth Daniel Riemer